OXFORD CLASSICAL MONOGRAPHS

*Published under the supervision of a Committee of the
Faculty of Classics in the University of Oxford*

The aim of the Oxford Classical Monograph series (which replaces the Oxford Classical and Philosophical Monographs) is to publish books based on the best theses on Greek and Latin literature, ancient history, and ancient philosophy examined by the Faculty Board of Classics.

STATIUS
SILVAE 5

EDITED
WITH AN INTRODUCTION
TRANSLATION, AND COMMENTARY
BY

BRUCE GIBSON

OXFORD
UNIVERSITY PRESS

OXFORD
UNIVERSITY PRESS

Great Clarendon Street, Oxford OX2 6DP

Oxford University Press is a department of the University of Oxford.
It furthers the University's objective of excellence in research, scholarship,
and education by publishing worldwide in

Oxford New York

Auckland Cape Town Dar es Salaam Hong Kong Karachi
Kuala Lumpur Madrid Melbourne Mexico City Nairobi
New Delhi Shanghai Taipei Toronto

With offices in

Argentina Austria Brazil Chile Czech Republic France Greece
Guatemala Hungary Italy Japan Poland Portugal Singapore
South Korea Switzerland Thailand Turkey Ukraine Vietnam

Oxford is a registered trade mark of Oxford University Press
in the UK and in certain other countries

Published in the United States
by Oxford University Press Inc., New York

British Library Cataloguing in Publication Data

Data available

Library of Congress Cataloguing in Publication Data

Data available

Typeset by SPI Publisher Services, Pondicherry, India
Printed in Great Britain
on acid-free paper by
Biddles Ltd, King's Lynn

ISBN 0-19-927715-X 978-0-19-927715-5

1 3 5 7 9 10 8 6 4 2

PARENTIBVS
OPTIMIS

PREFACE

The *Silvae* have gained in popularity in recent decades, in keeping with an increasing and welcome willingness among scholars to reassess post-Virgilian Latin literature. In addition to commentaries on books 2 by H.-J. van Dam (Leiden, 1984), 4 by K. M. Coleman (Oxford 1988), and 3 by G. Laguna Mariscal (Madrid, 1992), there have also been monographs such as A. Hardie's *Statius and the Silvae: Poets, Patrons and Epideixis in the Greco-Roman World* (Liverpool, 1983) and C. Newlands's *Statius' Silvae and the Poetics of Empire* (Cambridge, 2002), as well as the Oxford text of E. Courtney (Oxford, 1990) and the new Loeb text and translation by D. R. Shackleton Bailey (Cambridge, MA, 2003)—to say nothing of the burgeoning presence of Statius in journals. These are undoubtedly exciting times for scholars working on the *Silvae*. The present commentary on Book 5, which has received no commentary since F. Vollmer's edition of the whole of the *Silvae*, *P. Papinii Statii Silvarum libri* (Leipzig, 1898), owes much to the work of all these scholars, and aims to encourage consideration of a book which has perhaps received a little less attention than the rest of the *Silvae*.

The commentary originated in a doctoral thesis on *Silvae* 5. 1–4 submitted to the University of Oxford in 1995. I was very fortunate in my two supervisors, Robin Nisbet and Michael Winterbottom, who have allowed me to benefit so much from their learning, humanity, and wisdom over the years. I am also very grateful to Stephen Heyworth, who went far beyond the remit of a College adviser in commenting in great detail on the whole work more than once. Extensive and helpful written comments on the thesis were then kindly provided by my examiners, Gregory Hutchinson and Kathleen Coleman.

Since 1995, I have also benefited greatly from Kathleen Coleman's continuing guidance and Statian expertise, since she has calmly endured a decade of responding to successive drafts and importunate questions; it was a particular pleasure to be a near neighbour of hers in Cambridge, MA, when I spent part of the autumn term of 2002 on leave as a Visiting Scholar in the Department of the Classics at

Harvard. I am also very grateful to those who have read and offered valuable comments and suggestions on sections of the book, Miriam Griffin, Donald Hill, Gabriel Laguna Mariscal, Carole Newlands, Jonathan Powell, Robin Seager, and Tony Woodman: to all of them my thanks, though all errors that remain are of course mine. Many other colleagues and friends have also been generous, whether in answering questions, loaning or donating books and articles, or in providing help or support of varying kinds, including Rhiannon Ash, Dean Bowen, Ewen Bowie, Francis and Sandra Cairns, John Davies, Helen Dixon, Philip van der Eijk, Rolando Ferri, Rowland Gibson, Stephen Harrison, Tom Harrison, Marcia Hill, Fred Jones (who has also nobly provided the etching for the cover), Andrew Laird, Mohan Manuel, Chris Mee, Mark Molesky, Catherine Osborne, Michael Reeve, Richard Tarrant, Christopher Tuplin, Jonathan Williams, Alexei Zadorojnyi, and Max Zadow. I am also grateful to Hilary O'Shea and the staff of the Press for their patience and diligence. Here I gladly mention too the great debt I owe to Leofranc Holford–Strevens, who has acted as copy-editor in the last year: though I have at times been daunted by his suggestions and queries, he has made an enormous contribution to this book, liberally sharing with me his remarkable erudition and insights.

I should also like to thank the British Academy for the postgraduate studentship which enabled me to embark on my doctorate, Wadham College, Oxford for a Senior Scholarship during that period, and the Faculty of Arts of the University of Liverpool and the AHRC (*quondam* AHRB) for two semesters of research leave in 2002. I am also grateful to the University of Newcastle upon Tyne for financing a visit in 1997 to Madrid to consult the Matritensis, and to the School of Archaeology, Classics and Egyptology at Liverpool for providing funding for visits to libraries.

It is also a great pleasure to express my gratitude to Philippa Thomas for her cheerful serenity and encouragement. Lastly, I should like to thank my parents, David and Sheila Gibson, to whom this book is dedicated, for everything.

London
12 August 2005

CONTENTS

EDITIONS OF THE *SILVAE*

The following list records in chronological order the editions and translations of the *Silvae* cited in the apparatus and commentary. Citations from *Silvae* 1–4 in the commentary are taken from the edition of Courtney (Oxford, 1990); for the *Thebaid* and *Achilleid* I have used the editions of D. E. Hill (Leiden, 1983) and O. A. W. Dilke (Cambridge, 1954) respectively.

a	*editio princeps* (Rome, 1472)
b	*editio Parmensis* (Parma, 1473)
Calderini	D. Calderini, *Sylvarum libri quinque* (Rome, 1475)
Avantius	*Sylvae cum Domitii commentariis / Et auancii sui Emendationibus / Statii Thebais cum Lactantii Commentariis. / Statii Achilleis cum Maturantii Commentariis. Domitii Alie annotationes* (Venice, 1498)
Aldus	A. P. Manutius (ed.), *Statii Syluarum libri quinque Thebaidos libri duodecim Achilleidos duo* (Venice, 1502)
Bernartius	J. Bernartius, *P. Papinii Statii opera quae extant* (Antwerp, 1595)
Lindenbrog	F. Tiliobroga, *P. Papinii Surculi Statii opera quae exstant. Placidi Lactantii in Thebaida et Achilleida commentarius* (Paris, 1600)
Gevartius	J. Gevartius, *Publii Papinii Statii opera omnia* (Leiden, 1616)
Gronovius 1653	J. F. Gronovius, *P. Papinii Stati Opera* (Amsterdam, 1653)
Barth	C. Barth, *Publii Papinii Statii quae exstant* (Zwickau, 1664)
Markland	J. Markland, *P. Papinii Stati libri quinque Silvarum* (London, 1728; 2nd edn. Dresden and London, 1827)
Baehrens	E. Baehrens, *P. Papinius Statius: Silvae* (Leipzig, 1876)
Vollmer	F. Vollmer, *P. Papinii Statii Silvarum libri* (Leipzig, 1898)
Phillimore[1]	J. S. Phillimore, *P. Papini Stati Silvae*, 1st edn. (Oxford, 1904)
Slater	D. A. Slater, *The Silvae of Statius: Translated with Introduction and Notes* (Oxford, 1908)
Saenger	G. Saenger, *P. Papini Stati Silvae* (St Petersburg, 1909)
Klotz	A. Klotz, *Statius: Silvae* (Leipzig, 1900, second edition, 1911)

Phillimore[2]   J. S. Phillimore, *P. Papini Stati Silvae*, 2nd edn. (Oxford, 1917)

Mozley   J. H. Mozley, *Statius*, with English translation, 2 vols. (Loeb Classical Library; Cambridge, MA, 1928)

Iz.–Fr.   H. Frère (ed.) and H. J. Izaac (tr.), *Stace: Silves*, with French translation, 2 vols., (Paris, 1944, repr. 1961)

Colom–Dolç   G. Colom and M. Dolç, *P. Papini Estaci: Silves*, with Catalan translation, 3 vols. (Barcelona, 1957, 1958, 1960)

Marastoni   A. Marastoni, *P. Papini Stati Silvae* (Leipzig, 1961)

Traglia   A. Traglia, *P. Papini Stati Silvae* (Turin, 1978)

van Dam   H.-J. van Dam, *P. Papinius Statius: Silvae Book II. A Commentary* (Leiden, 1984)

Coleman   K. M. Coleman, *Statius: Silvae IV. Edited with an English Translation and Commentary* (Oxford, 1988)

Courtney   E. Courtney, *P. Papini Stati Silvae* (Oxford, 1990)

Laguna   G. Laguna Mariscal, *Estacio: Silvas III. Introducción, Edición Crítica, Traducción y Comentario* (Madrid, 1992)

Shackleton Bailey   D. R. Shackleton Bailey, *Statius: Silvae* (Loeb Classical Library; Cambridge, Mass., 2003)

ABBREVIATIONS

I. **Abbreviations used in the apparatus criticus**

Note: Scholars cited in the critical apparatus by year and page reference may be found in the bibliography at the end of the volume. Items which I have not been able to see are marked with an asterisk.

*Britannicus	*Commentarii Joannis Britannici in Juuenalem* (Brescia, 1501)
*Burmannus	Conjectures of his own recorded along with those of Heinsius in a copy of Lindenbrog's edition (see Baehrens, edn., p. xii)
Cruceus, *Antidiatribe*	E. Cruceus, *P. Papinii Statii Silvarum Frondatio sive Antidiatribe* (Paris, 1639); cited from F. Hand (ed.), *Iohannis Frederici Gronovii in P. Papinii Statii Silvarum Libros V Diatribe. Nova editio ab ipso auctore correcta interpolata. Accedunt Emerici Crucei Antidiatribe, Gronovii Elenchus Antidiatribes, et Crucei Muscarium,* 2 vols. (Leipzig, 1812), ii. 7–91
Davies, *Corpus*	In G. A. Davies and J. P. Postgate, 'Silvarum libri V', in J. P. Postgate (ed.), *Corpus Poetarum Latinorum,* ii (London, 1905)
Gronovius, *Diatribe*	J. F. Gronovius, *In Papinii Statii Silvarum Libros V Diatribe* (The Hague, 1637); cited from repr. ed. F. Hand (Leipzig, 1812), i
Gronovius, *Elench.*	J. F. Gronovius, *Elenchus Antidiatribes* (Paris, 1640); cited from repr. ed. F. Hand (Leipzig, 1812), ii. 122–271
Heinsius ooo	N. Heinsius, *Adversariorum Libri IV,* ed. P. Burman jr. (Harlingen, 1742)
*Heinsius	Conjectures recorded by P. Burman in a copy of Lindenbrog's edition (see Baehrens, edn., p. xii)
Krohn	Private communications addressed to Vollmer and Klotz reported in their editions
Laetus	Annotations made by Pomponius Laetus in a copy of the 1480 Florence edition of the *Silvae,* now

	preserved in the Bodleian Library (Auct. N. inf. 1. 6); see further Reeve (1977*b*), 217–18
Lipsius, *Elect.*	I. Lipsius, *Electorum Liber I* (Antwerp, 1580)
*Meursius	J. Meursius, *Exercitationes Criticae* (Leiden, 1599)
Meyer, Wolfgang	Private communications addressed to Krohn (see above)
*Morel	F. Morel, *In Papinii Surculi Statii Sylvas: Commentationes et coniectanea* (Paris, 1601 and 1602)
Postgate, *Corpus*	In G. A. Davies and J. P. Postgate, 'Silvarum libri V', in J. P. Postgate (ed.), *Corpus Poetarum Latinorum*, ii (London, 1905)
Salmasius, *Epistula*	In J. F. Gronovius, *Elenchus Antidiatribes* (Paris, 1640), 19–35; cited from repr. ed. F. Hand (Leipzig, 1812), ii. 108–21

II. Other works

AE	*L'Année épigraphique: revue des publications épigraphiques relatives à l'antiquité romaine*
Anth. Lat.	D. R. Shackleton Bailey (ed.), *Anthologia Latina I. Carmina in codicibus scripta*. Fasc. 1 (Stuttgart, 1982).
Barrington Atlas	*Barrington Atlas of the Greek and Roman World*, ed. R. J. A. Talbert, 2 vols. (Princeton, 2000).
BMC Ionia	B. V. Head, *Catalogue of the Greek Coins of Ionia*, ed. R. S. Poole (London, 1892)
BMCRE II	H. Mattingly, *Coins of the Roman Empire in the British Museum. Volume II. Vespasian to Domitian* (London, 1930)
CIG	*Corpus Inscriptionum Graecarum*, ed. A. Boeckh et al., 4 vols. (Berlin, 1828–77)
CIL	*Corpus Inscriptionum Latinarum* (Berlin, 1862–)
CLE	*Carmina Latina Epigraphica*: i–ii ed. F. Buecheler (Leipzig, 1895–7); iii, ed. E. Lommatzsch (Leipzig, 1926)
Collect. Alex.	J. U. Powell (ed.), *Collectanea Alexandrina: Reliquiae minores poetarum Graecorum aetatis Ptolemaicae 323–146 A.C.* (Oxford, 1925)
Diels, *DG*	H. Diels (ed.), *Doxographi Graeci* (Berlin, 1929)
Diz. Epig.	*Dizionario epigrafico di antichità romane* (Rome, 1886–)
FLP	E. Courtney (ed.), *The Fragmentary Latin Poets* (Oxford, 1993)
Garland of Philip	A. S. F. Gow and D. L. Page (eds.), *The Garland of Philip*, 2 vols. (Cambridge, 1968)

GL	*Grammatici Latini ex recensione Henrici Keilii*, 8 vols. (Leipzig, 1855–80; repr. Hildesheim, 1961)
Housman, *Class. P.*	*The Classical Papers of A. E. Housman*, ed. J. Diggle and F. R. D. Goodyear, 3 vols. (Cambridge, 1972)
H.–Sz.	J. B. Hofmann and A. Szantyr, *Lateinische Syntax und Stilistik* (Munich, 1965)
IG	*Inscriptiones Graecae* (Berlin, 1873–)
ILS	*Inscriptiones Latinae Selectae*, ed. H. Dessau (Berlin, 1892–1916)
I. Olympia	W. Dittenberger and K. Purgold (edd.), *Olympia. Die Ergebnisse der von dem deutschen Reich veranstalteten Ausgrabung, Textband V: Die Inschriften von Olympia* (Berlin, 1896)
Kaibel, *Epigr. gr.*	G. Kaibel, *Epigrammata Graeca ex lapidibus conlecta* (Berlin, 1878)
Kl. Pauly	*Der kleine Pauly: Lexikon der Antike* (Stuttgart, 1964–75)
K.–S.	R. Kühner and C. Stegmann, *Ausführliche Grammatik der lateinischen Sprache*, 2 vols. (Munich, 1962)
Krüger–Cooper	G. L. Cooper, III (after K. W. Krüger), *Greek Syntax*, 4 vols.: i–ii, *Attic Greek Prose Syntax* (Ann Arbor, 1998), iii–iv: *Early Greek Poetic and Herodotean Syntax* (Ann Arbor, 2002)
Laudatio Murdiae	*CIL* vi. 10230
Lausberg	H. Lausberg, *A Handbook of Literary Rhetoric. A Foundation for Literary Study*, tr. M. T. Bliss, A. Jansen, and D. E. Orton (Leiden, Boston, and Cologne, 1998)
LIMC	*Lexicon Iconographicum Mythologiae Classicae* (Zurich, 1981–97)
LSJ	H. G. Liddell and R. Scott, *A Greek–English Lexicon*, 9th edn. rev. H. Stuart Jones and R. McKenzie (Oxford, 1940)
LTVR	*Lexicon Topographicum Vrbis Romae*, ed. E. M. Steinby, 6 vols. (Rome, 1993–2000)
Meiggs and Lewis[2]	R. Meiggs and D. M. Lewis, *A Selection of Greek Historical Inscriptions*, rev. edn. (Oxford, 1988)
MRR	T. R. S. Broughton, *The Magistrates of the Roman Republic* (New York, 1951–2, suppl. 1960)
Neuer Pauly	*Der neue Pauly: Enzyklopädie der Antike* (Stuttgart and Weimar, 1996–2003).
N.–H.	R. G. M. Nisbet and M. Hubbard, *A Commentary on Horace: Odes, Book I* (Oxford, 1970); *A Commentary on Horace: Odes, Book II* (Oxford, 1978)

N.–R.	R. G. M. Nisbet and N. Rudd, *A Commentary on Horace: Odes, Book III* (Oxford, 2004)
OGIS	W. Dittenberger (ed.), *Orientis Graecae Inscriptiones Selectae* (Leipzig, 1903–5)
OLD	*Oxford Latin Dictionary*, ed. P. G. W. Glare (Oxford, 1968–82)
PIR[i]	*Prosopographia Imperii Romani* (Berlin, 1897–8)
PIR[2]	*Prosopographia Imperii Romani*, 2nd edn. (Berlin, 1933–)
PMG	D. L. Page, *Poetae Melici Graeci* (Oxford, 1962)
PMGF	M. Davies, *Poetarum Melicorum Graecorum Fragmenta*, i: *Alcman, Stesichorus, Ibycus* (Oxford, 1991)
RE	*Real-Encyclopädie der classischen Altertumswissenschaft* (Stuttgart, 1893–1980)
RIC II	H. Mattingly and E. A. Sydenham, *The Roman Imperial Coinage, Vol. II: Vespasian to Hadrian* (London, 1926)
SH	H. Lloyd-Jones and P. J. Parsons, *Supplementum Hellenisticum* (Berlin, 1983)
SVF	H. von Arnim, *Stoicorum Veterum Fragmenta*, 4 vols. (Leipzig, 1903–24); repr. as *Stoichi antichi: tutti i frammenti* with Italian translation by R. Radice (Milan, 2002)
Syll.[3]	W. Dittenberger (ed.), *Sylloge Inscriptionum Graecarum* (3rd edn. Leipzig, 1915–24, repr. Hildesheim, 1982)
Syme, *RP*	R. Syme, *Roman Papers*, 7 vols.: i–ii (Oxford, 1979), ed. E. Badian; iii (Oxford, 1984), iv–v (Oxford, 1988), vi–vii (Oxford, 1991), ed. A. R. Birley
ThLL	*Thesaurus Linguae Latinae* (Munich, 1900–)
TrGF	*Tragicorum Graecorum Fragmenta*, 5 vols. (Göttingen, 1971–2004)

General Introduction

Statius' Life and Works

EXISTING commentaries on books of the *Silvae* already provide admirable introductions to Statius' life and poetic output.[1] For convenience, however, I give the most important details here as well.

P. Papinius Statius was born in Naples (*Silv.* 3. 5. 12–13, 4. 7. 17–20); his father was a teacher of Greek poetry, at first in Campania and then in Rome (*Silv.* 5. 3. 146–77), and had competed in professional poetry competitions in Greece and in Italy (*Silv.* 5. 3. 133–45). Statius may have been born around AD 50, if vague statements in the 90s as to his approaching old age are legitimate evidence.[2] Statius himself also competed in at least three poetry competitions, winning at the Augustalia in Naples in his own father's lifetime (*Silv.* 5. 3. 225–7), and, after his father's death, at Domitian's Alban games (*Silv.* 3. 5. 28–31, 4. 2. 65–7, 5. 3. 225–30), though he was not successful in the Capitoline contest (*Silv.* 3. 5. 31–3, 5. 3. 231–3).[3] As well as the five books of the *Silvae*, also extant is an epic, the *Thebaid*, which took twelve years to complete (*Theb.* 12. 811–12), and was finished by early 93, since no mention is made of Domitian's Sarmatian campaign, which ended in a defeat of the Sarmatians in the January of that year.[4] A book and a half survive from the *Achilleid*, which was not completed. Since the poem is mentioned in some of Statius' last extant writings (*Silv.* 4. 7. 23–4, 5. 2. 160–3, 5. 5. 36–7), it is not unreasonable to suppose that its incomplete state was the result of Statius' death, traditionally assigned

---

[1] See van Dam (1984), 1–2, Coleman (1988), pp. xv–xx, Laguna (1992), 3–13. See also A. Hardie (1983), 58–65, Nauta (2002), 195–204.

[2] See *Silv.* 3. 5. 13 'patria senium componere terra' (Statius' plan to retire to his home town, Naples), 4. 4. 70 'uergimus in senium', 5. 2. 158–9 'nos fortior aetas | iam fugit'. Since all these poems date from the early nineties, this would imply that Statius was in his forties. While it has been suggested that *Silvae* 1–3 were published simultaneously after January 93, book 4 being published in AD 95 (see e.g. Coleman 1988, pp. xvi f., Laguna 1992, 8–10), note that Nauta (2002), 285–9, 444 has argued for separate publication of the first three books of the *Silvae* in AD 92, 93, and 94 respectively.

[3] For the dating of these contests, and of Statius' father's death, see the introduction to 5. 3.

[4] See Coleman (1988), pp. xvi f., Laguna (1992), 8.

to the year 96, the year of Domitian's own death. Lost works included the *Agave*, a libretto composed for the *pantomimus* Paris which is mentioned by Juv. 7. 87, and a fragment from the *De Bello Germanico*, which may or may not have been from a prize poem from Statius' Alban victory; the fragment survives as a result of quotation by Valla on Juv. 4. 94.[5]

The nature of the *Silvae*

It may be useful to sketch the insights into the *Silvae* offered by Statius himself.[6] One must naturally begin with the prose prefaces, but the 'poetics' exhibited in the poems themselves are also worthy of examination.[7]

Statius' concern with speed of composition is perhaps the most striking feature of the prefaces.[8] In the first preface Statius describes how the poems (*libelli*) came to him 'subito calore et quadam festinandi uoluptate' (1 pr. 3). When enumerating the contents of the book he emphasizes the swift composition of the individual poems, none of which took more than two days to compose (1 pr. 13–14).[9] In Book 2, Statius again comments on his rapid offering of consolation to Melior (2 pr. 7–12).

But speed is an unusual criterion for composition; accordingly Statius adopts a defensive position. In Book 1 he expresses the fear

---

[5] See Courtney (1980), 195–6, *FLP*, p. 360; Nauta (2002), 330. A. Hardie (1983), 61 argues that the *De Bello Germanico* fragment is more likely to come from a separate work referring to Domitian's German victory in 83 rather than from Statius' prize-winning poem.

[6] On the term *Silvae* see A. Hardie (1983), 76, van Dam (1984), 4 with nn. 41–2, Tanner (1986), 3041–2, Coleman (1988), pp. xxii–xxiv, Brown (1994), 11–13, 21–2, Nauta (2002), 252–4, Newlands (2002), 36–7. The term can suggest both Greek ὕλη, conveying the idea of 'material' from which a work of literature can be formed, and also miscellany and variety (cf. e.g. Gel. pr. 6).

[7] The limitations of using only the prefaces as a means to discovering Statius' attitude to the *Silvae* are recognized by A. Hardie (1983), 74; cf. Hutchinson (1993), 34: ' . . . so elaborately do these prefaces themselves play with modesty and with pride that their explicit description of the *Silvae* gives only a limited idea of what they are like.'

[8] On extempore poetic composition, see A. Hardie (1983), 76–85. Hardie, however, makes an important distinction between extempore writing and Statius' 'speed of composition' (85). See also Vessey (1986), 2761–5 for further discussion of Statius' *celeritas*. Woodman (1975), 276–80, 282–7, discussing Velleius Paterculus, usefully notes how claims of speed in composition can also reflect processes of selection and pruning of material.

[9] Thus 1. 1 was given to the emperor on the day after Domitian had dedicated the equestrian statue of himself (1 pr. 18–19), 1. 2 was written within two days (*biduo* 1 pr. 21), 1. 3 took one day (1 pr. 26), while 1. 5 was apparently produced within the span of a single dinner (1 pr. 29–30). See Nauta (2002), 249–51.

that the subsequent publication of the poems will not benefit from
the atmosphere of spontaneity which attended their inception (1 pr.
11–13): 'sed apud ceteros necesse est multum illis pereat ex uenia, cum
amiserint quam solam habuerunt gratiam celeritatis.' Similarly in
Book 2 he excuses himself to Melior on the grounds that late con-
solations are useless.[10] The excuse of speed is, moreover, linked with
a conception of the *Siluae* as representatives of a lesser kind of writ-
ing.[11] Thus in the first preface Statius asks why he is troubling with
the *Siluae* when he has the *Thebaid* to consider (1 pr. 5–7), while at 4 pr.
29–30 he concedes the frivolous nature of the *Siluae*: 'exerceri autem
non licet ioco?'

This concession needs, however, to be treated with caution. Even
the very passages where Statius seems most modest may hint at a
different attitude. Thus the comparison with the *Thebaid* is followed
by an acknowledgement that great poets wrote minor works such as
the *Culex* and the *Batrachomachia* (1 pr. 7–8). On the one hand, such
comparisons seem to set the *Siluae* firmly in their place. But they also
establish the *Siluae* as equal to minor works which were at the time
ascribed to Virgil and Homer;[12] the implication follows that the
Thebaid is on a par with other epics. Statius continues with the same
combination of modesty and assertion ('nec quisquam est inlustrium
poetarum qui non aliquid operibus suis stilo remissiore praeluserit',
1 pr. 8–9), cautiously acknowledging the *stilus remissior* and the levity of
such efforts (*praeluserit*), whilst simultaneously affirming that he is
acting in a manner characteristic of all other distinguished poets (*nec
quisquam est inlustrium poetarum*). The same preface also hints at the
seriousness attached by Statius even to the *Siluae*; after remarking on
the loss of spontaneity, and hence of the audience's goodwill, he
expresses his fears that the poetry will not succeed (1 pr. 14–15):
'quam timeo ne uerum istuc uersus quoque ipsi de se probent!' His
fear for the reception of his work again combines modesty with
assertion, since there is the strong implication that Statius *does* have
high hopes for his poems. Compare the closing remarks to the

---

[10] But contrast Statius' use of the opposite idea that a consolation should not be given
too early (*Silu.* 5. 1. 16 n.).

[11] Contrast the slow labour of the *Thebaid* (*Silu.* 3. 5. 35–6 and 4. 7. 26); see also *Theb.* 12.
811–12.

[12] Compare Mart. 4. 14 (discussed by Hutchinson 1993, 23), where Martial compares
Silius Italicus, his addressee, to Virgil, and suggests that he himself is following in the
tradition of Catullus.

prefaces to Books 2 and 4: at 2 pr. 27–9 Melior is told to make the book public if it pleases him; if not, he is to return the work to its author; similarly at 4 pr. 34–5 Marcellus is to defend the poetry if it pleases him; if not, Statius will take the blame. In both prefaces, the poet invites the involvement of the addressees in the subsequent reception of the book.[13] In accepting the possibility of criticism, Statius displays caution; but his desire for the book to be disseminated represents an attitude far from dismissive to his own work. We shall see below how this attitude is reflected in the poems themselves.

The very process of offering poems to others is itself a form of assertion: if the poems were poor, the honour conferred on the recipient would be meagre. Statius' remarks to Melior and Marcellus represent a cautious approach. Elsewhere, however, he is more confident. Thus at 3 pr. 1–7 Statius does not have to fear a negative response from Pollius ('securus itaque tertius hic Siluarum nostrarum liber ad te mittitur', 6–7), while at 3 pr. 23–5 he anticipates the recipient's particular pleasure in Statius' poem to his wife, since Pollius will realize that Statius wishes to withdraw from Rome to the company of his friend. At 3 pr. 13–15 he even remarks that the *pietas* of Claudius Etruscus towards his dead father *deserved* some consolation from him (*merebatur... aliquod ex studiis nostris solacium*);[14] the notion of desert is not consistent with an entirely dismissive attitude towards the poetry. A presence particularly vaunted in Statius' poetry is that of the emperor (1 pr. 16–17, 4 pr. 3–8 and 28–9); had he considered that the poems were entirely trivial, he would scarcely have attached so much importance to Domitian's appearances in the *Silvae*.

There are further elements in the prefaces that are similar. Thus at 1 pr. 19 and 22, and at 3 pr. 4, Statius refers to the boldness of his rapid composition;[15] the effect is also to suggest the ambitious nature of his work. Perhaps the most confident remark in all the prefaces is Statius'

---

[13] For similar requests for the involvement of others in corrections of a work prior to publication, cf. e.g. Mart. 6. 1, 5. 80, 12 pr. 22–6, Plin. 3. 10. 5, 3. 13. 5, and see the discussion by Nauta (2002), 124–8, 282–4.

[14] Compare *Silv.* 5. 1. 1–9 (where Statius comments on the similarly deserving *pietas* of Abascantus towards his dead wife Priscilla) and 5. 1 *epist.* 7–8, where Statius remarks on the need to commemorate his friend's grief.

[15] At 1 pr. 19, *ausus sum* is Sandström's conjecture for M's *iussum*; see further Håkanson (1969), 17–18. On *audacia*, see 5. 3. 135–6 n.; it is arguable that drawing attention to speed of composition is in fact a way of highlighting a virtuoso ability to write well, even in haste.

explanation of his decision to include more poems in his fourth book than in its predecessors: his critics are not to think that they have accomplished anything (4 pr. 25–7). This statement is far removed from the apparent anxiety expressed in the first preface. Elsewhere, a more complex attitude is maintained; thus at 2 pr. 24–6 Statius, referring to his poem on Lucan (2. 7), comments on his avoidance of the hexameter: 'ego non potui maiorem tanti auctoris habere reuerentiam quam quod laudes eius dicturus hexametros meos timui', 'I could not have had greater reverence for so great a poet than that I was afraid of my own hexameters when I was about to sing his praises.' What is the nature of Statius' fear? The key is provided by the accusative case (*hexametros meos*). Instead of constructions that would give the meaning 'to be afraid for',[16] Statius uses the accusative denoting what is feared (*OLD* s.v. 2). Rather than fearing *for* his hexameters, they are the very object of his fears. The danger may be that they will outdo the subject.[17] Thus at the very moment of offering a homage to Lucan, Statius hints that an offering composed in hexameters would involve his competing with Lucan.

This poem is an interesting example, since Statius declines to use the hexameter, the usual metre of the *Silvae*. A lesser metre, the hendecasyllable, is used instead.[18] Compare 4 pr. 22–4, on the use of the hendecasyllable in 4. 9 (addressed to Plotius Grypus): 'Plotio Grypo, maioris gradus iuueni, dignius opusculum reddam, sed interim hendecasyllabos quos Saturnalibus una risimus huic uolumini inserui.' Statius explains that while he will provide a more distinguished work for Plotius, he has for the moment produced a poem in hendecasyllables. *dignius opusculum* is revealing. The diminutive *opusculum* betokens modesty,[19] but *dignius* suggests that within the *Silvae* some poems possess a higher status than others. Hierarchy within the poems is confirmed by Statius' remarks on 2. 3, 2. 4, and 2. 5. At 2

---

[16] e.g. *timeo* followed by the dative (*OLD* s.v. *timeo* 1) or *pro* with the ablative (cf. *Silv.* 1 pr. 6–7 'quo adhuc pro Thebaide mea, quamuis me reliquerit, timeo'), both of which would give the meaning 'to be afraid for'.

[17] Contrast A. Hardie (1983), 85: '...and, for Statius, the hexameter was the natural vehicle of expression; but he did not trust his epic hexameters to do justice to Lucan the epic poet.'

[18] It is worth noting, though, that Statius employs the hendecasyllable for *Silv.* 4. 3, whose subject is the *Via Domitiana*. On Statius' use of the hendecasyllable, see L. Morgan (2000), 114–20.

[19] Compare Statius' use of the diminutive *libellus* to refer to single poems of the *Silvae*, and cf. Tanner (1986), 3036–41.

pr. 14–17, he singles out these poems: 'in arborem certe tuam, Melior, et psittacum scis a me leues libellos quasi epigrammatis loco scriptos. eandem exigebat stili facilitatem leo mansuetus, quem in amphitheatro prostratum frigidum erat sacratissimo imperatori ni statim tradere.' Here the comparison with epigram,[20] suggesting a particularly rapid composition, indicates that the poems are *leues libellos*. But by calling them *leues libellos*, it is implied that other poems in the collection are not *leues*, and are hence to be taken more seriously.[21]

Thus the prefaces do not simply present the *Silvae* as trivial *divertissements*: there coexists a more assertive and confident approach to the poems. This sketch of the complex attitude to his poetry exhibited in Statius' prefaces can now be supplemented by a survey of the evidence offered by the poems themselves.

The monumental qualities of the *Silvae* are particularly evident in the poems of consolation. In 5. 1, which contains a description of the actual tomb of Priscilla (222–46), Statius gives his own poem the status of an eternal *sepulchrum* (1–15), comparing physical monuments unfavourably with the lasting value of a poetic commemoration (11–15), and telling Priscilla 'haud alio melius condere sepulchro'.[22] The poem is itself a monument. Similarly at 3. 3. 31–42, when consoling Claudius Etruscus on the loss of his father, Statius contrasts his own durable *non arsura...munera* with such ephemeral offerings as spices; the poem will ensure that Etruscus' grief will last throughout the ages (38–9). At 5. 3. 47–63 Statius wishes to build a monument to his father, *par templis opus* (48), and to establish games in his honour. In the commentary I have argued that the language employed here, and the allusions to Horace and Virgil, indicate that the temple is a metaphor for the poem which Statius wishes to compose in honour of his father.

But consolation is not the only type of poem where Statius lays claim to immortality, whether for himself or for his subject. At 1. 1. 91–4 he affirms the eternity of the equestrian statue of Domitian, in terms of its resistance to the elements and the onset of time. Remarkably he uses a topos which typically characterizes poetic monuments

---

[20] On the influence of epigram in longer poems, see A. Hardie (1983), 119–36. On the contrast between epigrammatic style and longer works, see ibid. 85. See also Tanner (1986), 3036–44.

[21] On the word *libellus* in Statius and Martial, P. White (1974), 44–8 argues for the circulation of pre-publication *libelli* which were not of full book length, but see also Nauta (2002), 107–20, 280, 341.

[22] See also *Silv.* 3. 3. 216; Myers (2000), 106, Nauta (2002), 255.

and their invulnerability to physical decay (see Hor. *Carm.* 3. 30 and
Ov. *Met.* 15. 871–9, and indeed *Silv.* 5. 1. 10) as a means of affirming a
physical monument. The statue is thus inscribed in Statius' poem; its
immortality will be poetical as well as physical. Compare 1. 6. 98–102,
where Statius concludes a poem describing a single day (the Kalends
of December) with an affirmation of its immortality. The paradoxical
language of 'quos ibit procul hic dies per annos' (98), with the tension
between *hic dies* and *quos ... annos*, and the linking of the day's eternal
quality with the survival of Rome and the Capitol (alluding to the
terms of Virgil's promise of immortality to Nisus and Euryalus at *A.* 9.
446–9), suggest that the survival envisaged is literary commemoration
within the poem. Even more striking is 4. 3. 83–4, where the river
Volturnus gives thanks because Domitian will be read of as the river's
conqueror: 'quod tu maximus arbiter meaeque | uictor perpetuus
legere ripae'.[23]

One last (albeit modest) claim for poetic eternity is 2. 3. 62–3. After
describing Melior's tree, Statius offers the poem to his friend:

> haec tibi parua quidem genitali luce paramus
> dona, sed ingenti forsan uictura sub aeuo.

Here we have the familiar combination of modesty (Statius' allusion
to the small scale of his work) and assertion (the poem will perhaps be
a lasting gift). Indeed this claim for literary longevity is strikingly
expressed in a poem which Statius had previously characterized in
the preface as one of the *leues libellos* in the book.[24]

The description of 2. 3 as *parua ... dona* might be felt to evoke a
'Callimachean' concern with small scale work. The lines quoted do
not, of course, constitute a statement of poetic allegiance to Callima-
chus.[25] However, I hope to present a series of passages whose cumu-
lative effect may demonstrate that Statius is at least interested in
stylistic refinement.

---

[23] Gibson (1995), 8; cf. Newlands (2002), 308–9. Coleman ad loc. sees an allusion to an
inscription recording Domitian's achievement on the bridge. This interpretation does not
exclude a reference to the *poem's* survival as well.

[24] Cf. Nauta (2002), 254–5.

[25] On Callimachus and Roman poetry, see Wimmel (1960), Clausen (1964), Hutchinson
(1988), 277–354, Heyworth (1994), and Cameron (1995), 454–83. On Statius, see Thomas
(1983), 103–5 and Newlands (1991), who usefully identify Callimachean features in *Silv.* 3. 1;
see also Myers (2000), 135–7, Newlands (2002), 54, 140–2, 214–16. On grammatical study of
Callimachus, see Guhl (1969), 6–7, 29–30 (on Theon), and McNelis (2002), 81.

Statius twice refers to Callimachus by name. The first occasion is 1. 2. 252–5. Having invoked the assistance of the Muses, Statius notes that Philitas, Callimachus, Propertius, Tibullus, and Ovid would have wanted to praise the occasion of Stella's marriage to Violentilla. Although the statement is a bold one, since he is using the hexameter rather than the elegiac couplet, the effect is to suggest that Statius is writing in their vein. The juxtaposition of Callimachus and Philitas in 252–3 ('hunc ipse Coo plaudente Philitas | Callimachusque senex') enhances the sense of a programmatic element, since it recalls the opening of Prop. 3. 1. 1–2, where the poet asks for admittance to the *nemus* presided over by the same two poets. The second example is less significant. In the course of a passage describing his father's teaching, he notes (5. 3. 156–7) that his father taught Callimachus: 'tu pandere doctus | carmina Battiadae'. The importance of this passage is probably more biographical than literary, but the passage provides reasonable grounds for supposing that Statius himself was acquainted with Callimachus and the other poets on whom his father gave instruction.[26]

One aspect of Latin literary responses to Callimachus is a concern with stylistic refinement. Typically this is associated with works which have been produced slowly, as at Cat. 95, where Catullus compares Cinna's painstaking composition of the *Zmyrna* with more extensive, rapid, and worthless works. Statius similarly stresses the slow labour which characterized the *Thebaid*;[27] at 4. 7. 26 the epic is 'multa cruciata lima'. With the *Silvae*, one might not expect such criteria; Statius, as we have seen, makes much of his swift composition, and even requests his critics not to use an *asperior lima* when considering his poem on the death of Melior's favourite (2 pr. 10–12). But further examination is necessary, since Statius elsewhere within the *Silvae* does demonstrate a concern for a refined style. Thus at 1. 4. 36 he tells Rutilius Gallicus not to spurn praise offered 'tenuiore lyra'. For this phrasing, compare Virgil's 'tenui ... harundine' (*Ecl.* 6. 8), which itself suggests Callimachus' use of λεπταλέος in the *Aetia* prologue (fr. 1. 24 Pf.),[28] as a stylistic criterion. Although *tenuiore* here is an

---

[26] Hutchinson (1988), 353 with n. 145 notes the 'extremely probable' influence of Call. frr. 26–31a on Stat. *Theb.* 1. 557–668.

[27] See n. 11.

[28] Cf. e.g. Virg. *Ecl.* 1. 2 'tenui ... auena', *G.* 4. 6 'in tenui labor; at tenuis non gloria, si quem | numina laeua sinunt auditque uocatus Apollo', Ov. *Tr.* 4. 1. 15–16 'fertur et abducta Lyrneside tristis Achilles | Haemonia curas attenuasse lyra', Col. 10. 40 'Pierides tenui

expression of modesty, the word also has a strong 'Callimachean' resonance, particularly in view of its popularity as a Latin equivalent for λεπταλέος. Contrast Statius' description 'carmine molli' for his verse at 1. 5. 29, where the assessment is similar to *tenuis*, but without such noticeable overtones.[29] Note also 4. 4. 53–4 'tenues ignauo pollice chordas | pulso', and at 4. 7. 9 'Maximo carmen tenuare tempto', where, as Coleman has noted, there is a play on the contrast between *Maximus* and *tenuare*.

At 5. 3. 214, Statius remarks that his father taught him 'non uulgare loqui'. This avoidance of the language of the *uulgus*, that which is commonplace, recalls Propertius' use of *turba* (e.g. Prop. 3. 1. 12 and 3. 3. 24) and Horace's sacerdotal strictures against the *uulgus* in *Carm.* 3. 1.[30] The opposition of a poet and a crowd can be traced to *Epig.* 28. 4 Pf. σικχαίνω πάντα τὰ δημόσια; cf. the opening of the *Aetia* prologue, where Callimachus is opposed by the Telchines. Note also Apollo's instruction to eschew the well-worn path (fr. 1. 25–8 Pf.); in the *Silvae* this precept is directly expressed at 2. 7. 48–51, where Calliope tells Lucan to let others sing of such subjects as Troy, Odysseus, and the Argonauts ('trita uatibus orbita sequantur'); it is his task to sing of other subjects. Statius acts on this prescription at 5. 3. 80–5, where, using the device of *praeteritio*, he enumerates *exempla* of lamentation which he will not offer at his father's tomb, because they are 'nota nimis uati' (85). Compare also 2. 4. 9–10, where the belief that only swans sing of their death (referred to as 'Phaethontia uulgi | fabula') is rejected, since Melior's parrot did the same; *uulgi* denotes that, for Statius, the theme of dying swans is commonplace and to be avoided. See also 3. 3. 173–6, where Etruscus' *pietas* to his father deserves a song that shall outdo such examples. The surpassing of mythological *exempla* as a means of intensifying praise is a characteristic device; thus the *Silvae* begin (1. 1. 8–21) with the assertion that the equestrian statue of Domitian is greater in size than the Trojan horse.[31]

---

deducite carmine Musae'. See further Pfeiffer on Call. fr. 1. 23–24, and N.–H. on Hor. *Carm.* 1. 6. 9 and 2. 16. 38, Crowther (1978), 39–44, Myers (2000), 133.

[29] Note, however, the use of *mollis* in elegiac contexts (e.g. Prop. 3. 1. 19–20 'mollia, Pegasides, date uestro serta poetae: | non faciet capiti dura corona meo.')

[30] For Statius assuming a priestly role in the *Silvae* see 2. 7. 16–20, 3. 3. 13, 5. 3. 58–63.

[31] For similar eclipsing of previous *exempla*, compare *Silv.* 1. 3. 81–9, 2. 6. 25–33, 5. 1. 33–6. For the surpassing of poets, see 2. 7. 75–80 (in praise of Lucan) and 5. 3. 61–3.

I shall conclude this section by drawing attention to two more
indirect hints at 'Callimachean' poetics. By indirect, I mean that
although the passages are not concerned with poetry, they neverthe-
less might evoke a 'Callimachean' resonance. The first is 4. 3. 72–94,
where the river Volturnus thanks Domitian for his subjugation. Here
Statius expands on the familiar epic conceit of a river being subju-
gated by a bridge (e.g. Virg. *A.* 8. 728), and presents the river as
showing goodwill to his conqueror. In the course of his speech
Volturnus describes how he was previously 'turbidus minaxque'
(76), the first adjective suggesting the negative connotations of *turba*
and multitude.[32] However, Volturnus thanks Domitian for having
kept him within bounds (85); his flow is no longer polluted by mud,
and he is able instead to flow 'nitente cursu' (92). This recalls the
ending of Callimachus' *Hymn to Apollo* (*H.* 2. 105–13), where Phthonos,
who has condemned poets who do not produce vast works (οὐκ
ἄγαμαι τὸν ἀοιδὸν ὃς οὐδ' ὅσα πόντος ἀείδει, 106) on the scale of the
open sea, is rebuked by Apollo, who contrasts the filth of the Assyrian
river with the pure waters from a small stream which are offered to
Demeter. The allusion in Statius is confirmed by the last two lines of
Volturnus' speech, which repeat the motif of pure flow, and add the
theme of challenging the open sea (92–4):

> . . . sed talis ferar ut nitente cursu
> tranquillum mare proximumque possim
> puro gurgite prouocare Lirim.

Thus Domitian's epic subjugation of the river imposes a Callima-
chean aesthetic on it; instead of flowing with unchecked force, the
curbed river will be pure, a quality enabling it to challenge even the
open sea.[33]

The second example is *Silv.* 4. 6, a description of the small statue of
Hercules owned by Novius Vindex. At 4. 6. 37–8 the statue is
'paruusque uideri | sentirique ingens'; the epic figure of Hercules is
transformed into a small work of art. The paradox of grand subject
matter expressed on a small scale is also alluded to in 43: 'tam magna
breui mendacia formae'; the great care which attended the statue's

---

[32] Cf. Prop. 3. 3. 24 'medio maxima turba mari est', where *turba* punningly suggests
a dangerous *turbo*.
[33] Gibson (1995), 12–13; cf. Newlands (2002), 308.

creation (44–6) suggests the *labor* typically associated with 'Callima-
cheanism'.[34] Statius then evokes Callimachus (47–9):

> tale nec Idaeis quicquam Telchines in antris
> nec stolidus Brontes nec qui polit arma deorum
> Lemnius exigua potuisset ludere massa.

The Telchines, as Coleman notes, are associated with metal-working,
but they also recall the opening of the *Aetia* prologue, where they
complain that Callimachus has not written a lengthy epic.[35] Mention
of Brontes, the Cyclops, abusively called 'stolidus', may echo another
line of the *Aetia* prologue (fr. 1. 20), where the poet declares that
thunder (βροντᾶν) is not his preserve but that of Zeus. The reference
to Vulcan as the polisher of 'arma deorum' also evokes epic; the
overall effect of the passage is an affirmation of the artistic merit and
refinement of small scale work. *ludere* is perhaps a discordant note, as
Coleman comments, but the Callimachean qualities of the passage
seem confirmed by the reference in l. 51 to Hercules' role in the *Aetia*
in the episode of Molorchus (frr. 54–9 Pf.; cf. *SH* 254–69); moreover,
the poem concludes by comparing Vindex favourably with the pre-
vious 'epic' owners (Alexander, Hannibal, and Sulla), who would
have been unable to match the poetry with which Vindex will
celebrate the deeds of Hercules (99–109).

I hope to have shown that the 'poetics' of the *Silvae* are not confined
to Statius' well-known remarks on the quickness of his composition.
We should not uncritically accept Statius' *apologia*; there is ample
evidence in both the prefaces and the poems which allows a more
complex evaluation of Statius' attitude to his poetry. The frequent
combination of modesty and assertion (compare the end of *Thebaid* 12
where he tells his epic not to challenge Virgil, simultaneously suggest-
ing diffidence and rivalry), coupled with the poet's interest in the
work's more lasting qualities, and the traces of Callimachean poetics
that I have documented, would suggest that Statius, in common with
other Roman poets, did not regard his small-scale compositions as
mere trifles. This tension between caution and confidence is best
paralleled by Catullus' first poem, where, within a poem of only ten
lines, the poet expects poetry initially referred to as *nugae* to have a

---

[34] Cf. e.g. Call. *Epigr.* 27. 4, Cat. 95.
[35] Gibson (1995), 13; cf. Newlands (2002), 78.

lasting survival. With Statius, as with Catullus, we must not be too much convinced by protestations of levity.

The status of Book 5

Book 5 contains five poems. The first is an *epicedion* honouring the dead Priscilla, the wife of Abascantus, whose role as Domitian's *ab epistulis* involved him heavily in imperial correspondence.[36] The second is also concerned with public service, being addressed to the young Crispinus as he is about to embark on his career in public life. Both these poems are in keeping with the general tenor of the poems in the earlier books of the *Silvae*: they are addressed to men of some public standing and concentrate heavily on praise of the addressees and those associated with them. The third, the longest poem in the whole of the *Silvae*, is an *epicedion* for Statius' father, detailing his career as a teacher both in Naples and in Rome and his influence on Statius' poetry. The fourth, the shortest of the poems in the *Silvae*, is a complaint addressed in the first person to the god of sleep, Somnus, appealing for relief from insomnia. The fifth, which is incomplete, is an *epicedion* for a child in Statius' household. Though one might feel that 5. 3 and 5. 5 can perhaps be paralleled in *Silv.* 3. 5, where Statius addresses his own wife, all these last three poems are different from the first two in the book, in that they are not, as is usual in the *Silvae*, addressed to any patron or friend of Statius.

Markland suspected that the last book of the *Silvae* was published posthumously,[37] and the arguments have remained largely the same throughout the succeeding scholarship.[38] Most recently Laguna (1992), 11–12 has offered three reasons in favour of this hypothesis: (*a*) the contrast between the prose prefaces to the first four books and their counterpart in the fifth book, which only refers to the opening poem; (*b*) book 5 is longer than any of the other books of the *Silvae*,[39] even before we consider the likelihood that 5. 5 contained in excess of

---

[36] On the term *epicedion*, see p. xxxiii below.   [37] Markland on 5. 1 *epist.*

[38] See e.g. Vollmer (1898), 3 n. 7, Cancik (1965), 18, Newmyer (1979), 49, Bright (1980), 52.

[39] Laguna also notes the great disparity between the lengths of the individual poems: Book Five contains not only the longest poem of the *Silvae* (5. 3: 293 lines, without including any lacunae), but also the shortest (5. 4: 19 lines). Compare, however, the great diversity of length of poems in *Silvae* 2 and 4; Book 2, as well as containing a long *epicedion* (2. 1: 234 lines), also includes two poems of 37 and 30 lines respectively (2. 4 and 2. 5), whilst of the nine poems of Book 4, six are of 67 lines or less (4. 1, 4. 2, 4. 5, 4. 7, 4. 8, and 4. 9).

two hundred lines;[40] (*c*) it is unusual, in that only 5. 1 and 5. 2 are addressed to living individuals; Laguna argues that the more personal poems 5. 3, 5. 4, and 5. 5 represent a divergence from Statius' earlier practice of addressing poems to prominent figures, including the emperor.

The strongest of these arguments is (*a*). The absence of a proper preface to the whole book is certainly striking; it could further be argued that the opening letter to Abascantus was seized upon by an editor who wished to have some prose counterpart to the openings of the first four books. The availability of such a letter may further indicate that the process of editing took place at an early stage, since the letter would be unlikely to have survived for long on its own.[41] The possible counterargument that an original preface to the whole book was lost and then replaced by the letter to Abascantus is difficult, since it would suggest that Statius' preface disappeared from the tradition at an extremely early stage in the transmission, at a time when it was nevertheless possible for an editor to gain access to the letter.[42]

The second and third arguments are less decisive. Even adding another hundred or so lines to 5. 5 does not represent a great difference in the length of the book, which would then be in the region of 950 lines.[43] The length of the books of the *Silvae* would neverthless fall within a range of variation similar to that found within Statius' own *Thebaid* or Virgil's *Aeneid*.[44] As for the personal character

---

[40] Laguna (1992), 12 n. 37 demonstrates that the average length of a Statian *epicedion* (discounting 5. 5) is 222 lines. His sample of only five, however, includes one oddity (2. 6, 105 lines), so that caution is required when speculating on the probable length of 5. 5. See also Bright (1980), 52–3.

[41] Compare the presence in some of the *tituli* of *cognomina* and *nomina* which are not attested elsewhere. Coleman (1988), p. xxviii, who subsequently doubts whether the *tituli* are by Statius (a doubt I endorse), interprets this as evidence of their early date: 'It is likely that the full nomenclature derives from a contemporary source, if not from St. himself.'

[42] Note that the letter which was published 'de editione Thebaidos meae' (4 pr. 17–18) does not survive.

[43] Bright (1980), 70 notes that Cancik (1965), 18 commented on the unusual ending of book 5 with an *epicedion*, and wonders whether Cancik implies that there might have been other poems which followed. However, his own interpretation of the structure of Book Five (70–3) would suggest a rejection of this view.

[44] The books of the *Thebaid* range from 720 lines (*Theb.* 1) to 946 lines (*Theb.* 6). *Achilleid* 1, the only completed book of the *Achilleid*, has 960 lines. The books of the *Aeneid* range from 705 (*Aen.* 4) to 952 lines (*Aen.* 12). The books of the *Silvae* are as follows: 792 lines (Book 1), 773 lines (2), 763 lines (3), 724 lines (4), and 841 lines (5). I have not included any lacunae in these

of the poems in this book,[45] 5. 3 and 5. 5, the two poems in question, represent a continuation of and variation on Statius' earlier work on the genre of *epicedion*, so that the shift of focus is not especially startling, particularly as Statius had already included a poem to his wife in *Silvae* 3. 5.

Nevertheless, the absence of a proper preface is strong evidence for some form of posthumous publication. Acceptance of this need not, however, imply an abdication of critical responsibility. The nature of the collection of poems in *Silvae* 5 is still a legitimate area of enquiry. Though Statius may have not published the book himself, issues such as the ordering of the poems are at least worth raising. Even if the ordering is entirely editorial, the considerations which might have informed the editor's choice are still of interest.

A few simple points can be made.[46] First, the book observes a neat pattern, each *epicedion* being separated from the next by an intervening poem. This gives proper balance; to have placed all the laments at the beginning of the work would have led to an imbalance. Secondly, although 5. 1 and the other two laments (in which Statius explores the genre through *self*-consolation) are related, it is nevertheless the case that 5. 1 and 5. 2, as the opening of a book, are consistent with Statius' previous practice of addressing poems to other persons. Perhaps a projected book only contained two poems at the time of Statius' death; the editor may then have supplemented the first two poems with other material. *Silv.* 5. 3, as I argue in the introduction to that poem, appears to have been composed in two stages; it is also possible that it may never have been published by Statius, despite its qualities of self-affirmation.[47] Poem 5. 4 is certainly *sui generis* in the *Silvae*; so Statius may have been unwilling to include it in his published collections. Finally, 5. 5 may be unfinished (the result of death?) or it may be truncated as a result of manuscript damage: we cannot be sure. Certainty eludes us.

---

totals. On the lengths of ancient poetry books, see further Birt (1882), 289–307 and note especially the tabulation of Latin poets given on 292–3.

[45] Only 5. 3 and 5. 5 can with certainty be said to fall into this category.

[46] For more elaborate (and hence unconvincing) analyses of Book 5, see Vollmer (1898), 546 (introductory remarks on 5. 4), Cancik (1965), 18, Newmyer (1979), 58, 129–30, Bright (1980), 70.

[47] See p. 265 n.14 below.

'Consolation' and 'self-consolation' in *Silvae* 5

(i) *Background*

Amongst the many ancient responses to death, not only in literature but in funerary monuments and inscriptions, are the need to comfort the bereaved, and the desire to commemorate the dead.[48] As early as Homer, the need to provide comfort is represented, for example, with Achilles' meeting with Priam in the last book of the *Iliad*, where Achilles, the slayer of Hector, consoles Priam for his son's loss (*Il.* 24. 518–51, 599–620);[49] it is also in Homer that we find references to commemoration of the dead. In subsequent periods, these themes are found in both prose and verse. For example the funeral oration pronounced by Pericles at Thuc. 2. 35–46 combines these elements, although the actual consolations to the bereaved are somewhat muted (§§44–6).[50] One notable structural feature of this *epitaphios* is the placing of the praise of the dead (§§42–3) before the consolatory material: Pericles alludes to a possible effect of this when he remarks that parents who are too old to have more children are to be consoled by the fame of their dead offspring (§. 44. 4): ὅσοι δ' αὖ παρηβήκατε, τόν τε πλέονα κέρδος ὃν ηὐτυχεῖτε βίον ἡγεῖσθε καὶ τόνδε βραχὺν ἔσεσθαι, καὶ τῇ τῶνδε εὐκλείᾳ κουφίζεσθε. Here εὐκλεία need not merely be the reputation that will ensue in the future, but may also be the honour conferred on the dead by the oration; that praise is the purpose is specifically indicated (Thuc. 2. 34. 6 λέγει ἐπ' αὐτοῖς ἔπαινον τὸν πρέποντα. In Rome, we may note that a funeral oration was called a *laudatio funebris*.[51]

The rhetoricians also treat praise as an important element of consolatory speeches. Menander Rhetor distinguishes the speech of

---

[48] 'Consolation' in its various forms has a vast bibliography. Key general studies include Kassel (1958), Esteve-Forriol (1962), Scourfield (1993), 15–33, and Lillo Redonet (2001); for a survey of scholarship in the field since the late 19th c., see Lillo Redonet (2001), 21–6. For bibliography and discussion of consolations in Statius, see van Dam (1984), 63–9 and Laguna (1992), 241–56.

[49] For interpretation of this scene as consolation, see [Plu.] *ad Apoll.* 105 B–C; cf. Kassel (1958), 92, Scourfield (1993), 15–16.

[50] For a concise introduction to the ἐπιτάφιος λόγος, see Hornblower (1991), 294–6; see further Stupperich (1977), 33–56.

[51] On the Roman funeral oration, see Durry (1950), pp. xiv–xxii, Kierdorf (1980); note also Cic. *de Orat.* 2. 341 'nostrae laudationes, quibus in foro utimur, aut testimoni breuitatem habent nudam atque inornatam, aut scribuntur ad funebrem contionem, quae ad orationis laudem minime accommodata est.' On the development of funeral orations for women, see Durry (1950), pp. xx f., Esteve-Forriol (1962), 122–3.

consolation, the παραμυθητικὸς λόγος (413. 5–414. 30), and the fu-
neral speech, the ἐπιτάφιος (418. 5–422. 4), as well as describing
procedure for the μονῳδία (434. 10–437. 4), whose purpose is more
the expression of grief (θρηνεῖν καὶ κατοικτίζεσθαι, 434. 14), although
there is again an encomiastic element. The difference between the
παραμυθητικὸς λόγος and the ἐπιτάφιος is that the former is mainly
devoted to consolation, whereas the latter, which may include ad-
dresses concerning those long dead, need not include a consolatory
element; encomium predominates (418. 13–14). Note also the pre-
scriptions of Ps.-Dionysius (ii. 277–83 Radermacher), which, whilst
neither so strict nor so specific as those of Menander Rhetor, never-
theless combine praise and consolation.[52]

An important element of the consolatory tradition is the influence
of philosophic approaches to consolation. As Scourfield notes, con-
solatory themes are found in dialogues of Plato such as the *Phaedo*, but
formal philosophical consolation appears to have begun with the
influential Περὶ πένθους ('On Grief') of Crantor (*c.*325–275 BC),
which is now lost.[53] Another important lost work is Cicero's *Consolatio*
to himself for the loss of his daughter, Tullia; though Cicero read
Crantor (as attested by Plin. *Nat.* pr. 22), modern scholars have rightly
emphasized that Crantor's was one of many different philosophical
texts that he read while composing it (Cic. *Att.* 12. 14. 3, *Tusc.* 3. 76; cf.
Jerome, *Epist.* 60. 5. 2).[54] As well as other lengthier treatises such as
the Senecan consolations (*Dial.* 6, 11, 12) and Plutarch's *Consolatio ad
uxorem* and the *Consolatio ad Apollonium*,[55] mention should also be made
of the tradition of the letter of consolation, of which there are
examples in the Ciceronian corpus such as Cic. *Fam.* 4. 5, Ser.
Sulpicius Rufus' letter to Cicero on the death of Tullia.[56] However,
as will be seen, Statius often adopts positions diametrically opposed to
those found in philosophical consolation.

---

[52] On rhetorical approaches to consolation, see further Kassel (1958), 40–8.

[53] Scourfield (1993), 18–20.

[54] See Scourfield (1993), 20, Lillo Redonet (2001), 199–200.

[55] On prose treatises in Latin, see Lillo Redonet (2001), 115–18, 195–277; on Plutarch's
Consolatio ad uxorem, see S. B. Pomeroy (1999), 59–81, and on the *Consolatio ad Apollonium*, of
uncertain authorship, see Hani (1985), 3–39 (especially 3–12 on the ascription to Plutarch).

[56] For letters of consolation, see Scourfield (1993), 20–1, Lillo Redonet (2001), 110–15,
125–94.

Various verse examples are attested in Latin.[57] Neoteric interest in
lament is attested by Licinius Calvus' lament for Quintilia,[58] while
later examples include Ov. *Am.* 2. 6, a lament for the dead parrot of
Corinna, and 3. 9, on the death of Tibullus. Ov. *Pont.* 4. 11, is an
example of an approach to death which is more concerned with
consolation, and there is also the *Epicedion Drusi*, also known as the
Consolatio ad Liuiam.[59] The potential for such poetry to attract atten-
tion and interest in Rome is reflected in Tacitus' account of Clutorius
Priscus, who unwisely followed up a successful poem on the death of
Germanicus with a similar poem anticipating the death of Tiberius'
son Drusus (Tac. *Ann.* 3. 49).[60] In the case of Statius, it is also worth
noting that he was brought up in Naples, a city which is one of only a
few to set up public inscriptions of consolation.[61]

Statius' poems of lamentation (*Silv.* 2. 1, 2. 6, 3. 3, 5. 1, 5. 3, 5. 5) are
variously referred to. He himself calls *Silv.* 2. 1 an *epicedion* at 2 pr. 7–9,
2. 6 is called a *consolatio* at 2 pr. 20, while 3. 3 is described as
aliquod . . . solacium at 3 pr. 14–15; scholars have called the poems
consolations or *epicedia*. The manuscript titles of the poems cannot
be relied on,[62] so for convenience I shall refer to these poems as
epicedia; the apparent interchangeability of generic titles is in any case
suggested by Ps.-Dionysius *Opusc.* ii. 278 Radermacher.[63]

In terms of structure and arrangement of material, there are
certainly similarities between the Statian examples. Thus Esteve-
Forriol's analyses show that the typical scheme of the Statian *epicedion*
consists of an introduction, a *laudatio* (sometimes with a *comploratio*), a
description of the final illness and death of the deceased, and a final
section of *consolatio*.[64] These poems are offered in response to a

---

[57] For brief remarks on archaic and Hellenistic antecedents in Greek, see Esteve-Forriol
(1962), 1–13; cf. ibid. 27–31 for discussion of Horace's adaptation of motifs from early Greek
elegy in *Carm.* 1. 24, on the death of Quintilius Varus.

[58] See Licinius Calvus fr. 15–16 Courtney (*FLP*, pp. 207–9), Esteve-Forriol (1962), 21–6.

[59] On the *Epicedion Drusi*, see Esteve-Forriol (1962), Lillo Redonet (2001), 324–32.

[60] See Esteve-Forriol (1962), 55–6, who also discusses the poem which Tiberius himself
wrote on the death of L. Caesar (Suet. *Tib.* 70. 2 'cuius est titulus conquestio de morte
L. Caesaris').

[61] See Buresch (1894), 457–9, Lomas (1993), 177–81; cf. Leiwo (1995), 133–42, who notes
similarities between Neapolitan consolation decrees written in Greek and formulae used in
Latin consolatory decrees from nearby Puteoli.

[62] See Coleman (1988), pp. xxviii–xxxii. B.-J. Schröder (1999), 180–9 is less sceptical.

[63] Note that Statius' description of *Silv.* 2. 1 as an *epicedion* does not fulfil the strict
condition laid down by Proclus (ap. Phot. *Biblio.* 321ᵃ30), that the *epicedion* was properly a
poem delivered before the corpse. See further van Dam (1984), 67 and Laguna (1992), 252.

[64] See Esteve-Forriol (1962), 78–107; cf. Newmyer (1979), 64.

person's grief (see e.g. *Silv.* 2 pr. 12, 20; 2. 1. 1; 3 pr. 14; 5. 1 *epist.* 7; 5.1.3);
their setting is thus consolatory, though it should be remembered that
consolation can be effected through *allowing* lamentation.[65] *Silvae* 5
also explores the related theme of self-consolation in Statius' own
response to his grief for his father (5. 3) and for a child (5. 5). Rather
than deal with each of the three *epicedia* separately in the introduction
to each poem, I have chosen to group the three poems here, so that all
the general material relating to *epicedion* and consolation is gathered in
one place.

(ii) *Poem One*

In the prose letter that precedes the poem, Statius declares that he
cannot pass over Abascantus' tears for his wife, Priscilla ('ingratus
sum si lacrimas tuas transeo', *Silv.* 5. 1 *epist.* 7). This hints at a
commemorative purpose to the poem, and also raises the possibility
that not only Priscilla, but also Abascantus, are to be praised and
memorialized. In the poem, however, Statius goes on to declare his
wish to provide Abascantus with *solacia* (3), which seems to imply a
consolatory design; *Silv.* 5. 1, moreover, ends with a request to Abas-
cantus to give up his grief (247–8). However, in spite of the strength of
such a framing device, it is worth asking how consolation and praise
are balanced throughout the poem.[66]

There is little direct consolation. The concluding section (247–60)
consoles Abascantus, assuring him that he need not fear that his wife
will meet the traditional horrors of the Underworld; instead, she will
be welcomed among the heroines of Elysium (254–7), and will plead
with the infernal powers to grant longevity to Abascantus (259–62).
Priscilla's speech to her husband (177–93) also functions as consola-
tion, since she tells him not to grieve, and not to neglect his duties to
the emperor.

Absent, however, are the more rigorous arguments associated with
philosophical consolation (even at *Silv.* 2. 1. 209–19 the argument that
everyone perishes hardly counts as such). Contrast, for example,
Statius' answer to Abascantus' fears of the Underworld, the assurance
that Priscilla is in Elysium, with Seneca's stern dismissal of such
terrors as irrelevant poetic invention (*Dial.* 6. 19. 4). The argument
that death is annihilation (e.g. Sen. *Dial.* 6. 19. 5 'quod uero ipsum
nihil est et omnia in nihilum redigit') is wholly foreign to this poem,

---

[65] Cf. Konstan (2001), 64.   [66] On *Silv.* 5. 1, see Esteve-Forriol (1962), 94–9.

which suggests that Priscilla lives on, not only in Elysium, but also in her fine tomb (called a *domus* at 237).[67] Similarly, Statius does not suggest that, because there can be far worse calamities, a sense of proportion is needed (see e.g. Ser. Sulpicius Rufus at Cic. *Fam.* 4. 5. 4). The uncertainty of Fortuna is mentioned (143–4), but does not receive a sustained treatment. Nor does Statius offer Abascantus *exempla* of those who showed fortitude in response to bereavement;[68] indeed Abascantus is positively associated with such *exempla* of extreme grief as Niobe, Aurora, Thetis, and Orpheus (33–6, 202–4).[69]

There is a sense in which the poem, whilst ostensibly presented as a consolation, actually celebrates the very grief it is intended to assuage.[70] Abascantus is praised not just as the emperor's loyal *ab epistulis* (39, 76–107, 132–4, 207–8, 239–41) but also as a grieving and devoted husband (1–9, 20–42, 158–246). Despite the request to Abascantus to abstain from grief (247), the poem monumentalizes not only the dead Priscilla (15) but also Abascantus' grief for her, which is recorded in a manner which emphasizes his *pietas* (see 238 n. for Priscilla's tomb as an index of her husband's grief).[71] The hints in the introductory epistle that Abascantus' grief is a powerful inspiration for the poem (see above) suggest that Statius would regret a failure to record his friend's grief; compare *Silv.* 3. 3. 38–9 'uenturosque tuus durabit in annos | me monstrante dolor'.

Much of 5. 1 is thus devoted to praise. Statius' practice, however, differs from the recommendations of Menander and Ps.-Dionysius in that praise is restricted neither to the subject of the consolation nor to specific sections. Three persons are commended. First, and most obviously, Statius praises the dead Priscilla, whose strength of

---

[67] But note the tension in Sen. *Dial.* 6 between the view that death is annihilation (*Dial.* 6. 26. 7 'Nos quoque felices animae et aeterna sortitae . . . et ipsae parua ruinae ingentis accessio in antiqua elementa uertemur') and the encouragement to Marcia that her son will join his grandfather and other noble Romans in the heavens (*Dial.* 6. 25).

[68] Cf. e.g. [Plu.] *ad Apoll.* 106 b–c (where Antimachus' use of examples of others' misfortunes in his *Lyde* to console himself is noted), Cic. *Fam.* 4. 6. 1, Sen. *Dial.* 6. 14–16, and see further Münzer (1920), 376–408 (on examples in Cicero's *Consolatio*), Scourfield (1993), 117–18.

[69] For the idea of becoming an *exemplum* of inconsolable grief, contrast Sen. *Ep.* 63. 14 'tam immodice fleui, ut, quod minime uelim, inter exempla sim eorum quos dolor uicit'.

[70] Contrast the precept of [Plu.] *ad Apoll.* 117 F on the need to avoid those who stir up and share in grief διὰ κολακείαν, as opposed to those who offer nobler consolations; cf. Lucian, *Demonax* 24, for Demonax' refusal to join others in encouraging Herodes Atticus to mourn the death of Polydeuces.

[71] Contrast Mart. 1. 33. 3–4: 'non luget quisquis laudari, Gellia, quaerit, | ille dolet uere qui sine teste dolet.'

character and morality are commended at 45–74 and 117–34 (see also her final devotion and speech to her husband at 171–96). Secondly, Statius praises Abascantus, as noted above. Finally, as befits a poem addressed to a prominent servant of the emperor, the poet praises Domitian as well (37–41, 79–83, 189–91, 207–8, 239–46, 261);[72] compare his remark in the introductory epistle to this poem (5 .1 *epist.* 8–9): 'nam qui bona fide deos colit amat et sacerdotes.'

The paucity of direct consolation has been noted. But this does not mean that the overall effect of the work is not consolatory. Rather than using the typical philosophical arguments, Statius responds in a gentler and more sympathetic fashion; only at the end of the poem is Abascantus told not to grieve. The poem relies on description, not prescription.[73] Statius describes Priscilla's marriage, her concern for her husband's duties, her illness, and her death, all in a manner which reflects credit not only on her but on her husband. Abascantus is to be consoled by praise rather than by reasoned argument.

(iii) *Poem Three*

With *Silv.* 5. 3 and 5. 5, Statius does not write to console or to please others, but composes for himself. Nevertheless, the nature and function of praise is still an issue. As *Silv.* 5. 1 illustrates, a lament for a dead person need not solely be concerned with glorifying the deceased, but can also praise others. Similarly 5. 3 is not only a lament for the elder Statius, but also a presentation of the poet's own career and achievements.[74] As for consolation, its absence from much of 5. 3 is noticeable, and even 5. 3. 277–93, which has been seen as *consolatio*, is perhaps less confident in tone, as will be discussed in section (v) below.

In 5. 1 the eternal poetic memorial for the dead Priscilla was contrasted with Abascantus' attempts to commemorate his wife through the plastic arts, explicitly at 5. 1. 1–15, and implicitly in the subsequent account of the grandiose tomb he built for her (5. 1. 222– 46). This same motif appears in 5. 3: at 5. 3. 47–63 (see nn.) Statius' apparent desire to build a physical memorial to his father also suggests a metaphorical and poetic memorial. Thus Statius combines

---

[72] Cf. Leberl (2004), 231, 240–1 for remarks on the technique of praise of a courtier in *Silv.* 3. 4 and 5. 1 as a form of praise of the emperor.

[73] Compare Seneca's advice to Polybius (*Dial.* 11. 18. 7) that he will enjoy recalling his dead brother 'si tibi memoriam eius iucundam magis quam flebilem feceris'; cf. [Plu.] *ad Apoll.* 114 c–d, Kassel (1958), 89–90.

[74] On *Silv.* 5. 3, see Esteve-Forriol (1962), 100–5.

the themes of physical monuments and poetic memorial, evoking Hor. *Carm.* 3. 30.[75] As well as poetic commemoration of his father, there is also an element of Horace's monument to himself: at 5. 3. 61–3 Statius affirms his desire to match the poetry of Homer and Virgil, whilst singing of his father. The lament for his father thus functions as self-presentation and self-commemoration, not merely as a record of Statius' grief (though he is careful to record his sorrow, as at 35, 45, 64–79, 262, 275–6),[76] but also as an affirmation of his poetry. Such affirmation also occurs at 5. 3. 80–8, where Statius declines to use such conventional *exempla* as dying swans and the Heliades. This passage is a compliment to his father, but it is also a statement of the special qualities which Statius has invested in his poem;[77] compare 5. 3. 264–5, where Statius declares that his father could not have surpassed the laments which were offered to him.

Another aspect of praise in the poem is reflected glory. This works in two ways. First, Statius' account of his own successes reflects credit on his father; Esteve-Forriol (1962), 102–3 rightly includes ll. 209–38 as part of the vast *laudatio* of the father which dominates the poem. That Statius' achievements are a credit to his father is evident not only from his status as a pupil of his father, but also from allusion to the epinician theme of the great delight experienced by a father who sees his son's victory. But Statius' far more extensive praise of his father is also a source of reflected glory for himself. Even the epinician motif of victorious father and son can be used as a means of praising the son, as at Pi. *P.* 10. 22–6.[78] Glorification of his father throughout the poem affirms Statius' own poetic credentials; at 5. 3. 209–11 the Muses admitted Statius to the groves of poetry, when he affirmed his poetic ancestry ('cum stirpe tua descendere dixi, | admisere deae'). Compare 5. 2, where Statius devotes much attention to Bolanus, the father of Crispinus, in order to honour a young man who has not yet had the opportunity to accomplish much in his career.[79] Statius' use of his father in this poem thus enhances his own achievements.

---

[75] Mention of the pyramids in 5. 3. 49–50 (see n.) is the most specific allusion to Horace's poem, but the shared motif of the poetic monument in both passages is obvious enough.

[76] Cf. 5. 1 *epist.* 7 'ingratus sum si lacrimas tuas transeo', emphasizing the importance of recording the grief suffered by Abascantus.

[77] On the ambiguities of 'nota nimis uati', see 5. 3. 85 n.

[78] See 5. 3. 216–17 n.

[79] See the Introduction to 5. 2 (pp. 176–8 below).

For a poem about his father Statius would have had few models.[80]
Nevertheless two relevant accounts of fathers are those of Horace and
Ovid. Horace affectionately discusses his father's moral guidance in
S. 1. 4 and 1. 6,[81] texts which Statius may reflect in his praise of his
father's poetic instruction, although the moral element is absent in 5.
3. As for Ovid, the encouragement with which Statius' father greeted
his poetic ambitions differs greatly from Ovid's father's insistence on
both of his sons following a public career (*Tr.* 4. 10. 17–40). *Tr.* 4. 10 is
neverthless an important antecedent for *Silv.* 5. 3, since the earlier
poem is also an autobiography, presenting Ovid's career in a manner
not wholly dissimilar from Statius' presentation of himself in this
poem. For possible echoes of *Tr.* 4. 10 in *Silv.* 5. 3 see the notes on
73, 247, 253–4, and 264–5.

   Silv. 5. 3 is not merely a lament for Statius' father, but also a piece of
self-affirmation. By implication, Statius will continue the high stand-
ards that his father set.

(iv) *Poem Five*

The truncated state of *Silv.* 5. 5 is much to be regretted,[82] since in this
poem even more than in 5. 3 Statius confronts and juxtaposes his
poetic role as a provider of consolation with his own bereavement. In
two of his consolations addressed to others, he had briefly drawn
attention to his own losses (2. 1. 33–34 and 3. 3. 39–40), but in this
poem he offers a more sustained and challenging examination of the
issue. At first sight, Statius' poetic difficulties at the beginning of 5. 3
seem comparable to his lack of inspiration in 5. 5. But in 5. 3 Statius is
at least able to appeal to his father for inspiration, so that the problem
of a substitute for Apollo and Bacchus (5. 3. 5–18), who have deserted
him, is at least resolved; thus the poem ends with a request for the
father to visit him in dreams and give his son his habitual advice (5. 3.
288–90). In 5. 5, however, the issue of inspiration is not so neatly
solved; the initial picture of Statius' estrangement from Apollo and
the Muses (5. 5. 1–5) is not modified by the appearance of any
substitute source of inspiration for the poem; indeed Statius not

---

[80] On Statius' presentation of his father, see Önnerfors (1974), 136–43.

[81] See Hor. *S.* 1. 4. 105–29 (where Horace recalls how his father used to point out to him
persons whose conduct he should not imitate) and 1. 6. 71–90, where he again recalls the
guidance of Horatius senior, who had insisted on educating his son at Rome.

[82] For analysis of the structure of 5. 5, comprising only an introduction (1–65) and a
portion of the *laudatio* (66–87), see Esteve-Forriol (1962), 105–7.

only suggests that he has been abandoned by his divine supporters, but also raises the possibility that he has caused offence (5. 5. 3–8). Moreover he continues to allude to his loss of confidence in his own poetic ability (5. 5. 28–34, 49–52). Such allusions are made more pointed by Statius' recollection of his previous success as a source of consolation to others, thus inverting the allusions to his own loss of his father in consolations given to others. Whereas in 2. 1 and 3. 3 mention of his own bereavement serves as a kind of *captatio benevolentiae*, reassuring the addressee that Statius has experienced similar loss (*Silv.* 2. 1. 33–4, 3. 3. 39–42), the effect of his recollection of his previous role as a source of consolation in 5. 5. 38–48 is to undermine the very process embodied in the poem. The recollection assumes an ironic and disturbing resonance; the impression is of failure, since the poet who could console others is unable to respond to his own loss. This negative tone is confirmed by Statius' use of medical imagery in ll. 42–3, using the common imagery of consolation as a medicine offered in healing of a wound.[83] Statius' presentation of himself as a doctor unable to heal his own wound recalls the pathetic irony of Umbro, the Marsian who could not heal himself (Virg. *A.* 7. 756–60).[84] By alluding to this epic motif, Statius emphasizes his failure to cure himself by means of poetry.

Statius' relation to the *puer* (who is not named) stands in contrast with the *pueri* who feature in two of Statius' other consolations (2. 1 and 2. 6). A feature of this poem, at least in the text as we have it, is Statius' emphasis on paternal rather than erotic feelings towards the child. While 2. 1 does have a section comparing the ties of blood with those of adoption, introduced by Melior's belief that he was like a father to the boy Glaucias (2. 1. 81), Statius does not take much care to obscure potentially erotic aspects: thus there is an extended treatment of Glaucias' beauty (2. 1. 38–51) and in his account of the boy's dealings with Melior, Statius refers to the boy in such terms as *deliciae* and *curae* (2. 1. 71, and see van Dam).[85] In 2. 6 the erotic nature of Ursus' relationship with Philetos is first suggested by a similarly extensive description of the boy's beauty in ll. 21–47,[86] and more fully revealed at the end of the poem, where Statius expresses the

---

[83] See further on 5. 1. 16 below.
[84] For the motif of the doctor in need of healing, see e.g. *Il.* 11. 833–6, E. fr. 1086, Luke 4:23.
[85] Mart. 6. 28. 3 refers to Glaucias as 'cari deliciae breues patroni'.
[86] See further Vessey (1986), 2784 with n. 105.

hope that the Fates will grant Ursus the chance of loving 'another Phileton' ('alium tibi Fata Phileton, | forsan et ipse dabit' 2. 6. 103–4) in language which seems to recall Virg. *Ecl.* 2. 73 'inuenies alium, si te hic fastidit, Alexim', the conclusion of Corydon's amorous plaint for the boy Alexis. Although it is perhaps an inevitable consequence of the extreme youth of Statius' *puer* in this poem, indicated by such details as the account of his first attempts to speak (86) and the implication that the boy had but little time in which to enjoy the freedom granted to him, it is nevertheless true that the erotic element is absent from the poem (in spite of the manuscript title, 'Epicedion in puerum suum', which cannot be authentic). There is thus no account of the child's beauty, and there is not even much on his character, apart from a determined attempt in 66–9 to emphasize that there is no comparison between Statius' child and the stereotyped image of a precocious pretty boy from Egypt, a topos which Statius had previously used at 2. 1. 72–5.[87]

The nature of parenthood is a central theme of the poem. The motif is first established with Statius' admission that he was not the child's father ('non fueram genitor' 11), an admission which however instead of settling the issue serves to prepare the way for Statius to redefine what it is to be a father.[88] This is reflected by his challenge to real parents who have also lost children (13–14); Statius continues by noting that his grief will surpass even that aroused where there are ties of blood (22). The theme is resumed at l. 69, where Statius announces his own claim on the child ('meus ille meus'), and recalls his own presence and involvement in the child's birth, asking dramatically what more could have been done by the child's parents. The confrontation of natural and adopted parents is most tellingly realized in 73–5, where Statius explains how he gave the child his freedom when he was 'sub ipsis | uberibus'. In the remaining lines of the poem Statius describes his dealings with the child in a manner entirely suggestive of an affectionate father's participation in his child's earliest years; at 79–80 Statius' paternal feelings are again stressed, with especially pathetic effect, when he remarks that while the boy was alive he did not desire children of his own.

---

[87] On the signification of terms such as *deliciae*, *delicatus*, and *delicium*, see Nielsen (1990), who argues that in general such terminology does not in itself denote a sexual relationship. On such children, see further W. J. Slater (1974), Wiedemann (1989), 30–1, Pollini (2003).

[88] For the theme of surrogate parenthood in this poem, see Fantham (1999), 67–70.

Thus, throughout the poem as we have it, Statius gives prominence to his paternal feelings. In part, perhaps, as evinced by the comparison with Egyptian *deliciae* in *Silv.* 5. 5. 66–9, Statius wished to indicate that the association was not open to misunderstanding, but, as attested by the use of the same motif in 2. 1. 72–5, this is unlikely to be the sole reason for the emphasis here. Affection must undoubtedly have been a motive, but what needs examination is Statius' *use* of his paternal claims in this poem. The answer may lie in his challenge to other parents in 13–14, which is resolved by Statius' assumption of the status of a father. By presenting himself as a father he is at once able to justify his grief, and to express it. Comparison with 2. 1 is instructive: the section where Melior is treated as Glaucias' father is preceded by a question, which implies the possibility of criticism of Melior's opulent arrangements for Glaucias' funeral (2. 1. 69–70): 'quid mirum, tanto si te pius altor honorat | funere?' By contrast 2. 6 opens with invective against those who would set a limit to grief, followed by the statement that a 'plaga minor' is nevertheless capable of causing 'maioraque uulnera', which suggests, though paradoxically, that Ursus' loss is not quite of the same order, since we are informed that it is a 'plaga minor'. Yet on other occasions Statius uses the technique of amplifying the importance of the deceased: at 3. 3. 8–12 the grief and anguish of Etruscus are such that an onlooker might think that Etruscus had lost either a wife or a child; in fact it is his father whom he is lamenting. The effect is thus to make the loss of a father more terrible, by comparison with the kind of bereavement which is not in keeping with the natural scheme of things. A similar implication of an untimely death is revealed at 3. 3. 20–1 'celeres genitoris filius annos | (mira fides!) nigrasque putat properasse sorores', where Statius hints that Etruscus experienced the loss of his father in the same way one would react to the death of a person who had died young. A close parallel is furnished by 5. 3. 73, where Statius says that his father seemed to him to be 'uiridi . . . ceu raptus ab aeuo', thus evoking the pathos of an untimely death in a context where such a motif would not be expected. Contrast, however, Priscilla's comment on the appropriateness of her dying before her husband ('saluo tamen ordine mortis' 5. 1. 181), where she offers consolation to her husband. Statius thus increases the pathos of an early death in 5. 5, by stressing his own role as the child's father.

However, Statius' use of the same motif, the amplification of a bereavement, differs in the poems which are concerned with himself.

Whereas in 3. 3 and 2. 1 the comparisons with such extreme forms of bereavement as the loss of a child, or the loss of a young wife, serve as a kind of compliment to the survivor,[89] such a device has a different function in a poem where Statius is consoling himself. In poems of the former type, emphasis on the severity of the bereavement does not itself challenge or undercut the process of consolation; indeed, Statius' consolation is elevated by the magnitude of suffering which it seeks to alleviate. However, for Statius to exaggerate the nature of his own grief when writing in a genre where there is at least the expectation of consolation may call into question the efficacy and indeed the purpose of the poem. While it is true that in 5. 5 we lack a final section equivalent to the close of 5. 3, the tendency of both of these poems to present personal bereavement in a heightened rather than mitigated form, and thus in a manner which seems opposed to any consolatory aim, adds weight to Statius' own remarks on the difficulty he experienced in consoling himself (5. 5. 42–3); his allusion to the epic motif of the healer unable to cure himself is a valuable key to the understanding of both 5. 5 and 5. 3.

(v) *The Failure of Consolation?*
The failure of consolation is something for which we have parallels in epic. After the killing of Archemorus by the serpent in Book 5 of the *Thebaid*, the dead child is variously lamented both by Hypsipyle, his nurse, and also by his parents. Book 6 opens with the funeral and then offers an account of a consolation offered by Adrastus to Lycurgus, the father of the child (*Theb.* 6. 45–53):

> ipse, datum quotiens intercisoque tumultu
> conticuit stupefacta domus, solatur Adrastus
> adloquiis genitorem ultro, nunc fata recensens
> resque hominum duras et inexorabile pensum,
> nunc aliam prolem mansuraque numine dextro
> pignora. nondum orsis modus, et lamenta redibant.
> ille quoque adfatus non mollius audit amicos
> quam trucis Ionii rabies clamantia ponto
> uota uirum aut tenues curant uaga fulmina nimbos.

Here Statius does not merely say that Adrastus tries to console Lycurgus for his loss, but even gives an account of the type of

---

[89] See p. xxxv above for discussion of Statius' treatment of Abascantus' grief as a vehicle for praising him.

arguments that Adrastus uses, such as, for example, the general reflections on the melancholy nature of the human condition: *nunc fata recensens | resque hominum duras et inexorabile pensum*. These arguments are in fact more typical of philosophical consolation than the consolatory poems of Statius. Nevertheless, the consolation fails, even before its delivery is complete (*nondum orsis modus, et lamenta redibant*) and the person at whom it is directed is in no way consoled.

This example from the *Thebaid* illustrates that consolation is not always successful. In the *Aeneid*, Aeneas wishes to console Dido (Virg. *A.* 4. 393–6):

> at pius Aeneas, quamquam lenire dolentem
> solando cupit et dictis auertere curas,
> multa gemens magnoque animum labefactus amore,
> iussa tamen diuum exsequitur classemque reuisit.

When Aeneas meets Dido again in the underworld, he does indeed attempt to console her. He fulfils his wish to offer her consolation, but of course it is too late (*A.* 6. 467–71):

> talibus Aeneas ardentem et torua tuentem
> lenibat dictis animum lacrimasque ciebat.
> illa solo fixos oculos auersa tenebat
> nec magis incepto uultum sermone mouetur
> quam si dura silex aut stet Marpesia cautes.

If consolation directed at others can fail, then this is also a possibility when consolation becomes 'self-consolation'. Statius draws attention to this possibility in *Silv.* 5. 5, when he comments that his accustomed role is that of consoler, yet now, in the light of the loss of the child, he is unable to help himself (*Silv.* 5. 5. 38–48):

> ille ego qui (quotiens!) blande matrumque patrumque
> uulnera, qui uiuos potui mulcere dolores,
> ille ego lugentum mitis solator, acerbis   40
> auditus tumulis et descendentibus umbris,
> deficio medicasque manus fomentaque quaero
> uulneribus subitura meis. nunc tempus, amici,
> quorum ego manantes oculos et saucia tersi
> pectora: reddite opem, seras exsoluite grates.   45
> nimirum cum uestra modis ego funera maestis   46
>   *   *   *   *   *   46a
> increpitans: 'qui damna doles aliena, repone   47
> infelix lacrimas et tristia carmina serua.'

Here Statius seems to imply the possibility that consolation may fail.[90] If the attempt at consolation fails with Statius himself, then what are we to make of his claim at the beginning of this passage that he is at other times successful in his consolation? Even outside 5. 3 and 5. 5, the poems addressed to Statius himself, we find the poet hinting at the possibility of failure, an insurance policy perhaps, but one which nevertheless points to the difficulty of the task in hand. In *Silv.* 5. 1, where Statius is consoling Abascantus for the loss of his wife Priscilla, Statius uses the common figure that one cannot expect immediate consolation to be successful (5. 1. 16–29): even Orpheus would have been unable to soothe the bereaved husband's grief with his poetry:

>   licet ipse leuandos
> ad gemitus siluis comitatus et amnibus Orpheus
> 25   adforet atque omnis pariter matertera uatem,
> omnis Apollineus tegeret Bacchique sacerdos,
> nil cantus, nil fila deis pallentis Auerni
> Eumenidumque audita comis mulcere ualerent:
> tantus in attonito regnabat pectore luctus.
> 30   nunc etiam adtactus refugit iam plana cicatrix
> dum canimus, grauibusque oculis uxorius instat
> imber. habentne pios etiamnum haec lumina fletus?
> mira fides!

Even when writing a year later (5. 1. 17), Statius records that Abascantus' grief is still powerful in its effects. This suggests the magnitude of the task which Statius is attempting, but another effect might be to convey that consolation can fail. It is worth looking at the coda of 5. 1. This section, which Esteve-Forriol classes as *consolatio*, significantly opens with the theme of the continuation of grief (5. 1. 247–8):

> quid nunc immodicos, iuuenum lectissime, fletus
> corde foues longumque uetas exire dolorem?

This, after some two hundred and forty lines, perhaps comes as a surprise. The lines that follow (247–61) do, however, provide consolatory arguments of a kind, such as the reassuring remark that Cerberus does not bark at those who are good (250), and the news that Proserpina is giving instructions to the heroines of Elysium to

---

[90] On the *ille ego* figure used in this passage, see 5. 3. 10 n., 5. 5. 38–41 n.

welcome Priscilla into their number (254–7). Consolations such as these are far removed from the more austere arguments associated with philosophic consolations, as has been already seen. Nevertheless, it is a striking feature of the whole poem that explicit consolation is confined to these closing lines.

In the equivalent section of 5. 3, Esteve-Forriol sees the *consolatio* as beginning at verse 277.[91] Similar motifs are common to both 5. 1 and 5. 3: in both poems Cerberus does not bark at the deceased, both poems present a gentle journey on Charon's craft across the river Styx, and in both poems appropriate companions greet the newly departed. In 5. 1, the heroines of Elysium are to welcome Priscilla; in 5. 3 Greek poets are asked to greet Statius' father. Thus on the surface, the end of 5. 3 appears to be very similar to 5. 1.

However, there is a difference. 5. 3. 277–93 is not a confident exposition of what happens to one who has died. Instead it is a *prayer* to the infernal powers for Statius' father to receive the kind of reception confidently promised for Priscilla in *Silvae* 5. 1. Hence the continuous use of the jussive subjunctive and the imperative in this part of 5. 3, as Statius first addresses the Underworld powers, then the poets of Greece, and finally his father himself. This may be contrasted with Statius' use of the indicative mood in consolations addressed to others, where reassuring descriptions of existence in the underworld are presented as firm statements.[92]

This use of the language of prayer might hint that 5. 3 does not end like 5. 1 on a note of comforting certainty. The optimistic consolation of 5. 1 ended with Statius reassuring Abascantus that his wife is successfully pleading for a long life for her husband from the Fates and the lords of the Underworld (5. 1. 259–62). The very last words of 5. 1 are 'certae iurant in uota sorores.' *Silvae* 5. 3, on the other hand, ends with the poet's *request* to the underworld powers and to his father. This ending could be read reflexively—as a commentary on Statius' practice elsewhere. The poet generally offers reassurance to those

---

[91] Esteve-Forriol (1962), 104–5.

[92] For use of the indicative in such passages, see e.g. *Silv.* 2. 1. 191–207 (Statius tells Melior how Glaucias has already met Blaesus in the underworld), 2. 1. 220–34 (the indicative is used in describing Glaucias' freedom from care, although subjunctives are used in the final exhortation to Glaucias to cheer Melior), 2. 6. 98–102 ('*subit* ille pios', '*carpitque* quietam | Elysiam'), 3. 3. 205–7 ('talia dicentem genitor... *audit*, et immites lente *descendit* ad umbras', 5. 1. 258–62 ('sic Priscilla manes *subit*', '*rogat*', '*placat*', 'certae *iurant* in vota sorores').

whom he is consoling. But in 5. 3 the attempt at self-consolation lacks that confidence.[93]

What is more, uncertainty about the success of consolation is also exhibited in Statius' other *epicedion, Silv.* 5. 5. Consider Plutarch's *Consolatio ad uxorem*, where Plutarch consoles his wife for the loss of their daughter Theoxena. Whereas Statius, while admittedly not addressing his poem to anyone, takes on the role of a grief-stricken parent (even though, as he points out, the child was not his own), Plutarch's role in his *Consolatio* to his wife is that of a relatively disinterested observer. Rather than record his own response to the loss, Plutarch adopts some detachment in addressing his wife. He provides her with guidance on how she should cope with the loss of her daughter. The tone is naturally enough more philosophical than any of Statius' consolations. At one point Plutarch notes approvingly the report that his wife has not put on mourning garb or allowed her women to lament excessively (608 F). It is almost as if he were preaching to the converted. He is all but silent about his own feelings of grief at this calamity. This is the most striking difference from the approach taken in *Silvae* 5. 5. Plutarch, at the outset of his consolation, exclaims his willingness to set bounds to his own feelings of grief, but then states that excess of it in her will hurt him more than the bereavement itself (608 c ἂν δέ σε τῷ δυσφορεῖν ὑπερβάλλουσαν εὕρω, τοῦτό μοι μᾶλλον ἐνοχλήσει τοῦ γεγονότος).

In contrast to Plutarch's withdrawal from the role of the bereaved, Statius' response to the death of a child in *Silv.* 5. 5 centres on the continuation of his grief and, again, on the failure of his poetry. Whereas 5. 3 began with the explanation that Statius has to seek poetic inspiration from his father rather than from Apollo, 5. 5 goes a stage further in the rejection of traditional sources of inspiration. The poet affirms that he is 'Castaliae uocalibus undis | inuisus Phoeboque grauis' (*Silv.* 5. 5. 2–3). Instead of affirming any mastery over grief, Statius declares that his grief for a child who is not of his own blood surpasses the grief even of real parents (5. 5. 8–24):

> morientibus ecce lacertis
> uiscera nostra tenens animamque auellitur infans,
> non de stirpe quidem nec qui mea nomina ferret
> iuraque; non fueram genitor, sed cernite fletus

10

---

[93] For the puzzling examples of divine guidance with which Statius compares his own situation in respect of his dead father in 5. 3. 290–3, see the commentary ad loc.

liuentesque genas et credite planctibus orbi.
orbus ego. huc patres et aperto pectore matres
conueniant: crinemque rogis et cinnama ferte.
siqua sub uberibus plenis ad funera natos   15
ipsa gradu labente tulit madidumque cecidit
pectus et ardentes restinxit lacte fauillas,
siquis adhuc tenerae signatum flore iuuentae
immersit cineri iuuenem primaque iacentis
serpere crudeles uidit lanugine flammas,   20
adsit et alterno mecum clamore fatiscat:
uincetur lacrimis et te, Natura, pudebit,
tanta mihi feritas, tanta est insania luctus.

Here Statius draws attention to his own suffering in the attempt to
justify his own role as mourner. He even challenges others who have
been bereaved to see if their sorrow outdoes his. This is far from any
kind of consolatory purpose; the poet seems to go out of his way to
emphasize and magnify his own suffering. Now the motif of outdoing
even such terrible bereavements as the loss of a child can be paral-
leled elsewhere in Statius. Thus in *Silv.* 2. 1 we learn that the lamen-
tations of Atedius Melior for his *puer delicatus* went beyond those of
parents (2. 1. 23), and then, later in that poem, that it was not the boy's
parents but Melior himself who attracted attention in his grief (2. 1.
173–4):[94]

> erant illic genitor materque iacentis
> maesta, sed attoniti te spectauere parentes.

Similarly, as already mentioned, *Silvae* 2. 6 opens with a priamel
where, contrary to expectation, Statius remarks that though it is
bad to lose a child, a spouse, or a sibling, it is in fact possible for a
plaga minor, a lesser blow, to inflict deeper wounds (*Silv.* 2. 6. 1–8). Thus
in 2. 1 and 2. 6 Statius emphasizes that his friends' grief surpasses even
the grief of parents for a child. This technique gives commendation to
the bereaved, however extreme his feeling may be.

In *Silv.* 5. 5 Statius uses for himself a rhetorical strategy generally
employed for praising the devotion of friends, by giving an account of
his own suffering. Yet this account, used elsewhere as praise of others,
becomes in this 'self-consolation' an admission of possible failure.
Hence in 5. 5. 26–7 Statius refers to his work as 'discordesque modos

---

[94] Perhaps compare Hor. *Carm.* 2. 9. 9–17 (with N.–H.), where Valgius' grief for Mystes is
seen to surpass that felt by Nestor for Antilochus or by the parents and sisters of Troilus.

et singultantia ... orsa', and then in 5. 5. 33 he says 'scindo chelyn'. In the same verse (33–4) we hear: 'iuuat heu, iuuat, inlaudabile carmen | fundere', indicating that Statius does not consider that his poetry is *laudabile*. In such 'self-consolation' the conceit of the power of poetry is undermined, though we do not of course need to believe anything of the sort: in spite of his grief Statius retains his poetic mastery, which he exercises even in his assertions of the opposite. In *Silv.* 5. 1, the lament for Priscilla, Statius reassures Abascantus, her husband, by directly telling Priscilla that commemoration in his own poetry is the finest memorial which he could offer her: 'haud alio melius condere sepulchro' (*Silv.* 5. 1. 15). Here, however, in *Silv.* 5. 5, the bland reassurance that the poem is a monumental offering for the deceased seems called into question. And Statius does not merely hint that consolation is impossible; he also affirms that his works are of no quality (5. 5. 49–52):

> uerum erat: absumptae uires et copia fandi
> 50 nulla mihi, dignumque nihil mens fulmine tanto
> repperit: inferior uox omnis et omnia sordent
> uerba.

Again we may notice the same process of inflating the suffering, not diminishing it; the death of the child is described as a *fulmen*, suggesting not only the scale of the disaster but also the grandeur of the poetry which Statius would wish to write. Paradoxically, Statius' choice of the metaphor of thunderbolts already undermines the comment that follows: he goes on to say *inferior uox omnis et omnia sordent | uerba*, but in fact he has only in the previous line used language of the highest register, *fulmen*—a celestial thunderbolt—in describing the calamity.[95] And the claim of inferiority is then followed (5. 5. 56–7) by Statius' admission that his reaction will be regarded as excessive: 'nimius fortasse auidusque doloris | dicor et in lacrimis iustum excessisse pudorem'. The language of excess follows what was in fact a paradox-ical claim that Statius' words did not live up to his grief, a claim which was itself expressed by using the lofty metaphor of thunderbolts.

There then follows another passage where Statius again might seem to undercut his other consolatory poetry (5. 5. 59–65):

---

[95] One may compare the manner in which Ovid in the exile poetry claims to be losing his poetical abilities; see e.g. G. D. Williams (1994), 50–99 for a subtle critique of Ovid's poetics of decline.

quisnam autem gemitus lamentaque nostra reprendis?
o nimium felix, nimium crudelis et expers
imperii, Fortuna, tui qui dicere legem   60
fletibus aut fines audet censere dolendi!
incitat heu planctus; potius fugientia ripas
flumina detineas, rapidis aut ignibus obstes,
quam miseros lugere uetes. tamen ille seuerus,
quisquis is est, nostrae cognoscat uulnera causae.   65

Here note again the paradoxical position in which Statius now stands, because he is at once the person bereaved and the consoler as well. Now it is not uncommon to reproach those who would apply too firm a boundary to mourning. Thus, for example, at the beginning of *Silvae* 2. 6, Statius says that it is excessive severity to try to set bounds on a person's grief (*Silv.* 2. 6. 1–2). But here in 5. 5, the situation is different. Statius, the composer of consolatory poetry, is now reproaching those who would attempt to censure his lamentations. The effect is that he affirms, rather than assuages, his grief. And again he uses the grandest language in his attempt to affirm it. The claim that *omnia sordent uerba* is also refuted in this passage. Verses 59–60 recall the epic language of Dido's lament in *Aeneid* 4 'felix heu, nimium felix, si litora tantum | numquam Dardaniae tetigissent nostra carinae' (Virg. *A.* 4. 657–8), and the subsequent comparison between attempting to stop a person mourning and trying to stand in the way of fires or rivers in flood also recalls the language of epic: compare the similes on these themes at Virg. *A.* 2. 304–8 and at 12. 521–5. The use of the word *causa*, 'case', at the end of this passage suggests that Statius is making a complaint against what he has suffered at the hands of Fortune, but there might also be a hint that he is in fact making a case in favour of mourning. This would conflict with the conventional idea of forbidding the bereaved to mourn, which can be paralleled at the end of poems such as 2. 6, where Statius tells Flavius Ursus to cease his lamentations (*Silv.* 2. 6. 103–5) as well as in 5. 1, where Abascantus is told to grieve no more (5. 1. 247–8). But here in 5. 5 it is clear that Statius rejects the idea of setting a bound to grief, and hence is far more concerned with the perpetuation of lament, not its end through consolation.

In 'typical' consolation, the consoling voice shows considerable detachment from the predicament of his addressee. As we saw, Plutarch stands apart as he addresses his wife, even though the loss of their child was a blow which affected both of them. In *Silv.* 5. 3 and

5. 5, Statius uses some of the same devices which he used in other consolations. But in these poems Statius addresses and indeed commemorates, perhaps perpetuates, his own grief with some of the same devices that he elsewhere used to console others. I hope to have shown that these poems, whilst outwardly allied to the consolatory tradition of lamentation, also have an *anti*-consolatory aspect to them. That is achieved by the violent combination of consoler and consoled, since both are conflated into the same first-person voice.[96] This represents a striking approach to consolation.

The Text

The survival of all the poems of the *Silvae* except one (2. 7)[97] depends on the Matritensis (M), MS Madrid, Biblioteca Nacional de España 3678 (*quondam* M. 31).[98] M is a copy made in 1417 or 1418 for Poggio from a now lost manuscript containing Manilius, Silius Italicus, and the *Silvae* of Statius, which he had discovered in the vicinity of Lake Constance.[99] M was subsequently taken to Italy and is the source of

---

[96] In epic, compare the speeches of Creon on the occasion of the funeral of his son Menoeceus at *Theb.* 12. 72–92 and 95–103, and note such motifs as his uncertainty ('credo equidem', 77, discussed by Pollmann ad loc.) with regard to his son's afterlife among the gods, and the intensification of his grief ('accensaque iterat uiolentius ira', 93) after the first speech: at the end of the speech, Creon is dragged away by his comites, perhaps a hint at further extreme behaviour on his part (cf. *Theb.* 10. 816 'abducunt comites', with reference to Menoeceus' mother, and *Silv.* 5. 1. 199–200 n. below).

[97] *Silv.* 2. 7 is preserved in a 9th-c. florilegium in MS Laurentianus plut. 29. 32 (L): see Reeve (1983), 397, Courtney (1990), p. vii.

[98] Excellent discussions of the textual tradition of the *Silvae* are found in the commentaries of van Dam on *Silvae* 2, Laguna on *Silvae* 3, and Coleman on *Silvae* 4, as well as in Reeve (1983), 397–9. Reeve (1977*b*) is an indispensable guide to the 15th-c. transmission of the *Silvae* and the *recentiores*. See also Anderson (2000), a massive catalogue of manuscripts of Statius: note especially Anderson i, pp. xix–xxiii and 225–6 (nr. 316) on M, i. 574–84 for a list of editions and editors of Statius, i. 585–618 for a list of annotated early editions of Statius, ii. 830–2 for a list of other manuscripts and sigla, and ii. 979–1006 for observations on early criticism on Statius after the re-emergence of the *Silvae*.

[99] For a convenient if pessimistic glance at the *fortuna* of Statius down to the 6th c., see Hill (2002); cf. also Laguna (1992), 32–6. From late antiquity until the time of Poggio's discovery, there are only scattered traces of the *Silvae*. See Vollmer (1898), 34 for echoes found in Carolingian poetry, Billanovich (1958), especially 239–43, for possible echoes of the *Silvae* in the works of Paduan prehumanists in the early 14th c., Coulter (1959) for the possibility that *Silv.* 5. 4 may have been known to Boccaccio (cf. Carrai (1990), 29–33), Laguna (1992), 37, who cautiously notes similarities between Petrarch, *Rime* 223 and *Silv.* 5. 4 and between *Rime* 287 and *Silv.* 5. 3. 19–28, and Caruso (2003), who suggests that the *Silvae* may have been of interest to the grammatical tradition in the Middle Ages.

all the *recentiores* manuscripts. The first printed editions of the *Silvae* are an anonymous edition published in Venice in 1472, an edition which involved Puteolanus in Parma in 1473 ('correctum p. d. franciscum puteolanum'), and Domizio Calderini's Roman edition and commentary of 1475.[100] M itself was in due course taken to Spain; in 1757 it formed part of the collection of the thirteenth conde de Miranda, don Antonio López de Zúñiga y Chaves Chacón, which was sold to the Biblioteca Real, now the Biblioteca Nacional.[101] Subsequently, it did not receive serious attention until it was 'rediscovered' there in 1879 by G. Loewe and subsequently confirmed as Poggio's manuscript in 1899 by A. C. Clark.[102]

Though M's importance was recognized in 1899, a paradoxical consequence of this, however, was the onset of an extensive debate concerning the status of certain annotations made by Politian in a copy of the first edition of the *Silvae*, the so-called *exemplar Corsinianum* (Cors. 50 F. 37) now kept in the library of the Palazzo Corsini in Rome. Politian's annotations,[103] many of which are simply corrections of errors and references to Calderini's edition, also include references to readings found in a *liber Poggii*, most of which are also found in M. The few discrepancies, of which the most striking is Politian's claim that *Silv.* 1. 4. 86a, which occurs in M, is not found in the *liber Poggii*,[104] gave rise to the notion that Politian saw a manuscript that was not M (hence the use of the siglum A* in many

---

[100] The view advanced by Marastoni (1961), p. xliii, that the anonymous first edition is the work of Calderini, is decisively refuted by C. Dionisotti (1968), 180–3. On Calderini's scholarship, see further Dunston (1968), Fera (2002), 72–4.

[101] On the collection of the Miranda family, see Andrés (1979), who gives a full inventory (623–7). On the thirteenth conde, see ibid. 615–17. Andrés suggests (620–1) that the books may have been purchased by the eleventh conde, don Juan de Chaves Chacón, in 1691, when the library of the dead marqués de Liche, son of the famous conde-duque de Olivares, was put up for sale. M itself may have been taken to Spain from Italy in an earlier period; it is of interest to note that the sixth conde de Miranda, Juan López de Zúñiga, was viceroy of Naples between 1586 and 1595: see further ibid. 614.

[102] Clark (1899), 128–9.

[103] See the convenient collation of the annotations in Cesarini Martinelli (1975), 166–70.

[104] Courtney (1990), pp. xvi f. suggests that Politian overlooked this verse in collating the *liber Poggii*, and did not have the latter before him when he annotated the *exemplar Corsinianum*; he also notes the parallel case in Politian's collation of the *codex Bembinus* of Terence, where Politian wrongly affirmed that at Ter. *Eun.* 703–4 the words 'me et nil mentitam tibi? | iam satis certumst uirginem uitiatam esse' were missing from the manuscript, doubtless as a result of the eye going from the *esse* immediately preceding *me* in 703 to the *esse* at the end of 704: see further Ribuoli (1981), 16–17 with n. 7, 57. On this passage of the *Silvae*, see also Dunston (1967).

editions), but in recent years this debate has subsided into acceptance of the idea that Politian's *liber Poggii* was indeed M itself, on the basis that the similarities between Politian's annotations in the *exemplar Corsinianum* and the readings of M far outweigh the differences.[105] Courtney indeed remarks that Politian's readings should not really be recorded in a true *apparatus criticus*, except in cases where they are actually his own conjectures: 'ergo quae profert Politianus non adferenda sunt in apparatu uere critico nisi pro coniecturis uel, quod aliquotiens accidit, erroribus felicibus.'[106] In this edition I have followed Courtney's practice of using the siglum 'Politianus A' to denote annotations in the *exemplar Corsinianum* in the apparatus, 'Politianus B' to denote readings offered by Politian in his commentary, published for the first time by L. Cesarini Martinelli in 1978,[107] and 'Politianus C' to denote readings contained in *Epistulae* 6. 1 (dated 1 April 1494, and addressed to Philippus Beroaldus).[108]

There are of course further manuscripts of the *Silvae*, all descended from M, and in some cases derived from early printed editions.[109] In this edition, in keeping with other recent editors of the *Silvae*, I have usually used the siglum ς to refer to all manuscripts other than M, although in cases where a manuscript anticipates conjectures commonly assigned to later scholars I have referred to manuscripts of this type by name. The same siglum has also been used to refer to anonymous early critical work on the *Silvae*, such as marginalia in printed editions;[110] where it is possible to assign annotations to an individual, as in the case of Pomponius Laetus, names are used.[111] As for later conjectures, as far as possible I have attempted to check attributions and references in the original materials, although this has not always been feasible.

[105] See Reeve (1977*a*), 285–6, (1977*b*), 205–6, van Dam (1984), 10–11, Coleman (1988), p. xxxiii, Courtney (1990), pp. xi–xx, Laguna (1992), 46–7.

[106] Courtney (1990), p. xx.

[107] See also Cesarini Martinelli (1982), for publication of a lost portion of Politian's commentary, including comments on *Silv.* 5. 5.

[108] The letter may be found in *Angeli Politiani, et aliorum uirorum illustrium, Epistolarum libri duodecim*, ed. Andreas Cratander (Basel, 1522), 196–202, and in other later editions such as *Angeli Politiani et aliorum uirorum Illust. Epistolae cum praefatione in Suet. expositionem* (Amsterdam, 1644), 201–7.

[109] See Reeve (1977*b*), 203–14 for manuscripts independent of printed editions, and 215–17 for manuscripts derived from printed editions.

[110] Again, Reeve (1977*b*) is invaluable in this area.

[111] On Laetus' scholarship on the *Silvae*, see Reeve (1977*b*), 217–18, Scarcia Piacentini (1984), 494, 506–7, Fera (2002), 74–83.

SIGLA

M	Matritensis 3678 (quondam M. 31), anno 1417 uel 1418 scriptus
*M*¹	librarius sese corrigens
*M*²	manus Poggii librarium corrigentis
m	aliarum manuum correctiones
a	editio princeps, Venetiis 1472
b	editio Parmensis, Parmae 1473 ('correctum p. d. franciscum puteolanum')
ς	emendationes uel in editionibus antiquioribus sine indicio auctoris traditae uel in codicibus recentioribus factae, ex quibus separatim laudantur:
Q	Vat. lat. 3283, anno 1463 scriptus: uide Reeve (1977*b*), 225
I	Vat. lat. 3875, a Pomponio Laeto exaratus: uide Reeve (1977*b*), 207
H	Vat. reg. lat. 1976, de quo uide Reeve (1977*b*), 207–8
U	Vat. Urb. lat. 649, a Nicolao Riccio exaratus: uide Reeve (1977*b*), 203
Politianus A	Angeli Politiani adnotationes in exemplari Corsiniano (Cors. 50 F. 37) editionis principis factae
Politianus B	Angeli Politiani Commentarius in Siluas (de quo uide p. lii)
Politianus C	Angeli Politiani Epistula 6.1, 'ad Philippum Beroaldum suum'

SILVARVM LIBER QVINTVS

ECLOGA PRIMA

STATIVS ABASCANTO SVO SALVTEM

OMNIBVS adfectibus prosequenda sunt bona exempla, cum publice
prosint. pietas, quam Priscillae tuae praestas, est morum tuorum pars
et nulli non conciliare te, praecipue marito, potest. uxorem enim
uiuam amare uoluptas est, defunctam religio. ego tamen huic operi
5 non ut unus e turba nec tantum quasi officiosus adsilui. amauit enim
uxorem meam Priscilla et amando fecit mihi illam probatiorem; post
hoc ingratus sum si lacrimas tuas transeo. praeterea latus omne
diuinae domus semper demereri pro mea mediocritate conitor. nam
qui bona fide deos colit amat et sacerdotes. sed quamuis propiorem
10 usum amicitiae tuae iampridem cuperem, mallem tamen nondum
inuenisse materiam.

EPICEDION IN PRISCILLAM <ABASCANTI>
VXOREM

Si manus aut similes docilis mihi fingere ceras
aut ebur impressis aurumue animare figuris,
hinc, Priscilla, tuo solacia grata marito
conciperem, namque egregia pietate meretur
5   ut uel Apelleo uultus signata colore
Phidiaca uel rasa manu reddare dolenti:
sic auferre rogis umbram conatur, et ingens
certamen cum Morte gerit, curasque fatigat
artificum inque omni te quaerit amare metallo.

---

1 omnibus *M* : omnium *Phillimore*,[1,2] *cunctanter* : communibus *Saenger*   2 est *Barth* : et *M*
5 nec *M*[2] : uec *M*   6 priscilla ⟨ : priscillam *M*   10 usum ⟨ : uisum *M*

1 fingere *M* : pingere *Krohn*   ceras ⟨ : caeras *M*   4 meretur *M*[2] : moretur *M*
6 uel rasa *Schrader? (uide adnotationes)* : uel uata *M* : uel nata *M*[2] : -ue animata *aut* nouata
Phillimore[1] : uel secta *Winterbottom*

SILVAE BOOK FIVE

POEM ONE

STATIUS SENDS HIS GREETING TO ABASCANTUS

GOOD examples must be honoured with every enthusiasm, since they are useful to the public. The devotion which you show to your Priscilla is a part of your character, and cannot fail to win anyone over to you, especially a husband. For while it is a pleasure to love a living wife, love for a dead wife is a religion. I have not, however, jumped at this task like someone from a crowd of bystanders or someone just bound by a sense of duty. For Priscilla loved my wife, and by loving her made her more worthy in my eyes; in the light of this, I am ungrateful if I make no mention of your tears. Besides, I am always trying humbly to do honour to all members of the Sacred Household, because a person who worships the gods in good faith loves their priests as well. But although for a long time I had been wanting to achieve a closer kind of friendship with you, I would rather not have found the opportunity yet.

LAMENT FOR PRISCILLA THE WIFE OF ABASCANTUS

IF my hand were skilled in fashioning true wax likenesses, or in giving life to ivory or gold through hammering out shapes, that is how, Priscilla, I would create welcome solace for your husband, because, through his outstanding devotion, he deserves that you should be given back to him in his grief, your face adorned with the hues of an Apelles, or sculpted by the hand of a Phidias: this is how he tries to snatch your shade from the pyre, and wages a great battle with Death, and wears out the pains of artists, and seeks to show his love

10   sed mortalis honos, agilis quem dextra laborat:
           nos tibi, laudati iuuenis rarissima coniunx,
           longa nec obscurum finem latura perenni
           temptamus dare iusta lyra, modo dexter Apollo
           quique uenit iuncto mihi semper Apolline Caesar
15   adnuat: haud alio melius condere sepulchro.
           sera quidem tanto struitur medicina dolori,
           altera cum uolucris Phoebi rota torqueat annum;
           sed cum plaga recens et adhuc in uulnere primo
           nigra domus, quis tum miseras accessus ad aures
20   coniugis orbati? tunc flere et scindere uestes
           et famulos lassare greges et uincere planctus
           Fataque et iniustos rabidis pulsare querelis
           caelicolas solamen erat. licet ipse leuandos
           ad gemitus siluis comitatus et amnibus Orpheus
25   adforet atque omnis pariter matertera uatem,
           omnis Apollineus tegeret Bacchique sacerdos,
           nil cantus, nil fila deis pallentis Auerni
           Eumenidumque audita comis mulcere ualerent:
           tantus in attonito regnabat pectore luctus.
30   nunc etiam adtactus refugit iam plana cicatrix
           dum canimus, grauibusque oculis uxorius instat
           imber. habentne pios etiamnum haec lumina fletus?
           mira fides! citius genetrix Sipylea feretur
           exhausisse genas, citius Tithonida maesti
35   deficient rores aut exsatiata fatiscet
           mater Achilleis hiemes adfrangere bustis.
           macte animi! notat ista deus qui flectit habenas

---

11 rarissima *M* : carissima 5   15 haud 5 : aut *M*   17 uolucris *M* : uolucrem *Markland*   19 nigra *M* : aegra *Heinsius 576–7*   quis tum miseras accessus ad aures *Sandström (1878), 32* : quaestu (questu 5) miseramque accessus ad aurem *M* : *aliquid excidisse inter* questu *et* miseramque *coniecit Courtney (1984), 333* : quis tum miserandam accessus ad aurem *Adrian*   20 tunc *M*[1] : nunc *M, ut uid.*   21 uincere planctus *M* : iungere planctus *uel* uincere planctu *Heinsius 577*   22 iniustos *M*[2] : iu iustos *M*   28 comis *M* : choris *Lindenbrog (in observationibus, p. 478)*   30 adtactus *Phillimore*[1,2] : ad planctus *M:* ad tactus *Cartault (1904), 528*   cicatrix 5 : citatrix *M*   32 etiamnum haec *M* : etiamnunc 5   33 Sipylea feretur *Heinsius 577 et ad Ov. Fast. 4. 943* : si pelea fertur *M* : Sipyleia fertur 5   34 Tithonida 5 : cithonida *M*

for you in every kind of substance. But mortal is the commemoration fashioned by a skilled hand: I am trying with my immortal lyre to give you, most excellent wife of a distinguished husband, lasting obsequies that will not end in obscurity, provided that Apollo gives me his favourable assent, and Caesar, who always comes to me in company with Apollo. In no other tomb will you be laid to rest so well.

[16] Truly it is a late salve that is being prepared for so great a sorrow, when a second circle of the swift Sun is turning the year, but when the blow was recent and the home was still darkened by the first wound, how then could the wretched ears of the bereaved husband be reached? Then weeping, tearing clothes, exhausting the hordes of slaves and surpassing their lamentations and attacking the Fates and the unjust immortals with his wild complaints was his consolation. Even if Orpheus himself, accompanied by woods and rivers, were at hand to still his groans, and all his mother's sisters together, and every priest of Apollo and of Bacchus escorted the bard, neither the songs nor the strings heard by the gods of pale Avernus and the tresses of the Eumenides would have been able to comfort him at all: so great was the grief that reigned in his stricken heart. Even while I am singing, the wound that is now smooth shrinks from being touched, and a rain of uxorious tears stands ready to fall from his heavy eyes. Are these eyes wet with devoted weeping even now? What wonderful loyalty! More swiftly will the Sipylean mother be said to have drained her tears, more swiftly will Aurora's sad teardrops fail her, or the sated mother tire of breaking the stormy seas against Achilles' tomb. Bless your heart! The god who wields the reins of the world and directs human affairs (for he is nearer to us than Jove

orbis et humanos propior Ioue digerit actus,
maerentemque uidet, lectique arcana ministri.
40 hinc etiam documenta capit, quod diligis umbram
et colis exsequias. hic est castissimus ardor,
hic amor a domino meritus censore probari.
    nec mirum, si uos conlato pectore mixtos
iunxit inabrupta Concordia longa catena.
45 illa quidem nuptuque prior taedasque marito
passa alio, sed te ceu uirginitate iugata
uisceribus totis animaque amplexa fouebat,
qualiter aequaeuo sociatam palmite uitem
ulmus amat miscetque nemus ditemque precatur
50 autumnum et caris gaudet redimita racemis.
laudantur proauis et pulchrae munere formae
quae morum caruere bonis falsaque potentes
laudis egent uerae: tibi quamquam et origo niteret
et felix species multumque optanda maritis,
55 ex te maior honos, unum nouisse cubile,
unum secretis agitare sub ossibus ignem.
illum nec Phrygius uitiasset raptor amorem
Dulichiiue proci nec qui fraternus adulter
casta Mycenaeo conubia polluit auro.
60 si Babylonos opes, Lydae si pondera gazae
Indorumque dares Serumque Arabumque potentes
diuitias, mallet cum paupertate pudica
intemerata mori uitamque rependere famae.
nec frons triste rigens nimiusque in moribus horror
65 sed simplex hilarisque fides et mixta pudori
gratia. quodsi anceps fors ad maiora uocasset,
illa uel armiferas pro coniuge laeta cateruas
fulmineosque ignes mediique pericula ponti
exciperet. melius, quod non aduersa probarunt
70 quae tibi cura tori, quantus pro coniuge pallor.
sed meliore uia dextros tua uota marito

---

39 *punctum post* ministri *posuit Klotz*   44 catena M^1 : catenae M 45 nuptuque
M : nuptumque ς 46 iugata *Baehrens* : iugatum M 51 proauis et *Politianus A* :
proaui seu M : proauis seu ς : proauis aut *Heinsius* : proauis ex *Polster (1890), 16*   52 fal-
saque *Meursius* : falsoque M, *quod defendit Phillimore*[1,2] : falsaeque *Heinsius 220*   64 in
moribus ς : maioribus M 66 fors *Gibson* : metus M : Mars *Heyworth*   ad ς : et M : in
Baehrens   uocasset ς : uacasset M, *cf. 5. 2. 148*   69 melius M : doluit *Phillimore*[1,2]

is) notices all this, and sees you grieving and the secret thoughts of his chosen servant. From this too, that you love her shade and honour her obsequies, he takes note of your character. This is the most pure passion, this a love that deserves to be approved by our master the Censor.

[43] And it is no wonder that long-lasting Concord has joined you with an unbroken chain, fused with hearts brought together. She indeed had been married before and had undergone the marriage-ceremony with another husband, but she cherished you as if joined to you as a virgin bride, embracing you with all her heart and soul, just as when an elm loves a vine that is bound to it with coeval foliage, and mingles its leaves and prays for a rich autumn, and rejoices to be garlanded with dear clusters of grapes. Women are praised for their ancestors and the gift of beauty who lack personal virtue, and though they have much false glory, it is true glory that they lack: but in your case, although you had both lustrous ancestry and a blessed appearance, such as husbands would greatly desire, you had greater honour from within yourself, in that you knew only one marriage-bed and kept but one flame trembling within your inmost bones. Neither the Trojan seducer, nor the suitors of Ithaca could have sullied such a love, nor the fraternal adulterer who fouled a chaste marriage in return for Mycenaean gold. Though she were offered the wealth of Babylon, the massive treasure of Lydia, and the mighty wealth of the Indians, the Chinese, and the Arabs, Priscilla would prefer to die undefiled in virtuous poverty, setting her life in the scales against her reputation. And her countenance was not grimly fixed, nor was her character too severe, but her loyalty was straightforward and cheerful, and she combined virtue with charm. But if uncertain chance had called her to greater things, she would for the sake of her husband happily be enduring even armed bands, or thunderbolts, or the perils of mid-ocean. But it is better that it was not adversity which showed what your concern was for your marriage and how great was your anxiety for your husband. Instead, by a better way, your prayers won

promeruere deos, dum nocte dieque fatigas
numina, dum cunctis supplex aduolueris aris
et mitem genium domini praesentis adoras.
75   audita es, uenitque gradu Fortuna benigno.
uidit quippe pii iuuenis nauamque quietem
intactamque fidem succinctaque pectora curis
et uigiles sensus et digna euoluere tantas
sobria corda uices, uidit qui cuncta suorum
80   nouit et inspectis ambit latus omne ministris.
nec mirum: uidet ille ortus obitusque, quid Auster,
quid Boreas hibernus agat, ferrique togaeque
consilia atque ipsam mentem probat. ille paratis
molem immensam umeris et uix tractabile pondus
85   imposuit (nec enim numerosior altera sacra
cura domo), magnum late dimittere in orbem
Romulei mandata ducis, uiresque modosque
imperii tractare manu; quae laurus ab Arcto,
quid uagus Euphrates, quid ripa binominis Histri,
90   quid Rheni uexilla ferant, quantum ultimus orbis
cesserit et refugo circumsona gurgite Thule
(omnia nam laetas pila attollentia frondes
            *   *   *   *   *
nullaque famosa signatur lancea penna);
praeterea, fidos dominus si diuidat enses,
95   pandere quis centum ualeat frenare, maniplos
inter missus eques, quis praecepisse cohorti,
quem deceat clari praestantior ordo tribuni,
quisnam frenigerae signum dare dignior alae;
mille etiam praenosse uices, an merserit agros
100   Nilus, an imbrifero Libye sudauerit Austro:
cuncta ego si numerem, non plura interprete uirga

---

81 auster *s* : arctos *M*   82 togaeque *s* : rotagae *M*   83 paratis *Gibson* : iubatis
M : subactis *Avantius* : iugatis *Lohr (1876), 75* : probatis *Krohn* : sub actis *Macnaghten (1891), 136* :
iuuantis *Saenger* : uolentis *Watt (1988), 159* : gravatis *Shackleton Bailey*   84 pondus *Laetus,*
Avantius : tempus M   92 nam *M* : num *uel* ne *Politianus A*   laetas (*facile legitur* laceras)
M : Clarias *Heinsius 355–6* : claras *Otto (1887), 543 post hunc uersum lacunam coniecit Courtney*
(1984), 334   93 famosa *Salmasius ad SHA Alexandrum Seuerum 58. 1 (cf.*
Heinsium 356) : fumosa *M* : damnosa *Heinsius 356*   95–6 maniplos inter missus eques
M : maniplis intermixtus equos *Salmasius, Epistula ad Gronouium* : maniplo intermissus eques
Madvig (1834), 39   100 Libye *s* : librae *M*   101 cuncta ego *Courtney (1966), 99* :
cunctaque *M* : cuncta quid enumerem? *Heinsius 577*

the good favour of the gods for your husband, as you wearied them night and day, prostrating yourself as a suppliant at every altar, and adoring the kind genius of the lord who dwells among us.

[75] Your prayers were heard, and Fortune came with kindly tread: for attention fell on a devoted young man's diligent calm and spotless loyalty, a mind readied for its tasks, a watchful nature, and a cautious heart, worthy to unravel such great events, the attention of him who knows every affair of his people, and visits everywhere in testing his servants. And no wonder: he sees the regions of the east and the west, what the South wind, what the wintry North wind is about, and approves schemes of peace and war, and their very purpose. He placed on shoulders that were ready a massive burden, a weight that could scarcely be carried (for no other task in the sacred household is more varied), the dispatch of the orders of the Romulean lord into the great world far and wide, and the handling of the powers and means of command: to enquire what the laurel brings from the north, what news the wandering Euphrates, and the banks of the double-named Danube, and the standards on the Rhine bring, how far the world's end and Thule that resounds with retreating waves have yielded (for all the spears that are lifting high the foliage of victory * * * and no weapon is marked with the shameful feather). Moreover, should our lord distribute swords of loyal command, it is for Abascantus to reveal who should be a centurion, an equestrian sent among the infantry, who should command a cohort, who should have the more distinguished rank of senatorial tribune, and who is more deserving to give the signal of command to a bridled troop. Indeed he must know in advance a thousand turns of events, whether the Nile has submerged its fields, or whether Libya has been sweating under the rainy South wind. If I were to list everything, the winged

nuntiat ex celsis ales Tegeaticus astris,
quaeque cadit liquidas Iunonia uirgo per auras
et picturato pluuium ligat aera gyro,
105   quaeque tuas laurus uolucri, Germanice, cursu
Fama uehit praegressa diem tardumque sub astris
Arcada et in medio linquit Thaumantida caelo.
    qualem te superi, Priscilla, hominesque benigno
aspexere die, cum primum ingentibus actis
110   admotus coniunx! uicisti gaudia certe
ipsius, effuso dum pectore prona sacratos
ante pedes auide domini tam magna merentis
uolueris. Aonio non sic in uertice gaudet
quam pater arcani praefecit hiatibus antri
115   Delius, aut primi cui ius uenerabile thyrsi
Bacchus et attonitae tribuit uexilla cateruae.
    nec tamen hinc mutata quies probitasue secundis
intumuit: tenor idem animo moresque modesti
fortuna crescente manent. fouet anxia curas
120   coniugis hortaturque simul fallitque labores.
ipsa dapes modicas et sobria pocula tradit
exemplumque ad erile monet, uelut Apula coniunx
agricolae parci uel sole infecta Sabino,
quae uidet emeriti iam prospectantibus astris
125   tempus adesse uiri, propere mensasque torosque
instruit exspectatque sonum redeuntis aratri.
    parua loquor: tecum gelidas comes illa per Arctos
Sarmaticasque hiemes Histrumque et pallida Rheni
frigora, tecum omnes animo durata per aestus

          *   *   *   *   *

130   et, si castra darent, uellet gestare pharetras,
uellet Amazonia latus intercludere pelta,
dum te puluerea bellorum nube uideret

---

105 cursu *M* : curru *Casaubon, Barth*   106 uehit *Calderini* : uelut *M*   110 certe *Markland* : cene *M* : paene *Burmannus*   112 merentis *M* : ferentis *Baehrens*   113 Aonio ς : ausonio *M*   114 quam ς, *Barth* : quem *M*   115 cui ius *Calderini* : cuius *M*   117 hinc ς : hic *M*   120 fallitque *uel* fulcitque *Watt (1988), 168–9* : flectitque *M*   121 tradit *M*[1] : trabit *M*   122 monet ς : mouet *M*   123 parci ς : parti *M*   sabino *M* : Sabina *Heinsius ad Ov. Am. 2.4.15*   126 redeuntis ς : redeuntibus *M*   127 illa *M* : ire *Nodell (1787), 116, Schrader (uide Haupt (1876), 133)*   129 durata *M* : durare *Markland   post hunc uersum lacunam statuit Courtney*   132 puluerea *M* : puluereum *Baehrens*   nube *M* : <in> nube *Gevartius*

Tegean from the high stars with his divining wand does not tell of
more, nor Juno's maiden who floats down through the clear breezes
and binds the rainy air in a coloured arc, nor Fame, who carries your
victories, Germanicus, in rapid flight, having overtaken the day, and
leaves behind the slow Arcadian beneath the stars, and Thaumantis
in the middle of the sky.

[108] How you looked, Priscilla, in the eyes of gods and men
on the kindly day when first your husband was raised up to great
deeds! You certainly surpassed even his own rejoicing, when you
eagerly made your obeisance, pouring your heart out, prostrate
before the sacred feet of our lord who had done so much for you.
Not so much does she rejoice on the Aonian hill, she, whom the
Delian father has installed over the gapings of his secret cave, nor she
who has received from Bacchus the revered command of the first
thyrsus, and the standards of the enthralled throng. But in no way
did this disturb her serenity, nor was your virtue swollen by good
fortune: your mind keeps the same course, and your ways remain
modest, even though your fortune grows. Anxiously, she looks
after her husband's cares, and, encouraging him, also makes his
toils seem less. She herself gives him simple feasts and sober
cups, and reminds him of his master's example, like the Apulian
wife of a thrifty farmer, or a woman tinged by the Sabine sun, who
sees, as the stars now look out, that it is time for her husband to
return from his labours, and swiftly prepares the tables and
couches and waits for the sound of the team's return. I am speaking
of small things: accompanying you through the cold north and wintry
Sarmatia, the Danube and the pale chills of the Rhine, enduring in
her mind through all the heat of summer with you, * * * and she
would willingly, if the camp allowed it, wield quivers, willingly protect
her side with an Amazonian shield, provided that she saw you in
the dusty cloud of war beside the thunderbolt of Caesar's horse,

Caesarei prope fulmen equi diuinaque tela
uibrantem et magnae sparsum sudoribus hastae.
135   hactenus alma chelys. tempus nunc ponere frondes,
Phoebe, tuas maestaque comam damnare cupresso.
    quisnam impacata consanguinitate ligauit
Fortunam Inuidiamque deus? quis iussit iniquas
aeternum bellare deas? nullamne notauit
140 illa domum, toruo quam non haec lumine figat
protinus et saeua proturbet gaudia dextra?
florebant hilares inconcussique penates,
nil maestum; quid enim, quamuis infida leuisque,
Caesare tam dextro posset Fortuna timeri?
145 inuenere uiam liuentia Fata, piumque
intrauit uis saeua larem. sic plena maligno
adflantur uineta Noto, sic alta senescit
imbre seges nimio, rapidae sic obuia puppi
inuidet et uelis adsibilat aura secundis.
150 carpitur eximium fato Priscilla decorem,
qualiter alta comam, siluarum gloria, pinus
seu Iouis igne malo seu iam radice soluta
deficit et nulli spoliata remurmurat aurae.
    quid probitas aut casta fides, quid numina prosunt
155 culta deum? furuae miseram circum undique leti
uallauere plagae, tenduntur dura sororum
licia et exacti superest pars ultima fili.
nil famuli coetus, nil ars operosa medentum
auxiliata malis; comites tamen undique ficto
160 spem simulant uultu, flentem notat illa maritum.
ille modo infernae nequiquam numina Lethes
incorrupta rogat, nunc anxius omnibus aris
inlacrimat signatque fores et pectore terget
limina, nunc magni uocat exorabile numen
165 Caesaris. heu durus fati tenor! estne quod illi

---

133 Caesarei ϛ : Caesari *M*   134 uibrantem *M* : librantem *Markland*   139 not-
auit *M* : notabit *Barth*   144 tam dextro *M*¹ : dextro tam *M*   149 adsibilat
Markland, fortasse recte, etsi ipse repudiauit, praelato uel obsibilat *uel* obnubilat : adnubilat *M* :
aduersa flat *Cornelissen (1877), 277*   156 tenduntur *M* : tenuantur ϛ   158 coetus
M : questus *Polster (1890), 8–9*   161 numina *Heinsius* : flumina *M*

brandishing his divine weaponry and sprinkled with the sweat from his great spear.

[135] Up to this point my lyre is kindly. Now, Phoebus, it is time to lay aside your garlands and to blight my hair with gloomy cypress.

[137] What god joined Fortune and Envy in implacable kinship? Who ordered the cruel goddesses to be always at war? Has Fortune singled out no home without Envy at once fixing it with her grim gaze, and overturning joy with her savage hand? Their home used to flourish, cheerful and untroubled, without any sorrow; for how, though she is unreliable and fickle, could Fortune be feared, when Caesar showed such goodwill? The envious Fates found a way, and a terrible malignance entered their pious home. Just so are rich vineyards blasted by a malevolent South wind, just so does a standing crop deteriorate from too much rain, just so does an adverse wind envy a swift craft, and hiss at the favoured sails. Priscilla is robbed by Fate of outstanding beauty, just as a tall pine, the glory of the forest, loses its leaves, whether through some baneful lightning from Jove or through being uprooted, and, despoiled, makes no murmur in the breeze.

[154] What is the good of your virtue or your pure marriage-tie, and the deities you worshipped? The dark nets of death surrounded the wretched woman on every side, the Sisters' hard threads are drawn taut, and the last part of the finished strand is all that is left. Crowds of slaves, and the diligent skills of doctors were of no avail to her suffering; everywhere, however, her attendants feign hope with contrived expressions, but her weeping husband is what she sees. At one moment he is appealing, uselessly, to the obdurate powers of infernal Lethe, at another weeping anxiously at every altar, now he marks the doors, prostrating himself on the threshold, now he calls upon the divinity of Caesar that can be won over. Alas, the course of Fate is

non liceat? quantae poterant mortalibus annis
accessisse morae, si tu, pater, omne teneres
arbitrium: caeco gemeret Mors clusa barathro,
longius et uacuae posuissent stamina Parcae.
170   iamque cadunt uultus oculisque nouissimus error
obtunsaeque aures, nisi cum uox sola mariti
noscitur; illum unum media de morte reuersa
mens uidet, illum aegris circumdat fortiter ulnis
immotas obuersa genas, nec sole supremo
175   lumina sed dulci mauult satiare marito.
tum sic unanimum moriens solatur amantem:
'pars animae uictura meae, cui linquere possim
o utinam quos dura mihi rapit Atropos annos,
parce precor lacrimis, saeuo ne concute planctu
180   pectora, nec crucia fugientem coniugis umbram.
linquo equidem thalamos, saluo tamen ordine mortis,
quod prior; exegi longa potiora senecta
tempora, uidi omni pridem te flore nitentem,
uidi altae propius propiusque accedere dextrae.
185   non in te fatis, non iam caelestibus ullis
arbitrium: mecum ista fero. tu limite coepto
tende libens sacrumque latus geniumque potentem
inrequietus ama. nunc, quod cupis ipse iuberi,
da Capitolinis aeternum sedibus aurum,
190   quo niteant sacri centeno pondere uultus
Caesaris et propriae signent cultricis amorem.
sic ego nec Furias nec deteriora uidebo
Tartara et Elysias felix admittar in oras.'
haec dicit labens sociosque amplectitur artus
195   haerentemque animam non tristis in ora mariti
transtulit et cara pressit sua lumina dextra.
at iuuenis magno flammatus pectora luctu
nunc implet saeuo uiduos clamore penates,
nunc ferrum laxare cupit, nunc ardua tendit
200   in loca (uix retinent comites), nunc ore ligato

---

172 reuersa *M* : reuersae *Heinsius*   177 possim *M* : possem *Markland*   180
pectora ς : poctora *M*   181 mortis ς : mostis *M* : maestos *Calderini* : nostros *Korsch*
190 quo *M* : quod *Vollmer (1893), 840*   niteant *Lipsius Elect. 1.9* : niteat *M*   191 sign-
ent *Gibson* : signet *M* : signa *Markland* : signes *Baehrens*

hard! Is there something which is beyond Caesar's control? What great delays could be added to mortal years, if, father, you held sway over everything: Death would groan, confined in a dark abyss, and the Fates, unoccupied, would have set aside their spinning for a while longer.

[170] And now her countenance falls, her eyes flicker at the last, and her ears hear nothing, except when she recognizes only her husband's voice. Him alone her mind sees as it returns from the midst of death, him she bravely embraces with her weakened arms, turning to him with fixed gaze, and she prefers to fill her eyes not with a last sight of the sun, but with her dear husband. Then, as she dies, she consoles with these words the lover who shared her soul:

[177] 'You, the part of my soul that will survive, to whom if only I could leave the years which hard Atropos is snatching from me, hold back your tears, I beg you, do not beat your breast in wild lamentation, and do not torment the shade of your wife as it flies away. I may be leaving behind the marriage-chamber, but the ordering of death is preserved in that I am the first to die; I have lived a life that is worth more than long old age. For a long while I have seen you thriving in all your glory, I have seen you go closer and closer to the mighty hand of the emperor. Neither the Fates, nor any of the gods now have any power over you: all that I am taking with me. Go gladly on the path you have started, and tirelessly adore the sacred presence and the powerful godhead. Now (this is a command you yourself desire) give eternal gold to the dwelling-place on the Capitol, so that the sacred countenance of Caesar may shine out in hundredfold weight, showing the love of his own worshipper. In this way I shall neither see the Furies, nor wicked Tartarus, and I shall be blessedly received into the Elysian realms.'

[194] These are her words as she slips away, and she embraces her husband's limbs giving out her lingering breath into her husband's lips without sorrow, closing her own eyes with his dear hand.

[197] But the young man whose heart was burning with terrible grief now fills the widowed home with wild cries, now wanting to draw a sword, and now climbing up to high places (his companions can scarcely hold him back); now he falls on the wife he has lost, their

incubat amissae mersumque in corde dolorem
saeuus agit, qualis conspecta coniuge segnis
Odrysius uates positis ad Strymona plectris
obstipuit tristemque rogum sine carmine fleuit.

205   ille etiam certae rupisset tempora uitae
ne tu Tartareum chaos incomitata subires,
sed prohibet mens fida duci firmataque sacris
imperiis et maior amor.
                                    quis carmine digno
exsequias et dona malae feralia pompae

210   perlegat? omne illic stipatum examine longo
uer Arabum Cilicumque fluit floresque Sabaei
Indorumque arsura seges praereptaque templis
tura Palaestinis simul Hebraeique liquores
Coryciaeque comae Cinyreaque germina, et altis

215   ipsa toris Serum Tyrioque umbrata recumbit
tegmine. sed toto spectatur in agmine coniunx
solus, in hunc magnae flectuntur lumina Romae
ceu iuuenes natos suprema ad busta ferentem:
is dolor in uultu, tantum crinesque genaeque

220   noctis habent. illam tranquillo fine solutam
felicemque uocant: lacrimas fudere marito.
     est locus ante Vrbem qua primum nascitur ingens
Appia quaque Italo gemitus Almone Cybebe
ponit et Idaeos iam non reminiscitur amnes.

225   hic te Sidonio uelatam molliter ostro
eximius coniunx (nec enim fumantia busta
clamoremque rogi potuit perferre) beato
composuit, Priscilla, tholo. nil longior aetas

     202 agit *M* : alit *Heinsius 579, Markland*   conspecta coniuge segnis *M* : conspecto
coniugis igni *Barth*   205 certe (*i.e.* certae) ς, *Markland* : recte *M* : erecte *M*[1] : spretae
Appelmann (1872), 24 : reliquae *Polster (1890), 17* : fractae *Imhof (1859), 20–1*   207 sed ς :
sec *M*   duci *Calderini* : ducis *M*   firmataque *Winterbottom* : mirandaque *M* : firmandaque
Courtney (1968), 56–7 : iurataque *Markland*   211 Cilicumque ς : ciliciumque *M*
213 palestinis *M* : Palaestini ς   214 Coryciaeque ς : Corstiaeque *M*   et
M : at *Gronovius 1653* (*in notis, puncto interposito post* germina)   215 Serum ς : serium *M*
219 crinesque *M* : *fortasse* pectusque?   220 noctis *M* : sordis *Markland, qui*
noctem puluerem significare posse negat   226 fumantia *M, recte* : infamantia *Phillimore*[1,2]
nescio qua ratione usus, nisi fortasse conferebat St. Theb. 9.96–7 'haec infamantia bellum /
funera'   228 tholo *Polster (1890), 2–3* : toro *M*

mouths joined together, and, in his rage, stirs a hidden grief within his heart, just as the Odrysian bard, stilled when he saw his wife, fell silent after setting down his lyre beside the Strymon, and he lamented her grim funeral without singing. Abascantus would even have severed the certain span of his life, so that you should not go alone into the emptiness of Tartarus, but a greater love, and a mind that is loyal to his lord and encouraged by sacred commands, holds him back.

[208] Who could recount in fitting song the funeral rites and the grim gifts of that unhappy procession? Heaped up there in a great train every unguent of the Arabs and Cilicians flows, the Sabaean flowers, the harvest of the Indians soon to burn, and the incense snatched away from Palestinian temples, together with Hebrew perfumes, Corycian strands, and Cinyrean buds, and she herself reclined on a high Chinese funeral couch, shaded by a drape in Tyrian purple. But in the whole procession, only her husband is looked at, and the eyes of great Rome are turned to him as if he were carrying his young sons to their final pyre, such grief is there in his face, so much darkness is there in his hair and eyes. They say that she is released by a quiet end and lucky: they shed their tears for her husband.

[222] There is a place outside the City where the great Appian Way begins, and where Cybele first cast aside her laments in the Italian Almo, and no more remembers the rivers of Mount Ida. Here, Priscilla, your outstanding husband, covering you softly in Sidonian purple (for he could not endure the smoking pyre and the ritual cries), set you to rest in a blessed dome. Nothing will the long years

carpere, nil aeui poterunt uitiare labores:
230   sic cautum membris, tantas uenerabile marmor
spirat opes. mox in uarias mutata nouaris
effigies: hoc aere Ceres, hoc lucida Cnosis,
illo Maia nites, Venus hoc non improba saxo.
accipiunt uultus haud indignata decoros
235   numina; circumstant famuli consuetaque turba
obsequiis, tunc rite tori mensaeque parantur
adsiduae. domus ista, domus! quis triste sepulchrum
dixerit? hac merito uisa pietate mariti
protinus exclames: 'est hic, agnosco, minister
240   illius, aeternae modo qui sacraria genti
condidit inque alio posuit sua sidera caelo.'
sic, ubi magna nouum Phario de litore puppis
soluit iter iamque innumeros utrimque rudentes
lataque ueliferi porrexit bracchia mali
245   inuasitque uias, it eodem angusta phaselos
aequore et immensi partem sibi uindicat Austri.
    quid nunc immodicos, iuuenum lectissime, fletus
corde foues longumque uetas exire dolorem?
nempe times ne Cerbereos Priscilla tremescat
250   latratus? tacet ille piis. ne tardior adsit
nauita proturbetque uadis? uehit ille merentes
protinus et manes placidus locat hospite cumba.
praeterea, siquando pio laudata marito
umbra uenit, iubet ire faces Proserpina laetas
255   egressasque sacris ueteres heroidas antris
lumine purpureo tristes laxare tenebras
sertaque et Elysios animae praesternere flores.
sic manes Priscilla subit; ibi supplice dextra

230 sic cautum *Phillimore*[1,2] : sic catum *M* : siccatam ς   marmor *M*[1] : mamor
M   231 spirat *M* : saepit ς   232 effigies ς : effugies *M*   gnosis
M   233 nites *(uel* nitet*) Holford-Strevens* : tolo *M (i.e.* tholo*); sunt qui defenderint)* : loco *a* :
auro *Markland* : luto *Baehrens*: coli *Krohn* : solo *Saenger* : nitens *Courtney*   238 hac ς : haec
M   245 it *Gevartius in Comm. 230* : in *M*   angusta ς : augusta *M*   252 cumba *M* :
ripa *Markland*   253 laudata *M* : plorata *Markland*   255 heroidas ς : eoridas *M*

wear away, nothing will the toils of time be able to harm: such care has been taken with your body, the noble marble breathes out such opulence. Next, changed into various images you are made new: in this bronze as Ceres, in this one as the shining Cretan, in that one you gleam as Maia, and in this stone as a not impure Venus. The goddesses do not disdain to put on your beautiful face; slaves and the throng assigned to memorial duties stand around, then couches and assiduous tables are duly prepared. That is a home, a home! Who will call it a grim tomb? Anyone who saw this display of a husband's devotion would straightway deservedly exclaim, 'Here, I can tell, is a servant of the lord who recently founded temples for his eternal family and set his own stars amid another heaven.' So too, when a vast ship casts off from the Pharian shore on a new journey and has already stretched forth on either side countless ropes and the broad yard-arms of her sail-covered mast, and has set out on her way, a narrow skiff sails in the same water, and claims for itself a share of the unceasing South wind.

[247] Why are you now cherishing your excessive laments in your heart, most excellent of young men, and forbidding your long grief to depart? Can you be afraid that Priscilla will tremble at Cerberus' barking? He is silent for those who are good. Or do you fear that that the ferryman will be too slow in coming and will push her roughly away from the shallows? Those who are deserving he transports immediately, gently setting the shades in his welcoming craft. Besides, if ever there comes a shade who has been honoured by a devoted husband, Proserpine orders a procession of joyful torches, and tells the heroines of old to come forth from their sacred caves, and to dispel the gloomy shadows with bright light and to set garlands and Elysian flowers on her. This is how Priscilla goes down to the shades,

          pro te Fata rogat, reges tibi tristis Auerni

260   placat, ut expletis humani finibus aeui

          pacantem terras dominum iuuenemque relinquas

          ipse senex. certae iurant in uota sorores.

261 pacantem *Avantius* : placantem *M*   262 certae *M* : ternae *Nodell (1787), 117*

there she invokes the Fates on your behalf with pleading hand, and wins over the lords of grim Avernus for you, so that when you have filled your span of mortal life you may leave behind your master pacifying the earth and still a young man, when you yourself are grown old. Unswervingly the Fates swear to her prayers.

ECLOGA SECVNDA

LAVDES CRISPINI VETTI BOLANI FILII

Rvra meus Tyrrhena petit saltusque Tagetis
Crispinus; nec longa mora est aut auia tellus,
sed mea secreto uelluntur pectora morsu
udaque turgentes impellunt lumina guttas,
5 ceu super Aegaeas hiemes abeuntis amici
uela sequar spectemque ratem iam fessus ab altis
rupibus atque oculos longo querar aere uinci.
    quid si militiae iam te, puer inclite, primae
clara rudimenta et castrorum dulce uocaret
10 auspicium? quanto manarent gaudia fletu
quosue darem amplexus! etiamne optanda propinquis
tristia, ut octonos bis iam tibi circuit orbes
uita? sed angustis animus robustior annis,
succumbitque oneri et mentem sua non capit aetas.
15 nec mirum: non te series inhonora parentum
obscurum proauis et priscae lucis egentem
plebeia de stirpe tulit; non sanguine cretus
turmali trabeaque recens et paupere clauo
augustam sedem et Latii penetrale senatus
20 aduena pulsasti, sed praecedente tuorum
agmine. Romulei qualis per iugera circi
cum pulcher uisu, titulis generosus auitis

---

3 sed *Gronovius, Diatribe c. 30 §196* : et *M*   4 guttas *M* : guttae *Markland*
8–10 *interpunxit Shackleton Bailey (1987), 280*   11 etiamne optanda propinquis ς :
etiamne optanda propinqui *M* : etiamne optanda propinquant *Avantius* : et iamne
optanda propinquas *Phillimore*[1,2]   12 octonos ς : ottonos *M*   bis iam *M* : uix bis
Phillimore[1,2]: bis non *Saenger*   13 angustis ς : augustis *M*[1] : augustus *M*   18 tra-
beaque recens et *Krohn* : trabeque ac remis et *M* : trabeaque Remi nec ς : trabeeque et
remis *a* : trabeaeque et remis ac paupere clauo *b*   21 qualis *M*[1] : acialis *M*   iugera
M : munera *Markland*   22 uisu *M* : uisu et *Heinsius ap. Vollmer, Markland*

POEM TWO

PRAISE OF CRISPINUS THE SON OF VETTIUS BOLANUS

My Crispinus is journeying to the Etruscan countryside and the wooded tracts of Tages. It is not a long delay, nor is the place inaccessible, but my heart is torn with a secret wound, and my moist eyes propel swelling tears, as if I were to follow the sails of a departing friend across the stormy seas of the Aegean, and were exhausted while looking at the ship from tall cliffs, and complaining that my eyes were defeated by the expanse of air.

[8] What if the distinguished beginnings of your early military career and the sweet promise of the camp were already summoning you, noble youth? With what tears would my joys flow, what embraces should I give! Are even desirable things sad for your relations, when your life is already making the circuit of twice eight years? But your spirit is more robust than your slender years and submits to its burden, and your mind is not held back by its age. And no wonder: no inglorious line of ancestors produced you from plebeian stock, with obscure forebears and lacking in ancient lustre; you did not knock at the august seat and innermost shrine of the Latin senate as a newcomer sprung from equestrian blood or new to the robe of knighthood and the mean stripe, but with a throng of your family going before you. As a horse is awaited in the expanses of Romulus' circus, beautiful to look at and distinguished for its ancestral honours, whose lucky siring from a long pedigree has parents who have won

exspectatur equus, cuius de stemmate longo
felix demeritos habet admissura parentes;
25   illi omnes acuunt plausus, illum ipse uolantem
puluis et incuruae gaudent agnoscere metae:
sic te, clare puer, genitum sibi curia sensit
primaque patricia clausit uestigia luna.
    mox Tyrios ex more sinus tunicamque potentem
30   agnouere umeri. sed enim tibi magna parabat
ad titulos exempla pater. quippe ille iuuentam
protinus ingrediens pharetratum inuasit Araxen
belliger indocilemque fero seruire Neroni
Armeniam. rigidi summam Mauortis agebat
35   Corbulo, sed comitem belli sociumque laborum
ille quoque egregiis multum miratus in armis
Bolanum, atque uni curarum asperrima suetus
credere partirique metus, quod tempus amicum
fraudibus, exserto quaenam bona tempora bello,
40   quae suspecta fides aut quae fuga uera ferocis
Armenii. Bolanus iter praenosse timendum,
Bolanus tutis iuga quaerere commoda castris,
metari Bolanus agros, aperire malignas
torrentum nemorumque moras totamque uerendi
45   mentem implere ducis iussisque ingentibus unus
sufficere. ipsa uirum norat iam barbara tellus,
ille secundus apex bellorum et proxima cassis.
sic Phryges attoniti, quamquam Nemeaea uiderent
arma Cleonaeusque acies impelleret arcus,
50   pugnante Alcide tamen et Telamona timebant.
disce, puer (nec enim externo monitore petendus
uirtutis tibi pulcher amor: cognata ministret
laus animos. aliis Decii reducesque Camilli
monstrentur) tu disce patrem, quantusque negatam

---

24 demeritos *M* : emeritos ϛ *(uide Reeve (1977b), 219), Gevartius*   25 illi *Håkanson (1973), 78* : illum *M*   27 curia *M*[1] : cura *M*   30 parabat *M* : pararat *Courtney (1984), 337–8*   34 agebat *M* : habebat *Schrader (uide Haupt (1876), 133)*   37 uni *Heinsius 581* : illi *M*   39 exserto *Gronouius 1653* : exorto *M* : ex orto *b*   40 suspecta *Laetus, Politianus A* : suscepta *M*   43 metari ϛ, *nam hoc apud recentiorem codicem Q inuenitur* : metiri *M*   44 torrentum *Heinsius 581* : tot rerum *M* : tot ueprum *Calderini* : tot sentum *Krohn* totamque *Courtney, dubitanter* : tantamque *M*   48 Nemeaea *Politianus A* : nemea *M* : Lernaea *Markland* uiderent *M* : pauerent *Heinsius 581*   54 negatam *Gibson* : negantem *M* : natantem *Calderini* : nigrantem *Avantius*

favour—at his arrival all quicken their applause, and as he flies the very dust and the curved turning-posts rejoice at recognizing him—just so did the senate-house discern that you, distinguished youth, were born for itself, and enclosed your first steps with the patrician crescent.

[29] Soon your shoulders claimed as their own the customary Tyrian garments and the powerful tunic. But in fact your father set you great precedents for honours. For he, on entering his youth, straightway attacked Araxes with its quivers, bringing war, and Armenia which could not be taught to serve fierce Nero. Corbulo took the leading role in the rigorous warfare, but he too much admired Bolanus his comrade in war and partner of his labours during distinguished battles, and to one man was he accustomed to entrust his most bitter cares and share his fears: what occasion was favourable to deceptions, what were good occasions for open warfare, what promise was suspect, or what flight of the ferocious Armenian was genuine. Bolanus had foreknowledge of a route to be feared, Bolanus sought ridges that were suitable for safe encampments, Bolanus assessed the terrain, opened up the hostile delays of torrents and woods, fulfilled his revered commander's entire plan, and alone was equal to his great commands. Already the barbarian land itself knew the man, he was the second plume in battle, his helmet was closest to his leader. Just so, although they saw the Nemean arms and the bow of Cleonae was driving back their line, the astonished Phrygians nevertheless feared Telamon too when Hercules was fighting. Learn, youth—for you do not have to seek the beautiful love of valour from an outsider's guidance: let kindred glory provide your courage; to others let the Decii and the returning Camilli be shown. Learn of your father, how powerfully he entered Thule that

55   fluctibus occiduis fessoque Hyperione Thulen
intrarit mandata gerens quantusque potentis
mille urbes Asiae sortito rexerit anno
imperium mulcente toga. bibe talia pronis
auribus, haec certent tibi conciliare propinqui,
60   haec iterent praecepta senes comitesque paterni.
    iamque adeo moliris iter nec deside passu
ire paras. nondum ualidae tibi signa iuuentae
inrepsere genis et adhuc tenor integer aeui,
nec genitor iuxta; fatis namque haustus iniquis
65   occiderat geminam prolem sine praeside linquens,
nec saltem teneris ostrum puerile lacertis
exuit albentique umeros induxit amictu.
    quem non corrupit pubes effrena nouaeque
libertas properata togae? ceu nescia falcis
70   silua comas tollit fructumque exspirat in umbras.
at tibi Pieriae tenero sub pectore curae
et pudor et docti legem sibi dicere mores,
tunc hilaris probitas et frons tranquilla nitorque
luxuriae confine tenens pietasque per omnes
75   dispensata modos; aequaeuo cedere fratri
mirarique patrem miseraeque ignoscere matri
admonuit fortuna domus. tibine illa nefanda
pocula letalesque manu componere sucos
eualuit, qui uoce potes praeuertere morsus
80   serpentum atque omnes uultu placare nouercas?
infestare libet manes meritoque precatu
pacem auferre rogis, sed te, puer optime, cerno
flectentem <a> iustis et talia dicta parantem:
'parce precor cineri: fatum illud et ira nocentum

55 fluctibus *M* : noctibus *Phillimore*[1,2]   occiduis *M* : occiduo *Courtney (1988), 45*   fessoque *Calderini* : fessusque *M* : fesso usque *Vollmer* : fessamque *Phillimore*[1,2] : fissis *Courtney (1988), 45*   56 potentis *Heinsius 519, Markland* : potentes *M*   58 bibe *Heinsius 519* : tibi *M*   60 praecepta senes comitesque *Housman, Class. P. ii. 653* : comites praecepta senesque *M*   61 adeo *Markland* : alio *M* : animo *Waller*   65 occiderat *Saenger* : occidio et *M* : occidit et *ç* : occidit, heu *Calderini*   68 corrupit *M*[1] : corripit *M* : corripuit *ç*   73 tunc *M* : hinc *E. Baehrens (1873), 261*   74 tenens *M* : timens *Barth*   75 modos *Laetus, Behotius (1602), 2.11 (p. 92)* : domos *M*   79 praeuertere *M*[1] : praetertere *M*   81 meritoque *ç* : mertioque *M*   83 <a> iustis *Heinsius 462–3* : iustis *M* : uisus *ç, Postgate (1905), 133*   84 ira *Calderini* : ire *M*

had been denied by the western waves and tired Hyperion, bearing his orders, and how powerfully he ruled over the thousand cities of mighty Asia in the year assigned to him by lot, peace making his rule gentle. Drink in such things with readied ears, these things let your relatives strive to win you over to, these precepts let old men and your father's companions repeat to you.

[61] And at this very moment you are tackling the journey, and not with sluggish steps are you preparing to depart. Not yet have the marks of strong youth crept over your cheeks and your way of life is still unblemished, but your father is not beside you; for, engulfed by the unjust fates, he had fallen, leaving behind twin offspring without a protector, and he did not even take off the childish purple from your tender arms and clothe your shoulders in white raiment.

[68] Whom has unbridled youth and the rushed freedom of a new toga not corrupted? Just so does a plantation that has not experienced the pruning fork raise its leaves and breathe out its fruitfulness into shade. But you have Pierian concerns in your gentle heart, and modesty and a morality which has learnt to set laws for itself, and a cheerful integrity besides, and a tranquil expression, and a splendour which keeps to the right side of luxury, and a devotion bestowed in every way; the fortune of your house instructed you to give way to your brother, though he was your equal in age, to admire your father, and to pardon your wretched mother. Was it for you that that woman could prepare with her own hands unspeakable goblets and fatal decoctions, you who can turn aside the jaws of serpents with your voice and with your countenance please every stepmother? I should wish to harry her ghost and to rob the pyre of its peace with deserved curses, but you, excellent youth, I see turning me aside <from> just denunciations and preparing words such as these:

[84] 'Spare her ashes, I pray: that was destiny and the anger of the harmful Fates and a reproach to any god who looks into mortal hearts

85   Parcarum crimenque dei, mortalia quisquis
      pectora sero uidet nec primo in limine sistit
      conatus scelerum atque animos infanda parantes.
      excidat illa dies aeuo nec postera credant
      saecula. nos certe taceamus et obruta multa
90   nocte tegi propriae patiamur crimina gentis.
      exegit poenas hominum cui cura suorum,
      quo Pietas auctore redit terrasque reuisit,
      quem timet omne nefas. satis haec lacrimandaque nobis
      ultio. quin saeuas utinam exorare liceret
95   Eumenidas timidaeque auertere Cerberon umbrae
      immemoremque tuis citius dare manibus amnem.'
          macte animo, iuuenis! sed crescunt crimina matris.
      nec tantum pietas, sed protinus ardua uirtus
      adfectata tibi. nuper cum forte sodalis
100   immeritae falso palleret crimine famae,
      erigeretque forum succinctaque iudice multo
      surgeret et castum uibraret Iulia fulmen,
      tu, quamquam non ante forum leges<que> seueras
      passus sed tacita studiorum occultus in umbra,
105   defensare metus aduersaque tela subisti
      pellere, inermis adhuc et tiro, pauentis amici.
      haud umquam tales aspexit Romulus annos
      Dardaniusque senex medii bellare togata
      strage fori. stupuere patres temptamina tanta
110   conatusque tuos, et te reus ipse timebat.
          par uigor et membris, promptaeque ad fortia uires
      sufficiunt animo atque ingentia iussa sequuntur.
      ipse ego te nuper Tiberino in litore uidi,
      qua Tyrrhena uadis Laurentibus aestuat unda,

88 excidat illa dies aeuo *Avantius* : excitat illa die saeuo *M*   93 satis ς : fatis *M*
97 sed crescunt *M* : sic crescunt ς : decrescunt *Barth*   99–100 sodalis...palleret
Calderini : sodales...pallerent *M*   crimine ς : crimae *M*   101 iudice *M* : uindice
D. A. Slater (1908), 185 coll. Cons. ad Liuiam 185 'mutaeque tacent sine uindice leges'
103 legesque ς : leges *M*   110 et te *Shackleton Bailey (1987), 280* : nec te reus *M* : pro
te r. *Markland* : nec tunc r. *Leo* : nae te deus *Karsten (1899), 370* : tacite r. *Klotz* : Vecti (id est
Vetti) r. *Hardie Edinburgensis apud D. A. Slater (1908), 185–6, coniecta lacuna post 109* : nec se r.
Phillimore[1,2]   timebat *M* : tenebat *a*   114 qua ς : qui *M*

when it is too late and does not, right on the threshold, check attempts at crime and minds that are plotting unspeakable acts. Let that day be lost from time, and may later ages not believe. Let us be silent, certainly, and let us allow the crimes of our own family to be hidden, veiled in much darkness. He has exacted the penalty, he who has care for his people, at whose instigation Piety returns and revisits the earth, he whom every vice is afraid of. This vengeance is enough and lamentable for us. Why, if only it were possible to win over the savage Kindly Ones, and to keep Cerberus away from the timid shade, and to give the river of forgetfulness to your ghost more swiftly.'

[97] Bless your heart, young man! But your mother's crimes increase. And not only devotion, but high virtue did you aim at forthwith. Recently, when by chance your friend grew pale at a false accusation of undeserved infamy, and the Julian law stirred up the forum, and, girded with many a juryman, rose up and shook her chaste thunderbolt, you, although not previously experienced in the forum and in grim laws, but instead concealed in the quiet shade of study, undertook to ward off the fears of your terrified friend and to drive away the enemy's barbs, whilst still unarmed and a novice. Never did Romulus or the ancient Dardanian behold such youthful years at war in the toga-clad slaughter of mid-forum. Amazed were the senators at such efforts and at your endeavours, and the defendant himself was afraid of you.

[111] There is also equal vigour in your limbs, and your strength, ready for brave action, matches your mind and obeys its great commands. I myself have recently seen you on the bank of the Tiber, where the Tyrrhenian surge eddies in the Laurentine shallows,

115   tendentem cursus uexantemque ilia nuda
       calce ferocis equi, uultu dextraque minacem:
       siqua fides dictis, stupui Martemque putaui.
       Gaetulo sic pulcher equo Troianaque quassans
       tela nouercales ibat uenator in agros
120   Ascanius miseramque patri flammabat Elissam;
       Troilus haud aliter gyro leuiore minantes
       eludebat equos, aut quem de turribus altis
       Arcadas Ogygio uersantem in puluere turmas
       spectabant Tyriae non toruo lumine matres.
125   ergo age (nam magni ducis indulgentia pulsat
       certaque dat uotis hilaris uestigia frater)
       surge animo et fortes castrorum concipe curas.
       monstrabunt acies Mauors Actaeaque uirgo,
       flectere Castor equos, umeris quatere arma Quirinus,
130   qui tibi iam tenero permisit plaudere collo
       nubigenas clipeos intactaque caedibus arma.
           quasnam igitur terras, quem Caesaris ibis in orbem?
       Arctoosne amnes et Rheni fracta natabis
       flumina, an aestiferis Libyae sudabis in aruis?
135   an iuga Pannoniae mutatoresque domorum
       Sauromatas quaties? an te septenus habebit
       Hister et umbroso circumflua coniuge Peuce?
       an Solymum cinerem palmetaque capta subibis
       non sibi felices siluas ponentis Idumes?
140   quod si te magno tellus frenata parenti
       accipiat, quantum ferus exsultabit Araxes,
       quanta Caledonios attollet gloria campos,

---

117 Martemque *Markland* : armatumque *M*   120 patri *M* : puer *Markland* : patre
Unger (1868), 204   flammabat *Heinsius* : flagrabat *M* : inflagrabat *Unger (1868), 204* :
capiebat *uel* placabat *D. A. Slater (1907), 147–8*   121 leuiore *M* : breuiore *Gronovius*
1653 (in notis), Heinsius   123 turmas *Markland* : metas *M*   125 nam *M* : iam
Vollmer in commentario, parenthesis initio ante ducis *posito*   magni *Calderini* : magno *M, quod*
coniunxit cum animo (127) Vollmer in commentario   128 Actaeaque **ς** : acceaque *M*
129 equos **ς** : eques *M*   130 qui **ς** : quis *M*   iam *Polster (1884), 11* : tam *M*
131 nubigenas *Politianus B* : nubigeras *M*   caedibus **ς** : cedimus *M*   133 Arctoosne **ς** :
arctoosue *M*   134 aruis **ς** : armis *M*   137 umbroso *M* : undoso *Avantius*   Peuce
ς : pauce *M*   138 Solymum *Calderini* : solidum *M*   140 magno **ς** : magne *M*
141 accipiat *M* : aspiciat *a* : accipiet *hoc male attributum Politiano a quibusdam declarat Courtney*
(uide Cesarini Martinelli [1975], 169)   142 Caledonios *Politianus A* : calidonios *M*

pressing on your way and goading the flanks of your fierce horse with
bare heels, making threats with your face and right hand: if there is
any credence to my words, I was amazed and thought that you were
Mars. In the same way Ascanius, beautiful and brandishing Trojan
weapons, used to go hunting in his stepmother's lands on his Gaetu-
lian horse, and set wretched Elissa aflame for his father; no differently
did Troilus with a more nimble turn flee the threatening horses, or
the man whom the Tyrian mothers used to look at, not with hostile
eyes, from the high towers as he manoeuvred the Arcadian squadrons
amid the Ogygian dust.

[125] Come, then, for the favour of our great lord pushes you on,
and your joyful brother leaves clear footsteps for your prayers, rise up
with zeal and assume the brave cares of the camp. Mavors and the
Attic maiden will show you the battle-lines, Castor will show you how
to turn horses, Quirinus how to wield weapons on your shoulders,
Quirinus who has already allowed you to beat on your still tender
neck the shields born from clouds and the weapons that are kept
apart from slaughter.

[132] To what lands, to what world of Caesar's will you go? Will
you swim the Arctoan rivers and the broken streams of the Rhine, or
will you sweat in the heat-enduring fields of Libya? Or will you smite
the summits of Pannonia, and the Sarmatians who change their
homes? Or will the sevenfold Hister possess you and Peuce around
whom flows her shadowy husband? Or will you go to the ash of
Jerusalem and the captive palm-groves of Idume, planter of trees that
do not bring her good fortune? But if the land reined in by your great
parent were to receive you, how much will the wild Araxes exult,
what great glory will extol the Caledonian fields, when an ancient

cum tibi longaeuus referet trucis incola terrae:
'hic suetus dare iura parens, hoc caespite turmas
145   adfari uictor; speculas castellaque longe
(aspicis?) ille dedit, cinxitque haec moenia fossa;
belligeris haec dona deis, haec tela dicauit
(cernis adhuc titulos); hunc ipse uocantibus armis
induit, hunc regi rapuit thoraca Britanno.'
150   qualiter in Teucros uictricia bella paranti
ignotum Pyrrho Phoenix narrabat Achillem.
    felix qui uiridi fidens, Optate, iuuenta
durabis quascumque uias uallumque subibis,
forsan et ipse latus (sic numina principis adsint)
155   cinctus et unanimi comes indefessus amici,
quo Pylades ex more pius, quo Dardana gessit
bella Menoetiades. quippe haec <con>cordia uobis,
hic amor est, duretque precor. nos fortior aetas
iam fugit; hinc uotis tantum precibusque iuuabo.
160   ei mihi! sed coetus solitos si forte ciebo
et mea Romulei uenient ad carmina patres,
tu deris, Crispine, mihi, cuneosque per omnes
te meus absentem circumspectabit Achilles.
    sed uenies melior (uatum non inrita currunt
165   omina), quique aquilas tibi nunc et castra recludit,
idem omnes properare gradus cingique superbis
fascibus et patrias dabit insedisse curules.
    sed quis ab excelsis Troianae collibus Albae,
unde suae iuxta prospectat moenia Romae

    143 cum *M* : tum *Vollmer, fortasse recte?*   145 uictor; speculas (speculas *ς*) *Davies, Corpus* : uitae specula *M* : Vetti speculas *Polster (1890), 17* : uicum e specula *D. A. Slater (1908), 187 puncto post* adfari *notaque interrogationis post* aspicis *positis, nam confert Liv. 35.21.10* 'castella ucosque eorum peruastauit' : quas hinc speculas *Courtney (1968), 57* : *alii alia*   148 uocantibus *ς, Heinsius 584* : uacantibus *M, cf. 5.1.66*   149 thoraca M^1 : toraca *M*
150 uictricia *M* : ultricia *E. Baehrens (1873), 261*   paranti *Morel* : parentis *M*
153 subibis M^1 : subillis *M*   154 ipse *M* : ense *Heinsius 585*   sic *M* : si *Markland*
157 haec *Calderini* : et *M*   concordia *ς* : cordia *M*   159 tantum *Markland* : animum
M   160 ei *ς*? (*nam Calderini in editione sua scripsit* heu): et *M*   sed *M* : quod *Heinsius 585*   coetus *Gronovius 1653* : questus *M* : *fortasse cantus?*   165 recludit *M* : recludet
Courtney (1984), 338   166 properare *Saenger* : perferre *M* : superare *Baehrens* : proferre
Polster (1890), 18   cingique *b, Politianus A* : cingitque *M*   168 sed *ς* : si *M*

inhabitant of the savage land shall say to you: 'Here your father was accustomed to give laws, on this turf he addressed the squadrons in victory; he provided lookouts and forts far and wide (do you see them?), and surrounded these walls with a ditch; these are the gifts, these are the weapons he dedicated to the gods of war (you still see the inscriptions); this breastplate he himself put on when arms were summoning him, this one he seized from the British king.' In such fashion did Phoenix tell Pyrrhus of Achilles, who was unknown to him, when he was preparing victorious war against the Trojans.

[152] Happy Optatus, confident in your burgeoning youth, you who will endure whatever journeys and palisades you come to, perhaps yourself wearing a sword at your side (so may the divinity of the emperor be with you) and an untiring companion of your soul's friend, in the manner of dutiful Pylades, and of the son of Menoetius who waged Dardanian wars. Indeed you have such harmony, and such love, and I pray it may endure. As for me, braver years already are fleeing from me; hence only with prayers and blessings shall I be of help. Alas for me, but should it be that I summon my habitual gatherings and the Romulean fathers come to my poetry, you, Crispinus, I will be lacking, and through every row my Achilles will look around for you, absent though you are. But you will come back a greater man (the omens of bards do not turn out to be in vain), and he who now opens up for you the eagles and the camp will allow you to hasten your every step and be surrounded by the proud fasces and to sit in the curule chairs of your fathers.

[168] But what messenger is coming in swifter than Fame from the high hills of Trojan Alba, whence that god closest to us looks out on

170   proximus ille deus, fama uelocior intrat
        nuntius atque tuos implet, Crispine, penates?
        dicebam certe 'uatum non inrita currunt
        auguria.' en ingens reserat tibi limen honorum
        Caesar et Ausonii committit munia ferri.
175   uade, puer, tantisque enixus suffice donis.
        felix qui magno iam nunc sub praeside iuras
        cuique sacer primum tradit Germanicus ensem.
        non minus hoc, fortes quam si tibi panderet ipse
        Bellipotens aquilas toruaque induceret ora
180   casside. uade alacer maioraque disce mereri.

---

170 deus *M* : deis 5   172 *Klotz* certe *cum* 'uatum non inrita currunt / auguria'
coniungit, sed confer 164–5   175 uade 5 : unde *M*   178 fortis *M* : sortis *Heinsius,*
ita ut sortis *genetiuus partitiuus esse intellegatur*

the walls of his own Rome nearby, and fills your home with news, Crispinus? Certainly I said, 'The auguries of bards do not turn out to be in vain.' Look! Caesar is opening up a vast threshold of honours for you and is entrusting to you the duties of the Ausonian sword. Go, youth, be equal to such great gifts that you have striven for, happy you, who now are already taking an oath under our great protector, to whom sacred Germanicus is giving your first sword. This is no less a gift than if the Lord of War himself were to set before you his brave eagles and cover your face with his grim helmet. Go keenly, and learn to deserve greater things.

ECLOGA TERTIA

EPICEDION IN PATREM SVVM

IPSE malas uires et lamentabile carmen
Elysio de fonte mihi pulsumque sinistrae
da, genitor praedocte, lyrae. neque enim antra mouere
Delia nec solitam fas est impellere Cirrham
te sine. Corycia quicquid modo Phoebus in umbra,
quicquid ab Ismariis monstrarat collibus Euhan,
dedidici. fugere meos Parnasia crines
uellera, funestamque hederis inrepere taxum
sustinui trepidamque (nefas!) arescere laurum.
ille ego, magnanimum qui facta attollere regum
ibam altum spirans Martemque aequare canendo?
quis sterili mea corda situ <perfudit et omne
eripuit studium misero>, quis Apolline uerso
frigida damnatae praeduxit nubila menti?
stant circum attonitae uatem et nil dulce sonantes
nec digitis nec uoce deae. dux ipsa silenti
fulta caput cithara, qualis post Orphea raptum
adstitit, Hebre, tibi cernens iam surda ferarum
agmina et immotos sublato carmine lucos.
   at tu, seu membris emissus in ardua tendens
fulgentesque plagas rerumque elementa recenses,
quis deus, unde ignes, quae ducat semita solem,
quae minuat Phoeben, quaeque integrare latentem

5

10

12a
12b

15

20

---

3 praedocte *M* : perdocte *ς*   mouere *ς* : moueri *M*   6 monstrarat *Phillimore*[1,2] :
monstrabrat *M* : monstrabat *ς*   7 meos *ς* : mens *M, ut uid.*   Parnasia *ς* : pernasia
M   9 sustinui *Markland* : extimui *M*   trepidamque *M* : tripodumque *Saenger*
10–11 *interpunxi : alii punctum post* canendo *posuerunt*   10 ille *Markland* : certe *M*
12 *hic lacunam statuit suppleuitque Courtney (1984), 333*   corda *ς* : carda *M*   uerso *ς, Heinsius
148 et ad Ov. Her. 7.4* : merso *M* : maesto *Baehrens*   13 praeduxit *a* : produxa *M*
menti *ς* : menis *M*   14 sonantes *Calderini* : sonantem *M*   19 tendens *M* : tendis
Markland   21 semita *ς* : semina *M*

POEM THREE

LAMENT FOR HIS FATHER

YOU yourself, most learned father, grant me from the Elysian spring painful strength, a mournful song, and the striking of an ill-omened lyre. For neither is it right to disturb the Delian caves nor to stir up Cirrha in the usual way without you. Whatever Phoebus in the Corycian shade, whatever Bacchus on the Ismarian hills had shown me, I have unlearnt. The fillets of Parnassus have deserted my hair, and I have allowed the fatal yew to creep over the ivy and the trembling laurel to wither, an unspeakable thing! Am I that man who set out to exalt the deeds of great-hearted kings, emanating grandeur, and to equal Mars in singing? Who has <suffused> my heart with lifeless decay <and has snatched away from wretched me all my pursuits>, who has obscured my doomed mind with cold clouds, now that Apollo has turned? Astonished, the goddesses stand around the poet, making no sweet music either with their fingers or in song. Their leader herself, leaning her head against her silent lyre, is as she was when she stood beside you, Hebrus, after Orpheus had been carried off, looking at the throngs of animals who were now deaf, and the groves that did not move when the music was gone.

[19] But you, whether released from your limbs you take a high path and consider the shining regions and the elements of the universe, who God is, whence fires originate, what course leads the sun, what cause makes Phoebe wane and can also make her whole when

causa queat, notique modos extendis Arati;
seu tu Lethaei secreto in gramine campi
25   concilia heroum iuxta manesque beatos
Maeonium Ascraeumque senem non segnior umbra
accolis alternumque sonas et carmina misces:
da uocem magno, pater, ingenium<que> dolori.
nam me ter relegens caelum terque ora retexens
30   luna uidet residem nullaque Heliconide tristes
solantem curas; tuus ut mihi uultibus ignis
inrubuit cineremque oculis umentibus hausi,
uilis honos studiis. uix haec in munera soluo
primum animum tacitisque situm depellere chordis
35   nunc etiam labente manu nec lumine sicco
ordior, adclinis tumulo quo molle quiescis
iugera nostra tenens, ubi post Aeneia fata
stellatus Latiis ingessit montibus Albam
Ascanius, Phrygio dum pingues sanguine campos
40   odit et infaustae regnum dotale nouercae.
hic ego te (nam Sicanii non mitius halat
aura croci, nec sic tibi olet, si rara Sabaei
cinnama, odoratas et Arabs decerpsit aristas)
inferiis cum laude datis heu carmine plango
45   Pierio; sume <en> gemitus et uulnera nati
et lacrimas, rari quas umquam habuere parentes.
atque utinam fortuna mihi dare manibus aras,
par templis opus, aeriamque educere molem,
Cyclopum scopulos ultra atque audacia saxa

23 extendis *M* : expendis *Barth* : excedis *Phillimore*[1,2], *cunctanter*   28 magno *M, ut uidetur, Q, Auantius* : magna *M*[1] : magnam *ς* : dignam *Otto (1887), 544*   ingenium<que> *ς* : ingenium *M*   29 caelum *Heinsius ad Ov. Met. 8.172* : caelo *M*   me ter <iter> relegens caelo *Courtney cunctanter*, nam *deleto*   32 hausi *ς* : hausit *M*   33 in munera *ς* : immunera *M*   34 tacitisque ... chordis *Schrader (uide Haupt (1876), 133)* : tacitisque ... curis *M* : tactisque ... chordis *Polster (1884), 11–12*   35 labente *ς* : habente *M*   nec *Gronov. Diatribe c. 51 §336* : nunc *M, quod defenderunt Vollmer, Klotz*   41 hic *M* : his *Bernartius (in notis), quem secutus est Markland*   42 nec si tibi olet *Gibson* : ditis (dites *Calderini*) nec si tibi *M* : dites nec sic tibi *Aldus* : dites nec sicubi *Gronov. Elench. c. 7 §188*   43 et *Courtney, cunctanter* : nec *M* : uel *Barth*   decerpsit *M* : decerpat *ς* : decerpit *Baehrens*   *post hunc uersum lacunam statuit Leo (1892), 13–15, ita ut e textu recepto tantum* ditis *mutaretur*   44 inferiis cum laude datis *Krohn* : inferni cum laudae laci *M, quod defendit Vollmer, fine parenthesis post* laci *posito* : inserui cum laude loci *Calderini* : inserui cum laude locis *Bernartius (in notis)* : insertum cum laude locis *Markland*   heu *(uel* en*) Courtney* : sed *M* : te *Markland* : et *Heinsius 191, Krohn*   45 sume <en> *Klotz* : sume *M* : sume <et> *ς* : sume <hos> *Heinsius 191, Markland* : sume <o> *E. Baehrens (1873), 261*   et *M* : ut *Heinsius 191*   uulnera *M* : munera *Markland*   46 quas *ς* : quam *M*

she is hidden, and extend the measures of well-known Aratus, or whether in the secret meadow of the Lethaean field alongside the councils of heroes and the blessed shades you dwell next to the venerable ones of Maeonia and Ascraea, yourself a no less active shade, and make music in alternation and mingle your songs: give voice and inspiration, father, to my great grief. For traversing the sky again three times and three times unravelling her countenance the moon sees me inactive and consoling my sad cares with none of the Heliconians: from when your funeral fire glowed red on my face and I filled my weeping eyes with your ashes, my literary pursuits have had scant honour. With difficulty am I for the first time freeing my mind for these observances, attempting to clear off the mould from my silent lyre-strings, not with dry eyes and with a hand that even now is slipping, leaning against the tomb where you gently rest, protecting our lands, where after Aeneas' death Ascanius clad in stars heaped up Alba amid the Latin hills, hating the fields that were rich in Phrygian blood and the dowered realm of his inauspicious stepmother. Here, with offerings duly given (for not more gently wafts the breeze of the Sicanian crocus, nor is the scent so fragrant for you, if the Sabaeans have plucked the rare cinnamon, and the Arabian has plucked the perfumed herbs), I lament for you, alas, in Pierian song. Accept these laments and wounds and tears of your child, such as few parents have ever received. And would that I had the fortune to provide altars for your ghost, a work equal to temples, and to raise up an airy structure greater than the precipices of the Cyclops and the daring stones of

50 Pyramidum, et magno tumulum praetexere luco.
    illic et Siculi superassem dona sepulchri
    et Nemees ludum et Pelopis sollemnia trunci.
    illic Oebalio non finderet aera disco
    Graiorum uis nuda uirum, non arua rigaret
55 sudor equum aut putri sonitum daret ungula fossa,
56a sed Phoebi simplex chorus <
56b   > et frondentia uatum
    praemia laudato, genitor, tibi rite dicarem.
    ipse madens oculis, umbrarum araeque sacerdos,
    praecinerem reditum, cui te nec Cerberus omni
60 ore nec Orpheae quirent auertere leges.
    atque tibi moresque tuos et facta canentem
    fors et magniloquo non posthabuisset Homero
    tenderet et toruo pietas aequare Maroni.
      cur magis incessat superos et aena sororum
65 stamina quae tepido genetrix super aggere nati
    orba sedet, uel quae primaeui coniugis ignem
    aspicit obstantesque manus turbamque tenentem
    uincit, in ardentem, liceat, ruitura maritum?
    maior ab his forsan superos et Tartara pulset
70 inuidia, externis etiam miserabile uisu
    funus eat; sed nec modo se Natura dolenti
    nec Pietas iniusta negat mihi: limine primo
    fatorum et uiridi, genitor, ceu raptus ab aeuo
    Tartara dura subis. nec enim Marathonia uirgo

52 ludum *Markland* : lucum *M* : luctum *Saenger*   sollemnia ς : solemnia *M*
54 nuda ς : unda *M* : uda (*id est, oleo uncta*) *a* : uncta *Polster (1884), 12*   55 fossa *M* :
campo *Markland, coll. Verg. Aen. 8.596, 11.875*   56 *post* chorus lacunam statuit Holford-
Strevens et *M* : en *Shackleton Bailey*   57 dicarem ς : ligarem *M* : dicarent *uel* ligarent
Heinsius 587, Shackleton Bailey : litarent *Ellis (1885), 92*   58 araeque *Markland* : anima-
eque *M*   59 praecinerem *M* : praeciperem *Markland*   reditum *Markland* : gemitum *M*
61 atque tibi *M* : atque ibi me *Heinsius 587*   62–3 f. e. m. pietas aequare Maroni /t. e.
t. non posthabuisset Homero *temptat Courtney, cunctanter*   62 magniloquo ς : magnilo-
quio *M*   63 toruo *M* : docto *Markland* : nostro *Polster (1890), 5* : torno...Maronis
Postgate, Corpus : temptet et aeterno *Slater*   68 ruitura *Heinsius 587* : moritura
M   69 ab his *Schwartz (1889), 9–10* : aliis *M* : et his *Krohn* : ais *Vollmer*   pulset *Mueller
(1861), 19* : pulsem *M*   71 nec modo se *M* : nec mihi se *Calderini*   72 iniusta *M* :
in iusta (*id est, in ritus funebres*) *Boxhorn (1662), 65*   negat *Winterbottom* : dedit *M*   mihi *alii*
cum praecedentibus, alii cum sequentibus coniungunt

the Pyramids, and to surround your tomb with a great grove. There I should have surpassed the gifts of the Sicilian tomb and the competition of Nemea and the rituals of mutilated Pelops. There the naked strength of Greek men would not cleave the air with the Oebalian discus, the sweat of horses would not moisten the fields nor would the hoof resound in the crumbling furrow, but a simple chorus of Phoebus * * * and I should in due form dedicate the leafy garlands of poets to you, father, when I had praised you. I myself, with moist eyes as a priest of the shades and of your altar should foretell your return, from which neither Cerberus with all his mouths nor the laws which bound Orpheus could keep you. And perhaps, as I sang of your ways and deeds to you, your devotion would not place me behind grandiloquent Homer, and at the same time would be attempting to make me the equal of stern Maro.

[64] Why is a mother who sits bereaved on the warm burial mound of her son to inveigh more against the gods and the bronze threads of the sisters, or the woman who sees the flames of her husband in his youth and overwhelms the throngs standing around and the crowd that is holding her back, in order to rush into her burning husband, if she is able to? Perhaps a greater complaint from these persons assails the gods and Tartarus, perhaps the funeral, as it proceeds, is wretched even for strangers to see. But neither Nature nor Piety unjustly denies herself to me now as I grieve. You go to hard Tartarus, father, as if snatched away from your green years on the first threshold of the Fates. For no more sparingly had the Marathonian maiden lamented

75 parcius exstinctum saeuorum crimine agrestum
    fleuerat Icarium, Phrygia quam turre cadentem
    Astyanacta parens. laqueo quin illa supremos
    inclusit gemitus, at te post funera magni
    Hectoris Haemonio pudor est seruisse marito.
80   non ego, quas fati certus sibi morte canora
    inferias praemittit olor nec rupe quod atra
    Tyrrhenae uolucres nautis praedulce minantur,
    in patrios adhibebo rogos, non murmure trunco
    quod gemit et durae queritur Philomela sorori:
85 nota nimis uati. quis non in funere cunctos
    Heliadum ramos lacrimosaque germina dixit
    et Phrygium silicem atque ausum contraria Phoebo
    carmina nec fida gauisam Pallada buxo?
    te Pietas oblita uirum reuocataque caelo
90 Iustitia et gemina plangat Facundia lingua
    et Pallas doctique cohors Heliconia Phoebi,
    quis labor Aonios seno pede cludere campos
    et quibus Arcadia carmen testudine mensis
    cura lyrae nomenque fuit, quosque orbe sub omni
95 ardua septena numerat Sapientia fama,
    qui Furias regumque domos auersaque caelo
    sidera terrifico super intonuere cothurno,
    et quis lasciua uires tenuare Thalia
    dulce uel heroos gressu truncare labores.

---

76 fleuerat *Watt (1988), 169–70* : fleuerit *M*   77 Astyanacta *ς* : astranacta *M*   supremos *ς (uide Reeve (1977b), 219), Meursius* : supremo *M*   *post* 79 *lacunam coniecit Courtney (1968), 57*   84 durae *M* : dirae *Gronov. Diatribe c. 61 §393*   philomela *M²* : philomelia *M*   85 nota *ς* : nata *M* : trita *Baehrens*   in funere *M* : in funera *Markland*   cunctos *ς (hoc accipit Markland)* : cuncto *M* : iunctos *Heinsius 587, cunctanter* : ductos *Ellis (1892), 24*   86 dixit *M* : duxit *Markland*   87 ausum *M* : ausam *Postgate (1905), 133–4*   88 nec fida (id est, et infida) *M* : nec fido *a* : nec foeda *editioni Parmensi (b) perperam attribuitur (sed cf. Heinsium 587–8, Postgate [1905], 133–4)* : nec fissa *ς (uide Reeve (1977b), 219), Laetus, Auantius* : nec Lyda *Imhof (1859), 23–4* : nec bifida *Ellis (1892), 24*   gauisam Pallada buxo *M, plurimi ex recentioribus* : gauisum Pallade buxum *I* : gauisam Pallade buxum *Postgate (1905), 133–4*   92 cludere *anon. apud Gronov. Diatribe c. 50 §330* : ducere *M* : currere *Heinsius 588*   campos *M* : cantus *anon. apud Gronov. Diatribe c. 50 §330, Barth* : passus *Phillimore[1,2], cunctanter, coll. Sil. Ital. 4.391*   94 cura *ς (nam hoc marginale, quod exstat in exemplari Corsiniano, perperam Politiano attributum esse affirmat Courtney, coll. Cesarini Martinelli (1975), 169)* lyrae *Gronov. Diatribe c. 52 §339–43* : cydalibem *M* : oda labor *Schottius apud Gronov. Diatribe c. 52 §340* : chria liber *Ellis (1900), 259* : Ce[i]a fides (id est, Bacchylidis) *Phillimore[1], p. xx.* Pindaricum os *Saenger.* Pisa labor *Witjhof ap. Klotz*   96 qui *M¹* : quis *M*   domos *M* : dolos *Meursius*   98 quis...tenuare *Calderini* : qui...tenuere *M*   99 heroos *ς* : oroos *M* labores *Rothstein (1900), 516–18* : leones *M* : tenores *Calderini*

for Icarius, who was killed by the crime of savage rustics, than the mother who lamented Astyanax as he fell from the Phrygian tower. In fact the former stifled her last laments with a noose, but you shamefully served a Haemonian husband after the funeral of great Hector.

[80] I will not bring to my father's pyre the offerings which the swan, certain of its fate, sends ahead for itself in melodious dying, nor the song, most sweet to sailors, with which the winged Tyrrhenians on their black rock threaten sailors, nor the laments and complaints made by Philomela with broken voice to her hard-hearted sister: they are too well-known for a poet. Who has not spoken at a funeral of all the branches of the Heliades and their tearful resins, and of the Phrygian stone and of him who hazarded songs that competed with Phoebus, and Pallas who rejoiced in the disloyal boxwood? You it is who Piety must bewail, she who has forgotten men, and Justice who has been recalled to heaven, and Eloquence with her twin tongues, and Pallas, and the Heliconian band of learned Phoebus, those whose labour it is to enclose the Aonian fields in sixfold feet, and those who, measuring out their song on the Arcadian tortoiseshell, had a love for and name from the lyre, and those whom arduous Wisdom counts with sevenfold fame throughout the whole world, those who, standing on the terrifying buskin, thundered out Furies, and the halls of kings, and stars that turned away in the heavens, and those for whom it is sweet to refine their strength with licentious Thalia or to shorten heroic toils by a foot. For you embraced everything in your mind,

100	omnia namque animo complexus es, omnibus usus,
	qua fandi uia lata patet, siue orsa libebat
	Aoniis uincire modis seu uoce soluta
	spargere et effreno nimbos aequare profatu.
	exsere semirutos subito de puluere uultus,
105	Parthenope, crinemque adflato monte solutum
	pone super tumulos et magni funus alumni,
	quo non Monychiae quicquam praestantius arces
	doctaue Cyrene Sparteue animosa creauit.
	si tu stirpe uacans famaque obscura iaceres
110	nil gentile tenens, illo te ciue probabas
	Graiam atque Euboico maiorum sanguine duci:
	ille tuis totiens pressit sua tempora sertis,
113	cum stata laudato caneret quinquennia uersu
113a	<cumque soluta modis facundus uerba tonaret,>
114	ora supergressus Pylii senis oraque regis
115	Dulichii, pretioque comam subnexus utroque.
	non tibi deformes obscuri sanguinis ortus
	nec sine luce genus, quamquam fortuna parentum
	artior expensis; etenim te diuite ritu
	sumere purpureos Infantia fecit amictus

100 es *Saenger* : et *M*   usus *Wiman (1937), 15* : utor *M* : autor *Calderini*   101 uia *Markland* : uis *M*   102 seu ς : ceu *M*   104 semirutos *M, etsi Klotz hic* semrutos *legebat* : semiustos *Markland*   subito de *M* : Vesuuino e *Heinsius 588* : Vesuuino *Markland* 105 adflato monte *M* : adflato montis *Heinsius 588* : efflato monte *Leo (1892), 19*   solutum *Gibson* : sepultum *M* : adustum *Heinsius 588* : adesum *Markland*   107 quicquam praestantius arces ς : quitquam praestantias artes *M*   108 doctaue *Markland* : doctaque *M*   109 stirpe uacans *Laetus (uide Reeve (1977b), 218), Baehrens* : s. uetas *M, quod defendit Vollmer* : s. (nefas!) *Phillimore*[1,2] : stirpis egens *Adrian (1893), 42*   famaque ς : famaeque *M*   110 tenens *M* : tumens *Markland*   111 atque *M* : aque *Markland*   112 ille *M* : illa *Postgate (1905), 134*   pressit sua *Markland* : prestat sed *M* : praestabat *Elter ap. Vollmer, sed uide Håkanson (1969), 144* : praestant se *Vollmer, qui* tuis . . . sertis *esse parenthesin ducebat, inepte; cuius coniecturam suam fecit, sed rationem aspernatus, Postgate (1905), 134* sertis *Calderini* : seris *M*   113 *post hunc uersum lacunam posuit A. Hardie (1983), 7, quam exempli gratia suppleui (113a)*   114 senis ς : gregis *M* : ducis *D. A. Slater (1907), 157*   115 Dulichii *M* : Dulichii <est> *Heyworth*   pretioque *Saenger in apparatu critico* : speciemque *M, quod cum praecedentibus coniungit Klotz* : specieque *Calderini*   utroque *M* : utraque *(sc. specie) Calderini*   118 artior expensis *Auantius* : a. extensis *M* : et census tenuis *Saenger* : artior ex tantis *uel* ex celsis *Phillimore*[1,2]*, cunctanter*   119 sumere *Markland* : ponere *M*   Infantia fecit *Shackleton Bailey* : infantia legit *M* : Infantia adegit *Calderini* : Infantia uidit *Baehrens* : infantis adegit *Ellis (1910), 47–8*   amictus ς : amittus *M*

made use of everything where the broad path of diction lies open, whether you wished to bind your speech in Aonian measures or to scatter it in loosened tones and to match rain clouds in your unbridled utterance.

[104] Lift out your half-ruined countenance, Parthenope, from the sudden fall of dust, and place a lock that has been loosened by the burning of the mountain upon the tomb and upon the remains of your great pupil, than whom neither the Munychian citadels, nor learned Cyrene, nor vigorous Sparta created anything more distingushed. If you were lying in obscurity, lacking lineage and reputation, having no indications of your origin, with him as your citizen you would prove that you were Greek and that you were descended from the blood of Euboean ancestors. So many times did he press his temples with your garlands, when he sang the appointed quinquennial games in admired verse, <and when he eloquently thundered words released from metre,>, surpassing the speech of the Pylian ancient and of the Dulichian king, and binding his hair with both prizes. You did not have the shameful origins of an obscure pedigree, nor was your family without lustre, although the fortune of your parents became narrower through expenditure; for Infancy made you take up with opulent ritual the purple garments, given in honour

120   stirpis honore datos et nobile pectoris aurum.
        protinus exorto dextrum risere sorores
        Aonides, pueroque chelyn commisit et ora
        imbuit amne sacro iam tum tibi blandus Apollo.
        nec simplex patriae decus, et natalis origo
125   pendet ab ambiguo geminae certamine terrae.
        te de gente suum Latiis adscita colonis
        Graia refert Hyele, Phrygius qua puppe magister
        excidit et mediis miser euigilauit in undis;
129   maior at inde suum longo probat ordine uitae
129a   <Parthenope *   *   *   *>
130   Maeoniden aliaeque aliis natalibus urbes
        diripiunt cunctaeque probant; non omnibus ille
        uerus, alit uictas immanis gloria falsi.
            atque ibi dum profers annos uitamque salutas
        protinus ad patrii raperis certamina lustri
135   uix implenda uiris, laudum festinus et audax
        ingenii. stupuit primaeua ad carmina plebes
        Euboea et natis te monstrauere parentes.
        inde frequens pugnae nulloque ingloria sacro
        uox tua; non totiens uictorem Castora gyro
140   nec fratrem caestu uirides auxere Therapnae.
        sin pronum uicisse domi, quid Achaea mereri
        praemia, nunc ramis Phoebi, nunc gramine Lernae,
        nunc Athamantea protectum tempora pinu,
        cum totiens lassata tamen nusquam auia frondes
145   abstulit aut alium tetigit Victoria crinem?
            hinc tibi uota patrum credi generosaque pubes
        te monitore regi, mores et facta priorum

---

122 pueroque ς : puerique *M*   commisit *Axelson apud Håkanson (1969), 145–7* : summisit *M*
123 tibi ς : mihi *M*   125 ab *Barth* : et *M, quod accepit Klotz, nullo puncto post* terrae *posito* :
in ς   126 suum *M* : sua *Heinsius 496*   127 Hyele *Heinsius 496 et ad Ou. Met. 15.625* :
sele *M*   Phrygius *Avantius* : graius *(an grauis?) M, quod defendit Vollmer* : pronus *Waller
(1885), 54 : fortasse* Teucrus?   post 129 *lacunam statuit Markland, ut mentio urbis Neapolis fieret;
lacunam spreuerunt Ellis (1885), 94, Slater*   132 uerus *Laetus, Boxhorn (1662), 65* : uersus *M*
uictas *Bentley (uide Haupt (1876), 133)* : uictos *M*   133 ibi ς : ubi *M*   salutas *M* :
solutam *Heinsius 588–9*   135 festinus et audax *Lipsius, Elect. 1. 9* : festina sed ut dux *M*
137 Euboea *M* : Euboica *uel* Eubois *Heinsius 589*   140 auxere *Watt (1988), 170* :
clausero *M* : plausere *Calderini* : coluere *Håkanson (1969), 147–8*   141 sin *M* : sit *Calderini*
144 cum *M* : quin *Heinsius*

of your pedigree, and the noble gold worn at the chest. As soon as you were born, the Aonian sisters gave a favourable smile, and Apollo entrusted his lyre to the boy and imbued his lips with the sacred river, already favourable to you at that time. But not from a single homeland do you derive glory, and the origin of your birth hangs in doubt from an uncertain contest of two lands. You Grecian Hyele claims as her own by descent, she who has been adopted by Latin colonists, the place where the Phrygian steersman fell from the stern and wretchedly woke up amid the waves; but then greater <Parthenope> proves that you are hers by the long span of your life * * *, and other cities with other birthplaces share out Maeonides, and all prove him their own. But he is not genuine for all of them: the vast glory of falsehood nourishes the defeated competitors.

[133] And there while you advance in years and greet your life, you are at once keen for praise and bold in spirit, caught up in the contests of the ancestral lustrum that can scarcely be undertaken by men. Amazed at your youthful songs was the Euboean populace, and parents pointed you out to their children. Then your voice was often in the contest, and inglorious at no sacred event: not so often did green Therapnae glorify Castor victorious on the circuit or his brother, victorious in boxing. But if it is easy to have won at home, what was it to earn Achaean rewards, covering your temples now with the branches of Phoebus, now with the herb of Lerna, now with the pine of Athamas, when Victory, tired out so many times but nowhere unobtainable, never took away your garlands or touched another's hair?

[146] Because of this the hopes of fathers were entrusted to you, and noble youths were governed under your guidance, and learnt of

discere, quis casus Troiae, quam tardus Vlixes,
quantus equos pugnasque uirum decurrere uersu
150 Maeonides quantumque pios ditarit agrestes
Ascraeus Siculusque senex, qua lege recurrat
Pindaricae uox flexa lyrae uolucrumque precator
Ibycus et tetricis Alcman cantatus Amyclis
Stesichorusque ferox saltusque ingressa uiriles
155 non formidata temeraria Leucade Sappho,
quosque alios dignata chelys. tu pandere doctus
carmina Battiadae latebrasque Lycophronis atri
Sophronaque implicitum tenuisque arcana Corinnae.
sed quid parua loquor? tu par adsuetus Homero
160 ferre iugum senosque pedes aequare solutis
uersibus et numquam passu breuiore relinqui.
    quid mirum, patria si te petiere relicta
quos Lucanus ager, rigidi quos iugera Dauni,
quos Veneri plorata domus neglectaque tellus
165 Alcidae, uel quos e uertice Surrentino
mittit Tyrrheni speculatrix uirgo profundi,
quos propiore sinu lituo remoque notatus
collis et Ausonii pridem laris hospita Cyme,
quosque Dicarchei portus Baianaque mittunt
170 litora, qua mediis alte permissus anhelat
ignis aquis et operta domos incendia seruant?
sic ad Auernales scopulos et opaca Sibyllae
antra rogaturae ueniebant undique gentes;
illa minas diuum Parcarumque acta canebat,
175 quamuis decepto uates non inrita Phoebo.
    mox et Romuleam stirpem proceresque futuros
instruis inque patrum uestigia ducere perstas.

---

149 equos 5 : equus *M* : equum *Postgate (1905), 135*   153 Ibycus *Politianus A? (hoc in editionibus prioribus, quamquam marginale nunc legi non potest), etsi Politianus B legit* 'Obsitus' *cunctanter* : obsicus *M*   154 saltusque ingressa *M* : actusque egressa *Markland* : cantusque ingressa *Otto (1887), 545*   155 Leucade 5 *(uide Reeve (1977b), 219), laudat G. Merula (ut affirmat Courtney), Politianus AB* : calchide *(id est, Chalcide) M*   156 doctus *M* : docti *Markland*   157 atri 5 : ari *M* : arti *Baehrens*   161 uersibus *M* : uocibus *Markland*   166 mittit *M* : mitis *Phillimore*[1,2], *cunctanter*   168 ausonii 5 : ausoni *M*   169 Dicarchei 5 : dicarthei *M*   170 permissus *M* : permixtus 5   171 aquis *M*[1] : aquas *M*   domos *M* : animos *Markland* : dolos *Baehrens*   174 diuum 5 : duum *M*   canebat 5 : canebant *M*

the ways and deeds of the ancients, what was the fate of Troy, how slow was Odysseus, how great was Maeonides at describing horses and the battles of men in verse, and how greatly the old Ascraean and Sicilian enriched pious rustics, by what rule the changing sound of the Pindaric lyre comes back again, and Ibycus who entreated birds, and Alcman, sung in grim Amyclae, and fierce Stesichorus, and bold Sappho, heedless of Leucas, who entered the groves of men, and others whom the lyre has honoured. You were skilled in setting forth the songs of Battiades, and the recesses of shadowy Lycophron, and complicated Sophron, and the secrets of gentle Corinna. But why am I speaking of small matters? You were accustomed to bear an equal yoke with Homer, and to match his sixfold feet in freed lines, and never to be left behind by his swifter tread.

[162] What is surprising, if they sought you out, leaving their homes, those whom the Lucanian land sent, the acres of rugged Daunus, the home lamented by Venus and the land neglected by Alcides, or the maiden who watches over the Tyrrhenian main from the Surrentine pinnacle; those whom the hill sent that in the nearer bay is noted for a trumpet and oar and Cyme, once a stranger to her Ausonian home; and those sent by the Dicaearchean ports and the shores of Baiae, where fire, when it is given free rein deep below, gasps in the midst of the waters, and concealed fires stay in their homes? In the same way peoples from every direction would go to the rocks of Avernus and the dark cave of the Sibyl in order to pose their questions; she would sing of the threats of the gods and the deeds of the Parcae, no vain prophet despite her deception of Apollo.

[176] Soon you are giving instruction to the Romulean youth and future leaders, and firmly leading them in their fathers' footsteps.

sub te Dardanius facis explorator opertae,
qui Diomedei celat penetralia furti,
180   creuit et inde sacrum didicit puer; arma probandis
monstrasti Saliis praesagumque aethera certis
182   auguribus; cui Chacidicum fas uoluere carmen,
182a   *   *   *   *   *
183   cur Phrygii lateat coma flaminis, et tua multum
uerbera succincti formidauere Luperci.
185   et nunc ex illo forsan grege gentibus alter
iura dat Eois, alter compescit Hiberas,
alter Achaemenium secludit Zeugmate Persen,
hi dites Asiae populos, hi Pontica frenant,
hi fora pacificis emendant fascibus, illi
190   castra pia statione tenent; tu laudis origo.
non tibi certassent iuuenilia fingere corda
Nestor et indomiti Phoenix moderator alumni
quique tubas acres lituosque audire uolentem
Aeaciden alio frangebat carmine Chiron.
195   talia dum celebras, subitam ciuilis Erinys
Tarpeio de monte facem Phlegraeaque mouit
proelia. sacrilegis lucent Capitolia taedis
et Senonum furias Latiae sumpsere cohortes.
uix requies flammae necdum rogus ille deorum
200   siderat, excisis cum tu solacia templis
impiger et multum facibus uelocior ipsis
concinis ore pio captiuaque fulmina defles.
mirantur Latii proceres ultorque deorum
Caesar, et e medio diuum pater adnuit igni.
205   iamque et flere pio Vesuuina incendia cantu
mens erat et gemitum patriis impendere damnis,

---

178 opertae ς : oportae *M* : oportet ς, *a*   180 probandis *Powell* : probatur *M* :
probare *H, Lipsius Elect. 1.9* : rotare *Heinsius 589* : probatis *Baehrens* : probata *Wolfgang Meyer* :
probator *Ellis (1885), 96* : probatus *Vollmer*   181 monstrasti Saliis *Politianus B, Lipsius
Elect. 1.9* : monstrastis aliis *M*   certis *M* : certi *Vollmer*   *Schwartz (1889), 15 uel post
auguribus* 182 *uel post* flaminis 183 *latere lacunam suspicatus est, et Saenger post* cur *lacunam esse
credebat: fortasse lacunam post* carmen 182 *statuere possis*   182 uoluere ς : uolucre
M   183 cur... lateat *M* : cui... pateat *Postgate (1905), 135*   186 hiberas *M* :
hiberos ς   187 Zeugmate ς : zeumate *M*   188 asiae *M*¹ : aliae *M*   192 Nestor
M : Mentor *Saenger*   197 proelia ς : proeligia *M*   taedis ς : rhedis *M*
199 deorum ς : duorum *M*   202 concinis *M* : concipis *Markland*

Under your guidance the Dardanian enquirer after the concealed torch, who keeps secret the inmost recesses of the Diomedean theft, grew up and from you learnt of sacred matters as a boy. You showed arms to the Salii who have to be tested, and the prophetic heaven to certain augurs, and to the man for whom it is right to unroll the Chalcidian song * * * why the lock of the Phrygian priest is hidden, and the girt-up Lupercals trembled greatly at your blows. And now perhaps one from that flock is giving laws to the peoples of the Dawn, another holds in check the Iberians, and another keeps away the Achaemenid Persian at Zeugma. Some are controlling the wealthy peoples of Asia, some the Pontic regions, some correct the courts with rods that bring peace, others maintain the camps with loyal watchfulness; you are the source of their glory. Not Nestor nor Phoenix, who restrained his untamed pupil, nor Chiron, who broke in the son of Aeacus with a different song, even though he wanted to hear shrill bugles and trumpets, would have competed with you in shaping young men's hearts.

[195] While you were engaged in such things, a civil Fury from the Tarpeian hill stirred her sudden torch, and Phlegraean battles. The Capitol glowed with sacrilegious firebrands, and Latin cohorts assumed the fury of the Senones. Scarcely had there been any respite to the flames, and not yet had that pyre of the gods burnt down, when you, tireless and much swifter than the flames themselves, were singing consolations with pious lips for the temples that had been lost, and lamenting the captive thunderbolts. Amazed were the Latin notables and Caesar, the avenger of the gods, and from the midst of the fire the father of the gods gave his agreement. And already it was your intention to weep for the Vesuvian conflagration in pious song and to employ your lamentation for your country's losses, when the

cum Pater exemptum terris ad sidera montem
sustulit et late miseras deiecit in urbes.
210   me quoque uocales lucos Boeotaque tempe
pulsantem, cum stirpe tua descendere dixi,
admisere deae; nec enim mihi sidera tantum
aequoraque et terras, quae mos debere parenti,
sed decus hoc quodcumque lyrae primusque dedisti
non uulgare loqui et famam sperare sepulchro.
215 qualis eras, Latios quotiens ego carmine patres
mulcerem felixque tui spectator adesses
muneris, heu quali confundens gaudia fletu
uota piosque metus inter laetumque pudorem!
quam tuus ille dies, quam non mihi gloria maior!
220 talis Olympiaca iuuenem cum spectat harena
qui genuit, plus ipse ferit, plus corde sub alto
caeditur; attendunt cunei, spectatur Achaeis
ille magis, crebro dum lumina pulueris haustu
obruit et prensa uouet exspirare corona.
225   ei mihi, quod tantum patrias ego uertice frondes
solaque Chalcidicae Cerialia dona coronae
te sub teste tuli! qualem te Dardanus Albae
aspexisset ager, si per me serta tulisses
Caesarea donata manu! quod subdere robur
230 illa dies, quantum potuit dempsisse senectae!
nam quod me mixta quercus non pressit oliua
et fugit speratus honos, cum lustra parentis
inuida Tarpei canerem, te nostra magistro
Thebais urguebat priscorum exordia uatum;
235 tu cantus stimulare meos, tu pandere facta
heroum bellique modos positusque locorum

---

207 montem *ς* : monte *M*   209 Boeotaque *Baehrens* : biota *uel fortasse* luoca *M* (*etsi hic plurimi* biota *legerunt*) : luota *Politianus A* : lustrataque *Q*, *b*, *Calderini* : ignotaque *Ellis (1885), 96*   212 quae mos *Krohn* : quam uos *M*   213 decus M^1 : decum *M*   215 eras M^1 : erat *M*   217 confundens *Gibson* : confusus *M* : confessus *Sandström (1878), 38*   218 uota *m*? (*nam obscurissima littera* u *in margine adest*) : nota *M*   219 quam tuus *Politianus AC* : quam iuus (*uel* unis*) M* : qualis et *b*, *Calderini*   222 Achaeis *Imhof (1867), 2* : achates *M* : ephebis *Saenger*   223 haustu *Calderini* : hausti *M*   228 aspexisset *Håkanson (1969), 153* : uix cepisset *M* : excepisset *Cruceus Antidiatribe c. 7*   231 nam quod *M* : heu quod *Markland*   232 cum *Laetus*, *Markland* : qua *M* : quam *ς*, *Unger (1868), 181*   lustra *Markland* : dusce *M*, *ut uidetur* : dulce M^1 233 canerem *Gronov. 1653 (in notis)* : caperes *M* : caneres *Saenger* : colerem *Heyworth ante* te *editores aut notam exclamationis aut punctum ponere soliti sunt*   235 tu M^1 : tua *M*

Father uprooted the mountain from the earth, raised it to the stars, and hurled it down on the wretched cities far and wide.

[209] I too, beating at the groves of song and the valleys of Boeotia, on saying that I was descended from your stock, was admitted by the goddesses. For you did not only give me the stars and the seas and the lands, which it is right to owe to a parent, but you gave me this my glory of the lyre, such as it is, and were the first to give me speech which was not common and the hope of fame for my tomb. How you seemed, whenever I soothed the Latin fathers in song and you were present, a happy spectator of your own gift, alas, with what tears were you pouring forth your joys in the midst of prayers and pious fears and happy modesty! What a day of yours that was, and how my glory was no greater than yours! Such is the man who has fathered a son when he sees the young man on the Olympic sand; he himself is hitting harder, deep in his heart he himself is struck all the more; the rows of seats notice him, and it is he who is watched more by the Achaeans, while he covers his eyes with frequent handfuls of dust, and vows to die if the garland is captured.

[225] Alas for me that I wore on my head only the ancestral foliage, only Ceres' gift of the Chalcidian crown in your presence. How the Dardanian field of Alba would have looked on you if through me you had borne the garlands donated by Caesar's hand! What strength that day could have given you, how much old age it could have taken away! For as to the fact that the oak leaves with olive leaves mingled together did not cover me and the hoped-for honour deserted me, when I sang the invidious festival of the Tarpeian parent, with you as my master our *Thebaid* pressed hard on the beginnings of the ancient poets. You spurred on my song, you expounded the deeds of heroes and showed me the modes of war

monstrabas. labat incerto mihi limite cursus
te sine, et orbatae caligant uela carinae.
nec solum larga memet pietate fouebas:

240 talis et in thalamis. una tibi cognita taeda
conubia, unus amor. certe seiungere matrem
iam gelidis nequeo bustis; te sentit habetque,
te uidet et tumulos ortuque obituque salutat,
ut Pharios aliae ficta pietate dolores

245 Mygdoniosque colunt et non sua funera plorant.
    quid referam expositos seruato pondere mores?
quae pietas, quam uile lucrum, quae cura pudoris,
quantus amor recti! rursusque, ubi dulce remitti,
gratia quae dictis, animo quam nulla senectus!

250 his tibi pro meritis famam laudesque benignas
iudex cura deum nulloque e uulnere tristes
concessit. raperis, genitor, non indigus aeui,
non nimius, trinisque decem quinquennia lustris
iuncta ferens. sed me pietas numerare dolorque

255 non sinit, o Pylias aeui transcendere metas
et Teucros aequare senes, o digne uidere
me similem. sed nec leti tibi ianua tristis;
quippe leues causae, nec segnis labe senili
exitus instanti praemisit membra sepulchro,

260 sed te torpor iners et mors imitata quietem
explicuit falsoque tulit sub Tartara somno.
    quos ego tunc gemitus (comitum manus anxia uidit,
uidit et exemplum genetrix gauisaque nouit),
quae lamenta tuli! ueniam concedite, manes,

265 fas dixisse, pater: non tu mihi plura dedisses.

---

240 thalamis *Gibson* : thalamos *M*   241 seiungere *Calderini* : si iungere *M*
242 te *b* : et *M*   244 ut *M* : at *Calderini, fortasse recte*   250 laudesque benignas
M : cum laude benigna *Phillimore*[2], *cunctanter*   251 iudex *M* : index *a* : uindex
Aldus   tristes *Markland* : tristem *M*   *post* 251 *uersum deesse putauere Rothstein (1900), 502 et*
Krohn   253 trinisque ς, : crinisque *M*   255 o Pylias ς : opilias *M*   258 segnis
ς : segnes *M*   labe *M* : tabe *Gronov. Elench. c. 7 §188*   259 praemisit *M* : demisit
Schwartz (1889), 13   263 nouit *a* : uouit *M, ut uidetur*

and the placement of scenes. My progress falters in its uncertain path without you, and the sails of my bereaved craft are dark. Not only me did you cherish with vast piety: you were the same in your marriage-bed too. You knew marriage with but one wedding-torch, you had one love. For sure I cannot draw my mother back from the pyre that is already cold; you she feels and possesses, you she sees and greets your tomb at sunrise and sunset, in the same way as other women with feigned piety cultivate Pharian and Mygdonian griefs and weep for bereavements that are not their own.

[246] What am I to say of an open way of life that maintained its dignity? What piety you had, how you despised gain, how you cared for modesty, how great was your love for what is good! And again, when it was sweet to be at ease, what charm there was in your words, and how there was no old age in your mind! In return for these qualities the care of the gods who presided granted you fame and generous praise, not saddened by any blow. You are carried off, father, not lacking in years, not too old, having five years tenfold joined to three lustral cycles. But piety and grief do not allow me to count, you who are worthy to go beyond the Pylian limits of life and to match the old men of Troy, O worthy one to see me grow as old. But nor was the door of death grim for you, since its beginnings were gentle, nor did a sluggish dying send ahead your body in elderly decline to the imminent tomb, but a still numbness and death, like sleep, unravelled you and carried you below to Tartarus in seeming repose.

[262] What groanings then (an anxious band of companions saw me, my mother saw me too and recognized her example with joy), what laments I uttered! Grant me pardon, you shades, it is lawful to say this, father: you would not have given me more. That happy man

felix ille patrem uacuis circumdedit ulnis
uellet et, Elysia quamuis in sede locatum
268   abripere et Danaas iterum portare per umbras,
268a   <quem proli uentura suae praenoscere fata>
269   tempantem et uiuos molitum in Tartara gressus
270   detulit infernae uates longaeua Dianae;
       si chelyn Odrysiam pigro transmisit Auerno
272   causa minor, si Thessalicis Admetus in oris
272a   <coniuge ab infernis potuit gaudere reducta,>
273   si lux una retro Phylaceida rettulit umbram,
       cur nihil exoret, genitor, chelys aut tua manes
275   aut mea? fas mihi sit patrios contingere uultus,
       fas iunxisse manus, et lex quaecumque sequatur.
         at uos, umbrarum reges Aetnaeaque Iuno,
       si laudanda precor, taedas auferte comasque
       Eumenidum; nullo sonet asper ianitor ore,
280   Centauros Hydraeque greges Scyllaeaque monstra
       auersae celent ualles, umbramque senilem
       inuitet ripis discussa plebe supremus
       uector et in media componat molliter alno.
       ite, pii manes Graiumque examina uatum,
285   inlustremque animam Lethaeis spargite sertis
       et monstrate nemus quo nulla inrupit Erinys,
       in quo falsa dies caeloque simillimus aer.

---

post 268 *uersum huiusce modi deesse suspicatus est Housman, Class. P. ii. 654–5*   269–70 *ante* 266 *traiecit Saenger*   269 temptantem et *M* : quem tandem *Davies, Corpus* : Dardaniden *Saenger*   270 detulit *M* : rettulit *Markland*   271–2 si…si *Calderini* : sic…sic *M*   *post* 272 *uersum deesse suspicati sunt Heinsius ad Ov. Fast. 1.287, Postgate (1905), 135: lacunam hoc modo suppleuit Housman, Class. P. ii. 655*   273 si lux *Heinsius 593 et ad Ov. Her. 13.35* : silua *M* : sic lux *Vollmer*   rettulit *ς* : retulit *M*   275 sit *ς* : sic *M*   277 aecneaque *M* : aetneaque *ς* : Enn(a)eaque *Laetus (etsi a Reeve (1977b), 218 legitur Ennae), Gronov. Diatribe c. 59 §385–6* : Lethaeaque *Waller (1885), 56*   278 taedas *ς* : caedas *M*   279 ianitor *ς* : ianrior *M*   280 Centauros *Politianus A* : Centaurus *M*   hydraeque *ς* : bydraeque *M*   Scyllaeaque *ς* : scillaeque *M*   283 alno *D. A. Slater (1909), 249* : alga *M* : ulua *Markland*   286 inrupit *M* : inrumpit *ς* enfolded his father in empty arms and would have liked to carry him off, though he was situated in the Elysian land, and carry him again through Danaan shades, whom the ancient priestess of infernal Diana guided as he tried <to know in advance the fates that were coming for his own progeny> and directed his living steps into Tartarus. If a lesser reason sent the Odrysian lyre across to slow Avernus, if Admetus in the Thessalian lands <could rejoice, when his wife was brought back from the shades>, if a single day brought back the Phylaceidan ghost, why is neither your lyre nor mine to win anything from the shades? Let it be lawful for me to touch my father's face, let it be lawful to join hands, and let any decree whatsoever ensue.

[277] But you, monarchs of the shades and Aetnaean Juno, if I entreat for what is praiseworthy, take away the torches and tresses of the Eumenides; let the harsh doorkeeper make no sound from any of his mouths, and may remote valleys conceal the Centaurs and throngs of the Hydra and the Scyllaean monsters, and may the final ferryman invite an elderly shade from the banks, after dispersing the mob, and gently set him in the middle of his boat of alder-wood. Go, pious shades and throngs of Grecian poets, and shower a noble soul with Lethaean garlands, and show him the wood wherein no Fury has intruded, where there is a seeming daylight, and air most similar to the heavens.

inde tamen uenias melior, qua porta malignum
cornea uincit ebur, somnique in imagine monstra
290   quae solitus. sic sacra Numae ritusque colendos
mitis Aricino dictabat nympha sub antro,
Scipio sic plenos Latio Ioue ducere somnos
creditur Ausoniis, sic non sine Apolline Sulla.

288 *comma post* melior *ponit Köstlin (1876), 522, ita ut sensus sit* 'melior cornea uincit ebur', *sed quo modo potest cornea uincere, nisi re uera melior est? confer quoque 5. 2. 164:* 'sed uenies melior'   porta ς, *Laetus? (nam in margine scribit ille:* 'cornea porta mittit uera insomnia'*), Calderini :* parte *M*   289 monstra *Calderini :* monstrat *M*   293 creditur *M :* creditus *Heinsius* ausoniis *M :* Ausonio *Ker (1953), 6, quod coniugendum est cum* Apolline   sic non *Sudhaus ap. Vollmer :* nec non *M :* et non *Calderini*

[288] From there may you make a better journey however, where the gate of horn defeats the evil ivory, and in the appearance of a dream teach me as you used to. So did the gentle nymph in the Arician cave proclaim to Numa the sacred matters and rites to be observed, so is Scipio believed by the Ausonians to have experienced sleep full of Latin Jove, and so was Sulla not without his Apollo.

ECLOGA QVARTA

SOMNVS

CRIMINE quo merui, iuuenis placidissime diuum,
quoue errore miser, donis ut solus egerem,
Somne, tuis? tacet omne pecus uolucresque feraeque
et simulant fessos curuata cacumina somnos,
5   nec trucibus fluuiis idem sonus; occidit horror
aequoris, et terris maria adclinata quiescunt.
septima iam rediens Phoebe mihi respicit aegras
stare genas; totidem Oetaeae Paphiaeque reuisunt
lampades et totiens nostros Tithonia questus
10   praeterit et gelido spargit miserata flagello.
unde ego sufficiam? non si mihi lumina mille
quae piger alterna tantum statione tenebat
Argus et haud umquam uigilabat corpore toto.
at nunc, heu, si aliquis longa sub nocte puellae
15   bracchia nexa tenens ultro te, Somne, repellit,
inde ueni! nec te totas infundere pennas
luminibus compello meis (hoc turba precatur
laetior); extremo me tange cacumine uirgae
(sufficit), aut leuiter suspenso poplite transi.

---

1 *quidam editores comma post* iuuenis *ponunt, ita ut* iuuenis *non* Somnus *sed* Statius *sit, sed confer Silu. 3. 3. 208* 'salue supremum, senior mitissime patrum'   5 trucibus ς : trucibiss *M*
8 reuisunt ς, *Calderini* : reuisent *M* : recusent *a* : recursant *Markland* : renident *Baehrens* :
relucent *Krohn*   10 spargit *M* : tangit *Markland*   11 si *M* : sunt *Baehrens*
12 piger *Delz (1992), 251* : sacer *M* : uafer *Heinsius 188* : tamen *Saenger*   tantum *M* : tantum
<in> *Markland*   14 heu si aliquis *Barth* : heus aliquis *M* : fors a. *Markland* : nescioquis
Phillimore[2]   17 precatur *M* : precetur ς, *Heinsius*   19 aut...transi *M* : at...tran-
sit *Brandes (1885), 581*   leuiter *M* : leuior ς : limen *Saenger*   poplite *M* : pollice *Hoeufft*
(1807–8), 118–19

POEM FOUR

SLEEP

THROUGH what crime, young Somnus, most gentle of gods, or through what blunder have I deserved in my wretchedness to be the only one deprived of your gifts? All the cattle, the birds, and the wild beasts are silent, and the drooping tree-tops feign weary slumber, nor is there the same sound from the savage rivers; the trembling of the waters falls still, and the seas resting against the land are quiet. Returning already for the seventh time Phoebe again sees my sick eyes staying open; as many times do the Oetaean and Paphian stars return, and as many times does Aurora pass by my complaints, and sprinkle me in pity with her cool whip. How am I to endure? I could not, if I had the thousand eyes which sluggish Argus kept only alternately vigilant, and was never awake in his whole body. But now, alas, if someone of his own accord rejects you, Somnus, as he holds the enfolding arms of a girl throughout the long night, come from there. And I do not ask you to pour all your feathers over my eyes (a happier crowd prays for this); touch me with the extreme tip of your wand (it is enough), or pass by gently with lifted knees.

ECLOGA QVINTA

EPICEDION IN PVERVM SVVM

ME miserum! neque enim uerbis sollemnibus ultro
incipiam nunc Castaliae uocalibus undis
inuisus Phoeboque grauis. quae uestra, sorores,
orgia, Pieriae, quas incestauimus aras?
5   dicite: post poenam liceat commissa fateri.
numquid inaccesso posui uestigia luco?
num uetito de fonte bibi? quae culpa, quis error
quem luimus tanti? morientibus ecce lacertis
uiscera nostra tenens animamque auellitur infans,
10   non de stirpe quidem nec qui mea nomina ferret
iuraque; non fueram genitor, sed cernite fletus
liuentesque genas et credite planctibus orbi.
orbus ego. huc patres et aperto pectore matres
conueniant: crinemque rogis et cinnama ferte.
15   siqua sub uberibus plenis ad funera natos
ipsa gradu labente tulit madidumque cecidit
pectus et ardentes restinxit lacte fauillas,
siquis adhuc tenerae signatum flore iuuentae
immersit cineri iuuenem primaque iacentis
20   serpere crudeles uidit lanugine flammas,
adsit et alterno mecum clamore fatiscat:

---

1 sollemnibus ς : solemnibus M   ultro *Gibson* : ulla *M* : ultra *Barth apud Gronovium Diatribe*
c. 60 §387 : uti *Phillimore*[2], *cunctanter* : alta *Courtney, cunctanter*   2 nunc *Scriuerius, Io. Is.*
Pontanus apud Gronouium Diatribe c.60 §387 : nec *M*   8 tanti *Traglia* : tantis *M* : tantus
Politianus A   lacertis ς : lacestis *M*   9 animamque *perperam editioni Parmensi (b) attri-
buitur* : animaque *M*   11 iuraque *Gibson* : oraque *M*   12 orbi *esse genetiuum singularem
intellegebat Klotz, etsi alii esse uocatiuum credidere*   14 crinemque rogis et cinnama *Heinsius
(uide Lundström [1893], 40), alii alia* : cineremque oculis et crimina *M*   ferte *M, ut mihi aliisque
uidetur, etsi Souter, ut tradit Klotz, M* non ferte *sed* ferto *praebere credebat* : ferto *Politianus A*, ς *(uide
Reeve [1977b], 219)*   15 uberibus *M*[i] : uberi *M*   17 fauillas *Calderini* : papillas *M*
18 siquis *Hill* : quisquis *M*   20 flammas *Calderini* : malas *M*

POEM FIVE

LAMENT FOR HIS BOY

WRETCHED me! For I shall not begin of my own accord with solemn words, now that I am hateful to the sounding waters of Castalia and painful to Phoebus. What mysteries of yours, Pierian sisters, what altars have we polluted? Speak: after the punishment may it be permitted to confess faults. Surely I did not in any way place my footsteps in a grove that may not be entered? Surely I did not drink from a forbidden spring? What is the fault, what is the error, which we are paying for at so great a cost? With dying arms, lo!, and clinging to my inmost heart and my soul the infant is torn away, not, indeed, of my stock, or one who bears my name and rights; I had not been the father, but look on my weeping and bruised cheeks, and trust in the lamentations of one who has lost a child: I have lost a child. Here let fathers and mothers with bared breast assemble; bring to the pyres locks of hair and cinnamon. If anyone has carried her children beneath full breasts to their funeral with failing step, and has beaten her damp bosom and has quenched the burning embers with milk, if anyone has plunged a young man into his cremation when he is still marked with the bloom of gentle youth, and has watched the cruel flames creep over the first down as he lies there, let that person be present and grow weary with me in alternate wailing; he will be

uincetur lacrimis et te, Natura, pudebit,
tanta mihi feritas, tanta est insania luctus.
hoc quoque cum ni<tor>, ter dena luce peracta,
25 adclinis tumul<o pla>nctus in carmina uerto,
discordesque m<odos et> singultantia acerba
molior orsa ly<ra. satis> est atque ira tacendi
impatiens, sed nec solitae mihi uertice laurus
nec fronti uittatus honos. en taxea marcet
30 silua comis hilaresque hederas plorata cupressus
excludit ramis, nec eburno pollice chordas
pulso, sed incertam digitis errantibus amens
scindo chelyn. iuuat heu, iuuat inlaudabile carmen
fundere et incompte miserum nudare dolorem.
35 sic merui? sic me cantuque habituque nefastum
aspiciant superi? pudeat Thebasque nouumque
Aeaciden? nil iam placidum manabit ab ore?
ille ego qui (quotiens!) blande matrumque patrumque
uulnera, qui uiuos potui mulcere dolores,
40 ille ego lugentum mitis solator, acerbis
auditus tumulis et descendentibus umbris,
deficio medicasque manus fomentaque quaero
uulneribus subitura meis. nunc tempus, amici,
quorum ego manantes oculos et saucia tersi

24 cum *M* : dum *Gronovius Diatribe c. 60 §389*   ni<tor> *Gronovius Diatribe c. 60 §389* : ni *uel*
in *(uacat spatium fere uii litterarum) M*   ter dena ς : terdana *M*   25 tumulo ς, planctus
Unger (1868), 40, E. *Baehrens (1873), 251* : tumul *(uacat spatium fere uii litterarum)* nctus *M* : tumulo
luctus *a*   26 modos et ς : m *(uacat spatium fere xii litterarum)* singultantia *M*   acerba
Phillimore[1,2] : uerba *M*   25–8 *Courtney post* uerba (26) *grauiter distinxit, idem* dolor... |
impatiens *uncinis inclusit; Klotz post* molior *distinxit*   27 orsa *M* : ista *Shackleton Bailey*
ly<ra: satis> *Phillimore*[1,2] : ly *(uacat spatium fere xi litterarum)* est *M* : ly<rae uis> *Krohn* : ly<ra
dolor> *Sudhaus (uide* Vollmer *[1898], xvi); cf. Karsten (1899), 374; an* ly<ra
calor>? 31 ramis *M* : tremulas *Markland*   pollice *M* : pectine *Unger (1868),
46–7*   33 scindo ς : sciendo *M* : tendo *U, Phillimore*[2]   34 incompte ς : incomite
M   nudare *Markland* : laudare *M* : laxare *Unger (1868), 55–6, quod defendit
Håkanson (1969), 156–7* : clamare *Otto (1887), 546*   35–7 *sic interpunxere Phillimore*[1,2],
Mozley; iam Rothstein (1900), 506 hic interrogari suspicatus erat   35 sic merui *M* : si merui
Unger (1868), 58   37 placidum *M* : placitum *Markland*   manabit ς : manabat *M*
38 quotiens *M* : totiens *a*   blande *(quod laudat Baehrens) uel* blando *M* : blandus *Calderini* :
fando *Polster (1884) 14*   39 uiuos *M* : uiduos *Heinsius, frigide*   42 deficio ς : dificio *M*
43 subitura *Shackleton Bailey* : sed summa *M* : sed uana *Heinsius ad Ov. Pont. 4.11.20* : sed suntne
Polster (1878), 11 : sed nulla *Rothstein (1900), 506–7* : sessura *Phillimore*[1,2]*, cunctanter* : Dictamna
Saenger : (spes uana!) *Delz (1992), 252*   44 saucia ς : faucia *M*

conquered by my tears and you, Nature, will be ashamed, such wildness I have, so great is the madness of my grief. And when I <strive> at this, after thirty days have passed, I turn my <lamentations> into poems as I lie on the tomb, and I sound discordant <notes and> tearful beginnings on my bitter lyre. It is <enough>, and my anger is intolerant of being silent, but neither are the accustomed laurels on my head nor are there honours garlanded about my forehead; behold, the foliage of yew wanes in my hair and the lamented cypress keeps out the joyful ivy with its branches, and not with ivory thumb do I sound the strings, but with my erring fingers I tear at the uncertain lyre. It helps, alas, it helps to pour out a song that is not to be praised, and to lay bare a wretched grief in disarray. Have I deserved thus? Are the gods thus to look on me, unspeakable in song and appearance? Are Thebes and the new son of Aeacus to be ashamed? Will nothing calm now flow from my lips? I am that man who (so many times!) could gently soothe the wounds of fathers and mothers, who could soothe living grief, I, that gentle consoler of those who grieve, heard by bitter tombs and shades as they descend, am inadequate and seek healing hands and poultices to help my wounds. Now it is time, friends whose streaming eyes and wounded breasts I have wiped dry: give your help in return, and pay back your gratitude, late though it is. Certainly when your funerals in sad tones I * * *, reproaching me: 'You who grieve

45 pectora: reddite opem, seras exsoluite grates.
46 nimirum cum uestra modis ego funera maestis
46a   *   *   *   *   *
47 increpitans: 'qui damna doles aliena, repone
      infelix lacrimas et tristia carmina serua.'
      uerum erat: absumptae uires et copia fandi
50 nulla mihi, dignumque nihil mens fulmine tanto
      repperit: inferior uox omnis et omnia sordent
      uerba. ignosce, puer: tu me caligine mersum
      obruis. a durus, uiso si uulnere carae
      coniugis inuenit caneret quod Thracius Orpheus
55 dulce sibi, si busta Lini complexus Apollo
      non tacuit. nimius fortasse auidusque doloris
      dicor et in lacrimis iustum excessisse pudorem.
      quisnam autem gemitus lamentaque nostra reprendis?
      o nimium felix, nimium crudelis et expers
60 imperii, Fortuna, tui qui dicere legem
      fletibus aut fines audet censere dolendi!
      incitat heu planctus; potius fugientia ripas
      flumina detineas, rapidis aut ignibus obstes,
      quam miseros lugere uetes. tamen ille seuerus,
65 quisquis is est, nostrae cognoscat uulnera causae.
        non ego mercatus Pharia de puppe loquaces
      delicias doctumque sui conuicia Nili
      infantem, lingua nimium salibusque proteruum,
      dilexi; meus ille, meus. tellure cadentem

---

45 opem, seras (opem et seras *Unger [1868], 68–9) scripsi* : opem saeuas *M* : opes aequas *Cornelissen (1877), 293*   46 modis…maestis *van Kooten (uide Courtney [1966], 97), Klotz (1896), 79* : domus…maestus *M*   *post* 46 *lacunam statuit Baehrens, quem secuti sunt omnes fere editores excepto Vollmer*   47 increpitans *M* : increpitant *Vollmer, ita ut sensus uersus 46 repente frangatur, tamquam poeta uix loqui possit*   47 qui *M* : quid *F. Skutsch apud Vollmer*   doles *Politianus A* : dolens *M*   51 uox *ς* : nox *M*   52 mersum *Heinsius 595, Markland* : maestu *M* : maestum *ς* : maesta *ς*   53 durus *ς (uide Reeve [1977b], 219), Politianus AB (uide Cesarini Martinelli [1982], 198)* : duro *M*   58 reprendis *Politianus A* : rependis *M* : reprendit *ς*   59 nimium *ς* : nmium *M*   expers *M*[1] : etpers *M*   62 potius *M* : citius *Heinsius 595*   63 flumina *ς* : fulmina *M*   detineas *Boxhorn (1662), 66* : demneus *M*   65 causae *M* : curae *Markland*   66 puppe *M* : pube *Heinsius ad Ou. Met. 7. 56*   67 delicias *ς (uide Reeve [1977b], 219), Avantius* : aedituas *M* : nequitias *Markland*   68 nimium *Britannicus, Markland* : sumum *M* : eximium *Waller (1885), 57*

for the losses of others, keep back your tears, unlucky one, and conserve your grim songs.' It was true: my strength has been taken away and I have no abundance of speech, and nothing worthy of such a thunderbolt has my mind found. My whole utterance is too lowly and all my words are muddied. Forgive me, boy; you overwhelm me sunk in gloom. O, hard he was, Thracian Orpheus, if he found something sweet to sing to himself at the sight of his dear wife's wound, and Apollo, if he did not keep silent as he embraced the pyre of Linus. Perhaps I am said to be excessive and eager for grief, and to have gone beyond due shame in my tears. But who are you blaming our groans and laments? O too fortunate and too cruel, and outside your sway, Fortune, he who dares to pronounce a law for weeping or to set the boundaries of grieving! Alas, he spurs on lamentation; you may sooner hold back rivers that flee their banks or stand in the way of swift fires than forbid the wretched to grieve. However let that severe one, whoever he is, know the wounds of my case.

[66] I did not purchase a chattering darling from a Pharian ship nor loved an infant schooled in the banter of his native Nile too free in his speech and wanton in his wit: mine he was, mine. I raised him up from the ground as he came down, and cherished him, glorified with

70   suscepi atque auctum genitali carmine foui,
      poscentemque nouas tremulis ululatibus auras
      inserui uitae. quid plus tribuere parentes?
      quin alios ortus libertatemque sub ipsis
      uberibus tibi, parue, dedi, cum munera nostra
75   rideres ignarus adhuc. properauerit ille,
      sed merito properabat, amor, ne perderet <ullum>
      libertas tam parua diem. nonne horridus <inde>
      inuidia superos iniustaque Tartara pulsem?
      nonne gemam te, care puer? quo sospite natos
80   non cupii, primo genitor quem protinus ortu
      implicui fixique mihi, cui uerba sonosque
      monstraui questusque et murmura caeca resoluens,
      reptantemque solo demissus ad oscula dextra
      erexi, blandoque sinu iam iamque <cadentes>
85   permulcere genas dulcesque accersere somnos,
      cui nomen uox prima meum, cunctusque tenello
      risus et a nostro ueniebant gaudia uultu.

---

70 suscepi *Cancik (1972), 88* : aspexi *M* : excepi *Avantius*   auctum *Gibson* : unctum *M*
carmine *M* : aspergine *(uel flumine) Saenger (1907), 300, (1910), 562–3* : stramine *Baehrens* :
sanguine *Danielsson (1897), 43–5* : tramite *Delz (1992), 253–5*   71 poscentemque *M* :
pulsantem *Markland* : pascentemque *Otto (1887), 546*   74 tibi *M*[1] : ubi *M*   cum
Politianus A : heu *M*   75 rideres *M* : ridebas *ς*   ignarus *Avantius* : ingatus *M* : ingratus *ς*
76 <ullum> *ς* : *om. M* : <unum> *Baehrens*   77 <inde> *Baehrens* : *om. M* : <ipsos> *ς* :
<idem> *Phillimore*[1,2]   80 non cupii *Calderini* : concupii *M*   genitor *Gibson* : gemi-
tum *M* : genitum *Politianus A (uide Cesarini Martinelli [1975], 170)* : gremium *Heinsius 595,
Markland* : genetrix *Saenger* : mentem *Delz (1992), 255*   quem *Politianus A* : qui *M*
81 implicui fixique *Politianus A* : implicuit fixitque *M*   82 et *M*[1] : *om. M*   murmura
Markland : uulnera *M*   resoluens *Markland* : ne soluam *M* : resolui *ς* : resoluam *ς*
83 dextra *ς* : uestra *M* : nostra *ς, a*   84 <cadentes> *Baehrens* : *om. M* : <natantes>
ς   85 permulcere *Gibson* : excepere *M* : extergere *Lindenbrog (in obseruationibus, p. 479)* :
exceptare *Unger (1868), 140* : exsopire *Vollmer* : feci operire *Phillimore*[1,2], cunctanter   *post* 85
lacunam statuendam esse coniecit Courtney   86 tenello *ς* : tenebo *M*   cunctusque *Courtney,
cunctanter* : ludusque *M* : multusque *Boxhorn (1662), 66*

a song for his birth, and, as he asked for fresh air with trembling cries, I started him on his life. What more did his parents give him? Indeed I gave you, little one, another birth and freedom when you were still at the breast itself, although, still unaware, you laughed at my gift. Though that love may have made haste, rightly was it making haste, so that such small freedom should not lose a <single> day. Surely I should rudely assail the gods and unjust Tartarus <then> with my complaints? Surely I should lament for you, dear boy? While he was safe I did not want sons, he, whom I, a father, at his first birth embraced and drew to myself, to whom I showed words and sounds, interpreting both his complaints and his unclear murmurings, and leaning down I grasped and lifted him up to my kisses as he crawled on the ground, and in my gentle embrace I soothed the eyes that were now already <drooping>, and summoned sweet sleep, whose first utterance was my name, and for the gentle one all his laughter and joys came from my face.

COMMENTARY

Poem One

INTRODUCTION

Summary: *Epistle: Statius praises Abascantus' devotion to his dead wife, Priscilla, and explains his own wish to commemorate Abascantus' grief.*

Poem: Statius would wish to provide a physical memorial for Priscilla, though poetic commemoration is superior (1–15). The extent of Abascantus' grief; the emperor has noticed his devotion (16–42). Priscilla's virtues and her devotion to her husband (43–74). Abascantus' appointment and duties as ab epistulis (75–107). Priscilla's joy and support for her husband (108–34). Priscilla's final illness and her husband's pleas to the gods (135–69). Priscilla's farewell to her husband and her death (170–96). Abascantus' grief is only held in check by his devotion to the emperor; Priscilla's funeral (197–221). Priscilla's tomb on the Via Appia (222–46). Abascantus is to stop grieving; Priscilla is in Elysium (247–62).

For discussion of the poem as *epicedion*, see the section on consolation in the General Introduction, especially pp. xxxii–xxxiv.

T. Flavius Abascantus[1] held the post of *ab epistulis* under Domitian. Little else is known of him, although he does appear in inscriptions: *CIL* vi. 8598 and 8599 (inscriptions of two of his own freedmen), 2214 (set up by T. Flavius Epaphroditus, who was *aedituus* for Abascantus and Priscilla) and 8713, where another *aedituus* called T. Flavius (the *cognomen* is missing) is attested for a T. Flavius who may be Abascantus. The *Notitia Vrbis*[2] records baths of Abascantus in the region of the

---

[1] Abascantus would have received Domitian's *praenomen* 'Titus' on his manumission; the *praenomen* Titus is held by Abascantus' freedmen in *CIL* vi. 2214 and 8713 (if 8713 refers to Statius' Abascantus). For a contemporary Abascantus, note the L. Satrius Abascantus on whose behalf Pliny (*Ep.* 10. 11. 2) requested the *ius Quiritium* from Trajan.

[2] Nordh (1949), 74. 1. Weaver (1994), 339 compares the baths of Claudius Etruscus (*Silv.* 1. 5).

Porta Capena; these are perhaps attributable to the present Abas-
cantus, although the name is by no means rare and is regularly used
for slaves and freedmen; the Greek ἀβάσκαντος denotes 'secure from
enchantments, free from harm'.[3] Indeed the frequency of the name
provides good ground for rejecting the identification of the recipient
of the present poem with the imperial freedman T. Flavius Abascan-
tus, the *a cognitionibus*, who is the subject of a funeral monument set up
by his wife Flavia Hesperis (8628);[4] there is also another imperial
freedman named Ti. Claudius Abascantus (8411), who held the post
of *a rationibus*.

In ll. 85–107 Statius gives an account of Abascantus' duties as *ab
epistulis*, which, though invested with poetic and panegyrical colour, is
nevertheless an important piece of evidence. Statius begins by em-
phasising the arduous nature of the post (85–6), which includes
dispatching the 'Romulei mandata ducis' (87) throughout the empire,
the gathering of knowledge from all its four quarters (88–91) and
assisting in a variety of military appointments including the com-
mand of cohorts and cavalry (94–8). A. Hardie (1983), 186 suggests
that this last passage may indicate that Abascantus had a role to play
in the nominations to such posts.[5]

The office of *ab epistulis* itself appears to have emerged as a result of
the increasing demands of correspondence on the emperors.[6] Millar
(1992), 213 remarks that precedents are to be found even in the
Hellenistic monarchies; the first notable Roman instance is the
elder Pompeius Trogus, secretary to Julius Caesar: 'patrem quoque
sub C. Caesare militasse epistularumque et legationum, simul et anuli
curam habuisse' (Justin 43. 5. 12). The title itself is first attested in
inscriptions dating probably from the first half of the first century AD
(*CIL* vi. 4249, 8596, 8613), although the first major personality to have
held the post is Narcissus, the freedman of Claudius (Suet. *Cl.* 28). An
anecdote suggests the sensitive nature of the post; before his suicide,

---

[3] *ThLL* I. 47. 54–68; Stein s.v. 'Flavius' in *RE* vi/2. 2530. 12–17, Vidman (1980), 211,
Solin (1982), 844–7. For the frequency of identical nomenclature for imperial slaves and
freedmen, see Weaver (1994), 334–6.

[4] A. Hardie (1983), 185 is less sceptical, but see Weaver (1994), 343–60. On *CIL* vi. 8628,
see ibid. 339–42.

[5] See further *Silv.* 5. 1. 95–8 n., and Cotton (1981), 230–1 with nn. 10 and 11. The military
character of the post is stressed by A. R. Birley (1992), 42, 44, who also (42) offers a range of
quotations on the role of the *ab epistulis* in military affairs from the work of Eric Birley.

[6] For an overview of the various chancellery departments, see Lotito (1974–5), 290–2.
On imperial correspondence, see Millar (1992), 213–28.

Narcissus burnt letters of Claudius concerning his wife Agrippina
(D.C. 60. 34. 5). Travel with the emperor also seems to have been an
important aspect of the post,[7] which may lend further resonance to
Statius' assertion of Abascantus' knowledge of all four corners of the
empire, although Domitian seems only to have campaigned in person
on the northern frontiers.

A separate issue is the extent of the emperor's involvement in
imperial correspondence. Statius does not in this poem lay any stress
on Abascantus as a composer of letters; contrast the emphasis on
literary qualities in later periods, especially with holders of the office
of *ab epistulis Graecis*.[8] Significantly he only says that Abascantus has to
send (*dimittere*) his master's instructions. Moreover, Suet. *Dom.* 13. 1 is
evidence for Domitian's participation in the dictation of letters, with
him allegedly insisting on the use of the words *dominus* and *deus* in the
opening formula. On Domitian's correspondence, see further Cole-
man (1986), 3093–4.

Abascantus may have been one of the last freedmen to hold the
post of *ab epistulis*.[9] His tenure came at a time when there was already
something of a reaction against the excesses of the freedmen of the
last Julio-Claudians, a trend which continued under the Antonines,
especially Hadrian.[10] Although Tac. *Ag.* 40. 2 and 41. 4, as well as
Plin. *Pan.* 88. 1, might give the impression of a predominance of
freedmen in Domitian's administration,[11] Suet. *Dom.* 7. 2 mentions
the emperor's division of appointments between freedmen and mem-
bers of the equestrian order. One such equestrian appointment is Cn.
Titinius Capito, who held the office of *ab epistulis* in the successive
reigns of Domitian, Nerva, and Trajan (*ILS* 1448).[12]

---

[7] Millar (1992), 6, 85, 90–93.

[8] See ibid. 90–9 for some 2nd-c. AD instances of literary men in this post.

[9] On Statius' presentation of Flavian freedmen, see further Lotito (1974–5).

[10] Hadrian's impact is evinced by the erroneous ascription to him by *SHA Hadr.* 22. 8 of
the first equestrian appointments to the posts of *ab epistulis* and *a libellis*. Exceptions for both
of these positions can be found as early as the 'Year of the Four Emperors': Secundus, an
equestrian who was *ab epistulis* under Otho (Plu. *Otho* 9. 3), and Sex. Caesius Propertianus
(*PIR*² C 204), *a libellis* under Vitellius.

[11] Griffin (2000), 80 notes a parallel with the reign of Claudius in that the practice of
addressing literary works to imperial freedmen appears to have been revived under
Domitian (e.g. *Silv.* 5. 1, Mart. 8. 68).

[12] On Capito, see e.g. Syme, *RP* ii. 483, iii. 1346, v. 469, vii. 476, 587, A. R. Birley (1992),
45, who offers (ibid. 48–54) a convenient list of holders of the office of *ab epistulis* from Capito
onwards, with details of other offices held during their careers.

Given the dating of *Silv.* 5. 1 (no earlier than AD 94, given the
mention of the Templum Flauiae Gentis in 240–1),[13] the appointment
of Capito under Domitian has led to speculation on the fate of
Abascantus himself, particularly as Statius in this poem refers to
him as a *iuuenis*, which makes death as a result of old age an unlikely
reason for Capito's appointment to the post. Whatever the reason for
Abascantus' departure, it need not be assumed that he would auto-
matically have been put to death on leaving office: another *ab epistulis*
to be dismissed and survive was Suetonius, allegedly for offending
Hadrian's consort, Faustina.

A. Hardie (1983), 185–7 has argued that the present poem can be
interpreted against the background of the political uncertainties of
the final portion of Domitian's reign. On the basis of the execution of
Epaphroditus in 95, and the involvement of freedmen in the plot
which killed Domitian in 96 (Suet. *Dom.* 17. 1, D.C. 67. 15. 1), Hardie,
following Syme's[14] arguments for envisaging Domitian as looking for
support beyond the familiar and untrustworthy confines of his house-
hold, argues that the poem dates from a period of uncertainty prior to
Abascantus' dismissal, when he was perhaps weakened by the death
of his wife Priscilla, who had had a significant role in advancing his
career through her intercessions with the emperor. Hardie further
points to the emphasis on Abascantus' qualities of loyalty, which
would have served as a reminder to the emperor not to drop a trusted
servant, and notes that the poem carefully forestalls the usual criti-
cisms of freedmen as wealthy and corrupt. His hypothesis is thus that
the poem represents an attempt to state the case for Domitian's
retention of Abascantus.

Hardie's is certainly an impressive argument, but needs some
qualification,[15] since he seems close to arguing that the poem's
consolatory nature is really a cover for a political advertisement. He
cites the lateness of the *epicedion* and affirms an apparent lack of
intimacy between Abascantus and Statius. Both these points are
open to modification. Consolation was often given after the lapse of
some time (see 5. 1. 16 n.), while Statius' letter suggests quite a close
friendship, particularly as Statius is able to allude not only to the

---

[13] Vollmer (1898), 9.   [14] Syme (1958), ii. 597.

[15] Note that Weaver (1994), 357–8 has subsequently argued that the appointment of
Capito by Domitian may not in fact mean that Abascantus was either dismissed or
demoted; he points out (358 n. 129) that several instance of overlapping *pairs* of procuratorial
administrators are attested in the second century AD.

friendship existing between the wives of the two men, but also to Priscilla's favourable influence on Statius' own marriage (5. 1 *epist.* 5–6), a reference which seems enigmatic to us, although it was probably not so mysterious for Abascantus. Thus the seriousness of the personal and poetic purpose of this *epicedion* should not be discounted.

The tomb of Priscilla described in ll. 222–35 has been identified with the large tomb situated near the church of Domine, Quo Vadis? on the Via Appia Antica known as the Tomba di Priscilla (see FIG. 1). The identification is reasonable given the presence of thirteen external niches of *opus reticulatum* on the tomb, which would provide a setting for the statues of Priscilla in various divine guises described in ll. 231–3. Furthermore the Tomba di Priscilla is close to the Almo (compare 223 'quaque Italo gemitus Almone Cybebe | ponit)', and the inscription which mentions Priscilla, *CIL* vi. 2214, is recorded as having been found 'extra Portam Capenam', which would accord with the location of the tomb. The case for the identification of the Tomba di Priscilla with the tomb described by Statius in the

FIG. 1. View of the Tomba di Priscilla, showing *opus reticulatum*.
Photo: Bruce Gibson.

present poem is thus a good one, although absolute certainty is unobtainable.[16]

For architectural accounts of the monument, see Rivoira (1921), 139–40, Crema (1959), 326, Coarelli (1981), 15–16, Della Portella *et al.* (2004), 54–6. See also Canina's two drawings, one a picture of the ruins, the other an impression of the tomb in Roman times, in Canina (1853), ii, tab. 6. Rivoira describes it as an impressive structure, with two floors, the lower of which is a square of 20 m breadth, while the upper floor has a circular ambit-wall where the niches of *opus reticulatum* are to be found. Whereas it was possible to view the exterior of the monument in 1993, though the interior was unsafe, it is now (2005) closed pending restoration. It is topped with a medieval tower.

COMMENTARY

Statius Abascanto suo salutem

Unlike the other books of the *Silvae*, *Silvae* 5 has no general introduction to the whole book.[17] Instead the opening letter introduces only the first poem. The closest extant prose parallel is the letter and poem at the head of Martial's ninth book of epigrams; compare also, in verse, Cat. 65, which introduces poem 66.

The letter emphasizes Statius' friendship with Abascantus; for the importance of displaying genuine familiarity in situations of consolation, see Nauta (2002), 235. The imperial connection is here a subordinate reason (*praeterea*, 8) for the poem's composition. The end of the letter indicates that the motive for the poem is *amicitia*; see further Nauta (2002), 193–4. The personal reference to Priscilla's friendship with Statius' wife, Claudia (5–6), adds to the impression of a bond of affection between the two men.[18]

---

[16] See Coarelli (1981), 15.

[17] On the prose prefaces to the first four books of the *Silvae* see van Dam (1984), 51–4, Laguna (1992), 109–12 and Coleman (1988), 53–5, Nauta (2002), 281–3; see also useful remarks on prose prefaces in Lightfoot (1999), 222–4 and on dedicatory letters in Nauta (2002), 122–3. P. White (1974), 60–1 contrasts the stylized prefaces to the first four books of the *Silvae* with the greater informality found both in the letter at the start of Book 5 and in Martial's dedications. See the General Introduction (p. xxxviii above) for the relevance of this difference to the status of *Silvae* 5.

[18] Cf. Leberl (2004), 128–9, who, however, remarks (129) that 'Es muss daher offen bleiben, ob zwischen dem Dichter und dem *ab epistulis* ein dauerhaftes *patronus-cliens*-Verhältnis mit ensprechenden materiellen Folgen für Statius bestand, oder ob Abascantus das Epikedion mit einer einmaligen materiellen Zuwendung honorierte.'

1. omnibus adfectibus prosequenda sunt: cf. Plin. *Ep.* 3.
10. 3 'neque enim adfectibus meis uno libello carissimam mihi et
sanctissimam memoriam prosequi satis est'.

exempla: Abascantus' conduct towards his wife is a model for
others; compare *Rhet. Her.* 3. 6. 11, where one motive for praise is the
desire that others may recall a person's qualities: 'aut studio, quod
eiusmodi uirtute sit ut omnes commemorare debeant uelle'.[19] In the
poem, Abascantus becomes exemplary by surpassing or matching
other examples of devotion. This is particularly evident at lines 33–6,
where three examples of grief (Niobe, Aurora, and Thetis) are all
presented as inferior to Abascantus, but see also 7–8, where Abas-
cantus fights death, 23–8, where only Abascantus could be insensible
to the soothing songs of Orpheus, 101–7, where Abascantus is equal to
the messengers of the gods, and 202–4, where Abascantus' grief is like
that of Orpheus. The poem also commemorates the *exempla* set by
Priscilla, as at 57–9, where she would have remained insensible to the
advances of Paris or Thyestes.

publice: reference to the public advantage of an exemplary
marriage would have sounded a topical note under an emperor
who enthusiastically upheld public morality (5. 1. 42 n.).

2. pietas: a typical characteristic of bereavement (cf. Plin. *Ep.* 5.
16. 8, where Fundanus is intent only on his grief: 'expulsisque uirtu-
tibus aliis pietatis est totus') and a continuing theme in the poem (5. 1.
238 n.).

Priscillae tuae: the possessive adjective imparts an intimate
note.

est morum tuorum pars: compare Tac. *Hist.* 1. 14. 2 'ea pars
morum eius quo suspectior sollicitis adoptanti placebat', also in a
context of winning approval. M's *et* requires an ellipse of *est*; for
ellipses of *esse*, see Winter (1907), esp. 43, 56–62, K.–S. i. 10–15,
H.–Sz. 419–23 (§223); cf. van Dam and Iz.–Fr. on *Silv.* 2 pr. 22.
However, with an ellipse of *est* in the current passage, the first *et*
would have to be understood not as 'and', joining *pietas* to *morum
tuorum pars*, which would be a natural way of taking the conjunction,
but as 'both', looking forward to the second 'et' in the sentence; there
is also an imbalance between the ellipse of *est* in the first part of the
sentence and the clause with *potest* in the second. The sense would

---

[19] In the same section, ties of friendship are also cited as a reason for praise; Statius
mentions this additional motivation in 6–7.

have to be: 'the devotion which you show to your Priscilla [*is*] both a part of your character and cannot fail to win anyone over...'. With *est* (Barth), the transition is smoother and clearer.

3. praecipue marito: the reminder of his own status as a husband emphasizes Statius' fellow-feeling; his personal involvement is also brought out by *ego tamen* in 4.

amare: right at the outset, Statius characterizes the relationship between husband and wife as an emotional one: Dixon (1991) claims that from the time of the late republic, there existed a 'sentimental ideal' of family life in Rome, arguing that 'literature, art (especially funerary art), and inscriptions show that the *ideal* [her emphasis] of the affectionate, welcoming family unit pervaded many Republican representations of family life' (99); see also Treggiari (1991), 183–261.

5. nec tantum quasi officiosus: *officiosus* denotes one bound by the ties of duty (for its association with the obligations of a client owed to a patron, compare e.g. Mart. 1. 70. 2, 5. 22. 13); for the desire not to seem *officiosus*, cf. Mart. 10. 58. 13–14 'per ueneranda mihi Musarum sacra, per omnes | iuro deos: et non officiosus amo'. This poem, however, is not written only because of Abascantus' position: there is a personal link as well.

amauit: the emphatic position stresses the friendship between Statius' wife and Priscilla.

6. probatiorem: for the epithet, compare Plin. *Ep.* 6. 34. 1 'inde etiam uxorem carissimam tibi et probatissimam habuisti'.

7. ingratus sum: for *gratia* as a key term in patronage relationships, as regards both their reciprocity and their continued duration, see Nauta (2002), 25.

si lacrimas tuas transeo: for discussion of the poem's role as a commemoration not only of Priscilla but also of Abascantus' grief for her, see the Introduction (p. xxxv f., above).

7–8. latus omne diuinae domus: literally 'every flank of the divine house', i.e. all who are in the service of the emperor. Statius combines the metaphor of a house, *domus*, meaning the household, with a metaphor suggesting its members, *latus*, literally a side. For *latus* denoting a companion or supporter, perhaps similar to the English phrase 'right-hand man', compare V. Max. 2. 9. 6 'Claudius Nero Liuiusque Salinator, secundi Punici belli temporibus firmissima rei publicae latera', Mart. 6. 68. 3–4 'inter Baianas raptus puer occidit undas | Eutychos ille, tuum, Castrice, dulce latus' (cf. perhaps 2. 46. 8,

where the text is disputed), Juv. 3. 131–2 'diuitis hic seruo cludit latus
ingenuorum | filius'; note also *Silv.* 5. 1. 80 'et inspectis ambit latus
omne ministris' and Curt. 3. 5. 15 'cum ad perniciem eius etiam a
latere ipsius pecunia sollicitaret hostis'. Statius also describes proxim-
ity to the emperor in terms of the emperor's own *latus* (*Silv.* 3. 3. 65,
5. 1. 187); compare Sen. *Dial.* 6. 15. 3 'Seiano ad latus stanti', Mart. 6.
76. 1 'ille sacri lateris custos', Lactantius on *Theb.* 2. 312 'NVDVM
LATVS ab amicis desertum. regum enim semper latera stipatorum
satellitumque corona claudebat.' One may further note the use of the
title *legatus a latere* to denote papal legates of the highest rank, such as
Wolsey, who enjoyed precedence over the Archbishop of Canterbury
in England upon his appointment to the title in 1518; the Codex Iuris
Canonici 1917 can. 266 strikinginly describes the *legatus a latere* as
follows: 'Dicitur *Legatus a latere* Cardinalis qui a Summo Pontifice
tanquam *alter* ego cum hoc titulo mittitur, et tantum potest, quantum
ei a Summo Pontifice demandatum est'; cf. the Codex Iuris Canonici
1983 can. 385 for a more modern definition, with more emphasis on
ceremonial participation on behalf of the Pontiff.

8. pro mea mediocritate: for this kind of deference towards
the imperial family, compare e.g. Vell. 2. 104. 3 'caelestissimorum eius
operum per annos continuos VIIII praefectus aut legatus spectator,
tum pro captu mediocritatis meae adiutor fui' with Woodman ad loc.,
2. III. 3, *Pan. Lat.* 6(7). 1. 1 'quoniam maiestas tua hunc mediocritati
meae diem in ista ciuitate celeberrimum ad dicendum dedisset'; cf. V.
Max. 1 pr. 18–19 'mea paruitas eo iustius ad fauorem tuum decucur-
rerit'. Formulae of modesty are of course conventional at the opening
of works: see e.g. Isoc. 4. 13, *Rhet. Her.* 3. 6. 11 'ab eius persona de quo
loquemur, si laudabimus: uereri nos ut illius facta uerbis consequi
possimus', Quint. *Inst.* 4. 1. 8, Curtius (1953), 83–5.

10. usum amicitiae tuae: for *usus* denoting relations between
people, compare e.g. Ov. *Tr.* 3. 5. 1 'Vsus amicitiae tecum mihi
paruus', Tac. *Ann.* 2. 28. 1 'Flaccum Vescularium equitem Romanum,
cui propior cum Tiberio usus erat'. Nauta (2002), 247 emphasizes
Statius' desire for Abascantus' friendship, and also suggests that the
poem may have been written to order, in spite of the fact that
consolation is normally presented (as here) as a voluntary offering
to the bereaved.

11. The absence of a closing formula such as *uale* is paralleled in
the transmitted preface to book 2 of the *Silvae*, while the prefaces of
books 3 and 4 both have *uale* (the preface to book 1 is incomplete). The

letter could have ended with *uale*; for the disappearance of *uale* at the end of a letter, compare Quint. *Inst.* pr. 3, where H omits *uale*.

Epicedion in Priscillam <Abascanti> uxorem

1. similes . . . ceras: Statius would wish to offer Abascantus an artistic creation but considers himself unequal to the task (cf. Pi. *N.* 5. 1 Οὐκ ἀνδριαντοποιός εἰμ᾽ with Rosati (2002), 247, Hor. *Carm.* 4. 8. 1–12). *similis* denotes verisimilitude: cf. *Silv.* 3. 3. 200–2 'te lucida saxa, | te similem doctae referet mihi linea cerae, | nunc ebur et fuluum uultus imitabitur aurum', Sen. *Con.* 10. 5. 27, Mart. 1. 109. 18–20, Juv. 2. 6. These lines might suggest Ovid's story of Pygmalion (*Met.* 10. 243–97), but whereas Pygmalion asked that life be given to a statue, Abascantus tries to immortalize his wife in artistic representation (8–10). Ovid plays on this meaning of *similis* at *Met.* 10. 274–6:

> constitit et timide 'si di dare cuncta potestis,
> sit coniunx, opto,' non ausus 'eburnea uirgo'
> dicere, Pygmalion 'similis mea' dixit 'eburnae.'

docilis: for *docilis* with the infinitive, see *ThLL* v/1. 1768. 57 ff., and cf. *Silv.* 5. 2. 33 'indocilemque fero seruire Neroni'.

fingere ceras: if *fingere* is correct, the representations of Priscilla envisaged would be wax statues. However, given the pairing of painting and sculpture in 5–6, *pingere* (Krohn) is attractive, establishing the same pairing in 1–2. *pingere ceras* would signify encaustic painting, whereby pigments were burnt on using wax, a technique discussed by Plin. *Nat.* 35. 122–3; cf. Vitruv. 7. 9. 3 on the apparent use of wax in painting walls (but see Ling (1991), 201), and see Robertson (1975), 485, Bruno (1977), 109–11. Compare the pairing of encaustic painting and sculpture at *Silv.* 1. 1. 100–2.

2. animare, denoting the giving of breath, and thus life, to something (corresponding to Greek ψυχῶ), is especially appropriate, since Abascantus has tried to bring back his wife from death by means of artistic creation; *animare* hints that memorial art is an attempt to give some life to the deceased person. Compare *Silv.* 2. 2. 64 'si quid Apellei gaudent animasse colores', 4. 6. 28 'quid Polycliteis iussum spirare caminis', Virg. *G.* 3. 34 'stabunt et Parii lapides, spirantia signa', Prop. 3. 9. 9 'gloria Lysippo est animosa effingere signa', Mart.

11. 9. 2 (cited in 6 n.), Plin. *Ep.* 3. 6. 2 'uenae rugae etiam ut spirantis adparent'. See also *Silv.* 1. 1. 48–9 'uiuusque per armos | impetus', 1. 3. 47–8 'metalla | uiua', 2. 2. 66–7 'quod ab arte Myronis | aut Polycliteo iussum est quod uiuere caelo' (with van Dam), 3. 1. 95 'tot scripto uiuentes lumine ceras', 4. 6. 26–7 'laboriferi uiuant quae marmora caelo | Praxitelis', Juv. 8. 55 'illi marmoreum caput est, tua uiuit imago', 8. 103 'Phidiacum uiuebat ebur'.

4. meretur: at *Silv.* 3 pr. 14–15 Claudius Etruscus' *pietas* to his dead father deserved ('merebatur') some *solacium* from Statius, who also (3. 3. 173) indicates that Etruscus has requested the poem.

5. Apelleo ... colore: Apelles (*fl.* 330 BC), the most celebrated painter of antiquity, is the only one named by Statius (also at *Silv.* 1. 1. 100, 2. 2. 64, 4. 6. 29). He was noted for his encaustic painting, although the technique was not his invention (Plin. *Nat.* 35. 122–3). For accounts of his work and achievements, see Plin. *Nat.* 35. 79–97, Robertson (1975), 492–4. Of his qualities (see Quint. *Inst.* 12. 10. 6 with Austin's n., Cic. *Brut.* 70) the most relevant is his reputation for realism; cf. Petr. 83. 2 and Plin. *Nat.* 35. 95, who records that Apelles painted a horse at which real horses whinnied. Statius wishes that he could paint like Apelles, because he would then be able to give Abascantus a lifelike representation of Priscilla. The suggestion that Priscilla needs an Apelles to paint her is an obvious compliment to her beauty.

Though he did not invent the encaustic technique, Apelles did bring about technical innovations in the use of colour. Plin. *Nat.* 35. 97 refers to Apelles' use of an *atramentum* as a finish for his paintings, with the effect that the colours were more subtle; see Bruno (1977), 101, 106–7. Note also Plin. *Nat.* 35. 43, on Apelles' use of burnt ivory to create a dark pigment. Apelles' *color* (for *color* thus cf. Quint. *Inst.* 12. 10. 3) is also noted at Prop. 1. 2. 21–2 'sed facies aderat nullis obnoxia gemmis | qualis Apelleis est color in tabulis.'

6. Phidiaca ... manu: cf. e.g. *Silv.* 2. 2. 65–6 'si quid adhuc uacua tamen admirabile Pisa | Phidiacae rasere manus', Mart. 10. 89. 2 'Phidiacae cuperent quam meruisse manus'; for the use of χεῖρες and *manus* to refer to an artist's technique, see examples listed by Headlam on Herodas 4. 72. Phidias, a contemporary and friend of Pericles, most famous for his chryselephantine statues of Zeus at Olympia and Athena in the Parthenon (see further Robertson 1975: 292–322), is the natural counterpart to Apelles in the field of sculpture. These two artists feature in longer lists at *Silv.* 1. 1. 100–4, 2. 2. 64–7, 4. 6. 25–30; cf. Prop. 3. 9. 9–16.

uel rasa: M^2 corrects *uel uata* (M) to *uel nata*, which has been popular with editors. But Postgate (1905), 130–1 argues that *nata* cannot mean *renata*; the metaphor should indicate that Priscilla is reborn, not born for the first and only time. The prefix of *reddare* (cf. Mart. 11. 9. 2 'spirat Apellea redditus arte Memor') is, however, sufficient to convey the idea of rebirth when combined with *nata*: at *A.P.* 16. 257. 2 a statue of Dionysus by Myron is said to experience a second birth; cf. Coleman on *Silv.* 4. 6. 26. Nevertheless, it is odd to combine *nata* with the instrumental ablative *Phidiaca...manu*, since the phrase would almost be equivalent to 'made by Phidias' hand', whereas *nasci* is characteristically used to denote birth and other *natural* beginnings: note especially the examples cited by *OLD* s.v. *nascor* 8, 'To be produced spontaneously (as opp. to being made)', where the verb is used to effect a contrast with artificial processes.

Of the various conjectures *uiua* (Saenger) and *eburna* (Phillimore[2]) are to be rejected since a participle is needed to balance *signata* and to justify the instrumental ablative *Phidiaca...manu*, which is in parallel to *Apelleo...colore*. *Phidiacaue animata manu* (Phillimore[1]) is unattractive in the light of *animare* in l. 2; better is his *Phidiacaue nouata manu*, also suggested in his first edition, and defended by Ker (1953), 5.

To balance the Apelles and Phidias clauses, however, *signata* could be followed by a word more descriptive of an artistic process. Postgate's *Phidiacam uel nacta manum* answers this test, but demands further changes to the text and has a clumsy ring to it. *rasa*, ascribed by Klotz to Schrader, though the conjecture does not appear in the list of conjectures by Bentley and Schrader found in Haupt (1876), would refer to the process of smoothing the surface of a sculpture. This would provide an attractive counterpart to *signata*; cf. *Silv.* 2. 2. 65–6 (cited above), 4. 6. 27 'quod ebur Pisaeo pollice rasum'.

8. certamen cum Morte gerit: Heracles fought Death, and won back Alcestis from the dead (see e.g. E. *Alc.* 837–49; cf. Stat. *Silv.* 4. 6. 104 'penetrata tibi spoliataque limina mortis'). Here the struggle with Death is a hyperbolical characterization of Abascantus' grief and extreme efforts to commemorate his dead wife with memorial art. Cf. *Silv.* 3. 1. 172 'duram scio uincere Mortem', in a speech made by Hercules.

curasque fatigat: Abascantus exhausts the craftsmen with his requests for memorials for Priscilla. For *fatigo* in the sense of exhausting a skill, compare V.Fl. 8. 86–7 'omnem linguaque manuque fatigat | uim Stygiam', in an account of Medea's sorcery. *fatigo* can also denote mental or emotional exhaustion: cf. e.g. Sil. 1. 675 'inde agitant consulta patres curasque fatigant', *ThLL* vi/1. 347. 36 ff. For restless construction of memorials, compare Plin. *Ep.* 4. 7. 1 (see 231–4 n.); note also Cicero's intentions in constructing a *fanum* for his daughter Tullia (*Att.* 12. 18. 1): 'profecto illam consecrabo omni genere monimentorum ab omnium ingeniis sumptorum et Graecorum et Latinorum'. *fatigo* is also used at 72–3 below to describe Priscilla's continuous (and more successful) attempts to win divine favour for her husband.

9. inque omni te quaerit amare metallo: though *metallum* usually denotes either a mine, or a material produced from a mine (*OLD* s.v. 1 and 2), the word can be used more loosely to denote other substances, whether natural or manufactured (*ThLL* viii. 874. 68–875. 4). Since Statius has already raised the possibility of producing an image of Priscilla in wax or ivory (lines 1–2), a translation such as 'substance' or 'material' (Shackleton Bailey) seems appropriate for *metallum* here.

10. mortalis honos: for *honor* of memorial observances for the dead see *ThLL* vi/2. 2925. 23 ff. Plastic art is ephemeral, as Simonides pointed out to Cleobulus (*PMG* 581); but the dead Priscilla is reassured that poetry will provide an eternal commemoration.

agilis ... dextra: recalls the *manus ... docilis* in 1. *agilis* suggests speed, hinting that the artists' endeavours are not a measured and personal response to Priscilla's death. Contrast Statius himself, who explains why his offering comes so late (16–29), after indicating his personal involvement in the introductory epistle.

11. nos tibi introduces a note of solemnity after the pause at the end of the previous line, preparing for the formal statement of Statius' poetic and longlasting gift. Cf. *Silv.* 3. 3. 33–9, where Statius' poem for the father of Claudius Etruscus is contrasted with the spices burnt by Etruscus at the funeral:

> tu largus Eoa
> germina, tu messes Cilicumque Arabumque superbas
> merge rogis; ferat ignis opes heredis et alto   35
> aggere missuri nitido pia nubila caelo
> stipentur cineres: nos non arsura feremus
> munera, uenturosque tuus durabit in annos
> me monstrante dolor.

Note also Lucan's use of *at tibi nos* to effect a shift from the mortal fate of Curio's body to the poetic memorial offered by the poet himself (Luc. 4. 809–13):

> Libycas, en, nobile corpus,
> 810   pascit aues nullo contectus Curio busto.
> at tibi nos, quando non proderit ista silere
> a quibus omne aeui senium sua fama repellit,
> digna damus, iuuenis, meritae praeconia uitae.

For the contrast between material and poetic offerings see further 210–14 n. below.

laudati iuuenis points to an important element of the poem, praise of Abascantus; for its application to one bereaved, cf. *Silv.* 3. 3. 7 'cerne pios fletus laudataque lumina terge'. *iuuenis* emphasizes the pathos of Abascantus' loss, though Weaver (1994), 344–8 points out that Statius' usage of *iuuenis* covers a range of ages from seventeen to the mid-forties, and that most imperial freedmen appointed to high offices such as *ab epistulis* were already past fifty. Weaver suggests (351) that Abascantus may have been nearing fifty at the time of Priscilla's death.

rarissima coniunx: for the laudatory epithet, cf. *Silv.* 2. pr. 23, 4. 8. 32; Treggiari (1991), 231 notes its frequency in inscriptions referring to wives. *carissima* (*s*) might be felt to be too personal a mode of address for Statius to use in addressing Abascantus' wife, though it is striking that, as Dickey (2002), 134–6 notes, the superlative *carissimus* is more commonly used when addressed to friends and acquaintances, and the positive *carus* is more usual as a mode of address to relations, husbands and wives, and lovers.

12–13. longa ... iusta: a paradoxical phrase, since one would not expect *iusta* (funeral rites) to be long-lasting; the poem is thus likened to a perpetual funeral. When combined with *dare*, *iusta* also suggests that Priscilla deserves such an offering (cf. Cornelia's complaint at Luc. 9. 67–8 'numquam dare iusta licebit | coniugibus?'); for verbal play on the adjective *iustus*, 'just', and the neuter plural noun *iusta*, 'funeral rites', see also *Silv.* 5. 2. 83, Cic. *Flac.* 95 'iusta Catilinae facta sunt', Ov. *Met.* 2. 627 'iniustaque iusta peregit', Sen. *Oed.* 998 'bene habet, peractum est: iusta persolui patri'.

perenni ... lyra answers *mortalis* (10), poetry (*lyra*) being the eternal memorial given to Priscilla. For the ancient and familiar topos of literary immortality, see N.–H. on Hor. *Carm.* 2. 20 (pp. 335 ff.) and van Dam on *Silv.* 2. 3. 62–3; cf. Myers (2000), 106 on the relation between Statius' own poetic immortality and ecphrases of landscapes and architecture in the *Silvae*.

13. dexter: *dexter* is commonly used of the favour of the gods (*ThLL* v/1. 924. 19 ff.); here the goodwill of Apollo is a benign response to Statius' poetry, which, when coupled with imperial approval, will guarantee immortality to the memorial for Priscilla. For *dexter* referring to divine goodwill towards a literary work, compare Prop. 3. 2. 9, 4. 9. 72, Ov. *Fast.* 1. 6, *Aetna* 4; cf. Sil. 14. 467–8 'dexter donauit auena | Phoebus Castalia'. See also Quint. *Inst.* 4 pr. 5, where the favour of all the gods and of Domitian in particular is invoked; the emperor is asked 'dexterque ac uolens adsit'. For Domitian's support and involvement with poets, see Coleman (1986), 3100–5, who comments (3105) that 'Statius nowhere boasts of familiarity with the emperor, and always maintains a respectful distance'; cf. Nauta (2002), 327–55.

14. iuncto ... semper Apolline Caesar: for joint invocations of Apollo and the emperor compare Man. 1. 7–22, Calp. *Ecl.* 4. 87, V.Fl. 1. 5–21, and see Rosati (2002), 238–49 (esp. 246–8 on the present passage) for the emperor as a source of poetic inspiration. Domitian, who restored the temple at Delphi at his own expense (*ILS* 8905), was not the only emperor linked with Apollo; Suet. *Aug.* 70 records a private banquet attended by Octavian dressed as Apollo. On Augustus' links with Apollo, see further Virg. *A.* 8. 704, 8. 720, Prop. 2. 31, 4. 6, Ps.-Acro on Hor. *Ep.* 1. 3. 17, Serv. Auct. on Virg. *Ecl.* 4. 10, and Taylor (1931), 118–20, 131–4.

15. sepulchro: though physical memorials are ephemeral, here Statius offers Priscilla a metaphorical tomb, his poem, which will be eternal; see also 231–4 n. At *Silv.* 2. 7. 70–2, Lucan's poem will give a glorious sepulchre to Pompey:

> tu Pelusiaci scelus Canopi
> deflebis pius et Pharo cruenta
> Pompeio dabis altius sepulchrum.

Statius also calls his poem to Claudius Etruscus a *sepulchrum* (3. 3. 216). For this idea, see Prop. 3. 2. 17–22, Sen. *Dial.* 11. 18. 2, Tac. *Ann.* 4. 38. 2, on which see Woodman and Martin ad loc. and Sinclair (1991), Juv. 10. 146. Note also Mart. 1. 88. 3–6, a memorial of living trees for the dead Alcimus, which are more durable than Parian marble; the fragility of physical structures (including *monumenta*) is also expressed at Lucr. 5. 306–17. For the application of physical imagery to a poem see 5. 3. 47–8 n., and compare Hor. *Carm.* 3. 30. 1 'exegi monumentum', which is not a lament, but an assertion of the lasting qualities of Horace's poetry. The technique, however, is the same: Horace, who affirms the temporal nature of physical monuments, nevertheless refers to his literary work in physical terms; cf. Prop. 3. 2. 18 'carmina erunt formae tot monumenta tuae', Plin. *Ep.* 3. 10. 6, where a literary commemoration of the son of Vestricius Spurinna is intended to be an 'immortalem... effigiem'.

16. sera: the need not to give immediate consolation to the bereaved is most succinctly expressed at Cic. *Tusc.* 4. 63 'quodque uetat Chrysippus, ad recentes quasi tumores animi remedium adhibere'. Cf. Sen. *Dial.* 6. 4. 1, 12. 1. 2 (see below), Plin. *Ep.* 5. 16. 11, [Plu.] *ad Apoll.* 102 A, Kassel (1958), 52–3, Esteve-Forriol (1962), 128. Men. Rh. 419. 1–10 suggests that an *epitaphios* can be delivered without a consolatory passage if an interval of seven or eight months has passed, although close kin may require a full year: τούτῳ γὰρ οὐδὲ μετ᾽ ἐνιαυτὸν δίδωσιν ἀνάπαυλαν τοῦ πάθους ἡ μνήμη· διόπερ οὗτος σώσει καὶ μετ᾽ ἐνιαυτὸν τοῦ παθητικοῦ λόγου τὸν χαρακτῆρα. Sen. *Dial.* 6. 1. 7 notes that a third year has passed since Marcia's loss. The need not to offer consolation too soon is perhaps also reflected in the Statian *epicedia* by the placement of the more formal sections of consolation late in the individual poems themselves; cf. Men. Rh. 413. 6, 21–3, Konstan (2001).

In the *Silvae* compare the opening of 2. 1 (with Vollmer on 2. 1. 5 and van Dam on 2. 1. 1–13) and Statius' discussion of the poem at 2 pr. 7–12, where Statius points out that 'paene superuacua sint tarda solacia'; in Book 5 see also 5. 3. 29–31 (cf. 200–1) and 5. 5. 24. Nauta (2002), 247 suggests that Statius' claim that he has waited a year before consoling Abascantus is merely conventional, and that the poem may reflect an agenda unrelated to Priscilla's death a year before its composition; cf. A. Hardie (1983), 186.

struitur: *struo* can signify literary creation (*OLD* s.v. *struo* 3a), but *struitur* is striking, since Statius has previously distanced himself from the visual arts. Here he refers to the creation of his literary offering with a verb whose primary meaning is physical (e.g. Hor. *Carm.* 2. 18. 18–19 'sepulchri | immemor struis domos').

medicina dolori: the metaphorical use of words for healing is as old as Homer (*Od.* 22. 481 κακῶν ἄκος); cf. S. *Tr.* 1209 and E. fr. 1079. 1–2 οὐκ ἔστι λύπης ἄλλο φάρμακον βροτοῖς | ὡς ἀνδρὸς ἐσθλοῦ καὶ

φίλου παραίνεσις. For the philosophic tradition, see [Plu.] *ad Apoll.*
102 A and the parallels collected by Rutherford (1989), 19. In Latin
medicina also appears with *dolor* at Cic. *Acad.* 1. 11 'doloris medicinam a
philosophia peto' and [Quint.] *Decl. min.* 270. 27. Stat. *Silv.* 2. 1. 5
refers to his poem as 'cantus et uerba medentia', while Sen. *Dial.* 12. 1.
2 uses the metaphor in a similar discussion of the dangers of prema-
ture consolation: 'dolori tuo dum recens saeuiret sciebam occurren-
dum non esse, ne illum ipsa solacia irritarent et accenderent, nam in
morbis quoque nihil est perniciosius quam immatura medicina.' For
further examples of metaphorical usage see *ThLL* viii. 541. 40 ff. For
the application of the metaphor of medicine (φάρμακον) to music or to
λόγος in general and its Pythagorean origins, see Kassel (1958), 5.

   17. uolucris Phoebi rota torqueat annum: Markland argues
for *uolucrem*, citing parallels such as 'uolucris dies' (Hor. *Carm.* 3. 28. 6,
4. 13. 16), 'celeres...annos' (*Silv.* 3. 3. 20) and 'uelocibus annis' (Mart.
8. 8. 1), but to describe the year as swift when noting Abascantus'
extensive mourning seems inappropriate. The problem does not
entirely disappear if Phoebus' progress is 'swift', but there is less of
a contradiction than if the swiftness of the year itself is emphasized.
For the temporal usage of *torquere*, cf. *Ach.* 2. 110–11 'uix mihi bis senos
annorum torserat orbes | uita rudis'.

   18. uulnere: metaphors of wounding are commonplace: see 30
below (with n.), Esteve-Forriol (1962), 161, van Dam on *Silv.* 2. 1. 4.

   19. Although Vollmer (1893), 837, following Imhof, defends *nigra
domus quaestu miseramque accessus ad aurem* (M), the difficulties in con-
struing *quaestu/questu* (ς) and the confused sense that results militate
strongly against accepting it. Klotz gives a comprehensive account of
conjectures. Courtney (1984), 333–4 suggests a lacuna of two half-
lines, filling the gap as follows: 'nigra domus questu<que sonant
cuncta undique maesto, | quae uia solandi> miseramque...'. Al-
though such omissions occur, there is no need to posit a lacuna here.
Most successful are emendations of *quaestu*, such as Adrian's *quis
tum miserandam accessus ad aurem*, or Sandström's *quis tum miseras accessus
ad aures.*[20] These add rhetorical force to the passage: *tum* answers *sed
cum* in the previous line, anticipates the following *tunc* (if it is authen-
tic), and also emphasizes that only now, at the time of writing, is
Statius able to secure the attention of his friend. The choice is
between Adrian and Sandström; Sandström's *quis tum miseras... ad*

---

[20] For the adjectival interrogative *quis*, see *OLD* s.v. *quis* 5a and b.

aures is preferable, since it preserves the adjective *miser*, whereas Adrian is forced to emend to *miserandam* in order to retain M's singular *aurem*. For the plural *aures* compare *Theb.* 5. 731–2 'tunc pius Oeclides, ut prima silentia uulgi | mollior ira dedit, placidasque accessus ad aures'.

20. tunc (M¹): M's *nunc* cannot be retained in a sentence referring to an earlier stage of Abascantus' grief. *nunc etiam* (30) contrasts Abascantus' initial grief at the time of Priscilla's death with his present emotions, so that *tunc* is required here. Lines 20–3 describe four aspects of grieving at the time of Priscilla's death and funeral: weeping, tearing clothes, beating of the breast on the part of both Abascantus and his slaves (line 21), and verbal complaint directed against Fate and the gods (lines 22–3).

21. et famulos lassare greges et uincere planctus: *uincere planctus* is satisfactorily construed only if the *planctus* refer to the slaves, so that Abascantus surpasses their (possibly enforced) displays of grief; compare *Theb.* 6. 33–5 'planctusque egressa uiriles | exemplo famulas premit hortaturque uolentes | orba parens', where Eurydice mourns for her son Opheltes, and Luc. 2. 23–4 'nec mater crine soluto | exigit ad saeuos famularum bracchia planctus', from a simile in which Lucan contrasts the very first onset of grief at the moment of death with subsequent ritual mourning. Slater's translation, 'to outsorrow sorrow', misses the physicality of *planctus*, blows to the breast: cf. e.g. *Silv.* 3. 3. 176–7 'heu quantis lassantem bracchia uidi | planctibus', Sil. 2. 549–50, 'tunc Luctus et atri | pectora circumstant Planctus Maerorque Dolorque'. On self-inflicted violence in response to grief, see Denniston on E. *El.* 146 ff.

22. rabidis ... querelis: Statius does not conceal the frenzy and violence characteristic of the onset of grief. At *Silv.* 2. 1. 7–9 Melior's' initial antipathy to poetic lament is robustly expressed:

> odistique chelyn surdaque auerteris aure.
> intempesta cano; citius me tigris abactis
> fetibus orbatique uelint audire leones.

See further van Dam on *Silv.* 2. 1. 10–12. The savagery of grief is a topos as old as Homer (e.g. Achilles' desire to eat the raw flesh of Hector at *Il.* 22. 346–7). Such violence also occurs in more formalized practices such as weeping and the tearing of garments, as here.

pulsare: see *OLD* 7b for this transferred usage of *pulsare* signifying importuning with prayers or complaints. Cf. *Silv.* 5. 3. 69, 5. 5. 77–8 'nonne horridus <inde> | inuidia superos iniustaque Tartara pulsem?'; see also e.g. Luc. 9. 187–8 'omne quod in superos audet conuicia uulgus | Pompeiumque deis obicit', Esteve-Forriol (1962), 138–9.

23. solamen erat: Although Statius draws a contrast between his poem and Abascantus' violent grief, Abascantus is not criticized for acting inappropriately. Instead there is a sensitive recognition of the importance of the early stages of grief, whose value, paradoxically, is that of a *solamen*.

24. siluis comitatus et amnibus Orpheus is mentioned not only for his musical ability to charm even animals, trees, and rivers (e.g. A. R. 1. 23–31, 1. 492–515, Virg. *G.* 4. 510, Ov. *Met.* 10. 86–106, 11. 1–2, Sen. *Her. F.* 572–4, [Sen.] *Her. O.* 1036–60), but also for his grief at the loss of Eurydice; he thus becomes a symbol of the bereaved husband. Ironically Orpheus, who could win back his own wife from the dead, would not be able even to soothe the pain of Abascantus; cf. *Silv.* 2. 1. 11–12, where Orpheus would not console Atedius Melior.

25. omnis . . . matertera: Orpheus was the son of the Muse Calliope, by Oeagrus (A.R. 1. 24–5); the other eight Muses are here learnedly referred to as his aunts.

26. tegeret: for the figurative use of *tego* to denote protection and hence, as here, 'accompanying', see *OLD* s.v *tego* 5. For the association of Apollo and Bacchus see *Silv.* 5. 3. 6 n.

27. deis pallentis Auerni: Dis and Proserpine, the rulers of the underworld. *Auernus* (a lake in Campania, associated with the infernal regions because of its depth and because of the local volcanic activity) has a rich Virgilian resonance, and is mentioned not only in *Aeneid* 5 and 6 as the site of Aeneas' *katabasis*, but also at *G.* 4. 493 at the very moment when Orpheus loses Eurydice: 'terque fragor stagnis auditus Auernis'; cf. Ov. *Met.* 10. 51–2 'ne flectat retro sua lumina, donec Auernas | exierit ualles', Beloch (1890), 168–72, Frederiksen (1984), 76–7.

27–8. An elaborate conceit: the songs which won over the infernal powers (cf. Sen. *Her. F.* 575 'mulcet non solitis uocibus inferos') would have had no soothing effect on Abascantus.

mulcere is used of consolation at *Silv.* 5. 5. 39 'qui uiuos potui mulcere dolores' and 2. 1. 12 'mulceat insanos gemitus'.

28. Eumenidumque . . . comis: the 'hair' of the Eumenides is composed of snakes, and thus able to hear sounds. Note Luc. 9. 672

'uigilat pars magna comarum' (of Medusa) and Mart. 7. 1. 2 'Medu-
saeae ... ira comae' for exploitation of the paradox of the sentient
hairs (compare also the *Coma Berenices* in Call. *Aet.* and Cat. 66).

On the Eumenides and their snakes, see further *Silv.* 5. 3. 278–9
'taedas auferte comasque | Eumenidum', *Theb.* 11. 65–7 and N.–H. on
Hor. *Carm.* 2. 13. 35, where snakes enjoy the opportunity to hear the
dead Alcaeus recite his poems in the underworld.

29. regnabat ... luctus: the metaphor of dominion personifies
the grief; cf. *Silv.* 2. 1. 12–13: 'stat pectore demens | luctus', *Theb.* 2.
287, 3. 126, 10. 558, Virg. *A.* 6. 274 'Luctus et ultrices posuere cubilia
Curae', Sil. 2. 549 (see 21 n.).

attonito concisely expresses the shock of bereavement, as at Luc.
2. 21–2 'sic funere primo | attonitae tacuere domus'.

30. adtactus refugit iam plana cicatrix: with *ad planctus* (M)
it is hard to see how the wound flees 'to lamentations', particularly
given the physicality of *planctus*. Indeed *ad* presents great difficulty,
forcing *refugit* to be a verb of motion towards something. While *ad
tactus* (Cartault) is no better, *adtactus* (Phillimore) skirts the problem
neatly; translate *refugit* as 'shrinks from' or 'recoils'. The image is of a
wound which, though outwardly healed, is still sensitive to touch.
Contrast Ov. *Pont.* 1. 3. 15–16 (with Gaertner ad loc.) 'tempore
ducetur longo fortasse cicatrix: | horrent admotas uulnera cruda
manus', and Plin. *Ep.* 5. 16. 11; cf. *Silv.* 5. 5. 39, cited in 27–8 n., and
note the use of *refricare*, often used for rubbing wounds, to denote the
revival of painful feelings: see *OLD* s.v. *refrico* 2 and Fantham (1972), 17
who cites Cic. *Att.* 5. 15. 2, 12. 18. 1; cf. *Pis.* 82.

At *Dial.* 6. 1. 5 Seneca, having reminded Marcia of her dead
husband, remarks that he has shown her the *cicatrix* of her wound;
cf. *Dial.* 6. 8. 2, 12. 2. 2, 12. 15. 4.

31–2. uxorius ... | imber: for a rain of tears, cf. e.g. *Theb.*
5. 270, Cat. 68. 56, Ov. *Tr.* 1. 3. 18, Nonn. 16. 345, though the epithet
here is a bold one. *uxorius* can convey reproach, as at Virg. *A.* 4. 266–7
'pulchramque uxorius urbem | exstruis?' (and see Pease's note for
parallels), though Mercury's strictures to Aeneas are much more
obviously harsh than this reference to Abascantus' grief.

grauibus suggests not only the sadness of Abascantus, but also the
weight of the tears in his eyes.

33–6. Niobe, Aurora, and Thetis, celebrated grieving mothers,
will all be said to have spent less time in lamentation than Abascantus.
Niobe and Thetis are linked as *exempla* of grief at Call. *H.* 2. 20–4 (the

song for Apollo would cause their grief to abate); see further Hey-
worth (1994), 67–9. See also *Silv.* 5. 3. 9 n., 5. 5. 21–2 n. for further
allusions to the same hymn.

33. citius: for use with counterfactual examples, compare *Silv.* 2.
1. 8–9, where Statius tells Melior that his consolation would be given
a better welcome by tigers and lions that had lost their young, 3. 3.
87–8, and *Theb.* 12. 155–7, where Ornytus tells the Argive women that
they will win over Busiris and other mythical figures more swiftly
than they will persuade Creon to give back the bodies of their loved
ones. On Statius' use of the *adunaton* figure in general see Dutoit
(1936), 138–47.

genetrix Sipylea: Niobe, who lost her twelve children to the
wrath of Artemis and Apollo,[21] and was turned to stone on Mount
Sipylus (*Il.* 24. 602–17); see further Forbes Irving (1990), 146–8, 294–7.
The passage from Homer is relevant not only because Niobe is an
example of extreme grief, but also because its context is consolatory:
Achilles advises Priam not to spurn food on account of grief, since
even Niobe took food on the tenth day; cf. Scourfield (1993), 191.
Thus, although Niobe is primarily an example of extreme grief
surpassed by Abascantus' sorrow, the Homeric context also points
to the theme of consolation and acceptance of loss.

Sipylea feretur (Heinsius: *si pelea fertur* M): the repeated *citius*
demands some mythological personage as a counterpart to Aurora
and Thetis; *si pelea* is an easy corruption of *Sipylea*, proper names,
particularly when unfamiliar, being very susceptible to scribal error.

34. exhausisse genas: cf. *Theb.* 10. 168 'exhauritque genas',
where *genas* denotes cheeks, and not the eyes, in a description of
blood rushing to and from the cheeks of Thiodamas as he is inspired
by prophetic frenzy. Here the reference is to weeping; *exhausisse* also
suggests the erosion of the now stone cheeks of Niobe by her tears (cf.
Ov. *Met.* 6. 311–12 'ibi fixa cacumine montis | liquitur'); note also *Ach.*
1. 108 'pars exhausta manu, partem sua ruperat aetas' (the hollowed-
out mountain home of Chiron), Hor. *Epod.* 5. 30–1 'ligonibus duris
humum | exhauriebat'.

35. rores: the dew of early morning, associated with Aurora,
represents her tears for her dead son Memnon, who killed Antilochus
the son of Nestor and was then killed by Achilles in the closing stages

---

[21] For variations in the number of Niobe's children, see Apollod. 3. 5. 6 with Frazer, Gel.
20. 7, Ael. *VH* 12. 36.

of the Trojan War, as narrated in the cyclic *Aethiopis*; see also Apollod. *Epit.* 5. 3. The same conceit of the dewy tears of Aurora occurs at Ov. *Met.* 13. 621–2 'luctibus est Aurora suis intenta piasque | nunc quoque dat lacrimas et toto rorat in orbe'; for *ros/rores* denoting tears, see *OLD* s.v. *ros* 2b.

fatiscet: the primary significance of *fatisco* is to gape open, but the word can also signify exhaustion or weariness, as here: Statius uses *fatisco* six times thus (*Theb.* 1. 217, 4. 187, 11. 92, 12. 295, here, and *Silv.* 5. 5. 21). The deponent form is first attested at Pac. *trag.* 154 and Acc. *trag.* 330; the active voice first appears in Virgil (*G.* 1. 180, 2. 249). Pac. *trag.* 154 is the only other instance where the verb has a dependent infinitive.

36. hiemes: here, as at *Silv.* 5. 2. 5 (see n.), *hiems*, usually a storm, denotes a stormy sea. At. *Od.* 24. 47–9 Thetis and the divinities of the sea lament for Achilles: βοὴ δ᾽ ἐπὶ πόντον ὀρώρει | θεσπεσίη (48–9); cf. the much longer account of their lamentations at Q. S. 3. 582–664. Here Thetis hurls waves against the shore which was the site of her son Achilles' tomb (*Od.* 24. 80–4).

adfrangere: not found before Statius (*Theb.* 5. 150, 10. 47), this verb otherwise occurs only at Sid. Apoll. *Epist.* 2. 2. 17. . Its novelty is reflected by the retention of the prototypic *-a-* in the second syllable, since inherited compounds of *frangere* have an *-i-* in the second syllable (*defringere, effringere, infringere, offringere, refringere, profringere, suffringere*; for the change in vowel, see Sihler (1995), 39 (§ 41. 1), 59–61 (§ 65–6)), though it is worth noting that the only instance of *profringere* is in Statius (*Theb.* 10. 512).

37. macte animi: for this phrase see *Silv.* 5. 2. 97 n. The exclamation represents a sudden shift to Abascantus, here addressed for the first time in the poem. After a passage in which Abascantus' grief surpasses that of celebrated mythological *exempla*, it sounds the first genuinely positive note in the poem, signalling a move away from the sombre opening.

deus: Domitian; for discussion of divine honours rendered to Domitian, see Scott (1936), 88–101 (especially 96–8 on public cults of Domitian in the East), 113–25. Roman emperors had differing attitudes to deification within their lifetime, which also varied according to place. Tiberius, who scorned even lesser titles, could do nothing to prevent the deification of the reigning emperor in the East that had begun under Augustus (Tac. *Ann.* 4. 15. 3, 4. 37); note also the deification of Augustus in Latin poetry (e.g. Prop. 3. 4. 1, 4. 11.

60). Caligula (Suet. *Cal.* 22) assumed the title of a god but did not enjoy it for long. While Domitian did not assume divinity at the outset of his reign, *deus* seems to have been used with some degree of frequency. Suet. *Dom.* 13. 2 (cf. D.C. 67. 4. 7) notes that *dominus et deus* became a regular form of address after Domitian began a dictated letter with the phrase. The date of this is unclear in Suetonius, but Scott (1936), 102–12 concludes on the basis of the use of the words *dominus* and *deus* in Statius and especially Martial, as well as the scanty evidence of later historians, that the title probably came into currency in 86. B. W. Jones (1992), 108–9 and in his n. on Suet. *Dom.* 13. 2 strikingly rejects the Suetonian claim that the title was actually official; cf. Gradel (2002), 159–60, Nauta (2002), 382–3, Leberl (2004), 56–7. *Silv.* 1. 6. 83–4 would seem to provide some support for this view: 'et dulci dominum fauore clamant: | hoc solum uetuit licere Caesar', and L. Thompson (1984) argues that this passage may reflect imperial reticence about use of the title; cf. Nauta (2002), 401–2.

It is not impossible, however, that *Silv.* 1. 6. 83–4 might reflect no more than an isolated exception, with Domitian ostentatiously (and on only one occasion) refusing the titles which he had made his own; Griffin (2000), 81–2 points out that the Saturnalia (the setting for *Silv.* 1. 6) was in any case an occasion characterized by the reversal of social norms. The reference to the 'indulgentia maximi | diuinique principis' in the subsequently erased *AE* 1973, 137, an inscription of Puteoli celebrating the Via Domitiana (and thus dated to 95/6), would suggest that divine usages were entirely acceptable in addressing Domitian by the end of his reign; see further Flower (2001), 632. Mart. 10. 72 is illustrative of hostile reaction to the phrase *dominus et deus* during subsequent reigns, a reaction which may have encouraged communities (and individuals as well) to recant their use of such divine language when addressing Domitian, as in the case of the people of Puteoli, whose inscription was erased in its entirety (Flower (2001), 634–5).

38. propior Ioue: cf. *Silv.* 5. 1. 74 'domini praesentis', 5. 2. 170 'proximus ille deus'. This notion of the emperor as a god closer to human affairs than the Olympians (cf. *Collect. Alex.* 173, ll. 1–4, 174, ll. 15–19, from the ithyphallic hymn to Demetrius Poliorcetes ascribed to Hermocles) can be contrasted with the commonly expressed wish for an emperor's ascent to the heavens to be delayed (see e.g. *Silv.* 4. 2. 22, *Theb.* 1. 30–1, Hor. *Carm.* 1. 2. 45 with N.–H., Ov. *Met.* 15. 868–70, Luc. 1. 46). At *Silv.* 1. 1. 62 the 'forma dei praesens' has beneficial

effects on the construction of the equestrian statue of Domitian; for
the idea of the *praesens deus* (where *praesens* is equivalent to ἐπιφανής),
cf. e.g. Hor. *Carm.* 3. 5. 2–3 'praesens diuus habebitur | Augustus',
4. 14. 43–4 'o tutela praesens | Italiae dominaeque Romae', and *Ep.*
2. 1. 15 'praesenti tibi maturos largimur honores', where Brink's note
is invaluable. See also *Silv.* 4. 3. 128–9 'en hic est deus, hunc iubet
beatis | pro se Iuppiter imperare terris', Sauter (1934), 51–4, Scott
(1936), 137–8. In these Statian examples, the image of the present god
is not merely used for its own sake; on each occasion the emperor is
involved with events. Here the emperor's interest is in the personal
lives of his subjects.

Domitian is variously represented in relation to Jupiter by Statius.
Here and at *Silv.* 4. 3. 128–9 (see above), Domitian is explicitly
distinguished from Jove (cf. Mart. 13. 4 'serus ut aetheriae Germani-
cus imperet aulae | utque diu terris, da pia tura Ioui'), while at 1. 6.
25–7, the god and the emperor are strikingly differentiated whilst
both being referred to as Jove: 'ducat nubila Iuppiter per orbem | et
latis pluuias minetur agris | dum nostri Iouis hi ferantur imbres' (cf.
Mart. 7. 73. 4 'inde nouum, ueterem prospicis inde Iouem'); for a
similar use of a defining possessive to refer to Domitian, cf. Mart.
9. 91. 5–6 'quaerite qui malit fieri conuiua Tonantis: | me meus in
terris Iuppiter, ecce, tenet', 14. 1. 2 'dumque decent nostrum pillea
sumpta Iouem'. At 3. 4. 18, Domitian is described as 'Iuppiter
Ausonius' (though contrast the reference to Jupiter himself as 'Latio
Ioue' at 5. 3. 292), while at 1 pr. 17 the evocative phrase 'a Ioue
principium' is used to refer to Domitian with no qualification, except
perhaps its own literary resonance (see Arat. 1, Theoc. 17. 1, Cic. *Arat.*
1, Virg. *Ecl.* 3. 60, Germ. *Arat.* 1–2, V. Max. 1 pr. 16–17, Calp. *Ecl.*
4. 82, Quint. *Inst.* 10. 1. 46; see also Ov. *Met.* 10. 148–9 'ab Ioue, Musa
parens (cedunt Iouis omnia regno), | carmina nostra moue', *Fast.* 5. 111
'ab Ioue surgat opus'), which might contribute to the phrase being
read in a metaphorical way. Newlands (2002), 114 and 196 argues that
Statius' remarks on his wife's reaction to his defeat in the Capitoline
contest, 'saeuum ingratumque dolebas | mecum uicta Iouem' (3. 5.
32–3), represent a direct reproach to Domitian, but it is more likely
that Statius here is reproaching the god whom he would have praised
in the competition (hence *ingratum*), and not the emperor, who was
referred to as 'Caesar' only a few lines before in the context of Statius'
prize at the Alban competition, 'sanctoque indutum Caesaris auro'
(29). At *Theb.* 1. 22, 'bella Iouis' (also used at *Silv.* 1. 1. 79; cf. Mart.

9. 101. 14 'prima suo gessit pro Ioue bella puer', where Domitian is however initially compared to Hercules) is a subtle reference to Domitian's role in the attempted defence of the temple of Capitoline Jupiter against the Vitellians during the civil war (on these events, and also Domitian's rebuilding of the replacement temple of Jupiter after the fire of AD 80, see 5. 3. 196 n.); Statius goes on to suggest that Jupiter might yield possession of part of the heavens to Domitian (*Theb.* 1. 29–30). On Domitian and Jupiter, see further Sauter (1934), 54–78, Scott (1936), 133–40, Newlands (2002), 53–4, 229–30, 241–3, 313–14; on the Capitoline contest established by Domitian in the god's honour, see 5. 3. 231 n. below. The relationship between Jupiter in the *Thebaid* and Domitian is now an area of contention among scholars, some of whom have interpreted the god as a tyrannical figure analogous to the emperor; for an idea of the debate, see e.g. the contrasting work of Dominik (1994), 161–80 and Hill (1996).

39–40. Klotz's punctuation, with *hinc* beginning a new clause, is preferable to having no break at the end of 39; *arcana* should be construed as 'the secret thoughts' of Abascantus, rather than as an adjective agreeing with *documenta*. The point is not that Domitian keeps secret records on Abascantus, but that he is able to see into his heart.

39. lecti: a compliment to Abascantus (cf. *lectissime*, 247), as the emperor's choice is a mark of favour.

40. hinc could refer to *ista* in 37, but is better taken with the following *quod*.

documenta: found only three times elsewhere in Statius (*Theb.* 8. 296, 11. 657, 12. 689), though common in prose, *documentum* need not imply a written record, a meaning only attested in later Latin (*ThLL* v/1. 1809. 19–39). Here, with *capit*, the word denotes the emperor's acknowledgement of Abascantus' exemplary conduct (cf., though with different punctuation, Shackleton Bailey, 'and therefore he takes private proof of his chosen servant, in that you love the shade and pay tribute to her obsequies'). For the idiom *documentum . . . capere*, compare Cic. *Phil.* 11. 5 'ex quo nimirum documentum nos capere fortuna uoluit quid esset uictis extimescendum'.

quod diligis umbram: in the epistle Statius distinguished between love for a living wife and for a dead one, characterizing the last as *religio* (*epist.* 4). As he explains in the succeeding lines, this is the highest love, and thus worthy of imperial note. Cf. Statius' remarks on his wife's devotion to her dead first husband at *Silv.* 3. 5. 52–3: 'sic exsequias amplexa canori | coniugis'.

41. castissimus ardor: cf. Argia, the widow of Polynices, as she prepares to go to Thebes, where her husband has been denied a funeral (*Theb.* 12. 193–5): 'his anxia mentem | aegrescit furiis et, qui castissimus ardor, | funus amat'.

42. domino: 37 n.

censore: despite his allegedly chequered private life, on which see Suet. *Dom.* 22, D.C. 67. 3. 1–2, and the sceptical discussion of B. W. Jones (1992), 32–8, Domitian, as censor, attached great importance to private morality: see Suet. *Dom.* 8, Juv. 2. 30–1, *Silv.* 5. 2. 102 n., D.C. 67. 13. 1, Gsell (1893), 83 ff., Griffin (2000), 79–80. For the dating of Domitian's assumption of the office (AD 85), see Buttrey (1980), 38, Carradice (1983), 25–7, Martin (1987*b*), 192–3; by the end of the same year Domitian had taken the title of *censor perpetuus*. Statius also refers to the office at *Silv.* 4. 3. 14, in connection with Domitian's edict of 82–3 forbidding castration; cf. Leberl (2004), 280–91 on the treatment of Domitian as censor in Martial.

43–4. conlato pectore . . . concordia: For marital *concordia*, see also *Silv.* 1. 2. 240 'et insigni geminat Concordia taeda', 2. 2. 155 'non alias docuit Concordia mentes'. *conlato pectore*, 'with hearts brought together', points to the etymology of *concordia*; cf. Var. *L.* 5. 73 'concordia a corde congruente', Cic. *Tusc.* 1. 18 'aliis cor ipsum animus uidetur, ex quo excordes uecordes concordesque dicuntur', and see Maltby (1991), 147; for useful discussion of Statius' use of etymologies, see van Dam on *Silv.* 2. 2. 36–42, Laguna (1992), 27–9. On the concept of *concordia*, both as a political and as a domestic ideal, see further Dixon (1991), 107–8, who notes Livia's temple to Concordia in honour of her husband (Ov. *Fast.* 6. 637–40), and the use in legal texts of the phrase *bene concordans matrimonium*. For *concordia* as an ideal viewed retrospectively when the marriage is ended by death, compare Plin. *Ep.* 3. 16. 10, Tac. *Ag.* 6. 1.

inabrupta . . . catena: for *catena* used figuratively see *ThLL* iii. 606. 15 ff. For *catena* of the bond of love, cf. Tib. 2. 4. 3, Prop. 2. 15. 25; see further N.–H. on Hor. *Carm.* 1. 13. 18. *inabruptus* occurs only here in classical Latin. The image of the unbroken chain, referring to the married life of Priscilla and Abascantus, is ironic, since the link has been broken by death.

45. nuptuque: the ablative of respect is entirely unexceptionable (cf. e.g. Sen. *Dial.* 11. 15. 5 'minorem natu'), so that there is no need for the internal accusative *nuptumque* (5). Mention of the earlier marriage would not have seemed strange or tactless (cf. e.g. *Silv.* 1. 2. 138–9, 3. 5. 50–4, Humbert (1972), 102 ff.); prior marriages were often mentioned in sepulchral inscriptions (e.g. *CIL* vi. 7873, *CLE* 1578). By mentioning it, Statius enhances his very grand compliment (*ceu uirginitate*) to Priscilla in 46.

46. te ceu uirginitate iugata: *iugatum* (M) gives the slightly strange sense 'she used to cherish you when *you* had been married ... as if in her maidenhood'. *iugata* (Baehrens) establishes a connection between *ceu uirginitate* and the remainder of the sentence, if it is nominative, giving a participial phrase in apposition: 'she cherished you as if joined to you as a virgin bride', as in the translation. If *iugata* is ablative, the sense is perhaps more strained: 'she, as if her maidenhood were being yoked, used to cherish you ...'. As well as referring to marriage (see e.g. Muson. fr. 13a Lutz τῷ ὁμόζυγι), *iugare* can also be a technical term of viticulture; *iugata* anticipates the ensuing simile of the elm and the vine. See *ThLL* vii/2. 632. 68 ff.

47. uisceribus totis: for *uiscera* thus, cf. *Silv.* 3. 5. 30 '[me] uisceribus complexa tuis'; note also 5. 5. 8–9 (with n.) 'morientibus ecce lacertis | uiscera nostra tenens animamque auellitur infans'.

48–9. uitem | ulmus amat: the comparison between human love and the union of the elm and the vine would have been familiar. It first appears in Latin poetry in Cat. (61. 102–5, 62. 49); see further Mynors on Virg. *G.* 2. 221, Mart. 4. 13. 5. The image is not however confined to poetry, nor did it begin with it; *maritare* appears to have been a technical term of viticulture. Cato, *Agr.* 32. 2 has the following instruction: 'arbores facito ut bene maritae sint'; cf. Col. 4. 1. 6, 4. 2. 1, 5. 6. 18, 11. 2. 79. See further *RE* ix. A. 1. 552. 32–553. 18 s.v. 'Ulme' (M. Schuster), N.–H. on Hor. *Carm.* 2. 15. 5 and K. D. White (1970), 236 ff.

Statius reverses the usual mode of comparison, and compares the elm, normally paired with the man, to Priscilla, adding weight to the already emphatic description of her love for her husband in 47. Contrast the simile at *Theb.* 8. 544–7, where a rider and his horse are compared to an elm and a vine falling down together.

49. miscetque nemus: the simile echoes the language used to describe Abascantus and Priscilla, who were *mixtos* in 43. *nemus* signifies foliage: compare V.Fl. 3. 444, and note also *Theb.* 8. 545–6 'sed maestior ulmus | quaerit utrumque nemus' from the simile of the falling vine and elm (though Hill in his apparatus criticus suggests that *nemus* may denote 'truncus'). Cf. the similar use of *silua* to denote foliage at *Silv.* 3. 1. 185 and 5. 5. 30.

50. autumnum: the elm hopes for a rich autumn (for the epithet *diues* applied to autumn, cf. Sen. *Apoc.* 2), and thus a favourable vintage for the vine. For *autumnus* denoting 'the autumn harvest' (cf. Greek ὀπώρα, LSJ s.v. II), compare Ov. *Met.* 9. 92, 14. 660, Sen. *Thy.* 168, Mart. 3. 58. 7, 12. 57. 22, 13. 113. 1; see also the allied usages of *annus* (*OLD* s.v. 8) and *uer* (210–14 n.). This too is a sensitive extension of the simile (usually confined to an image of the intertwined plants), suggesting the delight of spouses in each other's good fortune, appropriate to the subsequent account of Priscilla's involvement in Abascantus' career. Compare also *Theb.* 8. 547, where the falling elm is 'inuita' as it crushes the grapes of the vine.

51–4. Whereas the poem began with the distinction between material and poetic memorials, a further distinction now emerges between true and false types of verbal praise. Ancestry and beauty are not enough but need to be aligned with other qualities: cf. *Silv.* 2. 7. 85–6, where Lucan's widow Polla has 'forma, simplicitate, comitate, | censu, sanguine, gratia, decore' and Prop. 2. 13. 9–12, where Propertius explains his preference for a *docta puella*. Note also Muson. fr. 13b Lutz, where Musonius advises against paying attention to lineage, money or beauty in considering marriage; cf. Treggiari (1984), 424–51, for further discussion of conventional criteria in determining whether to contract a marriage, and philosophical reaction against emphasis on factors such as wealth or beauty. Internal personal characteristics (*ex te*) are important; note as well that such a position is in keeping with more general precepts offered by epideictic manuals (e.g. *Rhet Her.* 3. 7. 13, Cic. *De Orat.* 2. 342, Quint. *Inst.* 3. 7. 12 and 15), which affirm the importance of character (*animus* or *uirtus*) over external characteristics. See also Esteve-Forriol (1962), 136.

51. laudantur evokes the *laudatio funebris* (for this near-technical usage of *laudare*, see Durry (1950), p. xviii): whereas some women have entire funeral orations devoted to their lineage and beauty, these qualities are only of passing importance to Statius. Cf. Sen. *Dial.* 12. 16. 3 'more aliarum, quibus omnis commendatio ex forma petitur', and contrast the emphasis on Cornelia's family in Prop. 4. 11.

52. morum ... bonis: for the philosophical distinction between types of *bona* compare Cic. *Tusc.* 5. 85: 'tria genera bonorum, maxima animi, secunda corporis, externa tertia, ut Peripatetici nec multo ueteres Academici secus'. For the neuter plural *bona* construed with a defining genitive, see e.g. *Silv.* 1. 3. 106 'bonis animi', 3. 5. 63 'formaeque bonis animique meretur' (where Statius' stepdaughter is said to have moral and physical qualities appropriate for a future marriage), 4. 4. 21–2 'dubium morumne probandus | ingeniine bonis', Ov. *Tr.* 1. 6. 34 'prima bonis animi conspicerere tui', Quint. *Inst.* 1 pr. 13, 1 pr. 27, 2. 5. 11, 2. 8. 3, 11. 3. 19, 12. 5. 2.

falsaque potentes: M here reads *falso*, which cannot be defended, since the balanced contrast of the previous line and a half, where the women are praised for qualities such as beauty and ancestry, but lack *morum ... bonis* is echoed in the sequel, where the women might win false praise for empty merits, but lack true praise. Phillimore absurdly attempted to defend M's reading on the ground that '*potentes* more Papiniano non cum genetiuo sed absolute positum, pro *nobiles*', but if *potentes* is simply equivalent to the noun *nobiles*, then what would adverbial *falso* modify? Moreover, it is artificial to suppose that Statian examples where singular *potens* is construed with a genitive (e.g. *Theb.* 1. 31 'undarum terraeque potens') or an ablative (e.g. *Theb.* 6. 154 'haec pietate potens') are of no account in considering whether or not the plural *potentes* can be so construed. Meursius conjectured *falsa*, which gives a pleasing variation in case between *falsaque* (sc. *laude*) *potentes* and *laudis ... uerae* in the next line, and is preferable to Heinsius' *falsae* (genitive, though the potential for its being read as a nominative plural does not help either).

53. laudis ... uerae: Cic. *de Orat.* 2. 342 remarks that external qualities 'non habent in se ueram laudem, quae deberi uirtuti uni putatur'. In the same passage Cicero continues by remarking that in *laudationes* external qualities are to be praised if they are not misused. Thus the ensuing reference to Priscilla's lineage and beauty functions as praise, since the context is one of moral praise as well. For the contrast between external circumstances, physical attributes, and character, see also *Rhet. Her.* 3. 6. 10. For *laudor* construed with an ablative compare Cic. *Phil.* 2. 69 'neque rebus externis magis laudandus quam institutis domesticis', Virg. *A.* 10. 449, Hor. *Carm.* 4. 5. 23, *ThLL* vii/2. 1045. 19–33.

53–4: quamquam et origo niteret: Weaver (1994), 338 and 350 suggests that Priscilla was from an equestrian family (since the *lex Iulia* would not have permitted a person of senatorial rank to be married to a freedman), noting also that Statius seems to make no mention of senatorial connections (contrast Crispinus' family at *Silv.* 5. 2. 17–21); cf. Nauta (2002), 233. Of the Priscillas collected by

Vidman (1980), 317 s.n. a considerable number are either freed slaves, or else married to freed slaves; cf. Kajanto (1965), 288. Lines 72–4 and 111–13 do, however, imply that she had sufficient access to the emperor to be able to advance her husband's career.

felix species: *felix* suggests that Priscilla's beauty is a matter of fortune, contrasting with the *maior honos* which comes from within her (*ex te*), her glorious devotion to her husband.

multumque optanda: perhaps an echo of Cat. 62. 42 'multi illum pueri, multae optauere puellae'.

55. maior honos: whereas a physical memorial to Priscilla was *mortalis honos* (10), her devotion to Abascantus is a greater kind of glory; cf. Tiberius' preference for 'haec mihi in animis uestris templa, hae pulcherrimae effigies et mansurae' (Tac. *Ann.* 4. 38. 2).

unum nouisse cubile: Statius refers to Priscilla as an *uniuira*, a wife married to one husband throughout her life. Despite the allusion to Priscilla's first husband (45–6), this startling utterance is less puzzling in the light of the previous description of Priscilla as 'ceu uirginitate iugata' (following Baehrens). Compare Horace's striking reference to Livia, in her second marriage to Augustus (she had previously been married to Ti. Claudius Nero), as 'unico gaudens mulier marito' (*Carm.* 3. 14. 5).

To be called *uniuira* was one of the highest compliments to a married woman, particularly in an age when divorce and remarriage were by no means uncommon. At Prop. 4. 11. 68, the dead Cornelia advises her daughter to have only one husband: 'fac teneas unum nos imitata uirum'; cf. Mart. 10. 63. 7–8 'contigit et thalami mihi gloria rara fuitque | una pudicitiae mentula nota meae'. Contrast the ironic description of a woman's eight marriages in five years as 'titulo res digna sepulcri' (Juv. 6. 229–30).

56. unum secretis agitare sub ossibus ignem: Here language which might be used of illicit passion, *secretis* and *ignem*, is applied to the married state in emphasizing Priscilla's fidelity. Cf. 'castissimus ardor', at 41 and *Theb.* 12. 194, *Silv.* 2. 2. 143–4 'quorum de pectore mixtae | in longum coiere faces', referring to Pollius Felix and his wife, Dido's use of *flamma* at Virg. *A.* 4. 23, and Luc. 5. 811 (of Pompey's wife, Cornelia) 'quamuis flamma tacitas urente medullas'. Pliny (*Ep.* 6. 7. 3) writes to his wife Calpurnia 'sed eo magis ad desiderium tui accendor'. Contrast Virgil's far more negative account of Dido's passion for Aeneas (*A.* 4. 66–7):

est mollis flamma medullas
interea et tacitum uiuit sub pectore uulnus.

For *agitare* used with *ignis* to refer to love, cf. Ov. *Met.* 6. 708
'arserunt agitati fortius ignes'.

57–9. Statius praises Priscilla's chastity by indicating that she
would have been immune to adulterous advances (cf. *Silv.* 3. 5. 8,
where Statius' wife would shun 'mille procos'). The examples given
are Paris (*Phrygius . . . raptor*), the suitors of Penelope (*Dulichiiue proci*) and
Thyestes, who seduced Aerope, the wife of his brother Atreus. Thus
two instances of adultery (Paris and Helen, Thyestes and Aerope) are
combined with Penelope, who was not won over by her suitors
(contrast Mart. 1. 62. 5–6 'iuuenemque secuta relicto | coniuge Penel-
ope uenit, abit Helene', said of a woman who betrayed her husband
for a young man).

Mycenaeo . . . auro is ablative of price, if the reference here is to
the conventional version of the story that Thyestes polluted the
marriage of Aerope and Atreus in return for 'Mycenaean gold', for
Aerope gave the golden ram to Thyestes, enabling him to overthrow
the kingship of Atreus (E. *El.* 720–6, Sen. *Thy.* 225–41). Taking
Mycenaeo . . . auro as instrumental ablative seems more difficult, since
the overall context of the passage refers to women being beset by gifts
in return for their chastity, and there is no no extant version of the
myth in which Aerope is given gifts by Thyestes. Vollmer suggested
that this passage and Hor. *Carm.* 1. 16. 17 may refer to another lost
version of the myth, perhaps related in Varius' Thyestes play.

60. Lydae . . . pondera gazae: the reference, if specific, is to
the wealth of Croesus, the king of Lydia (Hdt. 1. 30 ff.).

gazae is a borrowing of Greek γάζα, itself a borrowing of the Persian
word for royal treasure (Curt. 3. 13. 5, Serv. on *A.* 1. 119 and 2. 763). In
Greek the word first appears in the third century BC (e.g. Thphr. *HP*
8. 11. 5, *OGIS* 54. 22, and LXX *2 Esd.* 5. 17), and also occurs in
compounds such as γαζοφύλαξ. In Latin *gaza* denotes regal wealth,
not necessarily Persian, and is first attested in prose at Cic. *Leg. Man.*
66 and in verse at Lucr. 2. 37 and Cat. 64. 46. In Statius *gaza* occurs at
Silv. 1. 3. 105, 2. 2. 121, and here, and at *Ach.* 1. 959.

61. Statius' examples move from the more familiar geography of
Greece (57–9) and the Near East (60) to much more remote peoples.
The reference to the Arabs probably refers to the Sabaean kingdom

of south-western Arabia (211–14 n. below); for the Chinese (*Seres*) and
their contacts with Rome, see Ferguson (1978).

62. paupertate: for the dangers of a rich wife, cf. Sen. *Con.* 1. 6. 7
'impotens malum est beata uxor', Treggiari (1991), 329 ff. Juv. 6.
287–91 remarks that hard work and frugality maintained the moral
standards of old.

63. uitamque rependere famae: the image is of Priscilla
setting her life in the scales, in recompense for the safety of her
reputation, instead of yielding to material inducements to adultery.
Compare Luc. 2. 382 'patriaeque impendere uitam' and Juv. 4. 91
'uitam impendere uero'.

64. nimiusque in moribus horror: *nimius* suggests that, up
to a point, *horror* (severity) is desirable. Contrast the philosopher
Euphrates (Plin. *Ep.* 1. 10. 7), 'nullus horror in cultu, nulla tristitia,
multum seueritatis', where moral severity is praiseworthy, but phys-
ical *horror* is not.

65. simplex hilarisque fides: for the combination of moral
qualities and pleasantness of spirit compare *Silv.* 1. 2. 12, 1. 3. 81–2, 2.
3. 65, 3. 5. 17–18 (Statius' wife), 5. 2. 73, 5. 3. 246–9, Hor. *Ep.* 2. 2. 193
'simplex hilarisque', Vell. 2. 127. 4 (on Sejanus) 'uirum priscae seuer-
itatis, laetissimae hilaritatis' (where Woodman ad loc. notes that
hilaritas would be an official imperial virtue in the coinage of Ha-
drian), Sil. 8. 609–10 (a Brutus) 'laeta uiro grauitas ac mentis amabile
pondus | et sine tristitia uirtus', Jerome, *Epist.* 60. 10. 6 'grauitatem
morum hilaritate frontis temperabat', *CLE* 1307. 3–4 (from a hus-
band's epitaph for his wife) 'et proba iudicio cunctorum et amica
pudoris, | nec sine laetitia sermo, faceta loqui'; see also Plin. *Ep.* 1. 15.
4, 4. 3. 2, 7. 19. 7, 8. 21. 1 'ut in uita sic in studiis pulcherrimum et
humanissimum existimo seueritatem comitatemque miscere.'

66. anceps fors ad maiora uocasset: M here reads *metus et
maiora uacasset.* I shall postpone discussion of *metus* and deal with *et* and
uacasset first. The overall sense of the surrounding context is that
Priscilla would have been willing, if necessary, to undergo extreme
dangers for the sake of her husband. There is thus little to recom-
mend M's *uacasset*, when *uocasset* (ς) gives the sense of Priscilla respond-
ing to and meeting the demands of adversity; the confusion may in
part have arisen from the fact that *uocare* and *uacare* were originally
both spelt as *uocare* until at least the time of Domitian: see Housman,
Class. P. i. 301. As for M's *et*, joining *metus* (or whatever word might
stand in its place) and *maiora* is unsatisfactory, because the pairing of a

specific noun such as *metus* and the unspecific *maiora* is vague and unconvincing; *et* would also require the emendation of *uocasset* to the plural. Reading *ad* (ς) gives the sense that Priscilla would be spurred to perform greater deeds than the domestic virtues described in the preceding lines. The *maiora* to which Priscilla is called are listed in 67–9. For *uoco* and *ad* in similar contexts, compare e.g. Luc. 1. 387, 2. 476 'dumque ipse ad bella uocaret'.

M's *metus*, however, is more of a difficulty. *metus* is unconvincing in the light of the succeeding lines, where we hear that Priscilla would have endured perils on behalf of her husband. It is illogical for fear to call Priscilla to greater deeds; Sil. 4. 25–6 'haud segnis cuncta magister | praecipitat timor' refers to defensive preparations in anticipation of Hannibal, not to acts of heroism. The epithet *anceps* is not a negative, but rather an indication of uncertainty, of bifurcation, a puzzling concept to apply to *metus*, since Priscilla is spurred on to action, rather than being deterred from it. Although there are parallels for *anceps metus*, such as Petr. 89 v. 1 ('inter ancipites metus'), V.Fl. 3. 74 ('at Minyas anceps fixit pavor') and Sil. 3. 557–8 ('at Venus ancipiti mentem labefacta timore | affatur genitorem'), the contexts of these passages relate to the negative effect of fear, whereas in the present passage *metus* is offered as an explanation of Priscilla's readiness to undergo dangers on behalf of her husband. Translations reveal this difficulty: Slater translates *anceps metus* as 'doubting fear for thee', which strains the meaning of *anceps*, while Mozley has 'some dread crisis'; Shackleton Bailey offers 'some formidable danger'.

One possible emendation might be *anceps fatum*. *anceps* is quite frequently applied to words such as 'fortuna' (*Theb.* 6. 474–5, Virg. *A.* 4. 603, Vell. 2. 79. 3, Luc. 4. 390, Suet. *Caes.* 36; cf. Sen. *Phoen.* 629; 'casus' (e.g. Cic. *Fam.* 5. 12. 5) and 'euentus' (e.g. Liv. 4. 27. 6), but it is perhaps harder for *fatum*, usually something immutable, to be *anceps* (at Cic. *Rep.* 6. 12 'sed eius temporis ancipitem uideo quasi fatorum uiam', the use of *anceps* is explicable in terms of the bifurcation of fate, where Scipio Aemilianus is fated either to save the state or be slain by his relations). Stephen Heyworth suggests *anceps Mars* (cf. *Theb.* 9. 566–7 'sic anceps dura belli uice mutua Grais | Sidoniisque simul nectebat uulnera Mauors', Luc. 5. 67–8 'solus in ancipites metuit descendere Martis | Appius euentus', Sil. 15. 132 'et grauia ancipitis deposcit munera Martis', and see *OLD* s.v. *anceps* 6 for the epithet being applied to battles), but this seems too specific, since war is

strictly speaking the context of only the first example ('armiferas . . .
cateruas') of Priscilla's hypothetical bravery in 67–9. I therefore
suggest *anceps fors* (see above for examples where *anceps* is applied to
words such as 'fortuna'). *fors* elsewhere occurs as a noun in Statius at
Theb. 1. 327, 5. 718, 7. 403, 8. 250, 10. 73, 10. 384, 11. 283, 11. 481, 12.
382, *Ach.* 1. 810.

67–9. Statius praises Priscilla by describing how she would have
endured misfortunes in support of her husband: compare *Silv.* 3. 5.
18–22, where Statius, attempting to persuade his wife to leave Rome
for Neapolis, points out that she would have accompanied him on a
journey to such remote places as Thule or the source of the Nile. This
allows a grander type of encomium; contrast *Laudatio Murdiae* 20–5 on
the customary limitations imposed on praise by the habitual simpli-
city of women's lives: 'quom omnium bonarum feminarum simplex
simi|lisque esse laudatio soleat, quod naturalia bona propria custo|dia
seruata uarietates uerborum non desiderent, satisque sit | eadem
omnes bona fama digna fecisse et quia adquirere | nouas laudes
mulieri sit arduom quom minoribus uarieta|tibus uita iactetur'.

The topos of a friend's or a lover's readiness to endure extraordin-
ary privations on behalf of another is encountered in its simplest form
at Hor. *Carm.* 3. 9. 9–16, where two speakers each affirm their
readiness to die for their beloved, but it is often expressed in terms
of a willingness to countenance extraordinary dangers or journeys:
see e.g. *Silv.* 3. 3. 71–5 (Claudius Etruscus' father accompanied Calig-
ula to the north), Hor. *Carm.* 1. 22. 5 and 2. 6. 1 with N.–H., Sen.
Phaed. 613–16, Cairns (1972), 99, 123–4. Compare Cat. 11, where the
poet dismisses the offers of his friends Furius and Aurelius with the
remark that all they have to do is to pass on a final message to Lesbia.
The topos sometimes appears in a context of *recusatio*: Prop. 1. 6. 1–6
explains that though he would not fear to accompany Tullus on the
seas or to the ends of the earth, he is prevented from departure by his
mistress. For such offers see also Hor. *Epod.* 1. 11–14 (Horace's asser-
tion that he will follow Maecenas on campaign) and *Carm.* 3. 4. 29–36
(Horace would endure the ends of the earth in the company of the
Muses). The claim that Priscilla would follow her husband has more
weight, precisely because it is not made by Priscilla, but by Statius,
the observer of the marriage. At Luc. 8. 648–9 Cornelia, describing
her support for her defeated husband Pompey refers to herself as
'per undas | et per castra comes nullis absterrita fatis', while at Luc. 8.
75–6 Pompey tells Cornelia that 'laudis in hoc sexu non legum iura

nec arma, | unica materia est coniunx miser'. Cf. Sil. 3. 109–13, where Imilce expresses her wish to accompany her husband Hannibal, and 6. 500–11, where Marcia wishes to join her husband Regulus in returning to certain death in Carthage.

In the historians, compare Tac. *Ann.* 12. 51, on Zenobia's devotion to her husband Radamistus, *Hist.* 1. 3. 1, where 'secutae maritos in exilia coniuges' feature in a list of 'bona exempla' from the troubled period following Nero, and note also Vell. 2. 67. 2. who praises the 'in proscriptos uxorum fidem summam' during the triumviral proscriptions (cf. Sen. *Con.* 6. 4, 10. 3, V. Max. 6. 7. 2–3, App. *BC* 4. 39–40 [163–70] and Plin. *Ep.* 7. 19. 4 (on Fannia) 'bis maritum secuta in exsilium est, tertio ipsa propter maritum relegata'. Juv. 6. 94–102 inverts the theme of loyal wives, where wives will accompany their lovers at sea, but not their husbands.

67. armiferas: *armiger* and *armifer* are both found, *armiger* first occurring as an adjective at Acc. *trag.* 547 and as a noun on several occasions in Plautus. *armifer* is first found as late as Ovid (*Am.* 2. 6. 35, *Ars* 2. 5, *Ep.* 2. 84, *Fast.* 3. 681, 6. 421, *Met.* 9. 645, 14. 475, and *Tr.* 4. 10. 13). Statius uses both *armifer* and *armiger;* for his more general fondness for adjectives in *-fer*, see van Dam on *Silv.* 2. 1. 94–5. Quint. *Inst.* 1. 5. 70 notes that compound words are more suited to Greek than Latin; and in Greek, indeed, compounds in -φόρος are even more popular in prose than in verse, whereas in Latin, the equivalent compounds are more favoured in verse: see further Ahrens (1950), 241–4. Adjectives in *-ger* and *-fer* are often interchangeable in manuscripts: see e.g. Hill's apparatus criticus at *Theb.* 3. 420.

69. melius, quod non aduersa probarunt: cf. Plin. *Pan.* 31. 1 'cum secunda felices, aduersa magnos probent'. Ironically, adverse fortune has shown the extent of Abascantus' love for his wife. There is no need to accept Phillimore's emendation of M's *melius* to the almost masochistic *doluit*, with its improbable hyperbole that Priscilla grieved that her husband had not had the chance to experience real adversity: for ellipses featuring *melius* see Winterbottom on [Quint.] *Decl. min.* 305. 8, and for the immediacy of the repetion of *melius* with *meliore uia* in line 71 (a phrase also found at Luc. 9. 394), cf. e.g. Hor. *S.* 1. 1. 62–5, Virg. *G.* 1. 286–9 (three instances of forms of *melior* in four lines), 4. 90–2. For the idea of husbands and wives sharing in good and bad fortune alike, see Muson. fr. 13a–14 Lutz, Luc. 2. 346–7, Tac. *Ann.* 3. 34. 5 'male eripi maritis consortia rerum secundarum aduersarumque' (with Woodman and Martin), 12. 5, Plin. *Ep.* 3. 16. 6, D.C. 44. 13–14 (a story of Brutus' wife, Porcia, harming herself in order to show her resolution and her ability to share his secrets), Dixon (1991), 105–6.

70. tibi: *tua* in the next line confirms that the pronoun refers to Priscilla. The pronoun is most naturally taken as a possessive dative.

71–4. Priscilla's efforts to secure the success of her husband recall the delight of the elm in the vine's autumn vintage (48–50). Epic offers examples of attempts by women to obtain divine favour for their menfolk such as the robe offered to Athene by the women of Troy at *Il.* 6. 286–311 (cf. Virg. *A.* 1. 479–82, Luc. 2. 28–36, Stat. *Theb.* 10. 49–69); in an erotic context, compare Delia's prayers at Tib. 1. 3. 9–10.

74. genium domini praesentis: as noted by Scott (1936), 137, Domitian is here described in language (*praesentis*) which suggests the idea of a god's epiphany among mortals in order to rule over them benignly; see further 38 n. above. Domitian's *genius* is attested as having received sacrifice from the Arval Brotherhood: see *CIL* vi. 2060. 43 'Genio ipsius taurum', with Gradel (2002), 189–1, who notes that Domitian appears to have revived worship of the imperial *genius* after a period of abeyance under the earlier Flavians. Here Statius calls it *mitis* in a context where Priscilla is trying to win the emperor's favour; cf. e.g. 187–8 below (where Abascantus is told to worship it unceasingly), 1. 1. 58, 4. 2. 26 'ingenti genio', Plin. *Pan.* 52. 6 (addressed to Trajan): 'simili reuerentia, Caesar, non apud genium tuum bonitati tuae gratias agi, sed apud numen Iouis optimi maximi pateris', Sauter (1934), 41–5, Scott (1936), 118–19, and on the whole issue of cult of the emperor's *genius*, see Gradel (2002), 162–97.

75. audita es: Priscilla's devotions secure success for Abascantus: for prayers being granted in the course of poems, compare Virg. *Ecl.* 8. 109, Prop. 1. 8. 27–8, 2. 28. 59–62.

uenitque gradu Fortuna benigno: cf. *Silv.* 3. 3. 85–6 'praecelsaque toto | intrauit Fortuna gradu', Virg. *A.* 11. 42–3 ' "tene," inquit "miserande puer, cum laeta ueniret, | inuidit Fortuna mihi…" ', Luc. 4. 121–2 'paruo Fortuna uiri contenta pauore | plena redit'. Fortuna's arrival, at first sight paradoxical in the overall context of the poem, nevertheless highlights an important aspect of the consolation, praise of the successful career of Abascantus.

76–9. Statius identifies five qualities inherent in Abascantus' service to the emperor: his *quies*, his loyalty, his concern, his vigilance and his serious bearing, appropriate to the weighty duties of his office. Perhaps the most pertinent adjective is *nauam*, which has an air of paradox, since it denotes diligence (thus 'nauo labore' at Sil. 4. 485).

For positive instances of *quies*, compare *Silv.* 1. 3. 91 'fecunda quies', applied to the contemplation of Manilius Vopiscus in his villa, and 5. 1. 117, the inward calm of Priscilla even after her wedding day; see also Myers (2000), 120–5. In Abascantus' case *quies* might have political overtones, suggesting a convenient lack of political ambition, a dangerous attribute in an imperial servant. Cf. Tac. *Ann.* 14. 47. 1, where Memmius Regulus was able to survive Nero's dangerous praise 'quiete defensus et quia noua generis claritudine neque inuidiosis opibus erat'.

77. succinctaque pectora: the metaphor refers to the girding of clothing from below. Compare Quint. *Inst.* 12. 5. 1 (on the need for the orator's precepts) 'haec arma habere ad manum, horum scientia debet esse succinctus'. *succincta* also suggests readiness for action (*OLD* s.v. 1), reinforcing *nauam* in the previous line.

78–9. uigiles sensus: compare similar praise of Rutilius Gallicus and Claudius Etruscus' father at *Silv.* 1. 4. 55 and 3. 3. 98.

digna euoluere tantas | sobria corda uices: Abascantus' frenzied private grief (e.g. 'tantus in attonito regnabat pectore luctus', 29) is quite unlike his measured handling of the emperor's affairs. *euoluere* also appropriately (for an *ab epistulis*) evokes the unrolling a papyrus roll for reading (see e.g. *Silv.* 4. 3. 141, *OLD* 6); cf. *Silv.* 3. 3. 99, where the word refers to the activities of Claudius Etruscus' father, who was *a rationibus*. *euoluere* is used of Domitian at *Silv.* 1. 1. 41 'pectora quae mundi ualeant euoluere curas', in the description of his equestrian statue.

uidit qui: Statius relies on his account of Domitian's omniscience (cf. 37–9) to ensure that the grammatical subject of this passage is clearly understood. The delay in referring to the emperor even by a periphrasis until *Romulei . . . ducis* (87) contributes to the effect of grandeur.

80. inspectis . . . ministris: as at 37–40, the emperor's insights into his servants are emphasized. For *inspicio* thus, cf. Col. 11. 1. 7 'multisque prius experimentis inspiciendus erit futurus uilicus', Plin. *Ep.* 1. 10. 2, 5. 14. 5 'qui uir et quantus esset altissime inspexi'.

81. quid Auster: M's obviously corrupt readings at the end of lines 81–4 suggest damage to an earlier manuscript. In 81, M's *arctos* is a simple corruption influenced by *arcto* at the end of 88 (cf. e.g. the corrupt 'Hiberi' at the end of the line at Sil. 1. 387, followed by 'Hiberi' in the same *locus* at 1. 392), especially plausible in the light of *boreas hibernus* in the next line. *Auster* restores balance; the emperor devotes his attention to all four quarters of the earth (east, west, south and north, in that order); compare *Silv.* 3. 3. 95–7, where Claudius Etruscus' father's attentions are similarly expressed in terms of winds, and see Laguna's commentary.

82. ferrique togaeque: *ferri* is the usual metonymy of a sword representing war (*OLD* s.v. *ferrum* 5). For *toga* used to denote peace, cf. *Silv.* 1. 4. 48, 5. 2. 58, 5. 2. 108–9 'togata | strage fori'. The characterization of peace by the toga is found in Cicero, e.g. *De Orat.* 3. 167 'ex quo genere haec sunt, ... Liberum appellare pro uino, ... campum pro comitiis, togam pro pace, arma ac tela pro bello', *Off.* 1. 77 (= *Poet. fr.* 16 Traglia) 'cedant arma togae'; cf Ov. *Pont.* 2. 1. 61–2 'iuuenum belloque togaque | maxime', Vell. 1. 12. 3, Luc. 9. 199 'praetulit arma togae, sed pacem armatus amauit', Sil. 6. 617 'par ingenium castrisque togaeque', Plin. *Pan.* 4. 5 'alium toga sed non et arma honestarunt'. See also *Silv.* 5. 2. 108–9 n.

83. paratis: M's *iubatis* gives grammatical sense, but is by no means easy. The word primarily signifies endowment with a *iuba*, a mane. Markland scorns Calderini's explanation that the word is equivalent to 'fortissimis', through association with the mane of a lion. Nevertheless *iubatis* has found some support. Vollmer compared *Silv.* 1. 2. 2, where Apollo has 'umeroque comanti'. But Skutsch (1901), 199–200 argued that long hair, which might be suitable for Apollo, would not be appropriate for a Roman imperial servant. Though Klotz (1903), 286 cited the description of Achilles in Dares (c. 16, p. 16. 8M) as 'pectorosum ore uenusto, membris ualentibus, magnis, iubatum, bene crispatum', the same objection holds: *iubatus* is appropriate to Achilles, one of Homer's 'long-haired Achaeans', but not to Domitian's *ab epistulis*. This passage from Dares and *Silv.* 5. 1. 83 are, moreover, the only two cases where *ThLL* (vii/2. 1574. 13–26) finds *iubatus* applied to human beings: apart from a single reference in Var. *L.* 6. 6, where the word is used of a star, all other instances refer to animals, typically snakes or lions. Furthermore Sen. *Dial.* 10. 12. 3 uses *iuba* contemptuously of those who devote excessive attention to their hair: 'excandescunt, si quid ex iuba sua decisum est.' Cf. also Prudent. *Ham.* 134 'hirsutos iuba densa umeros errantibus hydris obtegit', a description of the devil. These last two citations make *iubatis* even less convincing, since a *iuba* is unlikely to win praise except in divine or heroic contexts. Politian's suggestion in his commentary that *iubatis* referred to the hair of young men was rightly ridiculed by Markland, since it is absurd to envisage Domitian entrusting cares of state to the management of a mere youth. Mart. 1. 31. 6 'dumque decent fusae lactea colla iubae', where *iuba* signifies the hair of a young boy, is thus irrelevant. It is also hard to see how *iubatis* is rhetorically relevant, if it is a mere description of Abascantus' shoulders. Indeed, any word like *iubatus* is going to strike the wrong note here, since Abascantus' shoulders are only going to receive a metaphorical burden from the emperor; Vollmer's citation of *Silv.* 1. 2. 2 'umeroque comanti' is thus irrelevant.

Of the numerous conjectures, *sub actis* (Macnaghten) joins the end of l. 83 to the preceding sentence, but this is padding. Macnaghten's explanation of 'mentem probat ille sub actis' as 'he judges not merely the act itself but the spirit which prompts it' blurs the progression of the rhetoric, since in the Latin Domitian judges first the *consilia* of war and peace, and then *ipsam mentem*; after beginning with practical *consilia*, it is odd then to move to *ipsam mentem* (which implies actual character) in the context of *acta*. Another strategy has been to replace *iubatis* with a genitive singular present participle, as with Saenger's *iuuantis* and Watt's *uolentis*. Although Watt asserts that there are thirteen instances in the epics where Statius ends a hexameter with some form of *uolens*, his criticism of Saenger's *iuuantis*, its weakness, can be applied to *uolentis* as well. *uolentis* is unnecessary; it can be taken for granted that the emperor's *ab epistulis* is a willing helper.

Avantius conjectured *subactis*, 'driven under (a yoke)'. For *subigo* construed with *iugum* see *OLD* s.v. *subigo* 3b; Vollmer argues that *molem immensam* and *uix tractabile pondus* (if M's *tempus* has been correctly emended) evoke the idea of a burden, so that *subactis* harmonizes with the language characterizing Domitian's delegation of duties. Though the metaphor of yoking can be used of imperial service (cf. *Silv.* 3. 3. 83 'tu totiens mutata ducum iuga rite tulisti', where Laguna argues that such language is taken over from love poetry) *subactis*, however, is too forceful, suggesting a compulsion which is inappropriate here; note that the word can be used for the subjugation of enemies (*OLD* 5). *iugatis* (Lohr) would mean 'joined', but it is only Abascantus who bears the emperor's burden.

Better is Krohn's *probatis* (perhaps compare the emendations and discussion of M's *probatur* at *Silv.* 5. 3. 180); for the emperor's testing of his servants, cf. 37–9 and 80 above. However, the repetition of *probatis* two words after *probat* is unattractive, especially when *probat* has previously emphasised Domitian's investigation of mental qualities;

the transition to *probatis*. . . . *umeris* unnecessarily labours and blurs the point through the intrusion of the physical (though metaphorical) *umeris*. I accordingly suggest *paratis*, indicating Abascantus' readiness and aptitude for imperial service.

84. Cf. Sen. *Dial.* 11. 7. 1, where the universe (*mundus*) is supported on the emperor's shoulders. In Statius, cf. *Silv.* 4. 4. 97–8, where Vitorius Marcellus is asked whether the poet's shoulders and neck can sustain the enormous weight of a projected imperial epic.

85–107. On the post of *ab epistulis*, see pp. 72–3 above.

85–6. sacra . . . domo: a poetic variant on the phrases *domus Augusta* and *domus diuina*, denoting the imperial household. The tribunician *potestas* assumed by Augustus made him (and later emperors) *sacrosanctus* (see Liv. 3. 55 for the Republican origins of this practice).

The importance of the emperor's *domus* is suggested by the prayer offered by Valerius Messala for Augustus and his home (Suet. *Aug.* 58. 2). The emperor's *domus* was considered divine: thus *CIL* iii. 231 begins 'Dis patriis et domu Aug.' There are also dedicatory formulae such as 'Numini domus Augusti' (e.g. *CIL* vi. 236) and 'genio domus Aug' (*CIL* viii. 6945). The *domus* is the subject of a cult in *CIL* vi. 30901, and there are also inscriptions attesting *cultores* and other holders of priestly offices. See further G. Calza in *Diz. Epigr.* ii. 2061 ff.

87–8. uiresque modosque | imperii tractare manu: Slater's translation 'to have in hand and to control all the strengths of the empire' not only ignores *modos* but applies an almost geographical meaning to *imperii*, which seems better taken as referring to the emperor's *imperium*, his right of command. Mozley's 'to handle all the powers and modes of empire' is a closer translation. Weaver (1994), 349 interprets this phrase and the succeeding lines as evidence for Abascantus actually travelling with Domitian on campaigns, but the indirect questions of lines 88–91 seem to point to knowledge of the far corners of the empire from a distance.

88–100: for the geographical sweep of Abascantus' responsibilities, compare the similar account of Claudius Etruscus' father's duties as *a rationibus* at *Silv.* 3. 3. 86–97.

88. laurus: cf. Σ Juv. 4. 149: 'antea si quid nuntiabant consules in urbem per epistulas, si uictoriae nuntiabantur, laurus in epistola figebatur, si autem aliquid aduersi, pinna.' These emblems of success or disaster could also be affixed to spears (Plin. *Nat.* 15. 133). See also e.g. Liv. 45. 1. 6, Pers. 6. 43–4, Sen. *Ag.* 390 (= 410 in Tarrant's edition and see his note), Mart. 7. 6. 5–10.

Arcto: the geographical reference is puzzling (cf. *Silv.* 5. 2. 133 'Arctoosne amnes', mentioned in close collocation with 'Rheni fracta . . . flumina'). Although Britain, in view of its northerly location, is a possibility, particularly in the light of Agricola's campaigns, the subsequent reference to Thule works against this hypothesis. Similarly, the Danube frontier (*binominis Histri*, 89) can be ruled out, as can the Rhine, referred to in 90. The succeeding references to three specific locations suggest that *Arcto* is only a vague expression for the northern frontiers.

89. uagus Euphrates: for *uagus* or *uagari* describing a river or its waters in flood, compare Luc. 10. 310, 327, Mart. 10. 85. 3–4, N.–H. on Hor. *Carm.* 1. 2. 18; note also *Silv.* 2. 7. 12 'docti largius euagentur amnes', Amm. 18. 7. 9 (*euagari* used of the Euphrates). The flooding of the Euphrates, though disputed by Hdt. 1. 193. 1–2 and by Polycleitus, *FGrH* 128 F 5, was widely recognized in antiquity (Plb. 9. 43, Cic. *ND* 2. 130, Str. 16. 1. 9–13 (C740–1), Luc. 3. 259–60, Plin. *Nat.* 5. 90, 18. 162, Minucius Felix 18. 3, Solinus 37. 2). The Euphrates could affect military operations as at e.g. Plb. 9. 43. 6 and in the Ammianus passage mentioned above; cf. the difficulties posed by the Tigris in flood (Amm. 25. 6. 12). Even in peacetime a ruler's concern could be exercised: Str. notes that Alexander inspected and cleared some of the irrigation canals, and remarks (16. 1. 10, C740) that good rulers will attempt to assist the inhabitants of inundated regions. See also 100 n. below.

binominis Histri: cf. Sil. 1. 326. The twin names of the Danube (Hister and Danuvius) are frequently alluded to in ancient literature. The Hister refers to the river in its lower course (Plin. *Nat.* 4. 79, Mela 2. 3. 57). Ovid has the same phrase at *Pont.* 1. 8. 11 'urbs, ripae uicina binominis Histri'; see Gaertner ad loc. and on 1. 2. 79. The Danube frontier was a source of recurrent trouble in this period; see *Silv.* 5. 2. 136n., B. W. Jones (1992), 135–9, 141–3, 150–5.

91. cesserit: a neat *double entendre*: the ends of the earth have not only yielded in battle (Agricola's victory at Mons Graupius), but they have also retreated (cf. Virg. *A.* 5. 629 'Italiam sequimur fugientem' with Williams's n., Prop. 2. 10. 17 'et si qua extremis tellus se subtrahit oris') as Roman power extends yet further. The reference to Thule in the next line evokes Agricola's circumnavigation of Britain (Tac. *Ag.* 38. 4) in AD 84. Tac. *Ag.* 10 illustrates the same sense of the

expanding frontiers of the known world (cf. Sen. *Dial.* 11. 13. 2 'hic
Germaniam pacet, Britanniam aperiat') suggested by *cesserit* here.

refugo circumsona gurgite: the waves noisily batter a rocky
shore, before being driven back (*refugo*); cf. Luc. 1. 411 'refugis...
fluctibus'.

92–3. Courtney (1984), 334 argues for a lacuna of one verse; the
present participle is not elsewhere treated as equivalent to a present
indicative until later antiquity (H.–Sz. 389 erroneously cite Prop. 3.
17. 27, where 'bene olentia flumina' is dependent on *dicam* in l. 21). If
there is a break in the text, the related subject matter of 92–3 indicates
that it cannot be long.

93. penna see 88 n. above.

94. fidos ... enses: the revolt of Saturninus and the more dis-
tant memories of the Year of the Four Emperors would have ensured
that references to loyalty would not have been considered formulaic;
contrast, in our times, 'Loyal Greetings' often sent by institutions to
the sovereign. Here, as at *Silv.* 5. 2. 177, *ensis* represents office; cf. 3. 3.
116, 4. 7. 45, Luc. 5. 61 'saeuum in populos puer accipis ensem', 10.
95–6 'sed habet sub iure Pothini | adfectus ensesque suos'.

95–8. Statius outlines an important duty of the *ab epistulis*, involve-
ment in appointments to equestrian military posts; higher offices were
appointed directly by the emperor, 'per epistulam sacram' (Veg. *Mil.*
2. 7). The nature of such involvement is debated. Cotton (1981), 230 n.
11 argues that 'the emperor is personally responsible for the appoint-
ments; he is the one who distributes "loyal swords". The *ab epistulis*
merely makes it known which job went to whom.' But this interpret-
ation ignores the force of *ualeat*, *deceat*, and *dignior*, which all hint at
evaluation rather than appointment. If Statius merely wanted to say
that Abascantus was responsible for informing those appointed of
their posts, it is curious that the language suggests assessment. The
varied indirect questions make it still more doubtful that *quis*, *quem*,
and *quisnam* are those actually informed. It is better to take *pandere* as
'to reveal (to the emperor)' with a series of indirect questions as its
objects.[22] Statius thus seems to suggest that Abascantus dispensed

---

[22] Cotton (1981), 230 suggests that the *ab epistulis* may have informed the commander-in-
chief of the appointee's commission. This may well be true, but the present passage is not
itself valid evidence for this hypothesis. It seems unlikely that anyone other than the
emperor could be alluded to so soon after *fidos si dominus diuidat enses*; there is, moreover,
the same difficulty that if the *ab epistulis* is informing the commander of the appointment,
why is there so much emphasis on evaluation, which suggests consideration of suitable

advice on appointments; perhaps compare Suet. *Ves.* 4. 1, where it is claimed that Vespasian owed the command of a legion in Germany to the influence of Claudius' freedman Narcissus, a post far higher in rank than the equestrian offices associated with Abascantus here.

There were typically three *equestres militiae* in the early imperial period; see Mattingly (1910), 64 ff. Suet. *Cl.* 25. 1 (see Hurley's notes ad loc.) describes Claudius' reforms in an area where no strict system had previously existed:

equestris militias ita ordinauit, ut post cohortem alam, post alam tribunatum legionis daret; stipendiaque instituit et imaginariae militiae genus, quod uocatur 'super numerum', quo absentes et titulo tenus fungerentur.

This order is only attested in two inscriptions (*CIL* xiv. 2960, and perhaps v. 4058). By the time of Trajan the order given here in 96–8, *praefectus cohortis, tribunus militum,* and *praefectus alae,* was usual.

As for the first office, Millar (1992), 286 n. 49 has convincingly suggested that M's *maniplos inter missus eques* refers to the rank of *centurio ex equite Romano*; cf. Zwicky (1944), 90–3, and see *Diz. epig.* ii. 197 (s.v. *centurio*) for relevant inscriptions. *inter* is postpositional, governing *maniplos*; see the examples collected at *ThLL* vii/1. 2146. 63–2147. 4.

95, 98. frenare ... frenigerae: whereas *frenare* applies the metaphor of bridling to a military command (cf. *Silv.* 3. 2. 105, 4. 4. 61, and note also *Theb.* 10. 245 'his tandem uirtus iuuenum frenata quieuit'), *frenigerae* (only occurring here in Latin) is not metaphorical. Since horses can be bridled, it is an easy transition to describe a military formation (cf. *Silv.* 4. 7. 47 'frenatae ... alae', Sil. 11. 264) or cavalrymen (e.g. *B. Afr.* 48. 1, 59. 4) as 'bridled'.

100. Nilus: as with the Euphrates (89 n.), much depended on the annual flood. Plin. *Pan.* 30–1 recounts a failure of the flood under Trajan, and the appeals of the Egyptians to the emperor.

sudauerit: *sudo,* which primarily denotes sweating, here indicates the process of becoming damp through the accumulation of moisture (*OLD* s.v. 3). This usage is typically employed in cases where moisture comes from within the affected object, as at Plin. *Nat.* 15. 14 (a precautionary measure in the preparation of olives): 'error collectam

persons before an appointment is made? The indirect questions (standing in place of names) also mean that this passage cannot support Cotton's thesis (231–2) that the *ab epistulis* may have issued blank forms to legates! E. Birley (1953), 142–3, 150 ff. suggests that confidential reports from superior officers would have reached the emperor through the *ab epistulis*.

[oliuam] seruandi in tabulatis nec prius quam sudet premendi'; cf.
Vitr. 7. 9. 3 'ceram . . . calfaciundo sudare cogat'. Here *sudauerit* refers
to the accumulation of rainwater on the land, so that the metaphor of
secretion from within is not strictly adhered to. Compare Enn. *scen.*
181 V. (= 165 Jocelyn) 'franguntur hastae, terra sudat sanguine',
where the verb is construed with an ablative. *sudauerit* also suggests
the hot climate; at *Silv.* 5. 2. 134 Crispinus is asked 'an aestiferis Libyae
sudabis in aruis'. For the frequent association of the south wind
Auster (called 'Libycus' at Sen. *Ag.* 480) with rainfall, see e.g. *Silv.* 3.
3. 86, *Theb.* 11. 520, Virg. *G.* 1. 462, *A.* 5. 696, Prop. 2. 16. 56, Tib. 1. 1.
47, Ov. *Ars* 3. 174, *Pont.* 2. 1. 26, Sen. *Med.* 583–4, Luc. 9. 320, Juv. 5.
101; the Greek name for the south wind, Notus, is also associated with
rainfall in Latin literature as at e.g. Stat. *Theb.* 1. 160–1. Although
Auster is puzzlingly described as rainbearing in Africa, before its
passage across the sea to Italy, the tempting emendation *aestifero* is
best avoided, despite *Silv.* 5. 2. 134 (see above), where the epithet is
applied to the land and not to the wind. *imbrifero* is supported by *Silv.* 1.
6. 78 'quas udo Numidae legunt sub austro', 2. 4. 28 'nec quas umenti
Numidae rapuere sub austro'. Abascantus' task is to ascertain
whether the rains have failed in north Africa.

101. cuncta ego si numerem: Statius rounds off the list by
suggesting that if he were to relate all Abascantus' duties, the epic
messengers Mercury, Iris and Fama would not have more to relate; in
105–7, Fama is used to bring in a compliment to Domitian (see
below). Courtney conjectured *cuncta ego* for M's *cunctaque*, following
on from Heinsius' *cuncta quid enumerem*, on the grounds that after the
list of Abascantus' various duties, it is odd to begin the summing up
with the copulative *-que*. The word-order of *cuncta ego si*, with *ego*
placed ahead of the *si-* clause to which it belongs, is entirely possible
(compare e.g. Cic. *Clu.* 166 'hoc ego si sic agerem', Virg. *A.* 4. 419
'hunc ego si potui tantum sperare dolorem', Ov. *Tr.* 3. 4. 13 'haec ego
si monitor monitus prius ipse fuissem'), and a further merit of Court-
ney's suggestion is that *ego* might be felt to echo the emphatic use of
ἐγώ in Homer's statement on the impossibility of describing the
whole multitude of common soldiers who fought at Troy at the
beginning of the catalogue of ships (*Il.* 2. 488): πληθὺν δ' οὐκ ἂν ἐγὼ
μυθήσομαι οὐδ' ὀνομήνω. Note also the appearance of *ego* (and indeed
cuncta) at Virg. *G.* 2. 42 'non ego cuncta meis amplecti uersibus opto';
for the motif of poetic inability, see further 5. 4. 11 n.

interprete uirga: the wand of Mercury, the ῥάβδος used by Hermes on his journey to Priam at *Il.* 24. 343 and when conducting the dead suitors to Hades at *Od.* 24. 2. Compare *Theb.* 1. 306–8 and Virg. *A.* 4. 242–4 (with Pease). For the epithet *interprete*, here applied to the wand, cf. Virgil's description of Mercury as 'interpres diuum' (*A.* 4. 378).

102. ales Tegeaticus: for Mercury thus, cf. *Silv.* 1. 2. 18 'uolucer Tegeaticus', 1. 5. 4 'uolucer Tegeaee'. Mercury is 'Tegean' since his birthplace was Mount Cyllene in Arcadia and Tegea was an Arcadian town. *Cyllenius* is used of Mercury at *Silv.* 2. 1. 189, *Arcas* at 2. 7. 6, 3. 3. 80, 5. 1. 107.

103. Iunonia uirgo: Iris, the daughter of Thaumas ('Thaumantida' in 107) and the Oceanid Electra (see Hes. *Th.* 265–6 and Serv. Auct. *A.* 3. 212). Iris is usually the messenger of Zeus in Homer (and Hesiod), although she is once sent by Hera to rouse Achilles to battle (*Il.* 18. 166–202). At A. R. 4. 753 ff. and at Call. *H.* 4. 66–7 and 157–9 she is the servant of Hera. Virgil reverses the usual association with Zeus, since his Iris is always the agent of Juno, except when at *A.* 9. 803–4 Jupiter instructs Juno that Turnus is not to remain within the walls of the Trojan stronghold. Ovid (*Met.* 1. 270, 14. 85) also associates Iris with Juno. At *Theb.* 10. 80–136 (note especially 'suamque | . . . Irin', 80–1) Iris is sent by Juno on a mission to Somnus. *Silv.* 3. 3. 80–1 'summi Iouis aliger Arcas | nuntius; imbrifera potitur Thaumantide Iuno' seems to imply an exclusive use of Iris by Juno.

104: in the *Iliad*, Iris is imagined as running on the wind (ποδήνεμος), though the noun ἶρις is used in singular and plural to denote a rainbow (*Il.* 11. 27, 17. 547). Hes. *Th.* 784–5 directly associates the goddess with the rainbow. This she sometimes travels on (e.g. *Theb.* 10. 83, Virg. *A.* 5. 609, Ov. *Met.* 11. 632, 14. 830, 838), and sometimes (as here) creates as she flies (Virg. *A.* 5. 658 = 9. 15 'ingentemque fuga secuit sub nubibus arcum', Sen. *Oed.* 315–16).

gyro: cf. *Theb.* 1. 311 'et ingenti designat nubila gyro' (Mercury's course through the air).

Whereas we now assign only the seven colours of the spectrum to the rainbow, to the ancients the rainbow had many more colours; *mille* frequently appears in descriptions. See e.g. Virg. *A.* 4. 701, Ov. *Met.* 11. 589, and esp. 6. 63–7, a simile, where Ovid comments on the difficulty in determining where colours of the rainbow end and begin. See also *Theb.* 10. 118–19, 136 for accounts of Iris' colourful appearance.

105. Germanice: After his first war against the Chatti in AD 83 (D.C. 67. 4), Domitian assumed the title of Germanicus, which, as suggested by Martin (1987*b*), 182–7, may both have been intended to recall use of the title by Germanicus Caesar, the nephew and adopted son of the emperor Tiberius, and to mark out Domitian's own achievements in Germany from the achievements of his brother and father in the East, especially in Judaea. Suet. *Dom.* 13. 3 'post autem duos triumphos Germanici cognomine assumpto Septembrem mensem et Octobrem ex appellationibus suis Germanicum Domitianumque transnominauit, quod altero suscepisset imperium, altero natus esset' mentions the assumption of the title in the context of Domitian's second triumph (Jones ad loc. sees this as a reference to the triumph over the Dacians in 86, not to the double triumph of 89), but documentary evidence indicates that the title was current from 83, when the title first appears in Domitian's coinage; see Carradice (1983), 21–3. Buttrey (1980), 52–6 argues that the title was conferred at some time between 9 June and 23 August 83 (cf. Citroni (1988), 11–12 with n. 13), though Martin (1987*a*) and (1987*b*), 7–10, who discusses papyrological evidence from Egypt, on which see also Martin (1988), argues that Domitian's decision to rename the month of September 'Germanicus' may indicate that he assumed the title in September of 83. In Statius, see *Silv.* 1. 1. 5, 1. 4. 4, 3 pr. 16, 3. 3. 165, 3. 4. 49, 4 pr. 5, 4. 1. 2, 4. 2. 52, 4. 9. 17. *Germanicus* is also used to refer to Domitian in the titles of *Silv.* 4. 1 and 4. 2. On Martial's use of the title *Germanicus*, see Leberl (2004), 245, 247, 303.

uolucri . . . cursu: Fama's power of flight is described at Virg. *A.* 4. 184–5 'nocte uolat caeli medio terraeque per umbram | stridens, nec dulci declinat lumina somno.' For the wings of Fame see further N.–H. on Hor. *Carm.* 2. 2. 7.

curru, conjectured by Casaubon and then by Barth (see the latter's note ad loc.), deserves consideration. The most relevant of Markland's parallels are *Silv.* 2. 7. 107–8 'at tu, seu rapidum poli per axem | Famae curribus arduis leuatus', 3. 4. 36 'ducam uolucri per sidera curru' (for *uolucris* as an epithet for *currus*, cf. Hor. *Carm.* 1. 34. 8, Virg. *A.* 10. 440, Claud. *Rapt. Pros.* 2. 247 'interea uolucri fertur Proserpina curru', where some MSS read *cursu*), and Hor. *S.* 1. 6. 23–4 'sed fulgente trahit constrictos Gloria curru | non minus ignotos generosis'. At Prop. 3. 1. 9–12 a winged chariot is associated with Fama, although triumphal imagery is also to the fore:

> quo me Fama leuat terra sublimis, et a me
> nata coronatis Musa triumphat equis,
> et mecum in curru parui uectantur Amores,
> scriptorumque meas turba secuta rotas.

Despite these parallels, however, there is no compelling reason to emend *cursu*. As with Fama's flight, her *cursus* can also be paralleled in *Aeneid* 4: 'protinus ad regem cursus detorquet Iarban' (*A.* 4. 196); cf. Stat. *Theb.* 6. 1–2 'nuntia multiuago Danaas perlabitur urbes | Fama gradu' and *Silv.* 4. 8. 36–7, where *cursus* is used of a letter bringing news 'protinus ingenti non uenit nuntia cursu | littera'. Note too the parallel for *uolucris* with *cursus* at Stat. *Theb.* 5. 167 'et in uolucri tenuis fiducia cursu' (of a hind). The point can also be made that since Fama is conventionally winged, she has little need for a chariot for aerial travel; indeed van Dam on *Silv.* 2. 7. 107–8 notes that that passage is apparently the only instance of Fama using a chariot.

105–7. Note the sudden change from mythical messengers to the recent victories of the emperor. The emperor is gracefully complimented when Fama, reporting his victories, is described as swifter than either Mercury or Iris. Domitian's appearance effects a neat transition to the climactic scene of Priscilla's joy at her husband's advancement which ensues.

106. praegressa diem: Fama ('malum qua non aliud uelocius ullum', Virg. *A.* 4. 174) overtakes the arrival of day, so hastily does she bring news of Domitian's victories. At *Silv.* 5. 2. 170–1 she is overtaken by an imperial messenger with news of Crispinus' appointment; cf. also Claudian, *Bell. Gild.* 1. 13 'rumoremque sui praeuenit laurea belli'.

107. Arcada . . . Thaumantida: these two divine messengers, and Triton, also appear at *Silv.* 3. 3. 80–2, where the dead father of Etruscus, who has served several emperors, is compared to those who have served only one god.

108. qualem te . . . Priscilla: Priscilla was last referred to in the second person in 75. The only subsequent apostrophe has been the brief address to Domitian in 105. Here, the apostrophe gives a sudden transition to Priscilla, after the detailed account of Abascantus' career. On such unprepared appearances of the second person in Statius, see Håkanson (1969), 43–4, Courtney (1971), 95–6, (1984), 330; on ancient and modern treatments of apostrophe, see Leigh (1997), 307–10.

108–10. the gods and men who see Priscilla suggest the idea of a wedding, attended by both groups. The marriage of Peleus and Thetis (*Il.* 24. 59–63, Cat. 64) is a famous case, but see also *Silv.* 1. 2. 238–40, where Hymen, Juno and Concordia participate in the nuptials of Stella and Violentilla. In particular the concentration on a single day in the present passage adds to the initial suggestion of a wedding day; for *benigno . . . die* compare *Silv.* 1. 2. 209–10 'quis tibi tunc alacri caelestum in munere claro, | Stella, dies!', 241 'hic fuit ille dies'. *cum primum* further confirms this impression, which is then challenged with the revelation that the occasion was not the marriage but Priscilla's response to the success of her husband (*ingentibus actis | admotus coniunx*). The use of language which might evoke a wedding day expresses Priscilla's extreme delight in her husband's service to Domitian. The technique is a subtle one; after the previous account of Abascantus' duties the poem goes back in time, seemingly to the day of the wedding, but really to the inception of Abascantus' career. This moment was already described in 75 ff., where Priscilla's prayers are answered (note the link between 'uenitque gradu Fortuna *benigno*' in 75 and '*benigno . . . die*' in 108–9). In this more emotive passage Abascantus' advancement is seen in terms of Priscilla's reaction, whereas 75–107 gave an account of the tasks required by the emperor.

For the intense emotion of 'qualem te . . . | aspexere', compare *Silv.* 3. 5. 37–9, where Statius describes seeing his own wife when very ill:

> qualem te nuper Stygias prope raptus ad umbras,
> cum iam Lethaeos audirem comminus amnes,
> aspexi, tenuique oculos iam morte cadentes!

Cf. Sil. 15. 356–8: 'urbe Sicana | qualem te uidi, nondum permitteret aetas | cum tibi bella, meo tractantem proelia uultu!'

110. certe (Markland): M's *cene*, as Courtney notes, recalls the line ending of *Silv.* 4. 2. 5 'noua gaudia cenae', but a sudden and unprepared reference to a meal cannot stand here. Markland emended to *certe*, while Vollmer favoured Burman's *paene* on the curious grounds that *uicisti* must in some way be qualified, otherwise Abascantus does not seem sufficiently delighted. However, this argument ignores one of the central themes of the poem, Priscilla's constant and remarkable concern for her husband (e.g. 50, 66 ff., 71 ff., 108 ff., 177 ff.): it is not inappropriate for her delight to exceed that of her husband, as it indeed surpasses the joys of the Pythia or of a Maenad in 113–16. Significantly it is Priscilla who expends so much energy in her prayers and devotions. *certe*, which emphasizes Priscilla's pleasure, thus flattering Abascantus, is preferable to the weaker *paene*, even though it would also be a compliment to his loyalty.

111. effuso . . . pectore: for such gestures of deference, cf. e.g. *Theb.* 10. 50 'ad patrias fusae Pelopeides aras'.

112. tam magna merentis: Slater translates ' . . . whereat with overflowing heart thou madest eager obeisance, prostrate at the knees of the hallowed Lord himself who had deserved of thee so well', construing the phrase as equivalent to the idiom 'bene mereor de aliquo', to deserve well of someone, or to behave well towards someone. *tam magna* would thus be almost adverbial. Even though there is nothing corresponding to 'de aliquo', such as 'de te', compare Caes. *Gal.* 1. 45. 1 'uti optime merentis socios desereret', and note too the regular appearance of 'coniugi bene merenti' in funerary inscriptions.

auide: the adverb is a little strange, because Priscilla is not eager or desirous, since her obeisance reflects gratitude rather than supplication. But for *auide* describing a reaction to an event that has already happened, cf. *Theb.* 4. 518.

112–13: As with the echo of *benigno* (see 108–10 n.), *domini* and *uolueris* recall the language used to describe Priscilla's appeals and entreaties to the gods and Domitian in 73–4. For *uoluo* in contexts of supplication or worship, cf. *Theb.* 11. 740, Prop. 3. 8. 12, Luc. 7. 379.

114. quam: an early emendation of M's *quem*, essential because *hiatibus antri* refers to the oracle of Apollo at Delphi, presided over by a priestess, the Pythia.

115. primi . . . ius uenerabile thyrsi: a formal periphrasis for leadership of the troop of Bacchantes; cf. *Theb.* 4. 379 'regina chori', E. *Ba.* 680–2. *primi . . . thyrsi* has a military resonance (cf. next n.), recalling the terms *primipilus* and *centurio primi pili*, applied to the senior centurion of a legion.

116. uexilla: 'thyrsi' (on which see Dodds on E. *Ba.* 25 and 113), though *uexillum* typically signifies the Roman military standard. *uexilla* emphasizes the martial aspect of *cateruae*, which can, as here, signify a crowd or a throng, but can also denote a military troop (e.g. 67 above, Virg. *A.* 8. 593, 12. 264).

117. hinc: M's *hic* is difficult; the word seems to demand some more precise antecedent. Moreover *hic*, since it would imply a particular moment (*OLD* s.v. *hic*² 5), would thus limit the succeeding compliments on Priscilla's moral qualities to the day of Abascantus' appointment, which is difficult with *probitasue secundis* | *intumuit*, which refers to a gradual increase in arrogance after attaining good fortune. In contrast, *hinc*, used either causally ('because of this') or temporally ('henceforth'), involves no such restrictions; thus Priscilla is not adversely affected by her husband's success (cf. Plin. *Pan.* 24. 2 'nihil <in> ipso te fortuna mutauit'; see also Cic. *Amic.* 54, Sal. *Hist.* 2. 47. 1 Maur. 'malae secundaeque res opes, non ingenium mihi mutabant', [Plu.] *ad Apoll.* 102 E–103 F), and her virtues continue undiminished. Cf. *Silv.* 3. 3. 106 (noted by Courtney) 'hinc tibi rara quies . . . '. Note also the similar qualities of Cornelia at Luc. 8. 155–8, who conducted herself in the same way both before and after her husband's defeat:

> tanto deuinxit amore
> hos pudor, hos probitas castique modestia uoltus,
> quod summissa animis, nulli grauis hospita turbae,
> stantis adhuc fati uixit quasi coniuge uicto.

The insistence that Priscilla's *quies* is unchanged is an amusing pendant to the preceding similes: neither the Pythia nor the Bacchantes, with whom Priscilla was compared, are usually associated with *quies*. Statius is careful to indicate that Priscilla's joy was not inappropriate to her married estate.

118. tenor idem animo: *tenor* is the quality of consistency and holding to a particular moral path, also praised in Crispinus at *Silv.* 5. 2. 63 'et adhuc tenor integer aeui'. Priscilla's *tenor* has already been demonstrated by her appeals to the gods and to Domitian, and her unswerving willingness to follow Abascantus, regardless of danger (67–9). The wifely virtues described in these lines are traditional: cf. e.g. *Laudatio Murdiae* 27–9 'quod | modestia probitate pudicitia opsequio lanificio diligentia fide | par similisque ceteris probeis feminis fuit', Lattimore (1942), 293–7.

119. fortuna crescente: in 75 Fortuna arrived auspiciously, and here the fortune of the couple is seen to increase, a preparation for the subsequent volte-face.

fouet anxia curas: cf. *fouebat* (47), characterizing Priscilla's love for her husband.

120. hortaturque: for *hortor* with a noun as direct object denoting what is encouraged, cf. *Silv.* 3. 5. 22, 4. 6. 56, *Theb.* 7. 798, Tac. *Ann.* 11. 3. 2, *ThLL* vi/3. 3011. 27–40.

fallitque labores: defending *flectitque* (M), Vollmer quotes Barth, 'ne nimis rigidi ad eum peruenirent', who implies that *flecto* denotes the softening or overcoming of the *labores*. This usage is typically found with persons as objects with the idea of persuasion (e.g. Virg. *A.* 7. 312 'flectere si nequeo superos, Acheronta mouebo'), but an abstract object is nevertheless possible, as is implied by Ov. *Met.* 1. 378 'si flectitur ira deorum'; cf. *Theb.* 1. 280 'belli deflecte tumultus'. However, in these examples, *flecto* has the sense of turning aside; here, the implication would be that Priscilla diverted her husband from his duties, which would, however, contradict *hortatur*.

fulcit, proposed by Watt (1988), 168–9, adds little to *hortaturque*, when the presence of *simul* raises the expectation that an idea different from *hortatur* is being added to the sentence. *fallit*, conjectured and rejected in the same article, is preferable, despite Watt's own argument that it is palaeographically more difficult. *fallit* would mean that Priscilla's efforts made her husband's toils seem less of a burden; cf. Hor. *S.* 2. 2. 12 'studio fallente laborem', where Porphyrio (cited by Watt) remarks 'ait studium ipsum effic<ere>, ne labor sentiatur', and note also *Theb.* 12. 230 'grauem luctu fallente laborem', Ov. *Tr.* 4. 1. 14 'fallitur ancillae decipiturque labor', Sen. *Apoc.* 4 'fallitque laborem'. Compare the support given by Statius' own wife (*Silv.* 3. 5. 35–6): 'longi tu sola laboris | conscia'.

121–6. This comparison between Priscilla and a Sabine or Apulian woman making preparations at home in anticipation of her husband's return is very similar to Hor. *Epod.* 2. 39–48, Alfius' idealistic evocation of the rustic virtue and simplicity of a Sabine or Apulian wife. While Statius closely echoes individual details (see notes on 121, 123, 125–6), he does not in any way replicate the overall irony of *Epod.* 2, which ends with a reminder that the speaker so eloquently praising the ways of the countryside is a money-lender, who is far too interested in making money (67–70); see further Mankin's and Watson's commentaries and Heyworth (1988), 71–2.

Such praise of chaste domesticity and frugality in a woman is commonplace; contrast the different context but similar sentiments of Augustus' speech to men who had fathered children at D.C. 56. 3. 3.

121. dapes modicas: a paradoxical phrase since *dapes* refers to an opulent feast, associated with the gods. Serv. *A.* 1. 706 remarks that 'dapes regum sunt, epulae priuatorum' and on *A.* 3. 224 and 8. 175 he associates the word with divine feasting. Paul. Fest. p. 59. 21 ff. Lindsay echoes this view: 'daps apud antiquos dicebatur res diuina quae fiebat aut hiberna sementi aut uerna. quod uocabulum ex Graeco deducitur, apud quos id genus epularum δαίς dicitur.' However, as in the present passage, *dapes* can appear in more modest contexts: in Statius compare Etruscus' father's 'exiguaeque dapes' at *Silv.* 3. 3. 107. Virg. *G.* 4. 133 and Hor. *Epod.* 2. 48 both refer to *dapes inemptae*, 'modest fare'; see also Hor. *Ars* 198 'ille dapes laudet mensae breuis', Ov. *Met.* 8. 683 'et ueniam dapibus nullisque paratibus orant'. Note also *Silv.* 1. 6. 94–5 'quis conuiuia, quis dapes inemptas, | largi flumina quis canat Lyaei?'. Though *ThLL* v/1. 36. 71–2 glosses 'inemptas' here as 'pretiosas', Vollmer's interpretation that the epithet means that the emperor rather than the people has paid for the *dapes* is preferable.

ipsa: Priscilla herself, and not some vast retinue of slaves, prepares her husband's meals; compare Ov. *Met.* 8. 635–6 on the household of Baucis and Philemon, where there are no slaves to join in tasks. A. Hardie (1983), 186, comparing Plin. *Pan.* 88. 2, suggests that this praise of Abascantus' frugality (cf. *Silv.* 3. 3. 107, cited above) may forestall the stock criticism of imperial freedmen as wealthy and corrupt; cf. 78–9 above.

sobria pocula: cf. Mart. 4. 8. 10 for Domitian's 'pocula parca', and (more frivolously) Tib. 1. 6. 27–8 'saepe mero somnum peperi tibi, at ipse bibebam | sobria supposita pocula uictor aqua.'

122. exemplum ad erile monet: Suet. *Dom.* 21 notes that the habitual frugality of Domitian's dining was a consequence of the magnitude of his midday meal. On the Flavian reaction against luxury under Vespasian, see Tac. *Ann.* 3. 55.

Apula: the Apulians were celebrated for austerity and virtue; see Hor. *Carm.* 1. 22. 13–14, 3. 5. 9, 3. 16. 26, and *S.* 2. 2, where the Apulian Ofellus is an advocate of plain living. Compare Var. *Men.* 554 'tetricam ducat Apulam bonis moribus'. Juv. 4. 27 would suggest that land was not expensive there (see further Courtney's note ad loc.).

123. sole infecta Sabino: Heinsius (on Ov. *Am.* 2. 4. 15) suggested *Sabina*, which is defended by Markland on the grounds that *Sabina* is parallel to the *Apula coniunx* in 122. Markland also cites Ov. *Med.* 13, where he considers 'rubicunda', applied to a Sabine matron, equivalent to 'sole infecta', and Hor. *Epod.* 2. 41–2 'Sabina qualis aut perusta solibus | pernicis uxor Apuli'. But the closeness of the parallel is itself an argument for retaining M's *Sabino*, which would then combine variation with allusion to the Horatian model; note that Horace too does not have two epithets in the nominative, but *Sabina* and then the genitive *Apuli*.

Like the Apulians, the Sabines had a robust reputation; see Cic. *Vat.* 36 'seuerissimorum hominum Sabinorum', Virg. *G.* 2. 167, 532,

Prop. 2. 32. 47–8, Hor. *Carm.* 3. 6. 37–44, Liv. 1. 18. 4 'disciplina tetrica ac tristi ueterum Sabinorum', Col. 1 pr. 19, Juv. 3. 85, 3. 169, 10. 299, Dench (1995), 155–8. Juv. 6. 164 cites Sabine women as an *exemplum* of chastity (cf. Mart. 1. 62. 1)), while Col. 12. pr. 10 laments the demise of women's interest in life on an estate, praising 'uetus ille matrum familiarum mos Sabinarum atque Romanarum'.

124–5. emeriti … uiri: *emeriti* embraces three meanings. Firstly, it denotes the serving out of a term of service (here, a day in the fields); this usage is frequent in military contexts, such as Liv. 25. 6. 16 'spes emerendi stipendia'. Secondly, *emeritus* can signify that something is worn out, or unfit for use, (e.g. Ov. *Fast.* 1. 665 'emeritum … aratrum', 4. 688 'emeritis … equis'). Finally, the basic sense of the verb, 'to deserve', from its cognate *mereor*, should not be forgotten. The present passage suggests all three uses: the husband has served his day in the fields, he is likely to be exhausted at the end of it, and he deserves the meal prepared for him by his wife. For the joy of returning home from the fields, compare E. *El.* 75–6.

125. tempus adesse uiri: a highly compressed phrase denoting the imminence of the husband's arrival; the wife sees that 'the time of her husband is at hand'; cf. Horace's 'lassi sub aduentum uiri' (*Epod.* 2. 44). Note also Tac. *Ann.* 3. 34. 2 'sed reuertentibus post laborem quod honestius quam uxorium leuamentum?'

125–6. Two subtle details heighten the sense of rustic simplicity and industry. *propere* indicates that the purpose of her meal is simple nourishment (cf. the wheat diet prescribed by Cato *Agr.* 56, and the *pultes* given to *redeuntibus* at Juv. 14. 171), and not luxury, which would require extensive preparation. The woman's wait for the *sound* of the returning plough shows that she is not idly looking out for her husband, but hears him while she is inside, engaged in various tasks.

For the return of the plough as a marker of the end of the day in agricultural societies, compare the Homeric βουλυτόνδε (*Od.* 9. 58), associated with the unyoking of oxen and hence evening. See also *Od.* 13. 31–5 (a simile in which Odysseus' desire to return home is compared to a ploughman's wish to return for his evening meal), Hor. *Carm.* 3. 6. 41–3 (with N.–R.) ' … sol ubi montium | mutaret umbras et iuga demeret | bobus fatigatis … '.

instruit: cf. the use of *exstruo* at Hor. *Epod.* 2. 43 'sacrum uetustis exstruat lignis focum'.

127. parua loquor: Statius shifts from praise of Priscilla's domestic life to her heroic character.

tecum: another unprepared change of address, this time to Abascantus. The last instance of apostrophe was Priscilla in 108, but the address to Abascantus returns the audience to the recipient of the poem just before the abrupt change to a more sombre tone in 135–6.

Note the repetition of *tecum* in 129, and compare V.Fl. 8. 50–1 'tecum aequora, tecum | experiar quascumque uias', where Medea assures Jason of her devotion

127–34. In the text as it stands, there is no verb which could govern the two clauses beginning with *tecum* in this sentence. The clauses appear to be in parallel to *uellet gestare pharetras* which follows, but this does not permit, as Vollmer argued, a verb of motion such as 'ire', to be implied, especially as *et* (130), if it means 'and', prevents the previous lines from being a participial phrase in apposition.

Nodell and Schrader suggsted that *illa* in 127 could be emended to *ire*, which, like *gestare*, would be governed by *uellet*. However, *illa* is required to show that the simile of the Apulian and Sabine women is complete: the deictic pronoun *illa* refers back to Priscilla. The unexpected apostrophe of Abascantus and the necessary change of subject from the first person *parua loquor* at the beginning of this line makes *illa* even more essential for clarity. *illa* also functions as an echo and reminiscence of the similar passage in 67–70 *illa uel armiferas pro coniuge laeta cateruas. . . .*

Courtney in his edition suggests either construing *et* in 130 as *etiam* (cf. Courtney (1984), 330) or positing a lacuna after 129. Though construing *et* as 'even' is possible (K.–S. ii. 8), there are two difficulties in this context: first, the difficulty involved in recognizing *et* as 'etiam', especially as it is separated from its clause by 'si castra darent', and secondly, the oddity of construing the adverbial 'omnes . . . per aestus' with the infinitive verbs 'gestare pharetras' and, even more so, 'latus intercludere pharetras'. A lacuna, however, would have contained a verb of motion governing the first part of the sentence, and perhaps even some examples of hot places to match the cold locations mentioned in 127–9 (cf. *Silv.* 3. 5. 19–21, where the north, Thule, and the source of the Nile are possible dangers). The rhetoric of the passage would thus be that 127–9 and the lacuna described Priscilla's willingness to travel, so that *et* ('and') introduces the new thought that Priscilla would have participated in battle.

For the topos of the willingness of a person to accompany a friend or beloved on perilous journeys, see 67–9 (with n.), a passage loosely evoked in 131–2.

Rheni frigora may recall Virg. *Ecl.* 10. 46–9, where Gallus laments the departure of his faithless Lycoris. Whereas Lycoris leaves her lover behind and travels to the snows of the Rhine and the Alps, the faithful Priscilla would have accompanied her husband on such a journey. Compare Statius' similar remarks to his wife at *Silv.* 3. 5. 19–22.

128. pallida: *pallor* and its cognates are often associated with death and the underworld (see van Dam on *Silv.* 2. 1. 204–5 and 217, Pease on Virg. *A.* 4. 26, N.–H. on Hor. *Carm.* 1. 4. 13; cf. André (1949), 145); the adjective may hint at Priscilla's impending fate, as well as evoking the appearance of the river in winter (cf. *Theb.* 7. 286–7 'pallida ... | bruma'). Statius' evocation of the cold Rhine in a potential situation of danger contrasts markedly with the whimsical language describing the river that Crispinus may swim in on his military travels (*Silv.* 5. 2. 133–4).

130–1. si castra darent: compare Prop. 4. 3. 45 'Romanis utinam patuissent castra puellis'; see also Prop. 2. 7. 15, Sen. *Con.* 9. 2. 1, and Luc. 2. 348, where Marcia asks to accompany her husband Cato to war. Augustus was reluctant to allow even legates to visit their wives (Suet. *Aug.* 24. 1). Note the senatorial debate on whether women should accompany provincial governors in AD 21; see Tac. *Ann.* 3. 33–4 with Woodman and Martin. On family separation in the lives of imperial officials, see Dixon (1991), 100–1.

pharetras: the bow is one of the weapons of the heroine Camilla at Virg. *A.* 11. 652, in a passage where she is called an Amazon (11. 648). The Amazons are an obvious mythological exemplar of fighting women: contrast *Theb.* 5. 144–6, where Hypsipyle compares the Lemnian women who would soon kill their husbands to Amazons. For the wish to bear arms, compare the list of heroines who would have preferred not to have been left behind at *Silv.* 3. 5. 46–9, and Arethusa at Prop. 4. 3. 43–4, who describes the Amazon Hippolyte as *felix*, while at *Pont.* 3. 1. 95–6 Ovid reassures his wife: 'non tibi Amazonia est pro me sumenda securis, | aut excisa leui pelta gerenda manu'. At *Silv.* 3. 5. 10 Statius' wife would have resisted any suitors by force: 'thalamosque armata negasses'. Contrast Priscilla's desire to fight with Statius' words to Celer (*Silv.* 3. 2. 95) 'etsi non socius, certe mirator essem'. For the *pelta* as characteristic Amazon equipment, cf.

e.g. *Theb.* 12. 528, Virg. *A.* 11. 662–3 'magnoque ululante tumultu | feminea exsultant lunatis agmina peltis', Sil. 8. 429, Plu. *Pomp.* 35. 5–6. The lunate shape is typical (for artistic representations see e.g. *LIMC* s.v. Amazon 120, 121, 246a), though for a comparison with ivy leaves see Xen. *An.* 5. 4. 12 with Poll. 1. 134.

132. puluerea bellorum nube: 'the dusty cloud of war', a combination of the clouds of dust arising from military activity (for *nubes* thus see e.g. Virg. *A.* 8. 593 'pulueream nubem', 9. 33 'hic subitam nigro glomerari puluere nubem', Sil. 5. 535–6, 13. 158) and the idea of 'clouds of weapons'; cf. e.g. *Theb.* 4. 846–7 'armorum sub nube', 9. 120 (with Dewar's n.), Virg. *A.* 10. 809 'nubem belli', Luc. 4. 488 'bellorum nube', Sil. 1. 311 'telorum... nube', 2. 37–8, 4. 550–1 'hinc pila, hinc Libycae certant subtexere cornus | densa nube polum', 5. 379 'atque atram belli castris se condere nubem', 7. 595, 12. 334. In prose compare Liv. 21. 55. 6 'obruti... uelut nube iaculorum a Baliaribus coniecta'. *nimbus* is similarly used at e.g. *Theb.* 9. 526–7 'nimbo | telorum', Virg. *A.* 7. 793 'insequitur nimbus peditum', Luc. 4. 776 'telorum nimbo', 2. 501–2 'crebroque simillima nimbo |... tela', Sil. 5. 215, 5. 656, 12. 177. Cf. the similar metaphors for war at *Theb.* 9. 488 'grandine ferri', Virg. *A.* 12. 283–4 'it toto turbida caelo | tempestas telorum ac ferreus ingruit imber', Sil. 5. 538–9: 'undanti circum tempestas acta procella | uoluitur atque altos operit caligine montes'. In Greek compare *Il.* 12. 156–8, 278–86, where stones thrown in battle are compared to the fall of snow; cf. also *Il.* 17. 243, where Ajax refers to Hector as a πολέμοιο νέφος.

133. fulmen: the emperor's horse is associated with his thunderbolt, giving an impression of violent and effective speed; cf. Tydeus' horse at *Theb.* 9. 218–19: 'hoc fulmine raptum | abstulit et similes minus indignatur habenas'. Ov. *Am.* 3. 4. 14 notes how he saw a horse 'fulminis ire modo', while Ammianus 31. 12. 17 likens Gothic cavalry to a *fulmen*. Hill on Ov. *Met.* 8. 289 notes Ovid's use of *fulmen* in descriptions of such animals as boars (cf. Mart. 11. 69. 9 'fulmineo spumantis apri sum dente perempta', Sil. 1. 421, and 12. 461, where the word is used in relation to a tiger); in Statius cf. *Theb.* 2. 470, 6. 868, 11. 530, *Ach.* 2. 124. As well as these animal associations, *fulmen* itself anticipates the *diuinaque tela* wielded by Abascantus, an extraordinary compliment but one appropriate to Priscilla's perception (*te... uideret*, 132) of the imaginary battle. The thunderbolt, an embodiment of the power of Zeus, frequently occurs in heroic contexts, such as *Il.* 13. 242, where Idomeneus, ἀστεροπῇ ἐναλίγκιος, is likened

to a thunderbolt whirled by Zeus on Olympus as a sign for mortals. In
Latin compare Lucr. 3. 1034 'Scipiadas, belli fulmen', Cic. *Balb.* 34,
Virg. *A.* 6. 842–3, Sil. 6. 248, where Regulus throws a spear 'fulmi-
neo... lacerto', 7. 106–7; note also *Theb.* 2. 571 'fulmineus Dorylas',
4. 94 'fulmineus Tydeus'. Closer to the spirit of the present passage,
and also illustrating the genitive after *fulmen* (cf. *Silv.* 2. 7. 67 'fulmen
ducis... diui') is *Silv.* 4. 7. 49–52, where Statius imagines Vibius' son
hearing of his grandfather's achievements in the campaign of 92/3
against the Sarmatians:

> ille ut inuicti rapidum secutus
> Caesaris fulmen refugis amaram
> Sarmatis legem dederit, sub uno
> uiuere caelo.

See further Coleman's notes on this passage for the association of
the *fulmen* with the emperor, and note also *Silv.* 3. 3. 158, where
anticipated punishment from the emperor is described as 'uenturi
fulminis ictus'.

134. magnae... hastae: the epithet shows that the spear is
wielded by the emperor; cf. *Silv.* 4. 6. 67 (of Alexander) 'seu clusam
magna Babylona refregerat hasta'.

sudoribus: the emperor's sweat drips from his spear onto Abas-
cantus. Vollmer thought this image tasteless, but the emperor's per-
spiration testifies to heroic exertions (cf. *Theb.* 9. 710 with Dewar, Plin.
Pan. 15. 4 'quis sudores tuos hauserit campus', *OLD* s.v. *sudor* 2).

135–6: after the account of the marriage and character of Pris-
cilla, there is a pause at the centre of the poem, before Statius returns
to her last illness and death, subjects which have been ignored for a
substantial portion of the poem's first half. For a similar and even
more self-conscious pause, compare *Theb.* 10. 827–8 'hactenus arma,
tubae, ferrumque et uulnera: sed nunc | comminus astrigeros Capa-
neus tollendus in axes', as Statius prepares to describe Capaneus'
final moments. For the use of *hactenus*, followed by *nunc*, to mark a
transitional moment in a text, cf. Virg. *G.* 2. 1–2 'hactenus aruorum
cultus et sidera caeli; | nunc te, Bacche, canam...', Prop. 4. 1. 119
'hactenus historiae: nunc ad tua deuehar astra'.

The straightforward division of the poem between the *alma chelys*
and the *maesta... cupresso* is not strictly accurate, since Priscilla's death
was confronted in the opening paragraph, while the second half of the
poem contains more positive features, such as the consolation that

Priscilla will not suffer the torments of the underworld. The simplification does have a function, however; the abrupt change to the *maesta . . . cupresso* mirrors the sudden transition from the felicity of Priscilla's marriage to her illness and death. For *tempus* as an indication of the need to alter a poem's direction, see Virg. *G.* 2. 542, Prop. 2. 10. 1; compare the usage of καιρός at Pi. *P.* 1. 81 ff.

For the presence of the cypress, a symbol of mourning, among poetic bay leaves see also *Silv.* 5. 5. 30–31, where it intrudes amid the poet's garland of ivy; compare the yew at 5. 3. 8–9. Note that *comam*, which here denotes hair, is used in a context where its other meaning of 'leaves' is suggested by the references to *frondes* and *cupresso*; cf. 5. 5. 29–30 n.

137–44. Although Fortuna is a familiar figure in literature (and indeed in epitaphs: see Lattimore (1942), 154–6), Inuidia is less frequently found, the only lengthy personification occurring at Ov. *Met.* 2. 760–82; for φθόνος and Inuidia in epitaphs, see Lattimore (1942), 148–9, 153–4. The pairing of Fortuna and Inuidia (cf. Sen. *Con.* 7. 6. 20; note also Luc. 1. 82–4) need not be so puzzling, despite Statius' exclamation; unfortunate happenings are commonly ascribed to Envy. Fortuna herself can be described in terms of enviousness, as at *CLE* 1814. 6 'I]nuida sed rapuit semper Fortuna probatos'. See Bernert on 'Phthonos' in *RE* xx/1. 961. 8 ff. for examples of this topos and van Dam on *Silv.* 2. 6. 68–70. In a funerary inscription at Thespiae (Kaibel, *Epigr. gr.* no. 497a, 1–2), a dead girl with the name of Kallityche ('fair fortune') comments on her fate, emphasizing the ironic resonance of her name: Γῆρας ἐρημώσασα πατρὸς νέκυς ἐνθ[άδε κεῖμαι | Καλλιτύχη, φθονερῷ δαίμονι χρησαμ[ένη. A similarly ironic configuration of good fortune and malevolent envy is found in the present passage. Compare the baneful onset of Inuidia at *Silv.* 2. 1. 120–4 and 2. 6. 68–70. Nauta (2002), 230 n. 134 sees the repeated references to Invidia and its cognates in this passage as punning on Abascantus' name and the Greek word ἀβάσκαντος, glossed by LSJ as 'secure against enchantments, free from harm'; for Statian puns on names see also Nisbet (1978), 8, Henderson (1998a), 17.

137. quisnam: For the same questioning of divine actions compare *Silv.* 2. 6. 58–9 (with van Dam) 'quis deus aut quisnam tam tristia uulnera casus | eligit? unde manus Fatis tam certa nocendi?' occurring, as here, at the beginning of a section with a similar shift from the qualities and character of Flavius Ursus' lost *puer delicatus* towards death and lamentation.

impacata consanguinitate: the phrase is almost an oxymoron, since *consanguinitate* would naturally presuppose a far more favourable connexion. Mozley's 'truceless kinship' suggests this tension admirably. *consanguinitas* only occurs eleswhere in classical Latin poetry at Virg. *A.* 2. 86–7 (Sinon's speech to the Trojans): 'illi me comitem et consanguinitate propinquum | pauper in arma pater primis huc misit ab annis.' Here, the effect of *consanguinitate* is even more striking in a hexameter consisting of only four words.

139. notauit: *notabit* (Barth) is unnecessary; *notauit* is a true perfect tense indicating that Fortuna acts first, singling out homes to be subsequently harmed by Inuidia.

140. figat: *figo* frequently indicates the fixed expression of the eyes, as at e.g. Virg. *A.* 1. 482 'diua solo fixos oculos auersa tenebat', but here the verb is used with *lumine* to denote staring at something; cf. Pers. 3. 80 'obstipo capite et figentes lumine terram'. *toruo ... lumine figat* is an etymological gloss of *Inuidia*, since the basic meaning of *inuideo* is looking askance (cf. Cat. 5. 12). Note also *Silv.* 4. 8. 16–17 'procul atra recedat | Inuidia atque alio liuentia lumina [*Markland*: pectora *M*] flectat'.

141. saeua ... dextra: compare the 'infausta ... dextra' of Lachesis at a similarly pivotal moment before Glaucias' final illness at *Silv.* 2. 1. 120.

142. hilares inconcussique penates: Priscilla had *hilarisque fides* (65). Just before the narrative of her illness and death, the audience is reminded of her *hilaritas*.

143. nil maestum: a terse gloss of the previous line, hinting at what is to come.

infida leuisque: although the instability of Fortuna is commonplace, these adjectives call to mind the opposite virtues of fidelity and loyalty associated with Priscilla (cf. 117–19).

144. Caesare tam dextro: Statius previously announced his intention to give a fitting poetic memorial to Priscilla, provided that his enterprise received the favour of Apollo and Caesar; for *dextro*, cf. 'modo dexter Apollo' (13). As the poem's narrative turns to unhappier events, the support of the two gods proves impotent against the effects of Fortuna and Inuidia. In 135–6, Apollo was instructed to wear cypress in token of mourning; now even Caesar is powerless against Fortuna.

145: inuenere uiam liuentia Fata: for the metaphor of a path to some (usually good) objective, compare Virg. *A.* 3. 395 (and 10. 113) 'fata uiam inuenient', ll. 128 'si qua uiam dederit Fortuna' and Luc. I. 33–4 'quod si non aliam uenturo fata Neroni | inuenere uiam'; see also *Silv.* 5. 2. 98–9 n. and Cic. *Rep.* 6. 12 (cited in 66 n. above). In Greek compare e.g. Hes. *Op.* 216–17 ὁδὸς δ' ἑτέρηφι παρελθεῖν | κρείσσων ἐς τὰ δίκαια, Pl. *Smp.* 184 B 5–6 μία δὴ λείπεται τῷ ἡμετέρῳ νόμῳ ὁδός, εἰ μέλλει καλῶς χαριεῖσθαι ἐραστῇ παιδικά and see further LSJ s.v. ὁδός III. For the role of the Fates in Greek and Latin epitaphs, see Lattimore (1942), 150–1, 156–7.

liuentia: blue-black, the usual colour of envy; note the personifications of *Liuor* at Prop. 1. 8. 29, Ov. *Am.* 1. 15. 1, *Rem.* 389, and see also André (1949), 174–5). Even the Fates were moved by the pervasive influence of Inuidia.

145–6. piumque ... larem: at a decisive moment, the hostile intervention of the Fates, the theme of Abascantus' piety returns, emphasizing Priscilla's unmerited death and Abascantus' grief. *piumque*, given prominence at the end of 145, is strikingly separated from its noun, *larem*, by the disturbing *intrauit uis saeua*; compare the similar arrangement but very different effect of *Silv.* 4. 8. 22–3 'uenit totiens Lucina piumque | intrauit repetita larem'. *larem* is a weighty word, evoking the tutelary deities of a Roman household (compare 'penates' in 142 and 'domum' in 140). This emphasis on home also suggests the earlier account of Priscilla's frugal domesticity (121–6).

At Sen. *Dial.* 11. 16. 5 Fortuna 'eas quoque domos ausa iniuriae causa intrare in quas per templa aditur'.

146–9: for the deleterious effects of wind and rain compare Cato *Agr.* 3. 2 'cogitato quotannis tempestates magnas uenire et oleam deicere solere', 28. 1 'caueto, quom uentus siet aut imber, effodias aut feras', Virg. *G.* 1. 311–34, 2. 333 'nec metuit surgentis pampinus Austros', Hor. *Carm.* 3. 1. 29–32. Note also the similes of well-tended olive trees destroyed by storm at *Il.* 17. 53–8, and V.Fl. 6. 711–16. Statius follows up these comparisons with a tree simile applied to Priscilla, though bad weather is not specifically mentioned (151–3).

The epithets *plena*, *alta*, *rapidae*, and *secundis* all stress good fortune, followed by calamity. *nimio* hints at an excess of good fortune (for the notion of continued luck as dangerous, compare e.g. Hdt. 3. 39–43, Virg. *A.* 4. 657 'felix, heu nimium felix'): the rich vine-harvest is overwhelmed by the malevolent south wind, and whereas a moderate amount of rain would benefit crops, an excess causes them to deteriorate (for *senescere* thus compare Col. 3. 18. 5).

For the south wind's effect, compare Prop. 4. 5. 61–2 'uidi ego odorati uictura rosaria Paesti | sub matutino cocta iacere Noto', *Silv.* 2. 1. 106–7 'uelut primos exspiraturus ad austros | mollibus in pratis alte flos improbus exstat', 3. 3. 128–9 'qualia pallentes declinant lilia culmos | pubentesque rosae primos moriuntur ad austros', *Theb.* 7. 223–4 'cum sole malo tristique rosaria pallent | usta Noto', and Jerome's metaphor for the death of Nepotianus (*Epist.* 60. 13. 2): 'marcescebat, pro dolor, flante austro lilium, et purpura uiolae in pallorem sensim migrabat', where, as Scourfield (1993), 176 notes, the south wind is treated as withering, in spite of its frequent assocation with rainfall (see 100 n. above). In this passage of Statius, it is perhaps more satisfactory if the wind is similarly regarded as dry and withering, so that the mention of rainfall in 148 is a separate and new point.

149. adsibilat: M's reading, *adnubilat*, is hard to defend, since, as Markland argues, Barth's gloss 'nubila velis objicit' cannot stand because clouds would not delay a ship. Markland suggested *obnubilat* and *obsibilat*, which he preferred. The prefix *ob-* in both instances suggests opposition to the ship's progress. However *obnubilat* is open to the same objection as *adnubilat*, since cloud will not impede the ship if there is a wind (*aura*).[23] With *obsibilat*, the wind changes direction, blowing from the point of the compass opposite to the ship's hitherto favourable course. But with both these conjectures the prefix *ob-* duplicates the sense of *obuia*. Better is Markland's rejected *adsibilat*, suggesting hisses of envy.

uelis . . . secundis: *secundus* is usually applied to winds, but its application to sails and voyages is not uncommon. (*OLD* s.v. *secundus* 9). Statius uses the phrase at *Silv.* 3. 1. 107.

150. carpitur: for the passive of *carpo* with an internal accusative of respect comparable to the Greek middle voice, see Ov. *Fast.* 2. 769–70 'carpitur attonitos absentis imagine sensus | ille; recordanti plura magisque placent.' For *carpo* referring to death and mutability, cf. 228–9 below, *Silv.* 2. 6. 78–9, where the word is used to describe Nemesis' destruction of the beauty of Flavius Ursus' *puer delicatus*, Sil. 5. 591 'atra, Sychaee, dies properato funere carpsit'. The word is also used in images of plucking, such as the flower 'tenui carptus . . . ungui'

---

[23] *aura* is the crucial word, as Markland saw, citing Sen. *Nat.* 5. 3. 1–2: 'quod tunc interim minime uentus est cum aer nubilo grauis est . . . nullum tempus magis quam nebulosum uento caret.' If *aura* were not the subject of the verb, a word such as *adnubilat* or *obnubilat* would not give rise to the contradiction.

at Cat. 62. 43; here, *carpitur* continues the imagery of waste in the natural world from the previous simile and anticipates the next simile of the pine tree that has lost its leaves.

151–3. alta . . . pinus: after the simple statement of the loss of Priscilla's beauty, she is likened to a lofty pine tree; contrast the palm shoot to which Odysseus compares Nausicaa (*Od.* 6. 162–7). The comparison also recalls the imagery of vine and elm (48–50). Tree similes are also applied to heroes, as at Virg. *A.* 4. 441–6 (see further Austin ad loc.), where Aeneas is likened to an oak resisting the blasts and buffets of the winds, and Luc. 1. 136–43, where Pompey is likened to an ancient and declining oak tree. Comparisons of heroes to falling trees are also common: see further Dewar on Stat. *Theb.* 9. 532 ff., Q.S. 1. 249–51, 1. 625–7. Here the simile adds further weight to the picture of Priscilla's moral steadfastness.

iam radice soluta: now loosened, the tree's roots are unable to support it; compare Luc. 1. 138–9 'nec iam ualidis radicibus haerens | pondere fixa suo est'.

deficit: the tree 'fails', as it loses its leaves; cf. Col. *Arb.* 1. 4.

remurmurat: despoiled of leaves, the pine is unable to rustle in the breeze. For *murmur* used of trees, compare Virg. *G.* 1. 359, Ov. *Met.* 15. 604.

154. quid . . . prosunt: for the uselessness of mortal possessions or virtues in death, compare e.g. *Silv.* 2. 5. 1–3, Sen. *Dial.* 11. 3. 5, Sil. 5. 261–4 and see Fedeli on Prop. 4. 11. 11–12. The emphasis is on Priscilla's moral qualities, rather than lineage or beauty (cf. 51–74). Three virtues are mentioned, her *probitas* (see 117), her *fides* (55 and 62), and her devotion to the gods (71), qualities which have all been important aspects of the praise and characterization of Priscilla.

155. furuae: *furuus* is especially associated with the underworld, and was applied to victims consecrated to the infernal powers, as at Sil. 8. 119–20; see also André (1949), 60. Note also Stat. *Theb.* 8. 10–11 'aut furuo Proserpina poste notarat | coetibus adsumptum functis', Hor. *Carm.* 2. 13. 21 'furuae regna Proserpinae'. The archaic flavour of *furuus* is noted by Gel. 1. 18. 4.

156. circum . . . uallauere: *uallo* has the positive sense of protecting a position with a defensive fortification or palisade (*uallum*); see e.g. *B. Alex.* 27. 5, 30. 2, Liv. 9. 41. 15 'castra uallantem Fabium adorti sunt', Tac. *Hist.* 2. 19. 1 'uallari castra placuit'; cf. Cic. *Mur.* 49 'Catilinam . . . uallatum indicibus atque sicariis', Lucr. 5. 27 'hydra uenenatis . . . uallata colubris'. The compound verb *circumuallo* (here *in tmesi*) however has negative connotations of siege and blockade, as at Caes. *BC* 3. 43. 2 'ex castello in castellum perducta munitione circumuallare Pompeium instituit', Sil. 1. 328 'castelloque urbem circumuallare frequenti', 7. 583. Priscilla was surrounded by the nets of death. In Greek, compare ἀμφικαλύπτω, used of reception in a house or city at *Od.* 4. 618 and 8. 511, but also used to describe the action of fate or death (*Il.* 5. 68, 12. 116, 16. 350, *Od.* 4. 180).

plagae are stationary nets used in hunting to prevent the quarry from getting through gaps: see e.g. Hor. *Epod.* 2. 31–2 'aut trudit acies hinc et hinc multa cane | apros in obstantis plagas', N.–H. on Hor. *Carm.* 1. 1. 28, Virg. *A.* 4. 131 'retia rara, plagae', Ov. *Met.* 7. 768 'summaque transibat positarum lina plagarum'; for more technical discussions of hunting-nets, see Grat. 24–60, Nemes. *Cyn.* 299–302, Opp. *Cyn.* 1. 147–52, 4. 379–92.

For net imagery (compare English 'caught in the toils'), cf. Lucr. 4. 1146–8:

> nam uitare, plagas in amoris ne iaciamur,
> non ita difficile est, quam captum retibus ipsis
> exire et ualidos Veneris perrumpere nodos.

Note also Prop. 3. 8. 37–38 'at tibi, qui nostro nexisti retia lecto, | sit socer aeternum nec sine matre domus', Ov. *Ars* 1. 270 'capies, tu modo tende plagas'.

tenduntur: the threads of Priscilla's life are stretched, and hence made taut, in order to facilitate cutting; for the motif of the thread of life in epitaphs, see Lattimore (1942), 159–61.

dura is a transferred epithet, being more applicable to the *sorores*, the Fates (Atropos is 'dura' at 178), but there is also an element of paradox, in that the 'hard' threads of Priscilla's life will nevertheless be cut.

157. exacti superest pars ultima fili: *exacti* indicates that the thread of Priscilla's life is complete, but it also suggests the use of 'exigo' in less metaphorical phrases denoting death as at Cic. *Tusc.* 1. 93 'qui exacta aetate moriuntur'. The image of the spinning of the Fates is thus expressed in language which itself suggests the ending of life. Note the English word 'span' for the term of life, and its etymological associations with spinning. Compare Virg. *A.* 10. 814–15 'extremaque Lauso | Parcae fila legunt', Claudian *In Eutrop.* 2. 461 'fila tibi neuerunt ultima Parcae'.

158. nil . . . nil: cf. 27–8 'nil cantus, nil fila deis pallentis Auerni | Eumenidumque audita comis mulcere ualerent'. Just as Abascantus' grief was not affected either by artistic images of Priscilla or the crowds of slaves, Priscilla's illness cannot be alleviated by the ministrations of slaves or doctors. The failure of the doctors (*medentum*) contrasts with the *medicina* of real consolation offered by Statius (16).

159–60. auxiliata: Markland noted the appropriateness of this word, since *auxilium* and its cognates can be applied to medical assistance. Cf. e.g. Ov. *Pont.* 1. 3. 23–4 'tollere nodosam nescit medicina podagram | nec formidatis auxiliatur aquis', Plin. *Nat.* 13. 125 '[ferulam] quibusdam tamen morbis auxiliari dicunt medici permixtam aliis', 27. 124.

comites: a vague and almost dismissive word here (but note Sen. *Con.* 2. 4. 3, where the *absence* of slaves and friends from a death bed evokes pathos), contrasting with *maritum*.

tamen establishes a link with the previous two lines describing the failure of attempts to cure Priscilla; the *comites* nevertheless behave as if the treatment could be successful.

spem simulant uultu: cf. Virg. *A.* 1. 209 'spem uultu simulat', describing Aeneas after his speech to his comrades on landing in Africa. But whereas Virgil contrasts the inner thoughts and external appearance of Aeneas, here the contrast is between the feigned behaviour of the *comites* and the raw emotion of Abascantus. Compare the behaviour of Tydeus' friends as he nears death (*Theb.* 8. 728–35) and see Hutchinson (1993), 93.

notat . . . maritum not only expresses Priscilla's concentration on her husband, a motif about to recur in 171–96, but also implies a lack of interest in the *comites*, although such disregard might be involuntary as Priscilla's strength wanes, the sick woman being able to recognize only her husband (cf. 171). The passage concisely suggests the ease with which those not directly affected by impending bereavement are able to give an impression of cheerfulness by hopeful smiles.

161–2. infernae . . . Lethes: cf. Sil. 1. 236. Lethe, mentioned as a proper noun in the *Silvae* on four other occasions (*Silv.* 2. 4. 8, 2. 6. 100, 2. 7. 101, 3. 3. 187) and as an adjective six times (2. 1. 194, 3. 2. 112, 3. 3. 22, 3. 5. 38, 5. 3. 24, 5. 3. 285), is never *named* by Statius in any context where forgetfulness is emphasized (but note *Silv.* 5. 2. 96 'immemoremque . . . amnem'). Here the river Lethe is used

metonymically for the underworld; cf. Virg. *G.* 2. 492, *A.* 7. 312
'flectere si nequeo superos, Acheronta mouebo'.

numina (Heinsius) is preferable to M's *flumina*. Abascantus would
appeal to the powers of the underworld, not to its rivers; cf. *Silv.* 3. 3.
186–7 'nec flectere Parcas | aut placare malae datur aspera numina
Lethes'. The simple corruption to *flumina* would have been facilitated
by the presence of *Lethes*; cf. *Silv.* 3. 3. 22 'Lethaea ad flumina'.

incorrupta: the underworld powers will brook no entreaty; com-
pare Virg. *G.* 4. 470 and Prop. 4. 11. 1–8.

162–4. omnibus aris: Abascantus' vain appeals contrast with
those of his wife in 72–4, where she persuaded the gods to grant her
husband success; cf. 'cunctis . . . aris' (73). At Tib. 1. 3. 29–30 'ut mea
uotiuas persoluens Delia uoces | ante sacras lino tecta fores sedeat',
Delia attempts to secure divine help when Tibullus is ill; cf. Luc.
2. 35–6 'et nullis defuit aris | inuidiam factura parens', from a passage
dealing with desperate attempts by Roman matrons to win the favour
of the gods at the outbreak of the civil war (2. 28–36):

> cultus matrona priores
> deposuit maestaeque tenent delubra cateruae:
> hae lacrimis sparsere deos, hae pectora duro   30
> adflixere solo, lacerasque in limine sacro
> attonitae fudere comas uotisque uocari
> adsuetas crebris feriunt ululatibus aures.
> nec cunctae summi templo iacuere Tonantis:
> diuisere deos, et nullis defuit aris   35
> inuidiam factura parens.

inlacrimat: this verb is best construed absolutely (cf. Virg. *G.* 1.
480 'et maestum inlacrimat templis ebur aeraque sudant'), rather
than with a dative 'omnibus aris'. Although the latter construction
is well attested (e.g. Ov. *Tr.* 5. 8. 5–6 'mala . . . | nostra, quibus possint
inlacrimare ferae'), 'inlacrimare' with the dative means 'to weep at',
with the notion of weeping *about* something. Construing 'omnibus
aris' with *inlacrimat* gives the unwanted implication that Abascantus is
weeping on account of the altars. But if *inlacrimat* is absolute, with the
prefix serving as an intensifier, 'omnibus aris' is then an ablative of
place.

signatque fores et pectore terget | limina: Vollmer, citing
Gronovius *Diatribe* 47, §315 'exegesis est et unum dicunt haec duo
signare fores et *limina tergere*', explains that Abascantus leaves behind

imprints and refers to *Theb.* 6. 904 'turpia signata linquens uestigia terra' and Sil. 4. 258 'et tremulos cuspis ductus in puluere signat'. However, it is hard to see how Abascantus can make any kind of imprint on the *limina*, the raised threshold of antiquity (on which see Coleman on *Silv.* 4. 8. 62). The difficulty is compounded because *pectore terget* | *limina* suggests a horizontal position (cf. Luc. 2. 30–1, cited above), a position which would make even less likely the possibility of the door being at the same time imprinted by Abascantus. It is better to take the phrases as referring to distinct (though doubtless repeated) actions, which are all part of the list which begins in l. 161. Abascantus sometimes calls on the infernal powers, he sometimes weeps, he sometimes presses against the doors of the temples (for the idea of marking temple doors, compare *Theb.* 10. 52–3 'pictasque fores et frigida uultu | saxa terunt', also in a context of desperate supplication for loved ones), he sometimes lies down prostrate as well, and sometimes calls upon Caesar for help. Though *tergeo* only rarely denotes pressing (its usual signification is wiping and hence cleansing), *Silv.* 2. 1. 193 'te uidet et similes tergentem pectore ceras', where the action described is the embracing of a wax image, is a close parallel to Abascantus' gesture of prostration here.

Slater, who translates '. . . anon imprints kisses on their gates' considers *signatque fores* as equivalent to 'signatque fores osculis', so that Abascantus kisses the doors; compare Mozley's 'leaves his imprint at the gates'. But this interpretation is needlessly reminiscent of the *exclusus amator*; Abascantus has no cause to honour the doors with such conspicuous veneration, since there is no reason to suppose that he is being kept away from Priscilla. There is no justification for supplying 'osculis' as an ablative of means.

164. exorabile: the emperor's willingness to yield to entreaty (see *Silv.* 5. 2. 94 n. for the signification of *exorare*) pointedly contrasts with the refusals of the powers of the underworld (161; cf. Virg. *G.* 2. 491 'inexorabile fatum', Hor. *Ep.* 2. 2. 178–9).

165. heu, durus fati tenor: whereas Priscilla's appeal to the emperor was followed by the favourable appearance of Fortuna, Abascantus' appeals are followed by a remark on the implacable nature of the Fates. *tenor* might ironically echo the praise of Priscilla's consistency (118). This emotional outburst also prepares for the succeeding observations on the inability of even the emperor to master death (cf. Sen. *Dial.* 11. 3. 5).

167. morae: Fate can be delayed, but not averted: cf. e.g. Hdt. 1.
91. 2–3 (Apollo could only delay Croesus' downfall by three years),
Virg. *A.* 7. 313–16:

> non dabitur regnis, esto, prohibere Latinis,
> atque immota manet fatis Lauinia coniunx:
> at trahere atque moras tantis licet addere rebus,
> at licet amborum populos exscindere regum.

Note also Bacchus' decision to delay the onset of the Argives at
Theb. 4. 677, and Jove's concession of a few more years' survival to
Carthage before its destruction at Sil. 17. 372. *morae* also exploits the
sound of *mortalibus* from the previous line.

168. arbitrium: contrast Statius' wish for Domitian, apostro-
phized as *pater*, to have *omne … arbitrium* with Lucan's delight (also
expressed with an apostrophe) that Caesar had no power over Pom-
pey's death (9. 1058–9): 'o bene rapta | arbitrio mors ista tuo'. At Cic.
S. Rosc. 131 *arbitrium* is associated with Jove 'cuius nutu et arbitrio
caelum, terra mariaque reguntur'. Note also the 'splendida … arbi-
tria' made by Minos when judging the dead (Hor. *Carm.* 4. 7. 21–2). In
186 Priscilla tells her husband that no *arbitrium* of the gods will be able
to harm him after her death.

omne: when mentioning what is not in the emperor's power,
Statius tactfully implies that Domitian can control everything else.
At *Silv.* 1. 4. 4–6 Fortuna blushes at the prospect of taking away
Rutilius Gallicus from Domitian; see Henderson (1998*a*), 43.

mors clusa: compare Virgil's similar image of the confinement of
Furor at *A.* 1. 294–6:

> Furor impius intus
> saeua sedens super arma et centum uinctus aenis
> post tergum nodis fremet horridus ore cruento.

barathro, the scene of Death's imprisonment, commonly signifies
the infernal regions, a usage found as early as Plautus. See further
Heuvel on *Theb.* 1. 85, and the full discussion of the word in Tuplin
(1981), 121–3, 138–9. For the idea of death being imprisoned, Vollmer
cites *CLE* 1385. 1 for a Christian application of this image: 'in tumulo,
mors saeua, iace'.

170–96: in 161 Statius broke off from his depiction of Priscilla's
final illness to describe Abascantus' reactions to the calamity. Now
attention returns to the dying woman. The precision of Statius'

approach is to be noted: in 160 Priscilla was watching her husband;
the next stage of her descent into death is marked by the falling of her
countenance (*cadunt uultus*) and the wandering of her eyes. For the
whole of this passage comparison with the deaths of Atedius Melior's
puer (*Silv.* 2. 1. 148–53) and of Atys in the company of his betrothed
Ismene is instructive (*Theb.* 8. 641–54):

ille tamen Parcis fragiles urgentibus annos
te uultu moriente uidet linguaque cadente
150   murmurat; in te omnes uacui iam pectoris efflat
reliquias, solum meminit solumque uocantem
exaudit, tibique ora mouet, tibi uerba relinquit,
et prohibet gemitus consolaturque dolentem.

prima uidet caramque tremens Iocasta uocabat
Ismenen: namque hoc solum moribunda precatur
uox generi, solum hoc gelidis iam nomen inerrat
faucibus. exclamant famulae, tollebat in ora
645   uirgo manus, tenuit saeuus pudor; attamen ire
cogitur, indulget summum hoc Iocasta iacenti
ostenditque offertque. quater iam morte sub ipsa
ad nomen uisus defectaque fortiter ora
sustulit; illam unam neglecto lumine caeli
650   aspicit et uultu non exatiatur amato.
tunc quia nec genetrix iuxta positusque beata
morte pater, sponsae munus miserabile tradunt
declinare genas; ibi demum teste remoto
fassa pios gemitus lacrimasque in lumina fudit.

170. nouissimus: a superlative often used of the last moments of
a person's life. See *OLD* 3 for parallels; note Dido's 'nouissima uerba'
at Virg. *A.* 4. 650.

error complements the sense of *cadunt uultus* (for which cf. *Silv.* 2. 1.
149 'uultu moriente', 3. 5. 39 'tenuique oculos iam morte cadentes'),
but adds the particular detail of the eyes' failure to focus at the last.
Compare *Theb.* 12. 777–8 'ille oculis extremo errore solutis | labitur',
V.Fl. 6. 277 'extremus cum lumina corripit error'; note also Virg. *A.* 4.
691 'oculisque errantibus', Esteve-Forriol (1962), 141.

171. obtunsae: *obtundo* can denote the deafening produced by
loud or repeated noise, as at *Rhet. Her.* 3. 9. 17 'nam si uehementer
aures auditorum obtunsae uidebuntur atque animi defatigati ab
aduersariis multitudine uerborum' (cf. Lucr. 5. 1054–5 'nec ratione
ulla sibi ferrent amplius auris | uocis inauditos sonitus obtundere

frustra', referring to those who are already deaf). Here, however, *obtunsae* indicates loss of hearing, without suggesting that noise was the cause; for this use of *obtundere* to denote the loss of one of the senses, cf. *Theb.* 7. 372 'et iam acies obtunsa negat', Plin. *Nat.* 22. 142 '[lens] aciem quidem oculorum obtundit'.

uox sola: compare Glaucias hearing only Melior at *Silv.* 2. 1. 151–2. At Prop. 2. 27. 13–16, the voice of a girl can save a dying lover.

172–3. illum unum... illum: cf. *Theb.* 8. 649 'illam unam', and for the anaphora compare Priscilla's fidelity in 55–6: 'unum nouisse cubile, | unum secretis agitare sub ossibus ignem'. Just as Priscilla was only concerned with her husband in life, so too at her death he is the only person she recognizes. Cf. *Silv.* 3. 5. 38–42, where Statius' describes his wife's presence during a serious illness and ascribes his recovery to her influence, and see Laguna ad loc. for parallels.

172. media de morte reuersa: with the possessive genitive *reuersae* (Heinsius), it would be Priscilla and not her mind that returned from the midst of death. However, this distinction is unnecessary: compare the *uirtus* of the tame lion at *Silv.* 2. 5. 17–18 'mansere animi, uirtusque cadenti | a media iam morte redit'. For the idea of *media mors*, cf. *Theb.* 8. 187, 729, 11. 554–5, Virg. *A.* 2. 533 'hic Priamus, quamquam in media iam morte tenetur', V.Fl. 1. 820, 3. 326–7, Sil. 5. 409, 7. 732 'e media iam morte renata iuuentus'. Note also Cat. 64. 149–50 'certe ego te in medio uersantem turbine leti | eripui', and see Fordyce ad loc. for this usage of *medius*.

173. mens: the use of this word with *uidet*, rather than a word denoting eyes, adds to the impression of Priscilla's failing senses.

fortiter recalls Priscilla's extreme devotion for her husband (67 ff., 127 ff.). Even as she faces her own death, Priscilla does not abandon her fortitude, which is contrasted with her physical weakness (*aegris*).

174. immotas obuersa genas: although Mozley construes *genas* as cheeks, translating 'turning to him her stiffened cheeks', it is preferable to follow Slater and Iz.-Fr. in rendering the word as eyes, though for caution in insisting on a rigid distinction between the two meanings, see Henderson (1998*b*), 239 n. 59. The key is *immotas*; whereas the eyes can, even in a serious illness, wander and view objects in different directions (hence 'nouissimus error', 170), the cheeks would not move even if a person was well; *immotas* only has any point if it refers to eyes. For a special case of *immotus* compare Ovid's description of the petrified Niobe's eyes (*Met.* 6. 304–5):

'in uultu color est sine sanguine, lumina maestis | stant immota genis, nihil est in imagine uiuum.'

See also *Silv.* 5. 4. 7–8 'aegras | stare genas'. The present phrase has an element of paradox in that the basic meaning refers to the turning of motionless eyes, an apparent contradiction. However, Priscilla's gaze is fixed, not because she is ill but because she is concentrating on her husband; she thus has to turn her whole head to see Abascantus. This small detail emphasizes the effort involved in Priscilla's last actions, and helps to explain *fortiter* in the previous line.

immotas obuersa genas might evoke two further passages from the *Aeneid*: *A.* 4. 331–2 'immota tenebat | lumina' and *A.* 6. 469 'illa solo fixos oculos auersa tenebat'; see Norden ad loc. for Greek parallels for this gesture and cf. *A.* 1. 482 'diua solo fixos oculos auersa tenebat' with Barchiesi (1998), 130–1, 138–9. The first passage describes Aeneas' fixed gaze as he prepares to leave Dido, the second Dido looking away from him in the underworld. In contrast, Abascantus does not leave Priscilla, who fixes her gaze on her husband; note the change from *auersa* to *obuersa*.

nec sole supremo: Vollmer notes the allusion to Dido's manner of dying (Virg. *A.* 4. 691–2): 'oculis errantibus alto | quaesiuit caelo lucem ingemuitque reperta.' Although dying persons commonly seek a last glimpse of the light (see Pease ad loc., Esteve-Forriol (1962), 141), the specific allusion to Dido is important. Whereas the Carthaginian queen has no husband to look at when she dies, Abascantus is beside his wife during her last moments.

Both Priscilla and Atys prefer a last glimpse of the beloved instead of seeing the light. Perhaps also compare the language of Anna's profession of affection to Dido at *A.* 4. 31 'o luce magis dilecta sorori'.

175. lumina . . . satiare marito: Priscilla literally sates her eyes (for this idiom cf. e.g. *Silv.* 4. 6. 34 'nec longo satiauit lumina uisu') with her husband, as opposed to the sight of him (cf. *Theb.* 8. 650 'et uultu non exatiatur amato', where the dying Atys looks on Ismene). Contrast the more favourable situations of *Silv.* 1. 2. 36 'amplexu tandem satiare petito', and Prop. 2. 15. 23 'dum nos fata sinunt, oculos satiemus amore'.

176. unanimum: cf. Virg. *A.* 4. 8 'cum sic unanimam adloquitur male sana sororem', where Dido addresses Anna. As Pease ad loc. notes, *unanimus* can characterise all kinds of affinities (cf. *Silv.* 5. 2. 155, *Theb.* 9. 169 with Dewar's n., instances where it is applied to friendship), even one so formal as allies in war. For husbands and wives cf. e.g. Cat. 66. 80 'unanimis . . . coniugibus', Sen. *Oed.* 773 'unanima coniunx'. It is also found in the epigraphic poetic corpus; to Pease's examples add *CIL* xi. 4978 (= *CLE* 1848, Spoleto).

solatur: for consolation given by the dying, compare *Silv.* 2. 1. 153, Mart. 1. 78. 3 'siccis ipse genis flentes hortatus amicos', Quint. *Inst.* 6 pr. 11 'ut me in supremis consolatus est', Plin. *Ep.* 5. 16. 4 'sororem patrem adhortabatur', Jerome *Epist.* 60. 13. 2 'lasso anhelitu tristem auunculum consolabatur'. This motif has an obvious role in a poem of consolation: Priscilla's reassurance anticipates the comfort which the poem seeks to provide; compare the consolations offered by the dead in funerary inscriptions, on which see Lattimore (1942), 217–20.

amantem emphasizes the sincerity of Abascantus' concern for Priscilla; for its application to married love compare Virg. *A.* 1. 352 'multa malus simulans uana spe lusit amantem', Ov. *Tr.* 1. 3. 17 'uxor amans flentem flens acrius ipsa tenebat'.

177. pars animae uictura meae: for this notion of another person as a part of one's own soul, ascribed by *Σ* Pers. 5. 22 to Pythagoras, see *Silv.* 3. 2. 7–8 with Laguna's n., N.–H. on Hor. *Carm.* 1. 3. 8 and 2. 17. 5, Ov. *Pont.* 1. 6. 16 with Gaertner's n., 1. 8. 2 'pars animae magna, Seuere, meae', Luc. 5. 757 'maneat pars optima Magni', Rutilius Namatianus 1. 426, 1. 493, Otto (1890), 25–6 (§111). In 176 Abascantus was *unanimus*; here the couple are *unanimi* since Priscilla addresses Abascantus as *pars animae . . . meae*. *uictura* may evoke 'uincere', to conquer or prevail, as well as 'uiuere', to live; compare the appearance of both verbs at Virg. *A.* 11. 160–1 'contra ego uiuendo uici mea fata, superstes | restarem ut genitor'; note also Cic. *Phil.* 14. 38 'si uiui uicissent qui morte uicerunt'.

178. Priscilla wishes her husband to receive a longer span of years as compensation for her untimely death; compare Cornelia's similar hopes (Prop. 4. 11. 95): 'quod mihi detractum est, uestros accedat ad annos.' See also *Epic. Drusi* 413, Sen. *Dial.* 10. 8. 4, *CIL* vi. 12652 col. a 23–6 'quodque mihi eripuit | mors inmatura iuuen- | -tae id tibi uicturo | proroget ulterius'. Priscilla's wish anticipates the end of the poem, where she appeals successfully to the Fates and to the powers of the underworld that Abascantus die only when he is 'senex' (262). For Atropos cutting off a span of years, cf. *Silv.* 3. 3. 127.

179. parce precor: see *Silv.* 5. 2. 84 n. and cf. [Sen.] *Her. O.* 1507 'parce iam lacrimis, parens'.

saeuo . . . planctu: Abascantus did not at once heed his wife's request; the fury of his grief at her death is made plain in 20 ff. and in 197 ff.

180. crucia: this request not to grieve is expressed in strong language. It is related to the theme of a dying person's consolation (and hence prevention of grief) expressed in 176 and also at *Silv.* 2. 1. 153. But whereas these examples are concerned with consolation and prevention of grief, here Priscilla directly states her wish not to be tormented by her husband's grief *as she is dying*. This is different from the well-attested topos of excessive lamentation being unwelcome to the departed, exemplified at *Silv.* 2. 6. 96 'quid caram crucias tam saeuis luctibus umbram'; see further van Dam on *Silv.* 2. 1. 153, 2. 1. 226–234 and 2. 6. 86, N.–H. on Hor. *Carm.* 2. 9. 9, Fedeli on Prop. 4. 11. 1. One parallel for a deathbed request is supplied by Maecenas in *Eleg. Maec.* 2. 15–16:

> hoc mihi contingat: iaceam tellure sub aequa.
> nec tamen hoc ultra te doluisse uelim.

But this example is not as clear as Priscilla's entreaty; she does not wish to be troubled while her 'umbra' is *fugientem*, which refers to the time *before* her death (cf. Luc. 2. 25, 5. 279 'anima . . . fugiente', Quint. *Inst.* 6 pr. 12 '. . . tuum fugientem spiritum uidi?', Sil. 1. 122; note also Luc. 3. 623 'effugientem animam'). This unusual reference to the torment caused to the dying woman by her husband's grief gives a potent insight into the emotions behind the consolations offered by one about to die.

Contrast Priscilla's wish for her husband to refrain from tears with Luc. 5. 281, where the chance to die amid a wife's tears 'coniugi inlabi lacrimis' is regarded as desirable by Caesar's troops.

181. mortis (ς) has generally found favour (M's *mostis* is meaningless); Calderini's *maestos* goes against the spirit of Priscilla's encouragement to her husband not to grieve in this speech, while *nostros* (Korsch, whose conjecture is mentioned in Saenger's edition) adds nothing to the meaning and gives an awkward word order. Compare Ov. *Ep.* 1. 101–2 (Penelope of Telemachus) 'di, precor, hoc iubeant, ut euntibus ordine fatis | ille meos oculos conprimat, ille tuos', Sen. *Ep.* 63. 14 'tamquam ordinem fata seruarent', Tac. *Ann.* 16. 11. 2 'seruauitque ordinem fortuna, ac seniores prius, tum cui prima aetas extinguuntur'.

182. quod prior: for the idea that those born first should die first, see Kassel (1958), 96, Scourfield (1993), 87 on Jerome, *Epist.* 60. 1.

3, and compare the similar use of *prior* or the adverb *prius* at Cic. *Amic.* 15, Sen. *Oed.* 72, Stat. *Theb.* 9. 634–5, Mart. 9. 51. 4. At Luc. 3. 741–51 the aged father of the mortally wounded Argus rapidly kills himself in order to predecease his dying son.

183. omni . . . flore: *flos* and its cognates are often associated with youth, as at Cat. 68. 16 'iucundum cum aetas florida uer ageret' (cf. *Il.* 13. 484 καὶ δ᾽ ἔχει ἥβης ἄνθος, ὅ τε κράτος ἐστὶ μέγιστον); see further *OLD* s.v. *flos* 8, *ThLL* vi/1. 934. 60–935. 74. The image of the flower is often applied to the dead in funerary inscriptions (see Lattimore 1942: 195–7); here, strikingly, it is Priscilla, as she dies, who speaks of her husband, who will survive, in such terms. The present passage evokes youth, particularly as Abascantus is 'iuuenis' at 11, 76 and 197, but also recalls 'florebant hilares inconcussique penates' (142), where the predominant overtone is success rather than youth. For *flos* used without any implications of youth, compare Enn. *Ann.* 308 Skutsch who describes the orator M. Cornelius Cethegus (*cos.* 204 BC) as 'flos delibatus populi Suadaique medulla', and Sen. *Ep.* 26. 2 '[animus] exultat et mihi facit controuersiam de senectute: hunc ait esse florem suum', where the word is applied to ripeness of years (but contrast *Ach.* 1. 625–6 'primumque imbelli carcere perdes | florem animi?', where the young Achilles addresses himself).

184. After expressing her general pleasure in her husband's good fortune in 183, Priscilla specifically mentions her delight in Abascantus' gradual progress in his service to the emperor, recalling her delight at his first advancement (108–16).

185. Cf. Sen. *Dial.* 12. 18. 6 'in me omnis fatorum crudelitas lassata consistat'. For the thought that bereavement renders the sufferer impervious to any further misfortune (which would be an odd conceit to use if the poem was designed to ensure that Abascantus remained in his post), see Quintilian's remarks about Fortuna (*Inst.* 6. pr. 15):

sed uel propter hoc nos contumacius erigamus, quod illam ut perferre nobis difficile est, ita facile contemnere. nihil enim sibi aduersus me reliquit, et infelicem quidem sed certissimam tamen attulit mihi ex his malis securitatem.

Thomas Hardy's *In Tenebris* opens with the same motif:

> Wintertime nighs;
> But my bereavement-pain
> It cannot bring again:
> Twice no one dies.

186. mecum ista fero: after the lofty language of the preceding line, Priscilla dismisses the power of the immortals in three words. The tone of *ista* has been ignored by translators; lengthy renderings such as 'I take with me their power to harm' (Mozley) and 'j'emporte avec moi leur puissance' (Iz.–Fr.) do not do justice to the brevity of *ista*, literally 'those things', a contemptuous reference back to *arbitrium*.

The phrase also ironically suggests the commonplace thought that a dead person can take nothing to the grave. See [Quint.] *Decl. min.* 260. 11–12 (with Winterbottom) and N.–H. on Hor. *Carm.* 2. 14. 21. Sometimes the deceased take with them their years: Petr. 43. 7 'quot putas illum annos secum tulisse', *CIL* vi. 12845. 5 'quadraginta duo mecum fero flebilis annos'. Cf. *CIL* vi. 5254. 2 'nullum dolorem ad inferos mecum tuli'.

limite coepto: for this image of the path of a person's career, compare *Silv.* 5. 2. 61 'iamque adeo moliris iter'; note also the phrase *cursus honorum*.

187. libens: Priscilla's request to her husband that he should gladly pursue his career is an implicit request not to grieve overmuch, and represents a rejection of his thoughts of suicide in 200–6. On the emperor's *latus*, see 5. 1 *epist.* 7–8 n.

188. inrequietus ama: Priscilla's words suggest both the description of her worship of the emperor in 74 ('et mitem genium domini praesentis adoras') and the 'molem ... et uix tractabile pondus' imposed on Abascantus by the emperor in 84. For the argument that bereavement should be subordinate to service to the emperor, cf. Sen. *Dial.* 11. 5. 2, 11. 7. 1 'Caesarem cogita', 11. 8. 1, 11. 12. 3–4.

189. Capitolinis ... sedibus: the golden statue will be *aeternum*, so that the Capitoline hill is a natural place for it. The Capitol can be associated with poetic immortality: cf. Hor. *Carm.* 3. 30. 7–9 (with N.–R.) 'usque ego postera | crescam laude recens, dum Capitolium | scandet cum tacita uirgine pontifex', Virg. *A.* 9. 447–9 'nulla dies umquam memori uos eximet aeuo, | dum domus Aeneae Capitoli immobile saxum | accolet imperiumque pater Romanus habebit'. Here Statius countenances a physical immortality of the kind rejected not only by Horace in the first two lines of *Carm.* 3. 30 ('Exegi monumentum aere perennius | regalique situ pyramidum altius), but also by Statius in this very poem (see e.g. 10 'sed mortalis honos, agilis quem dextra laborat').

A statue in a public place would commemorate the builder as well, as noted by Plin. *Ep.* 1. 17. 4 (on a statue of L. Silanus erected by the equestrian Cn. Titinius Capito): 'neque enim magis decorum et insigne est statuam in foro populi Romani habere quam ponere.'

190. centeno pondere: As befitting a ruler who apparently executed a woman for undressing in front of one his images (D.C. 67. 12. 2), Domitian imposed certain protocols on his imperial statuary, as noted by Suet. *Dom.* 13. 2: 'statuas sibi in Capitolio non nisi aureas et argenteas poni permisit ac ponderis certi' (see further Jones' commentary ad loc.). Cf. also Sil. 3. 623 'aurea Tarpeia ponet Capitolia rupe'. Plin. *Pan.* 52. 3 contrasts Trajan's choice of bronze with Domitian's use of gold and silver in statues of himself, though it is worth noting that the equestrian statue described by Statius in *Silv.* 1. 1 is in fact of bronze. Mratschek-Halfmann (1993), 214, 344 estimates that the cost of a golden statue weighing 100 pounds would have been 6m HS. Domitian's monuments did not long outlast him (Plin. *Pan.* 52. 3–5, Suet. *Dom.* 23. 1, D.C. 68. 1. 1). On imperial statuary in precious metals, see further Scott (1931), Whitehouse (1975).

niteant sacri ... uultus: M has *niteat*, but Lipsius and Markland preferred *niteant*. Markland argued that *sacri ... uultus* is nominative, citing extensive parallels (in his note on *Silv.* 4. 2. 54) for the plural, including *Silv.* 5. 1. 234 'uultus ... decoros', [Sen.] *Oct.* 841 'sanctos coniugis uultus meae', Luc. 8. 669–70 'ac retegit sacros scisso uelamine uoltus | semianimis Magni'. This last is perhaps the most relevant example, since, although the phrase is applied to Pompey, it may reflect imperial usage. Coleman on *Silv.* 4 pr. 6 notes that the emperor is only directly called *sacer* by Statius at *Silv.* 5. 2. 177 'sacer ... Germanicus', the usual procedure being to apply *sacer* to things associated with him; cf. Galán Vioque on Mart. 7. 1. 4. Thus the genitive *sacri ... | Caesaris* is unlikely to be right; the transmitted *niteat* should not be retained.

191. signent: if *niteat* is rejected, M's *signet* must also be emended. There are three possibilities: the imperative *signa* (Markland), which would pick up the tone of *da* in 189, *signes* (Baehrens) with *quo* in 190 as an instrumental ablative common to both of the following clauses, or perhaps *signent*, with *sacri ... uultus* as subject, so that the statue would show Priscilla's devotion to the emperor. No irrefutable argument can be advanced in favour of any one of these emendations, although *propriae* ('the emperor's own') perhaps makes the third person *signent* more likely. For *signare* denoting 'to signify' or 'to indicate', compare

Virg. *A.* 7. 3–4 (of Caieta) 'ossaque nomen | Hesperia in magna, si qua est ea gloria, signat' and Ov. *Met.* 14. 433–4 'fama tamen signata loco est, quem rite Canentem | nomine de nymphae ueteres dixere Camenae'.

192. Furias: Virgil locates the Fury Tisiphone in Tartarus at *A.* 6. 555 and 570–2 (where she calls on the 'agmina saeua sororum'). At *A.* 8. 667–9 Catiline in Tartarus trembles at the faces of the Furies.

193. Elysias . . . oras: cf. Lucr. 6. 763 'Acheruntis . . . oras'.

194. labens: *labor* sometimes occurs in descriptions of death with its literal idea of falling predominant, typically in battle scenes, as at Virg. *A.* 11. 818–19 (Camilla) 'labitur exsanguis, labuntur frigida leto | lumina', Luc. 7. 603–4 (Domitius) 'tunc mille in uolnera laetus | labitur', Sil. 5. 526–7 'labitur infelix atque appetit ore cruento | tellurem expirans'. Here *labens* means 'dying', with no hint of 'falling' or 'sinking'. Compare V.Fl. 5. 2–3 (and see *OLD* s.v. *labor*[1] 7c), where the death is also a result of disease:[24]

> Argolicus morbis fatisque rapacibus Idmon
> labitur extremi sibi tum non inscius aeui.

Contrast *labor* in another instance of sickness, where the death of a horse is only anticipated (Virg. *G.* 3. 498–500). Here the primary meaning is to the fore:

> labitur infelix studiorum atque immemor herbae
> uictor equus fontisque auertitur et pede terram
> crebra ferit.

The English colloquial idiom 'to slip away', applied to those dying quietly, has a similar metaphor.

For the collocation of *amplectitur*, and *animam* in 194–5, cf. 'te . . . | uisceribus totis animaque amplexa fovebat' in 46–7. For such dying embraces, cf. Tib. 1. 1. 60 'te teneam moriens deficiente manu', Ov. *Am.* 3. 9. 58 'me tenuit moriens deficiente manu', *CIL* ii[2]/14. 814. 14–16 'indignor misera[s] non licuisse frui | dulces anplexus morientis et oscula data | nec tenuit moriens deficiente manu'.

195. On the practice of 'catching' a dying person's last breath, see *Silv.* 2. 1. 150–1 and 3. 3. 19–20 with van Dam and Laguna respectively, Pease on Virg. *A.* 4. 684, Esteve-Forriol (1962), 141. Priscilla's

---

[24] Note the use of *labo* (short *a*) for the effects of disease at Lucr. 6. 1152–3 'morbida uis in cor maestum confluxerat aegris, | omnia tum uero uitai claustra lababant' and Luc. 6. 93–4 'inde labant populi, caeloque paratior unda | omne pati uirus durauit uiscera caeno'.

bestowal of her *anima* on Abascantus recalls her earlier address to him as 'pars animae uictura meae' in 177. *haerentem* and *non tristis* encapsulate, with great concision, the two themes of this scene. Even at the last moment of her life, Priscilla's great love for Abascantus causes her breath (*animam* here combines the notions of 'breath' and 'soul') to linger (*haerentem*) as she dies. *non tristis* recalls Priscilla's earlier attempts to dissuade her husband from sorrow; the poem offers Priscilla herself to Abascantus as an *exemplum* of refraining from grief.

196. cara pressit sua lumina dextra: Priscilla helps her husband to close her own eyes. Usually a loved one performs this act after, and not at the moment of, death; cf. e.g. Ov. *Ep.* 1. 113, 10. 120, *Epic. Drusi* 157–8, Luc. 3. 740, 5. 280, V.Fl. 1. 334 'et dulci iam nunc preme lumina dextra', where Alcimede tells the departing Jason to close her eyes, since she cannot anticipate his return, Mart. 10. 63. 6, and see further Fedeli on Prop. 4. 11. 64, Esteve-Forriol (1962), 141. Priscilla's participation in her husband's action points to the mutual nature of the marriage as demonstrated throughout the poem, but especially in the simile of the vine and the elm in 48–50. With *transtulit* and *pressit* Statius momentarily reverts to the past tense, after the dominance of the present tense in his narrative since 160. One reason may be that the actual moment of death is too painful to recall with the vivid tones of the present tense, which have hitherto re-enacted Priscilla's last illness. As the subsequent narrative shows, Priscilla's death elicited a violent response from her husband, and even at the time of writing attempts at consolation renew grief (30–2). Priscilla's death must be treated as a past event, if the poem's consolatory aim is to be achieved; cf. the appearance of the past tense 'qualis erat' in *Silv.* 2. 1. 157 after a passage (consisting mainly of present tenses) describing the dying moments of Glaucias (146–56).

197. iuuenis: at the decisive moment of Priscilla's death, *iuuenis* emphasizes the pathos of Abascantus' premature bereavement, and lends credence to his violent responses. See also 11, 183 n.

magno ... luctu: contrast 195, where Priscilla was *non tristis*.

flammatus: anger and hence grief can be described with fire imagery (e.g. *Theb.* 1. 249 'flammato uersans inopinum corde dolorem', Virg. *A.* 1. 50 'talia flammato secum dea corde uolutans', *A.* 9. 500–2 'illam incendentem luctus Idaeus et Actor | ... | corripiunt' and Tac. *Hist.* 2. 74. 1 'namque omnis exercitus flammauerat adrogantia uenientium a Vitellio militum'), but the same imagery is

also applicable to love; both emotions are evoked here. Abascantus'
flames of grief ironically recall Priscilla's 'unum ... ignem' (56).

198. implet ... clamore penates: compare e.g. *Theb.* 1. 592–3
'ipsa ultro saeuis plangoribus amens | tecta replet', Virg. *G.* 4. 460–1
'at chorus aequalis Dryadum clamore supremos | impleuit montes'
for shouting as a manifestation of grief.

**199–200: nunc ferrum laxare cupit, nunc ardua tendit | in
loca (uix retinent comites):** cf. 5. 3. 67–8 below (with n.), and
Claudius Etruscus' behaviour at *Silv.* 3. 3. 178–9 'uix famuli comit-
esque tenent, uix arduus ignis | summouet'. At *Theb.* 9. 76–81 Poly-
nices draws his sword for suicide but is checked by his 'comites' and
the words of Adrastus; at 11. 628 Antigone thwarts her father's search
for a weapon with which to kill himself. A curious parallel is Sil. 13.
390 'non comites tenuisse ualent', in a description of Scipio's grief for
his father and brother, where Silius makes no mention at all of any
attempt at suicide on the part of Scipio. V. Max. 4. 6. 2–3 refers to the
suicides of C. Plautius Numida and M. Plautius, following the deaths
of their wives; the former is another example of the intervention of
attendants to prevent suicide, though Plautius Numida was subse-
quently able to reopen his wound and bring about his death. At Luc.
9. 106–8 Pompey's widow Cornelia refuses a variety of deaths (which
she had previously wanted at 8. 654–6), preferring to die of grief; see
also Sen. *Phaed.* 258–60 and other *loci* collected by Winterbottom on
[Quint.] *Decl. min.* 260. 24. For suicide as a response to bereavement,
see van Dam on *Silv.* 2. 1. 23–5; note also Fraenkel (1932), on the topos
of different means of accomplishing suicide. Statius refrains from
direct allusion to Abascantus' wishes, but merely glances at them;
ardua tendit | in loca is especially discreet; for suicide by hurling oneself
from high places cf. Hor. *Epod.* 17. 70, Luc. 2. 155–6, 8. 654, Apul.
Met. 6. 12.

ore ligato, as Vollmer suggests, indicates that Abascantus is
kissing his dead wife. Cf. *Silv.* 2. 1. 172–3 'dilectosque premis uisus
et frigida lambis | oscula', 3. 3. 177 'et prono fusum super oscula
uultu'. There is also a hint that he is not lamenting loudly (contrast
198), hence preparing for the ensuing simile of the silent Orpheus:
more than one manifestation of grief is presented in this passage.

201. incubat: the characteristic word for a mourner leaning
over or lying on a dead person, as at Luc. 2. 27–8 'necdum est ille
dolor, nec iam metus: incubat amens | miraturque malum', 8. 727–8

'incubuit Magno lacrimasque effundit in omne | uolnus' and 9. 55–7 (Cornelia's speech):

> 'ergo indigna fui,' dixit, 'Fortuna, marito
> accendisse rogum gelidosque effusa per artus
> incubuisse uiro . . . '.

At *Silv.* 3. 3. 9, note the striking phrase 'incumbentemque fauillis'.

202. saeuus: there is a paradox in the juxtaposition of this word, suggesting violent grief (cf. 179 above), and *mersumque in corde dolorem* in the previous line. Abascantus' grief is violent, but it is internalized. Cf. the second half of Virg. *A.* 1. 209 'premit altum corde dolorem', and see 159–60 n. for a possible echo of the first part of the line, 'spem uultu simulat'.

agit: Heinsius and Markland favoured *alit*, on the analogy of Virg. *A.* 4. 2 'uulnus alit uenis' and other parallels. But *agere* is very frequently construed with a noun as a periphrasis for a verb cognate with the noun, as exemplified by Quint. *Inst.* 9. 3. 12 'unde eo usque processum est ut "non paeniturum" pro non acturo paenitentiam et "uisuros" ad uidendum missos idem auctor dixerit'; cf. e.g. Ov. *Ep.* 16. 304 'curam pro nobis hospitis, uxor, agas', *Met.* 12. 539–40 'Herculeae mirum est obliuia laudis | acta tibi, senior', Sen. *Her. F.* 27–9 'uiuaces aget | uiolentus iras animus et saeuus dolor | aeterna bella pace sublata geret', *ThLL* i. 1383. 50–70, 1384. 44–65, *OLD* s.v. *ago* 28. Since the construction is so common, *dolorem | . . . agit* need not be emended.

segnis: Shackleton Bailey's new Loeb prints Barth's conjecture *conspecto coniugis igne*, with a reference to Eurydice's funeral pyre, which is in any case referred to by *rogum* in line 204. However *segnis* is a striking description of Orpheus, who is 'slow', and hence physically 'stilled'. The epithet also draws attention to the contrast between Abascantus, who is *saeuus*, and Orpheus. One might expect Orpheus' reaction to his loss of Eurydice to be swift; compare the 'subita . . . dementia' affecting Orpheus at Virg. *G.* 4. 488, and the sudden ('subito') disappearance of Eurydice at *G.* 4. 499. *segnis* anticipates *obstipuit* and *sine carmine* in 204, referring to his poetic silence; the point of the comparison is that Abascantus, like Orpheus, was at first immobilized by grief, which utterly overwhelmed him. At Ov. *Met.* 10. 73–4, Orpheus sits beside the Styx for seven days.

203. Odrysius uates: mention of Orpheus prepares for Abascantus' wish to accompany his wife into the underworld (206). In

23–5, not even Orpheus would have been able to console Abascantus; here Abascantus' suffering is elevated yet further through a similar comparison. The earlier reference suggests a parallel between Orpheus and Statius, as poets; here, the simile now suggests an affinity between Orpheus and Abascantus, since both had lost their wives. For the silence of a poet compare *Silv.* 5. 3. 16, where Statius likens his own poetic silence at his father's death to that of Calliope after the death of Orpheus; contrast 5. 5. 54–5, where he declares that Orpheus or Apollo was 'durus' if he could sing after losing his beloved. Orpheus is usually cited for his unfailing song, even after his death (e.g. Virg. *G.* 4. 523–7, Ov. *Met.* 11. 51–3), but the shift of emphasis towards his inability to sing suggests the difficulty of artistic response to suffering; compare Daedalus' failure to represent his son's death in his engravings on the doors of the temple of Apollo at Cumae (Virg. *A.* 6. 30–3), and the refusals of Meliboeus and Moeris to sing at *Ecl.* 1. 77, 9. 66–7.

Strymona: for this Thracian river as the site of Orpheus' lamentations after his second loss of Eurydice, see Virg. *G.* 4. 508–9 'rupe sub aeria deserti ad Strymonis undam | flesse sibi'. There is perhaps a slight contradiction between this mention of the Strymon and the mention of the funeral pyre (*rogum*) in 204: one might assume that Eurydice's funeral had taken place before Orpheus' descent into the underworld since she had already crossed the Styx.

204. obstipuit: here and at Ov. *Met.* 10. 64 'non aliter stupuit gemina nece coniugis Orpheus', Orpheus' grief is accompanied by the same amazed silence which his own singing had previously provoked in others: Virg. *G.* 4. 481 'quin ipsae stupuere domus atque intima Leti', Ov. *Met.* 10. 42 'stupuitque Ixionis orbis'.

205. certae: M's *recte*, which would imply praise of Abascantus' desire for suicide, cannot stand since Statius praises Abascantus' loyalty to Domitian in 207–8; as genitive singular *rectae* (cf. Quint. *Inst.* 1 pr. 10 for this epithet applied to *uita*), referring to Abascantus' 'upright life', it would be mere padding. The correction of M^1, *erecte*, is however doubtful, since the adverb is securely attested with this meaning of 'boldly' only in Ammianus and Σ Cic. Bob. p. 154, 5 St. (*ThLL* v/2. 785. 75–786. 4). *spretae* (Appelmann) adds little: the context already indicates Abascantus' contempt for life. *fractae* (Imhof) simply doubles the metaphor of *rupisset*, with a consequent loss of clarity, while Polster's *reliquae* is tame. Better is *certae* (Markland), suggesting the magnitude of Abascantus' sacrifice in throwing away an assured future. If correct *certae* would also neatly anticipate the *certae . . . sorores* of 262 who accede to Priscilla's prayers for her husband's long life.

rupisset tempora: Statius suggests the commonplace idea of the threads of the Fates, which were severed at the end of a person's life (cf. e.g. Luc. 3. 19 'lassant rumpentis stamina Parcas'), without however using a word like *stamina*.

206. ne tu: Abascantus' extreme devotion is reflected by this apostrophe of Priscilla, now dead in terms of the poem's internal chronology.

Tartareum chaos (cf. *Theb.* 12. 772 and contrast *Elysium chaos* at *Theb.* 4. 520) suggests Abascantus' own anxieties for what is in store for Priscilla (cf. 249–52 below).

207. duci (Calderini) is preferable to M's *ducis. fidus* is normally construed with the dative, though there are very rare instances of the objective genitive, as at Virg. *A.* 12. 659–60 'praeterea regina, tui fidissima, dextra | occidit ipsa sua' (see also Prisc. *GL* iii. 216. 16–18, Arus. *GL* vii. 473. 23–4), a usage which may have been imitated by Statius himself (the manuscripts are not unanimous) at *Theb.* 6. 372–3 'quisnam iste duos, fidissima Phoebi [*Pω*: -bo *ex* −bi *B3* : −bo *DδO*] | nomina, commisit deus in discrimina reges?' However, the uncertainty here over whether *ducis* is grammatically possessive or objective genitive makes *duci*, the much commoner dative after *fidus*, preferable. The *mens* of course has to be Abascantus', since it is affected by the *sacris imperiis*, and it would in any case be very odd to describe the emperor as *fidus* to one of his freedmen.

firmataque: Vollmer and Iz.–Fr. defend M's *mirandaque* for different reasons. Whereas Vollmer argues that *sacris imperiis* is simply equivalent to 'imperatori', Iz.–Fr. compare τὴ]ν ἱερωτάτην αὐτοῦ ἐπιταγὴν in a proconsular inscription of Domitian's reign at Delphi (*Syll.*³ 821 D–E). The parallel is a good one, but whether or not the inscription is adduced here, *miranda* must be emended, since the *sacris imperiis*, which can hardly denote the emperor himself, can scarcely be described as admiring anything. An additional difficulty is the gerundive form: obligation is hardly appropriate to the *sacris imperiis*, an objection which applies to *firmandaque* (Courtney) as well; why *must* Abascantus' loyalty be supported or admired by the *sacris imperiis*?

iurata (Markland) not only accords well with praise for Abascantus as loyal, but also gives some point to the *sacris imperiis*, which are the commands which he must fulfil; for *imperia* thus cf. Virg. *A.* 8. 381

'nunc Iouis imperiis Rutulorum constitit oris', V.Fl. 1. 184–5 'at ducis imperiis Minyae … | puppem umeris subeunt'. Markland supplies convincing parallels for *iurata*: *Theb.* 2. 490–1 'exit in unum | plebs ferro iurata caput', 4. 305 'iurataque pectora Marti', Sil. 1. 9 'iuratumque Ioui foedus', and Man. 1. 907–9:

> nec plura alias incendia mundus
> sustinuit, quam cum ducibus iurata cruentis
> arma Philippeos implerunt agmine campos.

However Professor Winterbottom's *firmata* has the merit of suggesting imperial concern; Abascantus is encouraged not to end his life by the orders he receives from his master. For the frequent confusion of gerundive and past participle in manuscripts, see e.g. Brink on Hor. *Ars* 190, Ov. *Fast.* 2. 18 (with the apparatus of the Teubner edition of Alton, Wormell, and Courtney).

208. maior amor: cf. Priscilla's own instruction to her husband: 'inrequietus ama' (188).

quis carmine digno: Statius alludes to the difficulties of composing his own poem. Compare the modesty of '*temptamus* dare iusta' (13), and the address to the *Thebaid*, where Statius tells his poem not to attempt to challenge the *Aeneid* (*Theb.* 12. 816–17); it is of course arguable that such statements of modesty might encourage a reader to think the opposite.

Breaks in the flow of a poem, which with modern punctuation require a new paragraph, are not uncommon in the middle of a hexameter line; compare Virg. *A.* 7. 45, where the poet concludes the second exordium of the epic, and proceeds to begin his account of Latium in the same line. At *Silv.* 2. 1. 157 Statius breaks off in mid-line to begin his account of Glaucias' funeral with a similar rhetorical question asking how he is to describe the funeral obsequies.

209. dona malae feralia pompae: the juxtaposition of *dona* and *malae* points to the paradox of the funeral; gifts are lavished on Priscilla, but the occasion is a sad one. Cf. Plin. *Ep.* 5. 16. 7 (money intended for clothing and gems is spent on spices for the funeral of Fundanus' daughter).

210–14. For opulent funeral spices in Statius see *Silv.* 2. 1. 157–65 with van Dam, 2. 4. 34–6, 2. 6. 85–9, 3. 3. 34–7; cf. 3. 3. 211 'semper odoratis spirabunt floribus arae'. Statius typically lists more than one spice on such occasions; compare [Tib.] 3. 2. 23–4 'illic quas mittit diues Panchaia merces | Eoique Arabes, diues et Assyria'.

The function of such lists has been debated: van Dam questions
H. Lohrisch's description of the list at 2. 1. 160 as 'purely rhetorical',
but one might see emphasis being achieved in this passage through
the technique of λεπτολογία, or enumeration of details (Lausberg
§813). Van Dam himself suggests a personal interest in spices on the
part of Statius, and argues that the geographical names imply the
involvement of the whole world in the funeral and mourning for
Glaucias, whilst the spices themselves form a compliment to Melior's
wealth. Certainly the spices (and the dead Priscilla) form a back-
ground against which Abascantus will stand out (216); the passage
presents a spectacle of wealth, which nevertheless fails to capture
attention in the same way as Abascantus.

Although the funeral is unmistakeably opulent, there is no sugges-
tion that Abascantus is extravagant; contrast Pliny's pain at hearing of
Fundanus' expenditure on spices at the funeral of his daughter (*Ep.* 5.
16. 7–8), while at *Silv.* 2. 1. 163, Statius applies the adjective *prodigus* to
Melior, who wishes to burn all his wealth at Glaucias' funeral (con-
trast the miserly heir at *Silv.* 4. 7. 39–40: 'imminens leti spoliis et ipsum
| computat ignem'). Real funerals could be lavish: on Sulla's death the
women of Rome contributed enough spices to be carried in two
hundred and ten litters (Plu. *Sull.* 38. 3). More recent was the funeral
of Nero's consort Poppaea (Tac. *Ann.* 16. 6. 2): 'corpus non igni
abolitum, ut Romanus mos, sed regum externorum consuetudine
differtum odoribus conditur tumuloque Iuliorum infertur.' Plin. *Nat.*
12. 83 suggests that Poppaea's funeral outdid even Sulla's: 'periti
rerum asseuerant, non ferre tantum annuo fetu, quantum Nero
princeps nouissimo Poppaeae suae die concremauerat.' See also
Friedlaender (1921), ii. 361–2.

uer Arabum Cilicumque: cf. *autumnus* (50 n.), where the word
for the season denotes the products of that time of year; cf. Mart. 9.
12(13). 2 'cum breue Cecropiae uer populantur apes'. Arabian and
Cilician spices are also paired at *Silv.* 3. 3. 34–5 (a funeral): 'tu messes
Cilicumque Arabumque superbas | merge rogis'.

As for identification of these and other spices, van Dam on 2. 1.
159–162 remarks on Statius' alternation between vague and precise
epithets for spices, but continues, 'I think that we must assume that in
these enumerations, every item stands for one specific product, until
we are forced to admit the contrary.' Thus in his note, he suggests
that in our passage *uer . . . Cilicum* and *Coryciae . . . comae* are both refer-
ences to saffron. Similarly, he construes *uer . . . Arabum* and *Cinyrea*

germina as oil of myrrh. In his note on *Silv.* 2. 6. 86–89, van Dam also
remarks that '*Flores Sabaei* in 5. 1. 211 can refer to myrrh', citing V.Fl.
6. 709, where *flos Sabaeus* seems to signify some kind of liquid perfume
and [Sen.] *Her. O.* 376 'Sabaea...myrrha'. This method, however,
has the disadvantage of having Statius repeat himself needlessly; a list
of this length is likely to be more effective if repetition is avoided.

Though Laguna on *Silv.* 3. 3. 34–5 argues for precise references to
saffron and myrrh in that passage, phrases such as *uer Arabum Cili-
cumque* could represent a variety of spices, by way of introduction to
the list which follows. Arabia in particular, although itself only pro-
ducing frankincense, myrrh, and balsam, as noted by Miller (1969),
101–5, was often credited with spices which, though not native, came
from there, in the sense that Arabia was a port of call on the trade
route. Thus D.S. 2. 49. 3 ascribes Arabian origin to *costum*, cassia, and
cinnamon; see further Miller (1969), 7, and Raschke (1978), 652–5
(with nn.). The mention of the Arabians here could therefore refer to
a range of spices. The case of Cilicia is less clear, since saffron was
undoubtedly its most famous product, although Miller (1969), 116
notes that mountain nard was also found there.

flores Sabaei: also uncertain. Myrrh is certainly not to be ruled
out, but here again a non-specific reference is possible, particularly in
view of the very precise *Cinyrea germina* used to denote myrrh in 214,
alluding to the metamorphosis of Cinyra's daughter Myrrha into the
myrrh tree (Ov. *Met.* 10. 489–502). The Sabaean kingdom lay in the
south-western portion of the Arabian peninsula; see further von
Wissmann (1976), though 'Sabaean flowers' may signify goods
which came through Sabaean territory, as opposed to being
produced there. Statius also associates cinnamon (*Silv.* 4. 5. 32, 5. 3.
42–3) and incense (4. 8. 1; cf. V.Fl. 6. 138) with the Sabaeans; but
only frankincense is a local product. Plin. *Nat.* 12. 87 notes that
cinnamon was brought by sea to Africa; Miller (1969), 47 argues
that this confirms that the product was conveyed from India and
south-east Asia to East Africa, but see Raschke (1978), 652–5 for the
view that cinnamon actually originated in East Africa. Moreover,
V.Fl. 6. 709, referred to above, is evidence for not taking *flores Sabaei*
too literally.

Indorumque arsura seges is glossed by van Dam (on 2. 1.
159–62) as putchuk (Latin *costum*), a herb from northern India, whose
root was put to several uses, although he concedes that Statius is the
only author to mention it in the context of cremations; see further

Miller (1969), 84–6. This last detail should perhaps inspire caution. Van Dam himself on 2. 4. 34–6 notes that *amomum*—an Indian spice often confused with *cardamomum*; see Miller (1969), 67–9, 71–3—was frequently used in the preparation of funeral unguents (Juv. 4. 108–9 remarks that Crispinus wore enough for two funerals). In view of the considerable range of Indian spices known to the Romans, precise identification is unwise here; Miller (1969), 86–7 notes that sandal-wood was also used in funerals in India.

The future participle *arsura* here stresses the transience of such opulence, and recalls Statius' opening remarks on the difference between mortal and lasting honours paid to Priscilla; cf. *Silv.* 3. 3. 37–8 (with Laguna's n.), where an account of funeral spices at the funeral of Claudius Etruscus' father is followed by an assurance of the durability of Statius' poetic offering: 'nos non arsura feremus | munera'. Compare also *Silv.* 2. 1. 161–2 'quodque Arabes Phariique Palaestinique liquores | arsuram lauere comam', *Theb.* 6. 126 'inferias arsuraque fercula', 12. 572 'gens arsura rogis', Virg. *A.* 11. 77 'arsur-asque comas obnubit amictu' (the hair of the dead Pallas), Tib. 1. 1. 61 'flebis et arsuro positum me, Delia, lecto', V.Fl. 8. 236 'arsuras alia cum uirgine gemmas', a sinister foreshadowing of the death of Creon's daughter as a result of Medea's wedding gift, Mart. 10. 97. 1 'dum leuis arsura struitur Libitina papyro', *Alcestis Barcinonensis* 114 Nosarti 'arsurosque omnes secum disponit odores'.

praereptaque templis | tura Palaestinis: the prefix of *praer-epta* denotes that the frankincense was snatched before it could be used in the temples; cf. *Silv.* 4. 5. 31–2 'odoratisque rara | cinnama praeripiet Sabaeis', where, however, the force of the prefix is weaker. The reference is to the campaign of Vespasian and Titus against the Jewish revolt of AD 69–70 (cf. 5. 2. 138 n.).

Hebraeique liquores: probably gum of balsam, grown in the Royal Gardens of Judaea, which were praised by Plin. *Nat.* 12. 111 ff. for the quality and scarcity of the harvest; cf. J. *BJ* 1. 138, Miller (1969), 101, Schürer (1973–87), i. 288–9, 298–300, Raschke (1978), 901 n. 922.

Coryciaeque comae: a precise reference to the saffron crocus and its product; cf. Hor. *S.* 2. 4. 68, Luc. 9. 809 'Corycii pressura croci'. Plin. *Nat.* 21. 31 declared that Cilicia surpassed other lands for the quality of its saffron; within Cilicia, the saffron grown on Mount Corycus was the finest. Mart. 3. 65. 2 also refers to this same variety; see also Leigh (1994), 184–6. Ancient opinion was not unanimous, however; Thphr. *HP* 6. 6. 5 remarks on the sweetness of the saffron crocuses of Cyrenaica. The plant is mentioned in the list of ἀρώματα at Thphr. *HP* 9. 7. 3. Nowadays, Spain and especially Iran are the main producers of saffron; Finlay (2002), 246–70 offers an intriguing account of saffron in more recent times.

215. toris Serum: a play on the etymological relation between the Seres (the Chinese), and use of the adjective *sericus* to denote articles of silk; cf. *Silv.* 1. 2. 122–3 'querimur iam Seras auaros | angustum spoliare nemus', 3. 4. 89–90 (with Laguna's n.) 'et serica pectore ponunt | pallia', Sil. 6. 3–4 'primique nouo Phaethonte retecti | Seres lanigeris repetebant uellera lucis', 17. 595–6, Maltby (1991), 562. Thus Priscilla reclines on a 'Seric' bier; the coverlets are of silk. On the silk trade between Rome and China, see Ferguson (1978), 587–8, Raschke (1978), 622–37 (with nn.).

umbrata too exploits its etymology; Priscilla is shaded by the *Tyrio . . . tegmine*, and is herself an *umbra* (cf. 254). Purple is a common colour in descriptions of funerals from Homer onwards; the bones of Hector are covered with purple garments (*Il.* 24. 795–6).

217. solus: the postponement of this word to the end of the clause points to the contrast between the opulent funeral preparations for Priscilla, and the extreme grief of her husband, which is sufficient to divert the attention of the whole city. For the focus of attention on one (unexpected) individual, compare *Silv.* 2. 1. 173–4 'erant illic genitor materque iacentis | maesta. sed attoniti te spectauere parentes', and 5. 3. 222–3, where more attention is paid to an enthusiastic father who is watching his son at the Olympic games than to his son. Just as Priscilla set little store by riches in her lifetime (60–3), so too Statius suggests that Abascantus' grief was more significant than his expenditure. Compare *Silv.* 3. 3. 211–13, where Statius refers to the spices and fragrances which will be offered at the tomb of Claudius Etruscus' father, before continuing with 'et lacrimas, qui maior honos'. At *Silv.* 2. 6. 80–3 a similar list ends with Flavius Ursus' tears, which are more pleasing to the shade of the dead Philetos.

218. Abascantus' grief is compared to a father's loss of his sons. The pathetic detail of the *iuuenes natos* evokes the theme of premature death, particularly in time of war (e.g. Hdt. 1. 87. 4), when it falls upon parents to bury their children; cf. e.g. Virg. *A.* 11. 160–1 'contra ego uiuendo uici mea fata, superstes | restarem ut genitor', and for this motif in epitaphs, see Lattimore (1942), 187–91. The simile can be paralleled at *Il.* 23. 222–5, where Achilles' lamentation for Patroclus is likened to a father's grief for his son:

> ὡς δὲ πατὴρ οὗ παιδὸς ὀδύρεται ὀστέα καίων,
> νυμφίου, ὅς τε θανὼν δειλοὺς ἀκάχησε τοκῆας,
> ὣς Ἀχιλεὺς ἑτάροιο ὀδύρετο ὀστέα καίων,
> ἑρπύζων παρὰ πυρκαϊήν, ἁδινὰ στεναχίζων.

Note also Virg. *G.* 4. 477 'impositique rogis iuuenes ante ora parentum', *A.* 6. 308 (with Norden). See also Juv. 15. 138–40 and Winterbottom on [Quint.] *Decl. min.* 335. 4. In the *Silv.*, compare 2. 1. 23 (Melior's grief for Glaucias surpasses that of mothers and fathers), 2. 1. 173–4 (the boy's parents are affected by Melior's sorrow), 2. 6. 82–3 (Ursus' grief for Philetos could not be surpassed by the boy's parents), 3. 3. 10–12 (Etruscus' grief for his father is extreme enough to appear to be that shown for a young wife or a child), 5. 3. 64–74, 5. 5. 13, 18–20; cf. Esteve-Forriol (1962), 145, Fantham (1999), 67–70.

The simile heightens the sense of Abascantus' grief, but also hints that his grief is excessive. He is likened to a parent mourning a child, a death that violates the natural order, whereas Priscilla's last speech to Abascantus included the consolation that she should die first, being the older partner.

219. is dolor in uultu: *is ea id* is rarely used in the poets; for statistics on usage by authors other than Statius see Axelson (1945), 70 ff. *is* and *ea* are the forms most commonly used by Statius: *is* appears eight times in the *Thebaid*, once in the *Achilleid*, and three times in the *Silvae* (1. 6. 49, 5. 1. 219, 5. 5. 65). *is* is the only form used in the *Silvae* (discounting the prose prefaces). Here *is* is equivalent to *talis* (cf. Ov. *Tr.* 3. 13. 19 and see also Virg. *A.* 1. 529). Abascantus' expression at the funeral recalls his inability to conceal his suffering during Priscilla's final illness (160).

220. noctis: Markland asked how *nox* could refer to both *crines* and *genae*, and emended to *sordis* ('dust'). Dust as a sign of grief is often attested (see Markland's parallels from the *Thebaid* and elsewhere), but the reference seems a little too specific, particularly after *dolor*.[25] The transmitted text, however, can only be retained if it is acceptable for *noctis* to refer to dust in the case of *crines* and darkness in the case of *genaeque*. Emendation therefore seems called for, but *noctis* should not

---

[25] Ellis (1892), 22–3 notes that the Oxford MS of Statius has *color*, which he prefers to *dolor*; of *color* he remarks that 'with this would agree the blackness, perhaps produced by sprinkling ashes, of his hair and cheeks'.

be the only word under scrutiny. One could perhaps read *tantum pectusque genaeque | noctis habent*, 'there is so much darkness in his heart and in his eyes'.

221. felicemque uocant: the mourners declare that Priscilla is lucky because she is at rest (*tranquillo fine solutam*, 220), whereas her husband is tormented by grief. Hutchinson (1993), 95–6, sees this passage as manifesting a 'concern for ingenious paradox', but there is no need to see *felicem* as an apparent sign of heartlessness even at a first glance; the epithet is not really surprising or paradoxical, since it has been prepared for by *tranquillo fine solutam*.

felicem also suggests the more general idea of death as a blessing. Statius expresses this idea at some length at *Silv.* 2. 1. 220–6, where the dead Glaucias is *felix* (see Vollmer on 2. 1. 223). This notion is an ancient one: though not all the dead are blessed, Hesiod refers to μάκαρες θνητοί, and speaks of the dead heroes who live ἐν μακάρων νήσοισι (*Op.* 141, 171). At Hdt. 1. 32. 7 Solon pronounces on the need to distinguish between luck and happiness because the latter is only obtained by those who have died and are thus impervious to the vicissitudes of fortune: πρὶν δ᾽ ἂν τελευτήσῃ, ἐπισχεῖν μηδὲ καλέειν κω ὄλβιον, ἀλλ᾽ εὐτυχέα; cf. Cic. *Tusc.* 1. 115 (for the story of Elysius from Crantor's *Consolation*), Ov. *Met.* 3. 136–7, Otto (1890), 229 (§1143) . Note also the saying of Silenus that next best after not being born is to be born and to die as soon as possible (Arist. fr. 44 Rose, Cic. *Tusc.* 1. 114, [Plu.] *ad Apoll.* 115 B–E; cf. S. *OC* 1224–38, Sen. *Dial.* 6. 22. 3). In Latin see *OLD* s.v. *felix* 3b for the application of the word to the dead, and s.v. *beatus* 2 for examples of gods or Elysian spirits being so described. Note also Ammianus 25. 3. 21, where *beatus* means 'dead', without any overt allusion to Elysium: 'quem cum beatum fuisse Sallustius respondit, intellexit occisum'. For the particular paradox of lamentation for the living and felicitation of the dead, compare e.g. Thgn. 425–8, Bacch. 5. 160–2 with Maehler ad loc., Hdt. 5. 4. 2 (on the Thracian Trausi) τὸν μὲν γενόμενον περιιζόμενοι οἱ προσήκοντες ὀλοφύρονται, ὅσα μιν δεῖ ἐπείτε ἐγένετο ἀναπλῆσαι κακά, ἀνηγεόμενοι τὰ ἀνθρωπήια πάντα πάθεα, τὸν δ᾽ ἀπογενόμενον παίζοντές τε καὶ ἡδόμενοι γῇ κρύπτουσι, ἐπιλέγοντες ὅσων κακῶν ἐξαπαλλαχθείς ἐστι ἐν πάσῃ εὐδαιμονίῃ, E. fr. 449 (from the *Cresphontes*, and see Kannicht's edition for the popularity of this fragment in citations), Cic. *Tusc.* 1. 115, V. Max. 2. 6. 12, Quint. *Inst.* 5. 11. 38, [Plu.] *ad Apoll.* 107 C, Jerome, *Epist.* 60. 14. 4 with Scourfield (1993), 191–2, Kassel (1958), 76.

felix also implies that Priscilla is fortunate not to have lived to see her husband's grief. For the idea of being fortunate to die before seeing subsequent misfortunes, compare A. *Pers.* 712, Cic. *Brut.* 4–5, 329 'fortunatus illius exitus, qui ea non uidit cum fierent quae prouidit futura', *de Orat.* 3. 8, 12, *Fam.* 5. 16. 4 (cf. 5. 18. 1, Sulp. Ruf. *Fam.* 4. 5. 5), Virg. *A.* 11. 159 'felix morte tua neque in hunc seruata dolorem', Sen. *Dial.* 6. 20. 5, Sil. 2. 570 'felix, Murre, necis patriaque superstite felix', Tac. *Ag.* 45. 1–3, where Agricola is (45. 3) 'felix... etiam opportunitate mortis', Jerome *Epist.* 60. 17. 1 with Scourfield (1993), 196, 198–9, Kassel (1958), 82–3. Lucan's Cato offers a more complex variation on the motif, as he reflects on Pompey's death (9. 208–10):

> o felix, cui summa dies fuit obuia uicto
> et cui quaerendos Pharium scelus obtulit enses.
> forsitan in soceri potuisses uiuere regno.

For a very different and much more auspicious felicitation in which a husband is also the centre of attention (cf. 216 above 'sed toto spectatur in agmine coniunx'), contrast Stat. *Silv.* 1. 2. 236–7 'felices utrosque uocant, sed in agmine plures | inuidere uiro'. The Statian passages may themselves reflect Ovid's remarks to his wife at *Tr.* 5. 14. 9–10: 'quae te, nostrorum cum sis in parte malorum, | felicem dicant inuideantque tibi'.

222. est locus ante Vrbem: The ensuing *ecphrasis* of the site of Priscilla's tomb by the river Almo strikingly combines a contemporary and factual reference to the beginning (for *nascor* with the sense of 'incipio' see *OLD* s.v. *nascor* 11b) of the Appian Way, with a mythological reference to Cybele. The effect is not only to 'place' Priscilla's tomb in terms of geography, but to suggest a link with the gods, a connexion emphasized by the statues of her in the guise of various goddesses. On ecphrasis in general, see e.g. Fowler (2000), 64–107, who offers an extensive bibliography, at 65 n. 2; on Statian ecphrasis, see Newlands (2002), 38–43, 49–50.

Note that Ovid too uses the *est locus* figure at the start of his description of the Almo (*Fast.* 4. 337–8): 'est locus, in Tiberim qua lubricus influit Almo | et nomen magno perdit in amne minor'. For further examples of the figure, see Brown (1994), 12–13.

223. Cybebe: Cybele, represented by a sacred stone, was brought to Rome by sea from the Troad in 204 BC and received by Claudia Quinta (Liv. 29. 10–14, Ov. *Fast.* 4. 255–348). At the meeting of the Almo and the Tiber her image was annually washed (*lauatio*) on 27 March: see Luc. 1. 600 'et lotam paruo reuocant Almone Cybeben', Sil. 8. 363 'tepidoque fouent Almone Cybelen', Ammianus 23. 3. 7, Smith (1856), 105–6, Frazer on Ov. *Fast.* 4. 337, and Wissowa (1912), 319–27. Cybele's laments (*gemitus*) were for her lover Attis, who was driven mad after his infidelity with the nymph Sagaritis (Ov. *Fast.* 4. 229), but the next line also suggests the goddess's longing for her home on Ida. Cybele's abandoning of lamentation has an obvious exemplary purpose for Abascantus, particularly as the location is the site of Priscilla's tomb; cf. V.Fl. 8. 239–42, where Medea, abandoning her melancholy as she prepares to marry Jason, is likened to Cybele after the *lauatio* in the Almo.

224. non reminiscitur: at *Fast.* 4. 249–54, Ovid is told by Erato that Cybele did not come to Latium with Aeneas, since she took especial pleasure in her home on Mount Ida. Cybele's forgetting of the streams of Ida represents an acceptance of her new abode in Latium. Contrast the Trojans' remembrance of the rivers of the Troad in Virgil's *Aeneid* (e.g. *A.* 3. 302, 3. 350, 5. 634). For the emotional intensity of *reminiscitur*, compare Virg. *A.* 10. 782 'et dulcis moriens reminiscitur Argos', Stat. *Theb.* 12. 674.

225. hic: ecphrases of places characteristically refer back to the introductory phrase (*est locus* etc.) with a deictic pronoun or adverb; see Austin on Virg. *A.* 2. 21 and 4. 483. On deixis in the *Siluae*, see Nauta (2002), 258–69, 356–63.

225–8. Despite the repetition of the detail of the purple coverings from 215, this passage is not otiose, since the two passages describe different things: in 215, Statius recounts the public aspect of the funeral, and Priscilla's appearance in the procession, whereas the present sentence, with its apostrophe of Priscilla and its involved syntax, fractured by the parenthesis (where Statius puts the most emotive part of the sentence, Abascantus' inability to endure his wife's cremation), narrates the far more personal act of Priscilla's burial in the tomb. Compare Cat. 65: the whole poem is a single sentence, containing a central parenthesis on the poet's grief for his dead brother.

226. eximius coniunx: cf. *rarissima coniunx* (11).

fumantia busta: contrast Abascantus' inability to endure the flames of the pyre (cf. Nestor watching the pyre of Antilochus at Juv. 10. 252–3) and the equanimity with which Priscilla would have met *fulmineos ignes* at 68. Instead of being cremated, Priscilla is embalmed

(230–1), as Nero's wife Poppaea had been: Tac. *Ann.* 16. 6. 2, cited in 210–14 n. above, regards the practice as non-Roman, but note Lucr. 3. 889–93 who lists cremation, embalming ('in melle situm suffocari atque rigere | frigore', 891–2), and inhumation as means of dealing with the dead; cf. Toynbee (1971), 41–2, who argues that mummies found in the western portion of the empire had not been brought from Egypt.

227. clamoremque rogi: the *conclamatio* for the dead. Serv. *A.* 6. 218 quotes the elder Pliny's explanation of the practice (and also that of washing the body of the deceased in warm water) as a test to see whether any life yet remained; cf. Plin. *Nat.* 7. 173–7. Servius' language (phrases such as 'per interualla conclamentur' and 'post *ultimam* conclamationem') indicate that the practice was repeated: cf. Virg. *A.* 6. 506 'magna manis ter uoce uocaui', where *ter* recalls *Od.* 9. 64–6: Odysseus and his companions call on their dead three times before setting sail from the land of the Ciconians. The Homeric scholia offer two explanations for the practice: first, that calling on those dead in a foreign land is a substitute for taking them back home (Σ *Od.* 9. 65 καὶ ἐδόκουν κατάγειν αὐτοὺς πρὸς τοὺς οἰκείους [H]), and secondly, that calling on them is a test to determine whether any who have been left behind are still alive (Σ *Od.* 9. 64 [T] and 9. 65 [Q and V]). See further *RE* iii/1. 347. 63 ff. (s.v. *Bestattung*) (Mau), Dover on Ar. *Ra.* 1176, and Bömer on Ov. *Fast.* 3. 560 ff.

beato: for the assocations of *beatus* and *felix* with death, see 221 n.

228. composuit: *compono* frequently denotes burial; (*OLD* s.v. *compono* 4c).

tholo (Polster) is preferable to M's *toro*, since Statius is now describing the monument and not the bier on which Priscilla was placed in the funeral procession (215).

longior aetas: in view of Priscilla's untimely demise, this phrase might be expected to mean 'longer life'. However the next line shows that *aetas* refers to the passing of time.

229. aeui . . . labores: an almost paradoxical phrase, since time is naturally destructive, and needs to make no effort to achieve its effect. Here, where the aim is to praise Abascantus' memorial for his wife, Statius praises the imperviousness of the tomb. In an earlier passage, he had commented on the superior longevity of poetic commemoration (12–15). This passage applies to a physical monument the language of imperviousness to decay that is so often used to express *poetic* survival: see e.g. Virg. *A*. 9. 446–7, Hor. *Carm*. 3. 30. 4–5, Prop. 3. 2. 19–26, Ov. *Met*. 15. 872.

230. sic cautum membris (Phillimore): M's *sic catum* is meaningless. Phillimore's conjecture is preferable to *siccatam* (ς), which gives an inappropriate reference to the condition of Priscilla's corpse.

uenerabile anticipates the likenesses of Priscilla as various goddesses, and the attendants and funeral banquets in 235–7.

231. spirat opes: for *spiro* used of scents and vapours see *OLD* s.v. *spiro* 4. *opes* refers to the spices used to scent the tomb; for *opes* signifying the products of animals and plants, see *OLD* 4b.

231–4: On the Roman practice of decorating a tomb with likenesses of the deceased person as a god or goddess see B. Schröder (1902), 46–79 (especially 61–66), Altmann (1905), 281 ff., Cumont (1942), 66 n. 4, 302 n. 4, 415; see further van Dam on *Silv*. 2. 1. 191–3, 2. 7. 124–7 and 128–31 for adoration of the dead as divinities and portraits of them at home. Above all see Wrede (1981), who compares Statius' description of Priscilla's divine portrayals with surviving examples of the practice at 75–7. Note especially the mausoleum of Claudia Semne on the Via Appia, also built by an imperial freedman, M. Ulpius Crotonensis, for his wife, who is depicted as Fortuna, Spes, and Venus; on this see Wrede (1971).

mutata nouaris: despite the more favourable view of memorial images presented here, *mutata* hints at the disquiet expressed at the opening of the poem, when Statius announced that Abascantus deserved to have Priscilla restored to him, but in the form of artwork. *mutata* points to the inevitable change that has affected Priscilla, and perhaps has a didactic purpose for her husband. Recognition of the change wrought by death is a part of the process of consolation.

effigies: etymologically linked to *fingo* (used of artistic creation in line 1), *effigies*, held back until the end of the clause, tactfully indicates the unreality of Priscilla's presence at the tomb. Although Statius elsewhere praises images of the dead (cf. *Silv*. 2. 1. 191, 3. 3. 200–2 and the opening of this poem), at *Silv*. 2. 7. 124–31 Statius praises Polla for her concern to recall her dead husband Lucan not as a divinity, but in her heart ('ipsum sed colit et frequentat ipsum | imis altius insitum medullis'), before going on to discuss the 'solacia uana' which are offered by *uultus*. A preference for mental memorial is not uncommon; see Tac. *Ag*. 46. 3, where Agricola's wife and daughter are adjured not to show excessive devotion towards images of the dead man, but rather to concentrate on his mind (cf. Tac. *Ann.* 4. 38. 2 'haec mihi in animis uestris templa, hae pulcherrimae effigies et mansurae'). Pliny *Ep.* 4. 7. 1 drily notes Regulus' unceasing construction of memorials to his son, listing the various materials employed: 'hoc omnibus officinis agit, illum coloribus illum cera illum aere illum argento illum auro ebore marmore effingit.' The present passage is more tactful than Pliny's letter, but is less positive than the optimistic language of 229–30. Statius had already remarked on the supremacy of his own poem as a tomb for Priscilla in 15 (see n.): 'haud alio melius condere sepulchro.'

Ceres: for deifications of dead women as Ceres, see the list in Wrede (1981), 213–19.

lucida Cnosis: Wrede (1981), 76 argues that the reference here is to Diana rather than to Ariadne: 'Bei der "Lichtvollen von Knossos" ist eher an Artemis-Diktynna als an Ariadne zu denken, da *lucida* ein verbreitetes Epitheton für Diana ist.' However Ariadne could be *lucida* on account of Bacchus' transformation of her crown into a constellation (Ov. *Fast.* 3. 516 'aurea per stellas nunc micat illa nouem'); for depictions of the dead as mythological figures, compare the Severan statue of a Roman woman as Omphale in the Museo Gregoriano Profano at the Vatican discussed by Kampen (1996*a*) and Zanker (1999). *lucida* also suggests the shining appearance of the bronze figure on the tomb. The final syllable of *lucida* is scanned short, as is possible before *cn*; compare e.g. Hor. *Carm.* 1. 30. 1 'regina Cnidi', and see Housman, *Class. P.* iii. 1136–46.

illo Maia nites: Maia is one of the seven Pleiades, daughter of Atlas and Pleione; her child by Jupiter was Mercury. Ov. *Fast.* 5. 85–6 notes that her beauty surpassed that of her sisters, so that a compliment to Priscilla's beauty seems a likely effect of the comparison, although Maia is also 'sanctissima' at Cic. *Arat.* 270 (36); Wrede (1981), 75 and 77 suggests that Maia here could be a reference to the Bona Dea.

nites is a conjecture suggested to me by Leofranc Holford-Strevens. M's *tolo* could either be a doublet of *tholo* in 228, if Polster's conjecture there is accepted (see above), or a marginal correction of *toro* in 228 which has been displaced and wrongly applied. Although Klotz and Vollmer accept *tholo* here, it would be odd to refer to Priscilla's appearing as Ceres in bronze, then as *lucida*, before mentioning the niche in which a statue of her as Maia stood; the sequence produced would thus move from materials for the statues to the location of one of the images, before specifying the material of the final statue of Priscilla as Venus. Baehrens suggested *luto*, but its negative overtones (see *OLD* c and d) and comparative cheapness make it unlikely. The same objection applies to Saenger's *solo*. Somewhat more satisfactory is Markland's *auro*, which gives an air of opulence. In support of his emendation Markland notes that in l. 2 of the present poem Statius expresses the desire to 'aurumue animare figuris', comparing this with Claudius Etruscus' words to his dead father in *Silv.* 3. 3. 200–2:

> ... te lucida saxa,
> te similem doctae referet mihi linea cerae,
> nunc ebur et fuluum uultus imitabitur aurum.

Markland also cites Plin. *Ep.* 4. 7. 1 (see above) as evidence for the extravagance of some of the materials used.

Nevertheless, there is a problem common to all conjectures (including Markland's *auro*) which attempt to replace M's *tolo* with a material. The difficulty is that in the sequence of *hoc aere..., hoc..., illo..., hoc...saxo* it is natural to see the first three deictic pronouns as all referring back to *aere*; only with *hoc...saxo* is there a change of material. After the two instances of *hoc*, it would be natural for *illo* too to refer to another instance of *aere*. Hence Courtney's *nitens*, which opens up the quite separate possibility of replacing *tholo* with an adjective (compare *lucida* and *non improba*), represents a useful approach to the problem from another angle. However, *nitens* could only apply to Maia, and there is the further issue of the absence of a verb in this list. Holford-Strevens conjectures either *nites* or *nitet*, with the verb being common to all four instances; I have adopted the second-person form in the light of *nouaris* in 231. The suggestion that M's *tolo* be replaced with a verb is certainly a welcome approach to the problem.

Venus...non improba: for representations of deceased Roman women as Venus, see the catalogue in Wrede (1981), 306–23. Such statues often depicted the women as nude or partially clothed; see D'Ambra (2000). Such statuary tended to combine severe facial expressions with youthful beauty; see D'Ambra (1996), who on this passage remarks (222): 'Statius' description of the Venus portrait as *non improba* (not immodest) also implies that a statue of Priscilla as the nude or partially unclothed goddess did not offend and that the statue projected an image of pristine beauty, endowed with the feminine virtues of modesty and chastity.'

234–5: haud indignata ... numina: the gods accept and therefore approve not only the artistry but also Priscilla. For an extreme and paradoxical treatment of the theme of the gods reacting to their own images, compare Hildebert of Lavardin 36. 31–2, where the gods admire their statues in Rome: 'hic superum formas superi mirantur et ipsi | et cupiunt fictis uultibus esse pares.'

236–7: tori mensaeque parantur | adsiduae: cf. Claudius Etruscus' promise at *Silv.* 3. 3. 199–200 to offer 'adsiduas ... dapes et pocula sacris | manibus'. The *aeditui* were entrusted with funeral cult, maintenance of the tomb and the provision of funeral banquets; see further Wissowa (1912), 476–7, Toynbee (1971), 61–4. The language used of the banquets perhaps echoes the account of the Sabine woman's simple preparations for her husband at 125–6 ('mensasque torosque | instruit'), in a simile which was applied to Priscilla. Abascantus' concern to provide sumptuous feasts in honour of his dead wife contrasts with her modest preparations for him (121); a further difference is that Priscilla herself (*ipsa*, 121) arranges the meal, while Abascantus appoints others to the task.

237. domus ista, domus: such repetitions are an index of heightened emotion, often of a religious character: see Norden on Virg. *A.* 6. 46 'deus, ecce deus'. Cf. also e.g. Lucr. 5. 8, Virg. *Ecl.* 5. 64, V.Fl. 3. 271, Stat. *Silv.* 4. 6. 36, 5. 5. 69, *Theb.* 5. 133, 5. 751, *Ach.* 1. 528. The religious tone is appropriate to Priscilla's representation in divine guise, but the emphasis on *domus* also concentrates attention on the *domus* of Priscilla and Abascantus (see on 145–6 above), which thus continues even in death. For the idea of the grave as a home compare *Epic. Drusi* 73–4 'claudite iam, Parcae, nimium reserata sepulchra, | claudite: plus iusto iam domus ista patet' and Trimalchio's remark at Petr. 71. 7: ' ... ualde enim falsum est uiuo quidem domos cultas esse, non curari eas ubi diutius nobis habitandum est.' For this theme in funerary inscriptions see also Lattimore (1942), 165–7, who notes the popularity of the phrase *aeterna domus*.

238. hac merito uisa pietate mariti: Abascantus' monument to his wife is a visible sign of his *pietas* towards her (see *epist.* 2; 4, 32, 145–6 and 253). That the tomb might commemorate the qualities of Abascantus as well should not be surprising: Hopkins (1983), 207 n. 6 notes that in funerary inscriptions the name of the commemorator is sometimes more prominent than the name of the dead person being commemorated. The motif of pride in the magnificence of a monument is found in epitaphs: see Lattimore (1942), 227–8.

239–41. exclames: indefinite second person singular. Even though Priscilla was the last person to be addressed in the second person (231, and perhaps 233), she cannot be referred to here since it would be absurd for her to recognise (*agnosco*) that the builder of her monument is a servant of the emperor. These lines rely on the idea of a person unknown, perhaps in keeping with the addresses to ξένοι and *hospites* characteristic of funerary monuments and epigrams (see Lattimore (1942), 230–7), independently deducing that a servant of the emperor is responsible for the construction, since it is as lavish and as pious a creation as the temple which Domitian established for the deceased members of his family (Vespasian, Titus, Domitilla, and Domitian's own dead son).

The Temple of the Flavian Gens appears to have been completed around AD 94, since it is first referred to in Martial 9 (9. 1. 8, 9. 3. 12), published after May of that year (see Nauta (2002), 442). As a recent construction (*modo*), it would have attracted much attention. It was situated on the Quirinal, and would be the resting-place for Domitian's ashes, when his nurse Phyllis secretly mingled them with those of his niece Julia (Suet. *Dom.* 17. 3). See further Coleman on *Silv.* 4. 3. 19, Scott (1936), 61–82, B. W. Jones (1992), 87–8, Darwall-Smith (1996), 159–65, Davies (2000), 24–7, 158–68, Leberl (2004), 301–6. For the link between members of the imperial family and the stars compare e.g. *Silv.* 4. 2. 59, *Theb.* 1. 31, Mart. 9. 101. 22 and see further Vollmer on *Silv.* 1. 1. 94 ff.

caelo refers to heaven, the appropriate place for both divine beings and stars, but also adds weight both to Coleman's acceptance and to her interpretation of 'Flauiumque caelum' (*Turnebus*: caluum *M*) at *Silv.* 4. 3. 19, where she argues that *caelum* not only denotes heaven, but also refers to the temple itself, whose ceiling might perhaps have been decorated with the sky and stars; compare Prop. 3. 2. 20 'nec Iouis Elei caelum imitata domus'. The allusion would be not only to the transition of Domitian's dead relations into the abstract heaven of the gods, but also to their depiction in the starry heaven which was the temple's ceiling.

242–6. For the simile of a smaller ship contrasted with a larger one, compare *Silv.* 1. 4. 120–2, where Statius compares his own anxiety for Rutilius Gallicus to a small ship experiencing a storm alongside a larger one:

> immensae ueluti conexa carinae
> cumba minor, cum saeuit hiems, pro parte furentes
> parua receptat aquas et eodem uoluitur austro.

Here in *Silv.* 5. 1, the simile reinforces the implied comparison between Domitian's temple for his relations and Abascantus' tomb for Priscilla suggested by the direct speech of 239–41: Abascantus' efforts are like those of a small ship sailing alongside a large one. Henderson (1998*a*), 98 n. 216, discussing *Silv.* 1. 4. 120–2, compares Hor. *Epod.* 1. 1–2 'Ibis Liburnis inter alta nauium, | amice, propugnacula' (addressed to Maecenas), which seems an important parallel in this passage too for the idea of one of the emperor's helpers in a small ship. Note also *Silv.* 3. 3. 84 'inque omni felix tua cumba profundo', referring to Claudius Etruscus' father's successful career under various emperors, and cf. *Ciris* 479–80.

The simile evokes the magnitude of the ship not merely through the epithet *magna*, and the *innumeros utrimque rudentes* and the *lata... bracchia*, but also through the poetic resonance of the compound adjective *ueliferi* (cf. Prop. 3. 9. 35 'non ego uelifera tumidum mare findo carina') and *inuasitque uias*, which recalls the weighty words of the Sibyl to Aeneas at Virg. *A.* 6. 260 'tuque inuade uiam' as he embarks on his descent into the Underworld, the allusion adding a note of epic grandeur to the large ship's voyage.

soluit iter: *soluo* is the technical term for setting sail (*OLD* 4), usually construed with the ship as the object.

Phario: a favoured synonym for 'Aegyptius' (which is not found) in the *Silvae*, occurring ten times, usually with no particular reference to Pharos, the isle near Alexandria where the celebrated lighthouse was located. Here, at *Silv.* 5. 5. 66 ('Pharia de puppe'), and possibly at 3. 2. 22, where a ship brings in the 'Pharium...annum', the Egyptian harvest, a specific connexion with Alexandria does seem indicated.

it: with M's *in*, the absence of a verb of motion for the *phaselos* causes concern, particularly in view of the following *et* which indicates that something is missing; Housman's explanation (*Class. P.* ii. 653) that *et...sibi* is equivalent to *sibi quoque* is unconvincing. Vollmer placed a comma after *mali*, so that the subject of *inuasitque uias* is the *phaselos*, despite the presence of *-que*, which most naturally refers back to the previous lines (and note the *-que* in 244). A further effect of Vollmer's punctuation is that the whole sentence is governed by *ubi* in 242, with no main clause to go with *sic* in 242.

But if the *uias* are the journey of the *magna puppis* (with a comma after *uias*), *eodem* is given an antecedent, and is more effective. Accordingly it is preferable to accept Gevartius' *it*; the corruption to *in* would have been particularly easy before the ensuing *eodem...aequore*.

angusta phaselos: despite the primary meaning of *phaselos* in both Latin and Greek, an edible pod or a bean, which then comes to be used of boats, *angusta* ('narrow') is not redundant. *phaseli* could range from Egyptian vessels of clay (Virg. *G.* 4. 287–9 and Juv. 15. 127) or a lifeboat (*Silv.* 3.2.31) to a transport capable of carrying a cohort (Sallust, *Hist.* 3. 8 Maurenbrecher); see Fordyce on Cat. 4. 1.

247. quid nunc: the final section of the poem begins with a direct plea to Abascantus to end his grieving. *nunc* refers not only to the time of writing, with some quite considerable interval having elapsed from the time of Priscilla's death (compare *tunc* and *nunc* in ll. 20 and 30 for this contrast), but also refers to the 'time' of the poem, in that Statius has reached, after his description of Priscilla's marriage, death and tomb, a moment when it is at last appropriate to tell Abascantus to refrain from grief. Compare *iam* at *Silv.* 2. 1. 208–9 for a similar comment on the need to stop grieving near the end of a long poem: 'quin tu iam uulnera sedas | et tollis mersum luctu caput?'

immodicos...fletus: cf. Sen. *Ep.* 63. 2 'quaeris unde sint lamentationes, unde immodici fletus?', Luc. 8. 71 'immodicos castigat uoce dolores'; on immoderate grief see van Dam on *Silv.* 2. 6. 93–5.

lectissime: although *lectus* often indicates merely worthiness and quality (see *OLD* s.v. *lectus* 2), the idea of selection is important here, since Abascantus has been chosen by Domitian (75–88). Such imperial favour justifies the superlative form of the adjective.

248. foues: whereas *foueo* was used positively of Priscilla's love and devotion at 47 and 119, here *foues* refers to the questionable way in which Abascantus harbours an excessive sorrow.

uetas is even more pointed, implying that if Abascantus did not make a conscious effort, his grief would depart of its own accord. Similar strong language is addressed to Flavius Ursus at *Silv.* 2. 6. 94–5: 'quid damna foues et pectore iniquo | uulnus amas?' with the same conceit of grief being cherished (cf. Sen. *Dial.* 6. 1. 7 'et fit infelicis animi praua uoluptas').

249–52. nempe can introduce questions expecting an affirmative answer (*OLD* 2), but there may also be an ironic resonance as well (*OLD* 1b). Although van Dam on *Silv.* 2. 1. 184–8, a similar passage, in which Statius soothes Atedius Melior's fears for Glaucias in the underworld, remarks that 'Cerberus, the Furies and Charon are the best-known terrors of a descent into the Underworld', Abascantus' alleged fears are not to be taken seriously, particularly in the light of Priscilla's courage and her comment that she will go to Elysium (193). Thus *tremescat* momentarily evokes the traditional image of Cerberus terrifying the dead (e.g. Virg. *A.* 6. 401, Prop. 4. 5. 3–4, 4. 11. 25, Sil. 3. 35–6 'at Stygius saeuis terrens latratibus umbras | ianitor'), but after the earlier accounts of Priscilla's courage (66–9, 127–34, 173), it is hard to believe that Priscilla would fear anything. Abascantus' anxiety is groundless: compare *Silv.* 2. 1. 184, where Cerberus will not bark at Glaucias. Moreover, Statius only mentions the hound's bark, not its bite (on which see e.g. Hes. *Th.* 311 Κέρβερον ὠμηστήν, 772–3, Virg. *A.* 8. 297), and the description of Charon's craft as 'hospite cumba' adds an incongruous and homely touch to the dread helmsman of the Underworld and his boat, sinisterly called *auidae* at *Silv.* 2. 1. 186; cf. Virg. *A.* 6. 303, where Charon's *cumba* has the alarming epithet *ferruginea*. Similarly *placidus* is unexpected; Charon is normally described with adjectives such as *trux* (e.g. *Silv.* 2. 1. 186). The context of Statius' question to Abascantus and the shift away from a conventional literary treatment to a benign image of Charon are good grounds for detecting gentle irony in these lines.

An approach not used is the philosophical argument that the Underworld offered no reason for fear, since it was in any case mere fable (e.g. Cic. *Tusc.* 1. 10 with Douglas's n., Sen. *Dial.* 6. 19. 4, *Ep.* 24. 18). Juv. 2. 149–52 alleges that belief in the Underworld was extremely rare.

piis: for *pii* meaning 'the virtuous dead', see *OLD* 1b s.v. *pius* and cf. *Silv.* 2. 6. 98, Virg. *A.* 8. 670 'secretosque pios, his dantem iura Catonem', Mart. 12. 52. 11, Sil. 13. 552.

tardior: Statius assures Abascantus that Priscilla will not have to wait to reach Elysium. Contrast Virg. *A.* 6. 322–30, where the Sibyl explains to Aeneas how only those who are buried are taken across the Styx; others have a wait of a hundred years. At *A.* 6. 314 the waiting shades stretch forth their hands 'ripae ulterioris amore'. *tardior* also suggests Charon's reluctance to carry Aeneas (*A.* 6. 388–97); cf. *proturbet* in 251, which perhaps evokes Charon's rejection of some of his passengers at *A.* 6. 316 'ast alios longe summotos arcet harena'. Abascantus' imagined fears are cleverly assuaged by the immediacy of *protinus* (252).

253–4. pio laudata marito | umbra: an echo of 'laudati iuuenis rarissima coniunx' (11); the poem is thus framed by references to both husband and wife as recipients of praise. The phrase is also the final mention of Abascantus' *pietas* towards his wife. *umbra* is effectively held back until the start of the next line (cf. *effigies*, 232); like the juxtaposition of *Priscilla* and *manes* in 258, *umbra* reminds Abascantus of what has happened, in order that he can accept Priscilla's death.

254–7. Receptions of one newly dead in the Underworld by famous figures resident there are not uncommon. Thus in *Od.* 24. 1–204, the shades of the suitors encounter Achilles and Agamemnon in the underworld. Pl. *Ap.* 40 E 7–41 C 4 records Socrates arguing that death is worthwhile because it affords the chance to meet famous judges, poets, unjust victims, as well as those who fought at Troy. At Hyp. *Epitaph.* 35 Leosthenes and his troops encounter the heroes of the Trojan War, and Harmodius and Aristogeiton. In contrast Tib. 1. 3. 57–66 recounts the lover's heaven which he will encounter when Venus leads him to Elysium. Ov. *Am.* 3. 9. 61–4 gives the dead Tibullus rather different companions, the poets Calvus, Catullus, and Gallus (compare *Silv.* 5. 3. 26–7 and 284 for such poetic encounters). At *Silv.* 2. 6. 99–102 Glaucias is envisaged as meeting either his ancestors or the nymphs of Avernus and Proserpina; cf. Sen. *Dial.* 6. 25. 1–2, where Metilius will meet in the heavens not only the Scipiones and Catones, but also his grandfather Cremutius Cordus. A closer parallel is *Culex* 261–2, where the gnat describes its reception in Elysium in language similar to the present passage: 'obuia Persephone comites heroidas urget | aduersas praeferre faces.'

The detail of Persephone ordering the heroines to go forth is ultimately derived from *Od.* 11. 225–7, where Persephone sends the ghosts of wives and daughters of heroes to Odysseus. Statius' *iubet* and *urget* in the *Culex* recall *Od.* 11. 226 ὤτρυνεν γὰρ ἀγανὴ Περσεφόνεια.

ueteres heroidas: tautologous, since the heroic age is the distant past, but *ueteres* is a subtle compliment, suggesting that there may be recent heroines as well, whose number Priscilla might join. Compare Prop. 2. 28. 29–30, where Cynthia is told that if she dies she will have primacy 'Maeonias omnis heroidas inter' (see also Prop. 4. 7. 63 ff.). This interpretation is supported by Statius' use of the same phrase at *Silv.* 3. 5. 44–5, where he explicitly declares his own wife to be the equal of the heroines of myth: 'heu ubi nota fides totque explorata per usus, | qua ueteres, Latias Graias, heroidas aequas?'

Similar passages are found in Ovid: cf. *Am.* 2. 4. 33 'ueteres heroidas aequas', *Tr.* 1. 6. 33 'prima locum sanctas heroidas inter haberes', and see also *Pont.* 3. 1. 105–12, where Ovid compares his wife to mythical heroines.

sacris ... antris: are the abodes of the dead in Elysium, but there may also be a play on a less common meaning of *antrum*, a tomb (*OLD* s.v. *antrum* 4).

lumine purpureo does not denote a purple colour, but the brightness of the light shed by the torches; Virg. *A.* 6. 640–1 has the same phrase in an Elysian setting: 'largior hic campos aether et lumine uestit | purpureo....'; note the similar context of *CIL* vi. 30113 'patri date lucos | in quis purpureus perpetuusque dies'. For this sense of *purpureus* see *OLD* s.v. *purpureus* 3a, Isid. *Orig.* 19. 28. 5 'purpura apud Latinos a puritate lucis uocata'; cf. André (1949), 97–100. The offerings of flowers for Priscilla in Elysium mirror her husband's largesse of spices at her funeral.

258–60. Priscilla's appeals to the infernal powers are not only a counterpart to her appeals to the emperor (*supplice dextra* recalls *supplex aduolueris* in 73), but they are also contrasted with Abascantus' failure to win over the infernal powers at the time of his wife's illness and death (161–9). There Statius expressed the wish that the emperor might have held *omne ... arbitrium* (167–8); the success of Priscilla's intercessions is thus a great achievement. Her devotion to the gods and her efforts on behalf of Abascantus thus continue even after death; cf. *Silv.* 3. 1. 171–2, where Hercules assures Pollius Felix of long life, and 3. 3. 30, where the shade of Claudius Etruscus' father asks for long life for his son.

subit: compare *Silv.* 2. 1. 155 'manesque subibit', 2. 6. 98 'subit ille pios', where Ursus' *puer* reaches Elysium, 5. 3. 74, and Oedipus at *Theb.* 11. 622–3: 'subeam sic Tartara digna | morte'.

261. pacantem terras: cf. Augustus' boast at *Res Gestae* 5. 1 'mare pacaui a praedonibus'. Sen. *Suas.* 1. 4 indicates that *paco* can imply a more total and effective conquest than *uinco*: 'Memento, Alexander: matrem in orbe uicto adhuc magis quam pacato relinquis'. Pacifying was as much a merit as military victory for the Romans; compare Anchises' instruction to Aeneas at Virg. *A.* 6. 851–3.

261–2. iuuenemque relinquas | ipse senex: as Domitian is a god he is not subject to ageing. Domitian is also *iuuenis* at *Silv.* 4. 1. 33. At 4. 1. 46–7 Jove will ensure Domitian's 'longam ... iuuentam', while at 4. 2. 57–9 Statius expresses his wish that Domitian should far exceed the years of his father. At 4. 3. 149–52, the Sibyl foretells not only that the emperor will surpass the years of Nestor, Tithonus, and the Sibyl, but also that he will enjoy 'perpetua ... iuuenta'. Domitian's favourite Earinus expresses similar sentiments at 3. 4. 101–4. These examples all occur near the end of poems, as here. On such wishes for longevity in Statius, see further Scott (1936), 147–56, Geyssen (1995), 126–31; cf. Leberl (2004), 213–14.

senex reflects a change of tone from earlier in the poem. Previously Abascantus has been treated as *iuuenis* (11 n., 183 n.), but now attention turns from his past to his future, reinforcing Priscilla's own instruction to devote himself to the emperor (186–91), and his own resolution to continue in his duties rather than die with Priscilla (207–8).

certae sorores: Abascantus can be confident, since the malevolent Parcae (156, 169) who carried off Priscilla are now tamed and have assented to her prayers. *certae* in particular strikes an optimistic note, in contrast with the earlier vicissitudes of Fortuna, called 'infida leuisque' in 143. The poem thus ends by looking to Abascantus' future; this represents a final admonition against grieving for what is past.

Poem Two

INTRODUCTION

Summary: *Crispinus is departing for Etruria (1–7). His suitability for a public career (8–30). The achievements of his father Vettius Bolanus (30–60). The character and moral qualities of Crispinus (61–96). Crispinus' forensic success and warlike appearance (97–124). Exhortation to Crispinus; his likely travels and companion Optatus; Statius' inability to accompany him (125–67). The imperial messenger's arrival at Crispinus' home; Statius sends Crispinus on his way (168–80).*

Regardless of the reliability of M's title (*Laudes Crispini Vetti Bolani Filii*),[1] *Laudes* usefully underlines the fact that this poem does not offer allegiance to a single genre, but instead exploits aspects of the *propempticon* (an address to a departing friend or beloved), as well as more conventional techniques of praise.[2]

In Rome praise was often manifested on occasions of a public nature; an examination of the poem's relation to epideictic oratory (called *genus demonstratiuum* by Cic. *Inv.* 1. 7 in his threefold division of oratory) may be instructive. Epideictic oratory seems to have occupied a very minor position in republican times;[3] the principal use of the genre was in the *laudatio funebris*, though the literary merits of such speeches were censured by Cicero (*de Orat.* 2. 341).[4] Little attention is devoted to epideictic oratory in oratorical treatises; both Quintilian and the author of the *Rhet. Her.* give surprisingly little space to the topic, although Quintilian does argue that in Rome the possible

---

[1] On the titles, see p. xxxiii above.
[2] Cf. Seager (1983), 52: 'The alternation between directly propemptic and encomiastic elements is the principal structural device employed in the present example, though to posit any crude dichotomy between the two would do great injustice to the subtlety with which Statius handles his material.'
[3] On republican epideictic see G. Kennedy (1972), 21–3.
[4] On the *laudatio funebris*, see Kierdorf (1980).

applications of epideictic techniques are quite varied and suitable for public life ('sed mos Romanus etiam negotiis hoc munus inseruit', *Inst.* 3. 7. 2), giving as examples funeral orations, forensic oratory which can involve praise or censure of witnesses or the accused, and also some of Cicero's denunciatory speeches. A further use of praise in imperial times is the *actio gratiarum*, thanks given to the gods and emperor on the occasion of a consul's assumption of office, first alluded to by Ovid (*Pont.* 4. 4. 35–42); Pliny's *Panegyricus* is an extended example, given on his assumption of the consulship in AD 100.[5]

Statius' poem has little in common with this background. Crispinus is an unlikely candidate for praise, because of his youth and inexperience. Moreover the poem begins by excluding any suggestion of a public occasion (although it concludes with the arrival of the imperial messenger at Crispinus' house). *meus*, in the first line, sets a tone of intimate address and turns praise into a private concern.

The poem begins on a personal note with the announcement that Crispinus is about to depart on a journey to Etruria. Though Statius at once undercuts this, revealing that the journey will not be a long one, the emotional context is made more complex by the remarkable simile which ensues, in which Statius compares this unremarkable event to a more momentous kind of leavetaking, imagining the lament he would make if he were watching his friend depart on a ship (5–7). Thus from the outset Statius challenges generic conventions, by evoking a situation more typical of the propempticon *in a simile*.

The initial emphasis is on Crispinus' departure and Statius' response to it, and this in turn leads to the laudatory portions of the poem, which therefore spring from a personal connection. The overall structure could be represented concisely as a central section of praise of Crispinus' lineage and his own achievements in ll. 8–167, framed by two short scenes of leaving, Crispinus' imminent journey for Etruria (1–7), and the arrival of the imperial messenger which will precede Crispinus' official departure (168–80). Although the poem anticipates Crispinus' forthcoming career, since the initial journey to Etruria is subsumed into his official departure, Statius still speaks of his personal involvement even at the end of the poem, imagining Crispinus' absence from his recitations (160–3).[6]

---

[5] See further G. Kennedy (1972), 428–9, 543 ff.
[6] For discussion of the interchange of public and private aspects of the lives of Statius' addressees, see A. Hardie (1983), 142, 146 ff.

This combination of private emotion and a public context is recommended in the much later treatise of Menander Rhetor. When discussing the *propempticon*, Menander differentiates types of composition according to the standing of the speaker and the person addressed; this criterion determines the precise admixture of advice, encomium, and amatory material.[7] Nevertheless the dangers of too strict a generic approach are illustrated by the lack of agreement between Menander's precepts and Statius' poem. For example, there is no equivalent to Menander's suggestion of an introduction employing various *exempla* of the association of animals and famous friendships between heroes,[8] nor is there any account of the delights of the city which is being left behind. And although there are areas of agreement such as the need for tactful praise of a young man's appearance,[9] and approval of moral qualities,[10] Statius does not describe the marine deities who will accompany the ship, nor does the work end with a prayer.[11]

Comparison with *Silvae* 3. 2 is instructive. Lambasted as 'a protracted exercise on the conventional clichés',[12] it shares the thematic context of the present poem; Maecius Celer is about to depart on a visit to the East where he will be continuing his military career as a legionary legate.[13] As in 5. 2, Statius is affected by the prospect of his friend's departure; however, he begins the poem with an invocation of the assistance of the tutelary deities of the sea (1–49), and then describes the moments before the ship leaves the harbour. In 61–77 he breaks off to use the familiar topos of censure of the first men to travel on the sea, and then resumes further treatment of the ship's departure. In the lines which follow, we hear of the places likely to be visited by Celer, before the poem concludes with Statius' keen anticipation of his friend's return to Italy. Although space does not permit a lengthy defence of *Silvae* 3. 2 against the criticisms it has attracted,

---

[7] Menander 395. 5 ff.: εἶς μὲν ὁ δυνάμενος συμβουλὴν κατὰ μέρος δέξασθαι, τῶν λοιπῶν μερῶν δεχομένων καὶ ἐγκώμια καὶ λόγους ἐρωτικούς, εἰ βούλεται προστιθέναι καὶ ταῦτα ὁ λέγων... For a full discussion of Menander's precepts on the *propempticon* and this poem see A. Hardie (1983), 146 ff., who argues that Statius could have treated Crispinus according to the third of Menander's prescriptions for the genre, since his departure on a military posting would make him equivalent to a departing governor (the example given by Menander for an address from an inferior to a superior). Instead Statius chooses a more personal address, characteristic of an equal relationship, but with praise predominating over advice.

[8] Menander 396. 15 ff. [9] Ibid. 398. 14 ff. [10] Ibid. 397. 21 ff.
[11] Ibid. 399. 1 ff. [12] Quinn (1963), 241 n. 2.
[13] See Nauta (2002), 213 and n. 67.

the point that can be made without prejudice to either side of the argument is that Statius in *Silv.* 3. 2 is very much concerned with the precise moment of departure, as other writers of *propemptica* are; hence the attention given to such motifs as the ship's sailing away, and the appeal to the deities of the sea.

Silvae 5. 2 exploits the propemptic theme quite differently. As has been seen, Statius evokes the *propempticon* in a simile at the outset of the poem, but this move simultaneously suggests a more complex generic affiliation. There is also a challenging *absence* of much of the propemptic apparatus. Thus there is no lengthy prayer to invoke the goodwill of the marine gods, and no mention of a sea voyage, except in the simile. The poem does share with 3. 2 the theme of foreign service, although there is some difference between an account of places in the East likely to be visited by Celer, and a much more speculative examination of the possibilities open to Crispinus across the whole of the empire. Like his father, Crispinus would be able to serve anywhere, from Britain to the Parthian frontiers (132–51).

The possibilities for military service open to Crispinus reflect a further important feature of *Silvae* 5. 2, the young man's potential, which is throughout the poem exploited as a compensation for his youth and lack of significant achievements at the time of the poem's dramatic setting. Whereas Celer had already served in the East on the Parthian frontier, and had achieved some success there (*Silv.* 3. 2. 123–6), Crispinus' achievements are confined to forensic ability, and a *pietas* evinced in his dealings with his own family (5. 2. 74–110). Nevertheless Statius overcomes this paucity of laudatory material; to some extent, Crispinus' inexperience is an advantage, since there are therefore no bounds or limitations to his potential accomplishments.[14] But Celer, making his *second* trip abroad, can hardly be treated in the same fashion; a career in progress is more likely to be compassed by limitations than one which has not yet begun.

Another technique employed is the use of Bolanus, Crispinus' father, as a vehicle for praise. The technique is extremely ancient. Its simplest form is the patronymic; thus Homeric heroes are endowed with the same heroic qualities as their fathers. For the importance of ancestry within a Roman context, one may note for

---

[14] Compare Virg. *A.* 6. 879–81, where Marcellus, who died before he could fulfil his potential, is praised in sweeping terms for the victories which he would have won against any opponent.

example the practice of the consular *Fasti*, which gave the father's *praenomen* after that of the son, and Polybius' remarks on the importance of family *imagines* (Plb. 6. 53–4). Praise of a person's ancestry and parentage on a more elaborate scale is a familiar theme, and a standard recommendation of the rhetoricians (see e.g. *Rhet. Her.* 3. 6. 10, Quint. *Inst.* 3. 7. 10). But whereas praise of a person's ancestry can often be merely a gesture towards convention, in *Silv.* 5. 2 Bolanus has an extremely important role, since it is precisely his example which is to be adopted by his son; his deeds become a substitute for and an anticipation of Crispinus' future achievements. This is reflected in the structural position of Bolanus: whereas the conventions of epideictic posit treatment of ancestry at the beginning of the work, Bolanus occupies, if not a central position, at least an extensive part of the poem's first half, as well as receiving a vignette at 144–9 before the poem's conclusion. Thus Bolanus appears in portions of the poem where one might expect praise of Crispinus.

The only source for the life of Crispinus, as opposed to his father, is the present poem. Given the probable dating of Book 5 to AD 95 or 96,[15] it is apparent that if Crispinus was sixteen (5. 2. 12), his birth occurred around AD 79. Remarkably, in a poem of praise, the audience is reminded of Crispinus' singular and unfortunate upbringing; he was not only bereft of his father in his early youth, before coming of age (64–7), but also left in the care of a mother who, for reasons now obscure (see 78–9 n. below), made a murderous attempt on her son's life with poison. Statius' curious decision to mention an extremely inauspicious and indeed disgraceful incident in Crispinus' family history may have stemmed from the recognition that, since the notoriety of such a *cause célèbre* would have been unavoidable, the best policy would be to allude to the incident in a manner most favourable to Crispinus.

Statius makes much of Crispinus' successful defence of a friend on a charge of adultery brought under the *lex Iulia de adulteriis*. As has been suggested, the youth of Crispinus and his inexperience necessitate discussion of deeds which might not receive mention in an account of a person whose career was already in progress (contrast 3. 2, where Statius is able to refer to Celer's previous military experience on the eastern frontier), but the importance of forensic ability in

---

[15] This dating seems secured by Crispinus' anticipated attendance at a future recital of the *Achilleid* (163), Statius' unfinished epic on Achilles.

its own right is not to be underestimated. The *Laus Pisonis* places even
greater emphasis on the courtroom than this poem,[16] and gives only
the most perfunctory treatment of more warlike exercises, which
rapidly give way to an account of Piso's prowess at the *ludus latruncu
lorum* (*Laus Pis.* 178–208). Crispinus, however, though perhaps not so
proficient and experienced an orator as Piso, is much more emphat
ically presented as a candidate for military success than the other
older man; significantly the aninymous panegyrist pointedly declines
to recount the martial success of Piso's ancestors (*Laus Pis.* 22–4),
whereas continuity between Bolanus' and Crispinus' achievement
is central to the effect of this poem. Furthermore, the nature of the
Roman *cursus honorum* itself testifies to the importance of a mixture of
civil and military experience: it should not be forgotten that even the
magistracies associated with the command of military operations,
such as the consulship, were by no means devoid of civil functions;
note also the praise of Bolanus' civic achievements at *Silv.* 5. 2. 58.

This combination of military experience and less warlike duties is
reflected in the office of *tribunus militum*, for which Crispinus was
destined. The best description of the office in republican times is
given in Polybius' account of the Roman army in Book 6. Annual
elections yielded twenty-four tribunes (6. 19), who were assigned to
the customary four legions; once this process was completed it was the
duty of the tribunes to enrol troops into their respective legions and to
administer an oath of loyalty (6. 20–1); [17] Polybius also ascribes to the
tribunes the appointment of junior officers[18] and describes their
involvement in encampment (6. 26. 10, 6. 34). Only one pair from
the six assigned to one legion would have duties in the field at any one
time (6. 34); the tribunes were also involved in the giving of watch-
words and the inflicting of punishments on the negligent.[19] Thus even

---

[16] *Laus Pis.* 26–9 equates forensic success with military endeavours: 'nec enim, si bella
quierunt, | occidit et uirtus: licet exercere togatae | munia militiae, licet et sine sanguine
haustu | mitia legitimo sub iudice bella mouere.' The same metaphor of war is used at *Silv.*
5. 2. 105 ff. (see nn.) to describe Crispinus' performance in court. It has even been suggested
(though without discussion) by Laguna (1998), 18, 20 that the *Laus Pis.* is an early work of
Statius.

[17] Compare the oath administered to every man in the military camp, in order to
prevent theft (6. 34).

[18] But see Walbank on Plb. 6. 24. 1 for discussion of the role of consuls, whose *de iure* right
of appointment was probably devolved to subordinates, as argued by Mommsen (1887/8), ii.
120 n. 4.

[19] For the powers of the tribunes in the camp, see also Liv. 28. 24. 10, Vegetius 2. 7, *Dig.*
49. 16. 12. 2.

in republican times the conduct of operations in the field was not the sole function of the office,[20] although there was a required period of previous service in the legions for candidates for election.

Under the empire the tribunate assumed greater social importance, largely as a result of the reforms of Augustus, who made available various military posts, including the tribunate, to the sons of senators, the *laticlauii*,[21] so named from their right to wear the broad purple stripe on the tunic.[22] Of the six tribunes assigned to each legion, one would be a *tribunus laticlauius*, whose status appears to have been senior to that of his five colleagues.[23] Suet. *Aug.* 38. 2 is an important account of Augustus' new policy:

liberis senatorum, quo celerius rei publicae assuescerent, protinus uirili toga <sumpta> latum clauum induere et curiae interesse permisit, militiam auspicantibus non tribunatum modo legionum, sed et praefecturas alarum dedit; ac ne quis expers castrorum esset, binos plerumque laticlauios praeposuit singulis alis.

Although the passage evinces genuine concern for military experience, a simultaneous preoccupation with civil duties ('et curiae interesse permisit') is also apparent. Indeed in imperial times the lengthy period of previous military service required in the time of Polybius (five or ten years according to Plb. 6. 19. 1–2) gave way to a wholly different policy whereby the office could be held by those who had completed their eighteenth year, and in the exceptional case of Crispinus by a person of no more than sixteen years of age at the

---

[20] Thus Neumann in *Der Kleine Pauly*, v. 947. 24–53 s.v. Tribunus.

[21] For the office of *tribunus laticlauius* under the empire, see further Passerini in *Diz. Epig.* iv. 570 ff.

[22] It should, however, be noted that the sons of senators were not the only persons permitted to don the *latus clauus*; this privilege was given to ambitious young equestrians as well. Ovid was one such equestrian who did not go on to a senatorial career; see further Luck on Ov. *Tr.* 4. 10. 29–30, Talbert (1984), 76–8. It has been argued that Suet. *Aug.* 38. 2 and D.C. 59. 9. 5 (which records a decision by Gaius to allow equestrians who hoped for senatorial advancement to wear senatorial dress prior to holding any office) taken together imply that Augustus at some point restricted equestrians from wearing the *latus clauus* and confined it to the sons of senators; see e.g. Talbert (1984), 11–12, though in an extended note (p. 513) he is more cautious. At any event, there is no doubt that, in the time of Crispinus, ambitious equestrians could wear the *latus clauus*.

[23] Domaszewski (1967), 29: 'Unter den Tribuni legionis hat der senatorischen Standes, der Laticlavius, den höchsten Rang.' Domaszewski deduces this from *CIL* viii. 18078, where the *tribunus laticlauius* precedes the *praefectus castrorum* and the other tribunes.

time of appointment.[24] In the *cursus honorum*, the office was usually held after one of the various minor magistracies which comprised the vigintivirate (thus Hadrian was *Xuir stlitibus iudicandis* and then tribune, *SHA Hadr.* 2.2),[25] and would habitually lead to the quaestorship,[26] if a senatorial career was to be pursued (cf. Plin. *Ep.* 6. 31. 4 'tribuno militum honores petituro', D.C. 67. 11. 4 Ἰούλιος Κάλουαστρος, κεχιλιαρχηκὼς ἐς βουλείας ἐλπίδα).

Although prior office was not an invariable requirement for the aspiring *tribunus laticlauius*, Crispinus, in view of his age, is nevertheless an exceptional case. As for the future, not all *laticlauii* followed the desired route via the quaestorship to the senate. After the loss of a legion (probably *XXI Rapax*) to the Sarmatians in 92, the Roman army would have included twenty-eight legions.[27] With one *laticlauius* assigned to each legion annually, there would thus have been too many eligible candidates for the twenty quaestorships available each year,[28] and thus there are several instances of iterated military tribunates, as well as one example of the same person holding the office on three occasions, as well as slightly more unorthodox careers;[29] Trajan's 'stipendia decem' (Plin. *Pan.* 15. 3) would have been extraordinary.[30] With Crispinus we cannot be certain of his subsequent

---

[24] There appears to be no precise parallel for Crispinus' youth, though cf. Plin. *Paneg.* 15. 1, where Trajan is described as having been tribune 'teneris adhuc annis'. For the increasing involvement of children in public life under the empire, see Wiedemann (1989), 131–42.

[25] Compare also the career of Tacitus, who was *Xuir stlitibus iudicandis* in AD 76, and is then likely to have been a military tribune, before holding the office of *quaestor Augusti* under Titus: see A. R. Birley (2000), 236–8, who discusses the implications of Alföldy's realization that *CIL* vi. 1574 forms part of the historian's funerary inscription. See also *AE* 1950, 66, with Syme, *RP* v. 563–4, on C. Bruttius Praesens, who was *tribunus laticlauius* in AD 88 and 89 at about the age of 20, having previously been a *IIIuir capitalis*; he would go on to be quaestor in Baetica. Passerini (*Diz. Epig.* iv. 572) gives the epigraphic evidence for the few exceptions to this pattern; sometimes this order, which was most usual in the Flavian period, was reversed. On the vigintivirate, see further Mommsen (1887/8), i. 544, Talbert (1984), 13–14.

[26] Passerini (ibid.) cites *CIL* x. 6658 and ix. 2456 as instances where the quaestorship was held before the military tribunate. Mommsen (1887/8), i. 545 characterizes the office of military tribune as a *Vorschule* for young Romans aiming at a military career.

[27] Webster (1979), 113–14, B. W. Jones (1992), 152–3.

[28] J. M. Carter on Suet. *Aug.* 38.2. Talbert (1984), 30 notes *CIL* vi. 1538 as an example of a memorial for C. Vibius Maximus Egrilianus, who died at the age of 29 and is called *laticlauius* with no evidence of any public office.

[29] See e.g. *CIL* vi. 1440, where a *tribunus laticlauius* successively became *legatus missus ad principem, legatus pro praetore Africae, legatus pro praetore Asiae*, and finally *quaestor*; an even more military career is evinced by *CIL* iii. 4118, where the successive appointments after the tribunate were *legatus Augusti prouinciae Africae pro praetore*, and *legatus Augusti legionis XIII Gem.*

[30] For scepticism, see Syme (1958), i. 31, Campbell (1975), 18.

career, though he has been identified with C. Clodius Crispinus, *cos. ord.* 113;[31] Syme suggests that the *nomen* indicates adoption occurring after Crispinus' mother's attempt on his life.[32] Crispinus' brother was consul in 111.[33] It is not certain whether the M. Vettius Bolanus who restored the *sacrarium* of the Bona Dea was Crispinus' father or his brother (*CIL* vi. 65, 67).

Although the duties of the office in imperial times could involve real danger (Sen. *Ep.* 47. 10 remarks on the many young men of excellent pedigree who perished in Varus' campaign of AD 9), it seems that its functions remained, as they had been in republican times, predominantly administrative (Pliny was ordered 'rationes alarum et cohortium excutere', *Ep.* 7. 31. 2), despite the technical rank of the tribune as a deputy to the legate.[34] The period of service was brief, unlikely to have lasted more than a year. Tac. *Ag.* 5. 1, contrasting Agricola with his indolent contemporaries, suggests that most young men did not take the post seriously; cf. Plin. *Pan.* 15. 1–2. Even for those who did wish to, the opportunity may not have been there. Note the past tenses of Pliny's discussion of the military service for the young in the past at *Ep.* 8. 14. 5 'inde adulescentuli statim castrensibus imbuebantur ut imperare parendo, duces agere dum sequuntur adsuescerent; inde honores petituri adsistebant curiae foribus, et consilii publici spectatores ante quam consortes erant', to be contrasted with his more jaundiced view of military service for the young in his own time (8. 14. 7): 'at nos iuuenes fuimus quidem in castris; sed cum suspecta uirtus, inertia in pretio, cum ducibus auctoritas nulla, nulla militibus uerecundia, nusquam imperium nusquam obsequium, omnia soluta turbata atque etiam in contrarium uersa, postremo obliuiscenda magis quam tenenda.'

If the evidence is missing for an account of Crispinus' subsequent life, a clearer picture of his father Vettius Bolanus[35] can emerge. Though any connection with the M. Bolanus, a friend of Cicero commended by him to P. Sulpicius Rufus (*Fam.* 13. 77. 2–3), can only be putative, Vettius Bolanus appears to have originated in Mediolanum. Several Vettii are attested in the Cisalpine region, and a family connection with Etruria is possible in the light of

---

[31] *PIR* [2] C 1164; cf. Salomies (1992), 154.
[32] Syme, *RP* v. 644; cf. Nauta (2002), 216.
[33] *PIR* [1] V 324. On the issue of the brothers' ages, see *Silv.* 5. 2. 65 n. below.
[34] See Domaszewski (1967), 172 for the ancient evidence.
[35] *PIR* [1] V 323. The *praenomen* was probably Marcus.

Crispinus' projected journey there mentioned at the beginning of the poem.[36]

Though Statius praises Crispinus' distinguished ancestry in 5. 2. 15–28, Bolanus was the first of the family to reach the consulship.[37] Statius' remark (20–1) that Crispinus would embark on a senatorial career 'praecedente tuorum | agmine' may then imply either that there had been predecessors from the family in the senate who had not, however, risen as high as the consulship, or perhaps that there were maternal connections of greater lustre.[38] However, this second explanation is not without its own problems, given that the disgrace of Crispinus' mother would have reflected on her own family as well. If Crispinus' claims to distinguished ancestry did indeed depend on his mother's lineage, her disgrace might explain the vagueness of '*tuorum* agmine'.

Bolanus had a successful career, whose highlight was a suffect consulship in AD 66. Prior to that he was a legate under Corbulo on the Armenian frontier in 62 (Tac. *Ann.* 15. 3. 1); Tacitus does not echo the magnitude of Statius' praise for Bolanus' deeds during the campaign, but the association of Bolanus with Corbulo was an opportunity not to be missed for Statius.[39] On the basis of an inscription in the province of Macedonia, Anthony Birley suggests that Bolanus may have been a proconsul there between his eastern posting and his consulship; the inscription records a bequest made in AD 95 by M. Vettius Philo, to enable an annual celebration of Bolanus' birthday (19 October). This Vettius Philo may have received a grant of citizenship from Bolanus.[40]

In AD 69 Bolanus was sent by Vitellius to take over the command of Trebellius Maximus in Britain; here popularity with his troops seems to have accompanied an inability, or unwillingness, to take effective action in the province (Tac. *Ag.* 8. 1, 16. 5; *Hist.* 2. 65. 2, 2. 97. 1), though Roman intervention in the affairs of the Brigantes and the rescue of Queen Cartimandua would have taken place in his term of office (Tac. *Hist.* 3. 45), and, as noted by Hanson (1987), 18–19, it is necessary to apply some caution to Tacitus' presentation of governors

---

[36] A. R. Birley (1981), 62, Syme, *RP* vii. 597.   [37] Cf. Pistor (1965), 47.
[38] Compare *Silv.* 3. 3. 119–21, where the humble origin of Claudius Etruscus is redeemed by his mother's distinction. Note also Augustus, whose relationship with the *gens Iulia* was far more important than the family of his father Octavius.
[39] On the legates of Corbulo see Syme, *RP* iv. 138; cf. ibid. iii. 1012.
[40] A. R. Birley (1981), 63. However, Eck (1972–3), 240–1 and n. 28 is sceptical.

of Britain prior to his own father-in-law Julius Agricola. In any case Bolanus' difficulties would have been compounded by the departure of troops from Britain to fight for Vitellius in the civil war; Bolanus' own support for Vitellius seems to have been sufficiently unclear for Vespasian to have adlected him to the patriciate[41] on his return from Britain, which he probably left in late 70 or early in 71.[42] Bolanus' final public post was the prestigious governorship of the Roman province of Asia.[43] The time of Bolanus' death is not known, but it preceded Crispinus' assumption of the *toga uirilis* (*Silv.* 5. 2. 66–7).

COMMENTARY

1. Rura meus Tyrrhena petit saltusque Tagetis: cf. Tib. 2. 3. 1 'Rura meam, Cornute, tenent uillaeque puellam'. A. Hardie (1983), 147 suggests that the poem opens by alluding to Hellenistic models for the departure of a beloved to the countryside; see also Cairns (1979), 39–40. Note also Hor. *Carm.* 2. 6. 11–12 'et regnata petam Laconi | rura Phalantho', where it is Horace the aged poet who contemplates retirement in the Italian countryside.

A poem's first word can often be a significant marker of its subject, and hence its generic status; see e.g. Heyworth (1993), 85–6. Examples such as the opening word of Virgil's *Aeneid*, *arma*, are well known. Sometimes, a first word gives a misleading impression of subject and likely genre; the first word of Ovid's *Amores* is also *arma*. Statius uses the same technique, although the overall effect is a complex one. *rura* might conjure up the frivolous world of love poetry, but this impression is immediately undermined by the appearance of the Roman name Crispinus, which would be a highly unusual name for a beloved.[44] The succeeding lines (2–7) give the impression that the poem will be about Crispinus' departure to Etruria, but this is another false start before the real situation of the poem emerges

---

[41] Crispinus was entitled to wear the *luna patricia* (*Silv.* 5. 2. 28). Patrician status was also given by Vespasian to Agricola on his return from Britain (Tac. *Ag.* 9.1). On elevations to the patriciate, see further Eck (1970), 108–9, Talbert (1984), 30. The importance of the availability of patricians for certain priesthoods under the principate is discussed by Pistor (1965), 124–47, Griffin (2000), 35–6; note that Crispinus is mentioned in this poem as one of the Salii (129–31).

[42] A. R. Birley (1981), 64–5.

[43] Dated ibid. 65 n. 19 (following Kreiler) to AD 76. On Bolanus' coinage, see *BMC Ionia* 272–3 for coins from Smyrna (nos. 294–300).

[44] On the use of Greek names see e.g. Lyne (1980), 198–200.

(8–10), Crispinus' forthcoming departure for a public career abroad. Crispinus' initial journey to Etruria thus turns out to be a short visit prior to taking up a military appointment; on the shift in the poem from holiday to an official journey on a posting, see Seager (1983), 53.

Tages was said to be the grandson of Jove, uncovered by the plough of a rustic Etruscan, whereupon he gave various pronouncements to the Etruscan people; see Cic. *Div.* 2. 50 with Pease ad loc. and Wood (1980), who argues for the greater value of the later treatment of Lyd. *Ost.* 2–3 over Cicero's ironic presentation of the myth. Seager (1983), 52 sees reference to Tages as appropriate to the poem's prophetic foretelling of Crispinus' future career; mention of Tages is also suited to the subsequent praise of Crispinus' maturity beyond his years (13 and 68–70), for Cicero describes Tages in similar terms: 'is autem Tages, ut in libris est Etruscorum, puerili specie dicitur uisus, sed senili fuisse prudentia.'

3. sed: so Gronovius, *Diatribe* 30 §196 emends *et* (M). While *et* can be adversative (*OLD* s.v. *et* 14, *ThLL* v/2. 893. 4–894. 3, G. Friedrich (1908), 624–6, H.-Sz. 481 (§256d); for adversative καί, cf. Denniston (1959), 292–3), it is harder to accept here, since the subject changes from lines 2 to 3; indeed Phillimore (in both editions) punctuates with a semi-colon at the end of line 2. *sed* makes clear the striking contrast; the journey is not a long one, but Statius reacts as if he were sending his friend off on a long sea voyage.

secreto ... morsu: cf. Ov. *Met.* 2. 805–6 'quibus inritata dolore | Cecropis occulto mordetur'. For *morsus* denoting mental pain, *OLD* 6b, *ThLL* viii. 1509. 27–49.

4. udaque turgentes impellunt lumina guttas: *impello* can signify both striking or pushing against something, and also driving forward. Vollmer defends M's *guttas*, arguing that each tear swells up (*turgentes*) before being expelled by the eyes (*lumina*). Markland favours the other meaning: 'oculi enim non impellunt *guttas*, sed *guttae impellunt* et feriunt *oculos*.' He accordingly argues that *impellunt* would have to be emended to *expellunt*. But *impello* can signify the instigation of forward motion, as at Luc. 1. 213–14 'paruisque impellitur undis | puniceus Rubicon' (cf. Enn. *Ann.* 581 Sk. 'atque manu magna Romanos impulit amnis'), Plin. *Nat.* 21. 170 'urinam impellit', 24. 180. Thus *guttas* can be retained; translate *impellunt* as 'propel'. For a similar description of the onset of weeping, compare *Silv.* 3. 2. 52–3 'nequeo ... | claudere suspensos oculorum in margine fletus'. In the present passage, *turgentes* is applied to the tears; contrast Prop. 1. 21. 3 where the word describes eyes: 'quid nostro gemitu turgentia lumina torques?', V.Fl. 2. 464 'ad primos turgentia lumina [ς: surgentia flumina *V*] fletus'; cf. Cat. 3. 18 'flendo turgiduli rubent ocelli'.

5. Aegaeas hiemes: also found at *Silv.* 1. 3. 95; cf. e.g. *Theb.* 2. 45 'Aegaeo...gurgite', *Ach.* 1. 390 'Aegaeae...procellae', Hor. *Carm.* 3. 29. 63 'Aegaeos tumultus', Prop. 1. 6. 2 'Aegaeo...salo' (in a propempticon), Tib. 1. 3. 1–2 'Ibitis Aegaeas sine me, Messalla, per undas, | o utinam memores ipse cohorsque mei', Sil. 1. 468 'Aegaeo surgente ad sidera ponto'. See further *ThLL* i. 945. 1–67. The frequent association of the Aegean sea with tempestuous conditions (see e.g. Hor. *Carm.* 2. 16. 1–4 with N.–H., Prop. 3. 24. 12 'naufragus Aegaea...aqua') amplifies the pathos of Statius' complaint.

As the preposition *super* indicates, the *hiemes* are not storms, but stormy waves. Cf. *Silv.* 3. 2. 76 'inque hominem surrexit hiems', 5. 1. 36, Virg. *A.* 2. 110–11 'illos aspera ponti | interclusit hiems'.

6. uela sequar spectemque: *sequar* momentarily suggests accompanying the ship; cf. e.g. Hor. *Epod.* 1. 14 'forti sequemur pectore', Tib. 1. 3. 56 'Messallam terra dum sequiturque mari', and Dido's sinister 'sequar atris ignibus absens' at Virg. *A.* 4. 384 (note also Scylla's 'insequar inuitum' at Ov. *Met.* 8. 141). *spectem*, however, indicates that only the eyes 'follow'; cf. *Silv.* 3. 2. 100 'longisque sequar tua carbasa uotis', *Theb.* 4. 29–30 'stant in rupe tamen; fugientia carbasa uisu | dulce sequi', 5. 483 (see 7 n.), Virg. *A.* 6. 476 'prosequitur lacrimis longe et miseratur euntem', 8. 592 'oculisque sequuntur', Ov. *Ep.* 5. 55 'prosequor infelix oculis abeuntia uela'.

6–7. ab altis | rupibus: for watching the sea from on high, compare *Theb.* 4. 29, 5. 481, *Ach.* 1. 232–6, 2. 23, Cat. 64. 126–7, 64. 241–2. Such scenes of departure can be erotic, as at *Theb.* 4. 25–30, 5. 481–5, *Ach.* 2. 23–6, Ov. *Ep.* 13. 7–24, *Met.* 11. 454–73, Sil. 3. 128–57.

7. oculos longo...aere uinci: Compare the description of departing Argo at V.Fl. 1. 494–7:

> it pariter propulsa ratis, stant litore matres
> claraque uela oculis percussaque sole sequuntur
> scuta uirum, donec iam celsior arbore pontus
> immensusque ratem spectantibus abstulit aer.

Latin poets describe with great facility the disappearance of a ship from view; Valerius' 'celsior arbore pontus' is a splendid encapsulation of the optical effect. Compare *Theb.* 5. 483–5:

> prosequimur uisu, donec lassauit euntes
> lux oculos longumque polo contexere uisa est
> aequor et extremi pressit freta margine caeli.

See also *Silv.* 3. 2. 50–60, 79–80 (with Laguna ad loc.), Ov. *Met.* 11. 466–72. For the land disappearing from the view of those on a ship, see Ov. *Met.* 8. 139, V.Fl. 2. 6–16, Sil. 3. 156–7. Note also Albinovanus Pedo 12–14 (with Courtney, *FLP* ad loc., p. 319) where *aer* is an obstacle to the vision of mariners:

> atque aliquis prora caecum sublimis ab alta
> aera pugnaci luctatus rumpere uisu,
> ut nihil erepto ualuit dinoscere mundo.

Cf. Sen. *Nat.* 1. 3. 7: 'quia infirma uis oculorum non potest perrumpere ne sibi quidem proximum aera, sed resilit.' *ThLL* i. 1048. 72–83 gives examples where *aer* suggests immensity.

querar: A. Hardie (1983), 147 and n. 8 notes that *queror* is a technical term of the σχετλιασμός typical of a propemptic situation; cf *Silv.* 3. 2. 78 'iusta queror', where the context is also the departure of a ship. Note, however, that Statius' complaint is directed against the *aer*, and that he in fact forbears from direct σχετλιασμός; see Seager (1983), 52–3 on ll. 8–14 and 62 ff. for this strategy.

8. quid si: in the editions of Vollmer, Iz.–Fr., Phillimore[1,2], Mozley, Marastoni, and Traglia, *quid* appears as a separate question, so that the next sentence does not end until *quosue darem amplexus* in l. 11.[45] However Shackleton Bailey, (1987), 280 points out that *quid?* is always followed by another question, and accordingly argues that *quid* is part of a single question ending in 10 with *auspicium*. This punctuation usefully inserts an effective pause after *auspicium* and also gives force to the exclamations of 10 and 11, which are now in their own sentence. For *quid si* denoting 'supposing that', see *OLD* s.v. *quis* 13a: in Statius, see *Silv.* 2. 6. 21, 4. 9. 48, *Theb.* 1. 156, 1. 161, 7. 173, 10. 699, *Ach.* 2. 81; cf. *Ach.* 1. 767 'quid nisi'.

9. rudimenta: for *rudimenta* in a military context, compare Virg. *A.* 11. 156–7 (from Evander's address to his dead son Pallas) 'bellique propinqui | dura rudimenta', Liv. 21. 3. 4, Vell. 2. 129. 2, Sil. 1. 549 'naua rudimenta et primos in Marte calores'.

---

[45] Klotz punctuates with a comma after *quid*, but his sentence also runs on until *amplexus* in 11.

10. quanto . . . fletu: in spite of examples such as Apul. *Met.* 1. 12 'nam ut lacrimae saepicule de gaudio prodeunt', these are tears not of joy but of sadness at the prospect of Crispinus' departure, as indicated by *tristia* (12). For the combination of emotions, compare Ov. *Fast.* 6. 463; for the different idea of the pleasure inherent in lamentation, see *Silv.* 5. 5. 56 n.

manarent gaudia fletu: cf. Cat. 101. 9 'accipe fraterno multum manantia fletu'; here, strikingly, it is the abstract *gaudia* which are said to be wet with tears. Note that the imperfect subjunctives *manarent* and *uocaret* (9) imply that the conditional sentences referring to a possible military posting for Crispinus are contrary to fact; this will of course be refuted by the announcement of Crispinus' actual appointment at the end of the poem.

11–12. optanda propinquis | tristia: These lines have caused concern. If one could replace *propinqui* (M) with *uidentur*, the difficulties would disappear (since the point is surely that Crispinus' success is tinged with sadness), but *propinqui* is a highly unlikely substitute even if *uidentur* had been entirely lost as a result of damage, let alone as a corruption. Vollmer defends *propinqui* as an address to Crispinus' relations, but the vocative is intolerably sudden, particularly in view of *tibi* in the next line, while the genitive singular *propinqui* seems far too specific, since there is no other indication that Statius is a kinsman of Crispinus in the poem. *propinquas* (Phillimore) gives peculiar sense ('Do you approach even wished for sad things . . . ?'), even if his *et iamne*, for which there appears to be no parallel, is accepted ('And do you already approach wished for sad things . . . ?'). *propinquant* (Avantius) would give the following sense: 'Do even wished for sad things approach . . . ?'. With both of these conjectures *etiamne* is problematic. *propinquis* (ς) might seem difficult, because mention of the relatives is strange at the climax of a passage where Statius has been talking of how he would respond to Crispinus' departure; it is true, as has been observed, that the rest of the poem offers no evidence that Statius is a *propinquus* ('relation', not 'friend', as misleadingly translated by Mozley; see further 60 n. below). Nevertheless the abrupt introduction of a reference to the *propinqui* can be paralleled at 59–60 below. The sense is: 'Are even desirable things sad for your relations, when your life is already making the circuit of twice eight years?' The *optanda* are the hopes and expectations for Crispinus' career, which turn out to cause sadness (*tristia*), since his career will inevitably require his departure from Rome. For the paradox of a

desirable future career being a cause for concern, cf. Sen. *Con.* 2 pr. 4
'sed quoniam fratribus tuis ambitiosa curae sunt foroque se et honor-
ibus parant, in quibus ipsa quae sperantur timenda sunt', where,
however, the concern is for the danger and uncertainties of political
life, rather than for the sadness at partings imposed by postings
outside Italy envisaged here by Statius. Contrast also the opposite
idea of wishing for normally undesirable experiences at Sen. *Con.* 7. 6.
11: 'quam miseros putatis, iudices, esse quibus duo quae miserrima
sunt optanda fuerunt, tyrannus et raptor?'

12–13. ut octonos bis iam tibi circuit orbes | uita?: M's *ut*
('when') is entirely acceptable Latin, and is preferable to *et* (ς); with
et Statius would be additionally asking Crispinus whether he was
sixteen.

bis iam (M) has been questioned, but without good reason. With
bis non (Saenger), Crispinus' age is less than sixteen, which is unlikely
because appointment to a military tribunate at sixteen is in any case
highly unusual (see introduction above). *uix bis* (Phillimore) involves
additional emendation, and an unhappy verbal jingle.

circuit: 'making a circuit of' (cf. e.g. Virg. *G.* 1. 345 'terque nouas
circum felix eat hostia fruges'), not 'going through'. The tense is
present, since the contracted perfect *circuit* would have a long final
syllable: see further Vollmer ad loc.

orbis: for the meaning 'a year' compare e.g. *Theb.* 1. 505 'dimensis
orbibus anni', *Ach.* 2. 110–11 'uix mihi bis senos annorum torserat
orbes | uita rudis', Virg. *A.* 1. 269–70 'triginta magnos uoluendis
mensibus orbis | imperio explebit', 5. 46 'annuus exactis completur
mensibus orbis', *ThLL* ix/2. 912. 37–51. For the combination of the
number adverb *bis* with the distributive form *octonos* (giving sixteen),
cf. *Ach.* 2. 110 (cited above); Löfstedt (1958), 92 charts the increasing
popularity in post-Ovidian poetry of distributive forms over cardinal
numbers in such multiplicatives. For this way of expressing age, see
Sprenger (1962), 314–15.

**13–14. sed angustis animus robustior annis, | succum-
bitque oneri et mentem sua non capit aetas:** for the laudatory
motif of maturity beyond a young person's years, cf. *Silv.* 2. 1. 38–40
'hinc anni stantes in limine uitae, | hinc me forma rapit, rapit inde
modestia praecox | et pudor et tenero probitas maturior aeuo' with
Vollmer and van Dam ad loc., 2. 1. 109 'multumque reliquerat annos'
with van Dam, Hollis on Ov. *Ars* 1. 185–6, Curtius (1953), 98–101. The
descriptions of Ascanius at Virg. *A.* 9. 311 'ante annos animumque

gerens curamque uirilem' and of Germanicus at Ov. *Pont.* 2. 2. 71
'praeterit ipse suos animo Germanicus annos' are noted examples.
Other Statian instances are *Silv.* 2. 6. 49, 3. 3. 68, 4. 4. 45, *Theb.* 6. 756,
11. 34–5, *Ach.* 1. 148.

angustis: for *angustus* as an indication of temporal brevity cf. e.g.
Silv. 3. 1. 18 'angusti...menses', Virg. *G.* 4. 206 'angusti terminus
aeui', *ThLL* ii. 63. 35–44. The physical sense of *angustus* ('narrow') is
also suggested, particularly by *non capit*: Crispinus' age is not sufficient
to contain or hold back his mind; cf. the translations of Slater 'your
mind is too great for them [*sc.* years]' and Colom-Dolç 'la teva edat
sucumbeix al seu pes i no pot contenir el teu seny'.

robustior: for this contrast between the body (here referred to by
annis, physical age) and the mind (*animus*) compare e.g. *Silv.* 1. 4. 54–5
'animique in membra uigentis | imperium', Sal. *Cat.* 1. 2, 2. 8, Cic.
Rep. 6. 26, Sen. *Dial.* 6. 23. 2, *Laus Pis.* 259 'meis animus constantior
annis', Sil. 8. 465 'astu superauerat annos'. Here the superiority of the
mind is felicitously expressed in physical language (*robustior*); cf. Sil. 3.
603 'tum iuuenis magno praecellens robore mentis'. For the notion of
deeds beyond one's years, compare Sil. 4. 426–7 'iam credit puer
atque annos transcendere factis | molitur'.

succumbitque oneri: Crispinus' mind takes on itself the burden
of duty and responsibility imposed on him by a public career. The
metaphor (cf. Liv. 6. 32. 2 'cui succumbere oneri coacta plebes') is
agricultural, as at Prop. 2. 34. 47 'sed non ante graui taurus succumbit
aratro'.

15. non te series inhonora parentum: in fact Crispinus'
father Bolanus was the first of the family to be consul, holding a
suffect consulship in 66. Statius can either be referring here to
members of the family who had been in the Roman senate but
without reaching the consulship, or to distinguished maternal rela-
tions (though compare the more explicit distinction made at *Silv.* 4. 4.
75 'stemmate materno felix, uirtute paterna'); see further the intro-
duction to *Silv.* 5. 2 above. For the litotes in a reference to lineage,
compare *Silv.* 3. 3. 115 'nec uulgare genus', 5. 3. 117 'nec sine luce
genus'.

series . . . parentum: cf. *Theb.* 6. 268–9 'exin magnanimum
series antiqua parentum | inuehitur', where images of heroes are
carried in a manner analogous to the carrying of *imagines* at Roman
funerals. Here Statius praises Crispinus' lineage; contrast *Silv.* 3. 3.
43–6, where Statius excuses a *lack* of lineage; for the rhetorical

technique of praising or blaming such qualities as lineage or appearance according to need, see e.g. *Rhet. Her.* 3. 7. 13–14.

16. priscae lucis egentem: *egere* and *carere* are several times used in conjunction with *lux*. With *egere* the phrase normally denotes absence of light, as at Ov. *Met.* 1. 17 'lucis egens aer', Avien. *Arat.* 1558 'cedit uis inclita solis, | lucis egens' or V.Fl. 4. 427, where 'lucis egentem' refers to the blindness of Phineus. At *Theb.* 4. 486 'lucis egentes' is applied to the shades in the infernal regions, and this usage is more typical of *carere*. Lucretius was the first to use the phrase of the dead at 4. 39 'simulacraque luce carentum', repeated by Virg. *G.* 4. 472 and echoed at 4. 255 'corpora luce carentum'. Statius uses a familiar phrase but gives a different meaning to *lux*.

This transferred usage of *lux*, denoting nobility of lineage, is found in both prose and verse, as at *Silv.* 5. 3. 117 and Sil. 8. 246 'sine luce genus'. V. Max. 3. 3 *ext.* 7, on *nobiles* who 'in aliquod reuoluti dedecus acceptam a maioribus lucem in tenebras conuertant', inverts a trope employed by Cic. *Deiot.* 30: 'Deiotarus uestram familiam abiectam et obscuram e tenebris in lucem euocauit'; cf. Sen. *Ben.* 3. 32. 2: 'tenebras . . . natalium suarum clara luce discuteret'. In these last two passages *lux* denotes merit, not pedigree. At *Silv.* 1. 4. 69–70 'nec origo latet, sed luce sequente | uincitur et magno gaudet cessisse nepoti', the meaning of *lux* seems somewhere between the two ideas; see further Henderson (1998*a*), 82.

18. trabeaque recens: Krohn; M's *trabeque ac remis* is meaningless. But *trabeaque recens* might be felt to give an odd sense. If a person is *born* to equestrian stock, how can he also be *trabea recens*? Håkanson (1969), 127–8 argues that *recens* is equivalent to *recens a*, which could be translated as 'fresh from' comparing Tac. *Ann.* 4. 52. 2, where 'is, recens praetura' refers to Domitius Afer, who had been praetor in the previous year.[46] But the analogy between *recens praetura*, referring to a magistracy with a fixed term of office, and *trabea recens*, 'fresh from being an equestrian', is not satisfactory, especially as senators technically remained equestrians, as indicated by Cato's decision to deprive the ex-consul L. Cornelius Scipio of his horse during his censorship in 184 BC (Liv. 39. 44. 1, Astin (1978), 81). In any case, 'fresh from being an equestrian' would also be true of a person who was 'sanguine cretus turmali', and is therefore otiose, since it adds

---

[46] See also Koestermann on Tac. *Ann.* 1. 41 and 4. 52; cf. *Theb.* 4. 169 'Hydra recens obitu', translated somewhat tendentiously by Håkanson as 'fresh from death'.

nothing to what is in any case indicated by the subsequent 'aduena'. It is better if *recens* denotes a person new to equestrian status as well (for *recens* used with an ablative thus cf. e.g. Stat. *Theb.* 4. 169 'Hydra recens obitu', Tac. *Ann.* 1. 41. 3 'ut erat recens dolore et ira' with Goodyear ad loc.), suggesting a meteoric rise through the equestrian order to the senate. The *-que* in *trabeaque* thus corresponds to 'or' (on which see Fordyce on Cat. 45. 6, Kenney on Lucr. 3. 150), as in Mozley's 'no child of equestrian blood or but newly granted the robe of knighthood'. Instead of being either from a family of long equestrian lineage or (even worse) from a family of parvenu equestrians, Crispinus is the son of a senator, and therefore not an *aduena*.

On the *trabea*, said to have been worn by Roman kings (and especially linked with Romulus), and also worn by the Salii at their festival in March, see Serv. *A.* 7. 188, 612 (who distinguishes three kinds of *trabea*), D.H. 2. 70. 2–3, Ov. *Fast.* 1. 37, 6. 375, *Met.* 14. 828, Juv. 8. 259 with Courtney, Ogilvie on Liv. 1. 41. 6, Alföldi (1952), 36–53, Warren (1970), 60 and (1973), 592, 613–14, Wrede (1988). Its origins may lie in the account given by V. Max. 2. 6. 2 of the custom of wearing purple tunics to battle in order to conceal wounds from the enemy. The equestrian *trabea* was seen on formal occasions such as the *transuectio* on the Ides of July: see D.H. 6. 13. 4–5, V. Max. 2. 2. 9, Stat. *Silv.* 4. 2. 32–3 with Coleman, Mart. 5. 41. 5. The *trabea* also appears as equestrian mourning dress for Germanicus (Tac. *Ann.* 3. 2. 2; see also *AE* 1949, 215, l. 57). Domitian refused a senatorial decree that equestrians wearing the *trabea* should accompany his lictors when he held the consulship (Suet. *Dom.* 14. 3).

paupere clauo: exaggerated abuse, since the right to wear the *angustus clauus*, the narrow stripe on the tunic, was dependent on the equestrian property qualification of 400,000 HS (Pliny, *Ep.* 1. 19. 2 with Sherwin-White's n.). Contrast Statius' pleasant description of the equestrian Septimius as 'contentus <artae> lumine purpurae' (*Silv.* 4. 5. 42). For the senatorial laticlave, cf. *Silv.* 3. 2. 124 'notus adhuc tantum maioris lumine claui'.

20. aduena pulsasti: compare *Silv.* 4. 8. 62 'Romulei limen pulsare senatus', 5. 3. 210; a closer verbal parallel is *Ach.* 1. 10 'neque enim Aonium nemus aduena pulso' (Statius' renewed appeals to the Muses).

aduena: here 'newcomer'. Although *aduena* can be neutral, words denoting strangers or foreigners often assume negative overtones. Sometimes the precise implications of *aduena* are hard to determine;

thus at Cic. *De Orat.* 1. 249 (cf. *Agr.* 2. 94) 'ne in nostra patria peregrini atque aduenae esse uideamur', *aduenae* may be pejorative, but perhaps Cicero is merely expressing the fear that one may in one's own land be indistinguishable from a stranger. Note too Claudius' remark at Tac. *Ann.* 11. 24. 4 'aduenae in nos regnauerunt', when speaking in favour of extending senatorial privileges among the Gauls.

But Cicero and others also use the word as a direct term of abuse. Thus at *Tusc.* 5. 34 Zeno of Citium is called 'aduena quidam et ignobilis uerborum opifex'. Three of the four examples in Virgil have unfavourable overtones: at *Ecl.* 9. 2–3 Moeris laments the arrival of an 'aduena nostri | ... possessor agelli', while at *A.* 4. 591 Dido laments the humiliation she has suffered from the *aduena* Aeneas, who is also called 'improbus aduena' by Tolumnius at *A.* 12. 261. The fourth example in Virgil is *A.* 7. 38–9, where the narrator refers to the 'aduena ... exercitus' of the Trojans reaching Italy.

ThLL i. 829. 54 ff. also has an entry for the proper name Aduena, which frequently appears in inscriptions as a name for slaves, both male and female. The use of the word in servile names can hardly have increased its cachet.

21–6. The simile of the racehorse not only praises Crispinus, but also points to the glories which await him. As noted by Humphrey (1986), 156–7, the moment before the release of chariot teams from the *carceres* was a time of eager expectation, both from spectators and from the horses as well: see e.g. Enn. *Ann.* 79–83 Sk., Ov. *Met.* 2. 153–5, *Tr.* 5. 9. 29–30, Luc. 1. 293–5, Sil. 16. 314–16. Statius' focus on the moment before the race begins is an entirely appropriate parallel for Crispinus, who is on the threshold of a public career.

Mention of the physical attributes and breeding of the horse evokes Virgil's precepts on horses at *G.* 3. 75–94 on the desired appearance of the animal and 95–122 on breeding and competitive performance; note especially the description of the race at *G.* 3. 103–12. The references to racing also suggest the chariot race in *Theb.* 6. 296–549 and its precursor, *Il.* 23. 262–650. For epic similes referring to horses, see *Il.* 6. 506–11, A.R. 3. 1259–61, Enn. *Ann.* 535–9 (with Skutsch ad loc.), Virg. *A.* 11. 492–7, Stat. *Ach.* 1. 277–82, where heroes are compared to horses, typically going out from their stables into the open plain (the horse in Apollonius is eager for battle). Closer parallels are *Il.* 22. 162–4, where Hector and Achilles are likened to horses competing in a race, Grat. 227–9, where a hunting dog on the scent is compared to a four-horse team at the Isthmian Games, 'quam gloria patrum | excitat' (228–9), Luc. 1. 293–5, where Caesar, inflamed with still more passion for war by Curio's speech, is compared to a horse at Olympia waiting for the race to begin, and Sil. 15. 210–13, where Scipio is compared to a victorious horse at Olympia after his dream of his dead father. The emphasis in the present passage on ancestry and glory perhaps indicates a didactic as well as laudatory purpose in the simile. Note also Hor. *Carm.* 4. 4. 30–1 'est in equis patrum | uirtus', Plin. *Nat.* 8. 159 (on horses) 'nam in circo ad currus iuncti non dubie intellectum adhortationis et gloriae fatentur', Mart. 6. 38. 7–8 'acris equi suboles magno sic puluere gaudet, | sic uitulus molli proelia fronte cupit', where Regulus' son is likened to promising young animals.

21. Romulei: *Romuleus*, suggesting a continuity with the ancient past, is a synonym for *Romanus*; see *Silv.* 1. 1. 79, 3. 3. 165, 4. 2. 32, 4. 4. 4, 4. 6. 79, 4. 8. 62, 5. 1. 87, 5. 2. 161, 5. 3. 176 for varying degrees of specific reference to Romulus. Allusion to Romulus neatly projects the lineage of the horse (and therefore Crispinus) into the remote and distinguished Roman past.

23–4. cuius de stemmate longo | felix demeritos habet admissura parentes: *demereor* can take both an accusative of the person whose favour is won and an instrumental ablative; see e.g. Suet. *Ves.* 2. 3 'praetor infensum senatui Gaium ne quo non genere demereretur', *ThLL* v/1. 497. 13 ff. (and especially section 2b). However, the prepositional *de stemmate longo* cannot be construed in this way; in any case the parents of the young horse have won favour (*demeritos* is deponent) not because of their lineage, but because of their own successes, in keeping with the ancestral honours mentioned in line 22, so the phrase cannot be treated as analogous to *bene mereor de aliquo*. It is best to treat *de stemmate longo* as adverbial; the point is that the good fortune and quality (*felix admissura*) of the offspring comes from a long line of successful forebears. Translate 'whose lucky siring from a long pedigree has parents who have won favour'.

24. admissura: a technical term for the admitting of a male to a female animal, used by Varro and others not only of horses, but also of donkeys, goats, cattle, swine, and even peafowl; see *ThLL* i. 748. 24 ff. Here the meaning seems closer to 'siring'. Nevertheless the appearance of such a technical term is striking.

25. illi omnes acuunt plausus: *illi*, proposed by Håkanson (1973), 78 is preferable to M's *illum*. While *illum omnes acuunt plausus* is possible ('all their applause makes him keener'), since *acuo* can refer to the stimulation of animals,[47] the lines that follow refer to the way the horse is received by the audience, not to its actual behaviour. With Håkanson's *illi*, the thought moves from observable fact (Håkanson paraphrases 'when he enters all loudly applaud') to the hyperbole of the *puluis* and *metae* delighting in his arrival. Construe *omnes* as nominative and *plausus* as accusative; for *acuunt* conveying an intensification of applause compares V.Fl. 2. 172 'condensae fletus acuunt'; note too Virg. *A.* 12. 590 (on bees) 'magnisque acuunt stridoribus iras'. Håkanson's argument for construing *plausus* as accusative seems confirmed by *ipse* later in the line, the emphasis being appropriate to the conceit of not only the spectators, but even the *puluis* and *metae* responding to the horse. Moreover, with *illi*...*illum* there is a proper balance in sense: the spectators increase their applause at his arrival, and the very dust rejoices in his presence.

uolantem: for the hyperbole of a flying horse or chariot, cf. e.g. *Il.* 23. 372 οἱ δ' ἐπέτοντο κονίοντες πεδίοιο, Virg. *G.* 3. 107 'uolat ui feruidus axis', 3. 181, *A.* 12. 334; cf. *Theb.* 6. 521 '[Amphiaraus] uolat ocior Euro'. For the disturbance of dust or sand, see e.g. *Theb.* 6. 411, *Il.* 23. 365–6, S. *El.* 714–5, Virg. *G.* 3. 110, Grewing on Mart. 6. 38. 7.

26. incuruae . . . metae: the epithet alludes to the conical shape of the *metae* (cf. *Theb.* 6. 440 'flexae . . . metae'), the two turning posts at either end of the course, on which see further Humphrey (1986), 255–9, who notes (255) that, by the time of Augustus, 'the *metae* at each end of the arena consisted of not one but three cones on a high base'. Before the Secular Games of Claudius in AD 47 (Tac. *Ann.* 11. 11), the *metae* of the Circus Maximus had been made of wood and tufa; Claudius gilded them (Suet. *Cl.* 21. 3).

gaudent: for *gaudeo* with an inanimate subject see *ThLL* vi/2. 1708. 19 ff. Statius' fondness for personification using *gaudere* is noted by van Dam on *Silv.* 2. 2. 21–5. Here *agnoscere* heightens the effect: Statius ascribes not only emotion but recognition to the dust and turning-posts. The horse is recognized not because he has competed before, but because of his lineage. For this type of compliment, cf. *Silv.* 4. 2. 44–5, where Domitian would be recognized even by barbarian enemies and foreigners, 5. 2. 46 below.

---

[47] Courtney adduces Mart. Cap. 9. 925 (an auditory stimulus) 'tubas non solum sonipedes atque bella, sed agonas acuere certamenque membrorum nunc quoque compertum'; see also *ThLL* i. 461. 64 ff.

27. clare puer: as with *puer inclite* (8), this is a striking juxtaposition of words, because a *puer* can scarcely have had the chance to win such a reputation. Compare Hor. *Carm.* 1. 20. 5, where N.–H. argue for the *recentior* reading 'clare Maecenas eques' over 'care', on the grounds that *clarus* (normally reserved for senators) is an impressive compliment to the equestrian Maecenas, though see also Cairns (1992), 96. For the range of usage which can be covered by the use of *puer* as an address, see Dickey (2002), 191–6, who notes (192) that 'The addressee may be a baby, a boy, or a youth just old enough to enter battle, like Vergil's Pallas.'

28. luna: the ivory crescent placed on the strapwork of the *calceus patricius*, which confirms Crispinus' patrician status. For ancient explanations of the symbol, see Plu. *Quaest. Rom.* 76 (= *Mor.* 282 A–B); Isid. *Etymol.* 19. 34. 4 suggests that the emblem refers to the original complement of one hundred (C) patrician senators.

References to the shoe itself are scattered and confusing. Juv. 7. 192 (with Mayor, Courtney ad loc.) 'adpositam nigrae lunam subtexit alutae' and Hor. *S.* 1. 6. 27–8 'nigris medium impediit crus | pellibus' seem to refer to black straps (for *pellis* thus, cf. Mart. 1. 49. 31 'lunata nusquam pellis', Juv. 3. 149–50 'si toga sordidula est et rupta calceus alter | pelle patet'), while Mart. 2. 29. 7–8 refers to a red shoe: 'non hesterna sedet lunata lingula planta, | coccina non laesum cingit aluta pedem'. Isid. *Etymol.* 19. 34. 4 and 10 discusses the *calceus patricius* and the red *mulleus* separately. Alföldi (1952), 54–68 argues that they refer to the same shoe (cf. Talbert (1984), 219–20), but see Goette (1988), who documents the presence of three distinct types of shoes in iconographic evidence: *calceus patricius, calceus senatorius,* and *calceus equester.*

29. Tyrios ex more sinus: the *toga praetexta*, worn by children and holders of curule magistracies; see 5. 2. 66 n. below. The epithet refers to the border of the toga, 'Tyrian' because the crimson dye was extracted from the *murex*, a shellfish found in Phoenicia (Mayor on Juv. 1. 27) which yielded the highest quality; for the process of obtaining the dye, see Plin. *Nat.* 9. 133–5, André (1949), 92–3. Though André (1949), 103 argues that *Tyrius* can be used both as a technical term in Latin (referring to the Tyrian variety) and also in poetry to mean no more than 'purple', in a passage such as this it seems unnecessary to lose any of the prestige significance of *Tyrios ex more sinus*, whether or not Crispinus actually wore the Tyrian dye; for the significance of purple as a mark of status in Rome see Rheinhold

(1970), 37–61. The expensiveness of the Tyrian variety is indicated by
Plin. *Nat.* 9. 137, referring to Cornelius Nepos, who wrote that the
double-dyed (*dibapha*) variety was first seen in Rome in the consulship
of Cicero (63 BC) and could not be bought for less than 1000 denarii a
pound; for its appearance, note Plin. *Nat.* 9. 135: 'laus ei summa in
colore sanguinis concreti, nigricans aspectu idemque suspectu reful-
gens; unde et Homero purpureus dicitur sanguis'. Other instances of
Tyrian purple in Statius are: *Silv.* 1. 2. 151 'Tyrii moderator liuet aeni',
3. 4. 55 'Tyrios infundit amictus', 4. 4. 76–7 'iam te blanda sinu Tyrio
sibi curia felix | educat et cunctas gaudet spondere curules' (in a
similar passage anticipating the future career of Vitorius Marcellus'
son, Geta), 5. 1. 215, *Theb.* 6. 62, 7. 656 (see Smolenaars's n.) 'et rubet
imbellis Tyrio subtemine thorax', in a description of the Bacchic
priest Eunaeus, the only reference in Statius to Tyrian purple which
draws on the negative associations of purple as luxurious and hence
effeminate; for this moralizing tradition of hostility to purple and
ineffectual attempts at sumptuary legislation in Rome, see Rheinhold
(1970), 41–52. For further references and bibliography on Tyrian
purple see Grewing on Mart. 6. 11. 7; for a sense of more recent
fascination with ancient purples, see Finlay (2002), 390–434.

tunicamque potentem: Crispinus' tunic is 'powerful', because
as the son of a senator he wears the laticlave.

30. parabat: Courtney (1984), 337–8 argues against M's *parabat*,
because the *magna exempla* would have been performed before the
youth of Crispinus, who was probably born in 79 or 80, given the
dating of this poem, when he is sixteen, to the period between summer
95 and Domitian's death in September 96.[48] But the imperfect *parabat*
can be conative or even inceptive in meaning; the imperfect is
furthermore appropriate to the continuous nature of Bolanus' exem-
plary conduct. The perfect tenses after *parabat* occasion no difficulty,
since they are appropriate to the single completed actions which
make up the continuous process of Vettius' setting examples to his
son. Thus *parabat* should be retained.

31–2. iuuentam | protinus ingrediens: *ingredior* can be
used temporally, sometimes with *annus* in singular or plural as at
V. Max. 5. 4. 2 'uixdum annos pubertatis ingressum', but also with
less precise expressions. See further e.g. Tac. *Ann.* 3. 29. 1 'iam

---

[48] See p. 177 above, Vollmer (1898), 9, Coleman (1988), p. xxi. Bolanus' last post was the
governorship of Asia (for its dating, see p. 183 n. 43 above).

ingressum iuuentam', 6. 46. 1 'sed nondum pubertatem ingressus', *ThLL* vii/1. 1572. 1–15.

32. pharetratum...Araxen: the bow is the traditional weapon of Rome's eastern enemies; cf. e.g. *Silv.* 1. 4. 78–9 'arcu horrenda fugaci | Armenia', 3. 2. 126 'et Eoas iaculo damnare sagittas', 4. 4. 30–1, Hor. *Carm.* 2. 13. 17–18, Virg. *G.* 3. 31 'fidentemque fuga Parthum uersisque sagittis', 4. 290 'quaque pharetratae uicinia Persidis urget', Prop. 3. 4. 17, 3. 9. 54, 4. 3. 65–6, Sen. *Oed.* 118–19, Sil. 10. 11–12. For the Greek tradition of the Persians as archers, see Broadhead on A. *Pers.* 26, Hdt. 1. 136. 2, and Hordern on Tim. *PMG* 789, who notes that Persian inscriptions point to prowess with the spear as well. The river Araxes can symbolize both the frontier and the enemy:[49] cf. *Silv.* 1. 4. 79 'et patiens Latii iam pontis Araxes' with Henderson (1998*a*), 84 and n. 182, Virg. *A.* 8. 728 'et pontem indignatus Araxes', Prop. 4. 3. 35 'et disco, qua parte fluat uincendus Araxes', Luc. 1. 19 'sub iuga iam Seres, iam barbarus isset Araxes', 7. 188 'Armeniumque bibit Romanus Araxen', 8. 431 'cum primum gelidum transibis Araxen'. The river's association with bitter cold (cf. Sen. *Med.* 373, *Phaed.* 58, *Oed.* 428) and its history of resistance to bridges (Serv. Auct. *A.* 8. 728 notes previous attempts by Xerxes and Alexander) made it a potent symbol.

33. indocilemque fero seruire Neroni: like *docilis* (5. 1. 1 n.) *indocilis* can govern an infinitive: cf. *Theb.* 6. 313 'illi etiam ferus indocilisque teneri', Hor. *Carm.* 1. 1. 18 'indocilis pauperiem pati', Luc. 5. 539 'indocilis priuata loqui'. For the thought compare Hor. *Carm.* 2. 6. 2 'Cantabrum indoctum iuga ferre nostra' with N.–H.

As well as evoking Nero's treatment of Corbulo and the latter's suicide (D.C. 63. 17. 5–6), *fero*, ironically juxtaposed with *seruire*, is also an ingenious compliment to Vettius Bolanus, because Armenia is such a redoutable opponent that it is *indocilis* even to the savage Nero. Emphasis on the bellicosity of the Armenians also increases the glory of Bolanus.

34. rigidi summam Mauortis agebat: *summam Mauortis* is a variant on *summa belli*, denoting overall conduct of military operations: see e.g. Caes. *Gal.* 2. 4. 7 'ad hunc propter iustitiam prudentiamque suam totius belli summam omnium uoluntate deferri',

---

[49] Note that geographical features were represented in triumphal processions: see e.g. Hor. *Carm.* 2. 9. 20 with N.–H., Prop. 2. 1. 31–2, Ov. *Ars* 1. 220 with Hollis's n., *Tr.* 4. 2. 37–8, Flor. *Epit.* 2. 13. 88.

Liv. 29. 4. 3 'summae belli molem adhuc in Sicilia esse', *OLD* s.v. *summa* 6a–b. Slightly different is Virg. *A.* 12. 572, where Aeneas describes Ardea as 'hoc caput, o ciues, haec belli summa nefandi' (cf. Ov. *Pont.* 2. 1. 46 'belli summa caputque Bato'), where *summa belli* refers to the place or person at the centre of the war. Here Mars' attribute, *belli*, is replaced by his name; Statius uses the archaic and poetic form *Mauors* frequently in the epics, but only twice in the *Silvae*, here and at 128 below.

   Schrader conjectured *habebat* for M's *agebat* (Haupt records no discussion of the point), but although one might compare Liv. 4. 46. 3 ('donec castigantibus legatis tandem ita comparatum est ut alternis diebus summam imperii haberent'), the parallel is not for *summa belli*, much less *summa Mauortis*. *agebat* (cf. Nep. *Han.* 8. 3 'Antiochus autem si tam in agendo bello consiliis eius parere uoluisset, quam in suscipiendo instituerat ... ') suggests more activity than *habebat*, as is appropriate to the vigorous context ('rigidi ... Mauortis, ... comitem belli sociumque laborum').

   35. Corbulo: for Cn. Domitius Corbulo's eastern campaigns under Nero which culminated in the homage of Tiridates (AD 63), see Tac. *Ann.* 13. 35–41, 14. 23–26, 15. 1–17, 24–31, with Griffin (1984), 226–32, for a modern overview of Nero's eastern policy; on Corbulo's career and associations, see *PIR²* D 142, Syme, *RP* ii. 803–24. Corbulo's legendary status, the consequence of success on the notoriously difficult eastern frontier, is attested by Juv. 3. 251. He committed suicide in AD 67, having become too successful for Nero to tolerate (D.C. 63. 17. 5–6).

   Corbulo's daughter Domitia Longina (*PIR²* D 181) became Domitian's wife (Suet. *Dom.* 1. 3, D.C. 66. 3. 4), Domitian having taken her from her first husband L. Aelius Lamia Plautius Aelianus (*PIR²* A 205) prior to Vespasian's victorious arrival in Rome after the civil war; Lamia was subsequently killed by Domitian when emperor (Suet. *Dom.* 10. 2), allegedly for 'ueteres et innoxios iocos' relating to the imperial couple. Some asserted that there had been a liaison between Domitia and Titus (Suet. *Tit.* 10. 2), but she denied this vehemently and perhaps even with regret: 'sed nullam habuisse persancte Domitia iurabat, haud negatura, si qua omnino fuisset, immo etiam gloriatura, quod illi promptissimum erat in omnibus probris'. At the beginning of Domitian's reign, Suet. *Dom.* 3. 1 (cf. 13. 1) and D.C. 67. 3. 1–2 relate that Domitia committed adultery with the *pantomimus* Paris. After Domitian was dissuaded from executing her (D.C. 67. 3. 1) by one Ursus (probably L. Julius Ursus, consul for the first time in AD 84; see *PIR*² I 630, Syme, *RP* vii. 559, B. W. Jones (1992), 40–2), she was put aside before being recalled, though note the scepticism of B. W. Jones (1992), 34–5 about this scandal. However, the fate of Aelius Lamia, and the anecdote in Suet. *Dom.* 10. 4 about the younger Helvidius Priscus (*PIR*² H 60), executed after Agricola's death in AD 93 for writing a mythological farce on the story of Paris and Oenone which was a veiled reference to Domitian's marriage and his alleged intrigue with his niece Julia (Tac. *Ag.* 45. 1; see also Syme, *RP* vii. 575, B. W. Jones (1992), 38–40), point to the sensitivities which surrounded the marriage, even after the reconciliation. In spite of Domitia's continuing appearances in the *acta* of the Arval Brotherhood, and the divine honours paid to her in the east, on which see Scott (1936), 84–6, it is perhaps unsurprising that allusions to Domitia in Statius (who himself had been connected with Paris, as indicated by Juv. 7. 87, 'intactam Paridi nisi uendit Agauen'; cf. Martial's epigram for the dead Paris, 11. 13, only published after Domitian's death) and Martial are very rare: see Mart. 6. 3, with Grewing (1997), 84–6, where the poet hopes for the birth of an heir to the emperor, and Stat. *Silv.* 3. 4. 18–19 (the only reference to her in the *Silvae*) 'Iuppiter Ausonius pariter Romanaque Iuno | aspiciunt et uterque probant' in the poem addressed to Flavius Earinus. Though some traditions associated Domitia with complicity or knowledge of the plot that led to her husband's death (Suet. *Dom.* 14. 1, D.C. 67. 15. 2–4), B. W. Jones (1992), 37 notes that she continued to style herself as Domitian's wife even after his *damnatio memoriae*, if the brick-stamps from the 120s which mention 'Domitiae Domitiani' or 'D D' (*CIL* xv. 548–58) refer to her; contrast the inscription from Gabii of AD 140 which refers to a shrine in honour of her memory, *CIL* xiv. 2795. 1–2 (= *ILS* 272), where she is described as 'Domitiae Augustae, Cn. Domiti Corbulonis | fil(iae)', with no reference to Domitian.

   sociumque laborum: so Tiberius described Sejanus, according to Tac. *Ann.* 4. 2. 3; cf. Vell. 2. 127. 3 with Woodman, D.C. 58. 4. 3 κοινωνὸν τῶν φροντίδων. For other uses of the phrase, cf. Luc. 2. 346–7 'non me laetorum sociam rebusque secundis | accipis: in curas uenio partemque laborum', Plin. *Nat.* 8. 180 (on the ox) 'socium enim laboris agrique culturae habemus hoc animal' (note too Ael. *VH* 5. 14 τῶν ἐν ἀνθρώποις καμάτων κοινωνός), Tac. *Ger.* 18. 3 (on wives in Germany) 'admonetur uenire se laborum periculorumque sociam', Sil. 12. 378 'sociosque laboris Hiberos'.

37. uni: M's *illi* would refer to Bolanus, giving an awkward transition from 36, where *ille* denoted Corbulo. *uni* (Heinsius) is preferable (Courtney compares *unus* in 45), and complimentary to Bolanus, Corbulo's only adviser, and is supported by 'unam' in the description of Camilla's confidante, Acca, and 'uni' in Statius' description of Thiodamas, both cited immediately below. Cf. *Silv.* 3. 3. 95 'uni parent commissa ministro', on the duties entrusted to Claudius Etruscus' father.

37–8. curarum asperimma suetus | credere partirique metus: compare Enn. *Ann.* 270 'consilium partit' (and see further Skutsch's notes on *Ann.* 268–70 for the motif of the faithful subordinate), Virg. *A.* 11. 820–2 'Accam ex aequalibus unam | adloquitur, fida ante alias quae sola Camillae | quicum partiri curas', Stat. *Theb.* 8. 279–81 'quicum ipse arcana deorum | partiri et uisas uni sociare solebat | Amphiaraus aues'.

38–9. quod tempus amicum | fraudibus: with this and the succeeding indirect questions, which express the nature of the *metus*, supply *esset* or *essent* as required by the subject. The juxtaposition of *amicum* and *fraudibus* conveys admirably the manner in which misleading and favourable impressions are essential to the success of *fraudes*; cf. the use of *accommoda* at Virg. *A.* 11. 522–3 'est curuo anfractu ualles, accommoda fraudi | armorumque dolis'. For the wide semantic range of *fraudes*, which includes not only deceit and the injuries that may thereby arise, but also harm of a more general nature, see further Wheeler (1988), 63–5. For the phrasing *tempus amicum*, contrast the much more optimistic atmosphere of Hor. *Carm.* 3. 6. 41–4: 'sol ubi montium | mutaret umbras et iuga demeret | bobus fatigatis, amicum | tempus agens abeunte curru.'

39. exserto ... bello: *exorto* (M) is unsatisfactory, whether *exorto bello* is construed as ablative absolute (which leaves *bona tempora* in awkward isolation, 'what are suitable times, when war has broken out') or as a dative (it would be odd for Corbulo to be anxious about the right time for a war that has already broken out). A dative is, however, required, to balance the preceding *quod tempus amicum | fraudibus. exserto* (credited by Courtney to Gronovius, though ascribed by other editors to Livineius) presents no such difficulties, since the word can convey the idea of conspicuousness; *exserto bello* could be translated as 'open war', standing in contrast to *fraudibus*, with *exserto* construed adjectivally (cf. *apertus*), rather than with participial force. *ThLL* v/2. 1859. 24 compares Plin. *Nat.* 11. 58 (of bees) 'maxime rixa in conuehendis floribus exserta'.

40. suspecta fides . . . fuga uera: just as Corbulo invoked the advice of Bolanus concerning what ruses may be used against the foe, so too did Bolanus help to detect the enemy's deceptive stratagems. As with *amicum | fraudibus* there is a slight verbal play in *suspecta fides*, in that *fides* is supposed to be a pledge which is beyond doubt. Statius contrasts *suspecta fides* with the genuine flight of the Armenians, and pointedly juxtaposes their epithet *ferocis* (cf. Hor. *Carm.* 3. 2. 3 'Parthos feroces') with their flight. *uera fuga* obliquely refers to the usual Parthian cavalry tactic (here applied to the Armenians) of feigning flight and firing arrows over the shoulder at those in pursuit: see e.g. *Silv.* 1. 4. 78–9 (cited in 32 n.), Luc. 1. 230 'ocior et missa Parthi post terga sagitta', 8. 368–90 (Lentulus' scornful account of Parthian tactics), Sil. 10. 11–12; in a mythical context, cf. V.Fl. 6. 696–8. A Roman general would need to judge whether such retreats were genuine.

41–3. Bolanus . . . | Bolanus . . . | . . . Bolanus: Repetition of a name can occur in erotic contexts (N.–H. on Hor. *Carm.* 1. 13. 1), but is also possible as a means for emphasizing goodwill (F. M. A. Jones (1996), 110–11) or to convey a sense of loss (ibid., 112–13); here the triple repetition of *Bolanus* emphasizes his activities in their own right, since in the preceding lines we have only heard of him as Corbulo's adviser. In the following lines Corbulo recedes into the background, apart from the allusion in 45, where he is not referred to by name. Corbulo requires careful treatment in the context of praise of Bolanus, for although the association of Bolanus with Corbulo brings reflected glory to the former, the impression might also be given that Bolanus is a mere subordinate. A further difficulty to be overcome is the likelihood that Bolanus' achievements on this particular campaign were slight, as Tacitus' sole mention of him in the eastern campaign suggests (*Ann.* 15. 3. 1). Hence the stress on Bolanus' own activities.

41. iter praenosse timendum: without proper knowledge of the land, an army could be at the mercy of a treacherous guide (e.g. Ov. *Tr.* 4. 2. 33 'perfidus hic nostros inclusit fraude locorum'). Crassus was tricked by the Arab Abgaros into marching into a waterless plain (Plu. *Crass.* 21–2). Bolanus is credited with the foreknowledge necessary for a safe route (cf. Tac. *Ann.* 1. 61. 1, where Germanicus sends Caecina ahead 'ut occulta saltuum scrutaretur'), and the ability to detect treachery (*suspecta fides*), which could also manifest itself in invitations to conferences (e.g. Tac. *Ann.* 13. 38), assassination (e.g. Tac. *Ann.* 14. 24. 3 'conuictique et puniti sunt qui

specie amicitiae dolum parabant'), and straightforward defection (e.g.
Tac. *Ann.* 12. 14. 1–3).

43. metari: *metiri* (M) has been favoured by recent editors,
although *metari* (first found in the *recentior* MS Q[50]) has always been
offered respect. Indeed Vollmer notes that at *Theb.* 6. 676 and 679
metari and *metitur* seem to have almost the same meaning. The choice
between these two words in part concerns whether or not Statius is
referring to the measurement of fields or camps, or some other
activity. *metari* is usually associated with military camps (*ThLL* viii.
892. 24–66) and typically has *castra* as its object, as at Sal. *Jug.* 106. 5
'Sulla ... ortu solis castra metabatur'. Perhaps because *ThLL* does not
give any instance with *agros* or similar words as object, when *metari*
takes this particular meaning, later editors have favoured *metiri*.

Yet *metiri* is not straightforward. Although *ThLL* viii. 882. 55–72
gives examples where it is construed with *agros*, the passages often refer
to the distribution of land (e.g. Cic. *Fam.* 9. 17. 2, Liv. 31. 4. 2:
'decemuiros agro ... metiendo diuidendo crearet'),[51] which can
scarcely be envisaged as part of a frontier campaign, or as a compon-
ent of Statius' laudatory account of Bolanus' military career.[52] Alter-
natively, the word can simply denote motion, as at Hor. *Epod.* 4. 7
'Sacram metiente te uiam', *ThLL* viii. 887. 58–71; but mere motion
through fields scarcely warrants inclusion in a list of actions which are
praiseworthy precedents for the young Crispinus.

The sense of the passage requires a meaning which would har-
monize with the context, the list of the tactical skills demonstrated by
Bolanus. *castra* are mentioned in the previous line; for praise in this
respect compare e.g. Liv. 9. 17. 15, 35. 14. 9 (Hannibal's praise for
Pyrrhus' skill in encampments; cf. Amm. 24. 1. 3), Vell. 2. 111. 4 with
Woodman, Plin. *Nat.* 18. 32 (on Marius), Sil. 5. 552 'nulli uictus uel
ponere castra', from a passage where Viriasius is also noted for his
skills in siege warfare, Amm. 25. 4. 11, where Julian is praised for

---

[50] For the value of Q, see Reeve (1977*b*), 225: 'The manuscripts that have most to reveal
are G and Q , G through the person of its scribe and the primitiveness of its uncorrected
text, Q because already in 1463 there is not a page of it that does not bear the marks of
scholarly endeavour.' Note also the readings of Q reported at 5. 3. 28 and 5. 3. 209, and see
Anderson (2000), i. 447–8 (no. 637) for further information and bibliography on the
manuscript.

[51] Note also *CIL* i². 585. 97–8 '<agrum locum> ... me<tiun>dum terminosque statui
<curato>', with Crawford (1996), 140.

[52] Note, however, that this technical usage referring to land distribution is common both
to *metari* and to *metiri*.

'salubriter et caute castra metata'. But since we have already heard in this passage of Bolanus' skills in this regard (for the choice of location, *iuga*, cf. Luc. 3. 377–8 'haec patiens longo munimine cingi | uisa duci rupes tutisque aptissima castris'), it would seem best not to connect *agros* with *castris*. *Theb.* 7. 441–2, 'haud procul inde iugum tutisque accommoda castris | arua notant', is not a counterexample, since there one verb governs both *iugum* and *arua*, whereas here there are two different verbs.

Vollmer suggests that Statius may be referring to the planning of the route to be taken by the army (515): 'St. kann aber auch an Vermessung zu andern Zwecken, z. B. Marschrouten gedacht haben.' This is one possibility, but it is perhaps dangerous to seek such a precise meaning. Indeed Courtney's reference to a similarly striking phrase from the *Panegyricus Prosarius in secundum Consulatum Aetii* in Vollmer's edition of Merobaudes (*MGH AA* XIV; Berlin, 1905), p. 8. 2–8, '... aut <uiarum> spatia metiris...' suggests that this meaning would require a word more precise than *agros*. Moreover, mere measurement is not an activity particularly deserving of praise.

The solution may lie in a looser use of *metari*, perhaps translated as 'to assess' or by the English idiom 'to size up', although the notion of preparation may be involved as well. *ThLL* gives a variety of *notiones secundariae*, which include *ambiendi diligenterque examinandi* (viii. 893. 35–44) and *praeparandi* (ibid. 47–63). Note e.g. *Culex* 174 'metabat sese circum loca [serpens]', Iust. 37. 3. 5 'opportuna quaeque uictoriae suae metatus est', Nemes. *Cyn.* 6 'et late campos metatus apertos', where 'size up' might capture the sense of the word. In the section on *praeparandi* there are also examples which, though late, may be pertinent, such as Solinus 32. 23 '[crocodilus] metatur locum nido naturali prouidentia' and, in the Vulgate, Deut. 1: 33 'praecessit uos in uia et metatus est locus, in quo tentoria fingere deberetis'. In the present passage, preparation is a possible meaning for *metari*, and thus *metari* can be defended, not by citing the usual link with *castra*, but because the notion of preparation does involve a genuine tactical skill, the ability to assess terrain and to take appropriate measures; for this idea cf. Sil. 4. 90–1 'explorare locos consul collisque propinqui | ingenium et campis quae sit natura parabat'. This meaning is peculiar to *metari*, which is therefore to be preferred.

44. torrentum: *tot rerum* (M) must be wrong, since it is clumsy to have *rerum* immediately followed by *nemorum*, with *nemora* awkwardly singled out from the totality of *res*. *torrentum* (Heinsius) is a good solution of the difficulty.

Others, however, have retained *tot*. Calderini favoured *tot ueprum*, whilst Krohn proposed *tot sentum*, though there is no authority for these genitive forms in *-um* (the only instance of either word in the genitive plural is *ueprium* at Plin. *Nat.* 16. 178). In any case, although *nemora* may well delay and cause difficulties to a passing army, *uepres* and *sentes* in themselves are unlikely to present much of a problem. *torrentes*, however, could be a formidable obstacle to a force of any size in the ancient world (see 5. 1. 89 n.). Moreover, river-crossings and forests are obvious locations for enemy action (cf. e.g. Sil. 5. 2–3 'perque alta silentia noctis | siluarum anfractus caecis insiderat armis' for Hannibal's preparations prior to the battle of Lake Trasimene), which here seems implied by the epithet *malignas*; for such virtual personification compare Hor. *Carm.* 3. 1. 30 'fundusque mendax', Tac. *Ann.* 1. 61. 1 'fallacibus campis'. It is harder to see why the *morae* of *uepres* or *sentes* could be similarly dangerous.

totamque: Courtney suggests emending M's unobjectionable but bland *tantamque* to *totamque*, comparing *Silv.* 1. 1. 56 (toto *M* : tanto *ς*). *totamque* coheres with *implere*, since Bolanus is praised for accomplishing the whole of Corbulo's plan (*mentem*).

45. iussisque ingentibus: cf. 112, *Silv.* 5. 1. 109, *Theb.* 10. 384, and Virg. *A.* 7. 240–2, on the Trojans' mission on Italy:

> hinc Dardanus ortus,
> huc repetit iussisque ingentibus urget Apollo
> Tyrrhenum ad Thybrim et fontis uada sacra Numici.

The Virgilian echo and the emphatic *unus* (cf. Heinsius' conjecture *uni* in 37 above) at the end of the line exalt Bolanus' prowess.

47. ille secundus apex bellorum: the basic meaning of *apex* is the small rod at the top of a *flamen*'s cap, which was tied with wool (cf. Virg. *A.* 8. 664 'lanigerosque apices', Serv. on *A.* 2. 683, Serv. Auct. *A.* 10. 271). Here *apex* is the λόφος, the plume of the helmet (*cassis*). Compare *Theb.* 7. 292–3 'sic exit in auras | cassidis aequus apex', Virg. *A.* 10. 270, *ThLL* ii. 227. 13–18. *apex bellorum* also suggests the more metaphorical meaning of *apex* as the summit or pinnacle of something (e.g. Cic. *Sen.* 60 'apex est autem senectutis auctoritas'). There is a pleasing paradox, in that one would not expect to find a *secundus apex* of anything; the effect is to emphasize that Bolanus is all but equal to Corbulo.

proxima cassis: for *proximus* applied to a subordinate, cf. *Silv.* 1. 4. 6 'proxima ceruix' (Rutilius Gallicus), Ov. *Tr.* 4. 2. 28 'proximus ille duci'.

48–50. The simile refers to the participation of Hercules and Telamon in the first war against Troy, waged against Laomedon, who had attempted to cheat Hercules of his reward for rescuing his daughter Hesione from a sea-monster (see e.g. *Il.* 5. 638–51, Ov. *Met.* 11. 211–15, Apollod. 2. 5. 9). The story of her rescue had very recently been told at V.Fl. 2. 451–578, though, in contrast to the impressive Telamon described by Statius here (cf. *Theb.* 9. 68), in Valerius he is a 'passive observer' of the fight against the sea-monster (Hershkowitz (1998), 147). In both V.Fl. 3. 637–45 and A.R. 1. 1290–5 it is also Telamon who attempts to dissuade the Argonauts from leaving Hercules behind after the loss of Hylas. Having fought alongside Hercules at Troy, at the end of the war, when Priam was installed on his father's throne, he received Hesione in marriage; their son was Teucer. See Pisander fr. 11 Bernabé, Pi. *I.* 6. 27–35, *N.* 4. 25–7, S. *Aj.* 1299–1303, E. *Tr.* 799–818, esp. 804–6 ἔβας ἔβας τῷ τοξοφόρῳ συναρι|στεύων ἅμ᾽ Ἀλκμήνας γόνῳ | Ἴλιον Ἴλιον ἐκπέρσων πόλιν, Ov. *Met.* 11. 216–17 'nec, pars militiae, Telamon sine honore recessit | Hesioneque data potitur', Hyg. *Fab.* 89, Apollod. 2. 6. 4, who also writes that Telamon was the first to enter Troy, but avoided Hercules' wrath by building an altar to him (cf. Tz. ad Lyc. 469), 3. 12. 7.

An important passage for Statius here is Pi. *I.* 6. 41–54, where Hercules prays that Telamon may be granted a son by his wife Eriboea (for the form of her name, see Apollod. 3. 12. 7 with Frazer's notes), and foretells his achievements and his name, Ajax. The allusion is entirely appropriate to the situation of Statius' poem (for Statius and Pindar, see e.g. 5. 3. 151–2, Brożek (1965), Henderson (1998a), 109–11, 115–18), since it develops the comparison between Telamon and Bolanus, and foretells a glorious son. Statius follows this up in 51 with a reference to Virg. *A.* 12. 435–6: 'disce, puer, uirtutem ex me uerumque laborem, | fortunam ex aliis', which itself alludes to Ajax' farewell to his son, Eurysaces, at S. *Aj.* 550–1.

Like the preceding account of Bolanus, the simile maximizes the importance of a subordinate figure. Thus Hercules is not directly mentioned by name, but evoked through references to Nemea and Cleonae, and by the patronymic *Alcide*. In contrast, Telamon is identified by his own name, and the Trojans are moreover said specifically to fear him, whereas Hercules' *arma* they only see. *Telamona* is also emphatically placed towards the end of the sentence.

48–9. Nemeaea ... arma: Markland objected that *Nemeaea* and *Cleonaeus* refer to the fight against the same lion, since the two towns are in the same vicinity, and that Hercules fought the Nemean lion with his bare hands. By emending to *Lernaea* the *arma* become the 'spicula Herculis', the fearful arrows imbued with the venomous blood of the Hydra. Markland compares *Lernaea arma* (*Theb.* 5. 443‒4), *Lernaea tela* (Sen. *Her. F.* 1233, [Sen.] *Herc O.* 905), and *Lernaea spicula* (Sen. *Med.* 784). However, if the *arma* were arrows, this would consort oddly with *uiderent*, referring to the alarmed reaction of the Trojans; one would expect the *arma* to be significant because of their appearance as well as their effectiveness.

There are in any case specific traditions concerning Hercules and Cleonae. Pi. *O.* 10. 26‒30 tells of Hercules killing Eurytus and Cteatus on the road near Cleonae (cf. D.S. 4. 33. 3, Apollod. 2. 7. 2, Paus. 2. 15. 1, 5. 2. 1). More important for Latin literature is the *Victoria Berenices* in Book 3 of Callimachus' *Aetia*: see Parsons (1977), *SH* 254‒69, Thomas (1983). This section of the *Aetia* included the story of Hercules' visit to Molorchus on the way to killing the Nemean lion. Parsons (1977), 1‒4 gives other ancient versions of the story of Hercules and Molorchus. *SH* 259. 37 (= Call. fr. 177. 37 Pf.) refers to Cleonae (though not all letters are visible in the papyrus), which also appears as the location of Molorchus' home at Apollod. 2. 5. 1; see further Nonn. 17. 52, Livrea (1979), 40, (1980), 21‒2. Statius himself mentions Nemea and Cleonae together at *Theb.* 4. 159‒60: 'dat Nemea comites, et quas in proelia uires | sacra Cleonaei cogunt uineta Molorchi'; cf. *Silv.* 3. 1. 29‒31 (addressed to Hercules) 'non te Lerna nocens nec pauperis arua Molorchi | nec formidatus Nemees ager antraque poscunt | Thracia nec Pharii polluta altaria regis', and see Thomas (1983), 105, who argues that in *Silv.* 3. 1 Statius is responding directly to Callimachus, rather than through Virg. *G.* 3. In the present passage it is even possible that the epithet *Cleonaeus*, applied to Hercules' bow, is a learned reference back to a particular detail from Callimachus: Parsons (1977), 15 suggests that there may have been a conversation between Molorchus and Hercules about his famous bow (which he did not acquire at Cleonae): Statius' unusual epithet *Cleonaeus* would then allude not to the bow's origin, but to its mention in the conversation which took place at Cleonae. For another variation in the use of the epithet *Cleonaeus*. cf. Luc. 4. 612 'ille Cleonaei proiecit terga leonis', Mart. 5. 71. 3 'rura Cleonaeo numquam temerata leone', and see Kassel (1977), 51.

Perhaps the *Nemeaea . . . arma* are the skin of the Nemean lion, used by Hercules as armour (E. *HF* 361‒3, [Theoc.] 25. 278‒9, Hyg. *Fab.*

30. 2); the lion skin would certainly have had a striking visual effect (see e.g. V.Fl. 1. 34–5 'Cleonaeo iam tempora clusus hiatu | Alcides'). Note as well that the lion skin is mentioned in Hercules' prayer for Telamon at Pi. *I*. 6. 47–8 (discussed above). Another possibility is the club, which, according to Apollod. 2. 4. 11, Hercules cut for himself at Nemea (though Nigidius Figulus fr. 93 Swoboda says it was borrowed from Molorchus; see Parsons (1977), 1–2). Athen. 12. 512 F records the view of Megaclides that Stesichorus was the first poet to give Hercules his customary accoutrements of club, lion-skin, and bow, but cf. Suda s.v. Πείσανδρος (iv. 122. 16–17 Adler), which credits Pisander with being the first poet to give Hercules his club. On Pisander's treatment of the Nemean lion, see fr. 1 Bernabé.

48. uiderent: doubted by Heinsius, who suggested *pauerent* with no further explanation. But *pauerent* would entail three words referring to the fear of the Trojans, when two are adequate, as well as detracting from *timebant*, applied to Telamon in the next line; Statius is concerned with the Trojan reaction to Telamon, not Hercules, as a means of complimenting Bolanus.

51. disce, puer: compare especially Virg. *A*. 12. 435–6 (cited above); note also Stat. *Silv.* 4. 4. 74 'surge agedum iuuenemque puer deprende parentem', 4. 7. 43–4 'crescat in mores patrios auumque | prouocet actis', Sil. 6. 537–8 'tu quoque, care puer, dignum te sanguine tanto | fingere ne cessa', 13. 503–4 'uerum age disce, puer, quoniam cognoscere cordi est, | iam tua deque tuis pendentia Dardana fatis', addressed by the Sibyl to Scipio. Note that Crispinus is not offered anything equivalent to the doubt and uncertainty of Aeneas' 'fortunam ex aliis'. For Ascanius as a point of comparison for Crispinus, cf. the notes on 13–14, 118–20; for Ascanius in the *Aeneid*, see e.g. Petrini (1997), 87–110.

monitore: contrast the *imberbus iuuenis* of Hor. *Ars* 163, who is 'monitoribus asper'. Crispinus, however, does not even need the advice which Statius (and others) are giving him. For *monitor* in the precise sense of one set over the young, cf. *Silv.* 5. 3. 146–7 'hinc tibi uota patrum credi generosaque pubes | te monitore regi. . . .', *Theb.* 12. 205 'uirginei custos monitorque pudoris', Hor. *Ep.* 1. 18. 67 'protinus ut moneam, si quid monitoris eges tu', Sen. *Ep.* 94. 8.

53–4. aliis Decii reducesque Camilli | monstrentur: virtually *praeteritio*, since although the Decii and Camilli are said to be suitable models for others, they are effectively being mentioned to Crispinus as well. Similar is *Pan. Lat.* 10(2). 14. 2 'non necesse erit

Camillos et Maximos et Curios et Catones proponere ad imitandum;
quin potius uestra illi facta demonstret, uos identidem et semper
ostendat praesentes et optimos imperatoriae institutionis auctores',
though the context is praise of the imperial family, where the father
(Maximianus) is still living. Statius' *reducesque Camilli* recalls Luc. 7.
358–60 (Pompey's speech before Pharsalus):

> si Curios his fata darent reducesque Camillos
> temporibus Deciosque caput fatale uouentes,
> hinc starent.

For such lists of distinguished Romans compare e.g. Cic. *Sest.* 143,
Pis. 58, Virg. *G.* 2. 169–70, Hor. *Carm.* 1. 12. 33–48, and Man. 1. 777–
99. The Decii and Camilli were familiar exemplary figures: see e.g.
Sen. *Con.* 9. 2. 9 and 10. 2. 3, *Suas.* 7. 6, Otto (1890), 68 no. 311, and
(on the Decii) Litchfield (1914), 48 and n. 4. At Virg. *A.* 6. 756–853
Anchises tells his son of the sequence of Romans who will succeed to
his legacy, and among them are the Decii and Camillus: 'quin Decios
Drusosque procul saeuumque securi | aspice Torquatum et referen-
tem signa Camillum' (824–5). Although they are hardly heroes from
Aeneas' past ancestry, there is a sense in which Anchises the father is
telling his son to pay heed to them. Crispinus, on the other hand, does
not need such examples. As with *disce, puer* (51), an epic allusion is used
and surpassed.

The Decii Mures produced three consuls in successive generations
from father to son (*MRR* i. 135–6, 177, 192). The first two underwent
deuotio so as to secure Roman victories at Veseris (340 BC) and
Sentinum (295 BC). The third was consul in 279 BC and held com-
mand against Pyrrhus; some sources refer to a third *deuotio*, whilst
others report that this attempt was deliberately frustrated by the
Epirot king.

The dictator M. Furius Camillus was traditionally credited with
the recovery of the gold paid by the Romans to the Gauls for the
return of their city after the sack of 390 BC (*MRR* i. 95). *reducesque*
refers to his return from exile, since he had previously been pros-
ecuted by the tribune L. Appuleius. Although there were two consu-
lar Camilli in the fourth century BC (*MRR* i. 128, 138, 147), here and in
Lucan it is probably the celebrated Marcus who is referred to, as a
generic plural; cf. H.–Sz. 19 (§28). For the plural *Camilli*, cf. Virg *G.* 2.
169, Prop. 3. 9. 31, Mart. 9. 27. 6, Plin. *Pan.* 13. 4, 55. 6, *Pan. Lat.* 10(2).
14. 2 (cited above).

monstrentur: cf. 5. 3. 137 n.

54–6. quantusque negatam | fluctibus occiduis fessoque Hyperione Thulen | intrarit mandata gerens: whatever the correct text, this passage refers to Bolanus' spell as governor in Britain, on which see pp. 182–3; for the hyperbole, cf. Sil. 3. 597 'hinc pater ignotam donabit [*β* : denabit *Delz* : donabat *α*] uincere Thylen', a reference to Vespasian's time in Britain. For the admiring *quantus*, cf. e.g. Virg. *A*. 11. 283–4 'experto credite quantus | in clipeum adsurgat'.

M has *occiduis fessusque*, which is generally emended on the grounds that Statius would not describe Bolanus, whom he has been praising, as wearied by the sun. In any case the sun is an unlikely hazard for travellers to Thule, a place of darkness at *Silv*. 3. 5. 20 'super Hesperiae uada caligantia Thules' and 4. 4. 62 (see Coleman) 'nigrae litora Thules'.

There is at first sight a case for M's *negantem* ('resisting'), construed with the dative, a usage paralleled at *Silv*. 3. 1. 124 'saxa negantia ferro' and *Theb*. 2. 668–9, 3. 458 and 4. 124; cf. Prop. 4. 5. 5 'docta uel Hippolytum Veneri mollire negantem'. Construing *negantem* with *fluctibus occiduis*, one would envisage Thule as a bulwark enduring the waves of the Ocean. But, in a tradition that went back to Pytheas (see Roseman (1994), 120–1, 125–30), such remote seas were reputedly sluggish rather than tempestuous (though note *Silv*. 5. 1. 91): cf. Albinovanus Pedo 5 'pigris immania monstra sub undis', with Courtney, *FLP* ad loc., p. 318, Sen. *Suas*. 1. 1 (with Winterbottom) 'stat immotum mare quasi deficientis in suo fine naturae pigra moles', Tac. *Ag*. 10. 5 'sed mare graue et pigrum remigantibus perhibent ne uentis quidem perinde adtolli', *Ger*. 45. 1 'trans Suionas aliud mare, pigrum ac prope immotum'. Furthermore, if Thule is resisting the sun, then the dative *Hyperioni* (Imhof (1867), 3–4) would be required to balance the dative *fluctibus*; examples of a Hellenizing short final *-i* in Latin are rare (Mueller (1894), 496), even though there are Statian parallels (*Silv*. 4. 2. 28, *Theb*. 2. 599, 3. 521, *Ach*. 1. 285).

Some critics have supported Avantius' *nigrantem* (for the short first syllable, cf. e.g. Virg. *A*. 8. 353, cited below). Markland's claim that *nigrare* describes the effects of too much rather than too little sun (cf. e.g. Ov. *Ars* 1. 724 'debet et a radiis sideris esse niger', Sil. 9. 225 'corpora ab immodico seruans nigrantia Phoebo') is irrelevant, since *niger* and its cognates do not invariably refer to blackness caused by burning: see Virg. *A*. 8. 353–4 'credunt se uidisse Iouem, cum saepe nigrantem | aegida concuteret dextra nimbosque cieret', 11. 824 'et tenebris nigrescunt omnia circum', Stat. *Silv.* 2. 6. 82–3 'non saeuius atros | nigrasset planctu genetrix tibi salua lacertos', 4. 4. 62 (cited above). But *nigrantem* is nevertheless unsatisfactory. While Thule could be dark because of the setting sun, the waves would have no effect on either visibility or physical appearance, so that *fluctibus occiduis* cannot be an ablative of manner. *fluctibus occiduis fessoque Hyperione* is also unsatisfactory if treated as absolute: 'he entered dark Thule, the waves being western, and Hyperion being tired'.

A further problem concerns how M's *fessusque* is emended. Phillimore suggested *fessamque Hyperione Thulen*, but there is no reason why Thule should be *fessa*. With *fesso usque* (Calderini, Vollmer), *usque* would be intensifying; Mozley translates 'where Hyperion is ever weary'. Palaeographically, this is the simplest emendation of M's text; the absolute use of *usque*, however, without a further adverb or preposition, or a verb, seems less simple: though *usque* can be used in alternation with *semper* (*OLD* s.v. 5 cites Hor. *Carm.* 2. 9. 4 and Ov. *Ib.* 418), there is no parallel for its use as a modifier of an adjectival phrase such as *fesso . . . Hyperione* (at Mela 3. 36 'ideo sex mensibus dies et totidem aliis nox usque continua est', *usque* modifies the verb *est*, not the adjective, *continua*, referring to the whole repeated cycle of six-month days and nights).

Courtney (1988), 45 rids the text of *fessusque* and reads *negantem* | *fluctibus occiduo fissis Hyperione Thulen*. In itself *occiduo* is unobjectionable since *occiduus* is appropriate to the setting sun (cf. e.g. Sil. 1. 145 'occidui . . . solis'), but *fissis* represents a more serious difficulty. He translates 'Britain which resists the waves cleft by the setting sun', but even if the setting sun might be said, metaphorically, to 'cleave or "split"' waves (for the opposite idea of waves themselves "cleaving", note V.Fl. 1. 479–80, on damage to the Argo: "fissaque fluctu | uel pice uel molli conducere uulnera cera"), this is a difficult image when combined with the idea of Thule's literal resistance to the waves, which might arguably be much more obviously described as 'cleaving' in its effects.

This is a passage where complete certainty seems unobtainable. I suggest *quantusque negatam* | *fluctibus occiduis fessoque Hyperione Thulen* | *intrarit*. Translate: 'How powerfully he entered Thule that had been denied by western waves and tired Hyperion.' Thule had been denied to others (*negatam*—the word conveys a sense of difficult achievement as at Hor. *Carm.* 3. 2. 21–2 'Virtus, recludens immeritis mori | caelum,

negata temptat iter uia', Sen. *Phaed.* 224 'solus negatas inuenit The-
seus uias', Claud. *Bell. Get.* 69–70) because of the difficulties which
prevented ships from reaching it, darkness[53] and the western seas.
fluctibus occiduis is a pointed juxtaposition: Statius refers to the sluggish
seas as 'waves',[54] but they are *occiduis*, not only 'western', but 'falling',
and hence calm (cf. *Silv.* 5. 4. 5–6 'occidit horror | aequoris'). *negatam*
furthermore gives point to *quantus* and *intrarit*, emphasizing the diffi-
cult character of the voyage.[55]

56–7. potentis | mille urbes Asiae: the grand *mille* (cf. the
thousand ships that sailed to Troy, Fraenkel on A. *Ag.* 45, Virg. *A.* 2.
198, McKeown on Ov. *Am.* 1. 3. 15–16) is in keeping with the lofty
designation of a place by the number of its cities (compare e.g. the
hundred cities of Crete, *Il.* 2. 649, Hor. *Carm.* 3. 27. 33–4, Virg. *A.* 3.
106). Five hundred cities seems to have been a more conventional
number for the province of Asia: see J. *BJ* 2. 366, Ap. Ty. *Ep.* 58,
Philostr. *VS* 548, and cf. Aristid. *Or.* 23. 9, who remarks that no other
province has so many cities as Asia.

For the genitive singular *potentis* (Heinsius) agreeing with *Asiae*,
Markland's parallels include Man. 4. 680 'Asiam...potentis', Sen.
Tro. 7 'pollentis Asiae', *Ag.* 785 'potentis Asiae', Luc. 9. 1002 'Asiam-
que potentem'; add *Silv.* 1. 4. 80–1 'quid geminos fasces magnaeque
iterata reuoluam | iura Asiae?', from a similar passage lauding Ruti-
lius Gallicus' governorship of Asia.

58. imperium mulcente toga: cf. *Silv.* 1. 4. 48 'ferrum mulcere
toga'; on *mulcere*, see Henderson (1998a), 60 and n. 147. For the toga as
a symbol of peace, here also implying civil as opposed to martial
(*imperium*) administration, see *Silv.* 5. 1. 82 n. Tac. *Ag.* 9. 2 notes how
Agricola disproved the general expectation that military men were
unable to perform judicial functions well: 'Agricola naturali pruden-
tia, quamuis inter togatos, facile iusteque agebat'; he continues (§3) by
praising his conduct in Aquitania, both official ('seuerus et saepius

---

[53] For *fessoque Hyperione* cf. *Silv.* 2. 2. 48 'fessa dies' (with van Dam's n.). For the instrumental
ablative *Hyperione* without *a* or *ab*, cf. *Silv.* 3. 1. 53–4 'ictusque Hyperione multo | acer
anhelantes incendit Sirius agros', 4. 4. 27–8 'dum nimio possessa Hyperione flagrat | torua
Cleonaei iuba sideris', where a process of personification is implied not only by the epithets
multus and *nimius*, whcih can mean 'overbearing', but also by the passive participles denoting
Hyperion's actions, *ictus* and *possessa.*

[54] Note that *fluctus* can mean 'seas'; see e.g. Virg. *A.* 1. 755–6 'nam te iam septima portat |
omnibus errantem terris et fluctibus aestas'.

[55] *negatam* might suggest divine opposition to remote voyages; cf. Albinovanus Pedo
(Courtney, *FLP*, pp. 315–16, 319) 20–3, Tac. *Ger.* 34. 2.

misericors') and unofficial. *mulcente* suggests a similar leniency in
Bolanus' activities. For an account of the judicial role of proconsuls,
and the significance of assizes which a proconsul would have to tour,
see Burton (1975); for the particular assizes (*conuentus*) of the province
of Asia, see the discussion of a Flavian inscription from Ephesus
(Österreichisches Archäologisches Institut, Ephesus Inventory 3653)
in Habicht (1975).

bibe (Heinsius) is preferable to *tibi* (M); a suitable verb is needed
for *pronis | auribus*. The corruption is easy in the light of *tibi* in the
middle of the next line. For the image of drinking with the ears,
compare e.g. Hor. *Carm.* 2. 13. 32 (with N.–H.) 'densum umeris bibit
aure uulgus', Ov. *Tr.* 3. 5. 13–14 'et lacrimas cernens in singula uerba
cadentes | ore meo lacrimas, auribus illa bibi', Pers. 4. 50 'nequiquam
populo bibulas donaueris aures'.

60. haec iterent praecepta senes comitesque paterni: not
until Housman, *Class. P.* ii. 653, was M's *haec iterent comites praecepta
senesque paterni* emended, although Markland was uncertain about *sen-
esque paterni*, whilst Vollmer suggested that tutors or *paedagogi* might be
so designated.[56] Mozley translates '. . . these precepts let thy com-
rades and thy father's friends repeat'. But *senes* does not mean
'friends'. Housman accordingly conjectured *haec iterent praecepta senes
comitesque paterni*, explaining the corruption as the result of a scribe's
eye jumping from the final *-es* of *senes* to the *-es* of *comitesque*; the scribe
wrote *senesque* and placed *comites* in the margin, which was then
restored to the wrong place in the line; one might alternatively
argue that the two words ending in *-es* could simply have been
transposed in a scribe's mind, with *comites* being repositioned to
preserve the metre. The emended text could be translated 'the old
men and your father's companions'. *senes* would refer to the generality
of old men known to Crispinus, whilst the *comites* are specifically his
father's friends; cf. Prop. 3. 24. 9 'patrii . . . amici', Sen. *Con.* 2. 3. 20
'amici paterni', Luc. 9. 121 'patrios comites', Mart. 6. 25. 3, Plin. *Ep.*
5. 16. 3. Håkanson (1969), 129–30 defends M, arguing that the
distinction is between Crispinus' own companions and those of his
father. Comparing Hor. *Ep.* 1. 1. 54–5 'haec Ianus summus ab imo |
prodocet, haec recinunt iuuenes dictata senesque', he argues for a
link between the two passages. In fact Horace is discussing the need to

---

[56] Cf. Iz.–Fr.: 'les compagnons et les vieux serviteurs de ton père'.

abstain from cupidity, whereas Statius is encouraging Crispinus to repeat his father's glories; the link is therefore tenuous. Though Håkanson rightly notes the pairing of *iuuenes* and *senes* in the Horatian example, he does not deal with the problem of *senesque paterni*, and follows Mozley's error of allowing *senes* mysteriously to assume the significance of *comites*.

With the emended text the example set by the father is reiterated by his own contemporaries, whereas it is less appropriate for Crispinus' own coevals to instruct him on his father's achievements, deeds which occurred before their time. Hor. *Ep.* 1. 1. 54–5 is not a counter-example, because the issue there does not concern the accomplishments of an individual now dead, but a moral precept.

The slight rhyme of *propinqui* in line 59 and *paterni* helps to signal the closure of this section of the poem. For the pairing of kinsmen and friends, commonly expressed in terms of *amici* and *propinqui*, compare e.g. Sen. *Con.* 2. 3. 6, 2. 4. 6, 7. 2. 4, 7. 8. 2, Tac. *Dial.* 9. 3, *Ann.* 6. 19. 3, Juv. 14. 235–6.

61. adeo: M's *alio* is difficult because it makes Crispinus go 'elsewhither' in a poem which anticipates not only his journey to Etruria but also the official journey which will inaugurate his career; his destination is thus unclear, as noted by Seager (1983), 53. Markland argues for *adeo*, citing Virg. *A.* 5. 864 'iamque adeo scopulos Sirenum aduecta subibat' and 8. 585 'iamque adeo exierat portis equitatus apertis' (where Serv. ad loc. remarks that 'ADEO ad ornatum pertinet tantum'), Sil. 1. 20, 12. 534; see also Austin on Virg. *A.* 2. 567. *iamque adeo* ('at this very moment') is appropriate to the period just before Crispinus' career.

moliris iter: though *iter* evokes both the journey to Etruria and the official journey which will herald Crispinus' public career at the end of the poem, it also suggests the more metaphorical journey through life which Crispinus will take in imitation of his father; indeed the preceding passage has described the father's travels as well. Note also the *iter … timendum* so successfully avoided by Bolanus (41). *moliris iter* perhaps recalls Virg. *A.* 6. 477 'inde datum molitur iter' (see also *ThLL* viii. 1362. 44–52), imparting to Crispinus' future travels something of the solemnity and sense of destiny characteristic of Aeneas' journey in the underworld; cf. *Silv.* 5. 3. 269 'uiuos molitum in Tartara gressus'.

nec deside passu: litotes; far from lingering, Crispinus is hastening to embark on a public career.

62–3. nondum ualidae tibi signa iuuentae | inrepsere genis: although Crispinus has not yet grown his first beard (on which theme see Headlam on Herodas 1. 52, Bömer on Ov. *Met.* 9. 398, Eyben (1972), 691–5), he is still starting out in public life. What at first sight seems to be a statement that he is too young is in fact a compliment, in that Crispinus is on his way earlier than would be expected. Compare *Laus Pis.* 259–61, where the poet asks Piso to trust his *animus*, although he has only just begun to grow his first beard. Statius alters the usual topos of a young man dying before his first beard (cf. *Silv.* 2. 1. 52–5, 5. 5. 18–21 with n., Harrison on Virg. *A.* 10. 324–5), and uses the motif to denote the time at which Crispinus' *father* died, emphasizing how Bolanus' hopes of seeing his son grow up were frustrated by his own death; cf. Prop. 4. 1. 127–8 'ossaque legisti non illa aetate legenda | patris et in tenuis cogeris esse lares'. For *inrepere* with reference to hair, cf. Prudentius *praef.* 23 'inrepsit subito canities seni'; analogous is the usage of the word to denote the creeping onset of plant growth, as at *Silv.* 5. 3. 8, Col. 4. 4. 3 'nullis herbis inrepentibus' (of weeds), Drac. *De origine rosarum* 3 'sacrilega placidas irrepsit spina per herbas'.

63. tenor integer aeui: whereas Bolanus was praised exclusively in terms of his deeds in war and government, Crispinus, who has no similar achievements (because of his age), is praised for his moral quality. Having described his promise and illustrious forebears, Statius singles out a characteristic particular to Crispinus.

For *tenor* denoting moral quality, compare *Silv.* 3. 3. 147 'atque aeui sine nube tenor', Ov. *Ep.* 17. 14 'dumque tenor uitae sit sine labe meae'. *tenor integer aeui* appropriately combines, in a passage referring to Crispinus' youth and virtues, the moral tone of Hor. *Carm* 1. 22. 1 'integer uitae scelerisque purus' whilst evoking the use of *integer* in phrases to denote youth: cf. e.g. *Silv.* 2. 6. 46 'teneri sic integer aeui', Virg. *A.* 2. 638–9 'uos o, quibus integer aeui | sanguis' with Austin ad loc., Ov. *Met.* 9. 441. *tenor*, whose primary significance is even motion (*OLD* 1), is also appropriate to the language of travel in this passage.

64. nec genitor iuxta: a more direct intimation that Bolanus is dead. The instructions to Crispinus (59–60) to heed the advice of *propinqui* and *senes comitesque paterni* hinted at his absence. In 64–8 the implications of the father's absence are rendered more pitiful. After the euphemistic remark that Crispinus is not undertaking his journey with his father by his side, Statius laments his passing, before dwelling on the bereaved children and concluding with the affecting detail that the father died before he could witness his son assuming the *toga uirilis*. Crispinus' near-contemporary Hadrian similarly lost his father at the age of ten (*SHA Hadr.* 1. 4). For the motif of absent fathers and initiation into the adult world, see Petrini (1997), 5.

fatis . . . haustus iniquis: for *haurio* used to express destruction by abstract agents, cf. e.g. Sen. *Phaed.* 695–6 'quos hausit et peremit et leto dedit | odium dolusque', *Ag.* 414 'quis fare nostras hauserit casus rates', *ThLL* vi/3. 2571. 44–54. There may also be a hint at another usage of *haurio*, with Bolanus 'wounded' (*OLD* s.v. *haurio* 3b) by the Fates, before he 'falls' (*occidit*; cf. Hor. *Carm.* 1. 28. 7 'occidit et Pelopis genitor', Ov. *Met.* 5. 144–5 'occidit et Celadon Mendesius, occidit Astreus | matre Palaestina, dubio genitore creatus').

65. occiderat: Saenger emended M's nonsensical *occidio et* thus, though the Renaissance correction *occidit et* has tended to be favoured even in recent editions. Saenger's emendation is superior, since *occidit et* leaves an awkward sequence in ll. 64–5 of two participles *haustus* and *linquens* joined in a rather odd way by *et* immediately after the main verb. With *occiderat*, the pluperfect tense appropriately refers to Bolanus' death, before the perfect tenses *exuit* and *induxit* in ll. 66–7 refer to the actions which he was then unable to accomplish.

geminam prolem: for *gemina proles* referring to twins, cf. Virg. *A.* 1. 274 (Romulus and Remus), Ov. *Met.* 4. 514 (lion cubs), 6. 205 (Apollo and Artemis). P. White (1973), 282, however, argues (cf. Nauta (2002), 216) that this phrase does not mean that Crispinus and his brother were actually twins, citing *Il. Lat.* 177 'gemina cum prole suorum' (the sons of Nestor), and also *Theb.* 1. 394 'gemino natarum pignore fultus' (Adrastus' daughters) as cases where *geminus* does not refer to twin offspring, and arguing that Crispinus' brother cannot be his twin since his career is more advanced. But although 'certaque dat uotis hilaris uestigia frater' (126) is curious, since it implies that Crispinus' brother has started off his public career before Crispinus, White's argument that the *gemina proles* are not twins is difficult in the light of *aequaeuo . . . fratri* (75): if the brothers were not twins it is extraordinary that they are twice designated in a manner which might suggest that they were. Significantly Statius says little about the *certa . . . uestigia* given by the brother, who was perhaps only a little ahead of Crispinus.

sine praeside linquens: in fact the children were left in the care of their mother, who attempted to kill Crispinus. The defencelessness of fatherless children is an emotive motif which goes as far back as the laments of Andromache in the *Iliad* (22. 484–507, 24. 732–6).

66. nec saltem: 'and he did not even...' (cf. *Theb.* 9. 893 with Dewar's n., Mart. 1. 86. 8). *nec saltem* enforces the pathos of Bolanus' premature death, as do *teneris... lacertis* and *puerile*, emphasizing that Crispinus lost his father in boyhood.

ostrum: the purple-bordered *toga praetexta* (also mentioned in Book 5 at 5. 2. 29, 5. 3. 119–20), worn by children and magistrates as a sign of what is *uenerabile*; see Cic. 2 *Ver.* 1. 113 (where the garment denotes *ingenuitas*), Hor. *Epod.* 5. 7, Plin. *Nat.* 9. 127 (on the use of purple) 'fasces huic securesque Romanae uiam faciunt, idemque pro maiestate pueritiae est', [Quint.] *Decl. min.* 340. 13, Macrob. *Sat.* 1. 6. 7 ff.; for purple itself, see 5. 2. 29 n. The ceremony of exchanging the *toga praetexta* for the white *toga pura* of adulthood, whose importance is suggested by the younger Pliny's use of the term *officium* (*Ep.* 1. 9. 2), commonly took place at the Liberalia on 17 March (Ov. *Fast.* 3. 771–88); see further Wiedemann (1989), 86, 90, 114–16.

68. effrena: for the 'unbridled' qualities of youth cf. Cic. *Att.* 6. 1. 12 'sed alter, ut Isocrates dixit in Ephoro et Theopompo, frenis eget, alter calcaribus' (cf. *de Orat.* 3. 36, *Brut.* 204, with reference to rhetorical education); note also (from a longer horse simile) Stat. *Ach.* 1. 277–8 'effrenae tumidum uelut igne iuuentae | si quis equum primis submittere temptet habenis'. For the view that such excesses were simply a passing phase, see Sen. *Con.* 2. 6. 11.

68–9. nouaeque | libertas properata togae: *properata* hints that some were not mature enough to assume an adult role. Nero, who assumed the *toga uirilis* at thirteen (Tac. *Ann.* 12. 41. 1), would be a striking example. *libertas* suggests a superficial pleasure in the change of apparel.

69–70. nescia falcis | silua: for the metaphor of the pruning-hook (*falx*) as a check against misdeeds, compare Hor. *S.* 1. 3. 121–4:

> cum dicas esse pares res
> furta latrociniis, et magnis parua mineris
> falce recisurum simili te, si tibi regnum
> permittant homines.

For the application of the pruning metaphor to management of the young, cf. Cic. *Cael.* 76: 'etenim semper magno ingenio adulescentes refrenandi potius a gloria quam incitandi fuerunt; amputanda plura

sunt illi aetati, si quidem efflorescit ingeni laudibus, quam inserenda',
and contrast Quint. *Inst.* 2. 4. 10–11, who cautions against excessive
severity in education, likening its effects to the consequences of
dangerous pruning of young plants. See also Woodman and Martin
on *recidere* at Tac. *Ann.* 3. 53. 4. The theory of pruning as a means of
securing a balance between fruiting and growth is still prevalent in
horticulture.

70. silua comas: for this juxtaposition, see the note on 5. 5.
29–30.

tollit: for *tollere* used for the growth of plants, cf. e.g. Ov. *Fast.* 3.
854 'sustulerat nullas, ut solet, herba comas', Luc. 4. 128 'tollere silua
comas', Köves-Zulauf (1990), 88–9.

fructumque: as well as the pruning metaphor, Statius draws on
the idea of a person bearing fruit through later achievements. Cf. e.g
Cic. *Cael.* 76 'in adulescentia uero tamquam in herbis significant quae
uirtutis maturitas et quantae fruges industriae sint futurae', *Sen.* 9, 62, 70
(with Powell ad loc.) 'uer enim tamquam adulescentiam significat,
ostenditque fructus futuros; reliqua autem tempora demetendis fruc-
tibus et percipiendis accommodata sunt', Seneca, *Ep.* 104. 4, Plu. *An
seni res publica gerenda sit* 789 F.

exspirat: the primary notion of the word is the process of emit-
ting or exhaling; cf. Plin. *Nat.* 9. 115 where pearls (*uniones*) are said
'senescere...coloremque exspirare'. Because of the shade caused by
excessive foliage, the fruit is unable to ripen properly; perhaps com-
pare the slightly different metaphor at Quint. *Inst.* 1. 3. 5 'non subest
uera uis nec penitus inmissis radicibus nititur, ut quae summo solo
sparsa sunt semina celerius se effundunt et imitatae spicas herbulae
inanibus aristis ante messem flauescunt'.

71. Pieriae tenero sub pectore curae: to demonstrate that
Crispinus is not a youth who will be corrupted on attaining his
independence, Statius mentions his taste for poetry as the first of
the various qualities which distinguish him from other less promising
contemporaries. The nature of the *curae* is unclear; Statius does not
explain whether Crispinus' taste for literature extends to compos-
ition. The *Pieriae...curae* give a more rounded image of Crispinus'
character; thus far the poem has concentrated on his suitability for
public office and a military career in the footsteps of his father.
Here Statius shows something of his general character and *mores*; cf.
Plin. *Ep.* 2. 13. 6–7, where Pliny praises the literary pursuits of the
young Voconius Romanus, especially his letters (cf. *Ep.* 9. 28. 1), when

recommending him to a military commander, Priscus.[57] Myers (2000), 125–6 notes the increasing social importance of literary activity in this period.

By itself *tenero sub pectore curae* might have jokingly implied erotic interests (cf. 127 n.), evoking the behaviour of Crispinus' undisciplined contemporaries, but Pieriae shows that Crispinus' heart is given to literature!

72. docti legem sibi dicere mores: Crispinus' high moral qualities are an integral part of his character. For the combination of cultural interests and moral qualities, compare Plin. *Ep.* 4. 27. 5 'interim ama iuuenem et temporibus gratulare pro ingenio tali, quod ille moribus adornat', Sen. *Dial.* 11. 3. 5; cf. Tac. *Ag.* 4. 2 for praise of Massilia, where Agricola studied, as 'locum Graeca comitate et prouinciali parsimonia mixtum ac bene compositum'.

For the idea of setting a law for oneself, note the Stoic tradition that a wise man would need no law (*SVF* iii. 519; cf. ii. 326, where justice can only come from Zeus or ἐκ τῆς κοινῆς φύσεως), Cic. *Leg.* 1. 18, 1. 33. *Rom.* 2. 14 ὅταν γὰρ ἔθνη τὰ μὴ νόμον ἔχοντα φύσει τὰ τοῦ νόμου ποιῶσιν, οὗτοι νόμον μὴ ἔχοντες ἑαυτοῖς εἰσιν νόμος is the classic exposition of this thought in the Christian tradition, on which see Kühl (1913), 84–7, Fitzmyer (1993), 310–11; later examples include Bernard of Clairvaux, *Liber de diligendo deo* 13. 36 'Ubi dixit: Factus sum mihimetipsi gravis, ostendit quod lex ipse sibi esset, nec alius hoc quam sibi ipse fecisset' and Giovanni Pascoli, *Agape* 84 'Est, quicumque sibi est bene conscius, ipse sibi lex.' The negative notion more familiar today, that of being a 'law unto oneself', is paralleled at Man. 5. 495–6: 'ipse sibi lex est, et qua fert cumque uoluntas | praecipitant uires; laus est contemnere cuncta.'

73. tunc: if one reads *hinc* (Baehrens), all the qualities of Crispinus subsequently described are a consequence of his *Pieriae curae*, *pudor*, and *mores*. But the two lists are too disparate. *nitor* is especially difficult after *hinc*; it is hard to see how Crispinus' splendour, even if it is not luxury, can be a result of his literary and moral tastes; *nitor* is more naturally attributed to his position and background. *tunc* is preferable.

hilaris probitas: cf. 5. 1. 65 n.

frons tranquilla: for instances where *frons* is used in conveying character, see *ThLL* vi/1. 1355. 83–1359. 3.

---

[57] Syme (1958), ii. 632 rejects the identification of this Priscus with the jurist Neratius Priscus.

73–4. nitorque | luxuriae confine tenens: for *nitor* in the sense of 'splendour', often with overtones of wealth, cf. *Silv.* 1. 3. 92 'sanusque nitor' (where the thought is similar), 3. 3. 149 'testis adhuc largi nitor inde adsuetus Etrusci', 4. 8. 57–8 'largumque nitorem | monstret auus' with Coleman, *OLD* s.v. *nitor* 4, 5; for Statius' fondness for words cognate with *nitor*, see van Dam on 2. 2. 10 'nitidae iuuenilis gratia Pollae'. *luxuria*, here used in its abstract sense, also recalls the simile of the unpruned plantation in 69–70. *timens* (Barth), though defended by Håkanson (1969), 130–1 on the questionable ground that '*confine tenere* ought to mean "hold (be situated in) the boundary zone between this and that"' (131), gives the wrong sense; there is no reason why Crispinus' *nitor* should *fear* the borderline between *luxuria* and decent conduct. Instead it keeps to it (*tenens*, M). For the concept of kindred vices and virtues expressed in terms of the narrow boundary between them, cf. Liv. 22. 12. 12 'pro cunctatore segnem, pro cauto timidum, adfingens uicina uirtutibus uitia, compellabat', Cic. *Rep.* 1. 44 (with Zetzel) 'nullum est enim genus illarum rerum publicarum, quod non habeat iter ad finitimum quoddam malum praeceps ac lubricum', Sen. *Ep.* 120. 8 'sunt enim, ut scis, uirtutibus uitia confinia', Plin. *Pan.* 4. 5 'postremo adhuc nemo exstitit, cuius uirtutes nullo uitiorum confinio laederentur'; for the rhetorical background in Rome see further Radermacher (1916), who discusses the influence of Arist. *Rhet.* 1367[a] on such passages as Quint. *Inst.* 2. 12. 4, 3. 7. 25.

This passage is the only Statian occurrence of *luxuria*, as opposed to six instances of *luxus* (*Theb.* 2. 85, 2. 438, *Ach.* 1. 616, *Silv.* 1. 3. 92, 1. 6. 51, 2. 1. 158). Statius' predilection for *luxus* is in keeping with the practice of Lucan, Valerius Flaccus, Silius and Tacitus; for comparative statistics on usage in prose and verse authors, see *ThLL* vii/2. 1935. 25–43.

74–5. pietasque per omnes | dispensata modos: the succeeding lines exhibit differing forms (*per omnes ... modos*) of Crispinus' *pietas* towards his father, brother, and mother; cf. Cic. *Amic.* 11: 'quid dicam de moribus facillimis, de pietate in matrem, liberalitate in sorores, bonitate in suos, iustitia in omnes?' For *dispensare* meaning 'distribute' as an extension of its association with weighing out, cf. Sen. *Con.* 10. 4. 2 'sine satellitibus tyrannus calamitates humanas dispensat', Plin. *Pan.* 35. 4 'quae singula quantum gratiae tibi dispensata adiecissent!'

75–7. Though Courtney places a full stop at the end of 76, the infinitives in 75 are dependent on *admonuit* (77), as recognized in previous editions.

75. aequaeuo . . . fratri: 65 n.

cedere: Vollmer interpreted *cedere* as an allusion to Crispinus' waiving his inheritance rights in favour of his brother ('dem gleichaltrigen (Zwillings-?) Bruder trat er willig das Recht der Erstgeburt ab'), and though P. White (1973), 284 n. 19 rightly questions Vollmer's notion of an 'Erstgeburtsrecht', *cedere* could suggest the legal process of *cessio hereditatis* (Gaius *Inst.* 2. 35–6, 3. 85–6; cf. Walbank on Plb. 31. 28. 3, where Scipio Aemilianus is praised for conceding his share of a paternal inheritance to his brother). *cedere*, however, need not be so technical, and is better construed as 'defer to'. Vollmer cites *Silv.* 3. 3. 152–3 'huius honori | pronior ipse etiam gaudebat cedere fratri', but *pronior* and *honori* indicate that *cedere* refers to deference rather than to some specific financial transaction. Compare also *Silv.* 1. 4. 70 'et magno gaudet cessisse nepoti', and the poetic context of Mart. 12. 44. 3 'carmina cum facias soli cedentia fratri'. Nauta (2002), 307 with n. 58 raises the intriguing suggestion that the phrase here may be designed to counter suggestions of hostility between the two brothers which had arisen at the mother's trial.

76. mirarique patrem: cf. 'tu disce patrem' (54); Crispinus has already anticipated the advice to heed the example of his father.

miserae: referring to Crispinus' mother, a sympathetic focalization from Crispinus' perspective, but she cannot be depicted as wholly nefarious, since she is after all the mother of Crispinus. On focalization, see further Fowler (2000), 40–63.

77. fortuna domus: the phrase is first attested in verse at Virg. *G.* 4. 209, where 'stat fortuna domus' is applied to the successful and enduring bees; cf. *Silv.* 2. 1. 137 'haec fortuna domus', where the *fortuna* is auspicious, and there is a contrast with the cruel intervention of Fate which ensues. But at Liv. 26. 18. 11, Ov. *Met.* 13. 525, Sen. *Con.* 7. 3. 3, Sen. *Her. F.* 200, Apul. *Met.* 9. 39 the phrase occurs in unfavourable contexts; cf. Sen. *Con.* 5. 1 'domus meae fata claudo'. Here the *fortuna domus* gives Crispinus the necessary character to show *pietas* to the various members of his family.

illa nefanda: construe *nefanda* with *pocula* rather than *illa*, because the mother was called *miserae* in the previous line. Construing *illa nefanda* together, in itself perhaps too strongly archaic (and for the rarity in Statius of such line-endings with grammatical concord, see 109 n. below), would leave *pocula* as a very vague and unspecific counterpart to *letales sucos*; for *nefanda pocula*, cf. Luc. 6. 454–5 'noxia . . . | pocula'.

78. letales sucos: *letalis* corresponds to the Greek δηλητήριος.
Cf. e.g φάρμακα δηλητήρια in a fifth-century BC inscription from
Teos, Meiggs and Lewis² 30 A 1–2, and, for the context of such
decrees, see further Herrmann (1981). In Latin, *letalis* can refer to
poisons and poisonous substances, as at *Silv.* 4. 6. 72, Sen. *Med.* 269–70,
Plin. *Nat.* 11. 118, 34. 176, V.Fl. 2. 155 'letalesque dapes infectaque
pocula cerno' (an expression of fear of a stepmother's actions), Sil. 12.
123–4, Apul. *Met.* 4. 2, Sulp. Sev. *Dial.* 1. 16. 1; *letales suci* is also found
at Cyprian *ad Donat.* 11, p. 12. 24. D.C. 67. 11. 6 notes an upsurge in
the use of poisoned needles during Domitian's reign, so that mention
of poison may have sounded a topical note.

79–80. for the thought, compare the description of Glaucias at
Silv. 2. 1. 48–9 'cui sibila serpens | poneret et saeuae uellent seruire
nouercae'; cf. *Silv.* 2. 1. 140–5, Hor. *Epod.* 5. 13–14 'impube corpus,
quale posset impia | mollire Thracum pectora', [Sen.] *Oct.* 170–1. The
general stereotype of stepmothers is unfavourable: see Otto (1890),
245–6, nos. 1239–41, Watson (1995). The classic combination of
serpents and a stepmother is the myth of Hera sending snakes to
attack Heracles in his cradle (Pi. *N.* 1. 35–47), though Heracles
overcame the snakes not with his voice, but with his infant hands
(Mart. 14. 177).

79. uoce: evoking the practice of charming snakes by incantation
particularly associated in Italy with the Marsi, who had legendary
associations with Circe and Medea. See e.g. the description of the
Marruvian Umbro at Virg. *A.* 7. 753–4 'uipereo generi et graviter
spirantibus hydris | spargere qui somnos cantuque manuque solebat'
with Horsfall ad loc., Bömer on Ov. *Met.* 7. 203, van Dam on *Silv.* 2. 1.
48–9, Sil. 8. 495–7 'at Marsica pubes | et bellare manu et chelydris
cantare soporem | uipereumque herbis hebetare et carmine dentem',
Letta (1972), 53–9, 95–9, 139–45, Dench (1995), 159–66; note also the
persistence of traditions in the region, such as the snake festival of
San Domenico at Cucullo described by Ashby (1929), 115–22. As well as
Italy, powers over snakes are associated with such inhabitants of north
Africa as the Psylli, as at e.g. Nic. fr. 32 with Gow and Scholfield ad
loc., Luc. 9. 913–14, 9. 927–8, Sil. 1. 411–13, 3. 301–2, 5. 351–6.

Here Crispinus' own mother has attempted to poison him, a
stepmother's crime (e.g. Virg. *G.* 2. 128, Sen. *Con.* 9. 5, Watson
(1995), 13–14) and a snake's method of killing (cf. Juv. 6. 641 'tune
duos una, saeuissima uipera, cena?'). For similar exploitation of the
frisson engendered by a mother worse than a stepmother compare e.g.

Cic. *Clu.* 199 'nouerca fili', Sen. *Con.* 4. 6 'dum alterius uis esse mater, utriusque es nouerca' with Watson (1995), 4–5, 9. 6. 4 'quid extimuisti tamquam nouercam?', 9. 6. 17 'tolle matris nomen: post damnationem nouerca est'. See also Juv. 6. 627–42, on the dangers posed to *pupilli* by mothers eager to secure their inheritances (cf. Sen. *Con.* 7. 5. 4 'liceat mihi nutrire puerum: nec cum matre illi nec cum tutore conueniet'), a passage which culminates in Pontia, who poisoned her two sons (638–42; see also Mart. 2. 34. 6, 4. 43. 5, 6. 75 with Grewing). P. White (1973), 283–4 has suggested that Crispinus' mother is a historical example of this tendency, although the poem itself does not suggest her motive, and, as White himself acknowledges (284), this requires the sequence of murder attempt followed by the ceremony of the *toga pura*, whereas the poem has the opposite sequence. Vessey (1973), 179 speculates that Crispinus' mother may have been an inspiration for Polyxo, who urges on the women of Lemnos to kill their menfolk in *Theb.* 5.

praeuertere: for the word's pre-emptive quality, cf. Sil. 3. 329 'imbelles . . . annos praeuertere saxo'.

80. uultu placare: *uultu* might hint that Crispinus' appearance could inspire erotic interest, as well as assuage a stepmother's anger (for *placare* in an erotic context, cf. Mart. 4. 22. 1 'prima passa toros et adhuc placanda marito'). For the 'amorous stepmother' theme, cf. e.g. Sen. *Phaed.* 684 'placui nouercae', Mart. 4. 16, Watson (1995), 136–9.

81. infestare . . . manes: for *infestare* of personal animosity, cf. Sil. 2. 277 'ductorem infestans odiis gentilibus Hannon'. Here there is an element of paradox, because one might expect a ghost to trouble the living.

82. cerno: used figuratively; compare the Sibyl at Virg. *A.* 6. 87 'et Thybrim multo spumantem sanguine cerno'.

83. flectentem <a> iustis: for Heinsius' *a iustis* and for *flectere* meaning departure from a particular policy or course of action, compare Sen. *Med.* 203 'animum ab ira flectere', Tac. *Dial.* 19. 1 'quem primum adfirmant flexisse ab illa uetere atque derecta dicendi uia'. Here *flectentem* must have an object, and one different from Crispinus, unless *parce precor* is addressed to Crispinus himself. With *me* as the implied object, Statius imagines Crispinus turning him away from the *iusta*, with, as suggested by Heinsius 462–3, a pun on *iusta* meaning 'funeral rites', and the adjectival form, 'just words of censure', picking up on *meritoque precatu* in 81; see examples in

5. I. 12–13 n. above. This seems preferable to emending to *uisus* (ς, Postgate), since if Crispinus has a forgiving attitude to his mother, there is no need for him to turn his gaze away from her pyre.

talia dicta parantem: emphasizing that these are imaginary remarks; for direct discourse introduced by *talia* as a less faithful representation of speech, see Laird (1999) 90–4, Gibson (2001) 142–3.

84–96. The position of this speech almost exactly halfway through the poem suggests a role of some importance, particularly as speeches are uncommon in the *Silvae* (van Dam (1984), 507–8 puts the percentage of direct speech in the *Silvae* at 13%). The context of the speech ensures that it is the emotional summit of the poem. Crispinus attempts to absolve his mother from blame, declares his wish that her crime be never more remembered, and acknowledges the necessity of the emperor's condemnation. The speech ends with Crispinus' fears for his mother after death and his desire to intercede with the powers of the underworld. The unexpected apostrophe of his mother in the final line (*tuis*, 96) gives a highly effective conclusion.

As has been noted, Statius faced the problem of how to praise one so young and inexperienced as Crispinus. Crispinus' desire to save his mother, and his defence of his friend in court (99–110) are his only real achievements so far. This speech is moreover an index of character, proving the earlier assertion that Crispinus' *pietas* was 'per omnes | dispensata modos', to all members of his family (74–6). The speech also justifies mention of a rather unsavoury episode, since the *pietas* of Crispinus is not merely the conventional duty offered to a parent, but a duty to a parent who tried to kill him. Thus what at first seems an unsuitable anecdote becomes a vehicle for a very lofty compliment. Nauta (2002), 307 sees Statius as providing Crispinus with some favourable publicity, as a response to what would have been a public scandal.

84. parce, precor: a stock phrase: cf. Tib. I. 8. 51 (the first attested instance), Hor. *Carm.* 4. I. 2 'parce precor, precor', Ov. *Ep.* 7. 163, 16. 11, 18. 45, 20. 117, *Met.* 2. 360–1 (*bis*), *Fast.* 2. 451, 4. 921, *Tr.* 2. 179, 3. 11. 32, 5. 2. 53, *Pont.* 2. 8. 25, Luc. 6. 773 'ne parce, precor', 7. 540, Stat. *Silv.* 5. 1. 179, Mart. 7. 68. 2, 10. 82. 7, Sil. 9. 124, 17. 286, Juv. 6. 172; in inscriptions see e.g. *CLE* 971. 9 and 2028. The usual word-order is varied at *CLE* 1883. 2 'et tu, uiator, precor, parce tumulum Narcissi'. For the ritual tone of *parce*, see N.–H. on Hor. *Carm.* 2. 19. 7.

cineri: though literally denoting the deceased's ashes, *cinis* can have an element of personification, as at Calv. fr. 16 Courtney

(*FLP*, pp. 207–9) 'forsitan hoc etiam gaudeat ipsa cinis', Prop. 2. 20. 16
'si fallo, cinis heu sit mihi uterque grauis', Virg. *A.* 4. 552 'non seruata
fides cineri promissa Sychaeo', Mart. 12. 52. 4 'cuius et ipse tui flagrat
amore cinis'.

fatum illud: as *crimenque dei* in the next line indicates, blame is
shifted away from Crispinus' mother (see next note). *illud* is not,
however, an adjective qualifying *fatum*, but a pronoun, referring
back to the mother's crime: this use of *illud* with an ellipse of *esse* is
paralleled at *Silv.* 1. 4. 43 'hoc illud, tristes inuitum audire catenas'
(where *illud* refers back to the alarm of the senate and people at
Rutilius Gallicus' ill health, which is then explained in terms of his
mild ways), 1. 4. 52 'non illud culpa senectae'; for the construction
more generally (without an ellipse) cf. e.g. Virg. *A.* 3. 173 'nec sopor
illud erat', 4. 675 'hoc illud, germana, fuit?', *OLD* s.v. *ille* 11b.

85. crimenque dei: Compare Priam's refusal to blame Helen,
as opposed to the gods, for the Trojan war at *Il.* 3. 164, but for the
view that the gods are not responsible for mortal wrongdoing, con-
trast Zeus' speech at *Od.* 1. 32–43 (especially 1. 32 οἷον δέ νυ θεοὺς
βροτοὶ αἰτιόωνται) where Zeus blames Aegisthus for not heeding the
warning of Hermes. Compare also the related idea that the gods
might only be interested in vengeance after the event rather than
prevention (see e.g. Luc. 4. 807–9 'felix Roma quidem ciuisque
habitura beatos, | si libertatis superis tam cura placeret | quam
uindicta placet', Tac. *Hist.* 1. 3. 2 'non esse curae deis securitatem
nostram, esse ultionem'), perhaps reflected in l. 86 *sero* (cf. Sext. Emp.
Math. 1. 287 with Blank ad loc. for the proverbial ὀψὲ θεῶν ἀλέουσι
μύλοι, ἀλέουσι δὲ λεπτά).

86. nec primo in limine: the image is of crossing a threshold
and committing a crime (cf. English 'transgression'). For the meta-
phorical use of *limen* cf. Lucr. 3. 681, Virg. *Aen.* 6. 427, Luc. 2. 106 (all
referring to the 'threshold of life').

88. excidat illa dies aeuo: *aeuo* here denotes the whole course
of time. Compare *Theb.* 11. 577–9 (cited in 89 n.), Prop. 3. 2. 25–6: 'at
non ingenio quaesitum nomen ab aeuo | excidet: ingenio stat sine
morte decus'.

88–9. nec postera credant | saecula: though posterity is
typically incredulous (N.–H. on Hor. *Carm.* 2. 19. 2), even with regard
to crimes (e.g. Sen. *Thy.* 753–4 'o nullo scelus | credibile in aeuo
quodque posteritas neget'), Crispinus fears that an exception will be
made in his mother's case.

89. nos certe taceamus: *nos* denotes Crispinus and perhaps his brother, but not Statius (because of *propriae...gentis* in 90). *taceamus* recalls *infanda* (87). It is a ironic that Crispinus' wish for the crime to remain unknown is so convincingly thwarted by Statius' poem; cf. the similar paradox at *Theb.* 11. 577–9:

> omnibus in terris scelus hoc omnique sub aeuo
> uiderit una dies, monstrumque infame futuris
> excidat, et soli memorent haec proelia reges.

One may contrast Lucan's assurance to Caesar that he (and Lucan) will not be consigned to the shadows (9. 986): 'a nullo tenebris damnabimur aeuo'.

91. exegit poenas: on Domitian's strictness and his *censoria potestas* see 5. 1. 42 n.; Griffin (2000), 79, discussing the present passage, notes that Statius 'speaks of Domitian's justice in terms of punishment and fear'. Crispinus' wish to appeal to the Eumenides (94–5) reflects the fact that such pleas for mercy would have been wasted in the upper world. Suet. *Dom.* 11. 2 notes Domitian's tactic of declarations of clemency as a prelude to harsh judgements. For the honorific periphrasis for the emperor in the relative clauses in 91–3, perhaps compare e.g. Hor. *Ep.* 1. 18. 56–7 'sub duce qui templis Parthorum signa refigit | nunc, et si quid abest Italis adiudicat armis'.

92. Pietas: Statius draws on a complex tradition of the Golden Age, ultimately derived from Hesiod who describes the forthcoming departure of *Aidos* and *Nemesis* from the wickedness of the world (*Op.* 197–201), and places *Dike*, the personification of Justice (ἡ δέ τε παρθένος ἐστὶ Δίκη, Διὸς ἐκγεγαυῖα, 256), beside Zeus, warning him of transgressions as they are committed (*Op.* 256–62). These two separate strands are fused by Arat. *Phaen.* 96–136 (cf. Cic. *Arat.* fr. 16. 6 Soubiran, Germ. *Arat.* 96–139), who identifies *Dike* as a daughter of Astraeus (cf. Hes. *Th.* 378–82, where Astraios is the father of the winds and the stars), though also acknowledging the existence of other traditions about her parentage (98–100). This in turn gives rise to the common concept in Latin literature of the departure of Themis, or the *Astraea uirgo*, from the earth, as at e.g. Virg. *G.* 2. 473–4 'extrema per illos | Iustitia excedens terris uestigia fecit'; the theme is most clearly expressed at Ov. *Met.* 1. 149–50 'uicta iacet pietas, et uirgo caede madentis | ultima caelestum terras Astraea reliquit', while at Juv. 6. 19–20 *Astraea* and *Pudicitia* leave the world together. On the whole topic, see further Clausen (1994), 119–26.

Here *Pietas* is said to have returned to the world under Domitian's rule; cf. Mart. 6. 7. 1–2 'Iulia lex populis ex quo, Faustine, renata est | atque intrare domos iussa Pudicitia est'. For the panegyric motif of the return of such figures, see Virg. *Ecl.* 4. 6 'iam redit et Virgo, redeunt Saturnia regna', Calp. *Ecl.* 1. 43–4 'et redit ad terras tandem squalore situque | alma Themis posito', *Buc. Eins.* 2. 23 'Saturni rediere dies Astraeaque uirgo'; note also the more conditional way in which Amm. 22. 10. 6 and 25. 4. 19 speaks of the return of Iustitia under Julian. Here, Statius pays a compliment to Crispinus: he dispensed *pietas* to his family in 74–6, so that his actions also evince the return of the goddess. Note also Cat. 64. 398 on the driving out of *iustitia* from mortal minds, which is then exemplified by the failure of children to mourn their parents (400). Crispinus goes against this tendency, by mourning even a parent who has attempted to kill him (cf. Cat. 64. 401 'optauit genitor primaeui funera nati').

Statius is quite inconsistent in the names he employs, often treating *Pietas* as *Dike/Astraea*. He summons *Pietas* to make one of her rare visits to earth at *Silv.* 3. 3. 1–7 (see further Laguna), yet at 5. 3. 89–90 he refers to *Pietas* and *Iustitia*, whilst at 1. 4. 2 *Astraea* is mentioned. At *Theb.* 11. 458 *Pietas* has long been settled in a place apart, offended by both gods and mortals.

93–4. satis haec lacrimandaque nobis | ultio: in keeping with Statius' earlier remark that Crispinus forgave his mother (76), here he declares that vengeance on her is *lacrimanda* for him, showing that he does not revel in her punishment.

94. exorare: the prefix *ex-* indicates a successful entreaty, whereas *orare* would give no indication of success or failure. Note Paul. Fest. p. 253. 23–4 Lindsay: 'impetrare est exorare'; cf. Serv. *A.* 3. 370: 'orare est petere, exorare impetrare'. *exorare* is commonly used of appeals to divinities: cf. *Silv.* 5. 3. 274 and note also 5. 1. 164 'exorabile numen'.

95. Eumenidas: the Furies, avenging deities, frequently referred to euphemistically as 'the kindly ones'. They are most celebrated for their hounding of the matricide Orestes, in Aeschylus' *Eumenides*; it is a curious reversal that a son should wish to plead for their kindness towards his mother. The Eumenides are also mentioned in concert with Cerberus at Virg. *G.* 4. 483.

timidaeque auertere Cerberon umbrae: on Cerberus as a terror for the dead, see *Silv.* 5. 1. 249–52 n. The Greek accusative

Cerberon is used *metri gratia* for the Latin termination *Cerberum*, though in the nominative Statius always uses the form *Cerberus*.

96. immemoremque … amnem: Lethe, the river of forget-fulness. For the transferred usage of *immemor* compare [Sen.] *Her. O.* 936 'stabo ante ripas, immemor Lethe, tuas', Sil. 16. 476–7; note also Hor. *Carm.* 2. 7. 21 'obliuioso … Massico' (with N.–H.). *immemorem* also suggests Crispinus' hope that his mother's deeds will be forgotten.

tuis … manibus: This sudden address to Crispinus' mother is especially effective since she has been alluded to only twice before in the speech, *cineri* (84) and *timidae … umbrae* (95–6). Crispinus' wish to appeal to the Eumenides thus gives way to an emotional apostrophe.

97. macte animo: *macte* can denote future blessing wished on a god or a man[58] (e.g. Cato *Agr.* 132. 1 'Iuppiter dapalis, … eius rei ergo macte hac illace dape pollucenda esto', *Silv.* 1. 5. 63–4 'macte, oro, nitenti | ingenio curaque puer'), but can also have the sense of 'well done!', or 'splendid!', referring to the past (cf. English 'Bless you!' as an expression of thanks): compare e.g. Virg. *A.* 9. 641–2 (addressed by Apollo to Ascanius) 'macte noua uirtute, puer, sic itur ad astra, | dis genite et geniture deos', *Silv.* 4. 8. 25–6 'macte, quod et proles tibi saepius aucta uirili | robore', and the ironic *Theb.* 11. 681 'macte, potes digne Thebarum sceptra tueri'. *macte animo* is a development of the idiom *macte uirtute esto* (*OLD* s.v. *macte* 2); for *macte* with the ablative in Statius compare *Theb.* 7. 280, *Silv.* 1. 2. 201, 1. 3. 106, 1. 5. 63–4, 2. 2. 95, 3. 1. 166, 3. 3. 31 (the genitive occurs at *Theb.* 2. 495 and *Silv.* 5. 1. 37).

Here *macte* refers both to the future and the past; Crispinus is congratulated on his *animus*, but there is also the hope that he will be fortunate in the future; for the gloomy context for such a felicitation, compare *Silv.* 3. 3. 31 and 5. 1. 37.

sed crescunt crimina matris: Crispinus' mother's crime seems worse in the light of his *pietas*. Vollmer compares Sen. *Thy.* 514–15 'pessimam causam meam | hodierna pietas fecit'.

98–9. ardua uirtus | adfectata tibi: *adfecto* can denote travel (*OLD* s.v. 1), e.g. Virg. *G.* 4. 562 'uiamque adfectat Olympo'. Here the metaphorical path to virtue is evoked: compare Hes. *Op.* 286–92 (where Hesiod tells his brother of the paths to κακότης and ἀρετή), Xen. *Mem.* 2. 1. 21–34 (where Prodicus' account of Heracles' meeting

---

[58] The word does not appear to be used to address women; Cassiod. *Var.* 11. 40. 2 'macte, Indulgentia, quae soluis et praesules' is addressed to personified *Indulgentia*.

with Vice and Virtue is related), Sal. *Jug.* 1. 3 'ubi ad gloriam uirtutis
uia grassatur', Hor. *Carm.* 3. 24. 44 (with N.–R.) 'uirtutisque uiam
deserit arduae', Sil. 15. 102 (from the speech of Virtus to Scipio)
'ardua saxoso perducit semita cliuo'.

   99–100. sodalis … palleret: Calderini's emendation of M's
plurals *sodales* and *pallerent* to singulars is necessary. The singulars
pauentis amici in 106 and *reus* in 110 are decisive. For the greater credit
accruing to defending (especially for one's friends) rather than pros-
ecuting, see Mayer on Tac. *Dial.* 5. 5.

   101. succinctaque iudice multo: Tisiphone at the trial of the
dead is similarly described (Virg. *A.* 6. 570–1): 'continuo sontis ultrix
accincta flagello | Tisiphone quatit insultans'; she is also 'palla suc-
cincta cruenta' at 6. 555. *Pace* Vollmer, *iudice multo* refers not to the
centumviral court (on which see *Silv.* 1. 4. 23–5, 4. 4. 43–5 with
Coleman, 4. 9. 16, Plin. *Ep.* 9. 23. 1, Kaser (1996), 52–5, Nauta
(2002), 145; note also the scorn of Cic. *De Orat.* 1. 173), which tried
civil cases, but to the judges of the *quaestio de adulteriis* which had been
established by Augustus (see below).

   102. uibraret … fulmen: for the thunderbolt as a means of
retribution, compare e.g. Ov. *Met.* 1. 253 'iamque erat in totas
sparsurus fulmina terras', Mart. 6. 83. 3, 6. Dido deems a thunderbolt
an appropriate punishment for an adulterous passion (Virg. *A.* 4. 25)
'uel pater omnipotens adigat me fulmine ad umbras'. *fulmen* also
neatly suggests oratory characterized in terms of thunder and light-
ning; cf. e.g. *Silv.* 4. 9. 15 'quae trino iuuenis foro tonabas', Prop. 4. 1.
134 'et uetat insano uerba tonare Foro', Sil. 8. 409–10 (of Cicero)
'implebit terras uoce et furialia bella | fulmine compescet linguae'.
For *uibrare* in oratorical contexts, see Aßfahl (1932), 87.

   Iulia: the *lex Iulia de adulteriis* of 18 BC, an important component of
Augustus' programme of moral reform; see Syme (1939), 445, Raditsa
(1980), 310–19, Treggiari (1996), 887–93, Galinsky (1996), 128–32. The
inherent severity of this law and the renewed campaign of moral
invigoration instigated by Domitian (Suet. *Dom.* 8, D.C. 67. 12. 1,
Mart. 6. 2 with Grewing, 6. 7, 6. 22, 6. 91; cf. Leberl (2004), 285–7)
explain the hyperbole of the law wielding a *castum fulmen*. For the
personification, compare Juv. 2. 37 'ubi nunc, lex Iulia, dormis?',
ThLL vii/2. 1256. 38–41, and Socrates' celebrated personification of
the laws of Athens (Pl. *Cri.* 50 A 6 ff.); here the personification and the
use of language which might also evoke an avenging Fury (101 n.)

magnifies the achievement of Crispinus in successfully defending his friend.

104. tacita studiorum occultus in umbra: for *studia* undertaken in leisure as an alternative to a more active lifestyle, compare Hor. *Ep.* 2. 2. 78, Virg. *G.* 4. 563–4 'illo Vergilium me tempore dulcis alebat | Parthenope studiis florentem ignobilis oti', Mart. 9. 84. 3 'haec ego Pieria ludebam tutus in umbra'. For the *umbra* of education, compare Juv. 7. 173 'ad pugnam qui rhetorica descendit ab umbra', the 'umbraticus doctor' censured at Petr. 2. 4, and Seneca's reference to 'studia, ut sic dixerim, in umbra educata' at Tac. *Ann.* 14. 53. 4. The transition from the declamation schools to the courts was not easy (Quint. *Inst.* 2. 10. 9, 5. 12. 17). Sen. *Con.* 9 pr. 5 likens the process to going out of a shady and obscure place into blinding daylight, while Tac. *Dial.* 35. 5 notes that the subject matter of declamation was rarely relevant in court. Plin. *Ep.* 2. 14. 2, lamenting the state of the centumviral courts, sourly comments that 'audaces atque etiam magna ex parte adulescentuli obscuri ad declamandum huc transierunt'.

105. tela: for the metaphorical usage of *telum* in oratorical contexts, see Aßfahl (1932), 85.

106. inermis adhuc et tiro: strictly a raw recruit to the legions, *tiro* and its cognates are also applied to the early stages of an oratorical career. Compare e.g. Cic. *Div. Caec.* 47 'hominem non aetate sed usu forensi atque exercitatione tironem', Quint. *Inst.* 12. 6. 3 'nec rursus differendum est tirocinium in senectutem', Aßfahl (1932), 88. *tiro* not only anticipates the military imagery of 108–9 but also suggests Crispinus' military inexperience. For *inermis* denoting inexperience cf. Cic. *de Orat.* 3. 136 'ad rem publicam gerendam nudi ueniunt atque inermes', *Fin.* 1. 22; contrast Cic. *de Orat.* 1. 32 'quid autem tam necessarium, quam tenere semper arma, quibus uel tectus ipse esse possis uel prouocare integer uel te ulcisci lacessitus?' For the use of *arma* and *armatus* to denote oratorical skill cf. e.g. Cic. *de Orat.* 1. 32, Tac. *Dial.* 5. 5, Aßfahl (1932), 84. Note the correption of the last syllable of *tiro* to a short ⁻*o* (for Statius' practice in this regard, see Mueller (1861), 9–10) before the violation of Hermann's Bridge (whereby a sense-pause in a fourth-foot dactyl after the first short syllable is usually avoided).

107. tales ... annos: for praise of impressive youthful eloquence, cf. *Silv.* 1. 4. 71–2, 4. 4. 45 'et iuuenis facundia praeterit annos', 4. 9. 14–16.

aspexit: for the idea of statues being cognisant of legal proceedings going on around them cf. Mart. 2. 64. 8 'ipse potest fieri Marsua causidicus', Juv. 1. 128 'iurisque peritus Apollo'.

107–8. Romulus . . . Dardaniusque senex: a reference to the Forum Augusti, where statues of Romulus and Aeneas (carrying Anchises, who could be the *senex*, although *senex* can also denote 'ancient' referring to antiquity rather than old age; see further Coleman on *Silv.* 4. 9. 20) were at the centre of the two exedrae on either side of the temple of Mars Ultor; cf. Ov. *Fast.* 5. 563–6 (where Mars looks at the temple) 'hinc uidet Aenean oneratum pondere caro | et tot Iuleae nobilitatis auos; | hinc uidet Iliaden umeris ducis arma ferentem, | claraque dispositis acta subesse uiris', and see further Lugli (1965), 19–20 nos. 121, 126, Zanker (1968), 14–15, (1988), 201–10, Galinsky (1996), 204–6, *LTVR* ii. 290–1 (V. Kockel). According to Suet. *Aug.* 29. 1 the forum was built so as to provide further accommodation for legal business, particularly *publica iudicia* and *sortiones iudicum.* Crispinus may have pleaded before Domitian; Claudius (Suet. *Cl.* 33. 1; cf. Tac. *Ann.* 12. 43. 1) and Trajan (D.C. 68. 10. 2) are known to have sat in judgement in the Forum Augusti.

108–9. medii bellare togata | strage fori: a play on the usual association of the forensic arts with peacetime. Roman authors were fond of using military imagery for the activities of the courts; cf. e.g. *Silv.* 3. 5. 87 'nulla foro rabies aut strictae in iurgia leges', 4. 5. 51–2 'ensisque uagina quiescit | stringere ni iubeant amici', Ov. *Rem.* 152 'uade per urbanae splendida castra togae', Sen. *De Ira* 2. 8. 2 'inter istos quos togatos uides, nulla pax est'. *strages* ('slaughter') is stronger than the much more common *pugna*; see e.g. Quint. *Inst.* 5. 12. 22, 6. 3. 28, Aßfahl (1932), 95–6.

The martial language suggests Crispinus' forthcoming career; it is a neat compliment to use the language of military success about one who is destined for a posting abroad. The imagery exaggerates Crispinus' achievement; a successful defence of a friend in court is described as if it was a great military victory.

109. stupuere: cf. Sen. *Con.* 7 pr. 5 (on Albucius) 'memini admiratione Hermagorae stupentem ad imitationem eius ardescere'. Wonder is an appropriate reaction to the prodigious deeds of youth, hence Statius' astonishment at the sight of Crispinus on horseback (117 below); cf. *Silv.* 2. 1. 119 'ipse pater sensus, ipsi stupuere magistri', 5. 3. 136. See also Cicero's reflections on his early career at *Orat.* 107, and *Laus Pis.* 55 'quis non attonitus iudex tua respicit ora?' Senatorial admiration for Crispinus has already been intimated at 27 above.

temptamina tanta: for this kind of hexameter ending where the last two words share the same termination in grammatical concord, see Harrison (1991), (1995), who notes that in the *Silvae* there are only two instances, here and 5. 5. 74, 'munera nostra' (there are five in the whole of the *Thebaid*); at 77 above I have argued that *illa nefanda* is not a further example. Though *-men* can be a poetic shortening of the *-mentum* termination of nouns, as noted by Leumann (1947), 130, the first attested appearance of *temptamen* is at Cic. *Agr.* 2. 16; the only other occurrences before late antiquity are Ov. *Met.* 3. 341, 7. 734, 13. 19. *temptamina* adds a note of daring to *conatus*, the pairing adding to the grandeur of Crispinus' efforts.

110. et te reus ipse timebat: M's *nec te* cannot stand, since there is no rhetorical point in saying that the defendant was not afraid of his advocate.

Markland favoured *pro te*, arguing that the defendant is afraid 'quasi mutatis uicibus tu *reus*, ille *patronus* fuisset'. *timeo* can be construed with *pro* and the ablative, but the reader cannot be expected to deduce this imaginary reversal of roles from the laconic *pro te*. One might instead take *pro te* to refer to the defendant's fears for Crispinus (cf. Baehrens's *de te*), but there is no good reason why the defendant should have feared for Crispinus (if the trial were to have been politically motivated, it would not be tactful to allude to this after the event), especially in the light of such an impressive performance in court. Phillimore's *nec se*, combined with the first edition's *tenebat*, makes two changes to M's text and produces a feeble and imprecise sequel to the amazement of the senators.

Vollmer argues that *nec ... reus* refers to the plaintiff, by a kind of litotes, 'and the man who is not the defendant'. The presence of another word between *nec* and *reus* makes this less likely, as noted by Klotz, and there is moreover no parallel for *nec ... reus* as an equivalent for *accusator*.

nec tunc (Leo) sidesteps the difficulties of *te*, and *tunc* at least suggests a moment after which the defendant no longer feared a conviction. But the defendant's lack of fear, even if *rei* are conventionally frightened or wretched (thus *palleret* in 100 and *pauentis* in 106 above; see further N.–H. on Hor. *Carm.* 2. 1. 13) is a feeble sequel to the admiration of the statues and senators; *ipse* seems especially redundant.

A very weak conjecture, Karsten's *nae te deus*, may nevertheless be illuminating. Karsten recognized that the point of the passage is to describe extreme responses to Crispinus' brilliant oratory; Romulus and Aeneas had never beheld such a spectacle, and the senators were astonished by his efforts. Accordingly Karsten suggested that the third clause should be in parallel to the first two; in his search for a climax he emended to *nae te deus* so that even the emperor himself is afraid. This emendation, though improbable, since it would have been inappropriate to ascribe fear to Domitian, does, however, point to the need for a climax.

The one person, above all others, who would not be expected to fear Crispinus, is the defendant himself. *et te reus ipse timebat* (Shackleton Bailey) gives point to *reus ipse* and a striking apostrophe of Crispinus. Unusual behaviour from defendants is not without precedent: compare Sen. *Con.* 8. 1 'alii pro reis rogant, ego rogabo ream' and 9. 6. 19 'accusator insidias reae timui'.

111–24. The concluding section of praise for Crispinus emphasizes his physical qualities (cf. *Laus Pis.* 178–89), and hence his suitability for a military career. Physical attributes are one of the three subdivisions that can be praised or blamed in epideictic (see e.g. *Rhet. Her.* 3. 6. 10 with Caplan's note a, p. 174). His intellectual ability is not forgotten; in 111–2 his *uires* meet the needs of his *animus*. For the transition from one quality to another, cf. the progression from eloquence to physical prowess at *Silv.* 4. 4. 64–5, and the shift from Parthenopaeus' beauty to his courage at *Theb.* 4. 253 'nec desunt animi, ueniat modo fortior aetas'.

111. promptaeque ad fortia uires: Crispinus' strength is appropriately directed towards brave deeds. The *fortia* are anticipated rather than accomplished.

112. sufficiunt animo atque ingentia iussa sequuntur: for this idea, cf. Vell. 2. 127. 3 (on Sejanus) 'sufficiente etiam uigori animi compage corporis'; note also 45–6 above (and n.) 'iussisque ingentibus unus | sufficere' describing Bolanus' subordinate role under Corbulo in the East. Just as Bolanus was subordinate to Corbulo, so too is Crispinus' bodily strength subordinate to his intellect. See 13–14 and 68–72 (with notes) above for Crispinus' maturity.

113. ipse ego: the personal note suggests verisimilitude; Statius affirms his own autopsy of Crispinus' prowess. Cf. e.g. *Silv.* 1. 2. 85–90, Tac. *Dial.* 17. 4 'nam ipse ego in Britannia uidi senem'.

te nuper Tiberino in litore uidi: a neat imitation of Virg. *Ecl.*
2. 25 'nec sum adeo informis: nuper me in litore uidi', itself a response
to Theoc. 6. 34–5 καὶ γάρ θην οὐδ' εἶδος ἔχω κακὸν ὥς με λέγοντι. | ἦ
γὰρ πρᾶν ἐς πόντον ἐσέβλεπον, ἧς δὲ γαλάνα. The attempt at self-
assertion by Virgil's Corydon is transformed into an elegant compli-
ment from Statius to Crispinus. Though Virgil used *litore* to refer to
the area of water closest to the land, since there could otherwise be no
reflection (see further Clausen ad loc., *ThLL* vii/2. 1537. 52–1538. 11),
Statius alters the nuance of *litore*, which here denotes the river bank
(cf. e.g. Virg. *A.* 8. 83 'procubuit uiridique in litore conspicitur sus').
Statius may also be recalling Horace's autopsy of the Tiber in flood at
Carm. 1. 2. 13–16 'uidimus flauum Tiberim retortis | litore Etrusco
uiolenter undis | ire deiectum monumenta regis | templaque Vestae':
on the flooding of the Tiber and ancient explanations in terms of the
build-up of water at the mouth (possibly alluded to in 114 by Statius'
qua Tyrrhena uadis Laurentibus aestuat unda; cf. Hor. *Carm.* 2. 6. 3–4 'ubi
Maura semper | aestuat unda'), see further N.–H. on Hor. *Carm.* 1. 2.
13–14. Whether or not Statius is alluding to theories on the causes of
the Tiber's flooding, *uadis Laurentibus* refers to the estuary of the Tiber,
and the marshy land on the southern side of the estuary (note the salt-
pans in the region of Ostia mentioned by Liv. 1. 33. 9 'in ore Tiberis
Ostia urbs condita, salinae circa factae').

115–16. On riding exercises, see N.–H. on Hor. *Carm.* 1. 8. 6.
The description of Crispinus in these lines suggests the leisured
occupations of an aristocrat.

117. siqua fides dictis: an admission of the implausibility of the
comparison, which paradoxically adds weight to the poet's demands
for credibility; cf. *Silv.* 2. 1. 50, 2. 6. 29–30, Stinton (1990), 236–64,
Hutchinson (1993), 38 with n. 73. Contrast the more uncertain tone of
Ov. *Am.* 1. 3. 16 'tu mihi, siqua fides, cura perennis erit'. For *siqua fides*
see e.g. Virg. *A.* 2. 143, 3. 434, 6. 459, *ThLL* vi/1. 683. 53 ff.

Martemque putaui: *armatumque* (M) cannot be right, since if
Crispinus was *dextraque minacem* (116), he was carrying a weapon; it
would therefore be absurd for Statius to have thought that Crispinus
was armed. Markland's *Martemque*, defended by Håkanson (1969),
131–3, is preferable. Comparisons with Mars or Ares are of course
not uncommon in epic: see e.g. *Il.* 2. 479, 11. 295, 12. 130, 13. 298–300,
22. 132, A.R. 3. 1282–3, Virg. *A.* 12. 331–6, Stat. *Theb.* 12. 733–6
(where Theseus is likened to Mars), Sil. 1. 433–6, 4. 460, 17. 487–90;
note also, though the text is in doubt, Ov. *Tr.* 5. 7. 17 'uox fera, trux

uultus, uerissima Martis imago.'[59] An especially close parallel for confusion of a person's appearance with that of Mars is Calp. *Ecl.* 7. 83–4 where Corydon describes his impression of the emperor:[60] 'ac, nisi me uisus decepit, in uno | et Martis uultus et Apollinis esse putaui.'

For confusion of mortals with gods, cf. *Silv.* 3. 4. 26–30 with Laguna's n.

118. Gaetulo ... equo: neighbours of the Numidians, the Gaetuli were famous for their horsemanship (especially riding without bridle); cf. Luc. 4. 677–8 'Autololes Numidaeque uagi semperque paratus | inculto Gaetulus equo', Sil. 2. 64 'nullaque leuis Gaetulus habena'.

pulcher: *pulcher* is the characteristic epithet of Ascanius/Iulus in Virg. (see *A.* 5. 570, 7. 477–8, 9. 293, 9. 310), and evokes the beauty of a young hero; note also the use of *pulcher* to refer to Parthenopaeus at *Theb.* 4. 251–2 (see 122 n.). The adjective described the young horse to which Crispinus was compared in l. 22. It is also used by Statius in less heroic situations as well: note the use of the word to refer to Philetos (*Silv.* 2. 6. 35, 71) and Earinus (*Silv.* 3. 4. 16, 66). For the eroticization of young men in Statius, see La Penna (1996).

119. nouercales ibat uenator in agros: the *nouercales ... agros* are the north African lands of Dido where Ascanius hunted (Virg. *A.* 4. 156–9); *nouercalis* strikingly suggests that the relationship between Aeneas, and Dido was like a marriage, even though Virgil denies this (*A.* 4. 172). Elsewhere, Ascanius' stepmother is of course Lavinia: see *Silv.* 5. 3. 40 'odit et infaustae regnum dotale nouercae' (see n.), Juv. 12. 71 'atque nouercali sedes praelata Lauino'. On stepmothers, see 79–80 n. above.

120. miseramque patri flammabat Elissam: the line must refer to Ascanius' role in the development of Dido's passion for Aeneas. Statius draws attention to a difficulty in the Virgilian original, the age of Ascanius, since it is not the hunt which inflames Dido in the *Aeneid* but the substitution of Cupid for Ascanius by Venus (note *A.* 1. 660 'incendat reginam atque ossibus implicet ignem', 1. 688 'occultum inspires ignem fallasque ueneno'); the description of the

---

[59] Martis *Gothani manus secunda* : mortis *Gw* : mentis *Housman*.

[60] For parallels between Statius and Calpurnius Siculus, see Håkanson (1969), 133, Courtney (1987) argues for Calpurnian imitation of authors such as Statius, Martial, and Juvenal. The dating of Calpurnius Siculus is of course controversial.

supposed Ascanius at *A.* 1. 715–19 is scarcely suggestive of a youth who might lead a hunt:

> ille ubi complexu Aeneae colloque pependit
> et magnum falsi impleuit genitoris amorem,
> reginam petit. haec oculis, haec pectore toto
> haeret et interdum gremio fouet inscia Dido
> insidat quantus miserae deus.

Despite the unfavourable outcome of Dido's love, Ascanius' (and subsequently Parthenopaeus') ability to elicit an amorous response is not inauspicious in this simile. The similes must be viewed as praise of Crispinus, and not in terms of their epic antecedents; compare Pi. *P.* 10. 59–60, where Hippocles is complimented as a μέλημα for young maidens.

flammabat: M's *flagrabat* is unsatisfactory since the verb is usually intransitive; Prop. 1. 13. 23–4 'nec sic caelestem flagrans amor Herculis Heben | sensit in Oetaeis gaudia prima iugis' is no help, because *flagrans amor . . . Heben* means 'burning love for Hebe', not 'inflaming love for'; in this passage *flagrabat* would thus wrongly suggest that Ascanius was in love with Dido. *flammabat* (Heinsius) gives a transitive verb, with *patri* as a dative of advantage. Cf. Virg. *A.* 3. 330, 4. 54, Sen. *Tro.* 303–4 'iamne flammatum geris | amore subito pectus', V.Fl. 8. 300 'coniugio atque iterum sponsae flammatus amore' for *flammare* describing the effects of love. D. A. Slater (1907), 147–8 conjectured *placabat* (cf. 80 above, 'omnes uultu placare nouercas') alluding to Venus' plan to ensure Aeneas' safety whilst in Carthage (Virg. *A.* 1. 671–5), but *flammabat*, palaeographically closer to the near-synonym *flagrabat*, is preferable.

121. Troilus: though the killing of Troilus by Achilles is some-times takes place in the temple of Thymbraean Apollo (see Apollod. *Epit.* 3. 32 with Frazer's notes), here and at *Silv.* 2. 6. 32–3 '[qualem] nec circum saeui fugientem moenia Phoebi | Troilon Haemoniae deprendit lancea dextrae', Statius imagines Achilles pursuing Troilus, the youngest son of Priam and Hecuba, before killing him. Achilles' pursuit is also mentioned in Σ *Il.* 24. 257b (A), and at Virg. *A.* 1. 474–8, where one of the scenes of the Trojan War seen by Aeneas at Carthage depicts Troilus in flight from Achilles, having lost control of his chariot. However, whereas at *Silv.* 2. 6. 32–3 the Philetos whom Statius praises is dead, here the tone is more positive since Crispinus is alive; the description of Troilus in flight emphasizes his skill in avoiding his pursuer (*haud aliter gyro leuiore minantes* | *eludebat equos*), and

Achilles is only alluded to glancingly, with the epithet *minantes* applied
to his chariot-team. Like Ascanius and Parthenopaeus, Troilus is
another hero noted for youthful beauty (thus at S. fr. 619 Radt,
Troilus is given the epithet ἀνδρόπαις, which A. *Septem*, 533 had
used for Parthenopaeus), and there was a tradition that Achilles was
in fact in love with him: see Lyc. 307–13 (with Tzetzes' scholia), Serv.
A. 1. 474, N.–H. on Hor. *Carm.* 2. 9. 16.

122. quem: Parthenopaeus, from Arcadia, was the son of Ata-
lanta, and famed for fleetness of foot and beauty (*Theb.* 6. 565–8, 9.
699 ff. with Dewar's n.); cf. the memorable appearance of Partheno-
paeus in the Argive catalogue at *Theb.* 4. 251–3:

> pulchrior haud ulli triste ad discrimen ituro
> uultus et egregiae tanta indulgentia formae;
> nec desunt animi, ueniat modo fortior aetas.

He was one of the Seven who fought against Thebes, dying, in the
Thebaid, at the hands of Dryas: see *Theb.* 9. 841–76 with Dewar, who
notes variant mythical traditions of his death. For critical discussion
of the character of Parthenopaeus in the *Thebaid*, see e.g. Vessey
(1973), 294–303, Dewar (1991), pp. xxii–xxvii, xxx.

For such comparisons with Parthenopaeus, cf. *Silv.* 2. 6. 40–5, a
passage where Statius compares the youthful but manly appearance
of Philetos to that of Parthenopaeus. Parthenopaeus is also cited as
a type of extreme youth at Mart. 6. 77. 2 'tam iuuenis quam nec
Parthenopaeus erat'; cf. 9. 56. 7–8 'non iaculo, non ense fuit laesusue
sagitta, | casside dum liber Parthenopaeus erat' and 11. 86 where
a young man with a cough is called Parthenopaeus. On the resonance
of the Parthenopaeus story among Statius' contemporaries, see fur-
ther Dewar (1991), pp. xxxiv–xxxvii.

de turribus altis: for *altus* as an epithet for the towers on the
walls of Thebes, cf. *Theb.* 10. 742, 11. 219, 11. 291–2. Towers and city-
walls are obvious places for women to look on scenes of battle below:
for the Theban mothers, note especially *Theb.* 7. 240–2 'nondum
hostes contra, trepido tamen agmine matres | conscendunt muros,
inde arma nitentia natis | et formidandos monstrant sub casside
patres', at the beginning of the war. There are set piece examples of
teichoscopia such as Helen and Priam in *Il.* 3. 161–244, Antigone in the
war of the Seven against Thebes (E. *Ph.* 88–201, Sen. *Phoen.* 414–42,
Stat. *Theb.* 7. 243–373), and Medea watching the fighting against
the Scythians in V.Fl. 6. 575–601, 657–89. Note also briefer but

nevertheless powerful examples such as the πύργος to which Andro-
mache goes to get news of Hector and from which she later sees
Hector being dragged by Achilles' chariot (*Il.* 6. 371–3, 22. 462–4), the
Parthian matron and maiden seeing the young Roman from the walls
at Hor. *Carm.* 3. 2. 6–12 (where N.–R. have further examples), Amata
seeing the onset of the Trojans (Virg. *A.* 12. 595), prior to committing
suicide, and the Saguntine mothers watching the onset of Hannibal at
Sil. 2. 251–2.

123. uersantem in puluere turmas: Markland emends *metas*
(M) to *turmas*. There can be no question of construing *uersari* with *metas*
as the object round which one turns, for which *OLD* offers no parallel
(Vollmer (1893), 841 tries to argue that '*uersare metas* idem est quod
flectere gyros', but the physicality of *metas* militates against this). *metas*
would have to imply some kind of competitive race, and although
Parthenopaeus figures in the funeral games for the infant Arche-
morus in *Theb.* 6, winning the footrace, those games were held at
Nemea, whereas here the two learned epithets *Ogygio* (referring to
Ogygus or Ogyges, the ruler of the Ectenes who had been the first to
dwell on the site of Thebes, as discussed by Dewar on *Theb.* 9. 812)
and *Tyriae* (alluding to Cadmus' Phoenician origin) set the scene
before Thebes. Vollmer wrongly argues against *turmas* on the grounds
that Parthenopaeus is not presented as a leader here or in the *Thebaid*,
in spite of descriptions of him as a leader of Arcadian forces at *Theb.* 4.
246 ff., 4. 310, where he is called *dux*, and at 6. 618, where he is *rex*.
The martial setting supports *turmas* (Courtney compares *Theb.* 9. 849–
50 'etenim huc iam fessus et illuc | mutabat turmas', from the episode
culminating in Parthenopaeus' death), and the corruption to *metas* is
explicable in terms of the equestrian context. *uersantem in puluere turmas*
could denote actual battle or perhaps military manoeuvres prior to
combat.

124. non toruo lumine: such was Parthenopaeus' beauty that
he could win the favour of his enemies; cf. *Theb.* 9. 709–11, where
the local nymphs of Thebes are charmed by his appearance, 882,
where his death is 'ipsisque nefas lacrimabile Thebis', and 12. 807,
where both sides weep for Parthenopaeus. The litotes *non toruo* hints at
the opposite (and expected) reaction of hostility to an enemy from
mothers who might have lost, or who might lose their sons in battle,
an attitude exemplified in extreme form by Hecuba's desire to eat the
liver of Achilles (*Il.* 24. 212).

125. ergo age: this figure of encouragement (cf. e.g. *Silv.* 1. 2. 182 3. 1. 23, 4. 3. 107) marks the beginning of the final exhortation to Crispinus to achieve a glorious career.

magni: so Calderini for M's *magno*, which cannot stand alone in the parenthesis; Vollmer's attempt to retain *magno* by construing it with *animo* in 127 is unsatisfactory, since he has to emend *nam* to *iam* A break in the sense is much more natural before *nam* than after *iam*

indulgentia: by this time almost a technical term for imperial favour, which is reflected by the more frequent use of the term in the second century AD not only in official documents but also in the writings of the jurists, as noted by Gaudemet (1962), 7–15; cf. Waldstein (1964), 130–40. In Statius, cf. *Silv.* 1. 2. 174–5 'sic indulgentia pergat | praesidis Ausonii', a similar parenthesis also in the context of anticipating a future career, 3. 4. 64 'multa tibi diuum indulgentia fauit'; cf. Courtney on Juv. 7. 21. The word also appears in Pliny's correspondence with Trajan; see Sherwin-White on Plin. *Ep.* 10. 92. Cotton (1984) notes that the term was first used to refer to Julius Caesar (Cic. *Att.* [Balbus and Oppius] 9. 7a. 2 'et hoc Caesarem pro sua indulgentia in suos probaturum putamus'), and discusses the single attested instance from the reign of Titus (*AE* 1962, 288, ll. 6–7) before discussing the more extensive evidence from subsequent reigns. From Domitian's reign, note *CIL* ix. 5420, a letter of Domitian to the people of Falerio, where Domitian refers to Augustus as 'diligentissimi et indulgentissimi erga quartanos suos principis' (ll. 21–3); Cotton, ibid., 249 notes the parallel with Statius' reference to Domitian as 'indulgentissimo imperatori' at *Silv.* 1 pr. 18, and note also that *indulgentissimus* had also been applied to Tiberius, 'patri optumo et indulgentissimo' in *Senatus consultum de Cn. Pisone patre* 58–9: see Eck, Caballos, and Fernández (1996), 42–3 and 182 n. 497. See also Flower (2001), 631, who notes the use of *indulgentia* in *AE* 1973, 137 'indulgentia maximi diuinique principis', to refer to Domitian's role as benefactor towards the community of Puteoli, and the context of earlier usages of *indulgentia* by Titus and Domitian. Though Suet. *Jul.* 69 'nec tam indulgentia ducis quam auctoritate', commenting on the swiftness with which Caesar curbed legionary mutinies, implies a strong contrast between *indulgentia* and *auctoritas*, Syme (1958), ii. 755, noting that Hadrian was the first emperor to adopt *indulgentia* on his coinage, remarks that the tone of the word was 'benevolent, but conveying the benevolence of a master (cf. "clementia")'.

pulsat: 'pushes on' or 'impels' (*OLD* 8a), giving a paradoxical contrast to the mildness implied by *indulgentia*.

126. hilaris: Vollmer construes this as a dative of the older form *hilarus* (on which see Macrob. *Sat.* 1. 4. 16, W. A. Baehrens (1922), 108), but there is no reason why it should not be nominative in accordance with normal classical usage. The argument for the dative is that the *hilara uota* refer to the *optanda* of l. 11, but the alternative is for the brother to be *hilaris*, which need not entail any difficulty; for this type of characterization, cf. Crispinus' *hilaris probitas* (73). An adjective of this kind is more suitable when applied to a person rather than to prayers or good wishes; one might expect a word such as *benignus* or *bonus* as the complement to *uota*, whereas *hilaris* seems too light in tone. On Crispinus' brother see 65 n. and p. 181 above.

uestigia: for the metaphor of following in a person's footsteps, cf. e.g. *Silv.* 5. 3. 177, *Theb.* 5. 441–2 'audet iter magnique sequens uestigia mutat | Herculis', 12. 817 'sed longe sequere et uestigia semper adora', Hor. *Ep.* 2. 2. 80 'contracta sequi uestigia uatum', Plin. *Pan.* 15. 4, *OLD* s.v. *uestigium* 5c. Juv. 14. 36 'sed reliquos fugienda patrum uestigia ducunt' is a bitter comment on the idea of imitating one's own family.

127. fortes castrorum concipe curas: *cura* is often used in erotic contexts (cf. 71 n.); *curas*, combined with *fortes* and *castrorum*, gives a paradoxical variant of the *militia amoris* topos, since Crispinus' *curae* are for the military life and not for the lifestyle of a lover.

128. monstrabunt acies: for the didactic overtones of *monstro* see 5. 3. 137 n.

Actaeaque uirgo: 'the Attic maiden', Minerva; for her links with Domitian, see 5. 3. 91 n. On the epithet and its popularity in Greek and Roman literature, see Hollis on Call. *Hec.* fr. 1 (= fr. 230 Pf.).

130. iam tenero permisit plaudere collo: the Salii beat the shields with a staff; for their dances, see further Cirilli (1913), 97–102. To be a Salian, it was essential to be of patrician rank; see the references collected by Cirilli (1913), 57–9. There were two colleges of Salians, one associated with the Palatine hill (*Palatini*) and traditionally founded by Numa (Liv. 1. 20. 4, Plu. *Numa* 13), and one founded by Tullus Hostilius (Liv. 1. 27. 7, D.H. 3. 32. 4), associated with the Quirinal hill (*Collini*; they are also referred to as *Agonales* or *Agonenses*); for their names, see Var. *L.* 6. 14, D.H. 2. 70. 1. Cirilli, ibid. 34 suggests that Crispinus may have belonged to the *Collini*; this is attractive in view of the reference to *Quirinus* (Romulus) in 129, and perhaps also the word *collo* ('neck'), in 130, which might be felt to echo

the name of Crispinus' college. Under the empire, the two colleges
continued separately at least into the third century, to judge from
attestations in inscriptions; see Cirilli, ibid. 33–41. Virtually all patri-
cians are likely to have been Salians; indeed Scheid (1978), 640 notes
that there are numerous cases of patricians making no mention of
having been Salians in their *cursus*. Statius emphazes Crispinus' youth
(*tenero ... collo*), but in fact it was normal for the Salii to be appointed
(by the emperor, under the principate) when they were young (Cirilli
(1913), 59–60, Scheid (1978), 642), though the case of Marcus Aurelius,
appointed by Hadrian to the order in his eighth year (*SHA M
Antoninus* 4. 2–3), may be regarded as exceptional. Statius records
that his father gave instruction to the Salii at *Silv.* 5. 3. 180–1 (see note).

131. nubigenas clipeos: these are the curiously shaped shields
(Ov. *Fast.* 3. 377–8, Plu. *Numa* 13. 9–10) carried by the Salii in rituals in
honour of Mars (Liv. 1. 20. 4). The tradition was that a shield fell from
heaven during the reign of Numa (Ov. *Fast.* 3. 373–8, Plu. *Num.* 13. 2;
cf. Virg. *A.* 8. 664 'lapsa ancilia caelo', Liv. 1. 20. 4 'caelestia arma,
quae ancilia appellantur'). Plu. *Numa* 13 relates the tradition that one
Mamurius was required by Numa to produce eleven identical copies
so as to thwart any attempted theft of such a valuable sacred object;
cf. D.H. 2. 71. 2, Ov. *Fast.* 3. 373–92. The *ancilia* were naturally not
used in battle (*intacta caedibus arma*), to avoid pollution.

Though M has *nubigeras*, Politian in his commentary reads *nubi-
genas. nubiger*, found only in later Latin, according to Lewis and
Short who give one reference in Cassiodorus, literally means 'cloud-
carrying'. But 'born from a cloud' (reading *nubigenas*) is more appro-
priate to shields which fell from the sky. *nubigena*, usually applied to the
Centaurs, the progeny of the union of Ixion with a cloud (cf. *Theb.* 5.
262–3 'si quando profundo | Nubigenae caluere mero', Virg. *A.* 7.
674, 8. 293, Ov. *Met.* 12. 211, 541, Germ. *Arat.* 422, Luc. 6. 386–7), is
also used of Phrixus, the son of Nephele at Col. 10. 155. *Theb.* 1. 365
'nubigenas ... amnes' is however a good parallel for the literal (as
opposed to mythological) usage which is found here.

132–51. Statius mentions possible destinations for Crispinus.
The list is not to be considered either as exclusive or as indicative of
contemporary trouble spots, but evokes the sweep of the whole
Roman empire; cf. *Silv.* 1. 4. 72–93 for a similar list of *past* destinations
where Rutilius Gallicus had served. Overall, this passage emphasizes
travel more than military action; compare Maecius Celer's journey to
the East (*Silv.* 3. 2. 101–22) where the emphasis on sightseeing is even

more obvious: only after twenty lines of describing such marvels as the source of the Nile and the tomb of Alexander does Statius allow two lines to suggest the possibility of involvement in a Parthian war. Nevertheless travel even without fighting could be praiseworthy: cf. e.g. Plin. *Pan.* 15. 3 'cognouisti per stipendia decem mores gentium regionum situs opportunitates locorum, et diuersarum aquarum caelique temperiem ut patrios fontes patriumque sidus ferre consuesti.'

132. quasnam ... terras, quem Caesaris ibis in orbem?: this opens a series of rhetorical questions, following closely the exhortation to Crispinus in 125–7 to take up his career. *quem orbem?* 'to what region' (*OLD* 13) hints at even more impressive hyperbole: *orbis* can denote a continent (see e.g. Horsfall on Virg. *A.* 7. 223–4, Man. 4. 677, Luc. 3. 276, on the Tanais, the modern Don, 'nunc hunc nunc illum, qua flectitur, ampliat orbem'), and note that the world is often referred to as *orbis terrarum*; for the possessive *Caesaris* applied to *orbis* compare Sen. *Suas.* 1. 2 'resiste, orbis te tuus reuocat'.

133. Arctoosne amnes: the list of possible postings begins with the Northern rivers, a vague and unspecific reference to the northern frontiers of Roman dominion; cf. *Silv.* 1. 4. 89 'Arctoas acies' and the reference to Domitian's campaigns as 'Arctoos ... triumphos' at *Theb.* 1. 18. *Arctoos* suggests the remoteness and singular nature of such a posting. For fascination with the distant north compare e.g. Pi. *P.* 10. 31–48 (the Hyperboreans), Virg. *G.* 3. 349–83 (the Scythians); for this type of list of frontier peoples, cf. Mart. 12. 8. 8–10.

Rheni fracta ... | flumina: for the association of the Rhine with cold, cf. Virg. *Ecl.* 10. 47 'frigora Rheni'. Here the Rhine's streams are 'broken', because the ice has to be broken before the swimmer may proceed with his exercise. Cf. Virg. *A.* 9. 603–4 (Numanus boasts to the Trojans of how Italian children are brought up) 'durum a stirpe genus natos ad flumina primum | deferimus saeuoque gelu duramus et undis', Stat. *Theb.* 9. 797 (Parthenopaeus) 'protinus astrictos didici reptare per amnes', 10. 497–8 'rigidique natator | Oebalus Eurotae', Mart. 1. 49. 11–12 'quibus remissum corpus adstringes breui | Salone, qui ferrum gelat', Juv. 6. 522 'hibernum fracta glacie descendet in amnem' for swimming in similarly chilly conditions. There is an element of paradox in describing the river, rather than the ice, as broken; for *frango* signifying the breaking of ice see *ThLL* vi/1. 1243. 60–6. *fracta ... flumina* also draws on the idea of the river as broken in defeat: cf. Mart. 7. 7. 3 (with Galán Vioque's note) 'fractusque cornu

iam ter improbo Rhenus', where the horn of the river-god is broker
by Domitian's campaigns.

natabis: for swimming in a frontier river, compare *CLE* 427. 3–4
where a soldier boasts of swimming the Danube with his weapons
'Adriano potui qui iudice uasta profundi | aequora Danuuii cunctis
transnare sub armis' (cf. D.C. 69. 9. 6 where Hadrian's Bataviar
cavalry τὸν Ἴστρον μετὰ τῶν ὅπλων διενήξαντο). The importance of
swimming in military training is suggested by Plu. *Cat. Ma.* 20. 6 anc
Veget. 1. 10. Compare also Mart. 1. 49. 9–12, where he anticipates his
friend Licinianus' swimming in Spain. For an overview of swimming
in the ancient world, see Mehl s.v. 'Schwimmen' in *RE Suppl.* v. 847
10–864. 6.

134. sudabis in aruis: cf. Plin. *Pan.* 15. 4 'quis sudores tuos
hauserit campos', in a passage on the desire of posterity to pass on
Trajan's achievements as tribune. *Silv.* 3. 2. 123 'puer his sudauit
in aruis' (referring to Maecius Celer's previous tribunician service in
Egypt) lends support to *aruis* (*ς*). M's *armis* is impossible because of
aestiferis.

135. mutatoresque domorum: the Sarmatians are *uagos* at
Silv. 3. 3. 170; here a more vivid phrase describes their nomadic
condition. Cf. Str. 7. 3. 17 (C306): τῶν δὲ Νομάδων αἱ σκηναὶ
πιλωταὶ πεπήγασιν ἐπὶ ταῖς ἁμάξαις, ἐν αἷς διαιτῶνται· περὶ δὲ τὰς
σκηνὰς τὰ βοσκήματα, ἀφ' ὧν τρέφονται καὶ γάλακτι καὶ τυρῷ καὶ
κρέασιν· ἀκολουθοῦσι δὲ ταῖς νομαῖς μεταλαμβάνοντες τόπους ἀεὶ τοὺς
ἔχοντας πόαν, χειμῶνος μὲν ἐν τοῖς ἕλεσι τοῖς περὶ τὴν Μαιῶτιν,
θέρους δὲ καὶ ἐν τοῖς πεδίοις. Virgil's Libyan nomads are similarly
described (*G.* 3. 343–5):

> omnia secum
> armentarius Afer agit, tectumque laremque
> armaque Amyclaeumque canem Cressamque pharetram

136. quaties: this is the only martial verb used in the lines
describing Crispinus' future activities, but is explicable in the context
of the *iuga Pannoniae*, and the Sarmatians, and the recent wars along
this frontier, which would have secured a place in the public con-
sciousness.

Further up the Danube from Moesia, which neighboured the
Dacian kingdom, Rome faced the Marcomanni and Quadi on the
Pannonian frontier, as well as the nomadic Sarmatians known as
Iazyges who had moved to what is now Hungary in the first half of the

first century AD (Wilkes (1983), 259). In Domitian's reign there were at least two wars in this area: an unsuccessful war in 89 against the Marcomanni and Quadi which broke out because of Domitian's irritation at their failure to support him against the Dacians (D.C. 67. 7. 1, 67. 7. 2), and a second war in 92, in which the Suebi fought alongside the Iazyges against the Romans (D.C. 67. 5. 2). After the loss of a legion, probably *XXI Rapax* (Suet. *Dom.* 6. 1, B. W. Jones (1992), 152),[61] this war concluded with the emperor's ostentatious refusal of a triumph (*Silv.* 3. 3. 170–1 'quae modo Marcomanos post horrida bella uagosque | Sauromatas Latio non est dignata triumpho', Mart. 8. 15. 5, Suet. *Dom.* 6. 1). B. W. Jones (1992), 153–5 argues for a third war in 95/6 on the basis of increasing Roman military presence in the region, which may be the first phase of the Suebic war brought to an end under Nerva (*CIL* v. 7425, Plin. *Pan.* 8. 2–3). Thus the Danube frontier was certainly a posting with a high potential for active service. See further *RE* xiv/2. 1609 ff. (Franke) on the Marcomanni, in particular section VIII ('Markomannenkriege unter Domitian und Nerva'), Wilkes (1983), 269–70, Strobel (1989), 83–104, B. W. Jones (1992), 150–5, Bérard (1997), Griffin (2000), 64–5.

136–7. septenus . . . Hister: the numbering of the mouths of the Danube was a matter of controversy. Seven, which matches the number associated with the Nile (for parallelism between the Nile and the Danube, see Berger (1880), 346–7), is found in Str. 7. 3. 15 (C305), Ov. *Tr.* 2. 189, Mela 2. 8, V.Fl. 4. 718 'non septemgemini memorem quas exitus Histri' (which seems an acknowledgement of the contentiousness of the issue, as is perhaps V.Fl. 8. 186–7 'fundere non uno tantum quem flumina cornu | accipimus; septem exit aquis, septem ostia pandit'), Sol. 13. 1, Amm. 22. 8. 44. Den Hoeft *et al.* on Amm. 22. 8. 44 give an extensive list of sources such as Plin. *Nat.* 4. 79, who gave the figure as six, and Hdt. 4. 47. 2, who gives it as five; to their list should be added Σ A.R. 4. 303–6 which reports the view that there are three mouths; this is in keeping with the modern hydrography of the delta, the three branches being Chilia, Sulina, and Sfântu Gheorghe.

137. et umbroso circumflua coniuge Peuce: the isle of Peuce, lit. 'pine-tree'. Σ A.R. 4. 310 credits Eratosthenes with this

---

[61] But see Bérard (1997), 235 who suggests that *XXI Rapax* may have been disbanded, rather than annihilated in battle, following its involvement in Saturninus' revolt of AD 89 when it had been posted in Germany.

explanation of the name (see further Berger (1880), 344–6); note also Orph. *A.* 1189 where the unnamed νῆσον πευκήεσσαν in the western ocean associated with Demeter may be an allusive etymological glance back either to Apollonius or his scholia. Peuce was situated near the mouth of the Danube; see Mela 2. 98, Luc. 3. 201–2 'Sarmaticas ubi perdit aquas sparsamque profundo | multifidi Peucen unum caput adluit Histri', Plin. *Nat.* 4. 79, V.Fl. 8. 217–19. Its precise location is uncertain. Some scholars have identified it as the island now known as Ostrovul Sfântu Gheorghe (St George's Island), which lies between the southernmost Sfântu Gheorghe and the Sulina branches of the modern delta; see e.g. Forbiger (1877), iii². 746–7, *Kl. Pauly* iv. 678 (Christo Danov), Livrea on A.R. 4. 309, *Neuer Pauly* ix. 684 (Iris von Bredow), while the *Barrington Atlas* i, Map 23 (grid reference C3) places 'Peuke Nesos' in a bend lying to the south of the main southerly branch, though its reference (ii. 358) to the brief note in Kacharava and Kvirkveliya (1991), 219 does not seem to warrant such a location. More cautious is Bosworth on Arr. *Anab.* 1. 2. 2 (who incidentally suggests that the Peuce referred to by Arrian, at any rate, may in fact have been another island upstream), noting that the Danube course and its mouths have changed greatly over time, on which phenomenon see further Panin (1983). The island's physical geography is first described by A.R. 4. 309–13 Ἴστρῳ γάρ τις νῆσος ἐέργεται οὔνομα Πεύκη | τριγλώχιν, εὖρος μὲν ἐς αἰγιαλοὺς ἀνέχουσα, | στεινὸν δ᾽ αὖτ᾽ ἀγκῶνα ποτὶ ῥόον, ἀμφὶ δὲ δοιαί | σχίζονται προχοαί· τὴν μὲν καλέουσι Νάρηκος, | τὴν δ᾽ ὑπὸ τῇ νεάτῃ Καλὸν στόμα; cf. V.Fl. 8. 377–8 'gemino nam scinditur insula flexu | Danuuii', Amm. 22. 8. 45 (on the seven mouths of the Danube) 'quorum primum est Peuce cum insula supra dicta, ut interpretata sunt uocabula Graeco sermone, secundum Naracustoma, tertium Calonstoma...'. In the current passage the 'spouse' of Peuce is the river himself, in keeping with the story of the nymph Peuce and the river-god referred to by V.Fl. 8. 255–6 'gramineis ast inde toris discumbitur, olim | Hister anhelantem Peucen quo presserat antro'. According to Str. 7. 3. 15 (C305), the island was inhabited by a people of the Bastarnae called the Peucini; cf. Amm. 22. 8. 43 'Peuce prominet insula, quam circumcolunt Trogodytae et Peuci', but see also Babeş (1977), who argues that the Peucini did not inhabit the isle of Peuce.

Here, the epithet *umbroso* applied to Peuce's consort (*coniuge*), the Danube, is explicable in terms of the pine trees which grew on the island; for *umbrosus* applied to the recipient, rather than the cause of, shade, compare Tib. 2. 3. 72 'in umbrosa ... ualle'. For Peuce as a contemporary reference point for the Danube frontier, cf. Mart. 7. 7. 1, 7. 84. 3 'i, liber, ad Geticam Peucen Histrumque iacentem'. For *circumflua*, cf. Luc. 4. 407 'quos alit Hadriaco tellus circumflua ponto'.

138. Solymum cinerem: 'the ash of Jerusalem', referring to the sack of the city under Titus. Compare V.Fl. 1. 13, where Domitian's envisaged poem will include 'Solymo ac nigrantem puluere fratrem', and see Coleman (1986), 3090–1. The Latin name for Jerusalem, Hierosolyma (shortened to *Solyma* at Mart. 7. 55. 7 'Solymis ... per-ustis', 11. 94. 5) encouraged some to link the Jews with the Solymi (Tac. *Hist.* 5. 2. 3 'clara alii Iudaeorum initia, Solymos, carminibus Homeri celebratam gentem, conditae urbi Hierosolyma nomen e suo fecisse'), redoubtable inhabitants of Lycia in Homer (*Il.* 6. 184, 204; cf. *Od.* 5. 283), who dwelt in that region before the arrival of the Lycians from Crete (Hdt. 1. 173. 2).

palmeta: Tac. *Hist.* 5. 6. 1 mentions balsam (see *Silv.* 5. 1. 210–14 n.) and the palm as two particular plants of Judaea; cf. Virg. *G.* 3. 12 'Idumaeas ... palmas', Str. 16. 2. 41 (C763), Luc. 3. 216 'et arbusto palmarum diues Idume', Plin. *Nat.* 5. 70, 13. 26, 13. 44, Mart. 10. 50. 1, Sil. 3. 600 'palmiferamque senex bello domitabit Idumen', 7. 456, *Judges* 1. 16, 3. 13. The palm-groves of Herod the Great were especially famous (cf. J. *AJ* 15. 96); see Hor. *Ep.* 2. 2. 184 (the only other appearance of *palmetum* in poetry) with Brink, Schürer (1973–87), i. 298–300. Note also Flavian coins showing a palm tree and a Jewish woman mourning her people's defeat at the hands of Rome, some with legends on the reverse such as DEVICTA IVDAEA (*RIC* II, Vespasian, nos. 148b, 289, 419) and the more common IVDAEA CAPTA (*RIC* II, Vespasian, nos. 393, 424–7, 489–91, 595–6, 608, 620, 733, 762, 784; Titus, nos. 91–3, 128, 141), For such words derived from the name of a tree, see Mayer (1954), Leumann (1977), 335: in Statius, cf. *dumeta* at *Theb.* 1. 697, 4. 647, *nuceta* at *Silv.* 1. 6. 12.

139. non sibi felices: cf. J. *BJ* 4. 469 ὡς οὐκ ἂν ἁμαρτεῖν τινα εἰπόντα θεῖον εἶναι τὸ χωρίον, ἐν ᾧ δαψιλῆ τὰ σπανιώτατα καὶ κάλλιστα γεννᾶται. The East was noted for the opulence of some of its arboreal products, such as frankincense and other aromatic substances. *non sibi* indicates that the benefits of this wealth are not enjoyed *in situ*, but at Rome; for this idea perhaps compare the lines ascribed to Virgil in response to a plagiarist, *Anth. Lat.* 251 Shackleton Bailey 'hos ego versiculos feci, tulit alter honorem. | sic vos non vobis mellificatis apes'; further versions of the second line, all beginning with 'sic vos non vobis', are also found in later manuscripts of Donatus' *Vita* of Virgil. In spite of its originally aggrieved tone, *sic vos non vobis* has come to symbolize hard work deliberately undertaken for the benefit of others, and has enjoyed a long life in heraldic mottoes and the like even down to modern times, appearing as the edge inscription on the £2 coin struck to commemorate the Tercentenary of the Bank of England in 1994. For *felix* cf. e.g. V.Fl. 6. 138 'turiferos, felicia regna, Sabaeos', Mart. 13. 20. 1, 14. 89. 1 'Accipe felices, Atlantica munera. siluas', and see also N.–H. on Hor. *Carm.* 1. 29. 1 who discuss the similar designation of the Arabian peninsula as Arabia Felix.

ponentis: literally, 'planting' (*OLD* s.v. *pono* 4).

140. tellus frenata: the *tellus* is Britain, even though the river Araxes (see 32 n.), at the opposite end of the empire and the scene of Bolanus' eastern victories, will rejoice as well. Britain, which was only briefly mentioned in the earlier account of Bolanus' career (54–6), now features as the climax of the list of possible postings for Crispinus, a climax that is marked by the emphasis on the connection with Bolanus, the direct speech of the old Briton (144–9), and the simile which rounds off the passage in 150–1. For the metaphorical usage of *frenare*, compare e.g. *Theb.* 10. 245 'his tandem uirtus iuuenum frenata quieuit'.

141. exsultabit: an especially suitable verb to apply to a river; the principal reference is to jubilation, but the etymology points to vigorous leaping or springing, appropriate to the rising flood of a river, particularly one such as the Araxes, famed for the ferocity of its flow (*SH* 1171 explains the name Araxes with reference to ἀρασσω, 'dash against, smite'; cf. Isid. *Etymol.* 13. 21. 16 'Araxis amnis Armeniae . . . dictus quod rapacitate cuncta prosternit'). The river's joy is a neat inversion of its resentment of Roman dominion at Virg. *A.* 8. 728. For *exsulto* referring to liquids cf. Virg. *A.* 3. 557 'exsultantque uada atque aestu miscentur harenae', *A.* 7. 464 'exsultantque aestu latices.'

141–2. Araxes . . . Caledonios: a neat juxtaposition of the two most remote boundaries of the empire. Compare the pairing of geographical extremes at Virg. *Ecl.* 1. 61–3:

> ante pererratis amborum finibus exsul
> aut Ararim Parthus bibet aut Germania Tigrim,
> quam nostro illius labatur pectore uultus.

142. attollet: 'what great glory will extol the Caledonian fields'; cf. Luc. 6. 48 'nunc uetus Iliacos attollat fabula muros'. 'Caledonia' is usually used to designate an area north of the Forth and Clyde, as noted by Hind (1983), 373, but here may well be an exotic exaggeration (see also 144–9 n. below); Ogilvie and Richmond on Tac. *Ag.* 8. 1 suggest that Bolanus may have campaigned against the Brigantes and established forts in Yorkshire, but are sceptical at the possibility of further penetration northwards; cf. Hanson (1987), 18–19. For the context of increasing interest in Caledonia in the latter part of the first century AD, see Braund (1996), 149–50 (and n. 14), who notes that the first mention in Latin is Luc. 6. 67–8 'aut, uaga cum Tethys Rutupinaque litora feruent, | unda Caledonios fallit turbata Britannos'.

143. longaeuus: compare the *senex* who claimed to have fought against Julius Caesar in Britain (Tac. *Dial.* 17. 4); for ancient traditions of British longevity see Braund (1996), 42. For such visits to historic (and mythical) sites cf. e.g. Virg. *A.* 2. 27–30 (the Trojans survey the deserted Greek camp), Luc. 9. 961–79 (Caesar in the Troad), Sil. 12. 744–9 (the Romans view the deserted camp of Hannibal before Rome), Tac. *Hist.* 2. 70 (Vitellius views the battlefield at Bedriacum), *Ann.* 2. 53–61 (Germanicus' travels in the East, especially his visit to Actium (*Ann.* 2. 53), associated with his great-uncle Augustus and his grandfather Antonius), Rut. Nam. 1. 575–96 (Rutilius' travels in Etruria which his father had administered). Hunt (1984) discusses the role of ἱστορία as a motivation for travel, in relation both to pagan élites and to later traditions of Christian pilgrimage.

trucis . . . terrae: Britannia. For the ferocity of the Britons, cf. Hor. *Carm.* 3. 4. 33 'uisam Britannos hospitibus feros', Tac. *Ag.* 8. 1 'praerat tunc Britanniae Vettius Bolanus placidius quam feroci prouincia dignum est', 11. 4 'plus tamen ferociae Britanni praeferunt, ut quos nondum longa pax emollierit', *Hist.* 2. 97. 1 'perinde legati prouinciaeque cunctabantur, . . . Vettius Bolanus numquam satis quieta Britannia', Rut. Nam. 1. 500 'ferox . . . Britannus'.

144–9. Like Crispinus' speech (84–96), the second speech of the poem is imaginary. It provides a convenient recapitulation of the exploits of Bolanus, who dominated the first half of the poem. Here his presence in Britain is viewed as part of a process of civilizing; he gave laws, and protected the land. Only in the last line is direct conflict referred to; indeed Tacitus, writing after Domitian's death, would accuse Bolanus of 'inertia erga hostes' (*Ag.* 16. 5). Statius' emphasis on Bolanus' campaigning in north Britain in the present passage, including such conspicuous achievements as dedicating the breastplate of a slain enemy commander (149), may have sounded mixed notes in the Rome of Domitian's later years, in the light of Agricola's term as governor in Britain which concluded (probably in AD 84) with the decisive victory at Mons Graupius early in the reign. On the one hand Domitian gave honours such as the triumphal ornaments to Agricola (Tac. *Ag.* 40. 1), but he gave him no further command, moved according to Tacitus by jealousy towards his general (*Ag.* 39–41). Here, praise of Bolanus might thus be a revisionist attempt to place more emphasis on an earlier figure in the history of Roman campaigns in Britain, but we cannot of course know how this would have been interpreted only a few years after Agricola's achievements there. It is worth noting as well that Rome's most northerly forts in Scotland had already been abandoned: Hobley (1989) argues on the basis of numismatic evidence that the Romans had withdrawn by the middle of AD 88 at the latest.

The futurity of the speech is an important means of complimenting Crispinus; far from being a mere backward glance at his father, it recalls Bolanus' achievements in the context of those expected from Crispinus. Deictic forms add to the vividness; cf. e.g. Evander's speech to Aeneas (Virg. *A.* 8. 351–8).

144. hic: 'here', not 'this', although the word nevertheless contributes to the euphony of the ensuing polyptoton and anaphora of forms of adjectival *hic*.

dare iura: for *dare iura* and similar phrases denoting lawgiving, see e.g. Virg. *A.* 8. 670 'secretosque pios, his dantem iura Catonem', *OLD* s.v. *dare* 13c, *ThLL* vii/2. 682. 70–3. For the panegyric context, compare e.g. Virg. *G.* 4. 561–2 'uictorque uolentis | per populos dat iura', Hor. *Carm.* 3. 3. 43–4 'triumphatisque possit | Roma ferox dare iura Medis'. The governor of even a frontier province would not have conducted solely military matters. The settlement of disputes among the provincials would have been an important function; compare for example the role of Pontius Pilate in the Gospels. On provincial jurisdiction, see further Sherwin-White (1963), 13–23, Burton (1975).

caespite: turf was a versatile material. Hor. *Carm.* 2. 15. 17 (where N.–H. give further references) 'nec fortuitum spernere caespitem | leges sinebant' mentions its use in a modest dwelling, while at *Carm.* 3. 8. 3–4 'positusque carbo in | caespite uiuo' *caespes* denotes an altar. Here a fairly tall structure is envisaged (a military equivalent of the *rostra*), from which the commander could address his troops: cf. Tac. *Ann.* 1.

18. 2: 'congerunt caespites, exstruunt tribunal, quo magis conspicua sedes foret.' The Antonine Wall between the Forth and the Clyde was of turf (*SHA Antoninus Pius* 5. 4).

145. adfari: Bolanus was popular, but lacked presence (Tac. *Ag.* 16. 5): 'innocens Bolanus et nullis delictis inuisus caritatem parauerat loco auctoritatis'. His troops may have recalled his speeches fondly.

uictor: of the various conjectures proposed (see Klotz) for M's clearly corrupt *uitae*, this, by Davies, is the most convincing; it is to be construed with *adfari*. Waller's *late* would, when combined with *longe*, mean 'far and wide' (*OLD* s.v. *longe* 1b), but very little is added to the sense.

speculas castellaque: watchtowers and forts; cf. Tacitus' praise of Agricola's policy at *Ag.* 20. 3: 'quibus rebus multae ciuitates, quae in illum diem ex aequo egerant, datis obsidibus iram posuere et praesidiis castellisque circumdatae, tanta ratione curaque, ut nulla ante Britanniae noua pars inlacessita transierit'. However, it had been the dispersal of Roman forces in *castella* which had contributed to the early success of Boudicca's revolt: see Tac. *Ag.* 16. 1, where Richmond and Ogilvie differentiate *castella*, which were strategic posts for either a cohort of infantry or a cavalry *ala*, from the much larger *castra*, garrisoned by a whole legion. Juv. 14. 196 'dirue Maurorum attegias, castella Brigantum' uses *castellum* of British rather than Roman fortifications. Bolanus' watchtowers may have been similar to those constructed in the Agricolan era on the Gask ridge: see further Hanson (1987), 153–7.

148–9. hunc ...| induit, hunc regi rapuit thoraca Britanno: although *thoraca* is ἀπὸ κοινοῦ, being the object of both clauses in agreement with *hunc*, there are nevertheless two breastplates which have been dedicated in thanksgiving after victory to the gods of war (147). *hunc ... hunc* continues the sequence of deictic forms appropriate to the conducted tour given to Crispinus, and the contrast between the breastplate worn by Bolanus and that worn by his enemy is emphasized by *ipse* (148). Bolanus' achievement in taking the enemy commander's arms recalls the now unobtainable glory of the *spolia opima*; for Augustus' restrictions on the honour, see Harrison (1989), Rich (1996).

150–1. The simile refers to Phoenix, who had been a companion of Achilles, telling Achilles' son, Pyrrhus (Neoptolemus), about his father's achievements after he was brought from Scyros to fight in the Trojan war after his father's death; it is also an ingenious reversal of

Od. 11. 506–37, where Odysseus tells Achilles (who does not know
because he is among the shades) about Neoptolemus' exploits in the
closing phases of the Trojan war. Though in *Od.* 11. 509 Odysseus
speaks only of himself as bringing Neoptolemus to Troy, other texts
mention Phoenix as an envoy on this mission: see *Il. Parv.* arg. 2
Bernabé, S. *Ph.* 343–56, Apollod. *Epit.* 5. 11 (with Frazer's notes).
Phoenix' encouragement to Neoptolemus by telling him stories of
his father also recalls the Phoenix of the *Iliad*, who tells Achilles the
story of Meleager's anger and his failure to accept gifts at *Il.* 9. 528–99.
   Statius' simile not only mirrors the old Briton's reminiscences of
Bolanus in 144–9, but also more loosely evokes the poet's own role in
reminding Crispinus of his father.
   uictricia bella: for all his endeavours Achilles did not directly
bring about the fall of Troy, whereas his son Pyrrhus was involved in
the sack of the city. Similarly, Crispinus will not merely be a lesser
version of his father, but will achieve something of note for himself (cf.
180); note also that the first Trojan War was alluded to at 47–50 when
Bolanus was compared to Telamon.
   ignotum . . . Achillem: the final and most flattering compliment
to the memory of Bolanus, mentioned for the last time, here directly
compared to Achilles. Hitherto Bolanus has exerted a strong influ-
ence, and has been used to the full as a vehicle for praise of his son.
But by giving Bolanus his final appearance thirty lines before the end
of the poem, it is also the case that Statius gives Crispinus unchal-
lenged prominence in the lines that follow. *ignotum* is certainly appro-
priate in the simile, since Bolanus was in Britain between AD 69 and
71 (A. R. Birley (1981), 62–5), about a decade before the probable
birth of Crispinus in 79.
   152. Optate: nothing else is known of this friend of Crispinus; for
Statius' occasional habit of referring to mutual friends, see Coleman
on *Silv.* 4. 4. 20–4. *Optatus* is a *nom parlant* ('wished for'), which here
neatly plays on the μακαρισμός 'felix qui' at the beginning of the line
(on which see 176 n. below). On such names derived from the past
participle see Kajanto (1965), 75–7, Syme, *RP* iii. 1105–19: Optatus is
the third most common, with 770 instances; cf. Fortunatus (2430
instances) and Donatus (822). Bearers of such names, especially
those reflecting parental ambition, were often of modest backgrounds
(Syme, *RP* iii. 1106). The name is frequent in Africa; the connection
may have been stemmed from a *clientela* of Bolanus (ibid. 1109).
Alternatively, Syme suggests that Optatus may have been the

descendant of an eminent freedman such as the Optatus who commanded the fleet at Misenum under Tiberius (*ILS* 1986, 2815, Pliny *Nat.* 9. 62). The first consular Optatus was L. Burbuleius Optatus Ligarianus (*PIR*[2] B 174), governor of Cappodocia in AD 138.

153. quascumque uias uallumque subibis: for the topos of going on extreme journeys on behalf of another, see 5. 1. 67–9 n.

154–5. latus...| cinctus: for *cingo* denoting 'equipped with weapons', see e.g. *Theb.* 4. 41 'contentus ferro cingi latus', Ov. *Am.* 3. 8. 14 'ense latus cinctum', *Fast.* 2. 784 'ense latus cinxit', *OLD* s.v. *cingo* 2, *ThLL* iii. 1064. 12–14; here the word for a sword is omitted (in spite of Heinsius' *ense* for M's *ipse*; *ipse* is needed to express the fact that Optatus too might receive an imperial command). For the sword as an emblem of military office, cf. 174, 177, 5. 1. 94 n.

unanimi: 5. 1. 176 n.

156. Pylades: son of Strophius, and celebrated companion of Orestes (who was taken as a child to live with him after Agamemnon's death), who shared his friend's tribulations, both in avenging Agamemnon, and among the Taurians, and who would eventually marry Electra, the sister of Orestes. Not appearing in Homer, Pylades is first mentioned in *Nost.* arg. Bernabé helping Orestes to obtain vengeance against his mother Clytemnestra and Aegisthus, her lover, for Agamemnon's murder; as well as his appearances, sometimes silent, in fifth-century Attic tragedy (in extant works, A. *Ch.*, S. *El.*, E. *El.*, *IT*, *Or.*), see also Pi. *P.* 11. 15–37, Apollod. *Epit.* 6. 23–8, Pacuv. *trag.* 118–21 D'Anna, Hyg. *Fab.* 117, 119. His proverbial status as an example of a good friend is attested by Cic. *Amic.* 24, *Fin.* 2. 84 'hac Pyladea amicitia', Ov. *Rem.* 589–90 'semper habe Pyladen aliquem, qui curet Oresten: | hic quoque amicitiae non leuis usus erit', *Tr.* 1. 5. 21–2, 1. 9. 28, 5. 4. 25, 5. 6. 25–6, *Pont.* 3. 2. 33–4, V. Max. 4. 7 pr., Mart. 6. 11 (where the lack of contemporary equivalents to Pylades and Orestes is lamented), 7. 24. 3, 7. 45. 8–11, 10. 11, Juv. 16. 26–7 'quis tam Pylades, molem aggeris ultra | ut ueniat?'; at Hyg, *Fab.* 257. 1 he and Orestes are given as the first example of a series (which also includes Patroclus and Achilles) of those 'qui inter se amicitia iunctissimi fuerunt'. See also Otto (1890), 258 (§1307), and the discussion of Lucian, *Tox.* 5–6 in Ní Mheallaigh (2005), 82–5.

Statius' references to Pylades and to Patroclus gracefully compliment Crispinus, implying that he is senior to Optatus; compare the description of Philetos at *Silv.* 2. 6. 54–5 'dignus et Haemonium Pyladen praecedere fama | Cecropiamque fidem', where commentators have

seen 'Haemonium Pyladen' as an ingenious allusion to Patroclus, as a
Thessalian version of Pylades (who was not Thessalian, but came from
Phocis), though van Dam ad loc. oddly argues that in fact Achilles is
referred to. Cf. also *Theb.* 1. 475–7, where the friendship of Polynices
and Tydeus is likened to that between Pirithous and Theseus and
between Orestes and Pylades. For such groupings of exempla of
friendship cf. e.g. Ov. *Tr.* 1. 5. 19–24, 1. 9. 27–34 (which includes
Pylades and Orestes and Patroclus and Achilles), 5. 4. 25–6 'teque
Menoetiaden, te, qui comitatus Oresten, | te uocat Aegiden Eurya-
lumque suum', *Pont.* 3. 2. 33–4, Aus. *Epist.* 23. 19–22; note also that
examples such as Theseus and Heracles are recommended for a
propempticon by Men. Rh. 396. 16–18.

157. Menoetiades: Patroclus, the son of Menoetius (the patro-
nymic Μενοιτιάδης appears in the *Iliad* on nineteen occasions) and
companion of Achilles. Patroclus was brought by his father to live
with Achilles and Peleus after he killed a son of Amphidamas as a
child (*Il.* 23. 85–90). When the pair left to fight at Troy, Menoetius
told Patroclus to defer to Achilles, but also to offer counsel (*Il.* 11. 786–9),
while Achilles himself promised to Menoetius that he would bring
Patroclus back from the war alive, a promise that would be thwarted
(*Il.* 18. 324–32). The comparison of Optatus with Patroclus ingeni-
ously compares Crispinus with Achilles. To reflect the shift of interest
away from Bolanus' exploits, Achilles, previously compared with the
father in 151, is now an equivalent to his son Crispinus. Statius also
mentions the friendship of Patroclus and Achilles at *Silv.* 4. 4. 104–5.

158. nos fortior aetas: for *fortior aetas* as the season of young
manhood, when brave deeds are performed, compare *Theb.* 4. 253 (of
Parthenopaeus) 'nec desunt animi, ueniat modo fortior aetas', *Ach.* 1.
776–7 'utinam et mihi fortior aetas, | quaeque fuit' (where King
Lycomedes of Scyros laments his inability to join the war against
Troy), Ov. *Ep.* 1. 107 'Telemacho ueniet, uiuat modo, fortior aetas'.
Compare also Virg. *G.* 4. 559–66, contrasting Caesar Augustus, who
has been achieving great deeds, with the poet, who has stayed behind
in Naples working at his poetry, Stat. *Silv.* 4. 4. 69–71 'nos facta aliena
canendo | uergimus in senium: propriis tu pulcher in armis | ipse
canenda geres', and Mart. 9. 84. 1–4, where Norbanus' fighting on
the emperor's behalf is contrasted with Martial's own occupations in
poetic shade. The interpretation of what this passage (and others)
means for Statius' likely date of birth has been debated: see further
the General Introduction, p. xvii n. 2.

159. fugit: cf. Hor. *Ep.* 1. 20. 10 'donec te deserat aetas'. For *fugere* denoting the passing of time, both transitively and intransitively, cf. e.g. Catul. 68. 43 'fugiens saeclis obliuiscentibus aetas', Virg. *G.* 3. 66–7 'optima quaeque dies miseris mortalibus aeui | prima fugit', 3. 284 'sed fugit interea, fugit inreparabile tempus', Sen. *Ep.* 49. 9 'mors me sequitur; fugit uita', *ThLL* vi/1. 1484. 11–27, 1492. 11–25. As well as explaining Statius' inability to follow Crispinus, the reference to the passing of time is a reminder to the latter to seize his opportunities.

tantum: *animum* (M) is unsatisfactory. Little is added by saying that Statius will help Crispinus' mind or spirit (as opposed to merely saying 'Crispinus') with *uota* and *preces*. *tantum* (Markland) adds point to Statius' earlier complaint about the passing of his own *fortior aetas*: it is precisely because of this that he is only (*tantum*) able to offer *uota* and *preces*; for the offer of *uota*, cf. *Silv.* 3. 2. 99–100 'sed pectore fido | numquam abero longisque sequar tua carbasa uotis', with Laguna.

160. ei mihi: *et* (M) is impossible. The early correction *ei mihi* accords with Statius' sorrow at Crispinus' departure (compare the language of grief used at 3–4 and 10–12). For *ei mihi* followed by *sed*, cf. *Theb.* 12. 340: 'ei mihi, sed quanto descendit uulnus hiatu!'

coetus solitos . . . ciebo: M's *questus* is difficult, despite Sen. *Phoen.* 387 'dum tu flebiles questus cies' (applied to Jocasta's laments and not to poetry as such), and Vollmer's extraordinary argument that the word, suggesting the tragical nature of the contents, refers to Statius' readings of his epics. Now while *questus* might suit Statius' epicedia, these are not in question here, since the passage is clearly about future readings from the *Achilleid* (162–3). *cantus* might be a possible emendation of M's *questus* (cf. Sen. *Thy.* 917 'iam cantus ciet', Mart. Cap. 9. 918, Sidon. *Epist.* 8. 11. 3, verses 49–50, *ThLL* iii. 1055. 81–1056. 18), but better is Gronovius' *coetus*: the word can denote an assembly, but can also refer to a literary gathering, as at Suet. *Aug.* 85. 1 on the reading of Augustus' literary efforts 'in coetu familiarum, uelut in auditorio'. For the corruption, Courtney compares Perrotto's conjecture *coetu* for M's *questus* at *Silv.* 1. 2. 235, though his parallel of *Silv.* 1. 5. 5 'alios poscunt mea carmina coetus' is of less value, since the *coetus* in that passage are figures of inspiration, not the audience. Moreover, *coetus solitos* would accord well with Juvenal's account of Statius as a popular giver of recitations; despite the irony behind Juvenal's description (7. 82–7) of the citizenry's reaction, Statius' impact on his public is apparent. *coetus solitos . . . ciebo* conveys Statius' assurance that he is habitually able to muster an elite senatorial gathering to hear his poetry; for this kind of senatorial audience, cf. *Silv.* 5. 3. 215–17. On recitations, see P. White (1974), 43–4, who speculates that Statius may also have given recitations of his non-epic oeuvre, Markus (2000), (2003), 432–5, Nauta (2002), 203, 256–77, 356–63, Leberl (2004), 88–94.

162. cuneosque per omnes: *cunei* refers to rows of spectators (cf. *ThLL* iv. 1406. 26–62), but there is also a pleasing *double entendre*, appropriate to the martial Achilles, since *cuneus* can denote a formation of soldiers (*ThLL* iv. 1404. 37–1405. 83). The language humorously suggests Achilles hunting after an enemy; compare *Il.* 3. 449 ff. (Menelaus' search for the absent Paris), Virg. *A.* 12. 557–8 'ille ut uestigans diuersa per agmina Turnum | huc atque huc acies circumtulit'. A. Hardie (2003), 132 suggests that the theatrical language of *cuneos* here may imply the possibility of a grand performance in Domitian's Odeum.

163. meus...Achilles: the *Achilleid* is personified as Achilles; the same phrase occurs at *Silv.* 4. 7. 23–4. Compare *Silv.* 1. 5. 8–9 'paulum arma nocentia, Thebae, | ponite', 4. 4. 94 'magnusque mihi temptatur Achilles', 5. 5. 36–7 'pudeat Thebasque nouumque | Aeaciden', Callimachus *Aet.* fr. 1. 12 ἡ μεγάλη . . . γυνή.

164. uenies melior: Crispinus will be *melior* on his return, because he will have accomplished great deeds abroad. Cf. *Silv.* 5. 3. 288 'inde tamen uenias melior'.

164–5. uatum non inrita currunt | omina: the primary meaning of *uatum* is 'seers', since it was customary to seek propitiatory omens before starting a journey, but there is also a sense in which the poet has his own mantic function, since he has previously announced a glorious future for Crispinus. The almost direct echo of 164–5 in 172–3 (the only change in 172–3, 'auguria' for 'omina', is required by the metre since the second foot of 173 begins with a vowel, *en*) strengthens the identification of Statius as a *uates*, since his own comment on the status of prophecy in 164 is justified. By a pleasing paradox, the repeated lines also allude to quite different traditions in ancient poetry, concerning the vanity and uselessness of prophetic utterance. See Pease on Virg. *A.* 4. 65 'heu uatum ignarae mentes' for other examples, most notably the reviling of the prophet Mopsus by a crow at A.R. 3. 932–5; for the tradition of mere caution about the efficacy of prophecy, often expressed with a conditional clause such as Hor. *Ep.* 1. 20. 9 'quodsi non odio peccantis desipit augur', see further Fraenkel (1957), 358 and n. 3. Statius triumphantly surpasses such gloomy expectations; cf. the optimistic affirmation of Ov. *Pont.* 2. 1. 55 'quod precor, eueniet: sunt quiddam oracula uatum'.

inrita: Tacitus uses *irritus* of vain prodigies at *Ann.* 14. 12. 2: 'prodigia quoque crebra et irrita intercessere'; for the litotes *non inrita*, cf. *Silv.* 5. 3. 175, *Theb.* 7. 314 'et numquam manus inrita uoti', 11. 504–5 'di, quos effosso non inritus ore rogauit | Oedipodes', 11. 557 'non inrita uoui', Germ. fr. 4. 163 'tibi signa dabunt non inrita Pisces'.

currunt: for *currere* denoting the progression of events, see Sil. 7. 307 'heu fatis quae sola meis currentibus obstat', *ThLL* iv. 1518. 68–78.

165. omina: on favourable omens in propemptica see Cairns (1972), 130, 186 (with notes).

recludit: Courtney (1984), 338 argues for the future *recludet*, on the grounds that the poem has hitherto been concerned with the future career of Crispinus, but *nunc* establishes a contrast between current and more distant prospects (*dabit*, 167), which is satisfied by M's *recludit*.

166. properare gradus: the sense of this line and the next is that Domitian will grant to Crispinus the opportunities to follow his father in holding successive magistracies leading to the consulship; for *gradus* denoting honours or ranks, see e.g. Liv. 32. 7. 10 (tribunician opposition to Flamininus' standing for the consulship for 198 BC) 'nec per honorum gradus, documentum sui dantes, nobiles homines tendere ad consulatum, sed transcendendo media summa imis continuare', *OLD* s.v. *gradus* 8. However, M's *perferre* is difficult; translations such as Slater's 'will also grant to you to hold every preferment' and Mozley's 'shall grant thee to accomplish all the degrees of rank' do not reflect the basic meaning of *perferre* as 'to bring through' or 'to carry through'. In support of *perferre*, Klotz refers to Plin. *Nat.* 6. 25 '[Armenia] sic finem usque in Adiabenen perfert', but this is an entirely different geographical use of the word, as is indicated by *usque in*, and is in no way parallel to *omnes perferre gradus* here.

perferre, it is true, can denote enduring something (see *ThLL* x/1. 1359. 62–1362. 22), but it is hardly encouraging for Crispinus to be told of the burdens of office in such negative tones, especially when *perferre* is regularly used thus with words such as *labores* and *dolores* (*ThLL* x/1. 1360. 71–1361. 23). *ThLL* x/1. 1363. 65–1364. 6 does cite examples illustrating the sense of accomplishing orders and the like (including this passage), but examples where *perferre* is construed with words such as *mandata* (e.g. Ov. *Ep.* 11. 127–8 (= 129–30 Reeson) 'mandata sororis | perfer [*FGPVω* : perfice *ς*, *Slichtenhorst*]', Plin. *Ep.*

10. 81. 6 'Eumolpus respondit . . . non accusatorem se sed aduocatum Flaui Archippi, cuius mandata pertulisset') are not in any case parallel to *gradus*; one cannot 'carry out' *gradus* in this sense.

Baehrens notes Heinsius' conjecture *perque ire gradus*, which would give the correct sense, but the postponed *-que* does not inspire confidence here, especially in the context of the correlative *quique* and *idem* in ll. 165 and 166. He himself conjectured *superare* for M's *proferre*, but the only way in which Crispinus could 'surpass' all the usual stages of his career would be to omit them and proceed straight to the consulship, something which is not only at odds with the imminent appointment to a military tribunate, but which would have been extraordinary under the principate; to single out Crispinus as due for such remarkable advancement at such a young age would not only have been implausible, but perhaps also dangerous for both Crispinus and Statius. Polster conjectured *proferre* here, explaining the passage as 'dabit tibi, ut omnes, qui ad honores ferunt, gradus proferas et ita ad omnes provehare honores, quos amplexus est pater', but declining to give examples. Though *profero* can indeed be found with *gradus*, as at Plautus, *Men.* 754 'gradum proferam, progrediri properabo', Enn. *scen.* 213 V. (= 193 Jocelyn) 'procede, gradum proferre pedum', Stat. *Theb.* 12. 9–10 'uix primo proferre gradum et munimina ualli | soluere, uix totas reserare audacia portas', all of these instances refer to singular *gradus* in the context of literally moving forwards. It is harder to see how this idiom could work in the plural, and with *omnes* as an epithet; *proferre gradum* is an idiom used to refer to an individual advancing his or her own step, not advancing *through* some other set of (metaphorical) steps.

A better conjecture is Saenger's *properare*, also favoured by Shackleton Bailey. This gives a more pleasing sense of Domitian granting Crispinus the chance to progress swiftly along the *cursus honorum* (not, however, bypassing its stages) to eventual high office. For the motif of accelerated promotion, one can compare *Silv.* 1. 2. 174–6, where Venus predicts to Violentilla that Arruntius Stella will be consul 'ante diem' (176), through the *indulgentia* of Domitian. For *propero* thus, perhaps compare Hor. *Ep.* 1. 3. 28 'hoc opus, hoc studium parui properemus et ampli', but note too examples where *propero* is used with *gradus*, as at Varr. *Men.* 437 'per | aeuiternam hominum domum | tellurem propero gradum', Amm. 29. 6. 12 'illuc properato petierant gradu'; cf. Sal. *Jug.*105. 2 'itineris properandi causa', Sil. 3. 159 'properato . . . gressu', *ThLL* x/2. 1985. 51–9. These examples, it is

true, are all construed with singular objects of *propero*, but a case can
be made for *properare gradus* in the plural here on the basis that plural
gradus could be seen as synonymous with idioms for making journeys
(whilst at the same time evoking the usage of *gradus* to refer to the
stages of one's career): Domitian will grant Crispinus the opportunity
to hasten his every step (*omnes properare gradus*) on his path to high
office.

167. patrias . . . curules: the higher magistracies to be held by
Crispinus later in his career; as Campbell (1975), 18 points out, Statius
is not anticipating a merely military career for Crispinus. *patrias* not
only recalls Bolanus, but also evokes Statius' praise of Crispinus'
ancestry in 15 ff., emphasizing that he is no *parvenu*.

168–80. The final revelation of Crispinus' expected appointment
is heralded by the dramatic appearance of the emperor's messenger.
Crispinus is sent on his way, not on the journey to Etruria mentioned
at the outset of the poem, but to follow the commands of the emperor
and to achieve glory. The messenger's arrival at Crispinus' own home
gives an appropriate conclusion to the poem and a setting for his
imminent departure.

168. ab excelsis Troianae collibus Albae: cf. *Silv.* 4. 2. 65
'Troianae qualis sub collibus Albae', Mart. 4. 64. 13 'Albanos quoque
Tusculosque colles', 5. 1. 1 'Palladiae seu collibus uteris Albae'.
Domitian had a villa on the Mons Albanus: see Suet. *Dom.* 19, D.C.
67. 1. 2, B. W. Jones (1992), 27–8, 96–7 Darwall-Smith (1994). As
A. Hardie (1983), 11 and n. 70 notes, here and at *Silv.* 3. 1. 61, 4. 2. 65, 4.
5. 2, 5. 3. 38, 5. 3. 227, Statius associates Alba Longa with Troy (note
also Juv. 4. 60–1 'ubi quamquam diruta seruat | ignem Troianum et
Vestam colit Alba minorem', where Juvenal may be deliberately echo-
ing Statian practice); this arises from Ascanius' foundation of the city
(Virg. *A.* 1. 267–71, Liv. 1. 3. 3, D.H. 1. 66. 1).

169. suae iuxta prospectat moenia Romae: *moenia Romae* is
a famous Virgilian phrase (*A.* 1. 7): 'Albanique patres atque altae
moenia Romae.' For the possessive *suae*, cf. 'cui cura suorum' (91),
Luc. 3. 90 'miratusque suae sic fatur moenia Romae'. The emperor's
gaze perhaps recalls Juno looking down from the Mons Albanus
(Virg. *A.* 12. 134–7). The downward gaze of figures such as Caesar
or Hannibal can be malevolent: cf. Luc. 3. 88–100 with Henderson
(1998*b*), 197–9, Sil. 12. 567–70.

170. proximus: cf. 5. 1. 38 n.

170–1. fama uelocior intrat | nuntius: a simple but effective paradox; the messenger who is faster than fame or reputation is himself the bearer and agent of *fama*. Statius caps Virgil's celebrated description of *Fama* (*A.* 4. 173–4): 'extemplo Libyae magnas it Fama per urbes, | Fama, malum qua non aliud uelocius ullum.'

See also *Silv.* 5. 1. 105–7.

172. dicebam: for this aorist use of the imperfect tense to refer back to a single occasion, see Fedeli on Prop. 1. 9. 1 'dicebam tibi uenturos, irrisor, amores', H.–Sz. 317 (§177); for *dicebam* in a context of affirming the truthfulness of a prophecy, cf. *Silv.* 4. 3. 124.

173. reserat tibi limen honorum: the phrase suggests the more familiar *cursus honorum*, but *limen* is also appropriate to the transitional stage of Crispinus' life, as he prepares to embark upon his career. *reserat* and *limen* pick up the image of a door being opened from *recludit* (165).

175. For the exhortation to go and achieve greatness, contrast the ironic context of Hor. *Ep.* 2. 2. 37–8 'i, bone, quo uirtus tua te uocat, i pede fausto, | grandia laturus meritorum praemia', and see Brink's note on imperatives of verbs of motion combined with other verbs.

176. felix qui: in its earliest appearance in Greek literature this form of beatitude has a genuinely religious note; see *h. Hom.* 2. 480 ff. with Richardson's n. The formula is also used, in various guises, by the philosophers to denote the felicity of those who have reached the heights of philosophic contemplation; see Norden (1913), 100 with n. 1, Snell (1931), 74–5 (with notes) for examples both religious and philosophical. In Latin literature *felix qui* is common: see e.g. Virg. *G.* 2. 490 'felix qui potuit rerum cognoscere causas', Hor. *Carm.* 1. 13. 17–18 'felices ter et amplius | quos irrupta tenet copula' (with N.–H.), Stat. *Theb.* 10. 615 'felix qui tanta lucem mercede relinquet'; see also *Silv.* 5. 3. 266 ff. (with n.).

magno iam nunc sub praeside: Crispinus now enjoys the protection of the emperor, whereas he had previously been *sine praeside* after his father's death (65). For *praeses* applied to tutelary gods, see *OLD* s.v. 1b; for its use as divine language applied to Domitian, compare e.g. *Silv.* 1. 2. 175 'praesidis Ausonii', 3. 3. 183–4 'numina magni | praesidis', Mart. 6. 2. 5 'te praeside' (with Grewing ad loc.), Scott (1936), 133.

177. sacer: 5. 1. 190 n.

ensem: 5. 1. 94 n.

179. Bellipotens: Mars. The word is first attested at Enn. *Ann.*
198 Sk. (of the Aeacidae) 'bellipotentes sunt magis quam sapientipo-
tentes.' After Ennius the word is not applied to mortals until late
antiquity, in the works of Claudian and others. Virg. *A.* 11. 8 uses it of
Mars; in Statius see *Theb.* 3. 292, 3. 577, 8. 384, 9. 832, *Ach.* 1. 443, *Silv.*
1. 4. 34; cf. *Theb.* 2. 716 (Minerva). See further *ThLL* ii. 1815. 54 ff.;
note Tertullian's militant use of the adjective to describe Christ at *adv.
Marc.* 1. 6, 3. 14, and 3. 21.

179–80. toruaque . . . casside: cf. *Theb.* 2. 716–17 'cui torua
genis horrore decoro | cassis', 12. 189.

180. uade alacer maioraque disce mereri: the poem con-
cludes strongly. Crispinus is hastened on his way in a manner appro-
priate to a propempticon; at the same time the journey to Etruria
envisaged at the start of the poem is entirely forgotten, subsumed in a
grander concern with Crispinus' military career.

The imperatives *uade* and *disce* encapsulate the two principal
themes of the poem, action and example; the encouragement to
Crispinus to embark on his career is tempered with reminders of
the accomplishments of Bolanus. *disce* in particular looks back to
'disce puer' (51) and 'tu disce patrem' (54). Nevertheless, just as
Bolanus receded into the background after l. 151, so too the final
emphasis is not on his achievements, but on those which are expected
from Crispinus. This is the significance of *maiora*: Crispinus will
achieve yet greater things; cf. *Silv.* 3. 2. 127–8 'ergo erit illa dies, qua
te maiora daturus | Caesar ab emerito iubeat discedere bello', ad-
dressed to another young man, Maecius Celer. For the generalizing
maiora cf. Sil. 5. 14 'nec modicus uoti natum ad maiora fouebat'. *mereri*,
the last word of the poem, tellingly hints that moral qualities are also
required to ensure success.

Poem Three

INTRODUCTION

Summary: *Statius' grief at his father's death and loss of poetic inspiration (1–18). His father is either in the heavens or with the blessed in Elysium; he is to inspire Statius' composition of the poem; Statius' desire to commemorate his father with a temple and with games (19–63). The loss of a father can be as severe as the loss of a child or a spouse (64–79). Statius' desire to surpass ordinary laments; his father's mastery of every kind of literature (80–103). His father's origins in Naples and in Velia; his victories in poetic contests (104–45). His father's teaching of the Greek poets in Naples, and his move to Rome, where he gave instruction in religious matters; the subsequent distinction of his pupils in public life (146–94). His father's poem on the burning of the Capitol and his planned work in the eruption of Vesuvius (195–208). Statius' father's inspiration to his son's early poetic career, though he did not witness Statius' participation in the Alban and Capitoline contests; his support for the early stages of composition of the Thebaid; his devotion to Statius' mother (209–45). Statius' father's personal qualities; the extent of Statius' grief (246–76). Statius appeals to the infernal powers to grant his father admission to Elysium; his desire for his father to visit him in dreams (277–93).*

(For discussion of the poem as an *epicedion*, see the section on consolation in the General Introduction, especially pp. xxxvi–xxxviii.)

This poem raises a variety of chronological problems; most fundamental is the date of composition. At 5. 3. 29 Statius explains that the lament is being written three months after his father's death, which occurred at the age of sixty-five (5. 3. 253). This evidence must then be considered in the light of the other internal evidence of the poem, in order to establish Papinius senior's date of death. Thus we need to ascertain the dates of Statius' appearances in the Alban Games and the Capitoline contest (227–33). The interdependence of all these disputed dates does not help.

Whereas the Alban Games were held annually in March at the time of the Quinquatria, the Capitoline contest took place every four years, which may make it easier to date Statius' defeat. The time of year at which they were held may have been during May or early June.[1] The first contest was held in 86 (Censorinus, *De die natali* 18. 15). There are thus three possible contests during the reign of Domitian (86, 90 and 94). Coleman[2] argues that the *Alban* victory must belong to the period 90–2,[3] since Statius reveals (*Silv.* 4. 2. 66) that he received the prize from Domitian on a day when he sang of the emperor's victory over the Germans and Dacians; this she interprets as a reference to the emperor's successes in 89 against the Chatti (who had supported the revolt of Saturninus) and the Dacians. She further notes that in the two passages where both the Alban and Capitoline contests are named (3. 5. 28–33 and 5. 3. 227–33), the Capitoline contest is always placed second, and concludes that Statius lists the contests in the order in which they occurred. Such an assumption is entirely reasonable, if we are not to abandon the search for a chronology altogether. She argues that the Capitoline contest of 86 must be ruled out,[4] since if Statius' defeat followed the Alban Games, then only 90 and 94 are possible years.[5]

---

[1] See Nauta (2002), 197 with n. 12, who argues for a date in May, while Caldelli (1993), 56–8 argues for the first half of June. Cf. P. White (1998), 86 n. 6, Robert (1930), 31.

[2] Coleman (1988), p. xvii and on 4. 2. 66–67.

[3] See below for the argument that the victory cannot be later than the publication of the *Thebaid*, which could not have appeared after January 93.

[4] A. Hardie (2003), 144 suggests that Statius could have competed on two occasions in the Capitoline contest, in 86 and 90, arguing that Statius refers to the event in general terms at *Silv.* 3. 5. 31–3 and at 5. 3. 231–3. As noted above, however, the Capitoline contest is always mentioned after the Alban success, so that a reference to two Capitoline contests would destroy any sense of chronological sequence, and while *dolebas* (Calderini : *doleres* M) at *Silv.* 3. 5. 32 would be consistent with repeated defeats, it would also be satisfactory as an expression of continued grief even if Statius only entered the contest once.

[5] The Capitoline defeat could only have taken place in 86 if Statius' *Alban* poem had commemorated not the triumphs of 89, but earlier successes against the Chatti (Domitian took the title Germanicus in 83) and the disputed First Dacian War. If the first Dacian War was over in 85, this would be possible. The arguments of B. W. Jones (1992), 138–9 with nn. 76 and 77 in favour of dating of the First Dacian War to 84/5 are, however, questionable, particularly as he wrongly interprets the *Acta Fratrum Arvalium* as providing evidence for Domitian's stay in Rome during the first half of 86. Domitian is in fact never mentioned as present in the *collegium* in the *Acta* for 86 (see McCrum and Woodhead (1961), 12–13); contrast e.g. ibid. 25, l. 68 (May 87): 'adfuerunt imp. Caesar Domitian[us . . .' for the

As for 94,[6] this date is impossible, as Coleman has shown, since *Silvae* 5. 3, which mentions both contests, is written while the *Thebaid* is incomplete;[7] the epic was finished before January 93, the date of Domitian's Sarmatian victory, since there is no reference to that campaign in the epic's proem.[8] We are thus left with 90 for the Capitoline defeat. The same year is also most likely for the Alban victory, although it is theoretically possible for Statius, even if he did not win at Alba in 86 with a celebration of Domitian's earlier victories, to have sung of the same earlier victories in the years intervening between 86 and 90. It is most probable, however, that *Silv.* 4. 2. 66 does indeed refer to a song in honour of the double triumph of 89.

The date of Statius' father's death is much contested. Central to the issue are the interval of three months after the bereavement (*Silv.* 5. 3. 29), and the deceased's projected poem on the disaster of Vesuvius (5. 3. 205–8). Because the poem on Vesuvius seems only to have been projected (note the phrase *mens erat* at 206), it has been argued, most recently by Laguna, Brożek, and Nauta,[9] that the father's death belongs to the period immediately subsequent to the eruption of 79. But A. Hardie (1983), 13 and Coleman (1988), p. xviii suggest that 5. 3. 205–8 need not be evidence for the father's immediate death, since there was no reason why the composition of the poem could not be

emperor's presence. Syme, *RP* vii. 560 (cf. (1980), 1) speculates that Domitian may have campaigned on the Danube until late in 86. It is thus difficult to postulate the emperor's presence at an Alban festival in March 86, when he gave Statius his prize in person (*Silv.* 4. 2. 65–7). For this 'traditional' chronology of a Dacian campaign in early 86, following the defeat of Oppius Sabinus in winter 85/6, see Gsell (1893), 209–12.

[6] Van Dam (1984), 1 with n. 16 gives further bibliographical references to scholars who have dated the Capitoline failure to 90 or 94.

[7] Coleman (1988), p. xviii cautiously notes that the epic which Statius is completing with difficulty might not be the *Thebaid*. However, it is indeed 'reasonable to infer that St. meant the *Thebaid*', as opposed to the *Achilleid* or even the *De Bello Germanico*, since *te sine* (*Silv.* 5. 3. 238), and the shift from imperfect to present tenses in 5. 3. 234–8, emotively suggest a contrast with the times when Statius' father was helping with the epic before his death. Moreover, the nautical metaphor with which Statius describes the difficulties of finishing the poem (237–8 'labat incerto mihi limite cursus | te sine, et orbatae caligant uela carinae') may be thought curiously similar to the language used by Statius at the end of his *Thebaid* to describe the work's completion (*Theb.* 12. 809): 'et mea iam longo meruit ratis aequore portum'. The contrast between what it was like to write epic in his father's lifetime and after his death would be by no means so pointed if 237–8 described another work which had no assistance from the father.

[8] Coleman (1988), pp. xvii f.

[9] Laguna (1992), 4 and 8; Brożek (1994); Nauta (2002), 195–6. See also van Dam (1984), 1 with n. 10.

delayed.[10] Furthermore, if he had died soon after the eruption, it would have been effective for Statius to mention that his father's poem was cut off by death, as a means of eliciting pathos, by saying that his father had died in the aftermath of the calamity which had affected his native city of Naples. Rather, *Silv.* 5. 3. 205 ff. should be seen as a reference to unfulfilled, rather than unfinished, poetic ambition, which does not in itself constitute evidence for immediate death. Coleman further argues that Statius' poem on the death of Glaucias (*Silv.* 2. 1), which includes a reference to Statius' own bereavement (2. 1. 33–4), gives a synchronism with publication of Martial's epigrams on the same subject (6. 28 and 6. 29); this book of epigrams will have been published at some point in 90 or 91.[11] However, the wording of *Silv.* 2. 1. 33–4, 'et mihi, cum proprios gemerem defectus ad ignes | (quem, Natura!) patrem', need not imply that the father's death or the composition of Statius' lament was recent; Statius simply remarks that he too has experienced such a severe bereavement (cf. 3. 3. 39–40 'neque enim mihi flere parentem | ignotum; similis gemui proiectus ad ignem'). Nor can appeal be made to 2. 1. 35 'sed confer gemitus pariterque fleamus'; this passage refers to Statius' participation in Melior's grief, a particular characteristic of poetic, as opposed to prose, consolation (see van Dam ad loc.), which has already been implied by the suggestive line 'uix tenui *similis* comes offendique tenendo' (2. 1. 25). Thus although 2. 1 does not effect a synchronism of the death of Glaucias and the composition of 5. 3, much less the death of Statius' father, it is nevertheless evidence for the latest possible date for this last.

The problems of *Silv.* 5. 3. 29 are no less difficult. If Statius wrote no poetry in the three months after his father's death, there is then a conflict between the three months' silence and the composition of poems for both the Alban and Capitoline contests mentioned in 5. 3. 225–33. It is, moreover, likely that the poems cannot have been composed long in advance of the contests; A. Hardie (2003), 134 remarks in the case of the Capitoline contest that the topics for the

---

[10] Hardie notes that Martial's poetic response (4. 44) to the catastrophe was not published until 88, while Coleman suggests that whereas the elder Statius' poem on the Capitoline war could represent a swift demonstration of political allegiance to the Flavian cause, no such pressing reason existed for a work on Vesuvius.

[11] Coleman (1988), p. xviii suggests a date of the Saturnalia of 90 for the publication of Martial's Book 6. Citroni (1989), 222 n. 36, however, suggests that a later date is possible: see also Citroni (1988), Grewing (1997), 20–3, Nauta (2002), 442.

poetry contest were probably not given to the competitors very long in advance of the event, perhaps only on the day before when lots were drawn for the order of performance. The likely focus of the poetry event in the Alban contest may have been easier to predict, since the scanty evidence would seem to suggest a concentration on the martial achievements of Domitian,[12] but given the taste of the age for extemporary brilliance, it is unlikely that competitors would have had complete freedom to prepare a poem in advance of the competition.

A. Hardie (1983), 13–14 has attempted to avoid this difficulty by placing the father's death in September 90, *after* the Alban Games (which he dates to March 90), implying that the father was merely absent; more recently, Hardie (2003), 143–4 has revisited the topic, with the additional argument that 5. 3. 228–9 'si per me serta tulisses | Caesarea donata manu' is an allusion to the motif of the rejuvenation of the poet through acquisition of a garland (especially in the case of Hesiod),[13] so that had Statius' father been present he would have been rejuvenated. This hypothesis that Statius' father was still alive seems strange in view of the pathetic quality of *Silv.* 5. 3. 225 ff, and especially 230 'quantum potuit dempsisse senectae', the reference to old age strongly suggesting the onset of death which would have been reversed if only the father had lived to see the day of the victory, while the argument that there may be an allusion to motifs of old poets being rejuvenated does not in itself mean that Statius' father would have to be alive, but absent, at the time of the Alban contest. As Hardie himself remarks (144), 'If he had witnessed Statius' crowning, he would still be alive', and the motif of a missed opportunity for rejuvenation might well indeed be more suited to a situation where Statius' father was in fact dead at the time. Morever, since we are explicitly informed that Statius' father did not suffer a painful death (5. 3. 258–61), in a passage which implies that he enjoyed good health, it seems unlikely that his absence from his son's Alban victory was a result of illness. It is even more unlikely that he would have missed both competitions if he had been still alive.

We are thus left with three internal pieces of evidence from the poem: (*a*) the claim that it is written after three months' silence following the bereavement (5. 3. 29), (*b*) the father's projected work on Vesuvius (5. 3. 205–8) and (*c*) his absence from the Alban and Capitoline contests, which in all probability both took place in 90.

---

[12] A. Hardie (2003), 139–40.   [13] On which see Scodel (1980).

The real problem lies in establishing a concord between (*a*) and (*c*). As for (*b*), the planned poem on Vesuvius, there is no certain proof or refutation of the claim that the date of death is closely associated with the date of the eruption.

How, then, to reconcile or explain the mention of the Alban and Capitoline contests with the three-month interval before the poem's composition? Perhaps the most extreme solution is to regard 5. 3 as a conflation of two or more separate poems effected by a posthumous editor.[14] This hypothesis can, however, be countered with an appeal to the literary qualities of the poem, and in particular its ordered structure.[15] The mention of the Alban and Capitoline contests in no way constitutes a change of tone, being a natural progression from Statius' victory at the Neapolitan Games (which his father did witness); there is then a transition to an appreciation of his father's assistance in the composition of the *Thebaid*. The argument against the textual integrity of 5. 3 on the basis of length is unsatisfactory, since (discounting a few probable lacunae noted in the commentary which would admittedly lengthen the text), 5. 3 is only sixteen lines longer than 1. 2 (an epithalamium) and only thirty-one lines longer than 5. 1 (the longest *epicedion* after 5. 3).

Vollmer considered the dating of the poem to three months after the father's death to be a fiction.[16] This seems unlikely; if the poem were written long after the event, there would be little point in maintaining a fiction that only three months had passed, and it would indeed be more pathetic, and hence more likely, for the poet to assert that, even after several years, he could not recover from his father's death. Such a claim would accord well with the depth of grief manifested in such passages as, for example, 72–3 and 275–6. However, since Statius tells us that his poem is written three months after the father's death, this assertion should be taken at face value.

If we accept the validity of *Silv.* 5. 3. 29, then we must recognize that we do not possess the poem as it was originally composed. There is no need, however, for an excessively reductive approach, such as

---

[14] Thus Coleman (1988), p. xix: 'Since Book 5 is a posthumous collection...it is reasonable to suppose that two or more poems (or parts thereof) have been put together to form what is the longest poem in the *Silvae*.'

[15] On the structure of 5. 3 see Newmyer (1979), 19–24 and Esteve-Forriol (1962), 100–105, who note the careful ordering of the *laudatio* of Statius' father in 116–252.

[16] Vollmer (1896), 40, (1898), 9 n. 10; but see van Dam (1984), 15 and n. 30, Brożek (1994), 53.

the assumption that 5. 3 is a posthumous amalgam of two or more poems. Instead the references to the Alban and Capitoline poems can be regarded as later additions to the poem. Since the only irreconcilable conflict of evidence in the poem is between 5. 3. 29 and 5. 3. 225–33, the later passage should be seen as a partial revision by the poet.[17] Whether or not the revision was made with a view to publication is more uncertain; the evidence is lacking.[18]

To sum up, our only secure evidence for the dating of the death of Statius' father is the poem itself, which was, with the exception of 225–33, composed three months after the event. The father could not have died before the eruption of Vesuvius in 79, and was dead before the Alban Games of March 90. It is possible, but not certain, that the allusion to Aegeus' death just before Theseus' return home in *Silv.* 5. 3. 237–8 (see the n. ad loc.) might imply that he died at a late stage in the composition of the *Thebaid*; this need not contradict the reference to Statius' wife as the only person to support him throughout the epic's composition (*Silv.* 3. 5. 35–6).

---

[17] Cf. Brożek (1994), 54. Nauta (2002), 196–8 suggests that the insertion runs from 225 to 238, including the reference to the composition of the *Thebaid*. There is no need to follow Griset (1962), who discerns a clear difference between 1–224 and 225–93, arguing that 255–293, displaying a difference of tone and acceptance of the father's death, are composed later. Indeed if the original poem had stopped at 224, structural problems would have resulted; note also the natural tendency of an *epicedion* to veer towards acceptance of bereavement in its concluding stages. Furthermore the closing position of the poem exhibits signs of a *lack* of any such acceptance; such passages as 275–6 (Statius' wish to join his father, whatever the consequences) and the mention of *dolor* in 254 could be evidence for the poet's *reluctance* to be consoled, suggesting *recent* bereavement. A. Hardie (2003), 143 n. 87 argues that 'it is implausible that Statius should have failed to notice discrepancies within *Silv.* 5. 3 or to have made later additions without fully inserting them into his existing text', but the incomplete state of the *Achilleid* and the fact that the poems in Book 5 are demonstrably assembled by a posthumous editor mean that we cannot be so sure as to whether there might not have been inconsistencies in 5. 3.

[18] See Laguna (1992), 13 for the theory that the inclusion of Statius' recent successes is evidence for projected publication. However, the poem, even in its revised form, seems to be prior to the completion of the *Thebaid*. Given that Statius mentions his appearances in poetic contests, he would surely have mentioned the *Thebaid* (which was published by January 93) if it had been completed, doubtless rewriting 237–8. Adoption of this hypothesis thus requires the acceptance of further speculation to the effect that Statius then decided not to publish the poem in his remaining years.

COMMENTARY

1. Ipse: The initial concentration on Statius' father reflects the latter's importance as a source of poetic inspiration, a role fulfilled before his death (e.g. 213–14) and after death (288–90).

malas: referring to the tone of the work to be composed and its painful effect on Statius; cf. 5. 1. 209 'dona malae feralia pompae'.

uires: compare the appeal to Rutilius Gallicus (*Silv.* 1. 4. 22–3) 'ipse ueni uiresque nouas animumque ministra | qui caneris'. The *uires* are the necessary strength or inspiration (cf. Prop. 2. 10. 5, 2. 10. 11, Luc. 1. 66 (on Nero) 'tu satis ad uires Romana in carmina dandas', Tac. *Dial.* 21. 2) required for a successful composition; contrast Statius' *lack* of poetic voice after the death of his *puer* (*Silv.* 5. 5. 49–50): 'absumptae uires et copia fandi | nulla mihi'.

lamentabile carmen: the epicedion; Statius' father is summoned to assist the composition in the same way as Rutilius Gallicus ('qui caneris') is invoked in 1. 4.

2. Elysio de fonte: instead of drinking from such poetic springs as the Hippocrene or Castalia (on the poetic associations of water, see the notes on 5. 5. 2 and 5. 5. 7), Statius asks his father for Elysian water. This rejection of the usual poetic practice is also paralleled in *Silv.* 1. 4. 19–23, where instead of Phoebus, Pallas, the Muses, Mercury, or Bacchus it is Rutilius Gallicus who will inspire the song; cf. 1. 5. 1–8 (Naiads and Vulcan replace the Muses, Apollo, and Bacchus), and 2. 3. 6–7 (Naiads and Fauns, instead of Phoebus). At 5. 1. 13–14 the success of Statius' composition is dependent not only on Apollo, but also on the emperor. Compare Prop. 2. 1. 3–4 (inspiration comes from a girl, not Calliope or Apollo) and Ovid's rejection of Apollo and the Muses (though not Venus) at *Ars* 1. 25–30, Pers. *prol.* 1–7, Luc. 1. 66 (see previous n.); see also Rosati (2002), 240–6. Thus Statius emotively assigns to his father an inspirational role more typical of Apollo and the Muses.

At *Theb.* 3. 247 Jove swears by the 'Elysios . . . fontes', a more general reference to the realms of the dead and hence to the River Styx, the most potent oath for an immortal. Here *Elysio de fonte* does refer to Elysium, if not to a particular spring. Identification is difficult; although Virgil mentions Lethe in the context of Elysium (*A.* 6. 713–15, 748 ff.), the river of forgetfulness is not an obvious source for a poet's song. Nevertheless, waters are attested in the realms of the blessed, as at Pi. *O.* 2. 73 τὰ μὲν χερσόθεν ἀπ' ἀγλαῶν δενδρέων, ὕδωρ δ' ἄλλα φέρβει; cf. Virg. *A.* 6. 659 'plurimus Eridani per siluam uoluitur amnis', and 6. 674 where Musaeus mentions 'prata recentia riuis'. The phrase is also a subtle *captatio beneuolentiae*; Statius acknowledges that his father is one of the blessed dead of Elysium (compare 24–7).

2–3. pulsumque sinistrae...lyrae: compare 'laete lyrae pulsu' (Ov. *Fast.* 5. 667), where Ovid invokes Mercury. Whereas in the *Fasti* Mercury delights in the music of the lyre, Statius asks his father for inauspicious (*sinistrae*) music, appropriate to his theme. Just as Mercury gives instruction in elegant speech ('quo didicit culte lingua docente loqui', *Fast.* 5. 668), so does Statius' father (see 213–14).

3. genitor praedocte: this collocation encapsulates the twin themes of the poem, Statius' relation with his father, and his father's *doctrina*. M's *praedocte*, if correct, is the only instance of the word in classical Latin (the only parallel offered by *ThLL* x/2. 586. 71–5 is Coripp. *Iust.* 4. 56 'artificum praedocta manus'); later MSS have *perdocte* (the corruption is easy), while Markland favoured *praeclare*. *praerepte* (Schwartz (1889), 13) would be analogous to 'praerepti...alumni' in *Silv.* 2. 1. 1. But *praeclare* or *praerepte* would remove all mention of the father's *doctrina*, a central theme of the poem. Moreover, an allusion to learning is appropriate to a poetic invocation. As for *praedocte* and *perdocte*, M's reading deserves priority; see Vollmer's parallels for Statian adjectives with the intensifying prefix *prae-* (e.g. *praedulcis*, *Silv.* 5. 3. 82).

3–6. Compare Luc. 1. 63–6, where Lucan, with Nero as his guide, has no need to invoke Apollo or Bacchus. Statius more cautiously declares that it is not *fas* for him to invoke Apollo. For the taboo against the gods' being involved in death, cf. E. *Hipp.* 1396, where Artemis declares that she may not (οὐ θέμις) shed tears for the dying Hippolytus, and 1437–9 with Barrett ad loc.

mouere (ς): Vollmer defends *moueri* (M), which he oddly construes with the preceding *mihi*, as a dative of agent. Though he does offer parallels for a change of subject with two dependent infinitives (e.g. *Silv.* 1. 2. 55, 1. 4. 75, Virg. *A.* 5. 773, 11. 84), a crucial difference between these instances and the present passage is that here the passive form is neither encouraged by sense nor required by metre, and the parallelism between Statius' actions (*mouere* and *impellere*) would be lost. And construing *moueri* with the preceding *mihi* is unsatisfactory, since *mihi* is the indirect object of *da* and not a dative of agent. The greater clarity of *mouere* is preferable.

5. te sine: Statius asserts that he is unable to achieve anything without his father's presence: cf. 238 below, *Silv.* 4. 7. 21 (addressed to Vibius Maximus) 'torpor est nostris sine te Camenis', Lucr. 1. 22–3 'nec sine te quicquam dias in luminis oras | exoritur neque fit laetum neque amabile quicquam', Virg. *G*. 3. 42 'te sine nil altum mens incohat', *A*. 12. 882–3 'aut quicquam mihi dulce meorum | te sine, frater, erit?', Prop. 2. 30. 40 'nam sine te nostrum non ualet ingenium', Calp. *Ecl*. 3. 51–2 'te sine, uae misero, mihi lilia nigra uidentur | nec sapiunt fontes et acescunt uina bibenti'); for the use of language such as ἄνευ σέθεν and 'sine te' in religious contexts, see Norden (1913), 157 and n. 3, 159 and n. 1, 175, 349–50, N.–H. on Hor. *Carm*. 1. 26. 9, Fedeli (1983), 58–9.

   Corycia ... in umbra: after the two sites connected with Apollo, Delphi and Cirrha, a nearby town, Statius alludes to the Corycian cave of Mount Parnassus, sacred to Pan and the Nymphs (*CIG* 1728; for the Corycian nymphs, see A. *Eu*. 22–3, S. *Ant*. 1128–9, Call. fr. 75. 56 Pf., A.R. 2. 711–12, Var. At. fr. 7 Courtney (*FLP*, p. 241), Ov. *Met*. 1. 320, Nonn. 9. 287), and the refuge of the Delphians at the time of Xerxes' invasion (Hdt. 8. 36).[19] There was also a wood: at *Theb*. 7. 348 the 'Coryciumque nemus' refers to one of the districts of Parnassus. The *umbra* is that of either the wood or the cave (cf. *Silv*. 3. 1. 141 'Cirrhae ... opacae' and [Tib.] 3. 1. 16 'Castaliamque umbram'), but mention of Parnassus and the Muses also suggests the sheltered conditions of retirement (*OLD* s.v. *umbra* 5) and poetry. At *Silv*. 5. 2. 104 (see n.) Crispinus is 'tacita studiorum occultus in umbra' before his debut in the courts; cf. Mart. 9. 84. 3 'haec ego Pieria ludebam tutus in umbra'.

   6. Euhan: for the connexion between Bacchus and poetry, see van Dam on *Silv*. 2. 7. 7 and N.–H. on Hor. *Carm*. 2. 19. Bacchus and Apollo are mentioned together at *Silv*. 1. 2. 17–19 (with Mercury), 1. 2. 220, 1. 4. 19–21 (with Mercury and Minerva), 1. 5. 3, 2. 7. 7–8, 5. 1. 26; cf. Prop. 3. 2. 9, Ov. *Am*. 1. 3. 11, [Tib.] 3. 4. 44, Luc. 1. 64–5, Juv. 7. 64. Ovid refers to 'Ismariae ... Bacchae' at *Met*. 9. 642; for the Thracian mountain called either *Ismarus* or *Ismara* in Latin (Clausen on Virg. *Ecl*. 6. 30) and its associations with wine see Mynors on Virg. *G*. 2. 37.

   7. dedidici: the undoing of Statius' poetic learning indicates both the extremity of his grief, and his father's importance as a teacher. For *dediscere*, cf. the tame lion at *Silv*. 2. 5. 2–3: 'quid scelus humanasque animo dediscere caedes | imperiumque pati et domino parere minori?'

   7–9. Statius represents his loss not as the poetic gods' abandoning him, but as his losing the symbols of poetry; cf. Ov. *Tr*. 1. 7. 1 ff., where

---

[19] For the other Corycian cave in Cilicia, see Leigh (1994).

ivy is inappropriate for Ovid, and V.Fl. 1. 5–7 where Apollo is asked for inspiration, provided that the poets' tripod and laurel are as they should be.

8. uellera: 'fillets' or 'chaplets', the woollen symbols of priestly authority; cf. *Theb.* 4. 491–2 'uatisque horrenda canentis | nunc umeros nunc ille manus et uellera prensat', 8. 294–5 'atque is ubi intorto signatus uellere crinem | conuenitque deis'. The use of *uellera* here anticipates Statius' designation of himself as *uates* in l. 14; for Statian exploitation of the two meaning of *uates*, poet and seer, see Lovatt (2001), 115–17.

funestamque hederis inrepere taxum: ivy is perhaps an even older component of Dionysiac ritual than the vine (Dodds on E. *Ba.* 81); for its association with poetry compare Prop. 4. 1. 61–2: 'Ennius hirsuta cingat sua dicta corona: | mi folia ex hedera porrige, Bacche, tua.'

The yew is characteristically inauspicious, because of its dark green, almost black, foliage and its toxic qualities: 'taxus minime uirens gracilisque et tristis et dira, nullo suco, ex omnibus sola bacifera' (Plin. *Nat.* 16. 50); sleeping or eating in the shade of some varieties was said to be fatal (*Nat.* 16. 51, Dsc. 4. 79). On its literary associations (especially with the underworld), see Olck–Steier in *RE* v. A. 1. 90. 15 ff. and Bömer on Ov. *Met.* 4. 432, where yew trees ('funesta … taxo') adorn a path descending into the realms of Dis. At *Theb.* 8. 9–11 the yew has a part in Amphiaraus' initiation into the underworld:

> necdum illum aut trunca lustrauerat obuia taxo
> Eumenis, aut furuo [ω : fuluo *POS*] Proserpina poste notarat
> coetibus adsumptum functis.

Amphiaraus had previously returned his mantic emblems to Apollo (*Theb.* 7. 784–5): 'accipe commissum capiti decus, accipe laurus, | quas Erebo deferre nefas.' His abandonment of his tokens of his vatic status, and their replacement with purification by the yew, are paralleled by Statius' experiences here; the emblems of conventional poetic inspiration are lost or prove ineffectual as a result of his father's death. The expected and more naturalistic image of ivy creeping in among the yew is reversed, as an index of death's sway over the poet. Compare also Luc. 6. 644–5 'et nullo uertice caelum | suspiciens Phoebo non peruia taxus opacat' for the opposition of the yew to Phoebus.

inrepere: the word can be used neutrally, as at 5. 2. 62–3 'non-dum ualidae tibi signa iuuentae | inrepsere genis' (see n.), but can also have inauspicious assocations; cf. e.g. Col. 4. 4. 3, 'si mollis ac tenera humus nullis herbis inrepentibus humorem stirpibus praebuerit', Tac. *Ann.* 4. 8. 1: 'igitur Seianus maturandum ratus deligit uenenum quo paulatim inrepente fortuitus morbus adsimularetur.' Statius twice uses the word of sleep overcoming mortals (*Theb.* 1. 340, 8. 217).

9. sustinui (Markland): Vollmer defends *extimui* (M), arguing that *extimesco* can be construed with an infinitive instead of with *quod*. *ThLL* v/2. 2030. 13–21 gives examples where *extimesco* is construed with an infinitive, such as Tac. *Ann.* 11. 1. 2 'praecipuum auctorem Asiaticum interficiendi C. Caesaris non extimuisse in contione populi Romani fateri gloriamque facinoris ultro petere', but only in the sense 'to be afraid to do something', which cannot be correct here since Statius could hardly be the subject of the infinitives. Nor can *extimui* be considered as governing two indirect statements (*inrepere* and *arescere*). It would be peculiar to say 'The fillets of Parnassus abandoned me; I was afraid that the yew was creeping over the ivy and that the trembling laurel was withering'. *sustinui* is preferable, preparing for the indignant and shocked *nefas*.

trepidamque has caused concern; Markland favoured *partam*, while Vollmer argued that 'der Todesschauer des Trägers ist auf den Schmuck übertragen; die sonst so zähen Blätter des Lorbers erzittern und welken.' But the adjective can be treated as a learned allusion. Apart from its associations with fear, *trepidus* can also be-token physical movement (*OLD* 4), such as shaking or trembling. Call. *H.* 2. 1–2 evokes an atmosphere of expectation before Apollo's epiphany, describing the spontaneous movement of the laurel:

> Οἷον ὁ τὠπόλλωνος ἐσείσατο δάφνινος ὄρπηξ,
> οἷα δ᾽ ὅλον τὸ μέλαθρον·

Here, Statius inverts the positive significance of Callimachus' trembling laurel, and, by means of a pun on *trepidamque* is able to evoke Callimachus in the negative context of his grief. There is a further contrast between Statius' poem of grief, in which Apollo plays no part, and Call. *H.* 2. 17–24, where Apollo brings about the *cessation* of lamentation, causing even Thetis and Niobe to leave off mourning. For the withering of the laurel, cf. *Theb.* 8. 203 'ipsi amnes ipsaeque uolent arescere laurus', Cic. *Rep.* 6. 8, 'arescentibus laureis'.

10. Vollmer defends *certe ego* (M) as an anacoluthon, punctuating with a dash at the end of line 11; Courtney's full stop in 11 requires an ellipse of *sum* after *ego*. If there is an anacoluthon, the sense of what would have followed is relevant. Having indicated in the relative clause that he was accustomed to writing epic, Statius would hardly have repeated this material in the main clause of the sentence. Nor is it likely that yet another statement of the loss of his habitual poetic facility would have ensued, a point made elegantly and at some length in 5–9. The case for an anacoluthon after *certe ego* is not strong; the device in part depends on a clear sense of what might have followed.

ille (Markland) gives the familiar figure 'ille ego', most famously found in the rejected opening of the *Aeneid*, which records Virgil's progression through the lower genres of bucolic and didactic poetry towards epic, on which see Austin (1968); cf. e.g. Ov. *Met.* 1. 757–8 'ille ego liber, | ille ferox tacui!', Markland on *Silv.* 5. 3. 10. The figure occurs twice in *Silv.* 5. 5. 38–43, where Statius contrasts his former ability to console others and his present inability to assuage his own grief at the loss of his *puer*, before continuing with a simple statement of poetic inability. The effect of *ille ego* here in *Silv.* 5. 3 would be comparable, with Statius contrasting past achievements in epic, the highest genre, with his current poetic difficulties. For this use of the *ille ego* figure to describe a shift from better to worse, reversing the rejected *Aeneid* opening, Austin (1968), 110–11 compares Ov. *Tr.* 5. 7. 55–6 'ille ego Romanus uates (ignoscite, Musae) | Sarmatico cogor plurima more loqui', Stat. *Theb.* 9. 434–7, Sil. 11. 177–84. Note also *Theb.* 5. 34–6: Hypsipyle uses *illa ego* when she begins her poetic narrative of the Lemnian episode: 'o pater! illa ego nam, pudeat ne forte benignae | hospitis, illa, duces, raptum quae sola parentem | occului. quid longa malis exordia necto?'; see further Gibson (2004), 158.

In the present poem, there follows (12) an indignant rhetorical question as to the cause of Statius' *impasse*; a question mark at the end of l. 11 would also accord with such indignation.

magnanimum: the archaic genitive plural *magnanimum* (cf. *Theb.* 2. 733 'magnanimum . . . regum', 3. 349, 6. 268, Virg. *G.* 4. 476, *A.* 3. 704, 6. 307) is appropriate to the epic subject matter; compare *uirum* in a line describing Homer's poetry (149). *magnanimus* is a standard adjective for heroes or monarchs (recalling the Homeric epithets μεγάθυμος and μεγαλόψυχος); in Statius the epithet is for example applied to Theseus (*Theb.* 12. 795), Domitian (12. 814) and Achilles (*Ach.* 1. 1); see further Dewar on *Theb.* 9. 547.

11. altum spirans: cf. Hor. *Ep.* 2. 1. 166 'nam spirat tragicum satis et feliciter audet' with Brink ad loc., Sen. *Dial.* 3. 20. 2 'omnes quos uecors animus supra cogitationes extollit humanas altum quiddam et sublime spirare se credunt'.

Martemque aequare canendo: a reworking of Virg. *Ecl.* 5. 9 'Phoebum superare canendo'. Mars is paradoxically matched not in his own sphere, warfare, but in poetry. This use of *aequare* in contexts where a god is being equalled is rare, but compare Ov. *Tr.* 4. 8. 52 'aequantem superos emeruisse uirum', Sil. 1. 611 'et aequantem superos uirtute senatum', 13. 722 'nunc superos aequantem laude Camillum'; cf. Sen. *Ep.* 92. 30 'hic deos aequat'; see also below, 160–1 n.

The phrase also suggests an attempt to equal the loftiness of the subject, war (for *Mars* thus, see *OLD* 2a, 2b), with poetic grandeur. For the need to match the style of a work to its content, cf. Isoc. 4. 13 ὡς χαλεπόν ἐστιν ἴσους τοὺς λόγους τῷ μεγέθει τῶν ἔργων ἐξευρεῖν, Sal. *Cat.* 3. 2 'facta dictis exaequanda sunt'.

12–13. Courtney (1984), 333 argues convincingly for a lacuna of two half-lines in l. 12, rejecting the zeugma which arises if *praeduxit* is the main verb of both *quis* clauses, since in the first clause the accusative *corda* would be affected by ablative *situ* and in the second the dative *menti* would be affected by *nubila* in the accusative. Pinkster's comparison with the two uses of *donare* at Plin. *Nat.* 7. 121 'quo miraculo matris salus donata pietati est, ambaeque perpetuis alimentis', mentioned by *ThLL* x/2. 591. 4–6, is unconvincing as a parallel.

Indeed the difficulties of these lines as they stand in M are best demonstrated by contorted translations such as 'Who has doomed my spirit to decay? Who has drawn a cold shroud of mist about my blighted heart, and drowned my imagination?' (Mozley), 'Who has plunged my soul in barren lethargy? Who has darkened my sun, passed sentence on my mind, and enshrouded it in chill gloom?' (Slater), and 'qui a jeté sur mon génie une rouille stérile? Qui . . . a étendu un brouillard glacé sur mon esprit frappé de malédiction?' (Iz.–Fr.), all attempts to eliminate the zeugma by supplying verbs.

Apolline uerso: M has *merso* here, and although *mergere* can be used to denote the setting of heavenly bodies (*ThLL* viii. 831. 31–47), Håkanson (1969), 138–9 denied that the sun-god is indicated, on the grounds that *Apollo* is not used of the sun in Latin literature.

The phrase had been previously questioned; Heinsius and Markland favoured *uerso* (*ς*), while Baehrens proposed *maesto* (cf. 5. 5. 52–3 n. below). Håkanson nevertheless defended *merso*, arguing that Statius' inspiration has been hidden by the clouds.

But the *nubila* (13) make a reference to the sun more likely, particularly as the clouds are *frigida* (a natural consequence of an absence of sunlight). Even if, as Håkanson argues, Apollo is not the sun but Statius' inspiration, the clouds affecting Statius' mind are nevertheless imagery which might be used of the sun; because of this imagery Apollo assumes solar connotations as well. Compare especially Luc. 6. 465–7 'nunc omnia complent | imbribus et *calido praeducunt nubila Phoebo* | et tonat ignaro caelum Ioue', and the more paradoxical *Carm. adv. Marc.* 2. 33–4 'pondus apostolicum, fulgentis gratia uerbi, | *lumina praeducit menti*, neque cernere possunt.'

Statius thus extends the meaning of *Apollo*; the *context* implies the sun. However, *merso* needs emendation precisely because of this imagery; *merso*, if correct, would mean that the sun had already set. If the sun had set, the cold clouds affecting Statius would then be superfluous since he would be without the sun's influence anyway. The *nubila* are comparable to the darkness affecting Statius at *Silv.* 5. 5. 52–3; compare also the imagery of Virg. *A.* 12. 669 'ut primum discussae umbrae et lux reddita menti'. The citation from Lucan above would suggest that the image is of clouds affecting Statius' mind while it is still light, producing an overcast sky *during the daytime.* This impression would be lost if the clouds developed when it was already night. Baehrens's *maesto* is plausible; compare Statius' instruction to Apollo to assume a sad appearance at *Silv.* 5. 1. 136 'maestaque comam damnare cupresso'. On the other hand a word which explained *damnatae* would be useful. *damnatae* suggests that the poet has gone astray and been punished (cf. *Theb.* 4. 183 'mutos Thamyris damnatus in annos'); see also *Silv.* 5. 5. 2–8 where Statius suggests that he has offended Apollo and the Muses, and also uses the language of punishment. The parallel is a good one, since Statius in 5. 5 is confronting not only the issue of personal bereavement, but also his inability to compose poetry. *damnatae* here is a much briefer hint at ill-favour; a word suggesting hostility need not be inappropriate. *uerso* (*ς*) is attractive; Apollo had turned away from or against Statius (*OLD* s.v. *uerto* 7c, 8, and 13b; cf. Prop. 4. 1. 73 'auersus Apollo'). The sun imagery in the passage might also evoke the usage of *uerto* in the passive to denote the motion of heavenly bodies (*OLD* 1).

Words denoting cold occur in negative evaluations of speeches and other performances, denoting a failure to win a favourable reception; see Cic. *Att.* 1. 14. 1 where a speech of Pompey's is so described: 'itaque frigebat' (compare Cat. 44. 13–14 on the effect of a speech of Sestius' 'hic me grauedo frigida et frequens tussis | quassauit usque'). *frigida nubila* thus hints that, without his usual inspiration, the poet's literary productions may *frigere*, and fail to win approval. Compare the similarly negative tone of 'nil dulce sonantes', applied to the Muses in 14. *frigida* also emphasizes Statius' lack of inspiration (*calor*; cf. *Theb.* 1. 3, *Silv.* 1 pr. 3).

14–18. Statius's lack of inspiration is reflected by the silence of Calliope and the Muses, and the simile describing Calliope's reaction to Orpheus' death; cf. *Silv.* 2. 7. 36–40, where Calliope's grief continues until the moment of Lucan's birth. For such shocked silence compare 5. 1. 201–4, where Abascantus' grief is likened to Orpheus' first response to the loss of Eurydice; see also *Theb.* 8. 553 (the Muses mourn for the poet Corymbus of Helicon): 'sed amissum mutae [ω : mus(a)e *PDδO*] fleuere sorores'. For the inability to create art in response to suffering see further *Silv.* 5. 1. 203 n.

14. nil dulce sonantes: *sonantem* (M) cannot stand, since *et* would be unnecessary. With *sonantes* (Calderini), *et* links *attonitae* and *nil dulce sonantes*. For the silence of the Muses compare Calliope's 'silenti . . . cithara' (15–16).

15. digitis: the lyre, played with the fingers.

17. Hebre: Orpheus' head was thrown into the river Hebrus after he had been killed by the Ciconian women (Virg. *G.* 4. 520 ff. Ov. *Met.* 11. 50 ff.). Ovid also apostrophizes the river (11. 50). Orpheus' powers to affect such features of the natural world as wild beasts and even trees and rivers with his song is a frequent topos first found in Simonides fr. 62 Page (*PMG* 567). See also e.g. A.R. 1. 23 ff, Virg. *G.* 4. 510 'mulcentem tigris et agentem carmine quercus', van Dam on *Silv.* 2. 7. 43–7, Dodds on E. *Ba.* 560–4, N.–H. on Hor. *Carm.* 1. 12. 7, 9, 10 (p. 148–9). In 17–18 it is strikingly the *cessation* of Orpheus' song whose effects are described.

19. at tu: an abrupt return to Statius' father, after the apostrophe of Hebrus in l. 17. The repetition of *seu* in 19 and 24 is characteristic of prayer (Norden (1913), 144 ff., Pulleyn (1997), 100–6). Compare also *at tu* followed by *seu . . . seu* at *Silv.* 2. 7. 107–15, where Lucan's shade will either contemplate the universe or dwell in Elysium. The alternatives of either going to Elysium or joining the gods and looking down on the world are listed as consolatory motifs by Men. Rh. 414. 19–20; cf. 421. 16–17.

membris emissus in ardua tendens: compare the triumph-ant ascent of Pompey's shade and his contemplation of the universe at Luc. 9. 1–14, a passage which recalls Cic. *Rep.* 6. 15 ff. (in the *Somnium Scipionis*); note also Ov. *Met.* 15. 143–52, where Pythagoras describes the pleasures of looking down from heaven on earthly affairs below, and Stat. *Theb.* 12. 76–7, where Creon anticipates his dead son's dwelling among the gods above. The notion of the souls of the good going to heaven is found as early as Pl. *Tht.* 177 A 3–8 and is commonplace: see further van Dam on *Silv.* 2. 7. 107–11, Lattimore (1942), 32–5, Esteve-Forriol (1962), 157–8.

20. fulgentesque plagas rerumque elementa: as he as-cends, Statius' father will see the upper firmament. The *plagas* are regions of the sky rather than of the earth; *fulgentes*, denoting bright-ness rather than heat, is more appropriate to a celestial context. Ovid describes the original separation of the *liquidum caelum* from *spissus aer* (*Met.* 1. 23), and then assigns the loftiest station to the fiery element above the air (*Met.* 1. 26–7): 'ignea conuexi uis et sine pondere caeli | emicuit summaque locum sibi fecit in arce.'

21–3. Statius lists the theological (*quis deus*) and astronomical questions which his father will resolve if he has risen into the firma-ment. Such concerns, as indicated by the reference to Aratus, are *poetic* in character; the projected poem on the eruption of Vesuvius (205–6) may also reflect an interest in natural phenomena. Compare Virgil's stated wish to write of the stars (*G.* 2. 475 ff; cf. Prop. 3. 5. 23 ff.). Both Virgil and Propertius delay their astronomical careers. But whereas Propertius will begin his studies after the time for love has passed, Statius' father only undertakes such research after his own death; cf. the Platonic notion that true knowledge comes after death (Pl. *Phd.* 66 D 7–67 B 1). Astronomical insight can be a consolatory motif (Sen. *Dial.* 6. 25. 2, 11. 9. 8, 12. 8. 6, 12. 20. 2).

For indirect question in lists of astronomical or other technical subjects, compare e.g. Virg. *G.* 1. 1–5, 2. 479–82, *A.* 1. 743–6.

22. minuat Phoeben...integrare latentem: *minuat* and *integrare* represent the phases of the moon in terms of loss and gain; cf. Hor. *Carm.* 4. 7. 13 'damna tamen celeres reparant caelestia lunae'.

23. notique modos extendis Arati: despite *ThLL* v/2. 1974. 11–12 where *extendis* here is interpreted as 'nouos uersus carmini adicis' (cf. Sen. *Apoc.* 9. 5 'eamque rem ad Metamorphosis Ouidi adiciendam'), it is more likely that Statius is not saying that his father wrote additional verses for Aratus' astronomical poem, the *Phaenomena*, but that he 'extends the measures of Aratus', his father's now perfect knowledge of astronomy enabling him to surpass Aratus. As well as denoting the metres and hence the poetry of Aratus, *modos* also suggests the boundaries and limits of Aratus' works (cf. Man. 3. 3–4 'ducite, Pierides. uestros extendere fines | conor'); measurement is an appropriate image for the astronomical context.

24. secreto in gramine: for *secretus* in an Elysian context cf. Virg. *A*. 8. 670 'secretosque pios, his dantem iura Catonem', Sil. 13. 551–2; note also Maternus' praise of the 'nemora uero et luci et secretum ipsum' characteristic of poetry (Tac. *Dial*. 12. 1). Grass is also found in Virgil's Elysium (*A*. 6. 642), as are heroes and poets (*A*. 6. 660, 662). Mention of grass should not occasion surprise; its association with comfort in drier climates is suggested by e.g. Pl. *Phdr*. 230 C 2–5, and Ov. *Met*. 1. 633–4, where Io, now in bovine form, has to lie on 'terrae non semper gramen habenti'.

26–7. Just as Statius' father might pursue celestial and poetic interests in Aratus and astronomy, so too his hypothetical stay in Elysium is envisaged in terms of poetry, and meeting with Homer and Hesiod (see notes on 284 and 5. 1. 254–7, N.–H. on Hor. *Carm*. 2. 13. Pl. *Ap*. 41 A 6–8, where one advantage of dying is the chance to meet Orpheus, Musaeus, Hesiod, and Homer, Ael. *VH* 13. 20), here referred to by their places of origin. The home of Homer was disputed, but one tradition associated him with Maeonia (Lydia). There was also a view that he was the son of Maeon; see *FGrH* 4 F 5a–b, McKeown on Ov. *Am*. 1. 15. 9–10, Skiadas (1965), 34–6. Homer is *Maeonides* at 130; cf. e.g. *Silv*. 2. 1. 117 'Maeonium ... senem', Ov. *Ars* 2. 3–4 'mea carmina ... | praelata Ascraeo Maeonioque seni', *Laus Pis*. 232 'Maeoniumque senem Romano prouocet ore'. Hesiod himself mentions his home in Ascra in Boeotia (*Op*. 639–40); cf. e.g. *Ascraeus senex* in 151, Virg. *Ecl*. 6. 70, Sil. 12. 413.

26. senem non segnior: *segnior* puns on *senior* (cf. 258); the wordplay emphasizes the similarities between Statius' father and Hesiod and Homer. Isidore glosses *segnis* as 'sine igni, ingenio carens' (*Etym*. 10. 247); cf. Serv. *A*. 1. 423 'nam per contrarium segnem, id est sine igni, ingenio carentem dicimus', Maltby (1991), 557.

27. alternumque sonas: for *alternus* in contexts of poetic competition or alternation of songs, cf. e.g. *Silv*. 5. 5. 21, Virg. *Ecl*. 3. 59 'alternis dicetis; amant alterna Camenae', 7. 18–19 'alternis igitur

contendere uersibus ambo | coepere, alternos Musae meminisse
uolebant', Calp. *Ecl.* 2. 25, 4. 80, and 6. 2, *Buc. Eins.* 1. 20–1, *Il* 1.
604 Μουσάων θ', αἳ ἄειδον ἀμειβόμεναι ὀπὶ καλῇ, Theoc. 8. 61 δἰ
ἀμοιβαίων. One is reminded of the tradition of a contest between
Homer and Hesiod; it is a high compliment to assert that the poet's
father is their equal.

28. da uocem magno, pater, ingenium<que> dolori: in
contrast to the elaborate tone of his earlier request that his father
grant him *uires* and *carmen*, and *pulsus* for his lyre, Statius simply and
emotively petitions his father for the voice and the inspiration (*OLD*
s.v. *ingenium* 5a) for his grief (for such an appeal for inspiration from
one dead compare Lib. *Or.* 18. 5). The juxtaposition of 'pater' and
'ingeniumque' suggests the etymology of 'ingenium' (related to *gigno*);
see Isid. *Etym.* 10. 122 'ingeniosus, quod intus uim habeat gignendi
quamlibet artem', Maltby (1991), 303.

magno (usually ascribed to Avantius, but found in the *recentior* Q)
was perhaps the original reading of M, since *magna* looks like an
M¹ correction of *magno*. *magno* is preferable to *magnam*, found in
most later manuscripts, because 'uocem magnam' would most nat-
urally be an indication of loudness (*ThLL* viii. 128. 56–64). But volume
is scarcely an issue here, particularly as Statius combines his request
with one for *ingenium*. Furthermore the juxtaposition of *uocem* and
magnam would be inelegant. *magno* adds weight to the correct word,
dolori; the simplicity of the phrase need occasion no surprise in a line
where emotion is very much to the fore.

29. On the chronological problems of this poem, see the intro-
duction to *Silv.* 5. 3 above. On the need for an interval between
bereavement and successful consolation, see 5. 1. 16 n., while for the
conceit of the moon looking down on the poet's distress compare *Silv.*
5. 4. 7.

retexens, a metaphor of weaving, signifying going over and hence
unravelling what has already been woven; cf. Ov. *Met.* 7. 531 'Luna,
quater plenum tenuata retexuit orbem'. As Vollmer noted, *retexens* and
relegens must refer to opposites, and hence to the waning and waxing
of the moon; *relegens* has the sense of the moon's revisiting of its
travels, but the word can also be used in the sense of gathering up,
appropriate to a context where the imagery of *retexens* also suggests
weaving; cf. perhaps Ov. *Met.* 8. 173 'ianua difficilis filo est inuenta
relecto', referring to the thread given by Ariadne to Theseus in the
labyrinth. Heinsius on this passage of Ovid conjectured *caelum* for M's

caelo here, comparing *relego* with an object Stat. *Theb.* 1. 272 'Sicanios longe relegens Alpheos amores', *Ach.* 1. 23 'culpatum relegebat iter', Symmachus *Epist.* 2. 50 'cras igitur uiam nobis disce relegendam', 3. 62 'cum iter patriam relegere coeperimus'. Courtney in his edition suggested a more radical emendation of the earlier part of the line, suggesting deletion of the initial *nam*, and the insertion of *iter* after *ter*, to give *me ter iter relegens caelo*. This allows M's *caelo* to be retained as an ablative of place, but though the accusative *iter* is paralleled at *Ach.* 1. 23 and in the Symmachus passages quoted above (cf. V.Fl. 4. 54 'relegit-que uias') the jingle of *ter iter* is less attractive (at Prop. 2. 33a. 22 'ter faciamus iter' the words are not immediately juxtaposed). It is in any case hard to see why *nam* should be unsatisfactory (there is no real need to emend to *iam*): Statius has just asked his father to inspire him (line 28), and the *nam* is explanatory, introducing Statius' inability to compose in the three months since his father's death.

30. residem: Statius' mental inactivity is contrasted with his father's vigour ('non segnior') and the journeys and unravellings of the moon.

31. tuus... ignis: *ignis* commonly (e.g. 66–7 'quae primaeui coniugis ignem | aspicit', *OLD* s.v. *ignis* 3c), denotes the fire of a funeral pyre. Note the striking possessive *tuus*, and the suddenness of the unprepared transition to the scene of the funeral.

32. cineremque...hausi: Markland quotes Ov. *Met.* 8. 539 'post cinerem cineres haustos ad pectora pressant', arguing that here too *cinerem haurire* denotes physical gathering of the ashes (*cinerem relegere*). This is certainly true of Ovid (compare *Met.* 9. 35 'ille cauis hausto spargit me puluere palmis'), but the present passage need not exclusively have this meaning, particularly as *haurio* can denote taking in sights with the eyes or in the mind, as at Virg. *A.* 4. 661–2 'hauriat hunc oculis ignem crudelis ab alto | Dardanus' (where Dido does not envisage any physical contact between Aeneas and the flames of her funeral pyre), and Ov. *Met.* 15. 63–4 'quae natura negabat | uisibus humanis, oculis ea pectoris hausit'; see further *ThLL* vi/3. 2570. 49–82. For the visual and aural effect of a cremation, cf. *Silv.* 5. 1. 226–7. where Abascantus cannot endure the 'fumantia busta | clamoremque rogi'. A clearer sense of this passage might emerge if the text of 5. 5. 14, where M has 'cineremque oculis et crimina ferte', was more certain. Vollmer's hypothesis, that this passage describes ash sticking to Statius' wet eyes, seems extraordinary, though one should recognize the striking contrast between ash, which is very dry, and *oculis umentibus*.

33. uilis honos studiis: cf. Virg. *G.* 1. 506–7 'non ullus aratro | dignus honos'.

34. chordis (Schrader): although in l. 12 *situs* affected the poet's 'corda' (cf. Sen. *Dial.* 11. 18. 9 'haec . . . longo iam situ obsoleto et hebetato animo composui'), *corda* ('heart') is not an equivalent to *curis* (M); the former is the site of emotion, the latter is an emotion. Nor would Statius use his hand to remove such mental *situs*. Read *chordis*: *labente manu* and *tacitis* both suggest an attempt to play a lyre after a period of silence. *curis* could have been influenced by *curas* in 31.

35. nec lumine sicco: Klotz and Vollmer retained *nunc* (M), but *nec* (Gronovius, *Diatribe* 51) is preferable. *labente manu* indicates that Statius is still affected by grief; *nunc lumine sicco* would suggest the opposite. Statius elsewhere in the epicedia emphasizes the failure of mental wounds to heal even after some lapse of time (e.g. *Silv.* 2. 1. 3, 5. 1. 30); healing and recovery are indeed two aims of the genre. Thus *nec lumine sicco* is more consistent with the poet's extreme emotion. The detail picks up the 'oculis umentibus' (32).

36. adclinis tumulo: Statius' leaning against his father's tomb recalls his proximity to the flames and ashes of the pyre (31–2). The phrase occurs at *Silv.* 5. 5. 25, where Statius is also trying to respond poetically to bereavement.

molle quiescis glances at the commonplace tradition (Lattimore (1942), 65–74) of prayers for the earth to lie lightly on the deceased; cf. e.g. *Eleg. in Maec.* 141–142:

> nunc ego quod possum: TELLVS LEVIS OSSA TENETO
> PENDVLA LIBRATO PONDVS ET IPSA TVVM.

38. stellatus: a reference to the appearance of a starlike flame on the head of the young Ascanius (Virg. *A.* 2. 681–4).

ingessit: 'heaped up', a grand word, continuing the lofty tone set by *Aeneia fata* in 37: cf. Ov. *Am.* 2. 1. 13–14 'cum male se Tellus ulta est ingestaque Olympo | ardua deuexum Pelion Ossa tulit', *Met.* 5. 346–7 'uasta giganteis ingesta est insula membris | Trinacris', Stat. *Theb.* 4. 180 'summis ingestum montibus Aepy'.

Albam: see *Silv.* 3. 1. 61–4, where Statius describes his estate 'Dardaniae . . . sub collibus Albae', which had been endowed with a water supply by Domitian, and A. Hardie (1983), 12–13; cf. 4. 5. 1–28 for the simple pleasures of rural life.

39. pingues sanguine campos: the fields of Italy where Trojan blood has been spilt in the war between Aeneas and Turnus. For blood enriching the ground into which it is absorbed, see Virg. *G.* 1. 492, N.–H. on Hor. *Carm.* 2. 1. 29; contrast Luc. 7. 851, where any crop growing on the battlefield at Pharsalus will be *decolor*.

40. infaustae...nouercae: whereas at *Silv.* 5. 2. 119 (see n.) Ascanius' *nouerca* is Dido, the *nouerca* here is Lavinia. Stepmothers are typically unpleasant: see references in 5. 2. 79–80 n. above. For Lavinia compare Ovid's account of her plot against Dido's sister Anna (*Fast.* 3. 629–38), which gives an unfavourable impression of a Lavinia quite at odds with the passive figure presented in Virgil. Livy's account of Ascanius' removal from Lavinium to Alba Longa (1. 3. 3) lacks the personal sentiment ascribed to Ascanius here. Cartault (1903), 631 suggests that *infaustae* points to the blood shed in the war that Aeneas had to fight in Italy in order to marry Lavinia.

41–4. The parenthesis beginning with *nam* has inspired much discussion and emendation. It is perhaps useful here to give M's readings first of all:

> hic ego te nam sicanii non mitius halat
> aura croci ditis nec si tibi rara sabei
> cinnama odoratas nec arabs decerpsit aristas
> inferni cum laudae laci sed carmine plango

Vollmer (1896), 41–2 attempted to defend M by means of an extraordinary series of ellipses with the following sense: 'carmine meo non mitius halat aura Sicanii croci nec (mitius halant), si tibi dites Sabaei rara cinnama (decerpserunt) nec (mitius halant, si tibi) Arabs decerpsit odoratas aristas inferni cum laude laci.' Leaving aside the issue of whether M's 'inferni cum laudae [= laude] laci' is to be included in the parenthesis, such a varied series of ellipses is scarcely plausible. Vollmer's ellipses would be more convincing if the word-order of his paraphrase bore some resemblance to the text.

However, Vollmer's desperate defence of M happily draws attention to the wider extent of corruption and difficulty in this passage. Piecemeal attempts to emend one part of the text, such as *si tibi* (emended to *sicubi* by Gronovius, *Elench.* 7; cf. *sic tibi*, commonly ascribed to Avantius, but in fact not found until the Aldine edition of 1502) do not provide a satisfactory solution on their own. The real problem is how the two 'nec' clauses continue the sense of the comparative expression 'non mitius', which draws a contrast between

Statius' intangible poetry and possible physical offerings for his father. If *si* is accepted in 42, its clause is most naturally construed with the preceding *nam* clause. Furthermore, the two correlative instances of *nec* in the text as it stands cannot satisfy with *si* in only one clause; the postponement of the second *nec* after *odoratas* in line 43 makes it very hard to imagine an ellipse of a second *si*.

The problem is thus not confined to one particular part of a line. Emendation of a single word will not provide a satisfactory solution. A more comprehensive approach is thus called for, even if any solution obtained is more likely to be possible than probable.

This is why I have printed, *exempli gratia*, the following text of lines 41–3:

> hic ego te (nam Sicanii non mitius halat
> aura croci, nec sic tibi olet, si rara Sabaei
> cinnama, odoratas et [*Courtney*] Arabs decerpsit aristas)

Translate: 'For not more gently wafts the breeze of the Sicanian crocus, nor is the scent so fragrant for you, if the Sabaeans have plucked the rare cinnamon, and the Arabian has plucked the perfumed herbs.' I am treating M's *ditis* in 42 as a stock epithet which might have filled any omission by damage or haplography (*nec sic tibi olet, si* could have been reduced to *nec si tibi*).[20] In 43, Courtney's *et* (and Barth's *uel*) warrant serious consideration, whatever emendations are made in 42, since they offer an escape from the insufferable double *nec*. On the Sabaeans, see 5. 1. 210–14 n. above. Statius only refers to them as a people in the plural (2. 6. 86, 4. 5. 32 and here).

41–2. Sicanii ... croci: saffron. The Sicilian variety of the plant, also mentioned in the funeral of Melior's parrot at *Silv.* 2. 4. 36 and possibly at *Theb.* 6. 210 ('pallentique croco; see van Dam on *Silv.* 2. 1. 157–62), was not esteemed as highly as the Cilician variety (Plin. *Nat.* 21. 31). On the spices referred to in these lines see *Silv.* 5. 1. 210–14 n.

44. inferiis cum laude datis (Krohn): *inferni cum laudae laci* M, which Vollmer includes in the preceding parenthesis, on the grounds that the passage relates to Pliny's statement that the harvesting of

---

[20] For the interpolation of a common adjective subsequent to an omission, compare Prop. 3. 4. 22, where FP supplied *media* after *Sacra* had been omitted; the route of corruption is confirmed by the absence of any epithet in L.

cinnamomum does not occur without divine permission (Plin. *Nat.* 12. 89). However, quite apart from the oddity of the idea that Pliny's ethnographic detail is adequately conveyed by *inferni cum laude laci*, this does not satisfactorily account for 'inferni...laci'; the rare form 'laci' provides further cause for suspicion (recorded in *ThLL* vii/2. 860. 71–861. 17 in pre-Christian texts only here and at Sen. *Nat.* 3. 27. 10, where it is a variant for the more usual genitive *lacus*). Other attempts to emend M's *inferni cum laudae laci* have included Calderini's *inserui cum laude loci*, the first of a number of conjectures which emend *laci* to some part of *locus*. Difficulties remain, however, since Bernartius' *his...locis* (adopted by Markland) involves an extraordinary delay between *his* and *locis*, and *his...locis* itself is less effective than the transmitted *hic* in line 41, which neatly picks up the clause beginning with *ubi* in ll. 37–9, where Statius describes the location of his father's tomb. If one accepts Krohn's *inferiis cum laude datis*, Statius refers to his offering of poetry (this must after all be the force of the parenthesis in ll. 41–3, where Statius is implying that his poetry is more agreeable to his father than any spices); the point is then enforced by *carmine plango* at the end of l. 43.

For M's *sed* (l. 44), which if retained would be an extraordinary instance of postponement, Courtney conjectures *heu*, which is in keeping with the emotional character of the passage.

45. sume <en> gemitus et uulnera: Klotz's *en* is the most satisfactory completion of the line, although Baehrens's *o* is also possible. The deictic *en*, requiring closer participation than *o*, is more in keeping with the tone of the whole passage; Statius frequently emphasizes his father's presence in the poem.

Markland rejected *uulnera*, arguing that Statius' father would be unable to receive his son's *uulnera*. *munera* is easily corruptible to *uulnera* and could denote not only the gifts of the bereaved, but also their grief, though here one might take *munera* as Statius' poetic offering (cf. 33 above).. Markland cites several parallels, notably Ov. *Met.* 2. 340–1 'nec minus Heliades fletus et inania morti | munera dant lacrimas' and *Pont.* 1. 7. 29–30 'cui nos et lacrimas, supremum in funere munus, | et dedimus medio scripta canenda foro'. But though *munera* would imply Statius' poetic gift to his father as well as his lamentations, *uulnera* must be retained here. Emotional wounds (*OLD* s.v. *uulnus* 3) stand easily alongside groans and tears (all three words also suggest a poetic offering; cf. *dolori*, 28), whereas the sequence of groans, gifts, and then tears does not convince. *ut* (Heinsius) would mitigate the anomaly, but is too prosaic; *sume* (receiving requires giving) indicates that gifts are being given anyway.

Statius sets a high premium on his own poetic offering in this passage. For a more cautious assessment of poetry as a poor substitute for actual participation in funeral rites contrast Ov. *Pont.* 1. 9. 45–8. Statius is closer to Propertius (2. 13. 19–26), who argues that his poetry will be a sufficient *pompa* (25–6): 'sat mea †sit magna†, si tres sint pompa libelli, | quos ego Persephonae maxima dona feram.'

46. rari quas umquam habuere parentes: *rari* here means 'few' (*OLD* s.v. *rarus* 5b), but the word also suggests exquisiteness and excellence (e.g. *Silv.* 5. 1. 11 'rarissima coniunx', 2. pr. 23 'rarissima uxorum'; cf. Prop. 1. 8. 42, 1. 17. 16). Statius' boast also implies that few others grieve for their parents; compare 3. pr. 15–16 where he praises Claudius Etruscus 'cum lugeret ueris (quod iam rarissimum est) lacrimis senem patrem' (contrast Pub. *Sent.* H. 19 'heredis fletus sub persona risus est', Juv. 13. 134 'ploratur lacrimis amissa pecunia ueris') and see also 3. 3. 1–2 (on the rarity of Pietas' visits to the world), 3. 3. 14–15, 3. 3. 20–1 and 3. 3. 35, 5. 3. 254 n., Cat. 64. 400 'destitit extinctos gnatus lugere parentes'.

47–8. atque utinam . . . opus: the desire to have been able to provide a more magnificent memorial to the dead is found in the epigraphic corpus; see e.g. *CLE* 204. 1–2 'si pro uirtute et animo fortunam habuissem | magnificum monimentum hic aedificassem tibi', 1086. 7–10, 1088, 1246, Lattimore (1942), 229. Cf. Nauta (2002), 202–3, who argues that Statius' wish to do better for his father should be interpreted literally, in terms of modest financial means.

Statius' wishes, however, are expressed in ambiguous terms, since *par templis opus* also suggests something metaphorical and poetic. 'A work which is the equal of temples' (cf. the enigmatic Theoc. 7. 14 ἐπεὶ αἰπόλῳ ἔξοχ᾽ ἐῴκει) might be another building, but could also be a grand poetic offering for Statius' father. Cf. *Silv.* 5. 1. 1–15, where Statius initially wishes to build a physical monument for Priscilla, but then tells her that his poetry will be a memorial ('haud alio melius condere sepulchro', 5. 1. 15 and see n.), and 3. 1, the poem on the temple of Hercules Surrentinus, which Newlands (1991) has argued to be a poetic temple. At Virg. *G.* 3. 13 ff, the projected marble temple for Augustus is at the same time actualized as a poetic monument in the ensuing *ekphrasis*, while at Pi. *O.* 6. 1–4 (cf. the treasury of songs at *P.* 6. 7–14) the temple which is announced is also a metaphor for the ensuing epinician.

49. Cyclopum scopulos: Housman, *Class. P.* ii. 654 rejects Vollmer's notion that these are the basalt rocks in Sicily ('scopuli tres Cyclopum') mentioned by Plin. *Nat.* 3. 89, arguing that *scopulos* 'is just the word for the huge polygonal blocks of the Mycenaean masonry' of Tiryns, Argos, and Mycenae; for the association with the Cyclopes, he compares E. *Tr.* 1087–8, Sen. *Her. F.* 996–8, *Thy.* 407–8, Stat. *Theb.* 4. 151 'Cyclopum ductas sudoribus arces'. Although *scopuli* are projecting rocks, rather than walls, the argument is sound; Statius' aim is to surpass created monuments, not geographical features. *scopulos* suggests grandeur (the walls are like precipitous cliffs); compare Seneca's description of the tower from which Astyanax perished (*Tro.* 1075–6): 'haec nota quondam turris et muri decus, | nunc saeua cautes'.

49–50. audacia saxa | Pyramidum: Hor. *Carm.* 3. 30. 1–2 declares that his poetic oeuvre surpasses the pyramids: 'Exegi monumentum aere perennius | regalique situ pyramidum altius'; cf. Prop. 3. 2. 19–22 and Mart. 10. 63. 1–2 'marmora parua quidem sed non cessura, uiator, | Mausoli saxis pyramidumque legis' where *legis* points to Martial's exploitation of the theme in a memorial epigram, suggesting at once the survival of the monument and of his poetry. Statius' work will also outdo the pyramids; the Horatian text supports the interpretation of this passage as a reference not only to physical commemoration, but also to poetic edifice. In both Statius and Horace physical imagery expresses poetic qualities. In Horace *altius*, a word signifying dimension, is applied to the poetry; Statius' *ultra* may indicate the size of the construction envisaged, but also evokes his poetic superiority. *audacia*, applied to the Pyramids, which are 'daring' because of their great height, is also appropriate to the confident tone of this passage; compare *Silv.* 4. 7. 27–8 (with Coleman) where the *Thebaid* 'temptat audaci fide Mantuanae | gaudia famae'.

50. magno . . . luco: *lucus* here denotes a sacred grove (Serv. Auct. *A.* 1. 310 'arborum multitudo cum religione', *ThLL* vii/2. 1751. 52–1752. 70), equivalent to Greek ἄλσος, appropriate to the *arae* honouring his father's tomb.

51. illic answers *hic* (41), contrasting the actual tomb of his father on the Mons Albanus with the *arae* Statius wishes he could construct.

Siculi . . . dona sepulchri: the memorial games given by Aeneas in honour of Anchises in Sicily (Virg. *A.* 5). Statius has already evoked Virgil's description of Anchises' memorial: note *aras* (47; cf. *A.* 5. 48 'maestasque sacrauimus aras', 5. 54 'altaria') and *tumulum* (36 and 50;

cf. *A*. 5. 76, 5. 86, 5. 93). Just as Virgil's games in *Aeneid* 5 outdo those in *Iliad* 23, so Statius' offering to his father would have eclipsed the games for Anchises. On epic games, see further Lovatt (2005).

superassem: the confident tone continues, tempered only by the counterfactual conditional sentence. The various festivals which Statius would have surpassed are also important subjects for poetry (see below). For 'outdoing' (the rejection of familiar *exempla* and comparisons as inadequate) in Statius and elsewhere see 80–88 below, Curtius (1953), 162–5.

52. Nemees ludum: despite such parallels as [Theoc.] 25. 169 Διὸς Νεμέοιο παρ' ἄλσος and Virg. *G*. 3. 19 'lucosque Molorchi', M's *lucum*, which sits oddly between the *dona* and *sollemnia* (both referring to games), may be a corruption influenced by *luco* in 50. The connecting *illic* is also somewhat unsatisfactory if there are two groves in these lines. Markland's *ludum* is probably correct. There are two stories associated with the origin of the Nemean Games (see further Brown (1994), 30–56): in one, the games are established after Heracles' slaying of the Nemean lion (Call. *Aet*. frr. 54–9 Pf., *SH* 254–69), while in the other (which occurs in Statius, *Theb*. 6), the games are established to commemorate the death of the child Opheltes.

Statius' desire to outdo the games of Olympia and Nemea recalls Virgil's similar challenge (*G*. 3. 19–20): 'cuncta mihi Alpheum linquens lucosque Molorchi | cursibus et crudo decernet Graecia caestu.' Notice that Statius' own Nemean Games in the *Thebaid* also outdo other contests (*Theb*. 6. 253–4).

Pelopis sollemnia trunci: Pelops' shoulder was consumed by Demeter when his father Tantalus served him to the gods at a feast; it was replaced with ivory (Pi. *O*. 1. 26–7; cf. Apollod. *Epit*. 2. 3 with Frazer). Statius calls him *truncatus* (*Theb*. 4. 590). Virg. *G*. 3. 7 refers to 'umeroque Pelops insignis eburno' as an example for a hackneyed subject for poetry. See Pi. *O*. 1. 90–6 for the posthumous fame and involvement of Pelops in the Olympic games.

53. Oebalio...disco: cf. *Ach*. 2. 154 'Oebalios...discos'. The epithet, derived from the Spartan king Oebalus, the father of Tyndareus (Paus. 3. 1. 4), means 'Spartan', and is appropriate here in view of the Spartans' celebrated physical prowess.

finderet: for *findere* applied to the flight of the discus see *Silv*. 3. 1. 155–6.

54. Graiorum uis nuda uirum: as editors note, this phrase gives a Latin response to the etymological link in Greek between γυμνάσια, bodily exercises, and γυμνός ('naked'); cf. *Silv.* 3. 1. 146 'nec pudet occulte nudas spectare palaestras', 3. 1. 152–3 'nudosque uirorum | certatus', *Theb.* 4. 229 'nudaeque modos uirtutis', 6. 18 'concurrunt nudasque mouent in proelia uires', and for other examples of Greek etymologies in Statius, see van Dam on *Silv.* 2. 2. 36–42, Laguna (1992), 28–9. Lovatt (2005), 41–5 offers discussion on Statius' references to nudity during the games in the *Thebaid*. Though Greek athletics were indeed performed in the nude in historical times, a paraphrase such as 'Greek athletes' loses the subtlety of *Graiorum* and *nuda. uis nuda uirum* also recalls Virgil's 'odora canum uis' (*A.* 4. 132); Austin ad loc. notes Lucretian parallels and the link with Homeric phrases featuring ἴς.

55. putri sonitum daret ungula fossa: a close echo of Virgil's famous 'quadripedante putrem sonitu quatit ungula campum' (*A.* 8. 596) and 'quadripedumque putrem cursu quatit ungula campum' (*A.* 11. 875). The Ennian antecedents of these lines are noted by Macrob. *Sat.* 6. 1. 22; see Enn. *Ann.* 242, 263, 431 Skutsch, cf. *scen.* 184 V. (= 169 Jocelyn). Statius' imitation occupies only part of a line, substitutes two words (*daret* and *fossa*) and alters the case and metre of *putri* (here with a long first syllable), but retains the rhythm of the second half of *A.* 8. 596. *putri ... fossa* is best construed as local ablative, indicating the place where the sound occurs. *fossa* has aroused suspicion (Markland emends to *campo*), but Schwartz's explanation (quoted by Vollmer) of *fossa* as 'sulco, quem equi cursus effodere solet' is satisfactory; see also Ellis (1892), 24 who suggests that *fossa* may mean a piece of prepared ground, and compares the Greek word σκάμμα. Vollmer's parallels from the *Theb.* (4. 245, 6. 312, 7. 760 ff, 10. 549–50—but not 4. 559, where *fossa* simply denotes a trench or a ditch) refer to the effects of chariots, and are thus admissible, since the usual contest involving horses would be a chariot-race.

56–7. sed Phoebi simplex chorus: *simplex* here (see *OLD* s.v. 4) denotes the absence of elaborate procedures in the chorus' activities, in contrast to the athletic games envisaged in the preceding lines. As *sed* indicates, these lines are clearly to be seen as a continuation, setting the athletic festivals in contrast with the far superior honours which Statius would prefer to have offered to his father. However, there are difficulties, principally in the lack of a verb governed by *chorus*. As Shackleton Bailey in his discussion of the passage notes (p. 399), 'the ellipse of *esset* after *chorus*, followed by *et ... ligarem*, has a makeshift aura'. Clearly, there cannot be an ellipse of some part of *esse*

in the phrase 'sed Phoebi simplex chorus', if there is then a clause
with a first person verb joined in an entirely unconvincing way by *et*: it
would be natural for the subjects of the two clauses to be the same.
Shackelton Bailey's solution is to emend to the third person plural
ligarent in 57 (in fact conjectured by Heinsius 587), with the chorus as
collective singular subject of the plural verb, and to remove the
otherwise troubling *et* in 56, by emending to *en*. Shackleton Bailey
moreover takes the *chorus* to be the Muses, with them awarding the
prize to Statius' father.

However, there are problems with this approach. In the first place,
the notion that the *chorus* consists of the Muses is not straightforward.
This is because Statius has indicated his desire to surpass the games of
epic (51–2), which can only imply that there would be some kind of
competition taking place; this is confirmed by the fact that Statius'
father would receive a garland (not as participant, but as the presiding
figure invoked at the event). Yet it is not convincing that the Muses
should in fact be involved in a competition in singing: the example of
Thamyris was a warning against the dangers of attempting to surpass
the Muses. *Phoebi simplex chorus* might thus refer to mortal poets. One
might even wonder whether it is odd to imagine a garland being
awarded by a whole *chorus*: presumably a person can only be so
adorned once. Thus Shackleton Bailey's solution to the problem of
how to construe *sed Phoebi simplex chorus* is not satisfactory.

A better approach is offered by Leofranc Holford-Strevens, who
suggests the possibility of a lacuna after *chorus*. The missing passage
might well have referred to the competition between the poets, before
a description of Statius' father receiving a dedication; see below for
the potential difficulties of the first persons singular *dicarem* (ς) or
ligarem (M).

56–7. frondentia uatum | praemia: Statius combines the
notions of a garland as an athlete's reward, and the laurel as a
poet's emblem of Apollo; cf. Hor. *Carm.* 4. 2. 9 where Pindar is 'laurea
donandus Apollinari'.

57. dicarem: with *ligarem* (M), it is implied that Statius' father is
actually present at the memorial event, but better is *dicarem* (ς), since if
Statius is able to bind a garland about his father's head, then there is
no need for his return from the dead to be anticipated (regardless of
whether one reads *praecinerem* or *praeciperem* in line 59, line 60 clearly
shows that Statius is imagining such an outcome). However, as
conjectures such as the third person plurals *dicarent, ligarent* (both

Heinsius) and *litarent* (Ellis) show, the problem of continuity with what has gone before remains, especially if line 56 contains a lacuna. Indeed, one might well expect something other than a first person singular here, since *ipse . . . praecinerem* in 58–9 looks like a change of subject, with Statius moving on to describe his own imagined actions.

58. ipse madens oculis umbrarum araeque sacerdos: Markland argues that *umbrarum animaeque* (M) is tautologous; the singular *animae*, if it refers to Statius' father, is in odd collocation with *umbrarum* (for plural *umbrae* referring to one person, see *Theb.* 7. 710–11). In favour of *arae* Markland cites Virg. *A.* 8. 179 'tum lecti iuuenes certatim araeque sacerdos', Sil. 2. 150 'Alcidae templi custos araeque sacerdos'; note also Statius' earlier wish to build 'aras' (47). *araeque* is thus preferable. There is no need to accept Shackleton Bailey's decision to replace not *animae* but *umbrarum* with Markland's *arae*: with *animae*, *animae sacerdos* is an odd way for Statius to say no more than that he is his father's priest, whereas *umbrarum* is in fact more appropriate, with Statius also implying a more general power to affect the shades here.

59–60. praecinerem reditum: Markland emended M's *praecinerem gemitum* to *praeciperem reditum*. *OLD* explains *praecinerem* as leading the lament, but *praecinerem* is better taken as a reference to divination of the future (for *praecino* thus, see *ThLL* x/2. 440. 22 ff.), which accords well with *sacerdos* in the previous line. Although *praecipio* is also used in sacred contexts (*ThLL* x/2. 444. 29 ff.), there is no need to reject *praecinerem*, which has more of an air of prophecy. Read *praecinerem reditum* (cf. 288 'inde tamen uenias melior'). There can be no defence of *gemitum*, since, even if it were possible, there is no reason why Cerberus and the *Orpheae . . . leges* should keep a shade from receiving a lament; a return from the underworld, however, is precisely what they are supposed to prevent. Thus *praecinerem reditum* removes the difficulty of *auertere*, obelized by Courtney; for the dative with *auertere*, cf. Prop. 3. 24. 9 'quod mihi non patrii poterant auertere amici'. The epithet *Orpheae* refers to Orpheus' successful transgression of this prescription; for *lex* used thus see 276 n. below.

61. atque tibi: Markland argued that *tibi* obscures the fact that, although the song is dedicated to the father, Statius is also singing *about* his father to others. Nevertheless, *tibi* must be retained: the whole passage describes Statius' offering to his father; the praise implied by 'moresque tuos et facta canentem' is part of the offering to him. *atque ibi me* (Heinsius) is unnecessary.

62. magniloquo non posthabuisset Homero: though *magniloquus* can imply boastfulness (see *Theb.* 3. 192–3 'magniloquos luit impia flatus | Tantalis', *OLD* s.v. *magniloquus* 1b), here it characterizes Homer's grandeur (cf. Cic. *Fam.* 13. 15. 2 'Homeri magniloquentia'), without negative connotations. The subject of *posthabuisset* is *pietas*, *fors* being adverbial, equivalent to *fortasse*.

63. tenderet hints that it was harder to be considered the equal of Virgil than Homer (for *aequare* used of literary judgements, compare Quint. *Inst.* 10. 1. 101 'nec indignetur sibi Herodotus aequari Titum Liuium'). For the primacy of Virgil over Homer, cf. Prop. 2. 34. 65–6 'cedite Romani scriptores, cedite Grai! | nescio quid maius nascitur Iliade' and *Laus Pis.* 230–2, where Virgil challenges ('prouocat') Homer; contrast Domitius Afer's judgement (Quint. *Inst.* 10. 1. 86): ' "secundus" inquit "est Vergilius, propior tamen primo quam tertio." '. See also Statius' closing instruction to the *Thebaid* (12. 816–17). Statius mentions Homer and Virgil together at *Silv.* 2. 7. 33–5 (where the primacy of Lucan, appropriately, is affirmed) and 4. 2. 1–10 (especially 4. 2. 9 'nectat odoratas [adoratas *ς*] et Smyrna et Mantua lauros').

toruo, 'stern', is a curious epithet for Virgil (for its frightening qualities, cf. e.g. *Silv.* 5. 2. 179–80, where the word is used of Mars' helmet, *Theb.* 1. 712 'torua Megaera', Virg. *Ecl.* 2. 63 'torua leaena', *A.* 6. 467 'torua tuentem', applied to Dido), though cf. *Silv.* 2. 7. 75 'cedet Musa rudis ferocis Enni' with van Dam, 154 below 'Stesichorusque ferox', Hor. *Carm.* 4. 9. 7–8 'et Alcaei minaces | Stesichoriue graues Camenae'. The epithet could point to the grim content of the *Aeneid*. Conjectures such as *docto* (Markland) or perhaps *terso* ('refined'), whilst appropriate to Virgil, are less fitting to the context of this passage, where Statius is seeking to outdo the two leading writers of epic: *magniloquo* and *toruo* do at least encapsulate particular aspects of the two poets as epicists. Despite the awkward postponement of the subject, *pietas*, Courtney's transposition of 'non posthabuisset Homero' and 'pietas aequare Maroni' is doubtful, since 'magniloquo' would be transferred from 'Homero' to 'Maroni'. Slater's *temptet et aeterno* (cf. Mart. 11. 52. 18 'aeterno ... Vergilio'), gives an unsatisfactory conclusion to the preceding series of counterfactual conditionals ending in *posthabuisset* because of the present subjunctive, which would give an ideal conditional referring to the future. Notice that the temporal force of *posthabuisset* is weak here, anticipating the tendency for the pluperfect subjunctive to displace the imperfect

subjunctive in later Latin and Romance languages; there is little
between it and the imperfect subjunctives that predominate in this
passage. If there is a difference between *posthabuisset* and *tenderet*, the
pluperfect could be seen as aspectual, representing a once and for all
judgement on Statius and Homer, as opposed to a more continuous
process of trying to set Statius alongside Virgil conveyed by the
imperfect *tenderet*.

pietas: not Statius' *pietas* towards his father, but his father's *pietas*
towards him. Statius could hardly have said that his own *pietas* might
not have placed him second to Homer.

64–5. cur magis incessat: an indignant rhetorical question.

aena sororum | stamina: the threads of the Parcae are bronze,
an indication of the implacable and irreversible character of fate
('dura sororum | licia', *Silv.* 5. 1. 156–7); cf. Hor. *Carm.* 1. 35. 17–20
(with N.–H.):

> te semper anteit serua Necessitas,
> clauos trabalis et cuneos manu
>   gestans aena [aenos *Campbell*], nec seuerus
>   uncus abest liquidumque plumbum.

65. tepido: a pathetic indication that the remains of the pyre are
still warm as a mother laments over her son's remains; contrast the
different emotional effect of 'iam gelidis . . . bustis' (242). For *tepidus*, cf.
Silv. 3. 3. 181–2 'foedatusque ora tepentes | adfatur cineres' (with
Laguna's n.), *Theb.* 10. 822, where the dead Menoeceus' mother is
like a tigress bereft of her young who '*tepidi* lambit uestigia saxi', Ov.
Ep. 6. 90 'certaque de tepidis colligit ossa rogis' (Hypsipyle condemns
Medea's desecration of pyres), Sil. 8. 55 'et tepido fugit Anna rogo'.
For the motif of 'impositique rogis iuuenes ante ora parentum' (Virg.
G. 4. 477, *A.* 6. 308), see *Silv.* 5. 1. 218 n.

66. primaeui emphasizes the youth of the husband who has
died (cf. *Silv.* 2. 6. 2–3 'miserum est primaeua parenti | pignora
surgentesque (nefas!) accendere natos', Sil. 5. 423 'primaeuos
iuuenes', in a battle scene). Statius amplifies the effect of the *exempla*
which are likely to be used *against* him; the accumulation of pathetic
details heightens the extremity of his own situation.

67–8. The desire for suicide in response to bereavement is a
favourite theme of Statius, as is the restraint of *comites* or *famuli*.
Compare Abascantus at *Silv.* 5. 1. 199–200 (with n.), 2. 1. 23–5 (with
van Dam), where Statius himself is a *comes*, and 3. 3. 178 (Claudius

Etruscus mourning his father). Such restraint is typically described from the point of view of the *comites*; here the same action is seen through the eyes of the widow. Hence the emotive exaggeration of *uincit*.

Such interventions by attendants occur in epic at moments of distress; compare e.g. *Il.* 22. 461 (Andromache assisted by her ἀμφίπολοι when she runs to the walls of Troy), Virg. *A.* 4. 391 (Dido and her *famulae*), *A.* 9. 500–2 (Idaeus and Actor restrain the mother of the dead Euryalus; cf. *Theb.* 10. 816–17, where Menoeceus' mother is restrained). The epic precedents further elevate Statius' depictions of bereavement.

ruitura (Heinsius): *moritura* (M) makes for an impossible construction, since *in*, used with the accusative *maritum* needs a verb of motion to govern it. Seeming parallels such as Virg. *A.* 9. 400–1 'an sese medios moriturus in enses | inferat' and 9. 554–5 'haud aliter iuuenis medios moriturus in hostes | inruit' are in inadmissible, since they include verbs of motion. It is true that *in* can be glossed as *super* or ἐπί (*ThLL* vii/1. 737. 83–738. 49; cf. Liv. 1. 58. 11 'prolapsaque in uolnus moribunda cecidit', *OLD* s.v. *in* 7a, 'on to', sometimes without a previous verb of motion, and 7b for *in* governing the object on which a person falls), and *Theb.* 8. 470 'ille ingens in terga iacet' is an example where *in terga iacet* clearly comes to mean '(falls and) lies on his back', without an actual verb of motion governing *in terga*. In this case, however, it is harder to see how *moritura in ardentem maritum* could mean 'about to (fall and) die on top of her burning husband', especially when *in ardentem maritum* is really equivalent to *in ignes*; with *maritum* one might expect *ad*, but *ardentem* and *in* indicate that the widow would wish to rush *into* the burning flames of her husband's pyre (on this practice see Winterbottom on Sen. *Con.* 2. 2. 1). Heinsius' *ruitura* not only provides a verb of motion but also gives a sense of the speed which would be required to evade the 'obstantesque manus turbamque tenentem' in line 67.

69–70. pulset: M's *pulsem* cannot be retained. As Courtney (1984), 339 notes, *Silv.* 5. 5. 78 'inuidia superos iniustaque Tartara pulsem' is only relevant as a possible source of scribal confusion. Here Statius is anticipating possible criticism. With Mueller's *pulset*, the sense of the passage is that those who have lost children or a husband stir up greater ill will against the gods; this leads to Statius' reply, which begins with *sed* in 71, as noted by Courtney (1984), 339. For *inuidia* felt against the gods, compare also *Silv.* 3. 5. 41–2 'superique potentes | inuidiam timuere tuam', referring to his wife's devotion during his illness; for such reproaches in a context of lamentation, see further examples gathered by Esteve-Forriol (1962), 138–9.

In 69 M's *aliis* would be a curious way of referring to the specific types of bereaved person already described, even if there were no grammatical or metrical objection. It might be a gloss on *externis*, but is also an easy corruption of *ab his* (Schwartz); for the possible meaning of *ab* here, see *OLD* s.v. *ab* 20d (instances where agency is expressed by a noun followed by *ab* and an ablative) and 22 (where *ab* is translated 'on the part of, so far as concerns'), though in this passage *ab* is most likely to mean 'issuing from': compare Tac. *Ann.* 2. 36. 2 'quantum odii fore ab iis qui ultra quinquennium proiciantur?'

71–2. Boxhorn's *in iusta* has found general acceptance; for *in* with the accusative after *se dare* ('to devote oneself to') cf. Cic. 2 *Ver.* 2. 169 'bene penitus in istius familiaritatem sese dedit', Virg. *A.* 12. 633 'teque haec in bella dedisti'. *se . . . dedit in iusta* could mean 'took part in the funeral ceremonies', *iusta* commonly signifying funeral ritual (*OLD* s.v. *iustum* 3b). Since Statius does treat Pietas as equivalent to Δίκη or Astraea (*Silv.* 5. 2. 92 n., cf. 89–90 'Pietas oblita uirum reuocataque caelo | Iustitia'), *iusta* could point to Statius' association of Pietas with other representatives of justice. However, the dative *dolenti . . . mihi* is difficult if the construction is 'se dedit in iusta mihi dolenti', since *dolenti . . . mihi* would have to be an indirect object of *se . . . dedit*; the presence of the participle rules out the ethic dative.

Vollmer argued that *nec modo . . . nec* is equivalent to the clumsily prosaic 'non, modo non . . . sed ne . . . quidem'. If by that he meant 'non modo Natura sed ne Pietas quidem', Statius would be undermining his own case by asserting that not only Natura (whose absence would be expected, since Statius' father was not young) but also Pietas failed to participate in the funeral. This would be a curiously negative prelude to the confident declaration that, in Statius' eyes, his father's death was that of a young man. The same argument also militates against taking the sense of the phrase as *nec . . . nec*, with *modo* being construed independently as 'recently', since the result is a denial of the presence of Natura and Pietas at the funeral.

Statius is dealing with potential criticism. One method of countering such attacks is to use the argument of the other side. The reference to Natura implies a charge that Statius should not mourn too much what is only the natural order (cf. *Silv.* 5. 1. 181 'saluo tamen ordine mortis' with n.). The most effective rebuttal would be to assert

that Natura is by Statius' side at the funeral, implying that the death
of Statius' father is indeed against the natural order. The puzzle is
resolved when Statius explains that he considers that his father was
carried off in his youth. Professor Winterbottom suggests:

> sed nec modo se Natura dolenti
> nec Pietas iniusta negat mihi.

Neither Natura and Pietas 'denies herself' to Statius, because they
are present at the funeral. *dedit* could have arisen as a gloss on the
perhaps confusing *nec . . . negat.*

Pietas iniusta (preserving M's word division) is a pleasing juxta-
position; Pietas would have been *iniusta* to have stayed away.

73. uiridi, genitor, ceu raptus ab aeuo: as well as suggesting
youth (e.g. Ov. *Tr.* 4. 10. 17 'frater ad eloquium uiridi tendebat ab
aeuo', Galán Vioque on Mart. 7. 40. 5–6), *uiridis* can be a compliment
describing activity (particularly intellectual) in old age, as at *Silv.* 3. 1.
174 'teque nihil laesum uiridi renouabo senecta' (cf. Sil. 13. 126–7,
OLD s.v. *uiridis* 5b). The paradoxical motif of the flowering of old age
appears to have been commonplace (Sen. *Con.* 2. 6. 13). Statius
regarded his father's death as premature, so great was his grief; cf.
Mart. 10. 71. 7 'hos tamen ut primis raptos sibi quaerit in annis', Plin.
Ep. 1. 12. 12, 2. 1. 10 (on the death of the octogenarian Verginius
Rufus) 'quibus ex causis necesse est tamquam immaturam mortem
eius in sinu tuo defleam'. See also 255–7 n.

74. Tartara, here as at 261 and 269, denotes the underworld in a
general sense, and not the Virgilian place of punishment (the Sibyl
explains at *A.* 6. 563 that no one who is *castus* may enter the tower of
Tartarus). In the *Aeneid*, Aeneas does not take the path 'ad impia
Tartara' (*A.* 6. 543).

subis: cf. *Silv.* 5. 1. 258–60 n.

Marathonia uirgo: Erigone, the daughter of Icarius, who killed
herself on discovering that her father had been killed in Attica by
drunken rustics, called *saeuorum* in 75 because their crime was against
their benefactor who had given them wine. Erigone was the subject of
a poem by Eratosthenes (see the fragments in *Collect. Alex.*, Eratos-
thenes frr. 22–7, pp. 64–5). The *Erigone* appears to have enjoyed a
great reputation (thus [Longin.] 33. 5 διὰ πάντων γὰρ ἀμώμητον τὸ
ποιημάτιον); its likely contents are discussed by Keller (1946), 53–94,
Solmsen (1947), Merkelbach (1963), and Fraser (1972), ii. 903–5, while
Knox (1998), 76–7 discusses the influence of Eratosthenes on Nonnus'

treatment of Erigone's story in *Dionysiaca* 47. 34–264. Compare Statius' simile at *Theb.* 11. 644–7, where Ismene's anguish at the fate of her mother Jocasta is likened to Erigone's grief for her father and her preparations for suicide. See also Prop. 2. 33. 29–30, Hyg. *Fab.* 130, Apollod. 3. 14. 7; cf. Ov. *Met.* 10. 450–1, where Erigone and Icarius, now transformed into stars, hide their faces from the incest of Cinyras and Myrrha.

76. Phrygia quam turre cadentem: for the death of Astyanax compare E. *Tr.* 725, Ov. *Met.* 13. 415, and Seneca's evocation (*Tro.* 1068–76) of the *turris* (cf. *Silv.* 2. 1. 145). Though Odysseus is traditionally responsible, Lesches and Pausanias ascribe the murder to Neoptolemus (Frazer on Apollod. *Epit.* 5. 23). Since the murderer is not named, Statius' reproach to Andromache for having married Neoptolemus (79) is even more damning.

77. parens: the chiastic arrangement of 74–7 (*uirgo . . . Icarium, . . . Astyanacta parens*) delays allusion to Andromache.

quin: 'in fact'; having compared the grief shown by Erigone and Andromache, Statius contrasts Erigone's death with Andromache's survival.

supremos, an annotation in an undated edition (*c.*1481–2) of the *Silvae* in the Bodleian Library (Auct. N inf. 2. 27 (5)), is preferable to *supremo* (M), which adds little to *laqueo*. With *gemitus, supremos* denotes not only Erigone's groans as she dies by hanging, but also her last laments for her father. These two meanings of the adjective, referring firstly to the time of death and secondly to the rituals performed at a funeral, are well attested (*OLD* s.v. *supremus* 4 and 5).

78. inclusit is well translated by Mozley as 'stifled'; her laments are shut in as she suffocates.

78–9. at te . . . marito: a sudden and aggressive apostrophe of Andromache. Mention of Erigone's suicide implied that Andromache did not do as much when she lost Astyanax; for the brevity of maternal grief, cf. Ael. *NA* 1. 18 Θαυμάζουσιν ἄνθρωποι τὰς γυναῖκας ὡς ἄγαν φιλοτέκνους· ὁρῶ δὲ ὅτι καὶ τεθνεώτων υἱῶν ἢ θυγατέρων ἔζησαν μητέρες, καὶ τῷ χρόνῳ τοῦ πάθους εἰλήφασι λήθην τῆς λύπης μεμαρασμένης, with a subsequent contrast with the devotion of a mother dolphin which will share the fate of its young when captured and killed. Now Statius adds the new charge that she even married Neoptolemus, the son of Achilles. This treatment of Andromache refutes the two situations mentioned in 65–8 as worthy of great sorrow, the grieving mother and the widow who kills herself on her husband's pyre. Statius does not mention that Andromache was given to Neoptolemus as a result of the capture of Troy; *post funera magni | Hectoris* suggests a far more rapid transition to the new husband. Similarly, *pudor*, 'shame', also evokes another meaning, 'chastity'; thus Dido wishes for death 'ante, pudor, quam te uiolo aut tua iura resoluo' (Virg. *A.* 4. 27). *pudor* is an ironic reminder that Andromache has not retained her chastity. Contrast Andromache's fears at E. *Tr.* 665–8:

> καίτοι λέγουσιν ὡς μί᾽ εὐφρόνη χαλᾷ
> τὸ δυσμενὲς γυναικὸς εἰς ἀνδρὸς λέχος·
> ἀπέπτυσ᾽ αὐτὴν ἥτις ἄνδρα τὸν πάρος
> καινοῖσι λέκτροις ἀποβαλοῦσ᾽ ἄλλον φιλεῖ.

79. seruisse: cf. E. *Tr.* 660 δουλεύσω δ᾽ ἐν αὐθεντῶν δόμοις, Virg. *A.* 3. 326–7 'stirpis Achilleae fastus iuuenemque superbum | seruitio enixae tulimus'.

80–1. non ego quas fati certus sibi morte canora | inferias praemittit olor: Statius rejects the familiar topoi of endless sorrow in his lament, whilst at the same time enumerating them. The rejection of direct comparison with these types of grief magnifies his own loss.

On the song of dying swans (which not everyone in antiquity believed in), see D'Arcy Thompson (1936), 180–3, Fraenkel on A. *A.* 1444–5 (the earliest example), N.–H. on Hor. *Carm.* 2. 20. 10, and van Dam on *Silv.* 2. 4. 9–10 for *loci* and modern bibliography. Pl. *Phd.* 84 E 2–85 B 3 has Socrates affirm that such song is not a lament, but a celebration of the joys to follow after death. For the phrasing 'fati certus ... olor', cf. *Silv.* 3. 3. 175 'nec fati iam certus olor'. Statius also mentions the song of dying swans at *Theb.* 5. 341.

82. rupe quod atra: Statius sometimes (as here) locates the Sirens on a rock formation near Surrentum (cf. A.R. 4. 892, Str. 5. 4. 8 (C247), Mela 2. 69, Plin. *Nat.* 3. 62, Beloch (1890), 258, Frederiksen (1984), 89, 105); cf. *Silv.* 2. 2. 1, 2. 2. 116, 3. 1. 64. At 2. 1. 10 and 3. 3. 174 their home is Sicily; for the two traditions see Str. 1. 2. 12 (C22). The Sirens are mentioned with Philomela at [Sen.] *Her. O.* 189–93 as types of lamentation; they had been the companions of Proserpina (Ov. *Met.* 5. 551–63).

praedulce minantur: a neat encapsulation of the Sirens' contradictory nature; Circe warned Odysseus against the dangerous beauty of their song (*Od.* 12. 39–46).

83–4. An allusion to the tale of Tereus, his wife Procne, and her
sister Philomela; see Ov. *Met.* 6. 424–674, and Forbes Irving (1990),
99–107, 248–9 for discussion of variants in the myth, and on the
fragmentary *Tereus* of Sophocles, see Fitzpatrick (2001). After Tereus
discovered that his wife and her sister had killed his son Itys, he
pursued them; all three were changed into birds, the two women
becoming a swallow and a nightingale (Ov. *Met.* 6. 668–70), although
Ovid does not specify which woman becomes which bird. As van
Dam on *Silv.* 2. 4. 21 notes, the identification of Procne and Philomela
with particular birds is inconsistent in Latin literature, although the
Greek tradition seems to have made Procne the nightingale and
Philomela the swallow; cf. D'Arcy Thompson (1936), 20–2.

Van Dam maintains that Procne is the nightingale at *Silv.* 2. 4. 21
'quae Bistonio queritur soror orba cubili' (though no name is given
and the phrasing is ambiguous) and 3. 3. 175–6 ('saeuique marita |
Tereos'), and regards Philomela here as the nightingale; he argues
that unless there is specific reference to the swallow, any bird which
laments is the nightingale, since the swallow does not sing, whereas
the nightingale 'is singled out for special mention in *Am.* 2. 6 as a bird
which must lament (7–10).' But Ovid there does not identify Philo-
mela as the nightingale, or even comment on the quality of her song.

While the swallow is often associated with a twittering sound of
little musical quality (see D'Arcy Thompson (1936), 320–1), Aelian
includes the swallow in a list of singing creatures (*NA* 6. 19), and
remarks (1. 58 *fin.*) that, although the bird assails bees, men refrain
from killing the bird αἰδοῖ τῆς μουσικῆς, contenting themselves with
merely preventing it from nesting by the hives. Note also Virg. *G.* 4.
306–7 'ante | garrula quam tignis nidum suspendat hirundo', and the
simile applied to Odysseus' bow-string at *Od.* 21. 411 ἡ δ' ὑπὸ καλὸν
ἄεισε, χελιδόνι εἰκέλη αὐδήν.

Van Dam gives only one instance of the complaint of the swallow,
Ov. *Fast.* 2. 853–6, where Procne is a *hirundo* ('saepe tamen, Procne,
nimium properasse quereris', 855). Two further passages where Sta-
tius describes the complaint of swallows are *Theb.* 8. 616–20:

> sic Pandioniae repetunt ubi fida uolucres
> hospitia atque larem bruma pulsante relictum,
> stantque super nidos ueterisque exordia fati
> adnarrant tectis, it [*Markland* : et *Pω*] truncum ac flebile murmur;
> uerba putant, uoxque illa tamen non dissona uerbis.

and 12. 478–80:

> Geticae non plura queruntur
> hospitibus tectis trunco sermone uolucres,
> cum duplices thalamos et iniquum Terea clamant.

Several details identify the birds as swallows. Firstly, the swallow returns ('repetunt') to its haunts after the winter; Ov. *Fast.* 2. 853–6 and Col. 11. 2. 21 both date its return to the end of February. Secondly, 'truncum... murmur' and 'trunco sermone' not only refer to Tereus' violent extraction of Philomela's tongue (Ov. *Met.* 6. 555–60), but also denote the characteristically interrupted sound of the bird; they could hardly refer to the melismata of the nightingale. Thirdly, the bird frequents buildings ('tectis') in both passages; Ael. *NA* 1. 52 refers to this practice and calls the swallow φιλάνθρωπος. Ov. *Met.* 6. 668–9 distinguishes the birds according to their haunt: 'quarum petit altera siluas, | altera tecta subit'; see also Virg. *Ecl.* 6. 80–1 (with Hudson-Williams (1980), 127–30, Boneschanscher (1982), 148–51), *A.* 12. 473–7, D'Arcy Thompson (1936), 316. Hence, despite van Dam, the evidence does not rule out, but positively requires, a reference to a swallow at *Silv.* 5. 3. 83. While *queritur* is appropriate to either bird, the detail which secures identification of Philomela with the swallow is 'murmure trunco'.

The technique here is almost that of a simile, except that Statius gives *negative* examples, which his own song will not imitate.

85. nota nimis uati: cf. Choeril. *SH* 317, Virg. *G.* 3. 4 'omnia iam uulgata', Man. 2. 50 'omnis ad accessus Heliconos semita trita est', and the weariness of Juv. 1. 7–9 'nota magis nulli domus est sua quam mihi lucus | Martis et Aeoliis uicinum rupibus antrum | Vulcani'. A striking parallel, since it involves a father and his child, is *Theb.* 4. 537 'ne uulgata mihi', where Tiresias rejects the prospect of his daughter's giving a general account of the underworld, before asking that only Theban and Argive ghosts be summoned. The songs of dying swans, the laments of the Sirens, and the story of Procne, Tereus, and Philomela are *nota nimis* not only to Statius' father, a teacher and practitioner of poetry, but also to Statius, since these same three examples occur at *Silv.* 3. 3. 174–6. As in 3. 3, such *exempla* are to be surpassed; cf. also 2. 4. 9–10 'cedat Phaethontia uulgi | fabula: non soli celebrant sua funera cycni'.

85–6. quis non in funere cunctos ... dixit: *cuncto* (M) offers no sense, but *ductos* is conjectured and inadequately explained by Ellis

(1892), 24 as 'the Heliades assuming boughs at their brother's death'. *cunctos* (ς) is preferable, and far closer to M. Markland emends to 'quis non in funera cunctos | ... duxit' ('who has not led all the Heliades into funeral poetry?'). Though he cites parallels for 'ducere in carmina' (Man. 2. 9, 3. 1 ff., 5. 468), the only emendation needed is *cunctos*. For *in funere*, 'at a funeral', cf. Lucil. 954–5 Marx 'mercede quae conductae flent alieno in funere | praeficae' (echoed at Hor. *Ars* 431–2). *cunctos*, far from being colourless, emphasizes the weariness experienced in contemplating such hackneyed themes. *ramos* and *germina* allude to the twin aspects of the metamorphosis of Phaethon's sisters, the Heliades (see *Theb.* 12. 413–15, Ov. *Met.* 2. 345–66, V.Fl. 5. 429 'flebant populeae iuuenem Phaethonta sorores'); their bodies became trees, and their tears for their brother became amber.

87. Phrygium silicem: on Niobe see *Silv.* 5. 1. 33 n. As with the Heliades, metamorphosis is experienced as a consequence of grief.

87–8. ausum contraria Phoebo | carmina: Marsyas, who was flayed by Apollo after losing a musical contest against him. In the *Met.*, Ovid relates the tales of Niobe (6. 146–312) and Marsyas (6. 382–400) in the same book. Although the two incidents are separated by the intervening episode of the wrath of Latona against the Lycians, all three episodes deal with the anger of the family of Latona against those who would belittle them. Whereas Niobe is an example of personal sorrow, Marsyas is an instance where lamentation is inspired in others (*Met.* 6. 392–400); the tears shed for him became the river Marsyas. See further Courtney (1984), 339–40 on these *exempla*.

88. nec fida is equivalent to 'et infida'; cf. *Silv.* 1. 2. 254–5, Prop. 2. 28. 52 'uobiscum Europe nec proba Pasiphae', *OLD* s.v. *neque* 4a. The allusion is to the tradition that Minerva picked up the aulos (*buxo*) and, displeased by her inability to play the instrument without contortion, laid a curse on whoever did play it; see Prop. 2. 30. 16–18, Hyg. *Fab.* 165, Apollod. 1. 4. 2 with Frazer. *gauisam* signifies Pallas' pleasure at the fate of Marsyas, who lost with the aulos against Apollo's lyre. Cf. Ov. *Met.* 6. 384 'Tritoniaca ... harundine'.

89–90. On Pietas (a rare visitor to the world, *Silv.* 3. 3. 1–2), and Iustitia (Δίκη) see *Silv.* 5. 2. 92 n. Statius has already mentioned Pietas at 72. The association of Eloquence (*Facundia*) with Pietas and Iustitia need not occasion surprise, given the belief that an orator should possess moral standing, though Holford-Strevens (2000), 40 usefully suggests that the elder Statius is being praised for expertise in philosophy. Quint. (*Inst.* 12. 1. 1) affirms that an orator should be 'is qui a M. Catone finitur uir bonus dicendi peritus, uerum, id quod et ille posuit prius et ipsa natura potius ac maius est, utique uir bonus'; cf. Plin. *Ep.* 3. 3. 7 'proinde fauentibus dis trade eum praeceptori, a quo mores primum mox eloquentiam discat, quae male sine moribus discitur'. Compare the transition from Crispinus' *pietas* towards his mother to the *uirtus* he displayed in defending his friend in court, in a passage praising his eloquence (*Silv.* 5. 2. 97–110). *Facundia* also effects a shift towards praise of Statius' father for his literary qualities; it need not solely denote oratory: see Hutchinson (1993), 10 n. 14. It is unlikely that this isolated reference to Facundia would imply that Statius' father taught *rhetorica* as well as *grammatica*: Suet. *Gramm.* 4. 4–6 suggests that even in the past this was an unusual practice.

90. gemina ... lingua: Greek and Latin; for similar phrasing compare e.g. Hor. *Carm.* 3. 8. 5 'utriusque linguae', Plu. *Luc.* 1. 4, Quint. *Inst.* 1 pr. 1, 6 pr. 11, Mart. 10. 76. 6, Plin. *Ep.* 2. 14. 5, 3. 1. 7, Suet. *Aug.* 89. 2, *Cl.* 42. 1, *Gramm.* 1. 2, Ammianus 15. 13. 1, 18. 5. 1, Dubuisson (1981), Biville (2002), 77 n. 1. For bilingualism, see e.g. Balsdon (1979), 123–8, 131–5, Holford-Strevens (1993), Swain (1996), 39–42, Biville (2002).

Suet. *Gramm.* 29. 1 records the Sicilian Sextus Clodius teaching rhetoric in both languages: Kaster ad loc. notes that, apart from Livius Andronicus and Ennius, (*Gramm.* 1. 2), Suetonius does not mention any other *grammaticus* or *rhetor* as having given instruction in both languages. Statius' father taught only Greek literature, though he was learned in both languages. For praise of a teacher's learning in both languages, compare Suet. *Gramm.* 7. 1 (Antonius Gnipho). It was of course highly unusual for a teacher of Greek literature to give the kind of Roman religious instruction referred to at 178–84.

For the grief of Facundia, compare Cornelius Severus' tribute to Cicero 'ictaque luctu | conticuit Latiae tristis facundia linguae', cited at Sen. *Suas.* 6. 26 (= fr. 13. 10–11 Courtney, *FLP* p. 325); cf. Nep. fr. 58 Marshall 'ex quo dubito interitu eius utrum res publica an historia magis doleat'. Note also Elegia's grief for Tibullus (Ov. *Am.* 3. 9. 3–4), and the epigram ascribed to Plautus in which the poet is lamented by Comedy (Gel. 1. 24. 3).

91. Pallas: Pallas is also found with Apollo and the Muses at *Silv.* 1. 6. 1–2. Minerva is often associated with learning, as at Mart. 5. 5. 1 'Sexte, Palatinae cultor facunde Mineruae' (a reference to the Palatine library) and Juv. 10. 116 'quisquis adhuc uno parcam colit asse

Mineruam' (alluding to the studies of schoolboys; cf. Ov. *Fast.* 3. 829–
30), and with poetry, as at Ov. *Fast.* 3. 833 'certe dea carminis illa est'.
For Domitian's various links with Minerva (which, according to
Philostratus *VA* 7. 24, 26, included a claim to be her son), see Coleman
on *Silv.* 4. 1. 22, Scott (1936), 166–88, Girard (1981*b*), B. W. Jones
(1992), 100, Darwall-Smith (1996), 115–29, 152–3, 172–8, 227–33 (on
the equestrian statue of Domitian described by Statius in *Silv.* 1. 1),
Geyssen (1996), 45–7, Nauta (2002), 329, 333–4, A. Hardie (2003),
138–40; just before his murder, Domitian was said to have dreamed
that he was no longer under Minerva's protection (Suet. *Dom.* 15. 3; cf.
D.C. 67. 16. 1).

The Quinquatria, a festival of Minerva, was held at the emperor's
Alban villa (Suet. *Dom.* 4. 4; cf. D.C. 67. 1. 1–2).[21] According to
Suetonius, the festivities included hunting (*uenationes*) and acting (*scae-
nicos ludos*) as well as contests in poetry and oratory: see further Dar-
wall-Smith (1994), 156, A. Hardie (2003), 135–42. At *Silv.* 4. 2. 67
Statius recalls his own victory and how he was presented with 'Palla-
dio . . . auro' by the emperor; for the dating of his participation in the
Alban and Capitoline contests, see the introduction to this poem, pp.
261–2 above. Since Statius was successful at Minerva's festival, it
would be natural for him to call upon the goddess here.

92. labor: This line denotes practitioners of hexameter poetry,
which includes not only narrative poetry (epic in the modern sense)

---

[21] A. Hardie (2003), 135–6 suggests that the festival was known as the *Iuuenalia* on the
basis of a reference to the consul Acilius Glabrio's being summoned to τὰ νεανισκεύματα in
D.C. 67. 14. 3: ὅτι ὑπατεύοντα αὐτὸν ἐς τὸ Ἀλβανὸν ἐπὶ τὰ νεανισκεύματα ὠνομασμένα
καλέσας λέοντα ἀποκτεῖναι μέγαν ἠνάγκασε, καὶ ὃς οὐ μόνον οὐδὲν ἐλυμάνθη ἀλλὰ καὶ
εὐστοχώτατα αὐτὸν κατειργάσατο. While Dio does refer to the *Iuuenalia* of Nero in similar
terms at 61. 19. 1 (ἐπεκλήθη δὲ Ἰουοενάλια ὥσπερ τινὰ νεανισκεύματα), it is unlikely either
that Statius would not have alluded to *Iuuenalia* as the name of the festival (when he readily
refers to the Capitoline festival as *Capitolia* at *Silv.* 3. 5. 31) or that Domitian would have
reused the title of Nero's *Iuuenalia* so blatantly, when, as Hardie (2003), 126–7 shows,
Domitian had to overcome the opprobrium attached to Nero's attempts to institute
Greek festivals in Rome. It is more likely that Dio is confusing the two festivals (and note
that in the case of Nero's festival, Dio shows awareness of the actual Latin title), or possibly
that there may have been some section of the festival which included separate events for
boys. Moreover Dio elsewhere (67. 1. 2) refers to the Alban festival as τὰ Παναθήναια; see
also 54. 28. 3, where τοῖς Παναθηναίοις is likely to be a reference to the Quinquatria during
the reign of Augustus, as argued by Habicht (1995), 261–3). Cf. the possible reference in an
honorific inscription of Side in Asia Minor, published in Bean (1965), 69–70, no. 189, where
C. P. Jones (1998), 185–6 has argued that Παναθηναϊκὸν ἀγῶνα may refer to the honorand's
having gone to Rome for the Alban contest, though it is true that identification of the
emperor referred to in the inscription with Domitian is perhaps difficult in the lack of any
reference to his title *Germanicus*.

but also didactic (for the need not to see these as two separate strands
of literary activity see e.g. Gale (1994), 99–128): one may note the
agricultural as well as poetical implications of *labor* (cf. Virg. *G.* 1. 145
'labor omnia uicit'). Thus *Aonios... campos* not only denotes poetry,
through the usual association of *Aonius* with Helicon, the source of
poetic inspiration, but also evokes Boeotia and the Theban legend (cf.
Theb. 1. 33–4 'nunc tendo chelyn satis arma referre | Aonia')—thus
confirming Statius' own place in the poetic canon together with
Hesiod's *Works and Days*.

seno pede refers to the measurement in feet of both fields and
verses: Professor Winterbottom has suggested to me that *seno pede*
might reflect such usages as the *decempeda*, used for measurement by
the *decempedator* (Cic. *Phil.* 13. 37).

cludere campos: M's *ducere campos* is difficult: it either has to be a
shortened form of 'ducere campos in carmina' (cf. 85–6 n.), or else a
variant on the common 'ducere carmina', with *campos* denoting the
subject matter of the poems. An anonymous friend of Gronovius
(*Diatribe* 50) promisingly emended to *cludere cantus*. For *cludere* signify-
ing the enclosure of verse within the metre, cf. Hor. *S.* 2. 1. 28–9 'me
pedibus delectat claudere uerba | Lucili ritu nostrum melioris utro-
que', Ov. *Pont.* 4. 16. 36 'clauderet imparibus uerba Capella modis',
Pers. 1. 93 'cludere sic uersum didicit'. However, the presence of
carmen in 93 makes *cantus* unconvincing, as well as unnecessary (for the
poetical implications of *campos* see Prop. 2. 10. 2 'et campum Haemo-
nio iam dare tempus equo'; cf. Virg. *G.* 2. 541 'sed nos immensum
spatiis confecimus aequor').

cludere campos gives a play on the primary and the metaphorical
significance of *campus*. The literal sense of the phrase would be the
enclosure of fields; compare Sen. *Thy.* 232 'prata, quae cludit lapis'
and Hyg. *Agrim.* p. 72 Thulin 'ut quadraturae diligenter claudi pos-
sint'; see also Tac. *Dial.* 30. 5 where a similar rural metaphor is
heightened by the word *terminis*: 'neque oratoris uis et facultas sicut
ceterarum rerum angustis et breuibus terminis clauditur'.

93. Arcadia ... testudine: the lyre is 'Arcadian' since Hermes,
its inventor, was born in Arcadia (5. 1. 102 n.). *testudine* (literally
'tortoise') evokes the aetiology of the lyre, which Hermes fashioned
from a tortoise shell and the entrails of stolen cattle (*h. Hom.* 4. 24–54);
the lyre was given to Apollo in recompense for the cattle.

94. cura lyrae nomenque fuit (Gronovius, *Diatribe* 51) is the
most convincing reconstruction of M's *Cydalibem*: *lyrae nomen* alludes to

the designation of the lyric poets as *lyrici*. Emendations too closely linked to a single poet, e.g. *Pindaricum os* (Saenger) and *Cea fides* (Phillimore), are unsatisfactory because of the preceding plural *quibus*. Statius is not enumerating particular authors but types. *Chria liber* (Ellis (1900), 259) is unlikely; it would be strange to refer to poets who were only noted for the appearance of lines of their poetry in rhetorical exercises; cf. Cartault (1903), 676–7. Withof's *Pisa labor*, a less specific reference to epinician, is unlikely, given the presence of *labor* in 92 and the resulting difficulties of satisfactorily construing *nomen*.

95. Statius here denotes the Seven Sages of Greece, on whom see Pl. *Prt.* 343 A 1–5, D.L. 1. 13, 1. 30, 1. 40–2, Snell (1943), Burn (1960), 207–9. On the popularity of the Seven Sages in late antiquity, see Curtius (1953), 210–11. Courtney's suggestion that 93–5 be transposed to follow 99 is unnecessary; we need not expect a consistent separation of prose and poetry.

96–7. The tragic poets, who do not appear in the later list of poets taught by Statius' father; for the place of tragedy in Roman education, see Bonner (1977), 214–15.

Furias regumque domos: despite Vollmer's interpretation as either hendiadys ('the furious halls of kings') or a reference to Oedipus, *Furias*, if it evoked a particular play, would suggest the *Eumenides* of Aeschylus.

domos: Meursius' *dolos* (noted by Barth) is unnecessary. The palace was a frequent setting for tragic action, and *regumque domos* also denotes royal families, frequent subjects of tragedy; Leofranc Holford-Strevens suggests to me that *domos* might then be a learned glance at the frequency of words such as οἶκος in the *Oresteia*.

auersaque caelo | sidera alludes to the myth of Thyestes, a popular subject: as well as Seneca's play, there were notable dramas by Curiatius Maternus (Tac. *Dial.* 3. 4) and Varius (ibid. 12. 6); see Tarrant (1985), 40–3.

terrifico super intonuere cothurno: *super* is best construed, with Iz.–Fr. ('Ceux qui, montés sur le terrifiant cothurne, ont tonnés....'), as indicating height, the *cothurnus* being a large-soled shoe (cf. Juv. 6. 505–6 'breuiorque uidetur | uirgine Pygmaea nullis adiuta coturnis'). *terrifico* seems to concur with at least part of Aristotle's theory of the effects of tragedy as expressed at *Poetics* 1449[b]27–8: δι' ἐλέου καὶ φόβου περαίνουσα τὴν τῶν τοιούτων παθημάτων κάθαρσιν. On the literary uses of words such as *tonare*, see van Dam on *Silv.* 2. 7. 66.

98. lasciua ... Thalia: cf. *Silv.* 2. 1. 115–16 'laudaret gauisa sonum crinemque decorum | pressisset [ς : fregisset *M*] rosea lasciua Thalia corona'; van Dam ad loc. rightly suggests that Thalia denotes comedy here, although she can be associated with various genres (including elegy, Ov. *Ars* 1. 264) and sometimes with poetry in general (see e.g. Hor. *Carm.* 4. 6. 25 'doctor argutae fidicen Thaliae'); cf. Serv. Auct. *A.* 7. 37, who explains Erato as referring either to Calliope or 'pro qualicumque musa'. Even though the context (apart from the prior mention of tragedy) does not suggest comedy as much as *Silv.* 2. 1. 115–16 (where Statius had previously mentioned Menander), and although *tenuare* (Calderini; an obvious emendation of M's *tenuere*) might suggest the refinement of elegy no less than *heroos gressu truncare*, it is important to note *uel*, which indicates that *two* genres are alluded to: comedy and elegy.

99. labores: Vollmer's defence of M's *leones* as a reference to poetry in which heroes fight like lions ('Kühn nennt der Dichter die Verse, welche wie die Löwen kämpfenden Helden darstellen, selbst *leones*. . . .') has little to recommend it. However, the case for *tenores* (Calderini) is not strong. *gressu truncare* denotes the shortening of the hexameter by a foot to form the pentameter line (cf. Ov. *Am.* 1. 1. 3–4 with McKeown); for *gressus* as a metrical foot compare *Silv.* 1. 2. 250–1 'sed praecipue qui nobile gressu | extremo fraudatis opus [*M* : epos *Heinsius*]'. *heroos . . . tenores* seems a strange and unparalleled designation of metre (the plural *tenores* is only found once, at Quint. *Inst.* 1. 5. 22, in a discussion of accentuation), even if *tenor* can mean a consistent course (5. 1. 118 n.), and suggests, if anything at all, heroic tones. 'To cut off the heroic tones by a foot' is somewhat unconvincing.

With *labores* (Rothstein), 'quis . . . | dulce uel heroos gressu truncare labores' would mean 'or those for whom it is sweet to shorten heroic labours by a foot' (cf. *Silv.* 4. 7. 2–3 'fortis heroos, Erato, labores | differ'), but *truncare* ('to lop off') is a little strange with *labores*. No entirely satisfactory solution seems available for this crux.

100. The list of genres culminates with the assertion that Statius' father is the master of them all (for the theme of wide-ranging knowledge cf. Suetonius' remarks on Ateius Philologus and Eratosthenes at *Gramm.* 10. 4–5).

es (Saenger) is essential, since there is otherwise no indication that Statius' father is the subject of *complexus* (for *complector* thus cf. Sen. *Suas.* 6. 11 'et omnia complexus est quae a ceteris dicta erant', Sil. 13. 788 (of Homer) 'carmine complexus terram, mare, sidera, manes',

and contrast the modesty of Virg. *G.* 2. 42 'non ego cuncta meis
amplecti uersibus opto'); the entry of *et* (M) into the tradition may
account for the confusion which gave rise to *utor* (see next n.).

usus (Wiman) is probably correct; *utor* (M) cannot be right, given
the sequence *omnia... omnibus* and the complimentary passage that
follows, which must refer to the father.

101. uia lata patet: Markland's *uia* is far more appropriate to
epithet and verb than *uis* (M); compare e.g. *Silv.* 2. 1. 4 'magnaeque
patet uia lubrica plagae', Sen. *Phaed.* 1213 'patuit ad caelum uia'.
Contrast the narrow way of Call. *Aet.* fr. 1. 25 ff. Pf.

102. Aoniis uincire modis seu uoce soluta: cf. Lucan's
mastery of both prose and verse (*Silv.* 2. 7. 21–2): 'dum qui uos
geminas tulit per artes, | et uinctae pede uocis et solutae'.

103. et effreno nimbos aequare profatu: cf. Homer's de-
scription of Odysseus' oratory (*Il.* 3. 222 καὶ ἔπεα νιφάδεσσιν ἐοικότα
χειμερίῃσιν, quoted by Plin. *Ep.* 1. 20. 22; cf. 114–15 n.), *Laus Pis.* 57–8
'siue libet pariter cum grandine nimbos | densaque uibrata iaculari
fulmina lingua'.

104. exsere semirutos ... uultus: Markland questioned *semi-
rutos*, arguing that the adjective is properly applied to buildings.
Although *OLD* s.v. *semirutus* gives the meaning as 'half-demolished,
half in ruins', there is no need for Markland's *semiustos*: *semirutos*,
applied to the face of Parthenope, not only suggests the physiognomy
of the Siren, but also evokes the physical aspect of the city itself, so
that an image of the Siren is combined with an evocation of the
condition of her city; the destruction is the result of the eruption of
Vesuvius (*adflato monte* in the next line). Compare Virgil's treatment of
Mount Atlas at *A.* 4. 246–51, where the mountain is described in
terms of human features; Ovid employs similar techniques at *Met.* 9. 3
(the river Achelous) and 11. 157–9 (the mountain Tmolus).

Parthenope: the Siren Parthenope had her tomb at, and gave
her name to, the Cumaean settlement of Parthenope, which was later
renamed Neapolis according to Lutat. fr. 7 Peter (= Serv. Auct. *G.* 4.
563), memorial games being instituted in Parthenope's honour
(113 n.). At 111 the city is 'Euboean' since Cumae itself was a Euboean
colony; see Liv. 8. 22. 5, Str. 5. 4. 4 (C243), Vell. 1. 4. 2, Ridgway
(1992), 32–4. The archaeological evidence for the tradition of an
earlier Rhodian settlement at Parthenope mentioned by Str. 14. 2.
10 (C654) is contested: Boardman (1980), 192 suggests a Rhodian
settlement by 650 BC, but see Frederiksen (1984), 55 and 86–7.

Settlement of Neapolis took place in two stages: a first settlement, referred to by Livy as 'Palaeopolis' around 675 BC on the heights of Pizzofalcone as attested by the presence of Protocorinthian ware (Frederiksen (1984) 69, 85–6); there was then a later settlement near the site of the modern Naples ('Neapolis'). As Oakley (1998), 633–8 has pointed out, the name Palaeopolis, 'old city', would not have been used to refer to the earlier foundation until the second phase of settlement.

105. crinemque adflato monte solutum: Håkanson (1969), 142–3 argues that M's *sepultum* is absurd, since Parthenope is asked to place a lock buried beneath a mountain on the tomb of Statius' father. But the covering is only one of dust (*subito de puluere*), so that Parthenope might more reasonably be able to have access to her locks. Nevertheless, *sepultum* is redundant, since some kind of covering is implied by *subito de puluere* in 104. Both Markland and Håkanson favour Heinsius' *adflatu montis adustum* (Markland would emend to *adesum*, having conjectured *semiustos* in 104). This removes the superfluous *sepultum*, but means that the hair would already have been burnt when placed on the tomb of Statius' father. Contrast *Il.* 23. 140 ff, where Achilles cuts off the special lock he had grown in honour of Spercheios and explains his decision to give it to the dead Patroclus. *Burnt* hair is hardly a suitable offering.

I suggest *sepultum* be emended to *solutum*. *soluo* is commonly applied to hair, particularly when it is loosened as a sign of grief (which Parthenope could feel both for Statius' father and for her city); cf. e.g. Virg. *A.* 11. 35 'et maestum Iliades crinem de more solutae'. *adflato monte* is an instrumental ablative; the eruption caused Parthenope's hair to be disordered.

106. funus: not the funeral of Statius' father, since the poem is composed three months after his death (29–33). *funus* can signify a dead body; cf. Virg. *A.* 9. 490–1 'aut quae nunc artus auulsaque membra | et funus lacerum tellus habet?', Prop. 1. 17. 8 'haecine parua meum funus harena teget?' But here *funus* refers to his ashes, which would have been stored in a *cinerarium* at his tomb; note Serv. *A.* 3. 62 'nam proprie funus est incensum cadauer' (cf. Serv. *A.* 2. 539, Serv. Auct. *A.* 3. 22).

alumni: the primary resonance is 'foster-son', Statius' father being an 'adopted son' of Neapolis by virtue of his youthful migration thither (cf. 124–32); but the sense that he was a 'pupil' (*ThLL* i. 1797. 23–54), having had his literary successes in Neapolis, is also present.

Statius' request for Parthenope to tend his father's tomb recalls (and perhaps eclipses) the customary assocation of Naples with Virgil, for which see e.g. Virg. *G.* 4. 563–4 'illo Vergilium me tempore dulcis alebat | Parthenope studiis florentem ignobilis oti', Plin. *Ep.* 3. 7. 8, and the purported epitaph of Virgil noted at *vita Donati* 36, 'Mantua me genuit, Calabri rapuere, tenet nunc | Parthenope; cecini pascua, rura, duces', Hinds (2001), 247–50. For Statius' links with Naples, see further Leiwo (1995), 36–40.

107–8. quo non ... quicquam praestantius ... | ... crea-uit: Iz.–Fr., Mozley, and Vollmer imply that Neapolis is compared with Athens, Cyrene, and Sparta in terms of poets. But the passage is best interpreted as a comparison between Statius' father and *all* the famous offspring of the three cities, not merely poets. While *doctaue Cyrene* can evoke Callimachus, not only because it was his *patria*, but also because *doctrina* was one of his qualities, *Sparteue animosa* does not perforce refer to Alcman; *animosa* might evoke the military successes of the Spartans. Similarly Athens (*Monychiae ... arces*; cf. *Theb.* 2. 252–3 'Monychiis ... iugis', and also 12. 616, where, as noted by Klotz, manuscripts offer support for M's spelling here, *moniciae*, this orthography also being confirmed by Steph. Byz. s.v. Μωνυχία), although it could stand for any Athenian poet or several, is a general home of excellence; compare e.g. Pericles in the *epitaphios* (Thuc. 2. 41. 1) Ξυνελών τε λέγω τήν τε πᾶσαν πόλιν τῆς Ἑλλάδος παίδευσιν εἶναι. Vell. 1. 18. 1 also affirms the superiority of Athens in Greece. For the hyperbole of these lines, compare Statius' desire to match Homer and Virgil (62–3), and his father's equivalence to Homer and Hesiod (26).

109. stirpe uacans: Vollmer awkwardly defends *stirpe uetas* (M) by printing *stirpe uetas famaque* as a parenthesis, giving too much prominence to Parthenope's imagined reaction to the charge of ignoble origins, and unnaturally separating *tu* from *uetas*. Moreover Parthenope has to be temporarily imagined as bereft of her lineage and fame, since she subsequently proves her claim to Greek and Euboean descent by virtue of her association with Statius' father. Baehrens's *uacans*, very probably anticipated by Laetus, is sound.

famaque: though M's *famaeque* might be a partitive genitive governed by *nil gentile* in the following line, with *obscura* having almost adverbial force, the separation of *famae* from *nil gentile* is awkward. *famaque* (ς) is more elegant, the ablative being governed by *uacans*. The pairing of *stirpe* ('lineage') and *fama* ('reputation') is then matched by *nil gentile* and *obscura*, with effective chiasmus. The distinction is

perhaps between innate lustre and reputation won through achieve-
ment; even if Parthenope were without either type of fame, she
could still prove her Greek qualities by citing the career of Statius'
father.

110. tenens: *tumens* (Markland), despite such parallels as *Theb.* 8.
429–30 '(namque hae magnum et gentile tumentes | Euboicum duris
rumpunt umbonibus agmen)', strikes the wrong note; Parthenope's
swelling with pride (if she were able to) is not in keeping with her
modest desire to affirm her Greekness. M's *tenens* is preferable.

The Neapolitans appear to have been anxious to stress their Greek
antecedents, and their Greekness, as reflected perhaps in the institu-
tion of phratries; see Lomas (1993), 166–7. Str. 5. 4. 7 (C 246) notes the
retention of Hellenic culture in the city, even though he refers to its
inhabitants as Romans: πλεῖστα δ' ἴχνη τῆς Ἑλληνικῆς ἀγωγῆς
ἐνταῦθα σῴζεται, γυμνάσιά τε καὶ ἐφηβεῖα καὶ ὀνόματα Ἑλληνικά,
καίπερ ὄντων Ῥωμαίων; D.C. 55. 10. 9 attributes the foundation of
the *Augustalia* to a desire to follow Greek practice, while Vell. 1. 4. 2
contrasts the Neapolitans, who diligently maintained their heritage,
with the Cumaeans, who were influenced by their Oscan neighbours.
Note also praise of Naples as a centre of culture at Sil. 12. 31–2: 'nunc
molles urbi ritus atque hospita Musis | otia et exemptum curis
grauioribus aeuum'. On bilingualism in Naples and the use of
Greek in inscriptions, see Lomas (1993), 176, Leiwo (1995), 42–5,
167–72, and McNelis (2002), 74; on bilingualism as 'cultural capital',
see McNelis (2002), 71–3. Statius' counterfactual picture of Neapolis
needing to prove its genuine Greekness may reflect real anxieties over
the status and continuation of Greek culture in the city.

111. Euboico maiorum sanguine duci: the epic tone (cf. e.g.
Virg. *A.* 5. 568 'genus unde Atii duxere Latini', 8. 142 'sic genus
amborum scindit se sanguine ab uno') compliments both Parthenope
and Statius' father.

112. ille, referring to Statius' father, picks up *illo . . . ciue* (110).

pressit sua (sc. *tempora*): so Markland emended M's *prestat sed* (cf.
Håkanson (1969), 144–5), comparing *Silv.* 2. 1. 115–16 'crinemque
decorum | pressisset [ς : fregisset *M*] rosea lasciua Thalia corona'.

Though *praestabat* (Elter) could have been contracted to *praestat*,
leaving a gap conveniently filled by *sed*, Håkanson notes that *praestare*
is only used to denote the offering or giving of parts of the body in
inauspicious circumstances (e.g. Luc. 5. 770–1); the context of Mart.
11. 24. 2 'aurem dum tibi praesto garrienti', where Martial has to

listen to and praise the loquacious Labullus, does not counter this objection. Moreover, *praestantius* in 107 may have contributed to corruption here.

113. quinquennia: the victories were obtained at the *Augustalia* (Σεβαστά), the games held every four years in honour of Augustus, which were inaugurated in 2 BC (D.C. 55. 10. 9), replacing the annual funeral games which had been held for the Siren Parthenope; for imperial links with Greek festivals, see further van Nijf (2001), 318–20. *quinquennia* denotes this four- (not five-) year period under the inclusive system of reckoning time; cf. *Silv.* 2. 2. 6, 3. 5. 92, where *quinquennia* and *lustrum*, two words whose primary meaning is a period of five years, are similarly used. The competitions were gymnastic as well as poetic (Str. 5. 4. 7, C246), and were ἰσολύμπια (*IG* xiv. 748); the integration of the festival into the wider circuit of Greek games (cf. 141–5 below on Statius' father's successes in contests beyond Naples) is illustrated in *IG* xiv. 746 and 747, recording the achievements of pancratiasts across a wide spectrum of other contests as well, including the Isthmian, the Pythian, the Nemean, and the Olympic games, and the κοινὸν Ἀσίας at Smyrna; cf. Robert (1930), 53–5. For details of the events at Naples, see the fragmentary *I. Olympia* 56, with Geer (1935), Merkelbach (1974), and, for further *testimonia* and bibliography, see Buchner, Morelli, and Nenci (1952), 406–8, Miranda (1982), Leiwo (1995), 45–8. The games were held in the early part of August (Suet. *Aug.* 98. 5 records that Augustus was present shortly before his death on 19 August AD 14). The younger Statius was also successful in these games (225–7).

114–15. These lines seem to mark a transition from poetic to oratorical success. A. Hardie (1983), 7 argues that there may be a lacuna of a single line after 113 on the grounds that the change from verse to prose is too abrupt, particularly as *caneret* would still be the main verb in the phrases which follow; I have offered a suggestion for the possible content of the lacuna in the text.

The references to the Pylian and Dulichian leaders are to the Homeric characters Nestor and Odysseus, and to types of oratory associated with them. The association of Nestor with sweetness of style goes back to *Il.* 1. 249 τοῦ καὶ ἀπὸ γλώσσης μέλιτος γλυκίων ῥέεν αὐδή, while the grandeur of Odysseus' eloquence in Homer is illustrated by the comparison with words being poured forth like winter snows (*Il.* 3. 221–4). In Latin, Quint. *Inst.* 12. 10. 64 (see Austin's notes) distinguishes Menelaus, Nestor, and Odysseus as representing

three types of Homeric oratory, concluding with the following praise
of Odysseus: '...sed summam expressurus [est] in Vlixe facundiam
et magnitudinem illi uocis et uim orationis niuibus [et] copia uer-
borum atque impetu parem tribuit'; cf. Cic. *Brut.* 40, Plin. *Ep.* 1. 20.
22, Gel. 6. 14. 7 with Holford-Strevens (2003), 222 and n. 128. See
also *Paneg. Messallae* 48–9 'non Pylos aut Ithace tantos genuisse
feruntur | Nestora uel paruae magnum decus urbis Vlixem...',
Laus Pis. 57–64, where Piso surpasses the oratory of the Homeric
heroes; the author of the *Laus Pis.* assigns Quintilian's qualities of
brevity, sweetness, and vigour to Menelaus, Nestor, and Odysseus
respectively. Nestor's mellifluous oratory seems to have been pro-
verbial: see Otto (1890), 242 (§1224).

114. senis: Vollmer's defence of M's *gregis* as 'grex Pylio par,
Nestoreus, mellea facundia Nestoris praeditus' fails since the phrase
does not then denote Nestor himself. *ducis* (Slater) is possible, but is
not better than *senis* (ς), despite the argument of Håkanson (1969),
144–5 that *ducis* could easily have been corrupted to the synonymous
regis, in the light of the repeated *ora* in this line, with the unmetrical
regis subsequently being corrected to *gregis*. Contamination from *regis*
at the end of the line, however, does not guarantee that the word
displaced by *gregis* was a synonym of *regis*, so that *senis* deserves
consideration; even though the old age of Nestor is commonplace,
senis is less colourless than *ducis*, and there is little merit in having *regis*
accompanied by so close a synonym.

115. pretioque (Saenger): *speciemque* (M) cannot be defended. It is
unsatisfactory to construe *speciemque* with what has preceded (with
Iz.–Fr.), since it weakens the parallelism of *ora...oraque* in the pre-
ceding clause (though Dr Holford-Strevens has suggested to me that
the repetition of *ora* might itself be questionable, in which case the first
ora could have replaced a word such as *uerba*); it would also be odd for
Statius' father to surpass the *species* of Odysseus (especially in the light
of his explicitly inauspicious appearance at *Il.* 3. 217–20, just before
the passage on his oratory mentioned above), since the field of contest
is oratorical. Nor can *speciem* or *specie* (Calderini) be satisfactorily
construed with *subnexus*; the poet's father cannot be said to bind to
his hair the appearance of Nestor and Odysseus, despite Slater's
translation '...and wore the effigies of both in his circlet'.

pretioque...utroque would mean 'binding his hair with both prizes',
perhaps, as A. Hardie (1983), 7 suggests, denoting success in prose, as
well as the poetry prize mentioned in 112–13; alternatively, *utroque*

could look back to the nearest pair, Nestor and Odysseus. This interpretation is more promising in terms of grammar, although Statius would then seem to refer to two different prose contests. It is, however, unlikely that there should have been separate contests delineated according to the characterizations of the oratory of Nestor and Odysseus described above. On balance it is preferable to interpret *utroque* as denoting both verse and oratory, referring back to 112–13a. Indeed *utroque* is a further argument in support of the lacuna, since it might otherwise refer unhelpfully to success in Latin and Greek contests, when there is nothing in this passage (contrast of course *gemina . . . lingua* in 90 above) to imply competitions in both languages at Naples; a possible reference to Latin would also be unfortunate in a passage whose concern is to show how Statius' father is emphatic proof of the Greekness of Naples. Statius mentions his father's prowess in prose at 102 and 160, so that it is not unreasonable to see a compliment to his father's skill in both spheres.

It might at first glance appear that *supergressus* and *subnexus* present difficulties, since competing in the contests (regardless of whether a lacuna is accepted after 113) should logically precede binding the hair as a celebration of victory (*subnexus*, which is closely joined to the preceding and less problematic *supergressus* by *-que*). However, the Latin past participle does not always have to have strictly past sense; see Wackernagel (1920), 288–9, H.–Sz. 391–2 (§209a), K.–S. i. 758–60. There is thus no need either for Saenger's conjecture *subnectis*, which could not in any case follow *caneret* in 113 (and indeed *tibi* in 116 looks as if it should mark a shift from third person to second person singular), or for Vollmer's suggestion that *subnexus* should be construed as a main verb (with *est* omitted), which would also require *supergressus* to be a main verb, since the two participial clauses are joined by *-que*.

116. deformes: for the tone of moral censure see *ThLL* v/1. 368. 79–369. 39.

117. nec sine luce genus: compare the similar litotes at *Silv.* 5. 2. 15–21 (with 16 n.).

118. artior expensis: Statius' grandparents fell on hard times, as a result of heavy expenditure. The family may have lost equestrian status through failure to meet the property qualification (Iz.–Fr. 197 n. 5, Coleman (1988), xv; see also A. Hardie (1983), 6), though Nauta (2002), 199 suggests that their loss of wealth may have been the result of public benefactions expected of the local aristocracy (the *decuriones*) in Velia.

diuite ritu carefully counters the impression that the family was utterly without means. Wealth and poverty could both be used as encomiastic topoi, since the key was to see how such external circumstances might bear on a person's character (e.g. *Rhet. Her.* 3. 7. 14). Statius thus shows his father to advantage by simultaneously hinting at wealth and poverty.

119. fecit: with M's *legit* and *ponere*, this line has a curious sense, for Infancy is said to choose Statius' father to take off his purple garments. There is, however, no reason for this to be a matter of choice, since the exchange of the *toga praetexta* for the *toga uirilis* was a ceremony undergone by every freeborn youth who had survived childhood (it is mentioned in the case of Crispinus in 5. 2. 66–7 because of the pathos of Crispinus' father Bolanus' not being able to be there, not because it is in any way unusual). Shackleton Bailey's *fecit* would seem an improvement, but there is still something a little odd about its being Infantia who makes Statius' father cease to be a child.

A reference to the assumption of the emblems of childhood, however, may be preferable. This would also fit with the sequence of the passage, for Statius goes on to describe the reaction of the Muses at Papinius' birth (*protinus exorto* in line 121), and then Apollo's favour, before describing how he grew up in Naples and first began to essay poetry (134–7). If one accepts Markland's *sumere* for M's *ponere* in 119 (even though *ponere* is the proper word for the removal of garments: cf. Cic. *Amic.* 33 'quod summi puerorum amores saepe una cum praetexta toga ponerentur', *OLD* s.v. *pono* 6b), then lines 118–20 become an elaborate gloss on the earlier remarks on how Papinius' family was 'nec sine luce genus' (117), emphasising that the family was not without means. It is not necessary to see *diuite ritu* as implying an otherwise unattested ceremonial on assuming the emblems of childhood; the phrase might simply denote that when Papinius did so, his family celebrated in splendid fashion. When combined with *sumere*, Shackleton Bailey's *fecit* seems preferable to *legit*, since the problem of why Infantia actually has to choose Papinius to do anything still remains.

Infantia: the only parallel offered by *ThLL* vii/1. 62–7 for this personification is the much later *Sacramentum Gelasianum* 1. 44 (p. 73 Mohlberg) 'omnis in una pareat gratia mater infantia'.

120. nobile pectoris aurum: the gold *bulla* worn by equestrian children and dedicated to the Lares on coming of age (cf. Pers. 5. 30–1: 'cum primum pauido custos mihi purpura cessit | bullaque subcinctis Laribus donata pependit'). On the origins of the *bulla*, see Plin. *Nat.* 33. 10, Plu. *Quaest. Rom.* 101 = *Mor.* 287 F–288 B, Macrob. *Sat.* 1. 6. 7 ff. Pliny notes that equestrian children wore a gold amulet, while others wore one of leather; see also Juv. 5. 164–5.

121–3. For such divine interest in a young poet compare *Silv.* 2. 7. 36–41 and van Dam's note; see also Sidonius. *Carm.* 23. 204–9 where Sidonius refers to the Muses dipping the infant Consentius in the Hippocrene. For *protinus*, denoting an immediate reaction, note 2. 7. 36–38 'natum protinus atque humum per ipsam | primo murmure dulce uagientem | blando Calliope sinu recepit'.

121. exorto begins a short passage looking back over the father's birth and childhood, and his poetic initiation by the Muses and Apollo. This passage is in the tradition of such celebrated poetic initiations as Hesiod's encounter with the Muses on Mount Helicon (*Th.* 1–34) and Callimachus' meeting with Apollo at the beginning of the *Aetia* (fr. 1. 21–8 Pf.); see further Kambylis (1965).

122. Aonides: the epithet applied to the Muses here places this initiation on Mount Helicon: cf. e.g. Virg. *Ecl.* 6. 65 'Aonas in montis ut duxerit una sororum', *G.* 3. 11 'Aonio rediens deducam uertice Musas', Stat. *Theb.* 4. 182–3 'hic fretus doctas anteire canendo | Aonidas mutos Thamyris damnatus in annos'.

pueroque chelyn commisit: with *puerique…summisit* (M), Apollo not only exposed the boy's lips to the poetical waters of Mount Helicon (*imbuit amne sacro*: on the links between water and inspiration, see 5. 5. 7 n. below), but also dipped the lyre therein. The dative *pueroque* (ς) is attractive: Apollo gave the boy his lyre. Axelson's *commisit*, discussed by Håkanson (1969), 145–7, 'entrusted', is preferable to *summisit* ('sent to', *OLD* s.v. *submitto* 5, 6).

123. iam tum tibi blandus Apollo: M's *mihi* cannot be retained. Statius is referring to his father, who benefited because Apollo was *blandus* towards him. Since Statius was not alive when his father was born, he cannot be the person towards whom Apollo is *blandus*.

124. nec simplex patriae decus: *nec simplex* is equivalent to *duplex*, because Statius' father has two *patriae*. Praise of a person's *patria* was standard encomiastic practice. *Rhet. Her.* 3. 6. 10 includes *ciuitas* in its list of external characteristics; cf. Men. Rh. 369. 18–370. 28.

125. ambiguo geminae certamine terrae: for two cities to compete in claiming a person's birthplace is a mark of the highest honour, as Statius himself indicates in the following passage; cf. *Silv.* 2. 2. 133–7 where Pollius is associated with both Neapolis and nearby Dicaearchea (Puteoli). Most celebrated were the disputes over the birthplace of Homer; see e.g. Gel. 3. 11. 6–7, Lefkowitz (1981), 13; Heath (1998) notes that among more exotic traditions for Homer's origin was a claim that he was a Roman. There was also another such dispute over the origins of Alcman; cf. *A.P.* 7. 18. 5–6 (Antipater of Thessalonica) and 7. 709 (Alexander), *P. Oxy.* 2389 fr. 9 i, Vell. 1. 18. 3 'nam Alcmana Lacones falso sibi uindicant', Page (1951), 167–70. Here Statius makes a virtue of his father's departure from Velia, a city on the Lucanian coast to the south of Naples, asserting that both cities consider his father as one of their own. The implied comparison with Homer maintains the confidence of the earlier image of the elder Statius in the underworld engaging in poetic composition with Homer and Hesiod (26).

126. Latiis adscita colonis: cf. *Silv.* 2. 2. 136 'hinc adscite meis', referring to Pollius' adoption by the citizens of Neapolis. Here the Greek city is adopted by the 'Latin colonists' who chose to live there. Velia (*Hyele*, in Greek) received Roman citizenship and became a *municipium* as a consequence of the *lex Iulia* of 90 BC (Cic. *Balb.* 21, 55; cf. Kahrstedt (1959), 182–3, Musti (1966), 326–7, and note also Mingazzini (1954), 50–2 on an inscription recording the career of one Cornelius Gemellus recording his tenure of the offices of *gymnasiarchos* and also *duouir* and *quattuoruir*, suggesting a dating from the time of the change in the city's legal status to that of Roman *municipium*). Sp. Carvilius Maximus (*cos.* 293 BC) captured the city from the Samnites (Liv. 10. 45. 9), and an alliance between Rome and Velia at the time of the First Punic War is attested by Plb. 1. 20. 14 (cf. the treaty providing for Velian naval contributions attested in the Second Punic War at Liv. 26. 39. 5). Sources for Velian history are conveniently collected by Musti (1966). *adscisco* is a *mot juste* for acquisition of citizenship: cf. Cic. *Balb.* 27 'modo adsciscatur ab ea ciuitate cuius esse se ciuitatis uelit', *ThLL* ii. 764. 29–42. *Latiis* and *Graia* in the next line emphasize the twin nature of Velia as a part of both the Latin and the Greek world; note for instance that the epigraphic record at Velia shows inscriptions in both Greek and Latin (see further Musti (1966), 330, Lomas (1993), 176–7), and the persistence of the office of φώλαρχος, on which see Musitelli (1980). Similarly, Statius' father and Statius himself are equally at home in both cultures, as reflected in Statius' choice of examples and literary references throughout the poem, as when he remarks that Facundia bewails his father 'gemina lingua' (90). We are not told why the elder Statius left Velia; perhaps the city offered few prospects to a young man of promise. Str. 6. 1. 1 (C252) comments on economic decline in the time of Augustus, noting the poor soil and the consequent dependence of the inhabitants on the catching and salting of fish for a livelihood.

127. Graia refert Hyele: Hyele was founded by Phocaeans who had been defeated by the Carthaginians and Etruscans after their flight from Ionia to Corsica (Hdt. 1. 167. 3); see Gigante (1966), and for bibliography on the origins of Hyele see Boardman (1980), 189 n. 106. At Str. 6. 1. 1 (C252) the Phocaeans under Creontiades go first to Cyrnus and Massilia, before reaching Elea. Strabo also notes the different names given to the city: κάμψαντι δ' ἄλλος συνεχὴς κόλπος, ἐν ᾧ πόλις, ἣν οἱ μὲν κτίσαντες Φωκαιεῖς ῾Υελῆν,[22] οἱ δὲ ῎Ελην ἀπὸ κρήνης τινός, οἱ δὲ νῦν ᾽Ελέαν ὀνομάζουσιν. Heinsius' brilliant emendation of M's *sele* to *Hyele*, giving the Greek name for Velia, is supported by *Graia*, signalling the likely presence of a Greek name.

Phrygius: M's *graius* cannot stand; Vollmer's suggestion that Palinurus could be called *Graius* as a pointer to the Greek components of his name is unsubtle (and feeble when compared with Mart. 3. 78. 2 'meiere uis iterum? iam Palinurus eris') in a line where Statius has already used the word *Graia*. Avantius' *Phrygius* is an acceptable epithet for Palinurus; Baehrens's *Troius* would be closer to M, but would require an unparalleled scansion of the word as two long syllables with consonantal 'i'. Another possibility would be *Teucrus*. The combination of *Latiis, Graia,* and some word denoting 'Trojan' in these two lines is quite in keeping with the evocation of the *Aeneid* achieved through Statius' reference to Palinurus' death.

127–8. Statius closely echoes Virgil's treatment of Palinurus. Palinurus' own account to Aeneas of his misfortunes and death at *A*. 6. 347–71, where he declares that he fell from the ship without any divine involvement, is to the fore, as opposed to the narrator's account of Palinurus at *A*. 5. 833–71, where he is taken from his vessel by the god Somnus. Thus Palinurus falls (*excidit*, cf. *A*. 6. 339 'exciderat puppi'), is a *magister* (a term he uses of himself at *A*. 6. 353), is

---

[22] For the perispomenon, see Schulze (1933), 395–6,

miser (he requests Aeneas: 'da dextram misero' at *A.* 6. 370), and
survives amid the waves (*A.* 6. 355–8) until his death off the coast of
Velia, where his body was washed up (*A.* 6. 366 'portusque require
Velinos'). *euigilauit*, however ('he woke up', or possibly 'he stayed
awake'), evokes the narrative in *Aeneid* 5 where Palinurus is over-
whelmed by Somnus; allusions to both aspects of the story are thus
combined within the space of a few words.

Velia is close to Cape Palinurus (Str. 6. 1. 1 (C252) μετὰ δὲ ταύτην
ἀκρωτήριον Παλίνουρος). The Lucanians pacified the shade of Pali-
nurus by giving him a grave and cenotaph near Velia (Serv. *A.* 6. 378).

129. longo probat ordine uitae: *longo . . . ordine uitae* is equiva-
lent to 'longo ordine annorum (uitae)' (cf. Virg. *Ecl.* 4. 5 'magnus ab
integro saeclorum nascitur ordo'), the many years of residence in
Neapolis. Compare also *Theb.* 6. 380–1 'datur ordo senectae | Admeto
serumque mori' where 'ordo senectae' is the sequence of years of
old age.

Markland's lacuna after this line is sound, as there is no city to
balance Velia; since the contest is between between two cities, both
need to be named, particularly as Neapolis is assigned the better
claim. *maior* alone is intolerably weak, and *ibi* (133) needs a clear
antecedent. The lacuna may have included a reference to the city's
Euboean origins.

130–2. Statius compares the contest between Velia and Naples in
claiming his father as their own with the disputes over Homer's
origins. A. Hardie (1983), 8 suggests that Statius' father was offered
citizenship at Naples after his victory in the Neapolitan *Augustalia*.

Maeoniden: Statius appropriately alludes to Homer with a
patronymic form.

aliaeque . . . cunctaeque: the 'epic' repetition of -*que* in these
lines is equally apposite in a passage referring to Homer; compare the
grand context of the archaic genitive plural *magnanimum*, discussed in
10 n. above. For the hyperbole that all cities (*cunctae*) claim Homer as
one of their citizens, cf. *Certamen* 7–8 Ὅμηρον δὲ πᾶσαι ὡς εἰπεῖν αἱ
πόλεις καὶ οἱ ἔποικοι αὐτῶν παρ' ἑαυτοῖς γεγενῆσθαι λέγουσιν; note
also the verdict of Man. 2. 7–8 'patriam cui turba petentum, | dum
dabat, eripuit'.

diripiunt: *diripere* (literally 'to tear apart') can be pejorative when
signifying competition for favour; cf. Sen. *Dial.* 10. 7. 8 'diripitur ille
toto foro patronus', Juv. 6. 404 'quis diripiatur adulter'. There may be
gentle criticism at *Silv.* 2. 2. 133–4 'tempus erat cum te geminae

suffragia terrae | diriperent celsusque duas ueherere per urbes', but here the word is without censure (cf. *Theb.* 5. 721–2 'matremque auidis complexibus ambo | diripiunt flentes alternaque pectora mutant'). The indicatives *diripiunt* and *probant* are satisfactory, but the contemptuous tone of *aliaeque aliis natalibus* would suit jussive subjunctives (*diripiant* and *probent*). The corruption of subjunctives to indicatives is not difficult; for a similarly dismissive jussive subjunctive applied to other persons (contrasted with a specific individual) compare *Silv.* 5. 2. 52–4 'uirtutis tibi pulcher amor... | ... aliis Decii reducesque Camilli | monstrentur'.

probant: i.e. each argues its own case; cf. Ov. *Met.* 15. 499–500 'mirabere, uixque probabo, | sed tamen ille ego sum', *ThLL* x/2. 1469. 55–1470. 2.

uictas (Bentley), agreeing with *urbes*, is preferable to *uictos* (M) which has no obvious antecedent. The argument that the masculine plural might refer to the citizens of the cities is countered by *omnibus*, which refers back to the cities. Line 132 is framed by *uerus* and *falsi*; cf. *Silv.* 5. 1. 52–3.

134. protinus ... raperis: this line introduces a rapid narrative of the father's successes, in keeping with his ambitions (*festinus*) in 135. At Hor. *Carm.* 3. 25. 1–2 'Quo me, Bacche, rapis tui | plenum?' (see further N.–R.) *rapio* describes the onset of poetic inspiration from Bacchus (cf. *S.* 2. 1. 10 'aut si tantus amor scribendi te rapit'); *raperis* not only evokes the speed which characterized the elder Statius' participation in the contest, but also suggests an element of external inspiration in keeping with the divine favour enjoyed by the young poet (121–3).

patrii ... certamina lustri: 113 n.

135–6. laudum festinus et audax | ingenii: *festinus*, primarily signifying the elder Statius' desire for praise, may also carry a literary resonance; at *Silv.* 1 pr. 3–4 Statius' *libelli* are hastily produced, 'qui mihi subito calore et quadam festinandi uoluptate fluxerunt', whilst at 1 pr. 13 his poems possess a 'gratiam celeritatis'. Although these passages describe the circumstances of composition, style is at stake as well; speedy writing can provoke criticism (1 pr. 5–15).

audax ingenii: also found at *Silv.* 3. 2. 64, referring to the first person to send ships on the sea. For *ingenium* denoting something equivalent to innate talent note Ovid's verdict on Callimachus (*Am.* 1. 15. 14, with McKeown): 'quamuis ingenio non ualet, arte ualet'; cf. Prop. 3. 2. 25–6, Hor. *Ars* 408–18 with Brink, Ov. *Tr.* 2. 423–4 with

Luck. Though *audacia* and its cognates can denote stylistic daring (see *ThLL* ii. 1243. 8–19 s.v. *audacia*, 1248. 3–20 s.v. *audax*, 1250. 19–27 s.v. *audacter*, cf. Vessey (1971), 274), *audacia* can also refer to improvisatory daring (cf. *Silv.* 1 pr. 19, if Sandström's conjecture *ausus sum* is correct, and 22, 3 pr. 4), as argued by M. D. Reeve in Reynolds (1983), 398 n. 12; cf. Nauta (2002), 251. A reference to Statius' father's skill in improvisation seems appropriate here.

136. stupuit: *Silv.* 5. 2. 109 n.

137. monstrauere: parents regarded Statius' father as a suitable model for their children (cf. Tac. *Dial.* 7. 4 'quorum nomina prius parentes liberis suis ingerunt?') and would subsequently send their sons to be schooled by him (146). Contrast the negative examples pointed out by Horace's father at *S.* 1. 4. 105–26. For *monstro* thus, cf. *Silv.* 5. 2. 54, 5. 3. 237, 5. 3. 289, and Plin. *Pan.* 15. 4, where Pliny compares posterity's future wish to be shown places associated with Trajan's military service with Trajan's own experience of following in the footsteps of his predecessors: 'ut tunc ipsi tibi ingentium ducum sacra uestigia isdem in locis monstrabantur.' Note also Hor. *Carm.* 4. 3. 22 'quod monstror digito praetereuntium' and Juv. 14. 37 'et monstrata diu ueteris trahit orbita culpae'.

138. frequens pugnae: *ThLL* vi/1. 1299. 73 ff. gives only one other instance for the genitive with *frequens* denoting repeated action: Tertullian, *De ieiunio aduersus psychicos* 17 (p. 297 Reifferscheid and Wissowa, 4–5) 'conuiuandi frequentior'. *pugnae* anticipates the ensuing comparison made with Pollux' boxing; cf. military metaphors for oratory (*Silv.* 5. 2. 108–9 n.).

138–9. nulloque ingloria sacro | uox tua: another instance of litotes (cf. 124), to avoid repetition of the statement that the father was repeatedly successful in competitions (112). Such competitions were religious in character or origin; hence *sacra*.

139. uictorem Castora gyro: for the defining ablative with *uictor*, denoting the nature of the victory, cf. Cic. *ad Brut.* 1. 15. 10 (Shackleton Bailey) 'hoc bello uictores quam rem publicam habituri simus non facile adfirmarim', Tac. *Ann.* 3. 61. 2 'mox Liberum patrem, bello uictorem, supplicibus Amazonum quae aram insiderant ignouisse'. Castor and Pollux, whose most important cult site was Therapnae, are habitually associated with horse-racing and boxing: cf. e.g. Prop. 3. 14. 18 'hic uictor pugnis, ille futurus eques', Ov. *Am.* 3. 2. 54 'Pollucem pugiles, Castora placet eques', V.Fl. 1. 420–6.

140. auxere: M's *clausero* has been variously corrected. *plausere* (Calderini) cannot be accepted since the verb cannot take a direct object when it means 'to applaud'. *coluere*, suggested by Håkanson (1969), 147–8, imparts a religious tone appropriate to the two Spartan heroes; cf. *Silv.* 4. 8. 52–3: 'et uos, Tyndaridae, quos non horrenda Lycurgi | Taygeta umbrosaeque magis coluere Therapnae'. Nevertheless *auxere* (Watt), 'glorified' (*OLD* s.v. *augeo* 5a), is preferable. The thought of the whole passage is that Statius' father had many victories. The comparison, since it describes the athletic activities of both heroes, should suit this context, and should treat the heroes as victors, not as divinities. With *coluere* the comparison becomes imprecise; the word is appropriate to the Spartan heroes, but not to Statius' father. *auxere* suggests, in a manner appropriate to the epinician context, the analogous Greek usage of αὔξω denoting 'to glorify with praise'; compare Pi. *O.* 5. 4 τὰν σὰν πόλιν αὔξων, *P.* 8. 38 αὔξων δὲ πάτραν Μειδυλιδᾶν λόγον φέρεις.

On the apparently fictitious tradition of a verdant Therapnae, see Coleman on *Silv.* 4. 8. 53.

141. sin pronum uicisse domi: an anticipation of possible criticism that it is easy to win competitions held in one's home town; cf. A. Hardie (1983), 7. *pronum est* is a post-Augustan usage ('it is easy', *OLD* s.v. *pronus* 7b), construed with the infinitive or *ut*.

141–5. Vollmer, Håkanson (1969), 148–9, Clinton (1972), 79–80, and Laguna (1992), 4 rightly argue that the elder Statius was indeed successful in the Greek games described here. The Olympic Games do not feature in the list because they did not regularly include poetic contests (the isolympic status of the *Augustalia* is irrelevant): see Robert (1930), 54.

Clinton (1972), 79–82, suggests that *IG* ii^2. 3919. 2 (Eleusis), an honorific decree issued by the Areopagus, can be restored to Πόπλιον Παπίνιον Στ[άτιον]. The restoration is attractive. Clinton also suggests that the elder Statius may have taken part in the Eleusinian mysteries.

The contests indicated in 142–3 are the Pythian Games (represented by a garland of bay), the Nemean Games (celery), and the Isthmian Games (pine). Statius alludes to all three in a learned manner, naming the component plant of the victor's wreath only in the last example; for a similarly allusive list of competitions compare *Silv.* 3. 1. 140–3; note also the list of games at *Theb.* 6. 5–14, where Statius lists the Olympic, Pythian, and Isthmian festivals which preceded the foundation of the Neman games. The three phrases with *nunc* are all subordinate to 'mereri | praemia', *protectum tempora* being *ἀπὸ κοινοῦ*.

In 144–5 Statius again states a simple fact in a complex fashion, so as to avoid repetition. Instead of saying that Victoria always favours his father, Victoria is 'nowhere inaccessible' (*nusquam auia*); she has favoured no other competitor. As in 138–9, litotes varies the tone.

totiens lassata neatly transfers to the personified Victoria the weariness incurred by the elder Statius in gaining his triumphs; cf. *Silv.* 1. 5. 2 'nec lassata uoco totiens mihi numina Musas', Luc. 2. 727–8 'lassata triumphis | desciuit Fortuna tuis'. Mention of the Roman goddess Victoria, on whom see Hölscher (1967), also evokes, in this epinician context, the Greek goddess of victory, *Νίκη*. Statius' physical image of Victoria touching the hair of the victor (with a garland) recalls the description of a victor falling into the goddess' arms at Pi. *N.* 5. 41–2b: *τὺ δ' Αἰγίναθε δίς, Εὐθύμενες, | Νίκας ἐν ἀγκώνεσσι πίτνων | ποικίλων ἔψαυσας ὕμνων* (compare *I.* 2. 26 *χρυσέας ἐν γούνασιν πίτνοντα Νίκας*). *A.P.* 6. 313 (ascribed to Bacchylides) is an even closer parallel:

> *κούρα Πάλλαντος πολυώνυμε, πότνια Νίκα,*
> *πρόφρων Κραναῶν ἱμερόεντα χορὸν*
> *αἰὲν ἐποπτεύοις, πολέας δ' ἐν ἀθύρμασι Μουσᾶν*
> *Κηΐῳ ἀμφιτίθει Βακχυλίδῃ στεφάνους.*

The motif of Victory crowning an individual is also found in Roman coinage with triumphal motifs; note for example the aureus of Augustus in the British Museum where a *triumphator* in a chariot drawn by elephants is crowned by a winged figure; see further Hölscher (1967), 68–97 and especially, for this coin, 86.

146–7. hinc is causal; it is Statius' father's distinguished competitive record which encouraged parents to send their sons to receive his teaching. Parents could sometimes cause problems for instructors: Orbilius Pupillus wrote a treatise *Περὶ ἀλογίας* dealing with the difficulties occasioned by parental 'neglegentia aut ambitione' (Suet. *Gramm.* 9. 3, with Kaster ad loc.).

uota patrum: the children were the object of their father's prayers; cf. Ov. *Met.* 1. 272–3 'sternuntur segetes et deplorata colonis | uota iacent' and the analogous usage of *spes* (*OLD* s.v. *spes* 5) to denote the embodiment of another's hopes as at e.g. Virg. *G.* 3. 471–3 'nec singula morbi | corpora corripiunt, sed tota aestiua repente, | spemque gregemque simul cunctamque ab origine gentem.'

credi, **regi**, **discere:** historic infinitives; for the usage of this type of infinitive in Latin poetry, see further van Dam on *Silv.* 2. 1. 120–4.

te monitore: *Silv.* 5. 2. 51 n., cf. 4. 7. 25–6 'quippe te fido monitore nostra | Thebais'.

mores et facta priorum: *mores* could denote 'customs', but a moral tone is likely, particularly as Statius' father is a *monitor*. Cf. 61, 'atque tibi moresque tuos et facta canentem', where *mores* can only refer to moral conduct.

148–58. Statius lists four *categories* of literary knowledge. The first is mere knowledge of a work's plot, in this case the Homeric epics (147): what was the fate of Troy, and how did Ulysses come to be delayed in his return? The second category, the study of how an author achieves his effects, is the closest to evaluative criticism. Statius' father's pupils thus learnt something of Homer's technique in composing an epic. This is something quite different from mere knowledge of the events of a work, since judgement is involved.

Statius' third category is metre (*qua lege recurrat* | *Pindaricae uox flexa lyrae*, 151–2); his choice of poets is scarcely surprising, since all were practitioners of the lyric metres, the most difficult to analyse and compose. A fourth and final category is introduced in 156, exegesis (*pandere*), and once again the examples are highly appropriate, because of their difficulty and obscurity.

This list not only identifies the authors read by Statius' father's pupils, but also provides valuable insights into the nature of their studies. For other syllabus lists, cf. A. C. Dionisotti (1982), 100, 121–2, Holford-Strevens (2000), 49–52. The discussion of Statius' father's teaching and the intellectual and educational context of Greek grammarians in Rome given by McNelis (2002), who concludes (83) that 'the elder Statius' curriculum is consistent with the known activity of *grammatikoi* in Rome and Roman Italy during the early empire', is invaluable.

149. decurrere denotes the rapidity of the Homeric style (cf. Quint. *Inst.* 10. 1. 49 'narrare uero quis breuius quam qui mortem nuntiat Patrocli...?'). For *decurrere* cf. *Silv.* 2. 1. 113–14 'seu gratus amictu | Attica facundi decurreret orsa Menandri', Cic. *de Orat.* 1. 148 'ista, quae abs te breuiter de arte decursa sunt'. For the teaching of Homer in Rome by Greek *grammatici*, see McNelis (2002), 78–9. For Homer's primacy in education, see e.g. Bonner (1977), 212–13, A. C.

Dionisotti (1982), 121–2, and T. Morgan (1998), 71–8, 105–15, 313, who shows that not all parts of Homer may have received the same degree of attention.

150–1. quantumque pios ditarit agrestes | Ascraeus Siculusque senex: Statius alludes to agricultural didactic poetry.

pios evokes the moral tone of parts of Hesiod's *Works and Days*, such as Hesiod's instructions to his dissolute brother Perses (e.g. the link between virtue and prosperity, expressed at *Op.* 230 ff.). If *Siculus* below refers to Epicharmus, there could also be a glance at some of the philosophical works ascribed to that author.

Ascraeus ... senex: Hesiod (cf. 26–7 n.), author of the *Works and Days*; contemporary interest in Hesiod is reflected in Epaphroditus' commentary on the *Scutum* and Plutarch's commentary on the *Works on Days*; see McNelis (2002), 78.

Siculus: less certain, though Epicharmus has been suggested by Vollmer and Iz.–Fr., an identification accepted by Holford-Strevens (2000), 41 and McNelis (2002), 78. Columella 1. 1. 8 and 7. 3. 6 credits Epicharmus with the authorship of a treatise on remedies for cattle, while Plin. *Nat.* 1. 20–7 and 20. 89, 94 names him as a medical authority. D.L. 8. 78 gives the following summary of his works: φυσιολογεῖ, γνωμολογεῖ, ἰατρολογεῖ. See further Pickard-Cambridge (1962), 230–55; for study of Epicharmus in Rome, see McNelis (2002), 78–9.

151–2. As well as metrical responsion, *recurrat* and *flexa* suggest the propensity of Pindar's poetry to change direction abruptly; compare *P.* 10. 53–4 ἐγκωμίων γὰρ ἄωτος ὕμνων | ἐπ᾽ ἄλλοτ᾽ ἄλλον ὥτε μέλισσα θύνει λόγον. On Pindar and Statius, see *Silv.* 5. 2. 48–50 n. For *lex* applied to metre, see *ThLL* vii/2. 1248. 81–1249. 25. Holford-Strevens (2000), 41–2 argues that Statius is here reacting to Horace's claim (*Carm.* 4. 2. 11–12 'numerisque fertur | lege solutis') that Pindar's metrical practice was free of external responsion. For grammatical exegesis of Pindar in Rome, see McNelis (2002), 79; see also (on Theon, a grammarian who taught in Rome under Tiberius and Claudius) Guhl (1969), 14–15, 40–1. The list of poets which follow Pindar in lines 152–6 should be considered as further subjects for *recurrat*, with the names placed by metonomy for their verses; the implication is that Statius' father taught the metres of the other lyric poets as well.

152. uolucrumque precator: when the poet Ibycus was attacked (for *testimonia* of his life and death, see *PMGF*, pp. 236–9), he called on a flock of cranes as witnesses of his murder. The murderers subsequently betrayed themselves when one of them, on seeing some cranes, remarked that the avengers of Ibycus were at hand. Overheard, they were caught and punished. See *A.P.* 7. 745 (Antipater of Sidon), Plu. *De garrulitate* 509 F, and *Suda* ι 80 (= ii. 607 Adler), where the cranes of Ibycus are said to be proverbial. McNelis (2002), 79 notes that there is no other evidence for grammarians working on Ibycus in Italy. For an unconvincing attempt to discern a Statian allusion to Ibycus in the treatment of Adrastus' lineage in the *Thebaid*, see Delarue (1968), 24–31, with the sceptical discussion of Venini (1971), 14–17.

153. tetricis Alcman cantatus Amyclis: Statius' presentation of Alcman is indebted to the severe image of Sparta that was by his time canonical (for the epithet *tetricis*, see Dewar on *Theb.* 9. 615); on perceptions of Sparta during the Roman imperial period see E. Rawson (1969), 107–15. Cartledge (1979), 154–7, Forrest (1980), 71–3 discuss the less austere realities of Alcman's era; for the dating to the seventh century BC see Page (1951), 164–6. McNelis (2002), 80–1 notes that considerable evidence for commentaries on Alcman survives in Egyptian papyrus finds; for an attempt to discern traces of Alcman in the *Achilleid*, see Sirna (1973), 41–57.

Amyclae was traditionally said to be an Achaean city conquered by Dorian Sparta in the reign of Teleklos (Paus. 3. 19. 6, who records that it was henceforth a mere κώμη). Its assimilation is dated to around 750 BC by Cartledge (1979), 106–8 and Forrest (1980), 31–2. For its pleasant location see Plb. 5. 19. 2. Amyclae is mentioned in the fragmentary commentary on the lyric poets which includes Alcman (*P.Oxy.* 2506 fr. 1c. 8).

154. Stesichorusque ferox: Hor. *Carm.* 4. 9. 7–8 thought Stesichorus' verse severe: ' . . . et Alcaei minaces | Stesichoriue graues Camenae'. Such assessments may be linked to perceptions of Stesichorus as 'Homeric'; see [Longin.] 13. 3 and *A.P.* 9. 184. 3–4 (anonymous). Quintilian (who recommends the study of Stesichorus) remarks on this similarity 'ac si tenuisset modum uidetur aemulari proximus Homerum potuisse' (*Inst.* 10. 1. 62), having previously described the poet's epic subject matter: 'maxima bella et clarissimos canentem duces et epici carminis onera lyra sustinentem'. The presence of Sicilian and South Italian authors such as Stesichorus, Epicharmus, Sophron, and Ibycus in the list of texts taught by Statius' father may be a reflection of intellectual interest in the Doric dialect both in Italy and in Rome; see McNelis (2002), 84–6.

154–5. These lines contain two related difficulties: the meaning of *saltusque ingressa uiriles*, and the emendation of M's *calchide*. *Chalcide*, which could easily give rise to the alternative spelling *calchide*, has been defended as a generic term for a competition between poets. Iz.–Fr. 199 n. 5 modify Klotz's earlier hypothesis in his apparatus that the meaning is that Sappho would not have feared to compete with Homer and Hesiod, and suggest instead that *Chalcide* is a metonymy for a contest between Sappho and Alcaeus analogous to the legendary encounter between Homer and Hesiod in Chalcis. This explanation is, however, unconvincing, since neither is there any tradition of a contest involving Sappho, nor can such a complex metonymy of *Chalcis* be accepted. Vollmer quoted a letter from Buecheler referring to Steph. Byz. (685. 1–2 Meineke) where there is a reference to an island called Chalcis situated near Lesbos on which there is a city of the same name (see *RE* iii /2. 2090. 32–40 s.v. Chalkis 11 (Bürchner). Note too Holford-Strevens (2000), 43: 'If I were engaged to defend the manuscript reading, I should note that, like the more famous Chalcis in Euboea, Mytilene overlooked an εὔριπος (Xen. *Hell.* 1. 6. 22), and argue for a poetic transference of name. If the poet were Lycophron, a few might believe me; as it is, the more cautious critic will revert to the humanistic correction *Leucade*.'

Håkanson (1969), 150 supports *Leucade* (ς), which, though less close to *calchide* palaeographically, is nevertheless possible, and would refer to Sappho's suicide (traditionally a result of her passion for Phaon) by leaping into the sea from a cliff at Leucas in western Greece; cf. [Ov.] *Ep.* 15. 171–2 'pete protinus altam | Leucada nec saxo desiluisse time', Nagy (1973). Menander fr. 258 K. affirms that Sappho was the first to jump into the sea there, but Str. 10. 2. 9 (C452), the source for the Menander quotation, notes that older sources give Cephalus as the first to make such a leap. Photius, *Bibliotheca* 190 (153^{a-b}) gives Ptolemaeus Chennus' list of persons who jumped from Leucas, a list which curiously does not include Sappho. Statius' *saltusque ingressa uiriles*, even if the primary meaning of *saltus* here is not 'leaps' (see below), may be a learned allusion, glancing at the alternative tradition of a man having been the first to leap into the sea at Leucas. Note also the single fragment of the *Leucadia(e)* of Parthenius (fr. 14 Lightfoot, *SH* 625), which may have come from a poem on heroines who jumped into the sea; see Lightfoot (1999), 38, 156–7.

It is worth noting, however, that Wilamowitz (1913), 25–40 called into question the idea that Sappho was supposed to have killed herself in the Ionian Sea off western Greece, and suggested a locale near Chalcedon in the vicinity of Byzantium; for this reason (28–9) he favoured the reading *Chalcide* in the present passage, comparing Strabo 7. 6. 2 (C320) ἐκ τῆς Χαλκηδονιακῆς ἀκτῆς λευκή τις πέτρα προπίπτουσα and also Dionysius Periegetes 764 ἄχρι Θρηϊκίου στόματος, τόθι Χαλκὶς ἄρουρα. However, there seems no particular reason to connect Sappho with this Chalcis. As it happens, there are also Leucae Insulae near Lesbos (see Plin. *Nat.* 5. 140, Bürchner in *RE* xii /2. 2209. 9–17 s.v. Leuka 5), but it also seems unlikely that these are in any way connected with Sappho. But whatever toponym replaces M's *calchide*, *non formidata* would indicate that Sappho did not fear her leap from the rocks. There is no reason not to mention her death, particularly as the death of Ibycus has already been mentioned. *temeraria* would also fit this interpretation, suggesting her daring in choosing to die in this fashion.

As for *saltusque ingressa uiriles*, the primary meaning of *saltus* can hardly be 'leaps', despite *Theb.* 12. 20 'tandemque ingressa uolatus'; the secondary meaning of 'leaps' may perhaps be glanced at, but *non formidata* and *temeraria* in themselves are sufficient for an allusion to Sappho's death. For such phrasing, compare also the rather different 'planctusque egressa uiriles', applied to Eurydice, the mother of the dead Opheltes at *Theb.* 6. 33. Håkanson (1969), 149–50 defends Calderini's belief that the phrase refers to poetry (rejected by Markland), by comparing *saltus* at Man. 3. 1–4:

> In noua surgentem maioraque uiribus ausum
> nec per inaccessos metuentem uadere saltus
> ducite, Pierides. uestros extendere fines
> conor et indictos in carmina ducere cantus.

Critics have noted that *uiriles* recalls Horace's 'mascula Sappho' (*Ep.* 1. 19. 28). *saltusque ingressa uiriles* must refer to Sappho's status as the only woman among the *nouem lyrici*, the lyric poets of Greece. *A.P.* 9. 571. 7–8 (anonymous) goes further, calling her the tenth Muse: ἀνδρῶν δ' οὐκ ἐνάτη Σαπφὼ πέλεν, ἀλλ' ἐρατειναῖς | ἐν Μούσαις δεκάτη Μοῦσα καταγράφεται. The same thought occurs at *A.P.* 9. 506, ascribed to Plato (cf. Antip. Sid. *A.P.* 7. 14. 1–2, where Sappho is τὰν μετὰ Μούσας | ἀθανάταις θνατὰν Μοῦσαν ἀειδομέναν, 9. 66, Σ Dion. Thrax 21. 19 Hilgard where Corinna is the tenth Muse); at

Antip. Thess. *A.P.* 7. 15 (= *Garland of Philip* 73),[23] Sappho surpasses female poets by as much as Homer excels the males. For scholarly interest in Sappho, see McNelis (2002), 81.

156. quos alios dignata chelys: the 'other' poets are the remaining members of the canon of nine lyric poets, listed in *A.P.* 9. 184 and 9. 571. Statius does not mention Bacchylides, Anacreon, Simonides, and Alcaeus.

156–7. pandere doctus | carmina Battiadae: though Markland's *docti*, agreeing with *Battiadae*, is attractive, *doctus* (M) must be retained. *docti* would make *pandere* a historic infinitive in the second person, a usage only found at 5. 3. 235 (see n.). An *emendation* which would produce such a rare usage seems questionable, even if this poem offers the only other example. *pandere* and *doctus* neatly encapsulate the tendency of learned poetry to require explanation. The reference to Callimachus by his patronymic recalls Callimachus' own use of the form at *Ep.* 35 Pf. (*A.P.* 7. 415); for *carmina Battiadae*, cf. Cat. 65. 16, 116. 2. *pandere*, here poetic exegesis, can signify the setting forth of material; cf. e.g. 235 below, Lucr. 1. 55 'disserere incipiam et rerum primordia pandam'. For Callimachus and Statius, see the General Introduction, pp. xxiii–xxviii.

157. latebrasque Lycophronis atri: a recondite allusion to Lycophron's recondite *Alexandra*. *atri* (ς) could denote the melancholy tone of this work, filled with Cassandra's mordant prophecies of disaster, but more likely is a reference to the obscurity of the poet's style. Vollmer notes that *Suda* Λ 827 (= iii. 299 Adler) describes the *Alexandra* as τὸ σκοτεινὸν ποίημα, while Clem. Al. *Strom.* 5. 8. 50. 3 Stählin calls it a γυμνάσιον given by *grammatici* to schoolboys, who would be tested by its obscurities and difficulties. Compare Cic. *Fin.* 2. 15 'Heraclitus, cognomento qui σκοτεινός perhibetur' (cf. Clem. Al. *Strom.* 5. 8. 50. 2 St.), and μέλας at *A.P.* 11. 347 (Philip = *Garland of Philip* 61), an anti-Callimachean poem attacking the learned style:

> χαίροιθ' οἱ περὶ κόσμον ἀεὶ πεπλανηκότες ὄμμα
> οἵ τ' ἀπ' Ἀριστάρχου σῆτες ἀκανθολόγοι·
> ποῖ γὰρ ἐμοὶ ζητεῖν τίνας ἔδραμεν ἥλιος οἴμους
> καὶ τίνος ἦν Πρωτεὺς καὶ τίς ὁ Πυγμαλίων;
> γινώσκοιμ' ὅσα λευκὸν ἔχει στίχον· ἡ δὲ μέλαινα
> ἱστορίη τήκοι τοὺς Περικαλλιμάχους.

---

[23] Gow and Page ad loc. note that the epigram has also been assigned to Antipater of Sidon.

atri here suggests obscurity, but without censure. The word also complements *latebras*, for which applied to poetry, compare Cic. *Div.* 2. 111 (on the author of the Sibylline verses) 'adhibuit enim latebram obscuritatis, ut iidem uersus alias in aliam rem posse accommodari uiderentur'. *ThLL* vii/2. 995. 11–27 s.v. *latebrosus* gives examples from Christian Latin (referring to the problems of scriptural interpretation).

Though Lycophron is only otherwise named in Latin literature at Ov. *Ibis* 529–30, 'utque coturnatum periisse Lycophrona narrant, | haereat in fibris fixa sagitta tuis', possible allusions in Virgil have been identified: see Josifovic, *RE Suppl.* xi. 922. 20–925. 2, S. West (1983), 132–5. Scholarly interest in Lycophron in the early empire is reflected in the commentary composed by the grammarian Theon; see further Guhl (1969), 8–9, and also 31–2, where the fragments are assembled. Delarue (1968), 18–24 has argued for allusions to Lycophron's *Alexandra* in Statius' *Thebaid*, though Venini (1971), 9–14 is sceptical.

158. Sophronaque implicitum: For discussion of the mimographer's date (probably the end of the fifth century), life, works, and influence, see now Hordern (2004), 1–10, 26–9. The epithet, and the grouping of Sophron with Callimachus, Lycophron, and Corinna, imply that his works were not easily understood; for grammatical study of Sophron, see further McNelis (2002), 82. Continuing interest in Greek mime is also suggested by the fragments of popular mime from the imperial period, collected in Rusten and Cunningham (2002), 355–421. *implicitum* suggests intricacy; the image is of an object folded about itself. The word can be used of prose (e.g. Cic. *Fin.* 3. 3, Gel. 7. 2. 15), and poetry (e.g. Gel. 19. 9. 7 'Laeuius implicata et Hortensius inuenusta et Cinna inlepida...fecerunt').

tenuisque arcana Corinnae: the presence of Corinna in the company of Callimachus and Lycophron has no bearing on the debate over her date, on which see Page (1953), 65–84, M. L. West (1970). Since Sophron wrote in the fifth century BC, no conclusions on Corinna's date can be drawn from this passage. As with the other poets, Statius emphasizes Corinna's obscurity (*arcana*); Holford-Strevens (2000), 45 raises the possibility that *arcana* and *implicitum*, applied to Sophron, may refer to the difficulties of Sophron's Syracusan and Corinna's Boeotian dialects. McNelis (2002), 83 suggests that it is likely that *grammatici* in Rome worked on Corinna.

159. sed quid parua loquor?: the rhetorical question prepares for Statius' father's greatest achievement, his versions of Homer. *parua*

also points to a shift from lesser genres back to epic; compare the
climax introduced by *parua loquor* at *Silv.* 5. 1. 127. The absence of
tragic texts from this passage is noted by A. Hardie (1983), 10 and
Holford-Strevens (2000), 46–8.

   159–60. tu par adsuetus Homero | ferre iugum: the com-
parison between Homer and Statius' father (which first appeared in
26) is continued, with an image of the two men as a team of oxen
working together under the yoke. *ferre iugum*, which can denote
submission, (e.g. Hor. *Carm.* 1. 35. 27–8 'amici | ferre iugum pariter
dolosi', 2. 6. 2, quoted in 5. 2. 33 n.), when combined with *par iugum*
(*OLD* s.v. *iugum* 2b), denoting friendship, emphasizes the arduousness
of epic endeavour.

   160–1. senosque pedes aequare solutis | uersibus: Statius'
father 'equalled' Homer's hexameters by giving a prose version. For
aequare, see e.g. 11 (and n.) above, Virg. *A.* 2. 361–2 'quis cladem illius
noctis, quis funera fando | explicet aut possit lacrimis aequare labores?'
solutis uersibus, 'verses released from metre' (cf. *Silv.* 1. 4. 28–9 'seu plana
solutis | cum struis orsa modis', 5. 3. 102), appropriately placed to
produce enjambment across the verse-end (and hence producing a
'dissolving' of the verses), is a variant on the familiar *soluta oratio*,
denoting prose, and suggests that the paraphrases nevertheless retained
the qualities of poetry. Compare Quint. *Inst.* 1. 8. 13 (referred to by Ellis
(1885), 95) 'in praelegendo grammaticus et illa quidem minora praestare
debebit, ut partes orationis reddi sibi soluto uersu desideret et pedum
proprietates, quae adeo debent esse notae in carminibus ut etiam in
oratoria compositione desiderentur'; for an infelicitous instance of
paraphrase, see Sen. *Suas.* 1. 12 (Maecenas' censure of Dorion's render-
ing of *Od.* 9. 481–2). Suet. *Gramm.* 4. 5–6 gives 'paraphrasis' in a list of
'quaedam genera meditationum ad eloquentiam praeparandam' which
he says were less commonly practised in his own time.

   The elder Statius was not the only exponent of such prose render-
ings of poetry. Sen. *Dial.* 11. 11. 5–6 praises Claudius' freedman
Polybius for his ability to give a sense of the *gratia* if not the *structura*
of an original. Quint. *Inst.* 10. 5 discusses the *conuersio* of Greek prose
works into Latin, but also mentions Sulpicius' versions of poetry at 10.
5. 4. See also Bonner (1977), 255–6, T. Morgan (1998), 202–15 for the
role of paraphrase in education.

   161. numquam passu breuiore relinqui: Statius' father is
not 'left behind' by Homer, because his versions are equal to Homer's
poetry.

162. quid mirum: just as Statius' father left Velia for Neapolis, so too his students left their homes, in order to be taught by him. Whereas the reasons for the father's change of domicile are left obscure (126 n.), the motivation of his pupils is explicit (*te*). The ensuing list of places uses, on a small scale, the techniques of an epic catalogue, such as allusion and periphrasis, and devotes varying degrees of attention to each place; for discussion of Statius' catalogue technique in the *Thebaid*, see Georgacopoulou (1996).

patria . . . relicta: for this motif in catalogues cf. Juv. 3. 69 'Amydone relicta' and the use of *linquere* at Virg. *A.* 7. 670, 676, 728, 10. 168. Statius' father's reputation was sufficient for his pupils to leave their homes (for the desirability and difficulty of education at home, see Plin. *Ep.* 4. 13). Compare Tac. *Dial.* 7. 4, where Aper notes how foreigners and strangers in Rome 'requirunt ac uelut agnoscere concupiscunt' orators whom they have heard of in their own *municipia* and *coloniae*; contrast *Dial.* 10. 2, where Aper notes how infrequently visitors from Asia or Spain asked after the poet Saleius Bassus.

163. Lucanus ager: Lucania has the first place because of Statius' father's Velian origin.

rigidi quos iugera Dauni: Apulia is designated by Daunus, its legendary king (Hor. *Carm.* 3. 30. 11–12; see also N.–H. on *Carm.* 1. 22. 14). *rigidi* suggests stern and unbending moral qualities; Horace uses the word of the Sabines at *Ep.* 2. 1. 25, and of the Getae at *Carm.* 3. 24. 11. After Lucania and Apulia, Statius lists places much closer to Neapolis.

164–5. Veneri plorata domus neglectaque tellus | Alcidae: Venus' association with Pompeii is attested by *CIL* x. 787, whilst Hercules' patronage of Herculaneum, said to be founded by him, is recorded by D.H. 1. 44. 1 and Ov. *Met.* 15. 711 'Herculeamque urbem'; cf. Beloch (1890), 218–25. See also Mart. 4. 44. 5–6 'haec Veneris sedes, Lacedaemone gratior illi, | hic locus Herculeo nomine clarus erat'. The chiastic arrangement of the periphrasis emphasizes the patron deities. The contrast between *plorata* and *neglectaque* is surprising and effective.

165–6. e uertice Surrentino . . . profundi: for the temple of Minerva on the lofty *promuntorium Mineruae* (Capo Ateneo) (Ov. *Met.* 15. 709 and Plin. *Nat.* 3. 62) see *Silv.* 2. 2. 1–3, 3. 1. 109, Beloch (1890), 276–7, Frederiksen (1984), 89 with n. 31. See also the anonymous hexameter quoted at Sen. *Ep.* 77. 2: 'alta procelloso speculatur uertice

Pallas' (= Courtney, *FLP*, p. 462), to which *uertice* and *speculatrix* may allude; cf. *Silv.* 2. 2. 3 'speculatrix uilla profundi'.

Surrentinus appears only four times in the verse of the *Silvae* (and twice in the prefaces). The other three instances of the adjective are all in the neuter plural form, two of them (*Silv.* 2. 2. 82 and 4. 8. 9) at the beginning of the line, a position also employed by Hor. *S.* 2. 4. 55 and Mart. 13. 110. 1. At *Silv.* 3. 5. 102 the word occupies the fourth foot and most of the fifth. Here the ablative form is placed in the last two feet of the line, producing a spondee in the fifth foot; Ov. at *Met.* 15. 710 had deployed the four syllables of the ablative across the first three feet, effecting a caesura in the third foot. This is the only spondaic verse in the *Silvae* (Statius has five in *Theb.*: 4. 5, 4. 227, 4. 298, 9. 305, 12. 630): see Frank (1968), 397 and n. 3.

Minerva is *Tyrrhena* at *Silv.* 2. 2. 2 and 3. 2. 24; van Dam on 2. 2. 2 explains the epithet in terms of her temple's proximity to the Tyrrhenian Sea. But this does not preclude allusion to the Etruscan Minerva as well, as suggested by Iz.–Fr. on 2. 2. 2; see further Frederiksen (1984), 117, 124 (on Etruscan influence on Surrentum), Dench (1995), 157. The goddess's appearance is appropriate in view of her patronage of learning and teachers (91 n.), since it is she who sends the youth of Surrentum to study under the elder Statius.

mittit: *mitto*, also found at 169 below, is a characteristic word in catalogues, allowing the variation of saying that people are sent from a particular place instead of coming from it. Cf. e.g. Sil. 8. 359, 377, 567, 579, 606.

speculatrix uirgo profundi echoes the sound (though not the content) of *Silv.* 3. 2. 86 'fluctuet aut Siculi populatrix uirgo profundi'.

167–8. Statius closely follows Virgil's account of the funeral of Misenus, and the etymology of the cape named after him (*A.* 6. 233–5). Common features are the oar and the trumpet (*A.* 6. 233 'remumque tubamque'), and the hill (6. 234 'monte sub aerio') which bears his name. At *Silv.* 3. 1. 151, where Misenus is named, Statius mentions only the trumpet (cf. 4. 7. 19 where he is a *liticen*), whilst at 3. 5. 98 Misenus is designated by the oar. An alternative tradition made Misenus an attendant of Odysseus, comparable to the Baïos who was said to have given his name to Baiae: see Str. 1. 2. 18 (C26), 5. 4. 6 (C245). See further van Dam on *Silv.* 2. 2. 77, Beloch (1890), 190–202.

propiore sinu: the section of the Bay of Naples lying to the east of Punte di Miseno; the gulf is 'nearer', because it is closer to Neapolis than is Surrentum, which lies on the other side of the bay.

168. Ausonii pridem laris hospita Cyme: Str. 5. 4. 4 (C243)
claims that Cyme was the earliest Greek colony on the Italian main-
land, though Liv. 8. 22. 5–6 alleges that earlier settlement had taken
place on Pithecoussae (Ischia) before the move to the mainland; see
also Vell. 1. 4. 1, Ridgway (1992), 32–4. According to Strabo, a
composite force of Cymaeans and Chalcidians was led by Hippocles
of Cyme and Megasthenes of Chalcis. Frederiksen (1984), 59–60
argues that the Cyme was Euboean Cyme (as opposed to Aeolian
Cyme on the Anatolian coast); see further Sackett *et al.* (1966), Ridg-
way (1992), 32–3. Strabo mentions an agreement that one party
would lead the colony while the other would name it Cyme.

Archaeological evidence would seem to confirm that Pithecoussae
was the first Greek colony in Italy, founded by Euboeans from
Chalcis and Eretria. Pottery finds suggest settlement on Pithecoussae
(as opposed to trade) from about 775 BC; see Frederiksen (1984), 54
and n. 3, and cf. Ridgway (1992), 40–1 who points out the uncertain-
ties of the chronology of Pithecoussae, but notes that the main sites
were all 'operational' by 750 BC. As for Cumae, Ridgway (1992), 118–
19 notes that the earliest Protocorinthian finds from Cumae, aryballoi
and deep kotylai, are dated to 725 BC at the earliest.

Vollmer and Iz.–Fr. explain *Ausonii laris* as a reference to Apollo,
whose temple was at Cumae (Coleman on *Silv.* 4. 3. 115; there was also
a tradition that a dove sent by Apollo had directed the foundation of
Parthenope (Naples): see Vell. 1. 4. 1, *Silv.* 3. 5. 79–80, 4. 8. 48, *Laus Pis.*
91–2, Frederiksen (1984), 75 and n. 139). Slater translates 'Cyme that
welcomed long ago the Ausonian Lar', asserting (197 n. 2) that the
Ausonian Lar is Aeneas.

There are objections to both these interpretations. Firstly, *pridem*
suggests a state of affairs that has changed. Cyme is no longer a *hospita
Ausonii laris.* Furthermore, Apollo cannot be the *Ausonius lar* to whom
ancient Cyme would have been a stranger, since he is a Greek
divinity; it is moreover undesirable to anticipate the references to
the Sibyl and Apollo in the simile at 172–5. Mozley's translation
'Cyme, once a stranger to her Ausonian home' (cf. Mart. 1. 76. 2
'Flacce, Antenorei spes et alumne laris'), usefully conveys the correct
sense of Cyme having once been a Greek city, which then became a
part of Italy. The Greek name *Cyme*, rather than Latin *Cumae*, points
to this distinction; compare the treatment of Velia ('Latiis adscita
colonis | Graia refert Hyele') in 126–7, where the Greek name is used

instead of the Roman one. *Cyme* appears at *Silvae* 4. 3. 65, *Cumae* at 4.
3. 115 (see Coleman for other instances of the Greek form in Latin).

169–70. Dicarchei portus Baianaque mittunt | litora: in
Statius this metrical shortening of the adjective *Dicaearcheus* also occurs
at *Silv.* 2. 2. 3, 2. 2. 110, 2. 2. 135 and 3. 2. 22; the three consecutive short
syllables of Puteoli (whose Greek name was Δικαιάρχεια as indicated
at Plin. *Nat.* 3. 61 'Puteoli colonia, Dicaearchea dicti') cannot appear in
the hexameter.

The beaches (*litora*) of Baiae are also mentioned at *Silv.* 3. 2. 17 and
3. 5. 96 (see next note); cf. Prop. 1. 11. 2 'Herculeis ... litoribus', Ov. *Ars*
1. 255 'quid referam Baias praetextaque litora Bais' and Mart. 11. 80. 1
'litus beatae Veneris aureum Baias'. With Puteoli too, a particular
feature, the harbour, is singled out; cf. Sil. 8. 532–3 'naualibus acta |
prole Dicarchea', also in a catalogue. Str. 5. 4. 6 (C245) emphasizes the
city's importance in maritime trade: Ἡ δὲ πόλις ἐμπόριον γεγένηται
μέγιστον, χειροποιήτους ἔχουσα ὅρμους διὰ τὴν εὐφυΐαν τῆς ἄμμου·
σύμμετρος γάρ ἐστι τῇ τιτάνῳ καὶ κόλλησιν ἰσχυρὰν καὶ πῆξιν
λαμβάνει. See further N. Purcell in Frederiksen (1984), 319–49.

170–1. As well as beaches and luxury (see D'Arms (1970), 42–3,
119–20), Baiae was also noted for hot springs (Ov. *Ars* 1. 256, *Met.* 15.
713, Plin. *Nat.* 31. 4–5). The baths at Baiae employed such thermal
phenomena for heating water: see D'Arms 139–40 with nn. 109 and
111. Statius has briefer references to the waters at *Silv.* 3. 2. 17–18 'feta
tepentibus undis | litora', 3. 5. 96 'uaporiferas, blandissima litora,
Baias' (see Laguna), and 4. 3. 25–6 'aestuantes | ... Baias'.

permissus (M), 'given free rein', can be retained: *mediis alte
permissus anhelat | ignis aquis* could refer to thermal activity in the sea
(cf. Plin. *Nat.* 31. 5 'uaporant et in mari ipso quae Licinii Crassi fuere,
mediosque inter fluctus existit aliquid ualetudini salutare') or to
springs at the water's edge. Some baths appear to have used both
fresh and salt water; D'Arms, ibid. notes that the *thermae* of M.
Licinius Crassus Frugi (*cos.* AD 64) used both *aqua marina* and *aqua
dulcis* (*CIL* x. 1063, Pompeii). The early emendation *permixtus* (ς) adds
nothing, since *mediis* ... | *ignis aquis* already points to the miraculous
combination of heat and water (cf. Ov. *Ars* 1. 256 'et quae de calido
sulphure fumat aqua').

et operta domos incendia seruant is more difficult. Håkanson
(1969), 150–1 argues that the reference is to *naturales sudationes*, which
were found *above* Baiae in the *murteta* (Cels. 2. 17. 1, 3. 21. 6; see also Hor.
Ep. 1. 15. 5). If *mediis* ... | *ignis aquis* denotes activity at the surface

(since it would not otherwise be visible and miraculous), then *operta incendia* must be something different. Håkanson explains *operta* as an allusion to the covered buildings for heat treatments (Cels. 2. 17. 1: 'quarundam naturalium sudationum, ubi e terra profusus calidus uapor aedificio includitur'), but it is hard to see how these buildings constitute the *domos* of the *incendia*. More promising is Professor Hill's suggestion, that each clause refers to a separate aspect of the whole phenomenon. The first clause would then describe the effect of steam at the surface, resulting from the intermittent activity below (*alte permissus*); when the fires are dormant, they are *operta* and stay in their 'homes' below the ground.

172–5. By comparing his father's pupils to those who consult the Sibyl at Cumae, Statius also compares his father to the Sibyl; both have been favoured by Apollo. Less directly, the simile also confers some of the Sibyl's authority on Statius' father (compare the Sibyl's validation of Domitian's road at *Silv.* 4. 3. 124–63), so that he is described as educating future leaders (*proceres futuros*, 176) in an almost prophetic manner. Statius' topography is Virgilian, including *scopulos* (cf. the *arces* of *A.* 6. 9), the cave of the Sibyl (*A.* 6. 11, 42, 77, 157; cf. *Silv.* 4. 3. 117), and *opaca* (cf. *A.* 6. 10 'secreta Sibyllae', 13 'Triuiae lucos', and the tree with the golden bough, called *opaca* at 136). *opaca* also hints at the obscurity and mystery of the Sibyl (e.g. *A.* 6. 100 'obscuris uera inuoluens').

174. canebat points to poetry, common to the elder Statius and the Sibyl; *cano* denoting mantic utterance occurs in Virgil (e.g. *A.* 6. 99). Compare *carmen* at 182, and see Pease on Cic. *Div.* 2. 111.

175. decepto ... Phoebo: the Sibyl obtained a long span of years from the amorous god, whom she then cheated of his desire (Ov. *Met.* 14. 130–44, but contrast Serv. *A.* 6. 321, on the god's *pius amor* and the Sibyl's eventual demise); cf. *Silv.* 4. 3. 152 'et quantos ego Delium poposci', in the speech of the Sibyl.

uates non inrita: the litotes (see further 5. 2. 164 n.) here points to another prophetess, Cassandra, who was also pursued by Apollo and spurned his advances. Unlike Cassandra (Virg. *A.* 2. 247, Prop. 3. 13. 66 'experta est ueros irrita lingua deos'), the Sibyl did not lose her credibility. On the cult of the Sibyl, see Frederiksen (1984), 75–6.

176–7. In view of the reference to the civil wars in 195–8, Statius' father's move to Rome would have taken place before AD 69–70. Vollmer, arguing that his Roman pupils came to him rather than vice versa, ignores his own remarks at l. 162 n. on the difficulties of sending a son to be educated elsewhere (though one might note Plin. *Ep.* 4. 13. 3 where Pliny narrates a conversation with a *praetextatus* in Comum who had to be educated in Milan owing to a lack of teachers). But if pupils had really come from Rome to Naples to be taught by Statius' father, this fact would have been more clearly acknowledged. Compare the move to Rome made by the *grammaticus* Orbilius Pupillus after spending the first fifty years of his life in Beneventum (Suet. *Gramm.* 9. 2). Not everyone believed that Rome provided a better education than was available in the provinces: Suet. *Gramm.* 24. 2 claims that it was easier for M. Valerius Probus to study the *antiqui* from a *grammatista* in Syria, 'durante adhuc ibi antiquorum memoria necdum omnino abolita sicut Romae'. See Kaster ad loc. for a full discussion of the problems of this vexed passage, and the suggestion that Suetonius may have been exaggerating.

Romuleam stirpem proceresque futuros: the second phrase complements the first. Statius' father instructs the next generation of leaders, but their future is all part of one Roman design originating with Romulus, a message emphasized in 177, where Statius points out that his father's pupils will follow in their fathers' footsteps (for *uestigia*, cf. *Silv.* 5. 2. 126 n. and the exemplary role of Bolanus in the same poem). Cancik (1973), 183 suggests that Statius' Greek pupils learnt literature and that those in Rome learnt 'Kult, Sakralrecht und Divination' (for interesting speculation on his methods in religious education, see Cancik (1973), 189–90), but it need not be assumed that Statius' father did not teach Greek literature in Rome as well. As McNelis (2002) has shown, Greek literary studies did go on in Rome, and the poet's silence about them here may simply be the result of a desire not to repeat earlier material about the syllabus. Nauta (2002), 200–1 unconvincingly suggests that this section of Statius' poem refers not to religious instruction, but to Statius' father's teaching Latin poetry in Rome.

perstas: For *persto* with the infinitive denoting continuous persistence in a particular action, cf. *Silv.* 2. 3. 73–4 'Iliacos aequare senes et uincere persta | quos pater Elysio, genetrix quos detulit annos', *OLD* s.v. *persto* 3.

178–80. Curcio (1893), 8–9, citing this passage, argued that Statius' father gave instruction to Domitian in religious matters. Only the Vestals and the *pontifices* could see the ἱερὰ ἀπόρρητα (D.H. 2. 66. 3), which included the flame (178) and the Palladium (179). Curcio's case is confirmed by *Silv.* 1. 1. 32–6, where Statius imagines the emperor wondering whether the flame is burning, or whether Vesta is satisified with the Vestals; A. Hardie (1983), 11–12 with nn. 68 and 70 argues that *explorator* refers to Domitian's involvement as Pontifex Maximus in the investigation into the alleged incest of the Vestal Cornelia, treating *explorator* (178) as an echo of *exploratas . . . ministras* (1. 1. 36); cf. Coleman (1986), 3092–3, Geyssen (1996), 90–1.

Though the reference to Domitian is understated in these lines, Iz.–Fr. and Cancik (1973), 184 are wrong to question this hypothesis. One would not expect Statius to emphasize that the emperor was his father's pupil, implying a subordinate position. Equally, no reference to the emperor might be construed as a slight. Statius thus delicately alludes to the religious duties of the Pontifex Maximus, assigning to Domitian the first place in the list of pupils. Further arguments in support of the imperial identification are the shift from singular *puer* to the subsequent plurals designating religious groups (the Salii and Luperci), and the hint implied by 'creuit et inde sacrum didicit puer' (180), which, as well as denoting the acquisition of sacred knowledge, might suggest that Domitian began his instruction with the elder Statius while still a private citizen (he was born in AD 51), before continuing during his father's reign, when he would have learnt about matter that was *sacrum* as a son of the emperor.

178. facis ... opertae: the 'concealed torch' is the sacred fire (cf. 'Troicus ignis', *Silv.* 1. 1. 35) kept burning in the temple of Vesta.

179. penetralia, usually the innermost parts of a building, can figuratively denote the inner recesses of something (e.g. *Silv.* 3. 5. 56 'animi penetralibus imis', *Theb.* 9. 346 'atque animae tota in penetralia sedit'). Here *penetralia* is a metaphor for 'secret knowledge'; cf. Quint. *Inst.* 6. 2. 25 'sed promere in animo est quae latent et penitus ipsa huius loci aperire penetralia', Tac. *Dial.* 12. 2 'haec eloquentiae primordia, haec penetralia'. Uncertainty as to its origins may have been another 'secret' of the Palladium (see below).

The context also suggests a further, sacred meaning, since the Palladium would have been kept in the *penetralia* of the temple of Vesta (cf. Liv. 26. 27. 14 'Vestae aedem petitam et aeternos ignes et conditum in penetrali fatale pignus imperii Romani'). *penetralia* may even humorously point to the 'secret' reference to Domitian in these lines; if Statius' father had given instruction to Domitian on the Palladium, perhaps giving a solution to the arguments over authenticity, a reference to this esoteric tuition could be a private allusion between poet and emperor.

On the legend of the Palladium, a small image of Pallas Athena said to provide protection for the place where it was kept (and hence first stolen from Troy by Odysseus and Diomedes prior to the fall of the city in the Trojan War, as reported the *Ilias parua* ascribed to Lesches, *Ilias parua, argum.* 1. 17–18, 2. 1–2 Bernabé), see Frazer on Apollod. 3. 12. 3, *Epit.* 5. 13, Austin on Virg. *A.* 2. 163, and Ogilvie on Liv. 5. 52. 7, who discuss the ancient debate over the identity of the Palladium which was in Rome; see also Girard (1981a), 224–6, Dubourdieu (1989), 460–7. A particular concern was the origin of the Roman Palladium: if it had been stolen by the Greeks, whence had the Romans obtained the authentic version? Such anxiety over the status of the object was unsurprising, for several cities alleged ownership of the real Palladium: in Greece, Sparta claimed to have the genuine article, while Argos continued to display the Palladium on its coinage even into imperial times, and there were also rival claims in Italian cities such as Herakleia (near Thurii), Luceria and Lavinium: see Erskine (2001), 117, 140–4. Ov. *Fast.* 6. 433–6 remarks on the uncertainty of the subject:

> seu genus Adrasti, seu furtis aptus Vlixes,
> seu pius Aeneas eripuisset eam,
> auctor in incerto, res est Romana: tuetur
> Vesta, quod assiduo lumine cuncta uidet.

Austin documents a variety of ancient explanations, including the possibility that there were two Palladia or that there may have been a fake copy made which was stolen (D.H. 1. 69. 2–3; cf. 2. 66. 5, Serv. *A.* 2. 166), and a story that it was found at Troy by Fimbria in 85 BC (Serv. *A.* 2. 166; cf. App. *Mith.* 53, Erskine (2001), 237–45); this last story, however, contradicts the account of the Palladium's being saved from the burning temple of Vesta in 241 BC by L. Caecilius Metellus (see e.g. Cic. *Scaur.* 48, Ov. *Fast.* 6. 437–54, D.H. 2. 66. 4). Contemporary antiquarian interest in the Palladium is reflected at Sil. 13. 51–78 where Hannibal is told how Diomedes gave it back to Aeneas at Lavinium.

The Palladium appears to have been important in Flavian iconography, not only under Domitian, who made so much of his associations with Minerva, but even before Domitian's accession: for its appearance on coins, see e.g. *BMCRE* II, Vespasian no. 586 (Vespasian receives a Palladium from Victory), Titus nos. 200 (Vesta is shown holding a Palladium), 237 (a coin in honour of Domitian's consulship in AD 80 showing Vesta holding a Palladium), Domitian nos. 265 (Domitian himself holds a Palladium); see further Scott (1936), 178, 184–8, Geyssen (1996), 47, 51.

180–1. arma probandis | monstrasti Saliis: the *arma* are the *ancilia* which fell from heaven (Liv. 1. 20. 4, Ov. *Fast.* 3. 259–60); on the Salii, see further 5. 2. 130, 131 nn. M's *probatur* cannot be accepted. Baehrens's *probatis* is similar to *certis*, applied to the augurs in the next line. But the Salii can hardly be described as tested if they are still under instruction. The augurs are a different case; *certis* is proleptic, and is in any case an appropriate word for those engaged in divination.

probator (Ellis) only occurs once in poetry (Ov. *Pont.* 2. 2. 104), where it means 'one who praises'. Even the alternative sense of 'an examiner' (*OLD.* s.v. b) would leave it unclear whether the Salii or the *ancilia* are being put to the test. *probata* (Wolfgang Meyer) would mean that Statius' father taught the Salii how to recognize the genuine shield (see Ov. *Fast.* 3. 379–82 for Mamurius' construction of identical copies on the orders of Numa). This, however, is highly unlikely (the point of the copies is to prevent recognition); it is very doubtful that the identity of the true shield was known in the first century AD. Predicative *probanda* ('for testing') would not imply that Statius' father could discern the original shield, but the rarity of lines ending with two words in grammatical concord with the same termination (see 5. 2. 109 n.) inspires caution. More attractive is Jonathan Powell's *probandis*, referring to the Salians being tested in their studies. The lore of the Salii was particularly esoteric; the Salian songs were scarcely understood even by those who sang them (Quint. *Inst.* 1. 6. 40; cf. Cirilli (1913), 102–14); compare Ovid's request for someone to explain not only the *ancilia* but also the appearance of Mamurius' name in the Salian songs at *Fast.* 3. 259–60.

Statius' father's expertise in the lore of the Salii can be paralleled elsewhere: Macrob. *Sat.* 3. 12. 7 notes a commentary on the rites of the Salii of Tibur by one Octavius Herennius, while Quint. *Inst.* 1. 6. 40 famously described the archaic songs of the Salii as 'uix sacerdotibus suis satis intellecta'. For ancient study of Salian ritual, see further Cirilli (1913), 60–1.

181–4. The structure of these lines is difficult, although, from a purely grammatical point of view, there is no objection to *monstro* having a dependent indirect question in 183. Similarly 'cui Chalcidicum fas uoluere carmen' can be construed as 'monstrasti ei, cui

Chalcidicum fas uoluere carmen'. However the transition to *Phrygii...flaminis* in 183 is abrupt, even if it refers to the cult of Cybele (see below; the earlier *decemuiri* were involved in its arrival in Italy, Liv. 29. 10. 6), since one would expect a reference to Statius' father teaching the *quindecimuiri* about consultation of the Sybilline books, especially as he was an expert in poetry, and from the bay of Naples. Accordingly, I suggest the presence of a lacuna after 182. Schwartz's suggestion that it be placed after *auguribus* or *flaminis* does not help, since the abruptness of the *quindecimuiri* being taught about *Phrygii... coma flaminis* remains. Similarly Saenger's lacuna after *cur* is no solution, since, on the analogy of the Salians and the augurs, one would expect to hear of practical instruction, with Statius' father teaching *how* the duties were to be accomplished. *cur* is moreover essential for 'Phrygii lateat coma flaminis'.

After mentioning instruction in oracles, the lacuna might have then moved on to specific points of knowledge, such as the 'Phrygii...coma flaminis'. Cf. Cat. 66.1 1–6 for examples of the astronomer Conon's learning, expressed as indirect questions with *ut*. The *quindecimuiri* organized Domitian's Secular Games of 88 AD. Notable contemporaries in the college included Tacitus (*Ann.* 11. 11. 1) and Statius' friend Arruntius Stella (*Silv.* 1. 2. 177); see further Syme (1958), 65–6, 664, A. Hardie (1983), 45.

181. praesagumque aethera: one of the augural duties was the observation of lightning; see further Cic. *Leg.* 2. 21, Linderski (1986).

181–2. certis | auguribus: *certi* (Vollmer) is unnecessary. With *certis*, the augurs are certain to succeed as augurs, and indeed will have reliable knowledge as a result of their art. For *certus* applied to those who are expected to hold office (typically candidates for election) see *ThLL* iii 918. 21–7. *certis* could also allude to the custom that augurs held office for life (Plu. *Quaest. Rom.* 99=*Mor.* 287 D–287 E).

182. Chalcidicum...carmen: the Sibylline books are so called because they originate from Cumae, itself a colony of Euboean Chalcis (168 n.). The Sibylline books were consulted by the *quindecimuiri sacris faciundis* who visited the *sacrarium* in times of public need (Gel. 1. 19. 10–11); see further Boyancé (1964). A shortened form of this title appears at *Silv.* 4. 3. 142 (see Coleman's n.).

uoluere, denoting the unrolling of a book-roll, vividly portrays consultation of the Sibylline books.

183. Phrygii lateat coma flaminis: *Phrygius* might simply denote 'Roman' here, suggesting a Trojan origin for the covering of the hair: Serv. *A.* 2. 683 ascribes the institution of the *apex* to Ascanius at Alba Longa. Although prescriptions for covering of the head with the *apex* are usually associated with the *Flamen Dialis* (e.g. Gel. 10. 15. 16–18, Ov. *Fast.* 3. 397), all *flamines* were required to have their heads covered (Serv. *A.* 8. 664).

However, Cancik (1973), 186 considers the possibility that *Phrygii...flaminis* may refer to priests of Cybele; for the juxtaposition with the *XVuiri*, he compares the religious activities of Arruntius Stella at *Silv.* 1. 2. 176–7 'certe iam nunc Cybeleia mouit | limina et Euboicae carmen legit ille Sibyllae'. But he also notes the lack of evidence for the use of the title *flamen* in the cult of Cybele. If *Phrygii* were to be a specific reference to Cybele, there would then be a case for adopting Postgate's emendation of M's *lateat* to *pateat*, since, as pointed out by Cancik (1973), 186–7, uncovered, loose hair is a characteristic of the cult of Cybele.

183–4. Statius concludes the section with a joke, imagining the Luperci fearing his father's blows. The Luperci struck with goatskin all persons whom they met during the Lupercalia (Plu. *Quaest. Rom.* 68 = *Mor.* 280 B, *Romulus* 21. 7), especially women, in the belief that fertility was enhanced (Ov. *Fast.* 2. 441–6).

succincti, 'girt-up' and thus wearing clothes, adds to the humour; the Luperci ran naked at the Lupercalia (Virg. *A.* 8. 663 'nudosque Lupercos', Ov. *Fast.* 2. 267–380); here, when they are themselves struck, their garments are comically gathered together so that they can receive their punishment. Statius' father's pupils may have included the two youths who customarily participated in the Lupercalia (Plu. *Rom.* 21. 6). Compare the mock-grandiloquent tone of Mart. 10. 62. 10 'ferulae tristes, sceptra paedagogorum' and Horace's 'plagosum... | Orbilium' (*Ep.* 2. 1. 70–1). For the same paradox of one accustomed to use violence submitting to the blows of an instructor compare Ov. *Ars* 1. 11–16 (Chiron and Achilles).

185–90. As with modern institutions, the success of an education is sometimes measured by the subsequent fame of the recipients, or their ability to obtain positions of power and influence thereafter. Cf. Suetonius' accounts of pupils of various teachers at *Gramm.* 7. 2 (Antonius Gnipho) 'scholam eius claros quoque uiros frequentasse aiunt, in his M. Ciceronem, etiam cum praetura fungeretur', 10. 3 (Ateius Philologus), 13. 1 (L. Staberius Eros), 18. 3 (L. Crassicius), 27. 1

(Otalicius Pitholaus), 28. 1 (Epidius). For the value of Greek culture among Roman elites, see McNelis (2002), 87–91.

185. et nunc: the benefits of Statius' father's tuition are now evident as his pupils rise to the fore.

forsan indicates that the geographical locations do not refer to specific posts held by the elder Statius' pupils; note also the plurals in 188–9. Compare the list of possible postings for Crispinus at *Silv.* 5. 2. 132–42. Nevertheless, the general concentration on locations in the east may indicate that a significant number of pupils went there. In the earlier list, South Italian cities sent their sons to the elder Statius; his pupils are now administering the empire.

grege, a flock or herd, is a natural metaphor for pupils; the image is humorously continued in the next line where one pupil restrains (*compescit*) the Iberians. For *compesco* denoting the enclosure of animals cf. Paul. Fest. p. 35. 10 Lindsay 'conpescere est uelut in eodem pascuo continere', 63. 25–6, *ThLL* iii. 2061. 48–56; at V.Fl. 1. 338 'non leuiore Pholum manus haec compescuit auro', Aeson uses the word in referring to his defeat of the Centaur Pholus.

186. Hiberas: it is not immediately clear whether these are the Iberians of Spain (cf. *Silv.* 3. 3. 89 'quicquid ab auriferis eiectat Hiberia fossis', where mention of gold mining probably refers to Spain, 4. 6. 102 'pecoris possessor Hiberi', which seems to refer, as Coleman notes, to Geryon, Hercules' adversary in Spain), or the Iberians of Georgia in the Caucasus (cf. the μονὴ τῶν Ἰβήρων (Iviron) founded by Georgians on Mount Athos and the survival of the word *Virk′*, 'Georgians' in Armenian; it is the name of an ethnic Armenian political party in Georgia today). A reference to Spain might go well here as a contrast to the unspecific *Eois*, referring to eastern peoples, but the ensuing emphasis on particular eastern locations may indicate that *Hiberas* is a reference to the Transcaucasian Iberians. Inevitably, the temptation to connect the Iberians of Spain with the eastern Iberians proved inviting in antiquity: thus Str. 1. 3. 21 (C61) refers to a migration from the west to the Black Sea, while App. *Mith.* 101 remarks that there were divergent opinions on the direction of migration, and indeed a view as well that the nomenclature was simply a matter of coincidentally sharing the same name (cf. Str. 11. 2. 19 (C499) who refers to the fact that both Iberias had gold mines); see further Braund (1994), 20–1. Prisc. *GL* ii. 233. 19–234. 7 offers a discussion of the correct form of the name of the Iberians, and remarks as follows: 'nam proprie "Hiberes" sunt gens ab Hiberis

profecta, qui ultra Armeniam habitant, quorum singularis nomina-
tiuus "hic Hiber huius Hiberis" facit, et apud Graecos Ἴβηρ
Ἴβηρος. nam alterum Ἴβηρος Ἰβήρου dicunt.' Priscian's point might,
however, indicate not so much the existence of a firm rule in the
nomenclature of the two nations, as a hopeful attempt to impose
order on chaos, for there are even instances where the same authors
seems to use the two forms indiscriminately: thus compare Mela 3. 41
'perque Hiberas et Hyrcanis' with Mela 1. 13 'Hiberi, Hyrcani', and
V.Fl. 5. 166 'Armeniae praetentus Hiber' with 7. 235 'cui uadis
Hibero', all instances referring to the eastern Iberians, and note too
Horace's use of the noun *Hiberia* to refer to Spain at *Carm.* 4. 5. 28 and
to the eastern Iberia at *Epod.* 5. 21.

187. Achaemenium (suggesting wealth and luxury at Hor. *Epod.*
13. 8, and *Carm.* 3. 1. 44) contributes to the exotic sound of the line,
which ends with a Greek place name and the Greek accusative *Persen*.

Zeugmate: the town of Zeugma, comprising the two Seleucid
foundations of Seleucia and Apamea on the western and eastern
banks of the Euphrates (cf. Greek ζεῦγμα, a bridge), could symbolize
the boundary between Roman and Parthian power, as at Luc. 8. 235–
7; the name Zeugma would gradually supersede those of its constitu-
ent towns, though forms such as *Seleucia Zeugma* appear in inscriptions
at least until the end of the second century AD (Wagner (1976), 65–70).
It was the easiest crossing (Tac. *Ann.* 12. 12. 2; see also Plin. *Nat.* 5. 86,
Flor. *Epit.* 1. 46. 3–4); D. Kennedy (1998), 139–62 catalogues ancient
sources relating to Zeugma. In Statius' time, Zeugma was garrisoned
by the *legio IIII Scythica*; see Speidel (1998), especially 166–70. Vollmer
notes the oxymoronic effect arising from *secludit*, denoting separation,
and *Zeugmate*, related to the Greek word for a yoke. For recent
archaeological discoveries, see *Zeugma: Interim Reports* (2003).

188–90. hi . . . hi . . . illi . . . tu laudis origo: with this se-
quence the passage concludes effectively. The various achievements
of his father's pupils are all attributable to him.

189. fora . . . emendant: 'they correct the courts', with *fora*
representing those to whom justice is administered in court.

pacificis . . . fascibus: probably those of a praetor, the magis-
trate responsible for jurisdiction. The epithet first appears at Cic. *Att.*
8. 12. 4, after which it occurs at Ov. *Fast.* 4. 408, and twice each in
Luc. (3. 305, 7. 64 'pacificas saeuus tremuit Catilina secures'), Mart.
(8. 66. 11 and 12. 62. 8) and Statius (here and *Theb.* 12. 683), before
appearing more frequently in Christian Latin (*ThLL* x / 1. 14. 40–2 s.v.

pacificus). In Britain, the word was applied to King Edgar of England and to King James VI and I.

191–4. Statius concludes his account of his father's teaching with a series of mythological examples who could not match him. Just as the elder Statius was equal to such celebrated poets as Homer and Hesiod (26), so too is he compared with the instructors of mythology.

191. fingere: for *fingo* denoting the moulding of character, see *ThLL* vi/1. 773. 25–78.

192. Nestor: there is no need to reject M's reading in favour of *Mentor* (Saenger), the friend of Odysseus (*Od.* 2. 225, 22. 208–9), particularly since Homer's Nestor is often giving advice, not only to his fellow Achaeans in the *Iliad*, but also to the young Telemachus in the *Odyssey* (*Od.* 3. 254–328).

Phoenix: cf. *Silv.* 5. 2. 150–1 and n.

moderator: here contrasted with *indomiti... alumni*. For the word cf. Vell. 2. 102. 1: '... M. Lollii, quem ueluti moderatorem iuuentae filii sui Augustus esse uoluerat...'.

193. tubas acres lituosque: the trumpet is typically harsh-sounding (e.g. Enn. *Ann.* 451 Skutsch 'at tuba terribili sonitu taratan-tara dixit', 544 'inde loci lituus sonitus effudit acutos'), and can be a metonymy for epic, as at Prop. 3. 3. 41–2 'nil tibi sit rauco praeconia classica cornu | flare, nec Aonium tingere Marte nemus', Mart. 8. 3. 22 'dum tua multorum uincat auena tubas'.

194. frangebat: cf. Sil. 11. 481–2 'sic tunc Pierius bellis durata uirorum | pectora Castalio frangebat carmine Teuthras'; for *frango* applied to the process of breaking a person's spirits or emotions, see *OLD* s.v. *frango* 11 and 12.

Chiron: for Achilles' education from the centaur Chiron in the *Achilleid*, see Fantham (1999), 59–66. Achilles is a reluctant pupil of Chiron at Ov. *Ars* 1. 11–16, and at Stat. *Ach.* 1. 147–55, where the Centaur tells Thetis how he can no longer curb Achilles' bellicose excesses. Instead of describing Achilles learning to play the lyre, here Statius suggests that Achilles would have preferred to hear the warlike trumpet; cf. Sen. *Tro.* 832–5 for the effect of Chiron's songs of war on Achilles, and V.Fl. 1. 268–9 'te paruus lituos et bella loquentem | miretur', addressed by Peleus to Chiron. Chiron's song however in the present passage is not about war (*alio carmine*; contrast the rather different *Theb.* 1. 45 'atque alio Capaneus horrore canendus'). Achilles' subsequent taste for epic song is attested at *Il.* 9. 189 τῇ ὅ γε θυμὸν ἔτερπεν, ἄειδε δ' ἄρα κλέα ἀνδρῶν.

195. talia dum celebras: the shift in chronology back to the civil wars of AD 69 is effective; after describing the good government which his father has helped to foster, Statius recalls an earlier time of confusion and discord.

ciuilis Erinys: this almost paradoxical phrase also occurs at Luc. 4. 187; cf. 'tristis Erinys', used by Aeneas at Virg. *A.* 2. 337, V.Fl. 4. 617 'fraterna . . . Erinys' (and note Mart. 6. 32. 1 'ciuilis Enyo', with Grewing's n.). The Erinyes are commonly associated with kindred strife (or civil war in Latin literature): Hes. *Th.* 185 has them originating from the castration of Uranus by his son, and see also e.g. *Il.* 9. 571–2, 21. 412–13, *Od.* 11. 280, Sommerstein (1989), 6–13. Note too how the *Thebaid* opens (1. 56–87) with Oedipus' request to Tisiphone to stir up war between his sons (cf. the Fury who features in the prologue to Seneca's *Thyestes*, 1–121).

196–8. facem: Tisiphone carries a funeral torch at *Theb.* 1. 112–13; compare Allecto's torch thrown at Turnus (Virg. *A.* 7. 456); cf. 278–9 below. Here the torch anticipates the fire on the Capitoline in the next line, a fire which destroyed the temple of Jupiter Optimus Maximus; see Darwall-Smith (1996), 41–7. After Vespasian's replacement temple was subsequently burnt down in AD 80, during the reign of Titus, Domitian built another: see *Silv.* 4. 3. 16 'qui reddit Capitolio Tonantem', Mart. 6. 10. 2, Darwall-Smith (1996), 96–7, 105–10.

Phlegraeaque . . . proelia: in the closing stages of Vitellius' reign, after his attempted abdication, Vitellius besieged Vespasian's brother Sabinus and the young Domitian on the Capitoline (Tac. *Hist.* 3. 69–75), which fell on 19 December 69. Although Sabinus was captured and killed, Domitian escaped in disguise (*Hist.* 3. 74. 1, Suet. *Dom.* 1. 2). The conflict is here represented in epic terms as a gigantomachy (appropriate for a fight over the Capitoline, the home of Jove); compare 'bella Iouis' *Silv.* 1. 1. 79, *Theb.* 1. 22 and see also Mart. 9. 101. 13–14, and *Silv.* 4. 2. 56 (with Coleman's n. on artistic representations of military campaigns as gigantomachy). Luc. 7. 144–50 compares the preparations at Pharsalus to those which occurred before the battle of gods and giants; see also N.–H. on Hor. *Carm.* 2. 12. 7, Lovatt (2005), 114–18.

In fact Domitian's involvement in the siege was less distinguished; Suetonius records that he took refuge with the votaries of Isis, and, although the result of the war was not affected, the battle was certainly not a victory. J. *BJ* 4. 649 describes the escape of Domitian and others as δαιμονιώτερον. Statius is vague on the subject of

Domitian's participation, while Sil. 3. 609–11 alludes to the incident more directly, though even here the tone is still panegyrical:

> nec te terruerint Tarpei culminis ignes,
> sacrilegas inter flammas seruabere terris;
> nam te longa manent nostri consortia mundi.

sacrilegis: both Silius and Statius apply this epithet to the flames which burnt the temple of Jove (cf. Tac. *Hist.* 3. 72. 1 'id facinus post conditam urbem luctuosissimum foedissimumque rei publicae populi Romani accidit'); compare its appearance in a description of Hannibal's burning of Saguntum (*Silv.* 4. 6. 82), and at Mart. 9. 84. 1, 'sacrilegos...furores', with reference to Saturninus' revolt. As well as being an obvious epithet for flames which damaged a temple, *sacrilegis* also assigns responsibility to the Vitellians, an issue which was in doubt (Tac. *Hist.* 3. 71. 4): 'hic ambigitur, ignem tectis oppugnatores iniecerint, an obsessi, quae crebrior fama, dum nitentis ac progressos depellunt.' A panegyrical treatment naturally excises such uncertainties.

Domitian himself may have written a poem on the Capitoline war, though the evidence (Mart. 5. 5. 7–8) is ambiguous, since the poet may be the librarian Sextus. See Coleman (1986), 3089–90, Nauta (2002), 327 n. 2.

Senonum: the Roman Vitellians attacking the Capitol ('Latiae...cohortes') were like the Gauls who besieged the Capitol under Brennus, in 387/6 BC;[24] for the emotive resonance of the Gallic sack for later generations of Romans, see J. H. C. Williams (2001), 140–84. Tac. *Hist.* 3. 72. 1 notes that the temple of Jupiter Optimus Maximus, which was not captured by Lars Porsenna or the Gauls, was destroyed by Romans, 'furore principum excindi'.

199. necdum: normally consolation offered while the pyre was still aflame would be too early (*Silv.* 5. 1. 16 n.). But the elder Statius' haste to compose a poem on the burning of the Capitol demonstrates piety (202 *ore pio*), and energy: Statius' father is swifter than the flames themselves (201 *multum facibus uelocior ipsis*). Vollmer usefully suggests that Statius' father may have been inspired to imitate Lucan's lost work *De Incendio Vrbis* on the burning of Rome under Nero (*Silv.* 2. 7. 60–1); on this work, which may in fact have been in prose, see van Dam ad loc. and McGann (1975).

---

[24] On the discrepancy with the Varronian date of 390 BC, see Walbank on Plb. 1. 6. 1–2 and 2. 18. 6, Cornell (1995), 399–402.

rogus ille deorum: *rogus*, a funeral pyre, can metaphorically denote a large conflagration; see e.g. Man. 1. 745, Luc. 7. 814 (universal destruction by fire), Sil. 13. 319 (temple-burning).

deorum: the hyperbolical plural (since only one temple was destroyed), is answered (203–4) by 'ultorque deorum | Caesar'.

200. siderat: the fire sinks downwards into its own ashes; cf. Hor. *Carm.* 4. 13. 28 'dilapsam in cineres facem'.

202. captiua fulmina is the only hint at the Vitellian victory in the struggle for the Capitol (Tac. *Hist.* 3. 73).

203. mirantur: the reaction of leading Romans and the emperor is appropriate not only to the speed with which Statius' father composed his poem, but also to the mark of favour shown by Jupiter from the flames.

204. e medio . . . igni implies that the miracle occurred within the flames of the temple, although thunder in a clear sky is a frequent mark of Jupiter's goodwill (e.g. Ov. *Fast.* 3. 369).

adnuit: for *adnuo* in religious contexts, see *OLD* s.v. 3 and 6.

205. iamque: *iam* ('already') is puzzling, since it seems to draw attention to the *hysteron proteron* in these lines, with the *cum*-clause in 207–8 describing Jove's involvement in the eruption, which can only have preceded Statius' father's intention to compose a poem on the *Vesuuina incendia*. *cum* is thus best interpreted as explaining *damnis*: Statius' father was planning to write on the damage caused when Jupiter caused the eruption to take place. On the dating of the elder Statius' death, see the introduction above, pp. 262–6.

pio . . . cantu: whereas the elder Statius showed piety to the gods with his poem on the burnt temple of Jove, his piety here is towards his *patria* (206 *patriis . . . damnis*).

207. exemptum: the mountain is uprooted (see *OLD* s.v. *eximo* 1 for technical usages such as the extraction of plants from the soil and quarrying and mining). V.Fl. describes the mountain as 'broken off' (*prorupti*) in a simile (4. 507–9):

> sicut prorupti tonuit cum forte Veseui
> Hesperiae letalis apex, uixdum ignea montem
> torsit hiemps iamque eoas cinis induit urbes.

On the disputed effects of the eruption on Vesuvius itself, and the uncertain dating of the double cone known to modern times see Frederiksen (1984), 6–12.

sidera: a standard hyperbole for great height. In a volcanic context, cf. Virg. *A.* 3. 574 'attollitque globos flammarum et sidera lambit'.

209. me quoque: Statius at last mentions the benefits he himself derived from his father.

Boeotaque (Baehrens): the paradosis (*biota*) is uncertain; it may perhaps be read as *luoca*.[25] *Boeota* is thus possible (cf. Ov. *Am.* 1. 1. 15 'Heliconia tempe'), and could allude to Statius' 'Boeotian' work, the *Thebaid*, but is by no means certain.[26] Before Baehrens, the vulgate text was *lustrata* (*b*, Calderini, also found in the *recentior* Q).

210. pulsantem: as well as meaning 'striking the threshold', to gain entry (*Silv.* 5. 2. 20, Coleman on 4. 8. 62), *pulsantem* also recalls Statius' lyre-playing (2–3); cf. 1. 5. 1 'non Helicona graui pulsat chelys enthea plectro'. It suggests active efforts to win poetic initiation and a desire to seek out the company of the Muses. Contrast *Ach.* 1. 10, where Statius, already the poet of the *Thebaid*, is a well-known visitor: 'neque enim Aonium nemus aduena pulso'. Though the image of knocking in order to enter a grove may seem eccentric (perhaps compare Theoc. 3 where the komast is shut out from Amaryllis' cave only by fern, but behaves as if there were some more significant obstruction), the idea of beating at the doors of the Muses goes back to Pl. *Phaedr.* 245 A 5–6 ὃς δ' ἂν ἄνευ μανίας Μουσῶν ἐπὶ ποιητικὰς θύρας ἀφίκηται; cf. the translation of this thought at Sen. *Dial.* 9. 17. 10 'frustra poeticas fores compos sui pepulit' and note also Hor. *Ars.* 296–7 'excludit sanos Helicone poetas | Democritus'. Skutsch on Enn. *Ann.* 210 'nos ausi reserare' suggests that Ennius may also have used a metaphor of the Muses' doors, though the brevity of the fragment and Virgil's 'ingredior sanctos ausus recludere fontis' (*G.* 2. 175) makes certainty about the context impossible.

dixi: the omission of the subject of an accusative and infinitive construction in indirect speech after *dico* is rare, though found in all periods (*ThLL* v/1. 984. 42–80); see also H.–Sz. 362 §198. In Greek, it is possible to use a nominative and infinitive construction, the subject of the dependent infinitive usually being omitted, when the subjects of

---

[25] Usually M has no join between initial *b* and *i*; joins occur at 1. 2. 174, 1. 4. 53, 3. 1. 126, 3. 3. 122. 4. 9. 8, 5. 1. 89, and 5. 2. 12. The last example is perhaps closest in appearance to M here. Note that Politian A refers to *ant.* (a reference to the *liber Poggii*) as the source of the reading *luota.*

[26] For the corruption of proper names in M, compare e.g. 5. 1. 33, 5. 2. 138, 5. 3. 127, 5. 3. 153, 5. 3. 222; see also Courtney (1990), p. xxvi.

the two verbs are identical; see Krüger–Cooper i. 771–2 (§55.2.1), iii. 2499–2500 (§2.55.2.1); Statius' practice here may evoke the Greek construction.

211. deae: Statius' initiation by the Muses is like the welcoming of a stranger. On his reaching Helicon they ask who he is, the standard question addressed to strangers (e.g *Od.* 3. 69–74, Virg. *A.* 8. 112–14), and when Statius replies that he is his father's son, he is allowed access to Helicon. The Heliconian scene evokes other poetic initations such as the meeting of Hesiod and the Muses (*Th.* 22–34) and Gallus' encounter with the Muses and Linus (Virg. *Ecl.* 6. 64–73);[27] cf. Prop. 3. 1. 1–2 'Callimachi Manes et Coi sacra Philitae, | in uestrum, quaeso, me sinite ire nemus.' Note also Ennius' account of his descent from Homer, by means of the transmigration of souls (Enn. *Ann.* 9 Skutsch); Statius similarly credits his poetic facility to his father.

211–12. sidera... | aequoraque et terras: the components of the universe hyperbolically represent the existence which is owed to a parent. Contrast Cicero's explanation of the Roman punishment for parricide (*S. Rosc.* 71); the criminal is to be deprived of the elements from which all things derive their origin:

O singularem sapientiam, iudices! Nonne uidentur hunc hominem ex rerum natura sustulisse et eripuisse cui repente caelum, solem, aquam, terramque ademerint ut, qui eum necasset unde ipse natus esset, careret eis rebus omnibus ex quibus omnia nata esse dicuntur?

212. quae mos debere parenti: M's *quam uos* cannot be retained, even if *quam* is equivalent to *quantum*. Although the syntax is possible, the meaning is awkward in the light of *sed* in 213: 'It is not such a great thing for me to owe my life to my father, as it is to owe you [plural] to him, but you [the elder Statius] gave me the gift of poetry... '. The shift from singular *stirpe tua* (210) to plural *uos*, whomever *uos* refers to (the Muses have been mentioned, but not addressed), and then singular *dedisti* again is intolerable; there would furthermore be no need for the adversative *sed* (213), introducing poetry as a contrast, since poetry would already have been implied by *uos*. With *quae mos* (Krohn), Statius thanks his father for giving him *sidera...* | *aequoraque et terras*, which it is customary to owe to any parent, before mentioning his poetic skills, which were a special gift from this father.

---

[27] On a possible transposition of these lines, see Woodman (1997).

213. decus hoc quodcumque lyrae: the concessive *quodcumque* gives an air of conventional modesty, though *decus* suggests self-confidence; compare the lofty tone of Corn. Sev. fr. 13. 10 Courtney (= *FLP*, p. 325) 'abstulit una dies aeui decus' (on Cicero's death), and Virg. *Ecl.* 4. 11–12 'teque adeo decus hoc aeui, te consule, inibit | Pollio'. The same combination of assertion and self-effacement is found at 47–63 where Statius describes the type of poem he would present to his father.

hoc: as well as thanking his father for the gift of poetry, the demonstrative pronoun might also suggest the present poem, which Statius owes to his father's inspiration; cf. 28 'da uocem magno, pater, ingenium<que> dolori'.

214. non uulgare loqui: cf. the elder Seneca's praise of Scaurus' 'uerborum quoque non uulgarium grauitas' at *Con.* 10 pr. 2.

famam sperare sepulchro: as well as the conventional desire for his own posthumous fame, these words might also suggest Statius' desire for the immortality of the monumental poem being given to the father (cf. 49–50 n.); for a poem as *sepulchrum* see 5. 1. 15 n.

215. quotiens is used here with iterative subjunctives; this type of subjunctive becomes more prevalent in post-Augustan Latin. See further H.–Sz. 606 (§327) and K.–S. ii. 206–8.

215–16. Latios ... patres: a mild joke: Statius is able to tame the severe senators with poetry. *Latios* evokes an air of antiquity: cf. 'Romulei ... patres', used of a senatorial audience at *Silv.* 5. 2. 161. For *mulceo* describing the effects of song, cf. *Silv.* 5. 1. 27–8 (with n.) and Virg. *G.* 4. 510 (Orpheus) 'mulcentem tigris et agentem carmine quercus'. Even the hostile testimony of Juv. 7. 82–7 refers to Statius' 'uocem iucundam' (82) and to the effect on audiences of his *dulcedo* (84); see further Markus (2003), 432–3.

216–17. felixque tui spectator adesses | muneris: cf. (though in a very different context) Turnus' words prior to his combat with Pallas at Virg. *A.* 10. 443: 'cuperem ipse parens spectator adesset'. Here *spectator*, an onlooker at a gladiatorial contest or athletic competition, anticipates the subsequent epinician imagery with which Statius describes his own participation in poetic contests. For such imagery applied to Statius' father, cf. 134–45 and nn. Its recurrence testifies to the continuity of success from father to son, itself a theme of Greek epinician poetry; this adds point to Statius' assertion of lineage in 210. Pi. *P.* 10. 22 states that it is the highest happiness (εὐδαίμων δὲ καὶ ὑμνητὸς οὗτος ἀνὴρ γίνεται σοφοῖς) for a man to win success in athletic contests and to live to see his own son's success. *felix* here is equivalent to εὐδαίμων; see also Pi. *N.* 6. 15–26 for another instance of a victor following in an ancestor's footsteps. For a similar treatment of this fathers and sons theme in a martial context, cf. Alatreus and his father at *Theb.* 11. 36–7: 'felices ambo, sed fortunatior ille, | quem genuisse iuuat'.

But whereas Pindar praises the ancestor to add to the glory of the victor (in *P.* 10, Hippocles' victory is further enhanced by his father's felicity), Statius' victory adds to his father's glory. *tui . . . muneris* emphasizes that the father is watching his own achievement, the *munus* being the poetic skill which he has imparted to his son; similarly, Statius describes the day of victory as *tuus* (219); his own glory is not greater than his father's. *munus* can also denote a gladiatorial show (*OLD* s.v. *munus* 4), such shows being offered not only publicly, as one of the expected duties of magistrates, but also as a private funeral offering to a dead relation. In this sense, Statius' victories were a kind of offering to his father, which the father was able to witness while he was still alive. This passage thus combines motifs of Greek epinician and Roman gladiatorial spectacle. See further 220–4 nn.

217. confundens: M's *confusus* is unsatisfactory. The passive form combined with an accusative of respect (for there is no other way to construe *gaudia*) can only be rendered as 'With what weeping were you confused in your joys', which seems excessively abstract. An active form could mean 'pouring forth' or 'mingling', yielding a more satisfying image. With *confessus* (Sandström), the tears simply become a sign of joy, and not of the *mixture* of emotions central to this passage (see 218, 'uota piosque metus inter laetumque pudorem'). I suggest *confundens*; the present participle would be subordinate to the previous sentence. For the combination of such conflicting emotions, compare Virg. *A.* 12. 666–8, *Silv.* 5. 2. 10, 'quanto manarent gaudia fletu' (where *manarent* supports the case for a more visible image in this line), and Plin. *Ep.* 5. 17. 5 'tam notabiliter pro fratre recitante primum metus eius, mox gaudium eminuit'.

218. laetumque pudorem: 'happy modesty'. Statius' father is delighted by his son's efforts, but does not behave extravagantly.

220–4. This simile, which purports merely to refer to a Greek athletic contest, also suggests Roman gladiatorial combat (see 216–17 n.). Although the setting is Greek (witness *Olympiaca* and

Achaeis[28]), the event in which the son is involved (either boxing or the *pankration*) is significantly a single combat. Note also *harena*, 'sand' but also 'arena' (see Leigh (1997), 278–9 with n. 110), and the continued emphasis on the *spectatores* (*spectat* and *spectatur* in 220 and 222); see e.g. Leigh (1997), 234–91 on such vocabulary. Statius thus sustains the implications of *muneris* (217); his poetic successes are not merely a source of pride to his father, but are also in some sense an offering which he received whilst alive.

The father is the subject of all verbs in the third person singular in this passage. Vollmer's suggestion that *ille* refers to the son ignores the paradox that the father's involvement in what he is watching makes him become the focus of the other spectators' attention; contrast the parents of the dead Glaucias who become spectators at his funeral, instead of being the centre of attention, on account of Melior's extreme grief (*Silv.* 2. 1. 173–4): 'erant illic genitor materque iacentis | maesta, sed attoniti te spectauere parentes'; cf. 5. 1. 216–17 'sed toto spectatur in agmine coniunx | solus'. *ille* simply marks the change back to the father after a temporary interruption (*attendunt cunei*) to the sequence of singular verbs. The simile gives only the briefest reference to actual fighting; attention is devoted to the father.

There is a slight discrepancy between the simile and the passage immediately preceding it. After 'quam tuus ille dies, quam non mihi gloria maior' (219), one would expect *talis* to introduce a comparison between the glory of Statius' father and the glory obtained by the father of the Olympic victor. Instead the simile concentrates on the behaviour of the victor's father as a spectator.

But the simile refers further back than 219. A more obvious comparison is with Statius' father's conduct as a spectator (216–19). *talis* would then allude to this passage, and the *tertium comparationis* would thus be the fact that both individuals are the father of victors. However, more detailed comparison of the two passages reveals a contrast, and not a similarity. Statius' father experiences the usual emotions of hope and fear in 218, but he also feels *laetum . . . pudorem*. The spectator at Olympia, however, becomes a spectacle himself (cf. Hollis on Ov. *Ars* 1. 99 'spectatum ueniunt, ueniunt spectentur ut ipsae', Plin. *Pan.* 33. 3 'nemo e spectatore spectaculum factus miseras uoluptates unco et ignibus expiauit'), drawing attention away from his son; he is entirely lacking in *laetus pudor*. Though Håkanson (1969),

---

[28] I accept Imhof's emendation of M's *achates*, a confused reminiscence of Virgil.

152 n. 52 would argue that *corde sub alto* is common to *ferit* and *caeditur* on the grounds that the father need not be assumed to be making 'ridiculous gestures', Vollmer correctly maintained that *corde sub alto* only applies to *caeditur*; the father's gestures explain his ability to gain the attention of the crowd. Håkanson's view that he is the object of interest because he may have had 'a place of honour close to the arena' scarcely explains the striking effect of 'spectatur Achaeis | ille *magis*'. For such behaviour at spectacles compare Quint. *Decl.* 9. 9; note also the response of Alypius to a gladiatorial display (Augustine, *Confessions* 6. 8. 13) and see further Leigh (1997), 282–8.

crebro dum lumina pulueris haustu | obruit: the extravagant gesture fits the father's offer of *deuotio* in the next line.

prensa uouet exspirare corona: the concise syntax, where the ablative absolute technically stands in place of a conditional clause, 'if his son should obtain the garland', effectively produces a double wish, death in the circumstances of victory being the best possible one. Compare the story of Diagoras of Rhodes (Gel. 3. 15. 3), who died adorned with the garlands of his three sons, who had all triumphed on the same day in separate events at the Olympic games. Whereas Statius' father was *felix*, seeing his son's victory, the simile breaks off before victory is achieved; the comparison thus reflects favourably on the elder Statius and his *laetus pudor*. This final note of uncertainty perhaps also prepares for the forthcoming reference to the Capitoline disaster.

225. patrias . . . frondes: not only 'my country's garlands' (for *patrius* thus, see *ThLL* x/1. 758. 15–759. 24), Statius' victory in the Neapolitan Augustalia, but also 'my father's garlands' (cf. ibid. 762. 39–763. 45), since his father won the same competition (134–7). There the contest was described as *patrii . . . lustri* (134), *patrii* only indicating that Naples was his father's home, and an adopted one at that; here the adjective carries its full etymological force. Coming after the simile describing the father watching at Olympus, who is willing to die in order to secure his son's victory, this passage testifies to the extent of Statius' ambitions; after a series of lines alluding to the epinician ideal of a victorious father living to see his son succeed, *tantum* indicates that the poet is not satisfied with one victory, and would wish to achieve more for his father. The magnitude of these ambitions is comparable to Statius' plans for a 'par templis opus' (47–63).

226. This line repeats the content of its predecessor: the repetition heightens Statius' regret (*ei mihi* in 225) that he could only win one

contest. Statius mentions Ceres as a principal Neapolitan deity at *Silv.*
4. 8. 50–1, referring to the torchlit races in her honour; see further
Coleman ad loc. and Frederiksen (1984), 91 with n. 49 and 159.

227–8. Dardanus Albae | aspexisset ager: for Trojan asso-
ciations of the Mons Albanus, see *Silv.* 5. 2. 168 n. On the datings of
Statius' participation in the Alban and Capitoline contests, see above,
pp. 261–2). Mention of the Mons Albanus here is ironic because it is
the site of Statius' father's tomb (36–40). This point supports Håkan-
son (1969), 152–3, who emended M's *uix cepisset* to *aspexisset*; his
parallels are decisive: *Silv.* 3. 5. 37–9 'qualem te nuper... | ... | aspexi'
and 5. 1. 108–9 'qualem te superi, Priscilla hominesque benigno |
aspexere die'. A verb of seeing is also appropriate in the light of the
preceding passage describing Statius' father as a *spectator* and the
simile of the Olympic spectator becoming the centre of attention.

228. si per me serta tulisses: another suggestion that Statius'
own achievements confer glory on his father; cf. 219.

229. Caesarea donata manu: one reason for Statius' regret
that his father did not see his Alban success is that the event was
presided over by the emperor. The particular importance of this
triumph is indicated at *Silv.* 4. 2. 63–7 where Statius compares the
joy of dining with the emperor to his delight at receiving the Alban
prize. In both passages actual contact with the emperor is important
(4. 2. 67 'Palladio tua me manus induit auro'). Compare also 3. 5. 28–
31 (Statius' wife's reaction to his triumph).

231. mixta quercus ... oliua: on the Capitoline contest (*agon
Capitolinus*), see Caldelli (1993), Darwall-Smith (1996), 223–6, P. White
(1998), A. Hardie (2003), 126–34. There were three general categories
of competition (Suet. *Dom.* 4. 4): the *agon musicus*, the *agon equestris*, and
the *agon gymnicus*. Suetonius mentions a variety of contests ('certabant
enim et prosa oratione Graece Latineque ac praeter citharoedos
chorocitharistae quoque et psilocitharistae, in stadio uero cursu
etiam uirgines'), but does not mention the events for poetry in Latin
and in Greek, which Statius entered; for other events within the *agon
musicus* not mentioned by Suetonius but attested elsewhere, see Cal-
delli (1993), 69–70. The contest in oratory appears to have had praise
of Jove as its subject (Quint. *Inst.* 3. 7. 4 'an laudes Capitolini Iouis,
perpetua sacri certaminis materia, uel dubiae sunt uel non oratorio
genere tractantur?'), and White (1998), 87–8 suggests that the god was
also the subject in the poetic contests, citing *Silv.* 3. 5. 32, where
Statius refers to Jove as 'saeuum ingratumque' in the context of his

defeat in the Capitoline contest, and the hexameters which survive by the 11-year-old Q. Sulpicius Maximus, winner of the Greek poetry contest in 94 (*CIL* vi. 33976, *IG* xiv. 2012, *ILS* 5177). A. Hardie (2003), 126–32 shows how Domitian's inauguration of the Capitoline festival may reflect the influence of Nero's *Neronia* festival, and that the competition quickly became part of the circuit of contests (cf. *Silv.* 3. 5. 92 where Statius ranks the isolympic *Augustalia* of Naples as 'Capitolinis quinquennia proxima lustris'). The contests in music, poetry and oratory are likely to have taken place in Domitian's Odeum, while his Stadium (whose dimensions are reflected in the Piazza Navona of more recent times) was the site for the athletic contests; see Suet. *Dom.* 4. 4 'in stadio uero cursu etiam uirgines', 5, Darwall-Smith (1996), 221–3, A. Hardie (2003), 130–2. Winners received an oaken crown (Mart. 4. 54. 1, Juv. 6. 387, Caldelli (1993), 105–8), while the prize for the Alban Games was a gilded olive wreath (Mart. 4. 1. 5, 9. 23. 5). The oak was associated with Jupiter (e.g. Virg. *G.* 3. 332 'magna Iouis antiquo robore quercus', Mart. 11. 9. 1), in whose honour Domitian established the Capitoline contest, while the olive was linked to Minerva, the patron deity of the Alban Games (Suet. *Dom.* 4. 4, D.C. 67. 1. 2). Statius thus imagines the unobtained double victory in terms of the visual effect produced by wearing both wreaths simultaneously.

232. fugit speratus honos: Statius presents his defeat as something external to and independent from himself (compare the English idiom 'Success evaded him'). For *fugit* compare 7–8 'fugere meos Parnasia crines | uellera', where Statius presents his inability to compose poetry in similarly externalized terms.

232–3. cum lustra parentis | inuida Tarpei canerem: M has *qua dusce* [*dulce* M¹] *parentis | inuida Tarpei caperes*. Courtney adopts three emendations: *quam* (*ς*), *lustra* (Markland), and *caneres* (Saenger), to give *quam lustra parentis | inuida Tarpei caneres*. His text, however, does not solve the difficulties of this passage: there is no reason why the father should be singing of the Capitoline contest; the sense ('as for the fact that I was defeated—how you would be singing of the envious *quinquennalia* of Jove') is meaningless; it is scarcely plausible that Statius' father should have composed a poem on his own son's defeat. Much of the difficulty lies in the multiplicity of problems.

Markland suggested the following text, accepting Gronovius' *canerem* in 233:

> heu quod me mixta quercus non pressit oliua
> et fugit speratus honos, cum lustra parentis
> inuida Tarpei canerem.

It is unnecessary to emend *nam quod* ('as to the fact that') in 231; though *nam quod* in this sense might appear prosaic, there are verse examples: see e.g. Cat. 68. 33–4 'nam quod scriptorum non magna est copia apud me, | hoc fit quod Romae uiuimus', Ov. *Ep.* 20. 155–6 'nam quod habes et tu gemini uerba altera pacti, | non erit idcirco par tua causa meae'. *nam quod* might indeed be considered appropriate to Statius' defensive tone in excusing his defeat. *cum*, however, already anticipated by Laetus, represents an improvement on *quam*; the temporal clause explains the contest to which he is referring (cf. *Silv.* 3. 5. 31–2 'cum Capitolia nostrae | infitiata lyrae'). Exclamatory *quam* has little to recommend it; Klotz prints *et fugit speratus honos: quam dulce parentis | inuida Tarpei caperes!*, where *dulce* would have to be construed as adverbial ('how sweetly you would be taking ...', whatever that might mean), while Shackleton Bailey in his new Loeb edition (see also his critical appendix) prints *quam lustra parentis | inuida Tarpei caperes!*, with the idea that Statius is praising his father for the philosophic acceptance he would have shown if he had been alive to witness his son's defeat. But in spite of Shackleton Bailey's citation of Sen. *Oed.* 82–3 'regium hoc ipsum reor: | aduersa capere', philosophic acceptance of defeat seems odd in the present passage, where Statius has been concerned to express how his father would reacted with great joy to success in the Alban contest; note also that in *Silv.* 3. 5. 31–3, Statius praised his wife not for accepting defeat but for her chagrin: 'tu, cum Capitolia nostrae | infitiata lyrae, saeuum ingratumque dolebas | mecum uicta Iouem'.

The next two problems are related: *dusce* (M) and *caperes* (M). Emendation of the verb will in large part determine the fate of *dusce*; 'solution' of the passage is thus much harder. First, *caperes*. The second person could only refer to the father; the sense, however, remains opaque. Not even *cum ... caperes* is satisfactory, absurdly implying that Statius did not win when his father was involved in the competition. *caneres* is no better.

It is absurd to refer to the father, when Statius is speaking of his own defeat. Furthermore a second person verb spoils the emphatic *te nostra magistro* which follows (contrasting with *nam quod me*—a comma before *te* gives better sense). But the verb can be emended to the first person; *te* may even have influenced the corruption to the second person.

There is thus a case for a first person singular verb. Before proceeding, *dusce* (M) deserves consideration. Though *lustra* could have given rise to *dusce*, there are two other possible causes of corruption. Firstly, *magistro* (233) could have given rise to the gloss *duce*, which was then misplaced. *dusce* would be a desperate replacement of one form of nonsense with another. The second possibility is that *dusce* is influenced by *dulce*, sixteen lines below but also in fifth foot of the line.

As we have seen, the *cum*-clause should include some reference to Statius' participation in the games. *inuida* should give point to the clause; he found only ill favour with the god. *caperem* is unconvincing, and a word for 'praise' would be a desirable replacement for *dusce*, given that the poem is likely to have been in praise of Jove (see 231 n. above); no such word seems available (*facta...* | *inuida* would be strange). Stephen Heyworth suggests to me *cum lustra parentis* | *inuida Tarpei colerem*. Gronovius' *canerem*, however, is closer to *caperes*; for the accusative *lustra*, cf. 113 'cum stata laudato caneret quinquennia uersu'. For the sake of clarity, I repeat my printed text here:

> nam quod me mixta quercus non pressit oliua
> et fugit speratus honos, cum lustra parentis
> inuida Tarpei canerem, te nostra magistro

The comma before *te* is essential. The failure in the Capitoline contest is triumphantly redeemed by the father's encouragement for the *Thebaid*'s challenge to the epic poets; it need not be assumed that this carries any implication about whether or not Statius' father was alive at the time of the games, since Statius is simply switching the theme away from the inauspicious topic of the Capitoline contest to his father's earlier involvement in the *Thebaid*. The slight awkwardness of the transition between these two subjects may itself lend support to the idea canvassed in the introduction to this poem, that lines 225–33 may be a later addition.

233. te ... magistro: cf. 'te monitore' at 147 (on Statius' father's teaching) with n. *magistro*, however, has not the same corrective overtones as *monitore*. See also Cic. *Fam.* 11. 25. 1 'breuitatem secutus sum te magistro' and Sil. 4. 428–9 'te magna magistro | audeat'.

233–4. nostra ... Thebais: *nostra* is not merely a poetic plural ('my'), but also a recognition of his father's involvement ('our').

234. urguebat: *urg(u)eo* can denote pursuit (*OLD* s.v. *urgeo* 5b; contrast *Theb.* 2. 644–6 'Menoeten | proterrebat agens trepidis uesti- gia retro | passibus urguentem', where, as *retro* indicates, the process described is one of flight), implying Statius' challenge to the epic tradtion. *urguebat* reverses the more modest closing instruction to the *Thebaid* (*Theb.* 12. 816–17): 'nec tu diuinam Aeneida tempta | sed longe sequere et uestigia semper adora'; cf. Hinds (1998), 93–4 on the reversal of *Theb.* 12. 816, 'nec ... tempta' at *Silv.* 4. 7. 25–8.

235–7. These lines recall the description of the father's teaching in 146–61. But here, Statius' father's instruction enables his son to be a poet himself.

The language is nevertheless ambiguous. *cantus stimulare meos*, which establishes poetic instruction as the theme of these lines, must be taken as a historic infinitive. This passage seems an exception to the rule that the historic infinitive is not found in the second person (K.–S. i. 135). Nevertheless even an unparalleled rarity is preferable to construing *stimulare* with *monstrabas*; it is far more convincing for Statius to say that his father gave impetus to his poetry, than to say that his father *showed him how to* give impetus to his poetry. The remaining portion of the sentence can be construed in two ways. *pandere facta heroum* is either another historic infinitive clause, or an object clause dependent on *monstrabas* (for this construction see *OLD* s.v. *monstro* 2). With a historic infinitive, Statius' father gives instruc- tion on the deeds of heroes of a descriptive kind, similar to his teaching of Homer (148), where merely the content of a poem is taught. For *pandere* in a didactic context compare 156–7 'tu pandere doctus | carmina Battiadae'. Alternatively, with *pandere* dependent on *monstrabas*, *pandere facta heroum monstrabas* would mean 'you used to show/were showing me how to expound the deeds of heroes', so that Statius is claiming that his father taught him the techniques of epic.

The ambiguities continue. Thus *bellique modos*, the 'modes of war', can be construed either as an addition to *pandere facta heroum*, or with *positusque locorum*, as the object of *monstrabas*. *positusque locorum* has an air of paradox, perhaps referring, as Gatti in *ThLL* x/2. 92. 36–9 specu- lates ('an intellegas quomodo poeta locos ponere i. describere debeat'), to the procedures for topographical description; see also Curtius (1953), 200, who compares 'terrarumque situs' at Hor. *Ep.* 2. 1. 252 and Luc. 10. 178. The phrase might also have structural connotations, denoting the arrangement of subjects in a poem; for *locus* as a technical term for a topic, see *OLD* s.v. *locus* 24.

237–8. These lines refer to difficulties experienced by Statius in completing the *Thebaid* (Coleman (1988), xvii).

cursus (cf. Virg. *G.* 1. 40 'da facilem cursum') resumes the metaphor of a journey ('urguebat') from 234, while marine travel is a familiar image for literature (e.g. Pi. *P.* 10. 51–2 κώπαν σχάσον, ταχὺ δ' ἄγκυραν ἔρεισον χθονὶ / πρῴραθε, χοιράδος ἄλκαρ πέτρας, Virg. *G.* 2. 41 'pelagoque uolans da uela patenti', Prop. 3. 3. 23–4 'alter remus aquas alter tibi radat harenas, | tutus eris: maxima turba mari est', 3. 9. 3–4, 3. 9. 35–6, Liv. 31. 1. 5, Ov. *Met.* 15. 176–7, Quint. *Inst.* 12 pr. 2–4, Juv. 1. 149–50, Kambylis (1965), 149–55—for a metaphor derived from travel on *land* see Rutilius Namatianus 2. 7–8). Statius describes the *Thebaid* as having reached port at *Silv.* 4. 4. 88–9 'iam Sidonios emensa labores | Thebais optato collegit carbasa portu', echoing the metaphor of arrival in port used at the end of the epic itself: 'et mea iam longo meruit ratis aequore portum' (*Theb.* 12. 809). Contrast also *Silv.* 4. 4. 99–100 'fluctus an sueta minores | nosse ratis nondum Ioniis credenda periclis?', on the uncertainties and difficulties of imperial epic. The dark sails evoke the legend of Aegeus' death, who leapt into what became the Aegean Sea when his son Theseus did not remember to hoist white sails, the sign of success, on his return from slaying the Minotaur in Crete (Cat. 64. 202–50); cf. *Theb.* 12. 625–6 'Sunion, unde uagi casurum in nomina ponti | Cresia decepit falso ratis Aegea uelo'.

caligant echoes Catullus' use of *caligo* to describe Theseus' mental turmoil at 64. 207; other possible echoes of Catullus here are *uela* (64. 235) and *carinae* (64. 249). The allusion to Theseus' loss as he was nearing home might suggest that Statius' father died at a late stage in the composition of the *Thebaid* (on the chronological problems of the poem, see the introduction to *Silv.* 5. 3 above); this does not contradict *Silv.* 3. 5. 35–6 'longi tu sola laboris | conscia, cumque tuis creuit mea Thebais annis', addressed to Statius' wife.

The allusion to Theseus and Aegeus arrestingly effects a transition to the time of his father's death. Although images for poetry predominate in these two lines, the language equally well suggests Statius' journey through life (cf. Sen. *Con.* 2 pr. 4 'duobus filiis nauigantibus te in portu retineo'). The immediate transition to Statius' mother indicates that bereavement is as much a concern as poetry.

239. memet: Statius uses the intensifying suffix *-met* on twenty-four occasions in all poetry; see Fletcher (1961). Prisc. *GL* iii. 591. 24–592. 4 (cf. *GL* ii. 14. 12–17) explains that the suffix is used 'uel discretionis causa plerumque uel significatione', and continues by glossing *egomet* in Terence as 'ego et non alius' and *tute* in Cicero as 'tu ipse per te et non per alium'. Statius' usage is not entirely in accordance with this explanation, since the particularizing force suggested by Priscian is contradicted by *nec solum*; the sense would on this interpretation be 'not only did you cherish me (and me alone), but you also cherished your wife'.

240–1. una … unus: for the anaphora cf. *Silv.* 5. 1. 55–6 'unum nouisse cubile, | unum secretis agitare sub ossibus ignem' (Priscilla's second marriage is described as if she were *uniuira*). Similar language is here applied to Statius' father, as a compliment to his loyalty and devotion; for the application of such language to men, see Treggiari (1991), 235. Compare Abascantus' *pietas*, singled out for praise throughout 5. 1 and the dedicatory epistle.

241–3. Statius' mother's visits to the tomb are a counterpart to his own visit (29–40). In both passages the passing of time is noted; *iam gelidis … bustis*, with *iam gelidis* perhaps pointing to the supposed etymological assocation of *bustum* with *urere*, 'to burn' (see Maltby (1991), 88), is more emotive than the measurement of three months in lunar cycles given in 29–30. Here Statius is, for the only time in the poem, a spectator of another person's grief for his father.

244–5. Statius' mother's *pietas* towards her husband is contrasted favourably with the extravagant, but insincere, gestures of the votaries of Osiris and Attis. *ut* is perhaps a strange conjunction, however, since the natural reading would be to see the clauses describing Statius' mother and the foreign women as in parallel, with the implication that she too is insincere. However, one might argue here that content creates contrast: thus 'te sentit habetque' stands in contrast with 'ficta pietate' in 244–5; the similarity implied by *ut* would then lie in the amount of effort Statius' mother and the eastern women put in to their respective mourning, even though in the latter case such lamentation could be said to be insincere. Alternatively, emend *ut* to *at* (Calderini), which might be felt to be in keeping with the dismissive tone of 'aliae' and 'non sua funera plorant'.

Statius has two complaints against the followers of both cults; he questions the validity of their religion, and doubts their sincerity, since their lamentations are not occasioned by personal loss (*non sua funera plorant*). Contrast Encolpius' almost aesthetic criticism of lamenting the death of a stranger at Petr. 54. 1 (see also Friedlaender ad loc.): 'conclamauit familia, nec minus conuiuae, non propter

hominem tam putidum, cuius etiam ceruices fractas esse libenter
uidissent, sed propter malum exitum cenae, ne necesse haberent
alienum mortuum plorare.' The same criticism is envisaged at *Silv.*
5. 5. 47–8, where Statius is advised not to expend his tears on
'aliena … damna'; contrast 5. 3. 70–1, where the extreme pathos of
a funeral is measured by its ability to affect even strangers with grief.
Here such grief is trivial and pointless when set beside the pain of
bereaved relations; see also Hor. *Ars* 431–3 on hired mourners.

   Pharios … ficta pietate dolores: the Egyptian ritual in ques-
tion is the annual festival of the search and discovery (cf. Juv. 8. 29–30
'Osiri | inuento') of Osiris by his wife Isis, after he had been killed and
dismembered. Plu. *De Iside et Osiride* 39 = *Mor.* 366 c–f mentions four
days of mourning; see Gwyn Griffith ad loc. (p. 452). Statius was not
the first to censure this practice; Xenophanes of Colophon reputedly
told the Egyptians not to mourn if they were bewailing gods, and not
to believe in their gods if they mourned for them (Plu. *De Iside et Osiride*
71 = *Mor.* 379 B, *De superstit.* 13 = *Mor.* 171 D–E, *Amat.* 18 = *Mor.* 763
c–d). *ficta pietate* may glance at Xenophanes' criticisms.

   Statius' censure is striking in view of Flavian support for Egyptian
religion, on which see B. W. Jones (1992), 100–1, Darwall-Smith
(1996), 139–53. See also 196–8 n. above and note that at *Silv.* 3. 2.
101–22 Statius invokes Isis to protect his friend Celer on his Egyptian
travels. This passage, however, is part of a tradition of invective
against Egypt, which appears in several forms in Roman literature.
Virgil portrays the bestial gods of Egypt fighting against the gods of
Rome at Actium (*A.* 8. 698–9, cf. Prop. 3. 11. 41–2), whilst Luc. 8. 833
gives a recapitulation of Xenophanes; at Luc. 9. 158–61 Pompey's son
states his violent intentions against Isis and Osiris. Juv. 15. 1–13 also
attacks Egyptian religion; note also his censure of extravagant female
participation in eastern cults (6. 508–34).

   dolores | Mygdonios (cf. V.Fl. 8. 239 'Mygdonios planctus',
referring however to Cybele and not to her worshippers) are grief
for the dead Attis; cf. the simile of Phrygian lamentations at *Theb.* 12.
224–7. D.S. 3. 59. 1 ascribes Attis' death to the intervention of
Cybele's father Meion, who had discovered that his daughter was
with child. Paus. 7. 17. 9–12 mentions further versions of the legend,
including one given by Hermesianax, where Attis is killed by a boar
sent by Zeus. The cult of Attis is alluded to in derogatory tones at
[Lucian], *Am.* 42, where the involvement of women in such rituals as
τὸν δυσέρωτα κῶμον ἐπὶ τῷ ποιμένι is noted.

246–54. Statius reverts for the last time to his father's lifetime. Here he praises his father's moral qualities, which have previously been subordinate to literary concerns. Such character sketches typically occur at earlier stages in Statius' *epicedia*; contrast *Silv.* 2. 1. 39–40, 2. 6. 40–50, 3. 3. 106–10, and 5. 1. 53–74.

246. expositos seruato pondere mores: his father's *mores* are 'set out' (*expositos*), and hence open and without dissimulation. For *expositus* thus, glossed as 'patens, apertus', cf. Plin. *Ep.* 1. 10. 2 'est enim obuius et expositus', *ThLL* v/2. 1767. 17–45. Contrast *occultus* (e.g. Tac. *Hist.* 2. 38. 1 'occultior non melior', *Ann.* 6. 51. 3 'occultum ac subdolum fingendis uirtutibus').

pondere: equivalent to 'grauitate'.

247. quam uile lucrum: compare Priscilla's willingness to enjoy poverty rather than dishonourable wealth (*Silv.* 5. 1. 60–3). Though disdain for wealth is commonplace, *quam uile lucrum* might also evoke and counter the argument that poetry is useless since it does not secure financial advantage. Theocr. 16 provides the rejoinder that poetry brings about fame which wealth cannot confer (see further Gow on 16. 30–1). Statius thus affirms that his father had a poet's lack of regard for money; contrast Ovid's father (*Tr.* 4. 10. 21–4) who argued that Homer was poor when attempting to dissuade his son from literature in favour of a more lucrative career. For the moral tone (*pietas, pudoris, amor recti*) compare Maternus' defence of poetry (e.g. Tac. *Dial.* 12. 1 'sed secedit animus in loca pura atque innocentia fruiturque sedibus sacris'). Maternus is similarly contemptuous of the money available to an orator (e.g. *Dial.* 12. 2 'lucrosae huius et sanguinantis eloquentiae', 13. 6).

The phrase may also suggest that Statius' father was not avaricious as a teacher: for such praise compare Suet. *Gramm.* 7. 1 (on Antonius Gnipho) 'nec umquam de mercedibus pactus eoque plura ex liberalitate discentium consecutus', and 13. 2, where L. Staberius Eros is said to have taught the sons of victims of the Sullan prescriptions without charge; see also *CLE* 91. 3 'p[a]rce pudensque uixit omni tempore', from an epitaph for a schoolmaster, where *pudens*, incidentally, may be regarded as a preemptive strike against the traditional charge against schoolmasters of immorality, one that Statius disdains to acknowledge in this poem.

249. gratia: 'charm'. Priscilla (*Silv.* 5. 1. 65–6) had 'mixta pudori | gratia'; for such combinations see 5. 1. 65 n. For praise of a kindly nature in a teacher, cf. Suet. *Gramm.* 7. 1 (Antonius Gnipho).

animo quam nulla senectus recalls Statius' view that his father's death was premature (72–4). The phrase denotes two concurrent ideas. Firstly, Statius continues the characterization of *gratia quae dictis*: his father lost none of the vitality of youth in old age. Secondly, Statius affirms the continuity of his father's intellectual abilities. Intellectual deterioration was an aspect of ageing both recognized and feared; according to Solon fr. 27. 15–16 (West) the γλῶσσα and σοφίη begin to fall off in the ninth age of man. Juv. 10. 232–3 is more strident: 'omni | membrorum damno maior dementia', see further Powell (1988), 25 with n. 62. Conversely, the persistence of the mental faculties in spite of advancing years was valued; cf. Solon fr. 18 (West) γηράσκω δ' αἰεὶ πολλὰ διδασκόμενος, which is itself referred to at Cicero *Sen.* 49–50, where there is an enthusiastic list of elderly practitioners of such arts as astronomy and poetry. Sen. *Ep.* 26. 2 affirms that his *animus* is glad to have little to do with his *corpus*: 'exultat et mihi facit controuersiam de senectute: hunc ait esse florem suum. credamus illi: bono suo utatur.'

250–2. Though one might expect the adjective *tristem* (*M*) to go with a noun, Vollmer defended the transmitted text by arguing that *esse* is to be supplied, with *nulloque e uulnere tristem* [*esse*] as another object of *concessit*. This, however, cannot stand, since the lack of concord between *tibi* as the indirect object of *concessit* and the accusative *tristem*, which would also refer to Statius' father, is intolerable when combined with the absence of *esse*: for the usual construction with the complement in the dative, note e.g. Hor. *Ars.* 372–3 'mediocribus esse poetis | non homines, non di, non concessere columnae'. Emending to dative *tristi* is not without its difficulties, however, for it is hard to see what would be the basis for a reader even supplying *esse*. Krohn and Rothstein suggested a lacuna after 251, but Markland's conjecture *tristes* (agreeing with *laudes* in the previous line, the *-que* in line 251 joining *benignas* in 250 to the more elaborate *nulloque e uulnere tristes*) is a useful attempt to resolve the difficulty with minimum disturbance to the text: the sense would be that the gods granted Statius' father fame, and praise which was not marred by any wound: Shackleton Bailey translates as follows: 'the gods' protective care allowed you fame and generous credit unsaddened by any misfortune'.

253–4. Statius' father lived for sixty-five years; for enumeration of a father's age in *lustra* of five years, compare Ov. *Tr.* 4. 10. 77–8; this method of reckoning has particular point, since both *lustra* and *quinquennia* can refer to poetic contests (113, 134, perhaps 232). The *lustrum* is also used by Statius to compute ages at *Silv.* 1. 4. 53, 2. 6. 72, 3. 3. 146. On the tendency for ages to be rounded to numbers divisible by five, the period of the *lustrum*, and the resulting need for caution in determining a person's exact lifespan, see Wiedemann (1989), 15.

254. numerare: despite having given his father's age in *lustra*, Statius must not count his father's years and imitate a son who pays particular attention to his father's age in his eagerness to inherit. Ovid mentions the vice as a feature of the iron age (*Met.* 1. 148) 'filius ante diem patrios inquirit in annos'. Vell. 2. 67. 2 notes that during the triumviral proscriptions, sons showed no fidelity to proscribed parents, and concludes that 'adeo difficilis est hominibus utcumque conceptae spei mora'; cf. Juv. 3. 43–4 'funus promittere patris | nec uolo nec possum', Sen. *Con.* 6. 1. Statius ascribes unusual filial *pietas* to Etruscus (*Silv.* 3. 3. 20–1, 3. 3. 136); compare Mart. 7. 40. 7–8: 'sed festinatis raptum tibi credidit annis, | aspexit lacrimas quisquis, Etrusce, tuas.' See also 46 n.

255–7. Statius alludes to the longevity of Nestor (from Pylos) and Priam and Tithonus from Troy; for their proverbial status, see Otto (1890), 242 (§1223), 287 (§1469), and 349 (§1789) respectively. Statius' use of these *exempla*, see van Dam on *Silv.* 2. 2. 107–8, Laguna on 3. 4. 103–4, Coleman on 4. 3. 150–2, Taisne (1996), 217–18. Statius typically uses such examples in a prayer for long life, as at e.g. *Silv.* 1. 3. 110 'finem Nestoreae precor egrediare senectae'; their appearance here, where they are applied to Statius' *dead* father, underlines the presentation of his death as almost *mors immatura*, despite his thirteen *lustra*. An even more striking use of this same pairing occurs at *Theb.* 5. 751–2 'nam deus iste, deus, Pyliae nec fata senectae | maluerit, Phrygiis aut degere longius annis', when Amphiaraus assures his hearers that the dead child Opheltes would prefer his death (and deification) to long years; Nestor and Priam, indeed, were still alive at this point. Juv. 10. 188–288 castigates prayers for long life (cf. 12. 128 'uiuat Pacuuius quaeso uel Nestora totum'), and mentions, among others, the ill fortune of Nestor (10. 246–55) and Priam (10. 258–72).

255. transcendere: for this applied to age cf. *Silv.* 1. 4. 126 'Euboici transcendere pulueris annos'.

256. aequare: cf. *Silv.* 2. 3. 73 'Iliacos aequare senes'.

256–7. o digne uidere | me similem: after the familiar *exempla* of longevity, the sudden shift to Statius himself is an emotional conclusion to this passage.

257. me similem: Statius wishes that his father could have lived to see him as an old man, a hyperbolical extension of the wish that an old man may see his descendants grow up (e.g. *Silv.* 3. 1. 175 'concedamque diu iuuenes spectare nepotes'). *me similem* also hints at similar poetic achievement for Statius.

sed nec leti tibi ianua tristis: for examples of the *ianua leti*, see Bömer on Ov. *Met.* 1. 662; add Lucr. 6. 762–3 'ianua ne †poteis† Orci regionibus esse | credatur' and Sil. 11. 187–8 'ianua mortis | quod patet'. The door of death is typically open or closed, as at e.g. Virg. *A.* 2. 661 'patet isti ianua leto', as an index of the possible proximity of death, though note V.Fl. 3. 386 'patet ollis ianua leti', where the door of death is open for souls to *return* from the underworld to harass those who were their enemies whilst they were alive. Here, however, *nec leti tibi ianua tristis* indicates a concern with *how* his father died.

258–61. The desirability of an easy death is an ancient theme. Tiresias tells Odysseus of a θάνατος... ἀβληχρός when he is old (*Od.* 11. 134–6); contrast Dido's initial 'dolorem | difficilesque obitus' (Virg. *A.* 4. 693–4).

258. segnis... senili: 26 n.

labe: *tabe* (Gronovius *Elench.* 7) is unnecessary, in a passage describing disability rather than disease. For *labes* thus, cf. Lucr. 5. 930, Suet. *Aug.* 38. 3. *membra* confirms that *labes* is incapacity. *labe senili*, 'elderly decline', is effectively set beside *segnis*.

259. This line denote a long physical decline, leading to death (*instanti... sepulchro*).

praemisit: death can carry off a person's body before taking the soul. Compare Tiresias' description of Oedipus' condition at *Theb.* 4. 614–15 'iacet ille in funere longo, | quem fremis, et iunctae sentit confinia mortis' and note the English idiom 'a living death'. Such lingering existences were feared; Silius Italicus would choose suicide in preference to a long and debilitating illness (Plin. *Ep.* 3. 7. 1–2).

260. mors imitata quietem: on the kinship of Sleep and Death see 5. 4. 1–2 n.; for epitaphs referring to death as sleep, see Lattimore (1942), 164–5. *quies* often denotes death in poetry (*OLD* s.v. *quies* 3); for *quiescere* thus compare 36 above, Virg. *A.* 6. 371, 9. 445.

261. explicuit: the image is of death unfolding, or laying out a dead person. Although Luc. 5. 80–1 uses the metaphor of Apollo's slaying of the Python ('adhuc rudibus Paean Pythona sagittis | explicuit'), where the verb evokes the serpent's many coils, no such violence is signified here; indeed, the word describes the effects of sleep at *Theb.* 10. 141–2 'illius aura solo uolucres pecudesque ferasque | explicat'.

262–4. tunc . . . tuli: this last description of lamentation in the poem refers to Statius' laments as in the past. Although the process of consolation is not explicit, there has nevertheless been a move away from the inconsolable grief described in 29–46.

262–3. anxia uidit . . . gauisaque nouit: it is on this antithesis that the parenthesis depends. The *comites* (see 67–8n.) anxiously watch Statius' behaviour, but only his mother recognizes her own example (241–5) being matched by her son.

264–5. Statius amplifies Ov. *Tr.* 4. 10. 79–80 'non aliter fleui, quam me fleturus ademptum | ille fuit', and asks pardon of the *Manes* (though contrast Virg. *G.* 4. 469–70 'Manisque adiit regemque tremendum | nesciaque humanis precibus mansuescere corda', 4. 489 'ignoscenda quidem, scirent si ignoscere Manes' for the notion that this may not be easily obtained), since he sets himself on the same level as his dead father, for once assuming a position of equality.

fas dixisse: a neat juxtaposition, playing on the etymology of *fas* (associated with *fari*, 'to speak'; see Maltby (1991), 223). Such concern that extreme praise (whether of oneself or of another) should be *fas* is paralleled at Cat. 51. 1–2 'ille mi par esse deo uidetur, | ille, si fas est, superare diuos'; cf. Lutatius Catulus fr. 2. 3–4 (= Courtney, *FLP*, p. 77) 'pace mihi liceat, caelestes, dicere uestra, | mortalis uisus pulchrior esse deo'.

266–70. These lines refer to Aeneas' visit to Anchises in the underworld. Here Aeneas' apparent desire to rescue his father is Statius' amplification of *A.* 6. 108–9, where the hero merely asks the Sibyl whether he may visit Anchises: 'ire ad conspectum cari genitoris et ora | contingat'. Statius' treatment of this episode owes much to the same passage; a subconscious desire to rescue his father is revealed by Aeneas' *exempla* at *A.* 6. 119–23, where he cites Orpheus, Pollux, Theseus, and Hercules as mortals who have descended and returned, all of whom, save Theseus, secured permission for another person's return from the underworld. Indeed, Statius adopts Aeneas' technique on his own behalf in lines 266–76, since he too cites examples of those who have descended into the underworld, including Orpheus. The inclusion of Aeneas in Statius' own list is a tribute to the source of his argument. Other Virgilian echoes include *uiuos . . . gressus* (cf. *A.* 6. 391 'corpora uiua nefas Stygia uectare carina'), *molitum* (cf. *A.* 6. 477 'inde datum molitur iter'; see also *Silv.* 5. 2. 61, and for *molitum . . . gressus*, cf. *Theb*. 1. 457, 6. 705, *ThLL* viii. 1362. 52–7) and *longaeua* (*A*. 6. 628 'Phoebi longaeua sacerdos'); for the longevity of the Sibyl see 175 n.

The passage is, however, not without its problems. The change of subject from *ille . . . circumdedit* to *detulit uates* makes it impossible to construe 266–70 as one sentence with the ordering of the manuscript. A full stop after 268 is no improvement; with main clauses, the sequence of events is perhaps unsatisfactory, since we are told that the Sibyl escorted Aeneas (*detulit*) after we have heard of his meeting with his father; it is to be noted, moreover, that the Sibyl has only a very minor mention in Virgil (*A*. 6. 897) after Aeneas' meeting with Anchises. Thus Markland's emendation of *detulit* in 270 to *rettulit*, with the Sibyl bringing Aeneas back after his meeting with his father, is tempting but unlikely in view of the presence of *rettulit* in 273. Even more problematic, however, is the fact that *felix ille* in 266 has not been identified in a subsequent clause (expressions of beatitude typically include a relative clause): in this list of *exempla*, something is required in parallel to *Odrysiam chelyn* (Orpheus), *Admetus*, and *Phylaceida . . . umbram* (Protesilaus) in 271–3. Davies's emendation of M's *tempantem* at the beginning of 269 to *quem tandem* draws attention to this difficulty, but though *tandem* might be felt to be palaeographically close to *-tantem*, there is little reason to have the word here, when one would expect it to carry some weight or significance, as in an example such as Virg. *A*. 6. 472 'tandem corripuit sese', when Dido removes herself from Aeneas' presence in the underworld.

A more radical solution was provided by Saenger, who proposed placing lines 269–70 before 266 and also emending *temptantem* in 269:

Dardaniden uiuos molitum in Tartara gressus	269
detulit infernae uates longaeua Dianae:	270
felix ille patrem uacuis circumdedit ulnis	266
uellet et Elysia quamuis in sede locatum	267
abripere et Danaas iterum portare per umbras.	

With this emendation, the sequence is more satisfactory: the Sibyl escorts Aeneas, he meets his father, and wished he could carry him out even from Elysium. But the requirement not only to transpose lines but also to emend *temptantem* to *Dardaniden* (used in the nominative singular of Aeneas at Virg. *A*. 10. 545, 12. 775) inspires caution.

A more satisfactory solution to the need to define *ille* in 266 is provided by Housman's lacuna,[29] accepted by Courtney and Shackleton Bailey, which clarifies *ille* and *temptantem* and allows the change of subject from Aeneas to the Sibyl with *detulit*, whose clause now explains how Aeneas got to the underworld. The supplement has the further merit of reflecting the Sibyl's involvement before Aeneas' meeting with Anchises, with its references to Aeneas' desire to know the future: compare, as noted by Housman, *Silv.* 4. 3. 131–3: 'ex quo me duce praescios Auerni | Aeneas auide futura quaerens | lucos et penetrauit et reliquit'.

266. felix ille: for this type of formula, here used paradoxically since Aeneas' embrace of his father is frustrated, see *Silv.* 5. 2. 176 n. For such expressions of felicitation in cases which do not seem favourable, cf. e.g. *Od.* 5. 306–7, Virg. *A.* 1. 94–6, 3. 321 'o felix una ante alias Priameia uirgo'.

uacuis circumdedit ulnis encapsulates the frustration and pathos of Aeneas' meetings with both his parents in the *Aeneid*; see Virg. *A.* 1. 405–17 (Venus) and 6. 700–2, where Aeneas thrice tries to embrace the *imago* of his father. *circumdedit* recalls *A.* 6. 700 'ter conatus ibi collo dare bracchia circum', itself echoing Odysseus' attempts to embrace his mother at *Od.* 11. 204–9. Note also Sil. 13. 648–53, where Scipio is unable to embrace the shades of his mother, father, and uncle.

Statius suggests the contradictions of Aeneas' encounter. *circumdedit*, without a negative, implies that Aeneas did succeed in embracing his father, but the contrary impression is evoked by *uacuis... ulnis. felix* is puzzling (see above for paradoxical felicitations); in the *Aeneid* Aeneas' futile attempt to touch his father is preceded by tears (*A.* 6. 699; cf. Odysseus at *Od.* 11. 208), while his earlier meeting with Venus was also painful (*A.* 1. 405–9). For Statius, however, Aeneas was *felix* because he at least saw his father after death.

268. portare: Aeneas carried his father on his shoulders away from the sack of Troy (*A.* 2. 721–44).

umbras, as well as referring to the darkness under which Aeneas and his father fled from the Greeks (*A.* 2. 725 'ferimur per opaca

---

[29] Housman, *Class. P.* ii. 654–5 fills the lacuna as follows: 'felix ille patrem uacuis circumdedit ulnis, | uellet et, Elysia quamuis in sede locatum, | abripere et Danaas iterum portare per umbras, | <quem proli uentura suae praenoscere fata> | temptantem et uiuos molitum in Tartara gressus | detulit infernae uates longaeua Dianae.'

locorum'), also evokes the shades of the Greeks whom Aeneas briefly encountered in the underworld (*A.* 6. 489–93). At *A.* 6. 490 the Greeks see Aeneas and his arms 'per umbras'.

269. Tartara: see 74 n.

271–3. si … si … si: Though M has *sic … sic* in 271–2, where Calderini restored *si … si*, and *silua* in 273, where Heinsius conjectured *si lux*, repeated conditionals are desirable in these lines, since the rhetorical force of *cur nihil exoret* in 274 is dependent on a conditional sentence preceding it. Reading *sic* in 271 and 272, by contrast, makes the examples of Orpheus, Admetus, and Laodamia equivalent in merit to that of Aeneas, missing the point of *causa minor* in 272 (cf. *Silv.* 3. 3. 194 'hoc quanto melius pro patre liceret', where Claudius Etruscus dimisses Admetus' and Orpheus' claims for the recovery of their spouses). The effect is one of contrast: having mentioned Aeneas' visit to his father, Statius then cites *lesser* occasions for descents into the underworld. The full force of this pattern is thus dependent on reading *si* in 271, 272, and 273, imitating Aeneas' own use of such conditional sentences at Virg. *A.* 6. 119–21, where the hero justifies himself with a series of *exempla* for καταβάσεις introduced by *si* (see 266–70 n.).

271. pigro … Auerno: *pigro* denotes the torpor of the infernal regions, cf. *Theb.* 8. 17, 11. 588. The dative of motion may recall Virgil's famous 'facilis descensus Auerno [M^1P^1 : Auerni P^2R]' (*A.* 6. 126); both readings were known to Servius, who takes *Auerno* as dative, 'id est *ad Auernum*', and see further Austin ad loc., though Wellesley (1964) argues that *Auerno* is ablative of path. Cf. the local ablative at Ov. *Am.* 3. 9. 27 'hunc quoque summa dies nigro submersit Auerno'.

272–3. Heinsius proposed a lacuna between ll. 272 and 273; any attempt to forge a closer connection between these two lines is doomed, since *lux una*, referring to the one day allowed for Protesilaus, from Phylace (see e.g. *Il.* 2. 695, 700) and the first of the Greeks to die at Troy, to return to his wife Laodamia from the dead (see Vollmer and van Dam on *Silv.* 2. 7. 124 and 2. 7. 120–3 respectively), has no bearing on the tale of Admetus and Alcestis. Admetus, furthermore, cannot be the subject of either *transmisit* or *rettulit* (Hercules rather than Admetus restored Alcestis to him).

For the missing line Housman, *Class. P.* ii. 655 suggested:

> si Thessalicis Admetus in oris   272
> \<coniuge ab infernis potuit gaudere reducta,\>
> si lux una retro Phylaceida rettulit umbram   273

An alternative would be something as follows:

272   si Thessalicis Admetus in oris
                                 <Alcestin rursus superata Morte tenebat,>
273   si lux una retro Phylaceida rettulit umbram

Statius alludes to the conflict of Hercules and Death at *Silv.* 5. 1. 8.
All three *exempla* have negative aspects. Orpheus wasted his chance
to win back Eurydice (Virg. *G.* 4. 490–8), whilst Euripides' Admetus
himself comments on the censure he faces for allowing his wife to die
(*Alc.* 954–61). Laodamia is not only an *exemplum* of connubial devotion
(e.g. Ov. *Tr.* 1. 6. 20, *Pont.* 3. 1. 110), but is also, less auspiciously,
associated with a cult of the *imago* of her own husband; cf. *Silv.* 2. 7.
124–5 (Lucan's widow has no need to invest her husband with such a
cult), Ov. *Rem.* 723–4 'si potes, et ceras remoue: quid imagine muta |
carperis? hoc periit Laodamia modo'. See further Sarkissian (1983),
17–18, 42–4, Lyne (1998).

lux una might also be considered an inversion of the motif of one
day's causing destruction, being instead the one day when Protesilaus
was allowed to return: contrast e.g. A. *Pers.* 431–2 εὖ γὰρ τόδ' ἴσθι,
μηδάμ' ἡμέρᾳ μιᾷ | πλῆθος τοσουτάριθμον ἀνθρώπων θανεῖν, S. *Aj.* 131–
2, *OT* 438, *El.* 1149–50 νῦν ἐκλέλοιπε ταῦτ' ἐν ἡμέρᾳ μιᾷ | θανόντι σὺν
σοί, E. *Hec.* 285 τὸν πάντα δ' ὄλβον ἦμαρ ἕν μ' ἀφείλετο, fr. 420 (from
the *Ino*), Men. *Aspis* 415–18 (= Carcinus II, *TrGF* 70 F 5a), Lucr. 3. 898–
9 'omnia ademit | una dies infesta tibi tot praemia uitae', 5. 95, 5. 999–
1001, Corn. Sev. fr. 13. 10 Courtney (= *FLP*, p. 325–6) 'abstulit una dies
aeui decus', Ov. *Am.* 1. 15. 24 (with McKeown's n.) 'exitio terras cum
dabit una dies', *Fast.* 2. 235–6 'una dies Fabios ad bellum miserat
omnes, | ad bellum missos perdidit una dies' (cf. *Pont.* 1. 2. 4 'non
omnes Fabios abstulit una dies'), Sen. *Nat.* 3. 29. 9 'unus humanum
genus dies condet', Luc. 8. 332 'una dies mundi damnauit fata?', Stat.
Theb. 3. 148 'felices, quos una dies, manus abstulit una', 3. 191, Sil. 2.
4–5 'ter centum memorabat auos, quos turbine Martis | abstulit una
dies'. The motif of *abstulit una dies* is not unexpectedly found in
sepulchral inscriptions, perhaps under the influence of Virgil's 'abstu-
lit atra dies' (*A.* 6. 429): see *CLE* 405. 1, 1307. 7–8 'apstulit haec unus tot
tantaq. munera nob(is) | perfidus infelix horrificusque dies'. Here
Statius replaces *abstulit* with *rettulit*, and *una dies* with *lux una*.

For the apparent pleonasm of *retro . . . rettulit*, compare Lucr. 4. 310
'inde retro rursum redit', Virg. *G.* 1. 199–200 'sic omnia fatis | in peius
ruere ac retro sublapsa referri', *A.* 2. 169–70 'ex illo fluere ac retro

sublapsa referri | spes Danaum', 9. 794 'retro redit', 9. 797–8 'haud
aliter retro dubius uestigia Turnus | improperata refert', Phaed. 2. 1. 6
'feroque uiso rettulit retro pedem', Sil. 9. 506–7 'atque omnis retro
flatu occursante refertur | lancea'. Though Statius uses *retro* some
thirty times in the *Thebaid* (and not at all in the *Achilleid*), its only other
appearance in the *Silvae* is at 1. 4. 68.

274–5. nihil exoret: a pointed juxtaposition, since *exoro* usually
denotes *successful* appeals (*Silv.* 5. 2. 94 n.). Compare 'inexorabile
fatum' (Virg. *G.* 2. 491) for a similar negation of the force of *exoro*.

chelys aut tua . . . aut mea: the repetition of *chelys* from 271,
where it referred to Orpheus' poetry, emphasizes the similarities
between the myth and the situation of the poem; both involve the
attempt to triumph over death through poetry. *aut tua . . . aut mea*: cf.
'nostra . . . | Thebais' (233–4).

patrios contingere uultus: a reminiscence of Virg. *A.* 6. 108–9
'ire ad conspectum cari genitoris et ora | contingat [*M* : contingam
PR]', where Aeneas wishes to see his father Anchises in the under-
world. Whereas the Virgilian *contingat* is an impersonal verb construed
with an infinitive meaning 'may it happen that . . .', Statius varies the
verb's usage, for here *contingere* means 'to touch'. Silius also has this
usage of *contingere* at Sil. 13. 403 'adspectus orat contingere patrum',
13. 506 'patrios uisu contingere manes', referring to Scipio's wish to
encounter the shades of his father and uncle.

275. sit (ʂ): it is hard to see what M's *sic*, 'in this way', should refer
to, when the immediately preceding clause has shifted away from
examples of successful reunion after death to the *inability* of Statius or
his father to win over the infernal powers with their music. *sit* gives
better sense and parallels the ensuing jussive subjunctive *sequatur*.

276. et lex quaecumque sequatur: Statius invites upon him-
self whatever decree or condition the infernal powers may enact; cf.
Scipio at Sil. 13. 623–5, who tells his mother that he would have
wished to have seen her in the underworld even if he had had to die.
For *lex* thus see 59–60 above, Virg. *G.* 4. 487 'namque hanc dederat
Proserpina legem', the prescription that Eurydice follow her husband
on the ascent from the underworld, *A.* 12. 819 'nulla fati quod lege
tenetur', *Ciris* 199–200 'uos o crudeli fatorum lege, puellae | Dau-
liades, gaudete'. Mention of the *lex* of the infernal powers gives
a paradoxical sequel to Statius' use of *fas* with reference to his own
wish to surpass their authority. For *quicumque = quiuis*, cf. e.g. Virg.
A. 3. 654.

277. umbrarum reges Aetnaeaque Iuno: the plural *reges* (cf. *Silv.* 5. 1. 259) indicates that Statius' intercession on his father's behalf is addressed to the judges of the dead as well as Dis. The plural is otherwise inexplicable, since Proserpina is denoted by *Aetnaeaque Iuno*; it would be strange if *reges* referred only to Dis and his consort, who is then immediately referred to again.

Gronovius questioned *Aetnaeaque*, and conjectured *Ennaeaque*, in which he was anticipated by Laetus; the rape of Proserpina usually occurs near Enna in Sicily. In Claud. *Rapt. Pros.* there are several passages where manuscripts disagree between Aetna and Enna as the scene for the incident. J. B. Hall on Claud. *Rapt.* 1. 122 (see also Gruzelier ad loc.) notes that Aetna, the less common location (see his list of sources), is nevertheless favoured by most manuscripts, despite the popularity of Ovid's treatment which took place at Enna (*Met.* 5. 385–571);[30] Statius' influence on Claudian is well known (see e.g. Cerrato (1881), 356–93, Hall (1969), 108–10). There is thus no need to emend *Aetnaeaque*: note too that 'Aetnaeis . . . saxis' are mentioned in the context of a simile describing Ceres' grief at *Theb.* 12. 270.

The phrase is nevertheless recondite. Its origin lies in the association of Zeus with Hades. *Il.* 9. 457 refers to the infernal powers as Ζεύς τε καταχθόνιος καὶ ἐπαινὴ Περσεφόνεια, while Hes. *Op.* 465 recommends prayer to Διὶ χθονίῳ Δημήτερί θ' ἁγνῇ in order to secure a good crop from the land, Demeter here taking the role of a chthonic deity; cf. Diosc. *A.P.* 7. 31. 9 ἐν Δηοῦς, equivalent to εἰν 'Αΐδαο, and see further Farnell (1896–1909), iii. 320–3. In Latin literature this practice continues; the god of the underworld is referred to by such phrases as *Iuppiter Stygius* (Virg. *A.* 4. 638; see Pease ad loc.). His consort is similarly designated by such phrases as *Iuno inferna* (Virg. *A.* 6. 138, *CIL* x. 7576), *Iuno infera* (*Silv.* 2. 1. 147) and *Iuno Stygia* (*Theb.* 4. 526–7). Statius also revives the association of the queen of the underworld with Demeter: thus *Ceres inferna* (*Theb.* 5. 156) and *Ceres profunda* (*Theb.* 4. 459–60).

Both these elements are fused here; the tradition of 'an underworld Juno' is varied with an epithet appropriate to Ceres/Demeter. *Aetnaeaque* not only evokes the alternative tradition of the rape of Proserpina, but also refers to Demeter in her own right. Gelon planned to build a temple for Demeter at Aetna (D.S. 11. 26. 7), a project thwarted by his death.

---

[30] For other texts, see Hall (1969), 200 n. 1.

278. taedas auferte comasque: for the snakes of the Furies as 'hair', see *Silv.* 5. 1. 28 n.; for their torches, see 196–8 n., and contrast the 'laetas... faces' which Proserpina sends to greet the dead Priscilla as she is welcomed to Elysium (*Silv.* 5. 1. 254).

279. nullo sonet... ore: for *nullus* denoting *non ullus* compare 251 'nulloque e uulnere tristem'. At *Silv.* 5. 1. 249, Statius consoles Abascantus with the thought that Priscilla will not be troubled by the barkings of Cerberus (see n.); contrast 5. 2. 94–5 (Crispinus' wish that Cerberus could be kept away from his dead mother).

ianitor: Cerberus is the 'doorkeeper' of the underworld; cf. *Theb.* 2. 54, Hor. *Carm.* 3. 11. 16, Virg. *A.* 6. 400, 8. 296, Sil. 3. 36.

280. This collection of mythical creatures is Virgilian; Aeneas meets them (and others) before his arrival at the Styx (*A.* 6. 285–9).

Hydraeque greges neatly points to the many heads of the Hydra.

Scyllaeaque monstra: for the plural to denote the type of which the sea-monster Scylla is an example, cf. Virg. *A.* 6. 286 'Scyllae biformes'; cf. Lucr. 5. 890–4, where Centaurs appear as well:

> ne forte ex homine et ueterino semine equorum
> confieri credas Centauros posse neque esse,
> aut rabidis canibus succinctas semimarinis
> corporibus Scyllas et cetera de genere horum,
> inter se quorum discordia membra uidemus;

Cic. *ND* 1. 108 'quid, quod earum rerum, quae numquam omnino fuerunt neque esse potuerunt, ut Scyllae, ut Chimaerae' is similar in thought. Compare Manto's catalogue of monsters (*Theb.* 4. 533–5):

> quid tibi monstra Erebi, Scyllas et inane furentes
> Centauros solidoque intorta adamante Gigantum
> uincula et angustam centeni Aegaeonis umbram?

In Scipio's meeting with the shades in Silius, Scylla is mentioned with the Cyclopes and the horses of Diomede at Sil. 13. 440–1, and with Briareus, the Sphinx, the Centaurs, and the Giants at 13. 587–90.

281–3. For the affectionate portrayal of the usually truculent Charon, cf. *Silv.* 2. 1. 186–8 and 5. 1. 250–2 (see 5. 1. 249–52 n.). At 5. 1. 250–2, Statius adjures Abascantus not to fear that the boat will be late, while at 2. 1. 186–8 Charon helps the young Glaucias to board his vessel. Here the crowd gives way as Charon helps the old man onto his boat.

282. discussa plebe: for *plebes* referring to the dead, cf. *Theb.* 4. 608 and the *turba* (Virg. *A.* 6. 305) rejected by Charon at *A.* 6. 316 'ast alios longe summotos arcet harena'. The language is political; *discutio* can denote the forcible dispersal of an assembly (*OLD* s.v. *discutio* 3c), an impression enhanced by *plebe*.

283. uector: although Virgil does not use this word of Charon— he calls him *portitor* (*A.* 6. 298, 326; cf. *Theb.* 4. 479, 12. 559, *Silv.* 2. 1. 229) and *nauita* (6. 315, 385; cf. *Silv.* 2. 1. 186, 5. 1. 251)—it nevertheless recalls *Aeneid* 6: at *A.* 6. 391 Charon remarks 'corpora uiua nefas Stygia *uectare* carina'. Though *uector* is regularly used to denote a passenger on a ship (*OLD* s.v. 2a), here it is used etymologically to denote the boatman as a person who is 'conveying' the passenger; cf. Apul. *Met.* 6. 20 where *uector* is also used of Charon in the context of Psyche's *katabasis*.

in media componat molliter alno: M's *alga*, 'weed, seaweed', has been questioned. Markland considered *ulua* (cf. Virg. *A.* 6. 416 'informi limo glaucaque exponit in ulua'), but retained *alga* on the grounds that *alga* can signify weed on the banks of rivers as well as on the seashore. However, there are more serious difficulties, equally applicable to *alga* and *ulua*.

In the first instance, *componat* is not equivalent to *exponit* (used by Virgil of disembarkation in the passage quoted above; for *exponere* as the *vox propria* for bringing persons or objects onto the shore, see *ThLL* v/2. 1757. 36–1758. 29). *componat* can only mean that Charon 'sets his passenger to rest' (*OLD* s.v. *compono* 4b and 4c; the verb appears in funerary contexts); at Prop. 1. 11. 14 when Cynthia is described as 'molliter in tacito litore compositam' she should be imagined not as having disembarked, but as enjoying her repose on the beach. Superficially, *alga* might be possible; Charon could settle Statius' father on the seaweed at the conclusion of the journey; for 'molliter alga' perhaps compare Luc. 5. 520–1 'molli consurgit Amyclas | quem dabat alga toro', V.Fl. 1. 252 'molli iuuenes funduntur in alga'. But passage of the Styx does not mark the end of a soul's journey; in Virgil's topography of the underworld, Elysium is not situated beside the Styx. It follows that Statius' father would hardly rest on reaching the shore, but would continue his eventual progress to Elysium. However, Charon could have set his passenger at ease whilst the crossing itself was taking place (compare *Silv.* 5. 1. 252 'et manes placidus locat hospite cumba'). Furthermore, M's *media* is a curious epithet for *alga* (or indeed *ulua*): why should Charon set Statius' father down specifically in the middle of the seaweed (which itself seems an odd way to refer to the shore)? This last difficulty might encourage replacing *alga* with a word for a boat; there is at least a point to placing a person in the middle of a boat, since it is likely to be the most stable and comfortable place during travel.

Slater suggested *alno*, comparing *Theb.* 4. 479 'et plena redeat Styga portitor alno' and Juv. 3. 266 'nec sperat caenosi gurgitis alnum' as parallels for *alnus* as a boat from alder-wood; see further *ThLL* i. 1705. 77–1706. 22, where the earliest instance is Virg. *G.* 2. 451 (see also *G.* 1. 136). The parallel from the *Thebaid* is good, and this is a promising conjecture. Alternatively, and with the alteration of *media* as well, emend to *medio . . . alueo*, scanning *alueo* as a disyllable; for *alueus* denoting a ship, see *ThLL* i. 1790. 6–31. The scansion (the only possible means of incorporating *alueo* in a hexameter) may echo Virgil, who used the word with the same meaning and the same scansion in the same *locus* at *A.* 6. 412–13 'simul accipit alueo | ingentem Aenean', where the subject is Charon. Statius also uses this scansion in the sixth foot (but with a different meaning of *alueus*) at *Theb.* 9. 225: 'solito tunc plenior alueo'. For such recondite allusion cf. Statius' use of the Virgilian dative of motion *Auerno* in 271; such erudition might suit a tribute to his father and teacher.

284–7. This command to the blessed dead and to the Greek poets corresponds to the earlier account of the father's presence in Elysium (24–7).

284. ite: the imperative dramatizes this passage; the poem goes back in time to the moment of his father's arrival. Compare Priscilla's arrival among the welcoming heroines of old (*Silv.* 5. 1. 254–7 with n.), where there is, however, no comparable use of the vocative. Here Statius addresses the inhabitants of the underword directly.

Graiumque examina uatum: neither here nor at 24–7 (his father's meeting with Homer and Hesiod) does Statius mention Latin poets. This may be partly attributable to his father's academic interest in Greek poetry (146–61), but the omission also suggests the supremacy of Statius senior (note too that no Greek poet is actually named). Contrast Domitius Marsus' epigram on the death of Tibullus (quoted by Suetonius in his *Vita Tibulli*), where death sends Tibullus as a *comes* for Virgil in Elysium, in order that both the genres of epic and elegy be represented in the underworld.

285. inlustremque animam Lethaeis spargite sertis: *spargite* points to the etymology of *inlustris*, associated with *lustro* and purification; compare Ov. *Pont.* 3. 2. 73 'spargit aqua captos lustrali Graia sacerdos', *Theb.* 10. 777 'sanguine tunc spargit turres et moenia lustrat'. Moreover, *Lethaeis* further suggests purification by water. *inlustrem* might recall Statius' father's success in *lustra* (competitions); see 253–4 n.

Garlands (*sertis*) are a typical gift of welcome (cf. *Silv.* 5. 1. 257), but their poetic significance, both as the reward of victory and as a metaphor for verse itself (e.g. Mart. 8. 82. 4 'scimus et haec etiam serta placere tibi'), is resonant as well.

286. nemus: in his account of Elysium, Virg. *A.* 6. 656–65 locates practitioners of such virtues as poetry 'inter odoratum lauris *nemus*' (*A.* 6. 658). *nemus* and similar words can represent a place of retreat and hence poetic inspiration as at *Ach.* 1. 10, Prop. 3. 1. 2, 3. 3. 42, Tac. *Dial.* 12. 1; cf. *Silv.* 5. 5. 6 'numquid inaccesso posui uestigia luco?' The sense of retreat is enhanced by the statement that no *Erinys* has entered the grove; contrast the interruption to Statius' father's teaching (195–6), where an *Erinys* causes civil war. *nemus* may also suggest Statius' own *Silvae* (see General Introduction, p. xviii n. 6 above); for the metapoetic qualities of words like *silua*, see Hinds (1998), 11–14.

inrupit: there is no grammatical reason to emend M's reading; the perfect tense gives the sense 'No Fury has (ever) intruded'.

287. falsa dies caeloque simillimus aer: cf. Virgil's account of Elysium (*A.* 6. 640–1): 'largior hic campos aether et lumine uestit | purpureo, solemque suum, sua sidera norunt.'

288. uenias melior: instead of bidding farewell, Statius concludes by summoning his father from the underworld. Contrast the end of *Silv.* 5. 1, where Statius assures Abascantus that Priscilla will be acting on his behalf in the underworld, but with no hint of a further meeting during his lifetime. Cf. also 3. 3. 204, where Claudius Etruscus expresses his hope for 'adfatusque pios monituraque somnia' from his father, before final words of parting are offered by Statius to the latter. Closer to the spirit of this passage is the ending of 2. 1, where Glaucias is summoned from the underworld, since he alone can obtain whatever he asks for (228). Here, Statius expresses the hope that his father is not under the sway of the underworld, and may return to his son, even if it is only in sleep. Cf. 'sed uenies melior' (*Silv.* 5. 2. 164), which anticipates not only Crispinus' return from foreign service, but also his presence at one of Statius' recitations; *melior* here is harder to interpret than in the passage from 5. 2, but the sense would seem to be that when Statius' father finally comes to Statius, it will be better for Statius than the current circumstances of his grief. There is no need to adopt the punctuation of Köstlin (1876), 522 (accepted by Klotz), whereby a comma precedes *melior* so that it agrees with *porta*: since the gate of horn is said to surpass that of ivory (*uincere*), *melior* would be a redundant epithet.

288–9. The reference here to Aeneas' departure from the underworld by means of the gate of ivory, whence come false dreams (Virg. *A*. 6. 893–9 and see Austin ad loc. for parallels and discussions: cf. e.g. *Od*. 19. 562–7, Pl. *Chrm*. 173 A 7–8, Hor. *Carm*. 3. 27. 39–42), does not answer the problems of the celebrated Virgilian passage. Statius' father will leave from the gate of horn, because that is the place of egress for *uerae umbrae* (*A*. 6. 894). And just as Statius would wish to meet his father in the underworld, something that was accomplished by Aeneas, and by others (266–76), he requests that his father leave the underworld through the gate of horn, surpassing the ivory one used by Aeneas, so that here he even asks that his father outdo Virgil's hero. But our passage does not explain *why* Aeneas leaves by the ivory gate. Leofranc Holford-Strevens has suggested to me that Statius may be transcending the controversy over what Virgil's gate of ivory signified by requesting that his father leave the underworld through the gate of horn, and then adding the references to the feigned piety of Numa, Scipio, and Sulla (see 290–3 n.), to create a new puzzle of his own.

289–90. monstra: a final request for his father's guidance, a theme sustained throughout the poem. Statius began by invoking his dead father's assistance in the composition of the epicedion, then narrated his father's support and contribution to his own poetic career, and finally presents himself as still in need of instruction. Cf. *Silv*. 3. 3. 204 (with Laguna) where Claudius Etruscus asks his dead father for 'monituraque somnia'; cf. also Ennius' dream of Homer in the first book of the *Annales*, Esteve-Forriol (1962), 149. For the didactic force of *monstro*, see 137 n.; the verb is used of Statius' father at 181 and 237.

290–3. Statius' three examples of divine guidance, Numa's consultations with the nymph Egeria, Scipio's connections with Jove himself, and Sulla's claim of support from Apollo, curiously appear in the same order as the first three examples of feigned religion in both the Parisian and Nepotian extracts of Valerius Maximus 1. 2. 1–3. Whether or not Statius was familiar with this text, the use of these strange *exempla* needs to be considered.

Indeed Statius has already cited two examples of 'ficta pietate' at 244–5, setting his mother's grief for her husband alongside the feigned devotion offered to Attis and Osiris. Just as his mother's devotion was compared to inauspicious examples (if M's *ut* in 244 is retained), his father's guiding role is illustrated by instances which, though questionable and indeed doubtful in themselves, demonstrate the type of continuing association which Statius desires from his father after death. It might be argued that these examples imply a kind of scepticism about his father on Statius' part, but this would seem to accord ill with the positive way in which his father is presented throughout the poem. It may be better to see Statius as complimenting his father, imagining that he will surpass such spurious examples of divine guidance; one may compare *Silv.* 4. 6 where the statue of Hercules was previously owned by Alexander, Hannibal, and Sulla, but has now found a worthy owner in the person of Novius Vindex (4. 6. 106–9), also the end of a poem. There may even be an element of the literary man's disdain for lesser activities here: Numa, Scipio, and Sulla may have spuriously claimed to possess divine guidance, but Statius, as a poet, will hope to surpass this through his father's continuing poetical influence after death. One may perhaps compare Statius' request at the beginning of the poem for his father's inspiration (1–5).

At the same time, it is worth noting that the choice of examples may reflect the fact that Statius is only making a request here, and is not describing his father's future appearances with the same certainty as we find in poems addressed to others (see General Introduction, pp. xlv–xlvi); one can also contrast this passage with ll. 19–27, where Statius' description of his father either learning about the mysteries of the heavens or engaging in poetry with Hesiod and Homer seems more confident.

For Numa's association with Egeria (also called *nympha* by Ovid at *Met.* 15. 482, *Fast.* 3. 261–2), intended to convince his people to obey his dictates and to validate his religious innovations, see Liv. 1. 19. 5, 1. 21. 3, Plu. *Numa* 4. 1–3. *mitis* recalls the tradition that Numa desired his people to be less warlike (Liv. 1. 19. 2, Ov. *Fast.* 3. 277–84). The Arician valley in Latium was the resort of Egeria after her husband's death (Ov. *Met.* 15. 487–90) and the location of her eponymous spring (Ov. *Fast.* 3. 275). For cynicism with regard to Numa and Egeria, note the manner in which their meetings are referred to at Juv. 3. 12 'ubi nocturnae Numa constituebat amicae'.

On Scipio's nocturnal consultations with Capitoline Jupiter, see Gel. 6. 1. 6, who cites Oppius and Hyginus as authorities for the visits to the temple; see also Eutr. 3. 20. 2, *De Viris Illustribus* 49, Holford-Strevens (2003), 287 and n. 123. On the origins of this legend, see Walbank (1967) and Scullard (1970), 19 ff, who both suggest that the tradition of temple visitations was in existence by the middle of the second century BC; scepticism about Scipio's divine connections is evident in as early and as favourable a source as Polybius (10. 2. 8–13), who saw Scipio as wanting to make an impression on the people. *creditur* could be felt to glance at such scepticism. Markland compares this tale with Caligula's conversations with the moon and Capitoline Jupiter (Suet. *Cal.* 22. 4).

As for Sulla, Plu. *Sull.* 29. 11–12 relates that before the battle of the Colline Gate, he appealed to Apollo for victory, kissing a golden image of the god which he had always carried in battle. Sulla's taste for such images is also attested by Statius at *Silv.* 4. 6. 85–8 (Vindex's statue of Hercules had previously been a feature of Sulla's home). Sulla's continuing poor reputation is attested under the empire at e.g. Tac. *Hist.* 2. 38. 1 'nobilium saeuissimus Lucius Sulla'; Statius himself at *Silv.* 4. 6. 107 refers to 'saeui . . . uox horrida Sullae'.

Apollo's appearance in a context of inspiration suggests poetry. Note that the other two *exempla* are linked with poetry as well: Jupiter, through his patronage of the poetic competition which Statius was unable to win, and Egeria, since her spring is associated with the Camenae, the Latin Muses (e.g. Ov. *Fast.* 3. 275 'Egeria est, quae praebet aquas, dea grata Camenis'; at *Met.* 15. 482 Numa is *felix* not only because of his wife, but also because of the Camenae). Hence the similes end with the implication that Statius' father will be a quasi-divine patron of his son's literary endeavours. Statius initially declared that he could not ask Apollo for help (3–9); hence his request to his father for inspiration (3 and 28). In the *Thebaid*, cf. Thiodamas, who explains that his prophetic inspiration comes from his human predecessor Amphiaraus (*Theb.* 10. 189–91), in refutation of the narrator's own speculation that Apollo or Juno may have inspired him (*Theb.* 10. 162–3), and see further P. Hardie (1993), 111–13.

At the end of the poem, although there has been a movement away from his grief-stricken inability to compose, Statius still requests his father's assistance and inspiration, most tellingly indicated by the comparison with Apollo.

Poem Four

INTRODUCTION

Summary: *The poet asks Somnus, the god of sleep, why he alone is denied sleep, when it is enjoyed by the rest of the natural world (1–6). His insomnia has lasted for seven days and nights and is beyond endurance (7–13). Let the god come to him and give him at least some respite (14–19).*

The poem is an appeal to the god Somnus, and has affinities with the genre of the kletic hymn.[1] Thus there is a concluding plea for his presence (*inde ueni* in l. 16, which invokes the actuality of sleep, as well as the god), but other features of the genre are also present, such as the account of the god's power in 3–6 (for universal dominion, compare V.Fl. 8. 70 'Somne omnipotens', addressed by Medea to the god, and Venus' sway in Lucr. 1. 1–20), and the use of what is close to anaphora in ll. 7–10 (*septima* followed by *totidem* and *totiens*). However, Statius does not use all components of the hymn; thus there are no lists of locations and cult titles favoured by the god. In fact, the poem begins with reproaches; Somnus is asked what *crimen* or *error* has brought about the poet's misfortune, a clear indication of a perceived injustice.

The poem's opening reproach recalls another type of poem, the aubade, an address to the dawn or to the Morning Star.[2] A particularly important poem is Ov. *Am.* 1. 13, where Ovid asks Aurora to delay the onset of morning and thus a separation from his mistress. There are motifs shared by both poems: the Dawn ignores Statius' complaints in 9–10 (cf. *Am.* 1. 13. 47–8 'iurgia finieram, scires audisse: rubebat, | nec tamen adsueto tardius orta dies') and there are images of a lover fortunate in his mistress's arms: compare ll. 14–15 with *Am.*

---

[1] For a fuller discussion of the poem and the literary background see Carrai (1990), 11–27, Gibson (1996), on its hymnic features Laguna (1990), 124–5, 128, 135. The classic account of the *Du-Stil* (second-person address to a god) is Norden (1913), 143–63.

[2] Examples from Greek, Roman, and other cultures are collected by Hatto (1965), esp. 255–63 and 271–81; see also Cairns (1972), 137.

1. 13. 5–6: 'nunc iuuat in teneris dominae iacuisse lacertis; | si quando, lateri nunc bene iuncta meo est' and cf. *A.P.* 5. 172 and 173 (Meleager). But Statius' complaint is not made against Aurora but Somnus; Aurora is even sympathetic to the poet's suffering ('et gelido spargit miserata flagello', 10). Similarly the fortunate lovers are not concerned with repelling the onset of morning, but that of sleep.

The structure of the poem has been much disputed,[3] but it is perhaps dangerous to force so short and fluid a poem into too rigid a framework. An examination of changes of direction in the rhetoric and thought of the poem may be more valuable. Thus, after the opening complaint and description of the sleeping world, 'septima *iam* rediens' (7) marks the shift to an account of Statius' privations. 'unde ego sufficiam' (11) arrestingly heralds a change from description to entreaty, an entreaty intensified in line 14 with 'at nunc, heu', before the climax of 'inde ueni' (16), the simplest phrase in the poem. The poem ends on a paradoxical note; if Somnus is unwilling to assist, he is at least to pass by quietly (19), so as not to disturb Statius.

As with the motifs of Dawn poetry already mentioned, Statius' handling of other *topoi* is highly inventive. In the first instance he has transformed the whole notion of an appeal to the god of sleep. The first example of an attempt to persuade the god comes in *Iliad* 14, where Hera implores the assistance of Hypnos (233–41 and 264–9). Note also the appeals of Iris to the god of Sleep at Ov. *Met.* 11. 623–9, Stat. *Theb.* 10. 126–31, Nonn. 31. 132–96, and Juno's appeal to Somnus at Sil. 10. 337–50; see further Laguna (1990), 126–7. In these epic examples the intervention of Somnus is requested in order to further a particular device or policy. In the *Iliad* Hera has Hypnos overcome Zeus so that the Achaeans may succeed on the battlefield. In the *Metamorphoses* Juno dispatches Iris to ask Somnus to send Alcyone a dream so that she may know that her husband Ceyx is dead. In the *Thebaid* Iris, acting on Juno's behalf, asks for the Thebans to be overwhelmed by sleep so that they shall be easy prey for their enemies, while in the *Punica*, Juno asks that Somnus send a dream to Hannibal to deter him from a futile march on Rome. In Nonnos, Hera sends Iris (who is instructed to take the form of Hypnos' mother, Night) to win over the god, so that she can seduce Zeus, as a means of helping the Indians against Dionysus. In this poem, however, Statius appeals to Somnus without any intermediary, being solely concerned

---

[3] See H. Friedrich (1963), 52–4, Cancik (1965), 28, Newmyer (1979), 115.

with sleep, and only as a respite from sleeplessness.[4] Hence the much greater immediacy of his plea to Somnus.

On a smaller scale we can also see alteration to a familiar topos. In ll. 2–6 there is the habitual comparison between the isolation of a sleepless individual and the calm of the natural world (see 3–6 n.), yet the expected order, with the description of nocturnal calm coming first, is inverted because we have already been told ('donis ut solus egerem') of Statius' circumstances.

Although the poem is short, it nevertheless conveys a sense of a personality which comprehends a curious mixture of boldness and caution. Although Statius initially challenges the god, asking if he deserves his suffering, there is no further address to Somnus until the final sentence beginning in l. 14. Even here, Statius is immediately more defensive after his appeal ('inde ueni'), telling Somnus that Statius only requires to be touched with the 'extremo... cacumine uirgae'.

The poem mysteriously avoids giving a direct explanation of Statius' insomnia. Noise is not the cause; indeed Statius emphasizes that the world around him is quiet, and he avoids all impression of an urban setting.[5] Nor does Statius allude to the association of insomnia and literary creation.[6] Similarly, there is no context to suggest that Statius' insomnia is the result of love or grief.[7] This elusiveness may be a reason for the poem's unusual popularity among the *Silvae*.[8] *Silv.*

---

[4] Compare Medea's direct complaint of insomnia at V.Fl. 7. 9–20, which is not, however, addressed to Somnus.

[5] For the noise of the city see e.g. Hor. *Ep.* 1. 17. 6–7, 2. 2. 79, Sen. *Ep.* 56, Mart. 10. 74, 12. 57, 12. 68. 5–6, Juv. 3. 232–42. Note also *Silv.* 3. 5. 83–8, where Statius attributes his retirement to Naples to a desire to avoid the noise of Rome; cf. Mart. 12. 18. 13–16.

[6] For wakefulness as a prelude to literary composition, see Call. *Epigr.* 27 Pf., Cat. 50. 10–15, Cic. *Att.* 9. 10. 1, Plin. *Ep.* 3. 5. 8, 5. 5. 7, Lyne on *Ciris* 46, Laguna on *Silv.* 3. 5. 35, Coleman on 4. 6. 25–6; cf. *Theb.* 12. 811–12. Note too Paus. 2. 31. 3, on an altar at Troezen, where the people conducted sacrifices to the Muses and Hypnos, λέγοντες τὸν Ὕπνον θεὸν μάλιστα εἶναι φίλον ταῖς Μούσαις, and see Kambylis (1965), 109.

[7] Vollmer's argument (546) that Statius' insomnia is related to his laments in 5. 3 and 5. 5 is questionable in view of the uncertain status of Book 5 (see General Introduction). Laguna (1990) suggests that it might be caused by the loss of his wife, arguing that a link between Statius and Orpheus is established in ll. 3–10 (see discussion in the commentary below). A. J. Pomeroy (1986) argues that the poem is an erotic invitation to Somnus.

[8] See Mackail (1895), 188–9. Coulter (1959) boldly argues, on the basis of similarities with Boccaccio's *Elegia di Madonna Fiametta*, that the poem may have circulated independently before Poggio's discovery of M; see further Carrai (1990), 28–33, who suggests that the apparent echoes of Statius in Boccaccio may perhaps be attributable to this poem's having circulated independently in a manner comparable to *Silv.* 2. 7.

5. 4 has been at least a forerunner of, and sometimes a model for, several later works on sleep, such as Quevedo's *El sueño*, on which see Crosby–Lerner (1986); for the tradition of poetry addressed to Sleep in Italian literature, see Carrai (1990). Compare also the poems by Fyfe, Sidney, Daniel, Drummond, Wordsworth, Keats, Hartley Coleridge, and Warton in *The Oxford Book of Latin Verse*, ed. H. W. Garrod (Oxford, 1912), 493–500. For a modern and disturbing treatment of insomnia (owing nothing to Statius) see Sylvia Plath's *Insomniac*.

COMMENTARY

1–2. crimine quo ... quoue errore: for the distinction between deliberate and unintentional wrongdoing compare *Silv.* 5. 5. 7–8 'quae culpa, quis error | quem luimus tanti?', Ov. *Met.* 3. 141–2 'at bene si quaeras, fortunae crimen in illo | non scelus inuenies; quid enim scelus error habebat?' As noted by Laguna (1990), 126, this distinction is an ongoing motif in Ovid's exile poetry: cf. *Tr.* 1. 3. 37–8, 3. 1. 51–2 'in quo poenarum, quas se meruisse fatetur, | non facinus causam, sed suus error habet', 3. 5. 51–2, 4. 10. 89–90 'scite, precor, causam (nec uos mihi fallere fas est) | errorem iussae, non scelus, esse fugae', *Pont.* 3. 3. 75. At *Tr.* 2. 207, in a variation on this theme, Ovid obscurely ascribes his downfall to 'carmen et error'. See further Frank on Sen. *Phoen.* 203–15.

For 'crimine quo' cf. Cic. *Clu.* 61 'condemnastis Scamandrum, quo crimine?', 105, *Vat.* 41, *Cael.* 71, Luc. 2. 108 'crimine quo parui caedem potuere mereri', Juv. 6. 219–20 'meruit quo crimine seruus | supplicium?'

iuuenis is better taken with *placidissime diuum* than with *merui*; compare *Silv.* 3. 3. 208 'senior mitissime patrum'. The age and appearance of the god of sleep vary greatly in literature and artistic representations. Hesiod, *Th.* 756 has Night holding her child Sleep, the brother of Death, μετὰ χερσί, and this was presumably the tradition influencing the chest of Cypselos seen by Pausanias (5. 18. 1) at Olympia, where Sleep and Death are portrayed as infants in their mother's arms. In fifth-century vase paintings Sleep and Death are sometimes depicted as boys, and sometimes as bearded youths when carrying off the corpses of Sarpedon (cf. *Il.* 16. 682–3) and Memnon. In Roman times the god is variously portrayed as youthful or elderly; representation of the Endymion myth with an aged Somnus is found on some sarcophagi of the second century AD (*LIMC* s.v.

Hypnos 84, 89, 94–8). For discussion of the iconography of the god, see Vermeule (1979), 150, Laguna (1990), 137–8, Stafford (1991–3), Vaquerizo Gil and Noguera Celdrán (1997), 150–9.

The Latin literary tradition reflects the complexities of the artistic one. Virgil calls Somnus *leuis* as he descends from the heavens bringing a fatal sleep to Palinurus (*A.* 5. 838); the word might suggest the lightness of youth, but could equally well refer to the ease with which the god makes his journey. However, Ovid's Somnus is not young (*Met.* 11. 633–5, 646):

> at *pater* e populo natorum mille suorum
> excitat artificem simulatoremque figurae
> Morphea...
> praeterit hos *senior*...

In *Theb.* 10, where Statius imitates Iris' visit to Somnus in the *Met.* (ultimately derived from Hera's visit to Hypnos in *Iliad* 14), the age of the god is nebulous, although the languid description of his hair makes it unlikely that he is *senex* (*Theb.* 10. 110–11): 'manus haec fusos a tempore laeuo | sustentat crines'.

In this poem the god is gentle and youthful. For *iuuenis* applied to a god, cf. Ov. *Met.* 1. 530–1 'sed enim non sustinet ultra | perdere blanditias iuuenis deus'.

For the kinship of Sleep and Death, already mentioned, cf. *Il.* 14. 231, 16. 672, 682–3, Virg. *A.* 6. 278 'consanguineus Leti Sopor', Sen. *Her. F.* 1069, V.Fl. 8. 74, Stat. *Theb.* 5. 197, [Plu.] *ad Apoll.* 107 D–F with Kassel (1958), 77–8. For the similarity between sleep and death, cf. Virg. *A.* 6. 522 'alta quies placidaeque simillima morti', Sil. 15. 180 'nox similes morti dederat placidissima somnos'; note also Luc. 9. 818 'et socias somno descendis ad umbras' with the discussion of Hunink (1999).

placidissime diuum: compare Iris' words to Somnus at *Theb.* 10. 126–7 'mitissime diuum, | Somne' and Ov. *Met.* 11. 623 'Somne, quies rerum, placidissime, Somne, deorum'. Common to these addresses and the present poem is the use of a wheedling and flattering epithet as a *captatio beneuolentiae*. But the circumstances are not the same; whereas Iris in the epics asks Somnus to use his powers on others, this plea is more intense and personal, a simple request to be able to enjoy the benefits of sleep. *placidissime* also heightens the contrast between the god and Statius, who is *miser* (2); the speaker appeals that he too may become *placidissimus*.

For the appositional style of address in hymns, see N.–H. on Hor. *Carm.* 1. 10. 1, Norden, (1913), 148.

2. donis: for the 'gifts' of sleep, compare *Il.* 7. 482 καὶ ὕπνου δῶρον ἕλοντο.

3–6. This passage describing a scene of nocturnal calm recalls the contrast between Dido's insomnia and the peaceful sleep of the surrounding world at Virg. *A.* 4. 522–32 (see further Laguna (1990), 127–32):

> Nox erat et placidum carpebant fessa soporem
> corpora per terras, siluaeque et saeua quierant
> aequora, cum medio uoluuntur sidera lapsu,
525 > cum tacet omnis ager, pecudes pictaeque uolucres,
> quaeque lacus late liquidos quaeque aspera dumis
527 > rura tenent, somno positae sub nocte silenti.
529 > at non infelix animi Phoenissa, neque umquam
530 > soluitur in somnos oculisue aut pectore noctem
> accipit: ingeminant curae rursusque resurgens
> saeuit amor magnoque irarum fluctuat aestu.

For such scenes of universal sleep see Pease on Virg. *A.* 4. 522, and see also Gibson (1996), 457–60. Here Statius reverses the usual order; instead of beginning with a description of nocturnal calm, he places his own isolation first ('donis ut solus egerem'), adding to the urgency and intensity of the complaint. Note that in this passage he describes the sleeping world in the manner of an epic narrator; on the tension between the narrative mode and the speaker's situation in the poem (one might not expect an insomniac first person narrator to have omniscience about the calm conditions enjoyed everywhere else), see Gibson (1996), 460–3.

Although the *Iliad* (2. 1–15, 10. 1–16, and 24. 1–11) sets a precedent for the contrast between a sleepless individual and calm surroundings, the first extensive description of the sleeping world is Alcman fr. 89 (Page), where εὕδω is applied to a variety of natural features; see Page (1951), 159–61, cf. Alfageme (1978), Virg. *A.* 4. 522–7, where woods and seas are said to be asleep, Stat. *Silv.* 3. 2. 73 'ante rates pigro torpebant aequora somno'.

3. tacet omne pecus uolucresque feraeque: for the wording, compare e.g. *Theb.* 1. 339 'iam pecudes uolucresque tacent', Lucr. 4. 1197–8 'nec ratione alia uolucres armenta feraeque | et pecudes et equae maribus subsidere possent', Virg. *A.* 4. 525 (see previous n.),

Ov. *Met.* 7. 185–6 'homines uolucresque ferasque | soluerat alta quies', Sil. 15. 86.

4. simulant: a bold stroke; the trees 'feign' sleep, itself a kind of personification.

fessos curuata cacumina somnos: compare *Theb.* 10. 144 'demittunt extrema cacumina siluae' where the woods are affected by the journey of Somnus, on his way down to do Iris' bidding. Here too the *cacumina* are the tops of trees rather than mountains; despite the sleep of the ὀρέων κορυφαί and φάραγγες in Alcman fr. 89, it is more difficult to envisage immobile mountains as *curuata*, rather than the tops of trees.

fessos ... somnos stands in striking contrast to the divine Somnus, *placidissime diuum* (1). *fessos* is paradoxical ('tired sleep'), sleep being usually coupled with more positive adjectives such as *facilis* or *leuis* (N.–H. on Hor. *Carm.* 2. 11. 8).

5. nec trucibus fluuiis idem sonus: a curious observation, since rivers do not run more quietly at night, and one might expect their sound to be *more* noticeable in the stillness of night. Rather than artlessness, this detail is part of the attempt to cajole the god into granting Statius' request; Statius flatteringly conveys in these lines the extent of Somnus' power over the world, in keeping with an address to a god who enjoyed the Homeric epithet πανδαμάτωρ, as at *Il.* 24. 5 and at *Od.* 9. 373 (cf. Nonn. 31. 143, 158 Ὕπνε, τί πανδαμάτωρ κικλήσκεαι); cf. Hera's address to Hypnos as Ὕπνε, ἄναξ πάντων τε θεῶν πάντων τ' ἀνθρώπων (*Il.* 14. 233), and see further Gibson (1996), 459–60.

For the noise of rivers, cf. *Il.* 18. 576 πὰρ ποταμὸν κελάδοντα, Bacch. 9(8). 65 ποταμοῦ κελάδοντος, A.R. 3. 532 ποταμοὺς... κελαδεινὰ ῥέοντας, Virg. *A.* 12. 524 'dant sonitum spumosi amnes, et in aequora currunt', *Theb.* 4. 807–9 'iamque amne propinquo | rauca sonat uallis, saxosumque impulit aures | murmur'. *trux* can suggest either loudness or fierceness: both seem appropriate here. For *trux* applied to a body of water cf. Cat. 4. 9, Hor. *Carm.* 1. 3. 10.

There may also be a purely verbal play here. After the repetition of *Somne* and *somnos* in ll. 3 and 4,[9] *nec ... idem sonus* points to the change of sound as *somnus* gives way to *sonus*.

---

[9] For the framing of a pair of lines with a near-repetition of a word, see Wills (1996), 430–5, who notes that it is a common feature of elegy. His other Statian examples are *Silv.* 1. 2. 272–3, 2. 1. 151–2, *Theb.* 2. 451–2, 11. 566–7.

occidit: there seems to be no comparable usage for *occido* with reference to water falling. *ThLL* ix/2. 350. 23–7 cites instances where *occido* denotes the sinking of a flame (Lucr. 1. 668, Sen. *Oed.* 308, Petr. 22. 6).

5–6. horror | aequoris: for *horror* in a marine context, see *ThLL* vi/3. 2997. 68–75. Note *Theb.* 5. 364 'inde horror aquis'; cf. Luc. 5. 446, 564, V.Fl. 1. 652, Avienus *Arat.* 1397 'sali furit implacabilis horror'. Cognates of *horror* are also used in this manner; cf. e.g. Acc. *trag.* 412 (ap. Non. 422, 32) 'ut tristis turbinum | toleraret hiemes, mare cum horreret fluctibus', Cic. *Rep.* 1. 63, Ov. *Met.* 6. 704, 4. 135–6 where Thisbe 'exhorruit aequoris instar, | quod tremit, exigua cum summum stringitur aura'. Compare the Greek use of cognates of φρίξ, e.g. Antip. Sid. *A.P.* 10. 2. 1–2 θάλασσα | ... φρικὶ χαρασσομένη and Alciphr. 1. 10 Schepers τὴν θάλατταν μὲν, ὡς ὁρᾷς, φρίκη κατέχει; see further LSJ s.v. φρίξ, φρίκη, and φρίσσω.

6. adclinata: cf. *Theb.* 4. 61–2 'quaque obiacet alto | Isthmos et a terris maria inclinata repellit'. *adclinata* suggests a gentler image, as if the seas are resting against the earth.

quiescunt: cf. Virg. *A.* 4. 523–4 'saeua quierant | aequora', 7. 6–7, Sen. *Ep.* 107. 8, V. Fl. 2. 404–5. Contrast V. Fl. 2. 59–60, where the helmsman Tiphys asserts that nighttime, when breezes are stronger, is more suitable for swift progress on the sea.

7–10. At Ov. *Met.* 14. 423–5 Canens endures similar privations:

> sex illam noctes, totidem redeuntia solis
> lumina uiderunt inopem somnique cibique
> per iuga, per ualles, qua fors ducebat, euntem.

Statius' suffering surpasses the mythological suffering of Canens (who endured six nights, whereas for Statius, the *seventh* night is at hand, which was regarded as critical in ancient medicine: see Censorinus, *De die natali* 11. 6, van Dam on *Silv.* 2. 1. 146–7). While Ovid mentions night and sunrise, Statius mentions early evening and early morning (by referring to the *Oetaeae Paphiaeque...lampades*, the Evening and Morning Stars), and also night (*Phoebe*, the moon), as times of sleeplessness. His suffering therefore lasts throughout day and night. Moreover he modifies the typical characterisation of Aurora as indifferent ('nostros Tithonia questus | praeterit'), by introducing an attractive quality, sympathy, expressed with the oxymoron 'miserata flagello'. Furthermore the suffering of Canens seems to occur as a consequence of, or at least in parallel to, her wanderings; Statius' insomnia, by contrast, is isolated from any possible cause or attendant circumstance.

Laguna (1990), 130–2 sees these lines as an amplification of Virg. *A.* 4. 524 'cum medio uoluuntur sidera lapsu', and also sees similarities with descriptions of Orpheus' grief for the second loss of Eurydice, which lasted for seven months in Virg. *G.* 4. 507–10, and for seven days in Ov. *Met.* 10. 73–4. Perhaps note also the seven days mentioned by Evadne, during which time the Argive forces were left unburied (*Theb.* 12. 563–4 'septima iam surgens trepidis Aurora iacentes | auersatur equis'). However, the number seven can occur in such contexts without involving grief: for the combination of Aurora and the moon, cf. V.Fl. 1. 283–4 'septem Aurora uias totidemque peregerat umbras | Luna polo'.

7–8. aegras | stare genas: Vollmer translates 'krankhaft offen stehen'; cf. *Silv.* 5. 1. 174 'immotas obuersa genas'. For *stare* with reference to open eyes cf. Virg. *A.* 6. 300 (of Charon) 'stant lumina flamma', Ov. *Met.* 6. 304–5 (Niobe) 'lumina maestis | stant immota genis'.

8–9. Oetaeae Paphiaeque... lampades: cf. Cat. 62. 7 'Oetaeos... ignes' (with Fordyce's n.), and Virg. *Ecl.* 8. 30 'tibi deserit Hesperus Oetam'. Oeta is a mountain between Thessaly and Aetolia associated with Hercules and Hesperus, the evening star. Paphos was a city on Cyprus sacred to Aphrodite.

According to the elder Pliny (*Nat.* 2. 36–7) the single identity of the Morning and Evening stars was first noticed by Pythagoras:[10] '[Venus] praeueniens quippe et ante matutinum exoriens Luciferi nomen accipit ut sol alter diemque maturans, contra ab occasu refulgens nuncupatur Vesper, ut prorogans lucem uicemue lunae reddens. quam naturam eius Pythagoras Samius primus deprehendit Olympiade circiter XLII, qui fuit urbis Romae annus CXLII.' Cf. Var. *R.* 3. 5. 17, Cic. *ND* 2. 53. See also N.–H. on Hor. *Carm.* 2. 9. 10 and Le Bœuffle (1962). The planet Venus does not appear as Morning and Evening Star on the same day.

For poetic play on the double nature of the star, see 'Plato', *A.P.* 7. 670, Meleager, *A.P.* 12. 114, Cinna fr. 6 Courtney (*FLP*, pp. 218–19), Cat. 62. 35, *Ciris* 351–2. Here mention of the Evening as well as the

---

[10] For the variant tradition that the single identity of the stars was recognized by Parmenides, see Call. fr. 291 Pf. (= *Hecale* fr. 113 Hollis), fr. 442 Pf., D.L. 8. 14, 9. 22–3. Ibyc. fr. 50 Page is a testimonium ascribing this discovery to the poet.

Morning Star indicates that the poet has not been able to catch up on his sleeplessness during the day, since the Evening Star finds him wakeful when it appears. For the seriousness of total insomnia during day and night, see Cels. 2. 4. 2; cf. Juv. 3. 232 'plurimus hic aeger moritur uigilando'.

reuisunt: Markland conjectured *recursant*, glossed as 'id est, redeunt', comparing Virg. *A.* 1. 662 'urit atrox Iuno et sub noctem cura recursat'. But *reuiso* can be a synonym for *redeo*; cf. Lucr. 4. 1117 'inde redit rabies eadem et furor ille reuisit'. For *reuiso* used of the motions of celestial bodies, note also Lucr. 4. 393 '[sidera] quando-quidem longos obitus exorta reuisunt', 5. 636 'ad hanc [lunam] quia signa reuisunt'. *renident* (Baehrens) is weak because the mere shining of the planet does not involve it in the poet's torment. The preceding clause described the moon looking on at Statius in his torments; a similar idea is required here. *reuisunt* can be retained, since it is appropriate to heavenly bodies and can also convey the idea of going to see places or acquaintances again (*OLD* s.v. 2).

10. gelido spargit miserata flagello: for the whip of Aurora, cf. *Theb.* 8. 274 'et leuiter moto fugat astra flagello'.

Markland questioned *spargit*, asking how one could be sprinkled with a *flagellum*. He conjectured *tangit*, giving three parallels for its use with *flagellum* (*Theb.* 7. 579, 11. 150–1, Hor. *Carm.* 3. 26. 11). Nevertheless *spargit* can be retained. *gelido* clarifies and lends support to *spargit*: the whip is cold because it is early morning; *gelido* and *spargit* together suggest the dawn dew (cf. Ov. *Am.* 1. 13. 10 'roscida purpurea sup-prime lora manu'). *gelido* also contributes to the oxymoron *miserata flagello*. Aurora's cold whip, which typically compels persons to rise, to Statius seems a welcome gesture of pity, offering relief from his suffering. See also V.Fl. 7. 24, who compares the refreshing effect of dawn on the sleepless Medea to a shower reviving ears of wheat.

11. non si mihi lumina mille: if M's *si* is correct, there is an ellipse after *non*, which may best be taken as *sufficiam*. The sense of the passage would be 'unde ego sufficiam? non sufficiam, si mihi lumina mille <sint> ...'. Taking *non* with *si mihi lumina mille* would create anacoluthon, since there is no main clause, and give very odd word-order; there is, furthermore, no reason for Statius to say 'if I did *not* have the thousand eyes of Argus', since he does not possess them anyway.

sunt (Baehrens) is less effective: the ellipse of *sufficiam* between *non* and *si* is a more direct answer to 'unde ego sufficiam'. Furthermore, with *si*, Statius expresses his inability to endure his sleeplessness in language similar to that found in statements of poetic inability, as noted by Traglia (1964), 11. Hinds (1998), 34–47 offers a full discussion of the dynamics of the motif, which begins with *Il.* 2. 484–93. Virg. *G.* 2. 42–4 (cf. e.g. *A.* 6. 625–7) is one example that is close to our passage from Statius:

> non ego cuncta meis amplecti uersibus opto,
> non, mihi si linguae centum sint oraque centum,
> ferrea uox.

Instead of being unable to create poetry, Statius is unable to 'create' sleep without divine assistance. Virgil moreover has an ellipse of a main verb (after the second *non* and before the *si* clause), which is parallel to Statius' ellipse of *sufficiam*. For the use of *non si* and *nec si* by Statius in expressing impossibilities, cf. *Silv.* 2. 2. 36–42, 4. 2. 8–10, *Theb.* 12. 797–99, Laguna (1990), 133 and n. 34, Myers (2000), 133–4.

Markland questioned *mille*, suggesting *centum*, for which he cites Ov. *Met.* 1. 625, Phaed. *Fab.* 2. 8. 18 and Claudian *Stil.* 1. 312, where Argus has one hundred eyes, as well as Ov. *Am.* 3. 4. 19 where he has two hundred. The Aeschylean *Prometheus Vinctus* refers to Argus as τὸν μυριωπόν . . . βούταν (568); he is also πυκνοῖς . . . ὅσσοις (678–9), while Sil. 10. 345–7 'non mille premendi | sunt oculi tibi nec spernens tua numina custos | Inachiae multa superandus nocte iuuencae' also gives Argus a thousand eyes. Note also V.Fl. 4. 367–9, where Argus' eyes are compared to the limitless dots of interwoven purple. Despite the variations, *mille* should be retained. The greater the number of eyes Argus has, the more intense is Statius' complaint.

12. piger: M has *sacer*, which Vollmer unconvincingly glosses as 'weil von Hera bestellt'. An alternative explanation has centred on the negative significance of *sacer*, 'execrable, detestable' (*OLD* s.v. *sacer* 2c); cf. *Theb.* 2. 441–2, where Eteocles calls Oedipus *sacer*: 'et ex imis auditus forte tenebris | offendat sacer ille senex'. Delz (1992), 251 conjectures *piger*, arguing that *sacer* does not accord with the lighter tone of the poem. With this conjecture, an epithet often applied to Sleep (cf. e.g. *Silv.* 1. 6. 91, 3. 2. 73) is applied to Argus who is attempting *not* to fall asleep.

alterna tantum statione: Markland suggests 'alterna tantum in statione', comparing Ov. *Met.* 1. 627 'cetera seruabant atque in statione manebant', from Ovid's account of Argus. But *in*, though possible, is not necessary, because *statione* has an epithet; for the omission of *in* with the ablative of place, typically occurring when an adjective qualifies the noun, see K.–S. i. 353–4. Note also 'alterna . . . statione' (*Theb.* 1. 148).

14–15. at nunc heu: the exclamation marks a shift from the elaborate conceits that have gone before, and a return to the more immediate reproach and appeal which characterized the opening of the poem; cf. 'et nunc, heu' at *Theb.* 12. 80, where Creon moves from describing prospective honours for his dead son Menoeceus to asking what honour could be sufficient for him. Description of suffering now gives way to a direct petition. As well as appealing to the god's pity, *heu* has an ironic, even comic, resonance, as Statius consoles the god who has so regrettably been turned away by the lovers. The god who was previously envisaged as able to affect the whole world is now to be imagined as rejected by lovers.

The adversative *at* has two functions. While adversative particles may occur after the account of nocturnal calm in descriptions of insomnia, to heighten the isolation of the sleepless person (see *Il.* 24. 3, Virg. *A.* 4. 529); *at* also brings the audience back from the counterfactual *non si mihi lumina mille* to the realities of Statius' situation and his desire for sleep.

Statius also plays on the convention of the aubade, since it is Sleep rather than the Dawn who is repulsed by the lover. *longa sub nocte* tellingly evokes both the felicity of the lovers (though contrast Juvenal's bleak view of the insomnia of married life at 6. 268–9) and the extent of the poet's suffering.

16. inde ueni: As Friedländer (1932) remarks, this direct plea is anticipated by the whole poem. For *ueni* in appeals to divinities, cf. e.g. Pi. *N.* 3. 1–3 Ὦ πότνια Μοῖσα, μᾶτερ ἁμετέρα, λίσσομαι, | τὰν πολυξέναν ἐν ἱερομηνίᾳ Νεμεάδι, | ἵκεο Δωρίδα νᾶσον Αἴγιναν, Call. *H.* 5. 33 ἔξιθ᾽ Ἀθαναία, Virg. *G.* 2. 7 'huc pater, o Lenaee, ueni', Stat. *Silv.* 3. 1. 39, *Theb.* 10. 341. Note also V.Fl. 8. 74, 'nunc age maior ades', addressed by Medea to the god Somnus.

16–17. nec te totas infundere pennas | luminibus compello meis: for the wings of Somnus, compare Prop. 1. 3. 45 'dum me iucundis lapsam sopor impulit alis', Virg. *A.* 5. 861, Sil. 10. 354–5 'quatit inde soporas | deuexo capiti pennas'. For the request for only a modest favour, cf. Sil. 10. 343–8, where Somnus does not need to deal with Jove or Argus, but only send a dream to Hannibal.

totas: *pace OLD* s.v. *totus* 1b, *totas* here seems equivalent to *omnes* ('all', rather than 'the whole of his feathers'), a usage which was to become more common in later Latin: see H.–Sz. 203 (§108e); for another Statian example, see *Theb.* 1. 81 'huc ades et totos in poenam ordire nepotes'.

infundere pennas: *infundere* (used of nightfall at *Theb.* 2. 528 'nox et caeruleam terris infuderat umbram') here suggests the horn of Somnus, often represented in art (see *LIMC* s.v. *Hypnos* 9–10, 32–34, 44b, 49, 51–8, 66, 68, 70–3, 81, 94–6, 99, 104, 129–32, 152), and appearing four times in the *Thebaid* (2. 144, 5. 199, 6. 27, 10. 111; cf. Sil. 10. 351–2). *infundere pennas*, though a bold expression (the image is of pouring feathers; cf. perhaps the related use of *infundere* for hair spreading out, as at Ov. *Met.* 7. 183 'nudos umeris infusa capillos', Sen. *Oed.* 499 'infusis humero capillis'), neatly encapsulates two attributes of the god: his wings and his horn of Sleep.

17–18. turba . . . laetior: what is this 'happier crowd'? One explanation might be that Statius is only asking for a brief sleep; others, who are happier than he is (*miser*, 2), are accustomed to ask for a more substantial sleep. Another explanation might draw on the hints in the closing lines at the connection between sleep and death. However, if 'totas infundere pennas' were to refer to the deeper sleep of death, then why should the *turba* be *laetior*?

laetus can appear in Elysian contexts, such as Virg. *A.* 6. 638, 'deuenere locos laetos'. Even more relevant is the end of Horace's Mercury ode (*Carm.* 1. 10. 17–20), where we find a *turba* as well:

> tu pias laetis animas reponis
> sedibus uirgaque leuem coerces
> aurea turbam, superis deorum
>   gratus et imis.

On this interpretation, suggested in Gibson (1996), 465–6, Statius is reworking the Horatian model; the *turba laetior* are the blessed dead, who successfully appeal for sleep in Elysium.

precatur: there is logically no need for the jussive *precetur* (*ς*), favoured by Heinsius and Markland, though it perhaps has some rhetorical merit. Whereas the *turba laetior* expect to enjoy deep sleep, Statius only requires a brief respite.

18–19. extremo me tange cacumine uirgae | (sufficit): Statius evokes the beguiling of Palinurus by Somnus (Virg. *A.* 5. 854–6):

> ecce deus ramum Lethaeo rore madentem
> uique soporatum Stygia super utraque quassat
> tempora, cunctantique natantia lumina soluit.

Servius glosses 'uique soporatum Stygia' as 'morte plenum', and the fatal sleep of Palinurus is a reminder of the kinship of Sleep and Death (see 1–2 n.). In contrast, Statius wishes only to be touched by the tip of Somnus' wand. *sufficit* recalls 'unde ego sufficiam' (11); the indicative mood, as well as suggesting the modest nature of Statius' request, may hint that the appeal is at last successful, the poem ending with Statius falling asleep.

For the wand of Somnus, cf. V.Fl. 8. 84, Sil. 10. 355–6. Note also the *uirga* of Mercury (5. 1. 101 n.), used by him to subdue Argus (Ov. *Met.* 1. 716). Laguna (1990), 136–7 interprets Statius' request for Somnus' *uirga* in terms of Mercury's use of his *uirga* to bring souls to the underworld. Laguna argues that such a wish for death could be understood in the context of Statius' possible loss of his wife. However, the poem is striking precisely for its lack of clear contextual information. In any case Statius' request to Somnus (not Mercury) merely to touch him with the end of the wand is more naturally taken as wish for lighter sleep, as opposed to the deeper sleep caused by the *totas . . . pennas* (16).

19. aut leuiter suspenso poplite transi: Statius asks Somnus either to touch him with his wand, or to leave him. The poem ends with an ingenious joke: even if he will not send Statius to sleep, Somnus should at least go on his way quietly, without disturbing him. *suspenso poplite*, literally 'with suspended knee', is a variant on more common expressions for 'on tiptoe'; see e.g. Ov. *Met.* 8. 398 'institerat digitis, primos suspensus in artus', *Fast.* 1. 425–6 'uestigia furtim | suspenso digitis fert taciturna gradu', *OLD* s.v. *suspendo* 6b.

Poem Five

INTRODUCTION

Summary: *Statius' loss of poetic inspiration at the death of the child (1–8). His grief matches that of natural parents; the failure of his poetic powers, and his request for help from those friends he had previously consoled (8–65). The child was not a bought slave but born in Statius' household; Statius' involvement in his upbringing (66–87).*

(For discussion of the poem as an *epicedion*, see the section on consolation in the General Introduction, especially pp. xxxviii–xlii.)

The damaged state of M's transmission of this poem might constitute a powerful argument in favour of interpreting the abrupt end of the poem as merely the result of the ravages of time, manuscripts being particularly susceptible to damage at the end of a work, but it is at least worth asking whether the poem confronting us here is not an unfinished fragment. Certainly the poem is one of Statius' later works, as evinced by the reference to the *Achilleid* in *Silv.* 5. 5. 36–7, so that it is by no means impossible for the poem to be unfinished. However, we should perhaps not yield too much to the romantic allure of positing an unfinished 'last poem', especially attractive in the light of the poem's melancholy subject; no more can be said than the closing words of Courtney's apparatus: 'Vtrum textus mutilatus sit an carmen imperfectum reliquerit poeta incertum.'

COMMENTARY

1. Me miserum: as Statius himself notes, this arresting and simple introduction is not a typical opening for a lament. The hackneyed declaration of misery testifies to the poet's inability to respond to grief through poetry. The phrase is found in all periods, both in verse and prose: see *OLD* s.v. *miser* 1b, *ThLL* viii. 1106. 1–13, McKeown on Ov. *Am.* 1. 1. 25–6, Hinds (1998), 29–34. Though *miser* is often used of erotic suffering (e.g. Cat. 8. 1 'miser Catulle'), such assocations seem irrelevant here (see introduction. pp. xxxix–xl). One should not rush to call the emotion here self-pity; on the difficulties of applying such modern labels to the ancient world, see Konstan (2001), 64–71.

ultro: M's *ulla* seems redundant; there is little difference between Statius' being unable to begin, and being unable to begin 'anything'. Barth suggested *ultra* (Statius is unable to proceed further with poetry), but this meaning is covered by *neque... incipiam*. As an alternative, I suggest *ultro*. Statius cannot proceed 'of his own accord' (*OLD* s.v. *ultro* 5), since he is without the support of Apollo and the Muses (2–3; cf. 5. 3. 5–9). For *ultro* in a context of poetic inability, compare Catullus' apology at 68. 40 'ultro ego deferrem, copia siqua foret'; for its position at the end of a line, cf. *Silv.* 3. 3. 32–3 'Aoniasque tuo sacrabimus ultro | inferias, Etrusce, seni'.

2. nunc (Scriverius): M's *nec* cannot be accepted, since construing *uerbis* and *undis* as ablatives of manner in parallel is unsatisfactory; the literal *uerbis* and the metaphorical *Castaliae uocalibus undis* give the odd sense 'I shall begin with of my own accord neither with solemn words nor with the sounding waters of Castalia.'

Castaliae uocalibus undis: For *uocalibus*, cf. *Silv.* 1. 2. 6 'et de Pieriis uocalem fontibus undam', 5. 3. 209 'uocales lucos'; note also *Culex* 17 'Castaliaeque sonans liquido pede labitur unda'. With *nunc*, *uocalibus undis* is a dative dependent on *inuisus*; Håkanson (1969), 153–5 notes the contrast with Hor. *Carm.* 3. 4. 25 'uestris amicum fontibus' (and see now N.–R. ad loc.), addressed to the Camenae (cf. *Carm.* 1. 26. 1 'Musis amicus', with N.–H.). *nunc*, moreover, makes the point that Statius was previously pleasing to the poetic fountain and to Apollo, a situation which has now changed; contrast Ov. *Am.* 1. 15. 35–6 'mihi flauus Apollo | pocula Castalia plena ministret aqua' (with McKeown's n.).

Hdt. 8. 39. 1 describes the spring of Castalia at Delphi as near the τέμενος of the local hero Autonous: Αὐτονόου δὲ πέλας τῆς Κασταλίης ὑπὸ τῇ Ὑαμπείῃ κορυφῇ, while Paus. 10. 8. 9 reports that it was on the right side as one ascended from the gymnasium to the sanctuary, and its water was said to be καὶ πιεῖν ἡδύ. Pausanias goes on to note that some associated the name with a local woman, and others with a local man, Castalius, before noting that Panyassis (fr. 2 Bernabé) had made Castalia a daughter of Achelous: Παρνησσόν νιφόεντα θοοῖς διὰ ποσσὶ περήσας | ἵκετο Κασταλίης Ἀχελωΐδος ἄμβροτον ὕδωρ. However, Pausanias immediately afterwards (10. 8. 10) notes another tradition that the water of Castalia was a gift of the river Cephisus, which Alcaeus is said to have written of ἐν προοιμίῳ τῷ ἐς ᾽Απόλλωνα (= fr. 307d Lobel–Page; cf. fr. 307c). The association of Castalia with Apollo thus goes back as far as Alcaeus, and inevitably Castalia becomes linked with poetry; in later texts cf. e.g. Pi. *P.* 1. 39 Φοῖβε, Παρνασσοῦ τε κράναν Κασταλίαν φιλέων, Bacch. 3. 19–21 τόθι μέγιστον ἄλσος | Φοίβου παρὰ Κασταλίας ῥεέθροις | Δελφοὶ διέπουσι, Theoc. 7. 148 Νύμφαι Κασταλίδες Παρνάσιον αἶπος ἔχοισαι, Virg. *G.* 3. 292–3 'iuuat ire iugis, qua nulla priorum | Castaliam molli deuertitur orbita cliuo', Hor. *Carm.* 3. 4. 61–2 (Apollo) 'qui rore puro Castaliae lauit | crinis solutos' (cf. Stat. *Theb.* 1. 697–8 'seu rore pudico | Castaliae flauos amor est tibi mergere crines'), Prop. 3. 3. 13 'cum me Castalia speculans ex arbore Phoebus', Col. 10. 267 'antraque Castaliis semper rorantia guttis', Luc. 5. 125 'Castalios circum latices nemorumque recessus', Mart. 9. 18. 7–8 'quam dederis nostris, Auguste, penatibus undam, | Castalis haec nobis aut Iouis imber erit', 12. 2(3). 11–14 'laurigeros habitat facundus Stella penatis, | clarus Hyanteae Stella sititor aquae; | fons ibi Castalius uitreo torrente superbit, | unde nouem dominas saepe bibisse ferunt'. At *Theb.* 1. 565, Statius refers to 'Castaliis . . . fontibus' in connection with Apollo's slaying of the Python; cf. 8. 175–6 'hoc antra lacusque | Castalii tripodumque fides?' At *Theb.* 1. 697 (*pudico*, cited above) and at *Silv.* 2. 2. 38–9 (see van Dam's discussion ad loc.) 'reseretque arcana pudicos | Phemonoe fontes', *pudicus* is an etymological allusion to *Castalia* on the basis of Latin *castus*. Another tradition associated Castalia with Cadmus' slaying of a serpent which guarded the spring prior to the foundation of Thebes: see Ov. *Met.* 3. 14–130, Hyg. *Fab.* 6, 178. 5. On the literary associations of Castalia, see further Kambylis (1965), 138–9, Bömer on Ov. *Met.* 3. 14, and Parke (1978), and for discussion of the topography, see Amandry (1977) and (1978).

Whereas in *Silv.* 5. 3. 3–9 it was not *fas* for Statius, who has lost the symbols of poetry, to invoke Apollo without his father, here he asserts that Apollo and the Muses are actually opposed to him (cf. Mart. 2. 22. 1–2 'Quid mihi uobiscum est, o Phoebe nouemque sorores? | ecce nocet uati Musa iocosa suo'). For a general treatment of the Muses in Statius, see Rosati (2002).

3. Phoeboque grauis: cf. Virg. *Ecl.* 10. 75 'solet esse grauis cantantibus umbra'.

3–5. Instead of invoking the goodwill of the Muses; Statius asks what crime he has committed against them, using the strongest language (*orgia*, *incestauimus*, and *aras*). *incestum* can denote the pollution of religious ritual; Clodius was accused of *incestum* for his attendance at the festival of the Bona Dea in women's clothing (Cic. *Har.* 4, Vell. 2. 45. 1, Quint. *Inst.* 4. 2. 88). Far from presenting himself as a priest of the Muses (cf. e.g. Hor. *Carm.* 3. 1. 1–4), Statius asks whether he is one of the profane.

4. orgia: Statius asks if he has betrayed the secrets of the Muses, perhaps to the uninitiated. Cf. Prop. 3. 1. 4 'Itala per Graios orgia ferre choros', 3. 3. 29 'orgia [*Heinsius* : Ergo *O* : organa *Eldik*] Musarum'. *orgia* frequently refers to the worship of Bacchus (e.g. Cat. 64. 259–60), who may also be evoked here; on Bacchus' links with poetry, see *Silv.* 5. 3. 6 n.

5. dicite: far from requesting the Muses to sing or to grant a song, Statius asks them to name his crime, so that he may acknowledge it subsequently. Statius' request never receives a reply; the lack of an explanation for the loss of the child contributes to the sense of his isolation.

6–7. Contrast Propertius' request to enter the *nemus* of Callimachus and Philitas at 3. 1. 1 (cf. *Silv.* 5. 3. 209–11 with notes).

6. inaccesso ... luco: cf. Virg. *A.* 7. 11–12 'diues inaccessos ubi Solis filia lucos | adsiduo resonat cantu'. For the sacred connotations of *lucus*, see *Silv.* 5. 3. 50 n.; for woodland as a place of contemplation suitable for the production of poetry, compare 5. 3. 286 (with n.).

7. uetito de fonte: at Prop. 3. 3. 13–24 Apollo prevents Propertius from drinking the waters consumed by the epic poet Ennius; note especially ll.15–16: 'Quid tibi cum tali, demens, est flumine? quis te | carminis heroi tangere iussit opus?' Contrast Apollo's initiation of Statius' father in the poetical waters of Helicon at *Silv.* 5. 3. 121–3. In the proem to the *Achilleid*, Statius asks Apollo to vouchsafe him the waters of poetry, *if* the *Thebaid* had found favour (*Ach.* 1. 8–11):

> tu modo, si ueterem digno depleuimus haustu,
> da fontes mihi, Phoebe, nouos ac fronde secunda
> necte comas: neque enim Aonium nemus aduena pulso
> nec mea nunc primis augescunt tempora uittis.

For the symbolism of water, and its links with poetic inspiration, note also e.g. Hes. *Th.* 5–6, Pi. *O.* 6. 85–6, where Pindar drinks from Thebe, Call. frr. 2. 1, 696 Pf., *A.P.* 7. 55. 5–6 (Alcaeus of Messene),

9. 64, ascribed to either Asclepiades or Archias, [Mosch.] 3. 76–7 ἀμφότεροι παγαῖς πεφιλημένοι· ὃς μὲν ἔπινε | Παγασίδος κράνας, ὃ δ᾽ ἔχεν πόμα τᾶς ᾽Αρεθοίσας, referring to Homer and Bion, Lucr. 1. 927–8 'iuuat integros accedere fontis | atque haurire', Virg. *Ecl.* 6. 64–5, *G.* 2. 175 'ingredior sanctos ausus recludere fontes' (cf. perhaps Enn. *Ann.* 210, with Skutsch's note), Ov. *Am.* 1. 15. 35–6 (cited above), *Pont.* 4. 8. 79–80, Man. 2. 51–2, Stat. *Silv.* 1. 2. 259 'et sociam doctis haurimus ab amnibus undam', 1. 4. 25–8, 4. 7. 11–12; see further Kambylis (1965), 23–30, 66–8, 98–102, 110–22, 183–8, Crowther (1979), Knox (1985), Cameron (1995), 364–6.

quae culpa, quis error: cf. 5. 4. 1–2 (and n.) 'Crimine quo merui . . . | quoue errore'. Here as in 5. 4, there is an element of reproach in the pairing: *error* undercuts the possibility of real *culpa*.

8. tanti (Traglia): M's *tantis* gives the right sense, 'what is the fault, what is the error which I am paying for with so much', but the rather imprecise plural is not what one would expect, and is perhaps awkward in view of the natural tendency, in an unpunctuated text, to construe *tantis* with the following 'morientibus . . . lacertis' in the next sentence. However, Politian's *tantus* in the *exemplar Corsinianum* (in his commentary he approved the reading 'quem luimus tantis'; see Cesarini Martinelli (1982), 198) destroys the balance of 'quae culpa, quis error' in the previous line; one might even expect a subjunctive if *tantus* were correct, *quem* introducing a result clause constructed with *tantus*. Though an ablative might seem more suitable with *luo*, since it is the case commonly employed, as noted at *ThLL* vii/2. 1843. 19–20, while the genitive is rare (ibid. 1842. 12–20), in fact it is normal for *tanti* and *quanti* to be used in situations where an ablative of price might be expected. Thus *OLD* s.v. *tantus* 4 offers only two instances for ablative *tanto* in this sense, Man. 4. 403 (see Housman ad loc.) and Apul. *Met.* 9. 6; for the usage of *tanti* to denote price, see *OLD* s.v. 3a, K.–S. i. 390–1, H.–Sz. 72–4 (§57), and also Szemerényi (1956), 109–11 who suggests that *tanti* and *quanti* are relics of the old instrumental **quantād* and **tantād*. The corruption of singular *tanti* to plural *tantis* is an easy one, especially when the ablative *morientibus ecce lacertis* follows. The simplicity of *tanti* accords well with the bareness of the emotion throughout this opening section, and moreover, looks forward to the immediately ensuing description of the last hours of Statius' *puer*.

morientibus ecce lacertis: *morior* can be applied to parts of the body, both in the context of a person's death, as here, and to denote a separate process of mortification (*ThLL* viii. 1493. 64–1494. 4; *OLD* s.v. *morior* 1d). Compare e.g. Virg. *A.* 10. 463 'morientia lumina Turni'. The present passage is similar to Lucretius' description of the process of death throughout the parts of the body: 'inde pedes et crura mori' (3. 529). *morientibus* intensifies the emotion of the passage; a word which is metaphorically applied to the weakening arms of the boy is also appropriate in its primary meaning as well.

9. animamque: M's *animaque* is indefensible; *-que* cannot link *lacertis* and *anima*, since the boy can hardly be said to hold onto Statius' *uiscera* with *lacertis animaque*. *animamque*, wrongly credited to the Parma edition of 1473 (b) by most editors, is preferable, since the figurative language is concentrated (*uiscera nostra tenens animamque*); for this combination compare *Silv.* 5. 1. 47 'uisceribus totis animaque amplexa fouebat'; cf. 3. 5. 30 'uisceribus complexa tuis'.

uiscera can denote the organs beneath the diaphragm, as discussed by André (1991), 202–3, though note too *OLD* s.v. *uiscus*[1] s.v. 4, for *uiscera* denoting 'the innermost parts of the body regarded as the seat of thought, emotion', hence the translation used here, 'inmost heart'. Statius here and in the passages given above seems to develop the notion that a person, or his or her image, might be found in the *uiscera* of those dear to him or her (cf. Cic. *Phil.* 1. 36 'o beatos illos qui, cum adesse ipsis propter uim armorum non licebat, aderant tamen et in medullis populi Romani ac uisceribus haerebant!', Luc. 9. 71–2 'non imis haeret imago | uisceribus?'), with the idea that one can embrace with one's own *uiscera*. Here Statius varies this image, for the child embraces his *uiscera* and *anima*. Though *lacertis* might appear oddly literal in combination with the metaphorical use of *uiscera* and *animam* here, *lacertis* should be seen as effectively equivalent in meaning to *amplexa* and *complexa* in the other two passages from the *Silvae*; if it is possible to say that a person can embrace with *uiscera* and *anima*, it is not such a violation of language to hold another's *uiscera* and *anima* in one's arms. For *auello* denoting separation of a child from a parent, cf. Cat. 62. 21 and Virg. *A.* 4. 616 with Pease's n.

infans, if used strictly, would indicate that the child was very young, since the word is properly applied to those children unable to speak.[1] The child, however, had at least begun to talk, since

---

[1] In inscriptions, *ThLL* vii/1. 1347. 25–1348. 24 indicates that *infans* is used of children up to the age of 16 (for which see *CIL* vi. 6814. 3 'infanti dulcissimo', x. 2426. 3–4 'infa<n>s dulcissimus', both in funerary inscriptions); note also *CIL* v. 5032, where Iulius Ingenuus, a military tribune, an office often held at about the age of 20 (but contrast Crispinus in *Silv.* 5. 2 above), is called *infans*, perhaps by his father.

Statius' name was his first word (86). *infans* pathetically emphasizes and exaggerates the extreme youth of the child; cf. *CIL* iii. 6088 (Ephesus), a bilingual inscription recording the death of a child, Eppia, where *infans* is rendered in Greek as νηπία, with strong overtones of pathos and futility.

10–11. Vollmer believed that the poem is addressed to a legally adopted son, but l. 10 indicates both that Statius was not the boy's father by blood and that he had not adopted him, since the child had not assumed Statius' name, as was noted by Politian in his commentary: see Cesarini Martinelli (1982), 198.

iuraque: M's *oraque* would suggest the common theme of the desirability of family likeness (see e.g. Cat. 61. 214–18 with Fordyce's n., Gow on Theocritus 17. 44, and Coleman on *Silv.* 4. 8. 11). There is, however, an oddity here, in that one would expect the contrast to be between blood descendants of Statius (*stirpe*) and adopted ones (*nomina*), but *oraque*, referring to family likeness, would seem to be more appropriate to *stirpe* than to *nomen*. Accordingly, I suggest *iuraque*; an adopted child would have had Statius' name and rights (see *OLD* s.v. *ius* 10a).

ferret: cf. *Silv.* 1. 2. 272–3 (of an as yet unborn child): 'multum de patre decoris, | plus de matre feras'. For *fero* and *nomen* in the context of adoption, compare Cic. *Off.* 3. 74.

11–12. non fueram genitor: an emphatic summary of the previous line; though the pluperfect tense can be used loosely in place of a simple past, here *non fueram genitor* might be felt to be answered by the striking 'orbus ego' in line 13: the situation has changed, and Statius now considers himself like a father to the child, even though he had not begotten him. Cf. 79–80 'quo sospite natos | non cupii' and 80–1 n.

cernite fletus: Statius' tears and other gestures of lamentation prove his grief. Compare *Silv.* 3. 3. 7 (addressed to Pietas) 'cerne pios fletus'. This request recalls the forensic technique of a defendant or members of his family weeping in court in an effort to win over the judges, a technique spurned by Socrates in Plato's *Apologia*.

orbi is genitive singular, despite Vollmer and Lundström (1893), 39, who construed the word as vocative plural. Statius can hardly be addressing the *orbi*, bereaved parents, since he would then have no need to summon them in 13–14 ('huc . . . conueniant'). Håkanson (1969), 154–5 argues that *cernite* and *credite* are addressed to the Muses, but these imperatives are directed at the audience of the

poem (for the shift to an unspecified plural audience, cf. *Silv.* 2. 7. 19
'Lucanum canimus, fauete linguis' with van Dam; for changes of
addressee, see e.g. 5. 1. 37, 127, 239–41 nn.). Moreover, the Muses
are omniscient (see e.g. *Il.* 2. 485–6, Hes. *Th.* 26–8, Virg. *A.* 7. 645–6),
so that Statius has no need to convince them of his suffering. The
sequence of thought is 'I was not the father, but trust in the grief of
one has lost a child: I have lost a child.' The unspecific *orbi* appears to
contrast with *non fueram genitor*; Statius then turns the tables by point-
ing out that he is *orbus*. The defensive tone is similar to passages where
Statius confronts an imagined interlocutor (cf. 47–48, 5. 3. 69 ff).

13. patres ... matres: for comparisons with the grief felt by
parents for children, see *Silv.* 5. 1. 218 and n.

aperto pectore: the breast is exposed to be struck in lamenta-
tion; cf. *Theb.* 6. 136 'nudo ... pectore', where Eurydice bewails the
loss of her son Archemorus; see also the reactions of Hypsipyle (6. 178)
and of the maidservants (6. 219). 'aperto | pectore' occurs at Ov. *Fast.*
3. 15–16, but a parallel closer to the context of this passage is *Met.* 13.
688–9 (in the *ecphrasis* of the cup given by Anius to Aeneas): 'effusae-
que comas et apertae pectore matres | significant luctum'. In non-
funerary contexts, the breast may be exposed to win the pity of a son,
as in Hecuba's appeal to Hector at *Il.* 22. 79–89; compare also the
appeal of Phaedra's nurse to her mistress, referring to her 'cara ubera'
at Sen. *Phaed.* 246–9. The phrase anticipates the pathetic detail 'sub
uberibus plenis' in 15.

14. Earlier conjectures for this 'locus conclamatus' (Courtney), are
found in Lundström (1893), 39–41 and in Klotz's apparatus. The
transmitted text cannot be retained.

crinemque rogis et cinnama (Heinsius): M's *cineremque oculis et
crimina* cannot stand. The syllepsis of ashes and reproaches is unen-
durably strained, but it is also unclear on whose eyes the ashes should
be deposited and at whom reproaches should be directed, nor indeed
is there any indication why either of these operations ought to be
performed. *Silv.* 5. 3. 32 'cineremque oculis umentibus hausi' is not a
parallel, since the eyes are clearly those of the speaker; furthermore,
Statius is there developing the usage of *haurio* to denote taking in
sights with the eyes (see n.). Solutions of this passage have tended to
produce a text which is some form of request to the fathers
and mothers to join in the funeral rites for Statius' child. The best is
crinemque rogis et cinnama ferte (Heinsius, as reported by Lundström
(1893), 40, though Heinsius 594 suggests reading *cineremque rogis et*

carmina ferte), where locks of hair and cinnamon are brought as funeral offerings. But whatever text is read here, these lines are not an invitation to share in Statius' grief. Although Statius has summoned the parents to the funeral, a different aim is revealed in 21–2, where the agonistic quality of the encounter becomes apparent. Statius has challenged the bereaved parents to compete with him in expressing grief. It would scarcely be a contest if the parents were grieving for Statius' loss (on the undesirability of grieving for a stranger see 5. 3. 244–5 n.); the parents are summoned to express their own grief. They will, however, be defeated by Statius' tears (*lacrimis*, 22).

ferte: whether this or *ferto* is the reading of M is disputed; Souter, as noted by Klotz, gave the MS text as *ferto*, a reading otherwise credited to Politian and to the annotator of Auct. N. inf. 2. 27 (5), a Venetian edition of the early 1480s in the Bodleian library; see Reeve (1977*b*), 219). Note that the choice between *ferte* and *ferto* affects the punctuation of the passage: the subject of *ferte* is the mothers and fathers of l. 13, while the subject of singular *ferto* would be *siqua* in l. 15, so that a comma after *ferto* would be essential. As well as being the apparent reading of M, *ferte* allows a highly effective rhetoric in the new sentence following it in l. 15: Statius summons first mothers (*siqua*) and then fathers (emending *quisquis* in l. 18 to *siquis*, as suggested by Professor Hill) to compete with him in lamentation (21).

15. The mother's breast full of unused milk, since the baby is dead, is similar in its pathetic effect to the theme of possessions rendered useless by a person's death. At the funeral of Archemorus, his parents burn possessions destined for him (*Theb.* 6. 74–8); compare Andromache's decision to burn her husband's clothes (*Iliad* 22. 512–13), or Regulus' slaughter of his dead son's pets at Plin. *Ep.* 4. 2. 3–4. For milk as an offering to the dead see e.g. Hom. *Od.* 10. 518–19, 11. 27–8, A. *Pers.* 611–15, S. *El.* 895, E. *IT* 162, *Or.* 115, Virg. *A.* 3. 66–7, 5. 78.

funera natos: for this striking and emotive juxtaposition, cf. Cat. 64. 401 'optauit genitor primaeui funera nati', where, however, Catullus presents the opposite idea of a parent wishing for his son's death. Statius' plural *natos* implies the even greater calamity of a mother losing more than one child at the same time, who might be twins if they are still being nursed at the breast.

16–17. madidumque cecidit | pectus: Mozley and Slater both translate this phrase as 'teeming bosom' (compare Iz.-Fr. 'leurs mamelles pleines'), and would appear to be supported by *OLD* s.v. *madidus* 4, which cites this passage as an instance of the meaning 'full of liquid'. However, as well as the dampness caused by excess milk, *madidum* also evokes the effect of tears (*OLD* s.v. *madidus* 2a): for this image cf. Virg. *A.* 4. 30 'sic effata sinum lacrimis impleuit obortis'.

et ardentes restinxit lacte fauillas: *papillas* (M) is a psychological corruption inspired by *aperto pectore, sub uberibus plenis, madidumque cecidit pectus*, and *lacte* all occurring within the space of five lines. Vollmer's defence of it as a reference to *inflammationes mammarum* is not saved by his citations of Plin. *Nat.* 23. 63 and 27. 67: a mother extinguishing her dead child's ashes with milk is more in keeping with the extremes of suffering described in this passage than a digression referring to the medical condition of a bereaved mother; note also that this gives a variation on the epic convention of putting out a funeral pyre with wine (see e.g. *Il.* 23. 250, 24. 791, Virg. *A.* 6. 227 'reliquias uino et bibulam lauere fauillam'; cf. Stat. *Silv.* 2. 6. 90–1 'nec quod tibi Setia canos | restinxit cineres' with van Dam's n.). *fauillas* (Calderini) is moreover entirely concordant with *restinguo*. The juxtaposition of milk, usually given as a means of life (though see 15 n. above, for milk as a funerary offering), and ashes, an emblem of death, is especially effective; compare Hypsipyle's lament after discovering the death of Archemorus at *Theb.* 5. 617–19:

> sic equidem luctus solabar et ubera paruo
> iam materna dabam, cui nunc uenit inritus orbae
> lactis et infelix in uulnera liquitur imber.

18–20. Whereas the first example described the loss of a very young child (especially common in the ancient world, as a result of high infant mortality), Statius' second example has a particularly literary resonance, that of 'impositique rogis iuuenes ante ora parentum' (Virg. *G.* 4. 477, *A.* 6. 308); see *Silv.* 5. 1. 218 n. This is emphasized by *lanugine*, the first down on a young man's cheeks, a motif which frequently appears in epic with pathetic effect, as a foreshadowing of a future frustrated by death and as an emblem of youth's fragility (e.g. Virg. *A.* 10. 324, Ov. *Met.* 13. 754, Luc. 10. 135, *Theb.* 7. 655). In all these passages, *lanugine* is followed by either *malae* or *malas*; *lanugine malas* (M), emended to *flammas* by Calderini, is attributable to reminiscence of a common phrase. For the pathos of a young man dying before he grows his first beard compare *Silv.* 2. 1. 54–5 'cuncta in cineres grauis intulit hora | hostilisque dies', where 'cuncta' refers to the now futile hopes for the first beard of manhood,

5. 2. 62–3 (Crispinus' father did not live to see his son's first beard; see n.), Harrison on Virg. *A.* 10. 324–5, Lattimore (1942), 197–8.

19. immersit cineri is similarly vivid: *cineri* anticipates the final result of the cremation.

iacentis: for *iaceo* used of a person lying on a pyre, cf. *Silv.* 2. 1. 173–4 'erant illic genitor materque iacentis | maesta'.

20. serpere emphasizes the apparent slowness with which the body catches fire: by lingering on the one moment when the youth's *lanugo* is first set aflame, the pathos is heightened; for *serpo* denoting a gradual process, cf. Lucr. 6. 660 'exsistit sacer ignis et urit corpore serpens', *OLD* s.v. *serpo* 3a.

crudeles: for *crudelis* in a funerary context, compare Aeneas' address to the absent Evander at Virg. *A.* 11. 53 'infelix, nati funus crudele uidebis!': the epithet points to the pain for a father in seeing his son's funeral.

21–2. fatiscat: Slater, Mozley, Iz.-Fr., and Shackleton Bailey treat this word as denoting the exhaustion brought on by lamentation (exemplified by Niobe's decision to eat as a result of fatigue at *Il.* 24. 613). This is undoubtedly a possible interpretation of the word (*OLD* s.v. *fatisco* 2 cites this passage as an example of this meaning), but the primary meaning of the word, which is used of gaps or chinks, may also apply here, in a manner analogous to such Greek verbs as χάσκω. In drama, χάσκω can sometimes convey contempt, with perhaps an implication of speaking out of turn, as at S. *Aj.* 1226–7 σὲ δὴ τὰ δεινὰ ῥήματ᾽ ἀγγέλλουσί μοι | τλῆναι καθ᾽ ἡμῶν ὧδ᾽ ἀνοιμωκτεὶ χανεῖν, Ar. *Vesp.* 342 τοῦτ᾽ ἐτόλμησ᾽ ὁ μιαρὸς χανεῖν ὁ Δημολογοκλέων < ὅδ᾽ >, and cf. A. *Ag.* 919–20 μηδὲ βαρβάρου φωτὸς δίκην | χαμαιπετὲς βόαμα προσχάνῃς ἐμοί. Note also Call. *H.* 2. 24 μάρμαρον ἀντὶ γυναικὸς ὀϊζυρόν τι χανούσης, a reference to Niobe, where Williams ad loc. suggests that the verb may have been specially associated with Niobe, and argues that ὀϊζυρόν τι is adverbial, with χανούσης construed intranstively, and compare the use of *hiare* at Prop. 2. 31. 6 'marmoreus tacita carmen hiare lyra', with Heyworth (1994), 57–9. For Call. *H.* 2, see also the notes on *Silv.* 5. 1. 33–6 and 5. 3. 9 above. Such a meaning (and indeed a hint at Niobe) would be appropriate not only to the opening of the mouth indicated by *alterno . . . clamore*, but would also suggest the sense of stunned amazement at the magnitude of their loss. *alterno* emphasizes the competitive element of Statius' invitation; see *Silv.* 5. 3. 27 n. Poetry, however, is not so much to the fore as might be expected; *clamore fatiscat* and *lacrimis* scarcely suggest a poem of disciplined construction. Indeed Statius claims that his victory will be due to tears, which implies that it is in emotion and not in artistry that he wishes to challenge other mourners. He thus alludes to the poetic type of contest, but prejudges his win on emotional rather than stylistic or artistic grounds. For *uinco* in the context of poetry compare Virg. *Ecl.* 7. 69 'haec memini, et uictum frustra contendere Thyrsin'. For competitive mourning, compare Ov. *Am.* 3. 9. 53–8, where Tibullus' mistresses Delia and Nemesis exchange remarks at his funeral, while at *Theb.* 6. 178–9 Eurydice refuses to have Hypsipyle present at her son's funeral, 'et socium indignata dolorem'. The present passage differs from both these examples in that the mourners are not grieving for the same loss.

23. Madness and savagery are common characteristics of grief; see *Silv.* 5. 1. 22 n.

feritas suggests the fury of wild animals; cf. *Silv.* 2. 1. 8–9.

24–7. M's text is lacunose here, with spaces left in the middle of the line (M itself is not physically damaged). The lacuna has occasioned much debate, arising from Politian's remarks on the passage in the *exemplar Corsinianum*: 'codex uetustus intercisos habet hos uersus'. Courtney (1966), 95 argued that this meant that the manuscript seen by Politian could not have been M, but in his edition of 1990 (p. xvii) acknowledges that 'intercisos' could simply refer to a gap, rather than physical damage; cf. Dunston (1967), 98–9. On this hypothesis, Politian's marginal note in the *exemplar Corisnianum* does not provide an argument for the view that Politian's manuscript was different from M.

In this most difficult passage the lacunose reading of M is as follows (each asterisk denotes the approximate space of a letter):

> Hoc quoque cum ni✳ ✳ ✳ ✳ ✳ ✳ ✳terdana luce peracta
> 25   Adclinis tumul✳ ✳ ✳ ✳ ✳ ✳ ✳nctus in carmina uerto
> Discordesque m✳ ✳ ✳ ✳ ✳ ✳ ✳ ✳ ✳ ✳ ✳singultantia uerba
> Molior orsa ly✳ ✳ ✳ ✳ ✳ ✳ ✳ ✳ ✳ ✳est atque ira tacendi
> Impatiens sed nec solitae mihi uertice laurus
> Nec fronti uictatus honos en taxea marcet

Courtney's text is as follows:

> hoc quoque cum ni<tor>, ter dena luce peracta,
> 25   adclinis tumul<o et pla>nctus in carmina uerto
> discordesque m<odos et> singultantia uerba.
> molior orsa ly<ra (dolor> est atque ira tacendi

impatiens), sed nec solitae mihi uertice laurus
nec fronti uittatus honos. en taxea marcet...

nitor (Gronovius) seems appropriate in 24, since the following passage indicates Statius' difficulties in producing a poetic response to the child's death; compare the problems of composing a poem on his father's death at 5. 3. 33–4. Baehrens's *planctus* (which has replaced *luctus* as the vulgate text) and *tumulo* (ς) are also convincing in 25. In 26, there can be little argument over *modos et*. Line 27, however, is more difficult.

Courtney's text is not satisfactory. A number of objections can be made. Firstly, with no punctuation after 25, Courtney links *carmina* to *discordesque modos* and *singultantia uerba*; it is an odd mixing of categories to have a list comprising 'songs', 'notes', and 'words', when the last two are not equivalents but aspects of *carmina*. There is, moreover, no epithet for *carmina*. It is thus preferable to separate *carmina* from the next line by a comma; furthermore *molior orsa lyra* is feeble when placed on its own, and consorts oddly with the parenthesis which follows in Courtney's text.

However, construing *discordesque modos* and *singultantia uerba* with *molior orsa lyra* is not without difficulties; *orsa* and *uerba* have no conjunction, and *orsa* seems pointless after both *modos* and *uerba*. Indeed, Shackleton Bailey emends *orsa* to *ista* (followed by Krohn's supplement, *lyrae uis*), and ends the previous sentence with *molior*, but his translation 'It is compulsion to sing' reflects, by omitting it, the awkwardness of the deictic *ista*, which seems a rather unclear and unspecific way to pick up on the content of the preceding sentence. I have therefore adopted Phillimore's emendation 'singultantia acerba', where 'singultantia' is accusative plural agreeing with 'orsa', and 'acerba' is ablative singular agreeing with 'lyra'. The emendation is less unlikely than it might seem; the presence of *singultantia* would have increased the likelihood of corruption of *acerba* to *uerba*, particularly since the initial *a* of *acerba* could easily disappear by haplography after the last letter of *singultantia*; cf. (in the same *locus*) Virg. *A.* 7. 740 'moenia Abellae' with Servius and Horsfall ad loc, where the MSS read 'moenia bellae'.[2] This would intially have left *cerba*, which would

---

[2] Elision after the second syllable of a dactyl in the fifth foot in Statius is paralleled within *Silv.* 5 at 5. 1. 214; Eskuche (1890), 256 lists over sixty other Statian examples.

have been emended to *uerba* to restore sense to the passage.
A further argument against *uerba* is the blandness of the word.

If Phillimore's *satis* in 27 is adopted, *satis est* (cf. *Theb.* 1. 657) would
indicate that Statius is content to compose any poetry at all, regard-
less of quality, while *ira tacendi | impatiens* is an apologetic explanation
of Statius' decision to attempt poetic composition; cf. *iuuat* in a similar
context at 33–4 below. *dolor* (Sudhaus, Karsten) adds nothing new and
is not in parallel to *ira*, even if it were possible to translate Courtney's
parenthesis as 'Grief and anger are intolerant of silence', particularly
as the position of *est* before *atque* might suggest that *est* is part of a
separate clause. Another possibility would be *calor* (cf. *Theb.* 2. 391–2
'utque rudis fandi pronusque calori | semper erat', and for heat
in contexts of inspiration see 5. 3. 12–13 n.), 'There is passion and
my anger is intolerant of silence, but I have not the customary
laurels . . .', with the suggestion that Statius has the inspiration, but
not the appropriate divine support for his poem.

For the interval of time (in this case thirty days) marking a period
elapsing after a bereavement, and the importance of avoiding pre-
mature consolation, see 5. 1. 16 n. A month is only a brief interval.

25. planctus in carmina uerto: a striking encapsulation of the
topos that suffering produces songs, pointing to the closeness yet
distinctness of the two types of response to death; contrast the anti-
thetical pairing at 2. 1. 5–6: 'cum iam egomet cantus et uerba
medentia saeuus | confero [*a (ed. princ.)* : consero *M*], tu planctus
lamentaque fortia mauis'.

27. ira recalls the peremptory tone of the poem's opening; the
anger is directed at those gods who have allowed such a death to
occur; contrast the absence of complaint and anger (as opposed to
grief) in 5. 3, where Statius' father's death is not such a transgression
of the natural order.[3]

28. solitae: compare the language used by Statius to describe his
familiarity with Apollo at *Ach.* 1. 10–11 'neque enim Aonium nemus
aduena pulso | nec mea nunc primis augescunt tempora uittis',
a statement which follows an appeal to Apollo for 'fontes . . . nouos'
(*Ach.* 1. 9). In the present passage the emblems of poetic status are
withdrawn or unavailable; compare Statius' account of his own
poetic inability at *Silu.* 5. 3. 7–9 and see the notes ad loc. for the

---

[3] The passage where Statius is closest to anger in 5. 3 is 64–70, where he implies that his
father's death was like that of a young man or a child (e.g. 'cur magis incessat superos', 64).

infernal associations of the yew and the Dionysiac significance of ivy. Whereas in 5. 3. 8 the funereal yew is replacing ivy, in the present poem even the yew itself is wilting (*marcet*, 29)

29–30. taxea . . . silua comis: for *silua* denoting foliage removed from the bough, cf. *Silv.* 3. 1. 185 'populeaque mouens albentia tempora silua', *OLD* s.v. *silua* 3a. But it is worth at least speculating on the possible overtones of *silua*; since this is a passage where Statius is characterizing the quality and generic status of his poetry, a link with the title *Siluae* is not to be ruled out.[4] *silua* would not allude to 5. 5 as an individual poem (only the plural form appears to be found, and the word for a single poem used by Statius is either *libellus*, as at e.g. *Silv.* 1 pr. 16 'primus libellus', or *ecloga*, as at *Silv.* 3 pr. 20–1 'summa est ecloga qua mecum secedere Neapolim Claudiam meam exhortor', 4 pr. 19[5]), but to the Greek ὕλη, the 'matter' of which the composition was made up. By describing it as *taxea*, Statius comments on the funereal character of the poetry, while *marcet* might also suggest its inferior quality.

silua comis is a neat juxtaposition (contrast Seneca's censure of Maecenas' 'amne siluisque ripa comantibus' at *Ep.* 114. 5): cf. Ov. *Rem.* 606 'non flesset positis Phyllida silua comis', Luc. 4. 128 'tollere silua comas', 6. 643–4 'quam pallida pronis | urguet silua comis', Calp. *Ecl.* 1. 9–10 'graciles ubi pinea denset | silua comas', V.Fl. 1. 429 'siluasque comantes', 3. 402 'silua comanti', *Silv.* 3. 3. 98 (and *Theb.* 3. 257) 'siluarumque comas', 5. 2. 70 (and *Theb.* 6. 91) 'silua comas'; in Greek note the juxtapositions of ὕλη and φύλλα at Hes. *Op.* 420–1 τῆμος ἀδηκτοτάτη πέλεται τμηθεῖσα σιδήρῳ | ὕλη, φύλλα δ' ἔραζε χέει, Q.S. 10. 67–8 ὅτε δένδρεα μακρὰ καὶ ὕλη | φύλλα φύει. Here, *comis* might refer not just to hair but also to leaves; cf. *Silv.* 5. 1. 136, *Od.* 23. 195 ἀπέκοψα κόμην τανυφύλλου ἐλαίης, Cat. 4. 10–11 'ubi iste post phaselus antea fuit | comata silua' for possible exploitations of such double meaning. At Juv. 9. 12–13, hair is metaphorically described as a forest: 'horrida siccae | silua comae'. It is not impossible that this may be an allusion to Statius.

30. plorata is at first glance puzzling, since although the cypress was planted near graves, it would not itself be bewailed. It is, however, explicable as an allusion to a passage from Ovid's *Metamophoses*. When describing the assembly of trees which came to hear the song of

---

[4] On the term *Silvae*, see General Introduction, p. xviii n. 6.
[5] Though note that Politian does use the singular *silua* to refer to the poems of his *Siluae*.

Orpheus, Ovid gives an aetiology of the cypress tree, recounting how the boy Cyparissus (on whom see also Serv. *A.* 3. 680), beloved by Apollo, resolved to die after killing his pet stag (Ov. *Met.* 10. 106–42). Despite the entreaties of Apollo, he persisted in this design, and asked to be allowed to grieve in perpetuity, and accordingly was changed into the cypress tree. After the metamorphosis Apollo addresses the boy (*Met.* 10. 141–2): 'ingemuit tristisque deus "lugebere nobis | lugebisque alios aderisque dolentibus" inquit.'

plorata is a learned epithet, alluding to the paradox of the boy who mourns being mourned himself by Apollo. The image in 30–1 is of the cypress preventing the ivy from clinging to it; for *ramus* denoting foliage to adorn the head, compare *Silv.* 5. 3. 142 'ramis Phoebi' and *Theb.* 6. 818 'ramumque oblatumque manu thoraca repellit', where the word denotes the palm of victory.

cupressus: the cypress is mentioned as a tree of mourning at *Silv.* 5. 1. 135–6, where Statius directs Apollo to wear its foliage as a sign of grief.

31–3. eburno pollice: Lundström (1893), 47 explains that the thumb is 'ivory' because it holds the ivory plectrum used to play the instrument, comparing Prop. 2. 1. 9–10 'siue lyra carmen digitis percussit eburnis, | miramur, facilis ut premat arte manus', though one might wonder if *eburno pollice* could be viewed as a metonymy for the plectrum itself. Here, as in Propertius, the epithet conveys the refinement and quality of the music produced; it is opposed to *digitis errantibus*, suggesting confusion and disorder, in the next line. Similarly, *pulso* is the *vox propria* of musical activity (*OLD* s.v. *pulso* 4), whereas *scindo* and *amens* denote the violence and fury (23) which characterize Statius' grief.

33. iuuat, heu iuuat: for the repetition of *iuuat*, cf. *Theb.* 3. 354–5 'iuuat isse, iuuat, Thebasque nocentes | explorasse manu', Virg. *G.* 2. 437–8, Prop. 3. 5. 19–22, Ov. *Met.* 15. 147–8, Sen. *Ag.* 435–6, Wills (1996), 105. For *heu* as a separating word in repetitions cf. *Silv.* 3. 3. 25–6 'felix, heu nimium felix plorataque nato | uenit', Virg. *A.* 4. 657 'felix, heu nimium felix'. Other meanings of *iuuat* should not be overlooked; not only is it pleasing to Statius to compose, but it is helpful for him. *iuuo* commonly denotes the operation of medical remedies (*OLD* s.v. *iuuo* 3b), which recalls Statius' description of his poem of consolation for Abascantus as 'medicina dolori' (cf. 42 below, and 5. 1. 16 n.), so that the therapeutic, as well as the merely pleasurable aspects of poetry are suggested here.

nudare: Vollmer (and Gronovius before him) defended M's *laudare* by arguing that there is a reference to the *laudatio funebris*. But there is no reason to evoke the formal *laudatio funebris* in a context of poetic lament, especially for a child who does nothing which might possibly be praised. Corruption seems indicated; *inlaudabile* (first found here) in the previous line will have exerted an irresistible effect on any infinitive in the fifth foot of the next line. Håkanson (1969), 156–7 defends Unger's *laxare*, which has the merit of palaeographical similarity to *laudare*. Unger cited *Theb.* 6. 831 'et armiferas laxare adsueuerat iras', to which Håkanson adds *Theb.* 8. 215–16 'corda leuabat | exhaustus sermone dolor', and *Silv.* 2. 1. 14–15 'aegrumque dolorem | libertate doma'. Apart from the unhelpfulness of Håkanson's first citation, where it is *dolor* which is the subject and not the object of 'leuabat', there is a more serious objection to *laxare*: the verb is not remotely parallel to *fundere* earlier in the line. Statius has said that it is helpful to pour out song; the implication of this being that the opportunity to speak about his bereavement is a beneficial one. *laxare* by contrast, even if it is construed imperfectively, referring to the beginning of the process, looks towards a termination of the emotion experienced, and hence would anticipate a much later stage of the process of recovery. In the light of Statius' subsequent demand for the right to grieve, including in 59–61 an attack on those who try to set bounds to grief, a figure which indeed can occur at the beginning of a lament,[6] it is too early for him to be anticipating the *results* of 'inlaudabile carmen | fundere'.

A better solution is *nudare* (Markland), denoting the revelation of emotion (cf. 'ira tacendi | impatiens' in 27–8) which takes place when Statius pours forth his song; see e.g. Phaed. 3 *prologus* 47 'stulte nudabit animi conscientiam', *OLD* s.v. *nudare* 6b.

35–7. Editors' punctuation of these lines has been very varied. Punctuation of these lines as statments (e.g. Vollmer, Klotz, Iz.-Fr., Courtney) has the disadavantage that Statius, without any prior preparation, announces that he has deserved his wretched condition. This sudden revelation is scarcely in keeping with the almost confrontational tone of the poem's opening. Moreover, if this is an admission of guilt, why is there no explanation of the sin which the poet is acknowledging? Something stronger is required.

---

[6] e.g. *Silv.* 2. 6. 1–2, *Epic. Drusi* 7–8.

Punctuating each clause as a question (following Phillimore and Mozley) is stonger. Statius asks whether he has deserved his misfortunes, including the loss of his poetic inspiration. *aspiciant* and *pudeat* will thus be deliberative questions. For *merui* in a reproachful question, compare *Silv.* 5. 4. 1–3 'Crimine quo merui... | quoue errore miser, donis ut solus egerem, | Somne, tuis?'

35. nefastum (cf. *Silv.* 2. 1. 27 'infaustus uates', applied by Statius to himself as he sings the lament for Glaucias) recalls the religious crimes suggested by Statius as reasons for his misfortune at 3–8 above.

37. nil iam placidum manabit ab ore: *placidum* points to the gentleness of Statius' former role as a provider of consolation in the lines immediately following. *manabit* suggests tears as well as poetry (cf. 44 'manantes oculos'), recalling the tension between emotion and art described in 24–34.

38–41. ille ego: for this figure, most famously found in the rejected lines at the start of the *Aeneid*, see *Silv.* 5. 3. 10 n. above, where I have accepted Markland's conjecture *ille ego* in place of M's *certe ego*. Here Statius reverses the positive tone of the rejected opening of the *Aeneid*, with its upward progression towards epic, since Statius records a poetic decline, and his inability to compose a lament for himself. The bitterness of this is suggested by *quotiens*, which can be retained; there is no need to emend to *totiens*; the parenthesis adds to the intensity of Statius' lament.

38. matrumque patrumque: no poem is extant where Statius consoles parents for the loss of their children, although the death of a child is commonly mentioned, by way of comparison. Statius similarly claims to have consoled parents at *Silv.* 2. 1. 30–2. Although van Dam ad loc. concurs with the view that Statius did not include all his poems in the published books of the *Silvae*, Statius need not be *solely* thinking of poetic consolation in this passage, even if poetry is a central concern (e.g. 47–8 below); 44–5 could refer to other forms of consolation, metaphorical or otherwise. It may also be significant that Statius asks his friends for help; since we are not told that he is demanding poetry, it need not be assumed that *all* the assistance Statius claims to have rendered was poetical in character. For the idea that one should be able to console oneself with the arguments one has used with others, see [Plu.] *ad Apoll.* 118 B–C, Kassel (1958), 95.

39. uulnera: for the application of wound imagery to bereavement, see *Silv.* 5. 1. 18, 30 nn.; here the *uulnera* of the parents consoled by Statius anticipate his own wounds (*uulneribus*, 43).

uiuos: Boxhorn (1662), 65 remarked: 'vivi dolores sunt dolores viventium, propter amicos exstinctos'. But *uiuus* is a paradoxical epithet to apply to grief for one who is dead; *uiuos . . . dolores* suggests physical as well as mental pain, recalling the metaphor of *uulnera*. For *uiuus* denoting living parts of the body see *OLD* s.v. *uiuus* 2, and compare the English idiom 'to cut to the quick'; see also *Silv.* 5. 1. 30 'nunc etiam attactus refugit iam plana cicatrix'.

mulcere: 5. 1. 27–8 n.

41. auditus: for the idea of the dead being able to hear communications at the time of their funeral, compare *Silv.* 3. 3. 205–7:

> talia dicentem genitor dulcedine laeta
> audit, et immites lente descendit ad umbras
> uerbaque dilectae fert narraturus Etruscae.

See also 2. 1. 22 for the dead person's presence at his own funeral.

42. fomenta: a *fomentum* is a dressing or a poultice which might be applied to a wound, as at Tac. *Ann.* 15. 55. 3 'fomenta uulneribus nulla'. Its transferred use is attested at Cic. *Fin.* 2. 95 'uirtutis, magnitudinis animi, patientiae, fortitudinis fomentis dolor mitigari solet', Plin. *Ep.* 2. 7. 3 'grauissimo uulneri magno aliquo fomento medendum fuit'; cf. Hor. *Ep.* 1. 3. 26 'frigida curarum fomenta', Plin. *Ep.* 6. 7. 2 'gratum est quod nos requiris, gratum quod his fomentis adquiescis', and Seneca's derogatory use of the word at *Ep.* 51. 5 'fomenta Campaniae' in a passage on the enervating effects of pleasures.

43. subitura: M's *sed summa* cannot be retained; the adversative particle with *summa* is wrong, since there is no reason why Statius should not search for the best remedies. No solution is wholly convincing. Retaining *sed* (for this usage compare Ov. *Tr.* 5. 5. 24 'consumatque annos, sed diuturna, suos'), Heinsius suggested *sed uana*, but this perhaps too much anticipates an unfavourable outcome of Statius' search; cf. the parenthetical *(spes uana!)* of Delz (1992), 252. Markland's remark 'Latet epitheton τοῦ fomenta' seems plausible, and *sed* need not necessarily be retained, but *Dictamna* (Saenger) is eccentric, as noted by Håkanson (1969), 157. However, Håkanson's defence (158) of Rothstein's *sed nulla* is unconvincing, since he argues that the sense is 'sed nulla meis (*sc.* sunt)', despite the need to construe *meis* with *uulneribus*; his citation of Prop. 1. 5. 28 'cum mihi nulla mei sit medicina mali' is a parallel only for the thought and not for the syntax of *sed nulla*. Shackleton Bailey's *subitura* in his Loeb edition is the best solution to date: Statius seeks remedies that will help his wounds. For *subeo* thus, Shackleton Bailey compares Sil. 1. 566 'defessis subeant rebus'; cf. Virg. *A.* 2. 467 'ast alii subeunt', Liv. 28. 13. 8 'cum . . . integri fessis subirent', *OLD* s.v. *subeo* 6c.

43–5. Statius asks his friends to return the favour which he has done them by consoling them for their losses in the past; he also presents himself as a giver of consolation at *Silv.* 2. 1. 30–4, where he also alludes to his own loss of his father.

seras . . . grates: M has *saeuas* here. Though *saeuus* can be used of a person giving untimely consolation, as at *Silv.* 2. 1. 5–6 'cum iam egomet cantus et uerba medentia saeuus | confero', where Statius is *saeuus* in offering healing words to Melior, it is harder to see here how Statius' friends should be repaying him with *saeuas . . . grates*. There are two possibilities for emendation here. With *dignas*, Statius asks for a worthy recompense from those friends he has helped; cf. e.g. Virg. *A.* 1. 600–1 'grates persoluere dignas | non opis est nostrae', 2. 537–8 'persoluant grates dignas et praemia reddant | debita', Stat. *Theb.* 7. 379 'dignasque rependere grates', 11. 223 'dignas sed pendere grates'. Even more pointed, though, and closer to the transmitted text is Unger's *seras*, Statius' friends being reproached for their lack of appreciation for his support at the time of their own bereavements.

46–8. Baehrens's lacuna after 46 has found almost universal acceptance, except from Vollmer, who emended to *increpitant*, explaining the incompleteness of line 46 as the poet breaking off because of the interruption in the next line. This argument would be more convincing if the interruption began immediately in 47; instead, the verb of speaking, 'increpitant', would rather reduce the spontaneity of the passage.

46. Vollmer argued that in M's *uestra domus . . . funera* the genitive *domus* is equivalent to 'domestica', but this is a straining of usage; nor can the phrase mean 'funera uestrarum domorum'. Van Kooten and Klotz emended to *modis . . . maestis*; the corruption of *modis* to *domus* is certainly possible (cf. *Silv.* 5. 2. 75), but since a lacuna is inevitable in the following line there can be no certainty about emendations, even if they are very plausible.

Although the text of 46 appears corrupt, the sense of the lacuna is probably that one person upbraided Statius for his shedding of tears for others. Mozley restored the sense as folows: 'Doubtless when I in sad strains <bewailed> your losses <one among you spake> rebuking . . .'. It is, however, unlikely that a person being consoled would reproach the bringer of succour; it is more likely that an uninvolved interlocutor would be the source of such unfeeling criticism.

47. On the theme of grieving for another person's loss see *Silv.* 5. 3. 244–5 n.

48. infelix: the epithet appears puzzling, since *uerum erat* in 49 indicates that the remark occurred in the past. Three possible meanings may apply here; Statius could be 'inauspicious' or 'ill-omened', because he was acting as if he were bereaved, when he was not. Another view might be that *infelix* is here used to denote how misguided Statius was in seeking to console others when he would be faced by his own bereavements; cf. Lucr. 5. 1194–5 'o genus infelix humanum, talia diuis | cum tribuit facta atque iras adiunxit acerbas!', Virg. *A.* 5. 465 'infelix, quae tanta animum dementia cepi?', *ThLL* vii/1. 1364. 24–50, and note the English idiom 'Unhappy man!' *infelix* might also hint at a literary criticism from an opponent; for this sense of *infelix* compare Sen. *Con.* 7. 1. 27 and *Suas.* 2. 22; see also Hor. *Ars* 34, where the word is applied to the unsuccesful endeavours of a craftsman.

repone . . . serua: i.e. 'store away for later use' (*OLD* s.v. *repono* 9).

49. uerum erat: this answers and affirms the objection raised against Statius in the previous lines, which were 'true' in the sense that Statius should have stored up his poetic powers, since he is in need of them now.

uires: for this used to describe the strength needed by a poet, cf. 5. 3. 1 n.; for poetic inability expressed in terms of physical weakness, see 5. 4. 11 n.

49–50. copia fandi | nulla: *copia fandi* is Virgilian, found e.g. in the repeated line 'postquam introgressi et coram data copia fandi' (*A.* 1. 520, 11. 248); its appearance here in a personal and emotional context contrasts with the formulaic character of Virgil's usage. Statius' phrase also suggests *infantia* in its literal sense, so that the loss of his *infans* (9) paradoxically brings about the condition of *infantia*.

50. dignumque nihil . . . fulmine tanto: though one does not need to take this expression of poetic weakness seriously, *dignumque nihil* and *fulmine* encapsulates the tension implicit in the whole poetic process of Statius' lament for his *puer*, hinting at the two aims of expression of grief and creation of art. The aesthetic element is not in itself problematic; for the need and importance of poetic commemoration compare *Silv.* 5. 1. 15 'haud alio melius condere sepulchro', but 5. 1 is a poem where Statius is concerned with another person's bereavement and not his own. The linguistic force of the

words is strange. By saying that he found that he could compose
nothing worthy of such a disaster, it is implied that the disaster has
positive qualities in itself which deserve appropriate commemoration;
one might have expected Statius to have said that he could say
nothing worthy of his child (a familiar topos in memorial services
for persons of all ages in our own time) rather than nothing worthy of
the catastrophe. Furthermore, the statement conflicts, or at least
consorts oddly, with Statius' earlier affirmation of the usefulness of
producing poor poetry (33–4), and may even imply that Statius is
indeed concerned with recording rather than recovering from his
own grief (compare *Silv.* 5. 1 *epist.* 6–7 'post hoc ingratus sum si
lacrimas tuas transeo', where *lacrimas* indicates the need to commem-
orate not only Abascantus' wife, but also his grief). Compare Statius'
desire to build altars for his father and to match the poetry of Homer
and Virgil at *Silv.* 5. 3. 47–63, revealing the same type of poetic
ambition in a similar context. For *fulmen* denoting a great catastrophe
compare 2. 1. 30–31 'me fulmine in ipso | audiuere patres' with van
Dam ad loc., *ThLL* vi/1. 1528. 44–59. Lastly, there is an irony in Statius'
expression 'dignumque nihil . . . fulmine tanto': Statius is saying that
his poetry cannot reach the heights of grief, yet the very expression of
that failure still uses the grand metaphor *fulmine*.

51. repperit: the image of search as a metaphor for poetic
creation is also implied by *reperio* at Plaut. *Capt.* 1033; see also Quint.
Inst. 5. 10. 116, 10. 2. 5 and 11. 2. 3. Compare *inuenit* in 54 below,
perhaps giving life to the metaphor behind the rhetorical terms
εὕρεσις and *inuentio*; cf. e.g. *Rhet. Her.* 1. 2. 3 'inuentio est excogitatio
rerum uerarum aut ueri similium quae causam probabilem reddant',
Arist. *Rhet.* 1355ᵇ25–6 Ἔστω δὴ ἡ ῥητορικὴ δύναμις περὶ ἕκαστον τοῦ
θεωρῆσαι τὸ ἐνδεχόμενον πιθανόν.

inferior uox: the epithet denotes lack of quality but also implies
generic hierarchy; by writing the present lament for his *puer* Statius is
not responding as well as he would wish to the *fulmen* which has
overwhelmed him. The literal meaning of *inferior* gives rise to the
same metaphor of 'lowliness' as does *humilis*, used to characterize
literature and language from the time of Cicero (e.g. Cic. *Brut.* 274).
Compare Seneca the Elder's account of Asinius Pollio's disdain for his
own declamation, where *inferior* is also used to categorize a kind
of literary production not held in high regard by its creator (*Con.* 4
pr. 2): ' . . . siue—quod magis crediderim—tantus orator inferius id
opus ingenio suo duxit, et exerceri quidem illo uolebat, gloriari

fastidiebat.' At *Theb.* 10. 446 Statius refers to his own 'inferiore lyra', but there the comparison is not with his own poetry but with Virgil, as is indicated by the remarks on Nisus and Euryalus which follow.

omnis . . . omnia: for such repetitions of an adjective with variations in number or gender, cf. e.g. *Theb.* 7. 59–60 'adeo uis omnis et omne | uulnus' with Wills (1996), 282–5.

sordent: the image is of filth or dirt; compare the *situs* which affects Statius' lyre after his father's death at 5. 3. 34. *sordeo* itself appears to be first used as a term of literary criticism here, but cognates are attested as early as Plaut. *Mil.* 1001. See also Call. *H.* 2. 108–12 where Apollo's reply to Phthonos spurns the Euphrates as a carrier of dirt, preferring instead the πίδακος ἐξ ἱερῆς ὀλίγη λιβὰς ἄκρον ἄωτον. As a term of criticism *sordes* and its kin appear to have included several evils: at Sen. *Con.* 4 pr. 9 'nec, si qua sordidiora sunt aut ex cotidiano usu repetita, possunt pati' the phrase 'ex cotidiano usu' implies a desire to avoid what was commonplace or even vulgar (cf. *OLD* s.v. *sordidus* 4b), but contrast Tac. *Dial.* 21. 4 (where the text is admittedly uncertain), where an antithesis is drawn between the *nitor* and *altitudo* which Flavian readers might recognize in Caelius' speeches, and the *sordes* and other stylistic vices which typify (for the speaker) *antiquitas*, *sordes* being a counterpart to *nitor*, which suggests deliberate stylistic brilliance. Statius' usage seems akin to this passage; *sordent | uerba* does not imply actual vulgarity or use of lowly words, but simply unsuccessful and inglorious composition.

52–3. ignosce, puer: the boy is asked to forgive Statius for writing a poor poem about him; this represents a slight shift from 50, where Statius was seeking a response which was appropriate to the disaster rather than to his *puer*, whereas here he wishes to give the child a fitting tribute.

mersum: as Courtney notes, M's *maestu* is a corruption induced by the appearance of *maestus* at the same position of the line in 46. There is thus no need to be restricted to such colourless emendations as *maesta* or *maestum* (ς). *mersum* (Heinsius) is more evocative of Statius' bereavement; for *maestus* and *mersus* as variants, see Ov. *Tr.* 3. 11. 38, and note too 5. 3. 12, where Baehrens conjectured *maesto* for M's *merso*. The metaphor of immersion is commonly used in contexts of sorrow, as at Cat. 68. 13 'accipe, quis merser fortunae fluctibus ipse' (from a passage where Catullus continues by referring to the deleterious effects of his brother's death) and Virg. *A.* 6. 511–12 'sed me fata mea et scelus exitiale Lacaenae | his mersere malis'; a closer parallel from Statius is *Theb*. 10. 735 'illi atra mersum caligine pectus | confudit sensus', describing the fears and anguish of Creon for his son Menoeceus. The combination of *mersum* with *caligine* also recalls another usage of *mergo*, where the verb denotes a process of concealment; compare Virg. *A*. 6. 267 'pandere res alta terra et caligine mersas', echoed by Statius himself at *Theb*. 6. 510–11 'tandem caligine mersum | erigit adcursu comitum caput', used to describe the darkness which affects a person who has fainted or is close to losing consciousness. In the present passage *caligine mersum* combines two ideas, at once implying the metaphorical darkness which has overwhelmed Statius, and also suggesting an almost physical response to bereavement (consistent with *obruis* in the following line); compare the 'night' which affects Andromache when she learns of her husband's death at *Iliad* 22. 466–7: τὴν δὲ κατ' ὀφθαλμῶν ἐρεβεννὴ νὺξ ἐκάλυψεν, | ἤριπε δ' ἐξοπίσω, ἀπὸ δὲ ψυχὴν ἐκάπυσσε. Moreover, *caligine* itself can be metaphorical, denoting the poetic darkness which has affected Statius since the child's death; compare the *nubila* which affect Statius' *mens* as a result of his father's death at *Silv*. 5. 3. 13.

   obruis: an extremely resonant word. *obruo* can denote the overwhelming of a ship by the waves or drowning (*ThLL* ix/2. 153. 3–13); this would concur with the imagery of *mersum*. *obruo* can also denote the onset of darkness (ibid. 151. 39–49), in keeping with a more physical interpretation of *caligine mersum* in the previous line: compare Lucr. 5. 650 (where *caligo* also occurs) and 6. 864 for *obruo* in descriptions of nightfall.

   53. a durus: for this juxtaposition, cf. Virg. *Ecl*. 10. 47–8 'a! dura niues et frigora Rheni | me sine sola uides'. Here, Statius reproaches both Orpheus and Apollo for being able to sing after their bereavements. For a less specific version of such reproaches to survivors, cf. [Tib.] 3. 2. 3–4 'durus et ille fuit, qui tantum ferre dolorem, | uiuere et erepta coniuge qui potuit'.

   uiso…uulnere: Ovid locates Eurydice's wound in her ankle (*Met*. 10. 10); cf. Virg. *G*. 4. 458–9 'immanem ante pedes hydrum moritura puella | seruantem ripas alta non uidit in herba'; an alternative tradition of uncertain origin which may go back to the *Orpheus* of Lucan is attested in the *Liber monstrorum* 3. 3 p. 264 Porsia (= p. 306 Orchard, Luc. fr. 5 Morel): 'hydra anguis armatus fuisse describitur, quae Eurydicen coniugem Orphei in ripa fluminis capite truncauit et demersit in gurgitem et sicut Scylla monstris ita et haec serpentibus praecincta fuisse fingitur.' Though Courtney, *FLP*, p. 353 casts doubt on the attribution to Lucan, Orchard (2003), 92 points out that other specific references to Orpheus and Lucan in the *Liber monstrorum* (1. 5 and 2.7) make it likely that this passage of the *Liber* too is derived from the same work. For the emphasis on the first moment when Orpheus was confronted by the sight of Eurydice, compare 5. 1. 202 'conspecta coniuge', which refers to his backward glance when leading his wife from the Underworld, causing him to lose her for a second time. See the next note.

54. inuenit: see 51 n. above.

Thracius Orpheus: used by Virgil at the same position in the line in a passage where the poet Linus is also mentioned (*Ecl.* 4. 55–7). Orpheus' lamentations for his wife, which eventually moved the infernal powers to grant her return to life, are an essential and common feature of the legend (e.g. Virg. *G.* 4. 464–6, Ov. *Met.* 10. 11–48). For Orpheus' ability to lament his wife here, contrast *Silv.* 5. 1. 202–4 (with nn.), where, in a simile, Orpheus is explicitly said to have been unable to lament his wife in song when he saw her ('sine carmine fleuit', 5. 1. 204).

55. dulce sibi (cf., in the same *locus*, Virg. *G.* 4. 509, 'flesse sibi') modifies the force of the whole sentence; thus, as well as hinting that Orpheus was indulging in poetry when he might have been expected to be silent (cf. *Silv.* 5. 1. 202–4 above), Statius suggests that Orpheus was indeed *durus*, if he actually found pleasing material for his song. Thus the possibility of Orpheus' distaste for his own poetry is linked with Statius' censure of his own poem.

That Orpheus might not find his own poetry agreeable is paradoxical, since he is the poet who is able to soothe and charm not only all creatures but even trees (e.g. Virg. *G.* 4. 510, Ov. *Met.* 10. 90–106), as well as the infernal powers. Virgil implies that Orpheus' aim was to console himself, after he lost his wife for the first time (*G.* 4. 464 'ipse caua solans aegrum testudine amorem'); the persistence of Orpheus' laments however implies a lack of success.

busta Lini: though Snijder on *Theb.* 3. 144–5 argues that *busta* here means 'corpse' (cf. *Theb.* 12. 246–8 'haud procul, exacti si spes non blanda laboris, | Ogygias, Argia, domos et egena sepulcri | busta iacere reor'), the plural *busta* would be an odd way to refer to the single corpse of Linus and is more likely to denote his pyre (which would of course include the corpse before cremation began), as in my translation, or his tomb (Shackleton Bailey).

Apollo's grief for Linus is a closer parallel to Statius' experience, since it is the grief of a father for a son. By mentioning Orpheus and Linus in close collocation, Statius seems to allude to Virg. *Ecl.* 4. 55–7. That passage, however, treats Linus as a poet; see also *Ecl.* 6. 67–73, where Linus initiates Gallus into poetry, Ross (1975), 21–3. There were various traditions concerning Linus. An Argive legend (Paus. 1. 43. 7, see also Call. frr. 26–31 Pf., Lactantius on Stat. *Theb.* 1. 570, Brown (1994), 174–5) made him the son of Apollo and Psamathe, who was exposed and killed by hounds. This is the legend followed by Statius here and at *Theb.* 1. 575–90, and at 6. 64–5 where the death of Linus appears on a coverlet used at the funeral of Archemorus: 'medio Linus intertextus acantho | letiferique canes'. The second tradition was the Theban legend that Linus was a successful musician who aroused the wrath of Apollo and was killed by him (Paus. 9. 29. 6–9, see also *Σ Il.* 18. 570 (Tb), Brown (1994), 177). In the same passage Pausanias also mentions a later tale of another poet called Linus, the son of Ismenius, who was killed by his pupil Heracles; cf. Apollod. 2. 4. 9 with Frazer's notes. Linus' death was associated with a lament for him, αἴλινος, a tradition which appears to go back as far as *Il.* 18. 570 λίνον δ᾽ ὑπὸ καλὸν ἄειδε (see Edwards ad loc.); cf. Hes. fr. 305 Merkelbach and West:

> Οὐρανίη δ᾽ ἄρ᾽ ἔτικτε Λίνον πολυήρατον υἱόν·
> ὃν δή, ὅσοι βροτοί εἰσιν ἀοιδοὶ καὶ κιθαρισταί,
> πάντες μὲν θρηνεῦσιν ἐν εἰλαπίναις τε χοροῖς τε,
> ἀρχόμενοι δὲ Λίνον καὶ λήγοντες καλέουσιν.

Hdt. 2. 79 refers to the lament for Linos taking place not only in Greece, but also in Phoenicia, and Cyprus and Egpyt, but with different names being applied to Linus, Maneros being used in Egpyt; Lloyd ad loc. notes that modern scholars have suggested that the cry αἴλινος was perhaps of Semitic origin, denoting 'woe unto us', rather than 'a cry of woe for Linus', as was believed in Greece, but see also M. L. West (1997), 262–3 who speculates that the lament may originally be related to a north-west Semitic god called Lim. At any event, Statius' *non tacuit* in 56 may allude to the more traditional association of Linus with lament. Poems ascribed to Linus circulated in antiquity; for fragments and further discussion, see M. L. West (1983), 56–67.

Thus in mentioning Orpheus and Linus together (for the pairing, cf. Quint. *Inst.* 1. 10. 9, Tac. *Dial.* 12. 4) Statius follows Virgil (whose

Linus is a musician), but also alludes to his own treatment of Linus in
the *Thebaid*, who is killed at a much younger age. Pausanias testifies to
a similar intermingling of the poet and infant at 2. 19. 8 where he
notes that in Argos there were attested graves for both persons.

56. nimius ... auidusque doloris: for the genitive after *nimius*
compare 5. 3. 252–3 'non indigus aeui, | non nimius'. The epithet will
be answered by the repetition of *nimium* in 59; instead of defending
himself against the charge of excessive grief, Statius accuses his
detractors of excessive good fortune and excessive cruelty.

auidus implies deliberate desire for something, so that this paradox-
ical phrase suggests the peculiar pleasure sometimes experienced in
grief; compare e.g. 33–4 above, *Silv.* 2. 1. 15 'iam flendi expleta
uoluptas' (with van Dam), *Theb.* 6. 72 'inde ingens lacrimis honor et
miseranda uoluptas', and the delight of the bereaved women of
Thebes at *Theb.* 12. 793–4 'gaudent lamenta nouaeque | exultant
lacrimae', Plin. *Ep.* 8. 16. 5 'est enim quaedam dolendi uoluptas',
Od. 10. 398 πᾶσιν δ' ἱμερόεις ὑπέδυ γόος, 16. 215 ἀμφοτέροισι δὲ τοῖσιν
ὑφ' ἵμερος ὦρτο γόοιο.

58. reprendis: M has *rependis*. A verb of measuring or weighing
might seem appropriate, since Statius is said to have exceeded the
limits of *pudor*; note also that the emphasis on excess here is heigh-
tened by the repetitions of *nimius*. *rependis*, however, is difficult because
of the force of the prefix *re-*, implying that the action is being
reciprocated. Vollmer argued that the word simply denotes a process
of weighing or judgement, but, aware of the implication of the prefix,
also argued that an ellipse of some word like *damnis* is required to give
the sense: 'Das *re-* erklärt sich durch ein zu denkendes *damnis*.' This
argument would be more convincing if *rependo* were solely construed
with a dative of the thing something is weighed against. However,
rependo is also found with multiple accusatives denoting objects
weighed against each other; Vollmer himself cites *Theb.* 10. 890–1
'Lernam Thebasque rependit | maestus ... Tirynthius', a passage
where the two accusatives are opposed to one another, and thus not
parallel to this passage where *gemitus* and *lamenta* are not being con-
trasted. Thus since two accusatives appear in this line, a combination
which when used with *rependo* would normally not require a dative, it
is unlikely that Vollmer's suggestion that *damnis* is to be understood is
correct. Other meanings of *rependo* are even less satisfactory in sense
(*OLD* s.v. *rependo* 2–6), since the verb would then denote repayment or
compensation.

Accordingly, Politian's *reprendis* is to be accepted; the idea of reproach is explained in the following lines where Statius condemns the person who would set a limit to his grief. *reprendit* (*ς*) might also be possible; it is noticeable that Statius refers to his imagined critic in the third person in ll. 60–1, where the second person is reserved for Fortuna. In ll. 62–4 it is arguable whether the subject of the verbs is Statius' opponent or simply the so-called ideal second person (corresponding to French *on*), though the latter possibility is more likely in view of the shift to the third person *ille seuerus* in 64 to refer again to Statius' opponent.

59. nimium felix: for parallels see Pease on Virg. *A.* 4. 657–8 'felix, heu nimium felix, si litora tantum | numquam Dardaniae tetigissent nostra carinae'. In Statius, compare *Silv.* 2. 7. 24 'felix heu nimis et beata tellus' and 3. 3. 25–6 'felix, heu nimium felix plorataque nato | umbra uenit'.

nimium crudelis gives the line its point: such happiness would be tainted by cruelty; at 2. 6. 1 Statius used the phrase 'saeue nimis' to introduce a similar tirade against a person who should attempt to impose restrictions on grief; compare *Epic. Drusi* 7–8, and note the similar use of *leges* to denote the limits of mourning: 'et quisquam leges audet tibi dicere flendi? | et quisquam lacrimas temperat ore tuas?' *crudelis* is an epithet applicable to Fortuna herself (e.g. Cic. *Mil.* 87); here the person who is free of Fortuna himself assumes her less favourable qualities.

expers might appear slightly paradoxical, since the attainment of *felicitas* might well be attributable to Fortuna, but the sense is clear enough, since the person has not suffered at the hands of Fortuna. Taken with *audet* in 61 there may even be the implication that such pronouncements may call down retribution on the speaker; cf. Niobe's rash 'maior sum quam cui possit Fortuna nocere' at Ov. *Met.* 6. 195. Statius' own role as a source of consolation is not so dissimilar, since in his consolations to others he advises a cessation of grief (e.g. *Silv.* 2. 1. 208–9, 5. 1. 247)

60. imperii, Fortuna, tui: compare the wording, but not the sense, of *Silv.* 1. 4. 5–6 'erubuit tanto spoliare ministro | imperium Fortuna tuum'. The dominion of Fortuna is commonplace (e.g. Sal. *Cat.* 8. 1 'sed profecto fortuna in omni re dominatur', Boethius, *Cons. Phil.* 2. 1 'Fortunae te regendum dedisti; dominae moribus oportet obtemperes.').

62. incitat heu planctus: I have followed translators who have tended to construe the subject of *incitat* here as the *nimium felix* of line 59, with *planctus* as accusative plural. It would of course also be possible to construe *planctus* as nominative singular, with *me* as the implied object, though the point of the first interpretation (trying to prevent lamentation actually increases it) is perhaps sharper.

fugientia ripas has been variously explained: *OLD* s.v. *fugio* 3b cites this passage as an example of a transitive usage denoting 'to speed past or away from', but Slater and Iz.-Fr. interpret the phrase as describing the rivers which have burst their banks; cf. Shackleton Bailey's new Loeb translation: 'More easily might you hold back rivers as they flee their banks'. Their translations gain support from the second part of l. 63, which describes a situation of considerable difficulty, the attempt to check a swiftly spreading fire. Far more violence is evoked if the rivers are breaking their banks, rather than merely flowing past them, and this is in keeping with Statius' frequent portrayal of the violence of grief, with which the rivers and fires are compared. The drama of flood is an inspiration for similes in all periods (e.g *Il.* 16. 384–93, Virg. *A.* 2. 304–8, where fire is also mentioned). Statius uses here the familiar device of the *adunaton* as a means for expressing the impossibility of a task. Rivers flowing back to their source are commonly used in such passages; see Dutoit (1936), 16–18, 168. For the impossibility of putting out a fire, see Prop. 3. 19. 5–6 'flamma per incensas citius sedetur aristas, | fluminaque ad fontis sint reditura caput' where the motifs of fire and rivers appear together.   ·

63. detineas: Boxhorn's emendation of M's meaningless *demneus* is more precise than Calderini's *deuincas*, indicating that an attempt to check the flow of the rivers is envisaged.

rapidis . . . ignibus: the epithet suggests a sudden and terrible conflagration such as a forest fire; cf. Sil. 5. 511 'rapidoque inuoluitur aesculus igni'. Virgil also has the combination of fire and flood at *A.* 12. 521–5 where Aeneas and Turnus are simultaneously compared to both phenomena; whereas Virgil used *rapidus* to describe the flow (*decursus*) of the river, Statius uses it of the fires. *rapidi* is also applied to the fires of the funeral pyre, as at e.g. Ov. *Tr.* 1. 7. 20 (see Luck ad loc.) and *CIL* xi. 5836.

65. quisquis is est: on the usage of the pronoun *is* in Statius and in poetry, see 5. 1. 219 n. *quisquis is est* (or the neuter *quidquid id est*) is not uncommonly found at the beginning of a hexameter as in the well known Virg. *A.* 2. 49 'quidquid id est, timeo Danaos et dona ferentes'; cf. Stat. *Theb.* 3. 612 (where the phrase is used contemptuously of Apollo by Capaneus), Lucr. 3. 135, 5. 577, 5. 1252, Ov. *Ep.* 19. 203, 20. 217, *Met.* 13. 468, *Tr.* 3. 12. 43, *Ibis* 9, *Pont.* 1. 1. 21, 1. 6. 25, 2. 9. 77, 3. 3. 73, Pers. 3. 95, 6. 65, Mart. 6. 68. 11, Juv. 7. 162. At *Silv.* 1. 6. 49, 'quisquis is est' occurs in a hendecasyllable. In the present passage, the tone of *quisquis* is dismissive.

   nostrae cognoscat uulnera causae: *cognosco* is a technical term for the judicial investigation of a case and is regularly found with *causa* (*ThLL* iii. 1506. 44–1507. 60, *OLD* s.v. *cognosco* 4b); Statius will cite the 'wounds of his case' as evidence in his complaint against Fortune. The legal terminology recalls *legem* in l. 60; note also *censere* (see *OLD* s.v. *censeo* 5) in 61.

   66–9. Compare *Silv.* 2. 1. 72–6, where Statius emphasizes that Melior's *delicatus* Glaucias was not an expensive purchase from abroad, but was a slave born and reared in his master's home; cf. Fantham (1999), 69. Contrast Petr. 75. 10–11, where Trimalchio reveals that he was not a *uerna* but purchased, before going on to allude to his sexual involvement with master and mistress. Censure of the purchase of young boys is found as early as the second century BC: Plb. 31. 25. 5 records the disapproval expressed by Cato, who sourly noted that pretty boys could command a higher price than fields.

   Petronius represents Trimalchio as having Alexandrian boys in his service (e.g. 31. 3); the detail of their singing is a hyperbolical treatment of their celebrated volubility and wit, noted here and in *Silv.* 2. 1 by Statius and by other authors. See e.g. Mart. 11. 13. 3, Quint. *Inst.* 1. 2. 7; cf. the insults offered to Vespasian by the Alexandrians (D.C. 66. 8. 2, 7), W. J. Slater (1974), 134. An idea of the type of repartee engaged in by such boys may be gleaned from D.C. 48. 44. 3, who notes that a ψίθυρος at the wedding of Octavian and Livia tactlessly alluded to Livia's previous husband, who was also present at the ceremony. From D.C. 67. 15. 3 it emerges that such boys were a feature of Domitian's court as well; one of them unwittingly removed the emperor's private list of those he intended to have put to death, with the result that the document fell into the hands of Domitia. The conspiracy to kill the emperor was thereby hastened. In neither case, however, does Dio specify the nationality of the boys. If such boys were a notorious feature of the imperial court, Statius' defence of his own *puer* may have had contemporary resonance. Although *loquaces* itself in the present passage is harmless, *doctumque* implies a lack of spontaneity, or even a studied acquaintance with bad habits (cf. *Silv.* 2. 1. 74 'compositosque sales meditataque uerba'), on the part of foreign-born boys which will be contrasted with the child's innocent laughter at Statius' gift of freedom in 74–5.

Pharia de puppe: for obloquy of Egypt, compare Statius' treatment of Egyptian religion at *Silv.* 5. 3. 244–5, with notes above; cf. Balsdon (1979), 68–9. Juvenal reverses the usual opposition of *uerna* and foreign-born slave when he refers to Crispinus as 'uerna Canopi' at 1. 26.

68. infantem: Statius plays on the literal meaning ('not speaking') in the words which follow, indicating that such a boy would be far too talkative. *sales* (wit) are usually a positive quality, as is evinced by Cat. 86. 4, who, when comparing Quintia with Lesbia, notes that the former is entirely without *sal*; compare Lucr. 4. 1162 'paruula, pumilio, chariton mia, tota merum sal', and Catullus' rejoinder to Marrucinus Asinius (12. 4–5) that his theft of *lintea* cannot be called *salsum*.

nimium is probably the best available emendation of M's meaningless *sumum*; other conjectures are documented by Klotz and Lundström (1893), 58.

proteruum: the word's negative force here (contrast the more relaxed invocation of 'ridens Iocus et Sales proterui' at *Silv.* 1. 6. 6) is well illustrated by Martial's description of himself at 10. 9. 2 as 'et multo sale, nec tamen proteruo', thus appropriating to himself wit and charm, whilst repudiating any charge of shamelessness.

69. meus ille, meus: after the involved syntax of the previous lines, where Statius has said what the child was not, the sudden shift to this simple exclamation indicates emotion (for a harsher view, see Fantham (1999), 69), with the idea that the child was like a genuine son. On *geminatio*, often characteristic of religious utterances, see *Silv.* 5. 1. 237 n. Here it would be hard to argue that the effect is a religious one. Compare *Ach.* 1. 528 'meus iste, meus', where the inspired Calchas tells Thetis not to conceal her son Achilles so as to prevent his participation in the Trojan war; again there is an air of paradox in the forcefulness and even paternal nature of the language used to exert a claim against a real parent.

cadentem: for the idea of birth as falling, compare e.g. *Silv.* 1. 2. 109 (cited below), *Theb.* 1. 60–1 'si de matre cadentem | fouisti gremio', 2. 617 'procidit impulsus nimiis conatibus infans', 4. 281 'et feta uiridis puer excidit orno', V. Fl. 1. 355–6 'celer Asterion, quem matre

cadentem | Peresius gemino fouit pater amne Cometes' with Spalten-
stein's n.

70. suscepi: M's *aspexi* has inspired doubt since Avantius, who
emended to *excepi*. There are two difficulties. In the first place, *tellure* in
the previous line is hard to construe with *aspexi*, and cannot satisfac-
torily be taken with *cadentem* since one would expect an accusative
with *ad* to denote the place one falls to; *tellure* by contrast could only
denote 'on the ground', as an ablative of place, if M's reading is to be
retained. Secondly *aspexi* merely indicating that Statius was a witness
to the birth seems remarkably passive when compared with the
emotional intensity of *meus ille, meus* and *quid plus tribuere parentes*.

excepi is the simplest solution; compare Venus' words to Cupid on
her patronage and support for Stella at *Silv.* 1. 2. 109–10 'tellure
cadentem | excepi fouique sinu'. *tellure* would thus be an ablative of
separation; the presence of *foui* in the present line makes this an
impressive parallel.

Cancik (1972), 88 conjectured *suscepi*, comparing the similar use of
tollo at *Silv.* 2. 1. 78–81, where Statius describes how Melior raised up
the boy Glaucias at his birth, and considered the boy to be his own
offspring: 'raptum sed protinus aluo | sustulit exsultans ac prima
lucida uoce | astra salutantem dominus sibi mente dicauit | amplex-
usque sinu tulit et genuisse putauit'. But although *OLD* s.v. *suscipio* 4
seems to treat the word as a technical term to denote acknowledge-
ment of paternity, Shaw (2001), 31–56 has decisively shown that there
is no ancient evidence for the common misconception that *tollere* and
suscipere liberos are idioms specifically referring to rituals associated
with the acknowledgement of children at birth; cf. Köves-Zulauf
(1990), 1–94. Nevertheless *suscepi*, here denoting an informal moment
when the child is lifted up at birth, as the context indicates, perhaps
has an edge over *excepi*, which has a more general meaning of support
and protection. Since Statius explicitly remarks in 72 that the child's
real parents could have done no more, it would be appropriate for
Statius to present himself as raising the child with a gesture similar to
that of Melior.

unctum genitali carmine foui: this text has been defended by
Vollmer and Lundström (1893), 59 as a reference to a genethliacon
which Statius composed for the child's birth. But both Lundström
and Vollmer treat *unctum* as a reference to the *lustratio*, the ceremony
which was performed on the ninth day of a boy's life (the eighth day
for a girl), on which see further B. Rawson (1991*a*), 13–15. This day,

however, would not have been the child's birthday, so that it is even more difficult to accept the extraordinary imagery of M's text; as Köves-Zulauf (1990), 55 n. 198 notes, there is also a difficulty in referring to the child's first breath and cries after a reference to the *dies lustricus*. Köves-Zulauf (1990), 55–9 sees *unctum* as referring to anointing and washing of a new born child and suggests that one way to explain *genitali carmine* would be to see it as an 'einen Ablativ des begleitenden Umstands' (58), but the presence of the passive participle means that it is odd to suppose that we are supposed to understand the ablative *genitali carmine* with *foui* and not as an instrumental ablative with *unctum*. Köves-Zulauf, ibid. absurdly suggests that with an instrumental ablative, 'so wäre hier das Lied die metaphorische Entsprechung des Mittels, mit dessen Hilfe das *fovere* im realen Leben geschah, d.h. entweder das *gremium* der versorgenden Person (a), oder die Windeln, in die das Kind durch die Hebamme gelegt wurde (b)'. The difficulties of *unctum genitali carmine* remain, however.

Emendations have tended to concentrate on M's *carmine*, such as *aspergine* and *flumine* (Saenger), *stramine* (Baehrens) and *sanguine* (Danielsson), *tramite* (Delz); Shackleton Bailey's Loeb prints the suggestion of Håkanson (1969), 162–3, *geniali* [Axelson] *gramine*, which is oddly translated as 'festal oil'. None of these is entirely convincing. An alternative strategy may to be to emend *unctum*. I suggest *auctum*, denoting 'magnified'; Statius cherished the child and glorified him with a song of welcome on his birthday.

71. poscentem: Heinsius and Markland emended to *pulsantem*; Markland ad loc. offers extensive parallels for the idea of sounds striking the air. However, the epithet of *auras*, 'nouas', has little point if the baby is merely striking the air that is new to him with his cries,[7] as opposed to asking for new breath, so that *poscentem* can be retained; *poscentem* may also be linked to ideas of the child's cries as being interpreted as a sign of whether the child was suitable for rearing (see below), so that the child's request for air is in effect a request for life as well.

tremulis ululatibus is Virgilian (*A*. 7. 395); Statius' use of the phrase to describe a baby's crying stands in contrast with Virgil's

---

[7] Though there was debate in antiquity as to whether or not the embryo breathed prior to birth (see Aetius 5. 15 (= Diels, *DG* 425–6), Debru (1996), 169–76), it is likely that *nouas* here simply refers to the child's beginning to breathe after birth.

depiction of women inspired with a Bacchic frenzy; slightly different is
Statius' description of the infant Glaucias' first cries at *Silv.* 2. 1. 79–80
(cited above). For the importance of a child's first crying, cf. Macrob.
Sat. 1. 12. 20 'et Mercurium ideo illi in sacris adiungi dicunt quia uox
nascenti homini terrae contactu datur', 22, Ambros. *Hexaem.* 4. 4. 14
'constitue partum feminae, obstetrix utique eum primo cognoscit,
explorat uagitum, quo nati uita colligitur, attendit, utrum masculus
sit an femina'. The strength of the child's cries was seen as an indica-
tion as to whether it was worth rearing, as at Soran. 2. 10 [79] (p. 57,
27 ff. Ilberg) εἶτα λοιπὸν ἐκ τοῦ τεθὲν ἐπὶ γῆς εὐθέως αὐτὸ
κλαυθμυρίσαι μετὰ τόνου τοῦ προσήκοντος· τὸ γὰρ ἕως πλείονος
ἀκλαυστὶ διάγον ἢ καὶ παρέργως κλαυθμυρίζον ἐνύποπτον ὡς διά
τινα περίστασιν τοῦτο πάσχον; cf. Muscio 1. 76 (p. 28, 10–11 Rose)
'uocemque solidam statim ut cadat emittat, maxime cum adpunctus
fuerit aut molliter digitis pressus, uocem mittat', Caelius Aurel. *Gynaec.*
115 (p, 40, 1013–14 Drabkin and Drabkin) 'firmior significatio nutribilis
fetus approbatur si terre depositus statim dederit uagitum congrua
fortitudine uocis'; for further discussion, see Köves-Zulauf (1990),
4 with n. 10, 59.

   72. inserui uitae: a bold usage, perhaps linked to idioms where
inserere is used in connection with joining a family (though of course
this child was not adopted, as indicated in lines 10–11): cf. e.g. V. Max.
9. 7. 2 'neque oportere clarissimae familiae ignotas sordes inseri', 9. 15
tit. 'De iis qui infimo loco nati mendacio se clarissimis familiis inserere
conati sunt', Suet. *Tib.* 3. 1 'insertus est et Liuiorum familiae, adop-
tato in eam materno auo', *Claud.* 39. 2 'neminem unquam per
adoptionem familiae Claudiae insertum'. Here the sense is that
Statius sets the child on his path in life by allowing the child to be
reared in his household.

   73. alios ortus: Metre rules out the singular *alium ortum*, but the
plural may convey a tone of grandeur; cf. Ov. *Met.* 5. 494 'Pisa mihi
patria est et ab Elide ducimus ortus'. For the phrasing, cf. (with a
different sense) V.Fl. 5. 308 'aut alios duris fatorum gentibus ortus'.
Vollmer assumed that this line proves that Statius adopted the boy,
but see 10–11 above; *alios ortus*, appropriate to the assumption by the
child of his master's *nomina*, is best taken closely with *libertatemque*,
indicating that the child was freed, which Statius regards as a
second birth.

   73–4. sub ipsis | uberibus is pointed; while the child was still at
his mother's breast, a most potent image of parental love, Statius was

nevertheless able to give it more than its parents, picking up on *quid plus tribuere parentes* in the previous line. Having said that he could not have been outdone by the child's parents, Statius goes on to indicate how he outdid them in generosity; the force of *quin* is equivalent to English 'indeed', surpassing what has been said before (*OLD* s.v. *quin* 2). The motif of outdoing a child's natural parents in affection is given a much fuller treatment at *Silv.* 2. 1. 87–105, memorably introduced with the aphoristic 'natos genuisse necesse est, | elegisse iuuat' (87–8). See van Dam and Vollmer ad loc. for discussion of this theme, which became particularly important in the context of imperial adoptions, as at e.g. Plin. *Pan.* 89. 2 'cumque eo qui adoptauit amicissime contendis, pulchrius fuerit genuisse talem an elegisse', addressed to Trajan's natural father.

74–5. munera nostra | rideres ignarus adhuc: though M has *ingatus* in 75, *ignarus* (Avantius) is nevertheless preferable to *ingratus* (*ç*), which attributes the wrong motive to the child. Without *ignarus* it might appear that the child's motive for laughter was contempt; for dismissive responses to modest gifts (particularly those of poets) see e.g. Virg. *Ecl.* 2. 44, 56–7, Ov. *Am.* 1. 8. 57–62, *Ars* 2. 268. *ignarus* indicates that the child's laughter is spontaneous, affectionate, and natural, since he is unaware of what Statius has done for him; compare the language used to denote the extreme youth at which Glaucias was freed by Melior at Mart. 6. 29. 3–4: 'munera cum posset nondum sentire patroni, | Glaucia libertus iam Melioris erat.' The child thus laughs at Statius not because of mercenary motives, but through affection. A smiling infant was regarded favourably (e.g. Cat. 61. 212–13, Virg. *Ecl* 4. 60).

75–7. The brevity of the child's life is emphasized in these lines, particularly through the repetition of the verb *propero*, with the idea that Statius barely had enough time even to love the child.

<ullum>: Lundström (1893), 60 cited Claudian *In Ruf.* 1. 244–5 'Effugeret ne quis gladios neu perderet ullum | Augusto miserante nefas' in support of completing the lacuna with *ullum*. Vollmer's preference for Baehrens's *unum* as 'schärfer' rests, however, on a superfine and indeed subjective distinction, especially as *unus* with a negative can denote either 'more than one', as at *Theb.* 8. 152–3 'iam Fama nouis terroribus audax | non unum cecidisse refert' or 'not one', as at Apul. *Met.* 11. 19 'nec fuit nox una uel quies aliqua uisu deae monituque ieiuna'; see further *OLD* s.v. *unus* 2a. The greater precision of *ullum* here is perhaps preferable.

libertas tam parua recalls *parue*, addressed to the child in 74, stressing the age at which the boy received his freedom, but also has a temporal aspect as well, implying that the freedom did not last for long, being broken off by death. Compare *CIL* ii. 1235. 8 (Hispalis) 'quisq(ue) legis titulum sentis quam uixerim paruom', from the epitaph of a child whose full age of one year, eight months, and twelve days is given at the start of the inscription; the adverbial *paruom* evokes the brevity of the child's life, but also perhaps hints at its diminutive physical stature.

horridus suggests the uncouth manner (see *OLD* 4a and b) in which Statius will voice his complaints; compare *incompte* (34) and contrast with Seneca the Elder's assessement of Ovid's talent 'habebat ille comptum et decens et amabile ingenium' (*Con.* 2. 2. 8).

<inde>: M's lacuna is more satisfactorily filled with *inde* (Baehrens), which at least establishes a connection with the preceding sentence, than *ipsos* (ς). Such a conjecture cannot, however, be proved; Shackleton Bailey suggests either *omnes* or *ergo* in his new Loeb edition.

78. inuidia: here equivalent to *querelis*. Cf. *Silv.* 5. 3. 69–70 (accepting Mueller's emendation *pulset*) where *inuidia* is the subject of *pulso* in a similar passage of reproach of the gods, and note the same combination of *superos* and *Tartara*. The use of *inuidia*, with its overtones of envy, to signify mortal complaint against the gods reverses the often personified image of *inuidia* acting against mortals (see e.g. 5. 1. 137–41). *pulsem* might also carry a poetic resonance here (cf. 5. 3. 2–3 'pulsum ... lyrae'); Statius asks if he is to assail the gods in song.

pulsem: for *pulsare* denoting complaint, cf. also. *Silv.* 5. 1. 22–3 'Fataque et iniustos rabidis pulsare querelis | caelicolas solamen erat'.

79–80. quo sospite natos | non cupii: perhaps a reminiscence of Aeneas' words to Evander at Virg. *A.* 11. 56–7 'nec sospite dirum | optabis nato funus pater'; cf. *A.* 8. 470–1 'maxime Teucrorum ductor, quo sospite numquam | res equidem Troiae uictas aut regna fatebor', Mart. 2. 91. 1–2 'Caesar, | sospite quo magnos credimus esse deos'. Statius expresses his paternal feelings for the child in terms of a lack of any desire for children. Such disregard for childlessness is a potent means of characterizing his affection for the boy.

80–1. primo genitor quem protinus ortu | implicui fixique mihi: M's reading is a useful place to begin discussion:

> primo gemitum qui protinus ortu
>   implicuit fixitque mihi

Two difficulties arise at once. Reading *qui* with third persons singular necessitates a change of subject and viewpoint. Throughout the remainder of the passage Statius is describing his relation to the child, as he experienced it. Previously the boy was referred to with the ablative absolute *quo sospite*, and in the second part of l. 81 he will be referred to as *cui*. Only in the last two lines of the poem as we have it (86–7) is any action or emotion described from the viewpoint of the child. It is thus problematic to have him as the subject of such emphatic verbs as *implicuit fixitque*.

Secondly, *gemitum* cannot be correct. Though Lundström (1893), 61 compared *Ach.* 1. 380–1 'dum repetit monitus arcanaque murmura figit | auribus', as well as such phrases as *animo figere* and *in animis fixum tenere aliquid* (cf. *Silv.* 3. 5. 56–7 'fixamque animi penetralibus imis | nocte dieque tenes'), *gemitum* is unacceptable, particularly as it cannot easily be the object of *implicuit*; Vollmer's defence that *implicuit* denotes the movement of the body which accompanies the infant's crying is no solution to this difficulty. As Markland notes, corruption could have been induced by *gemam* in 79; a further argument is that *gemitum* needlessly anticipates the *questus* of l. 82.

Heinsius and Markland emend to *gremium* (Markland has *gremium* as the object of first-person verbs, *adplicui fixique*, and also emends *mihi* to *meum*). It is, however, hard to see how with first-person verbs Statius can enfold the *gremium* of the child when the *gremium* is characteristically the place where a child is held by another person (see *OLD* s.v. *gremium* 1; cf. André (1991), 183); third-person verbs are little better. Though the ablative *gremio* might appear an improvement, it is unlikely since its placement in the midst of the ablative *primo . . . ortu* is inelegant.

The other solution to have found favour with later editors is Politian's *genitum*. This, combined with correction of *qui* to *quem* and with first person verbs in l. 81, at least gives unobjectionable sense; Statius embraced the child at his birth. However, the combination *primo genitum quem protinus ortu* is emphatically repetitive. *primo* is in any case duplicated by *protinus*, without the need for an entirely redundant *genitum*. A more recent suggestion is Delz's *mentem* (retaining the transmitted third-person verbs), so that the child has an immediate affect on Statius' affections: Delz compares *Silv.* 2. 1. 79–80 'ac prima lucida uoce | astra salutantem dominus sibi mente dicauit', 2. 1. 102–3

'et te iam fecerat illi | mens animusque patrem', as well as *Culex* 200
'hoc minus implicuit dira formidine mentem'. This suggestion does
not, however, meet the objection raised against M's text above, that
the third-person verbs applied to the child go against the prevailing
focus of this passage on Statius' actions and responses to the child.

Unless obelization is used, a bolder approach to the text is re-
quired, if only to illustrate some of the difficulties of this crux. A
conjecture which may shed some light is Saenger's *genetrix* (retaining
M's third-person verbs). Although there can be no justification for
mentioning the child's mother at this point, this conjecture does at
least remind us that the actions described could be those of a parent.
Accordingly I suggest the following text:

> primo genitor quem protinus ortu
> implicui fixique mihi

The sense is that Statius did not want children while the boy was
alive, whom, from the moment of birth, he would embrace as a
father. *genitor* continues and makes explicit the implications of 'natos
| non cupii', as well as referring to the earlier occasions in the poem
where Statius presents himself as a father to the child; *genitor* here
might also recall and answer 'non fueram genitor' in l. 11 above.
Compare *Silv.* 2. 1. 81 'et genuisse putauit', describing Melior's feel-
ings for Glaucias; if *genitor* is correct, Statius would be representing the
same emotions in himself. See also 4. 8. 13‒14 'quaeque sibi genitos
putat attollitque benigno | Polla sinu' and *Theb.* 6. 166‒7, where the
mother of Archemorus bitterly laments her child's closer ties to the
nurse who caused his death: 'illa tibi genetrix semper, dum uita
manebat, | nunc ego'. For the child's real mother to use *genetrix* to
denote the nurse is as bold a usage as *genitor* here would be.

81‒2. Statius' instruction to the child recalls his father's role in his
own education; appropriately, for a poet, Statius describes how he
helped the child to speak (compare Statius' father helping him to 'non
uulgare loqui' in *Silv.* 5. 3. 214). On elementary language education,
see Bonner (1977), 165‒72, who notes that reading was taught through
the learning first of letters, then syllables, and finally whole words.

82. monstraui: for the didactic tone cf. 5. 3. 137 (with n.), 180‒1,
237, 289.

murmura: Courtney accepts M's *uulnera* here, but although *cae-
cum* is found with *uulnus*, it is hard to envisage how Statius 'inter-
preted' the child's hidden wounds. *murmura* (Heinsius, Markland) is

preferable; for *murmur* with *caecus* cf. Virg. *A.* 10. 98–9, 12. 591 and Sil. 9. 281; for *caecus* applied to other types of sound see *ThLL* iii. 46. 4–9. Statius uses *murmur* of babies at *Silv.* 2. 1. 104, 2. 7. 37, *Theb.* 5. 614, and 6. 165. *Theb.* 5. 613–15 'ubi uerba ligatis | imperfecta sonis risusque et murmura soli | intellecta mihi?' is also a striking parallel for a child's sounds being understood (in this case not by the dead baby's mother but by his nurse Hypsipyle). Compare Augustine's account of how he learnt to speak (*Conf.* 1. 8. 13), where he explicitly denies deliberate adult involvement in the process, whilst still noting the infant's desire to communicate through sounds if not words: 'non enim docebant me maiores homines, praebentes mihi uerba certo aliquo ordine doctrinae sicut paulo post litteras, sed ego ipse mente, quam dedisti mihi, deus meus, cum gemitibus et uocibus uariis et uariis membrorum motibus edere uellem sensa cordis mei, ut uoluntati pareretur, nec ualerem quae uolebam omnia nec quibus uolebam omnibus'; cf. *Conf.* 1. 6. 10 'eram enim et uiuebam etiam tunc, et signa, quibus sensa mea nota aliis facerem, iam in fine infantiae quaerebam.'

resoluens: M's *ne soluam* has correctly been understood as a corruption of some part of *resoluo* (*resolui* ʒ, *resoluens* Markland); no compelling arguments are available to distinguish between the two possibilities, although the participle is perhaps preferable since it does not need to be construed with *cui.* For *resoluo* denoting interpretation, compare *Theb.* 1. 66–7 'si Sphingos iniquae | callidus ambages te praemonstrante resolui'; see also Virg. *A.* 6. 29–30 'Daedalus ipse dolos tecti ambagesque resoluit | caeca regens filo uestigia'.

83. dextra: as Courtney notes, M's meaningless *uestra* was corrected to both *dextra* and *nostra*. The corruption of *nostra* and *uestra* is common, but ablative *dextra* is preferable; *nostra* is otiose (*erexi* makes it clear whose kisses these are), and the rarity of lines ending with two words in grammatical concord with the same termination (see 5. 2. 109n.) makes *oscula nostra* less likely.

84–5. The mutilated state of the text makes certain restoration of these lines almost impossible. Courtney's decision not to fill the lacuna at the end of l. 84 is understandable, since, at the end of a manuscript which has already shown considerable signs of damage in the present poem, no restoration can be made with confidence. *cadentes* (Baehrens) would describe the child's eyes as he falls asleep. *natantes* (ʒ) would describe the child's eyes as 'swimming' just before sleep; for the image, see Virg. *G.* 4. 496 and *A.* 5. 856, and note also *Theb.* 11. 558 'cerno graues oculos atque ora natantia leto', *Epic. Drusi*

93 'lumina caerulea iam iamque natantia morte' where the figure *iam iamque* also appears. Politian in his commentary suggested that a word like 'solebat' might be missing here (see Cesarini Martinelli (1982), 198), but the change of subject from Statius (*erexi*) to the child seems difficult here, and even if the subject remained the same with *solebam*, the temporal emphasis on the verb effected by *iam iamque* would seem very strange, since there is nothing to suggest that the passage would have gone on to reveal that at the moment when Statius was in the habit of lulling the child to sleep something else surprising happened. Lundström (1893), 62–3 tried to fill the lacuna in 84 with perfect tenses, suggesting either *paraui* or *tetendi* (additionally canvassing Lindenbrog's *extergere* at the beginning of 85). The same objection however arises; when Statius has previously listed a whole series of actions (*implicui fixique mihi, monstraui, erexi*), why should this particular one be marked out by *iam iamque*? Unger (1868), 140 attempted to conjecture *pandique* for M's *blando*, but there is no basis for this emendation; for the gesture of taking a child into the lap see van Dam on *Silv.* 2. 7. 38 (where *blando sinu* also occurs). Mention of the *sinus* here is a further argument against *gremium* or *gremio* in 80.

As for M's *excepere*, an infinitive is essential here, parallel to *accersere*; whether or not it is historic depends on whether a main verb is added in line 84 or 85. Phillimore's admittedly tentative *feci operire* was accepted by Slater, and more recently by Shackleton Bailey, giving the sense 'I made you cover your eyes and summon sleep', but this requires the assumption on the part of the reader that *te* is to be understood, and gives a slightly strange sense, as if Statius were stressing his own role in making the child fall asleep; it is odd for Statius to make the child cover his eyes, and even odder for Statius to make him summon sleep. Moreover, if we read *iam iamque cadentes* or something like it, there is in any case no real reason for Statius' involvement in the process of the child falling asleep anyway, which would make Lindenbrog's *extergere* difficult; if the child's eyes were to be *iam iamque cadentes*, wiping them would hardly encourage sleep. Unger's *exceptare* might accord with the physicality of *sinu* but can hardly have *genas* as its object. Vollmer's *exsopire* would be a neologism, but in any case the sense that Vollmer argues for of completing the process of sending the child to sleep ('meine Vermutung *exsopire* fügt zwar den vielen Singularia bei Statius ein neues hinzu, gerade *ex*-(völlig) passt aber trefflich zu *iam iamque cadentes*, "die schon zufallenden"') makes the following *dulcesque accersere somnos* entirely otiose. No conjecture convinces here, but the sense should perhaps be that

Statius soothes the child's eyes as he is about to fall asleep. I accordingly suggest *permulcere*, as at Ov. *Met.* 1. 716 'languida permulcens medicata lumina uirga'; cf. perhaps Stat. *Theb.* 11. 700 'et meliora meos permulcent sidera uultus'. This is admittedly a long way from M's *excepere*, but the damaged state of the transmission in this part of the poem might encourage a more radical approach.

For the summoning of sleep, compare 5. 4, and also Prop. 3. 17. 13–14 'quod si, Bacche, tuis per feruida tempora donis | accersitus erit somnus in ossa mea'.

86. cui, which would be a somewhat abrupt sequel to historic infinitives in the previous lines, may support Courtney's suggestion of a possible lacuna after 85.

uox prima: a child's first word was as significant in antiquity as it is now. Herodotus 2. 2 records how Psammetichus of Egypt kept two children in isolation from all human speech, so as to determine which nation was the most ancient. When the children's first word proved to be the Phrygian word for 'bread', the antiquity of that people was thereby proven, thus testifying to the importance attached to first words.

cunctusque: M's *ludusque* cannot stand here, in spite of Shackleton Bailey's attempt to retain it by translating 'ludusque tenello | risus' as 'my play [was] your baby laughter. *tenello*, commonly ascribed to Calderini but also found in the Parma edition of 1473, is a good emendation of M's absurd future, *tenebo* (for *tener* of a very young child, cf. e.g. Ov. *Fast.* 4. 512 'et tener in cunis filius aeger erat' with Fantham's n.), but if *ludus* is retained, how is the reader to understand that the *ludus* is that of Statius, when the *risus* in the next line is the child's (see next n.); contrast the clarity of 'cui nomen uox prima meum' in this line. Lundström (1893), 63 attempted to gloss M's text as 'risus meus puero ludus erat', but this would be more convincing if one read predicative dative *ludo*, unsatisfactory in view of the adjacent *tenello*, and in any case how would Statius' laughter be understood to be the child's play? Courtney tentatively suggests *cunctusque*, which would then give the sense that all the child's laughter and joys (*gaudia* in the next line) came from Statius' face; this is preferable to the slightly less precise *multusque*, conjectured by Boxhorn.

87. risus: the laughter is the child's, as is confirmed by the final clause of the poem as we have it: the child's joys come from Statius' smiling face. Vollmer ad loc. suggests comparison with *Silv.* 2. 1. 36 ff. and 2. 6. 34 ff. to see how the poem might have continued. On the role of play in Roman childhood, see B. Rawson (1991*a*), 19–20.

BIBLIOGRAPHY

This bibliography does not include works cited in the section of Abbreviations, nor does it include most standard commentaries referred to in the text. Items which I have not been able to see are marked with an asterisk.

ADRIAN, G. (1893). *Quaestiones Statianae* (Diss. Würzburg).

AHRENS, J. C. (1950). '*-fer* and *-ger*: Their Extraordinary Preponderance among Compounds in Roman Poetry', *Mnemosyne*, 4th ser. 3: 241–62.

ALFAGEME, I. R. (1978), 'El sueño de la naturaleza: Alcmán *FR.* 89 Page', *CFC* 15: 13–52.

ALFÖLDI, A. (1952). *Der frührömische Reiteradel und seine Ehrenabzeichen* (Baden-Baden).

ALTMANN, W. (1905). *Die römischen Grabaltäre der Kaiserzeit* (Berlin).

AMANDRY, P. (1977). 'Notes de topographie et d'architecture delphiques, VI. La fontaine Castalie', *BCH Suppl.* 4: 179–228.

—— (1978). 'Notes de topographie et d'architecture delphiques, VII. La fontaine Castalie (compléments)', *BCH* 102: 221–41.

ANDERSON, H. (2000). *The Manuscripts of Statius*, 2 vols. (Washington, DC).

ANDRÉ, J. (1949). *Étude sur les termes de couleur dans la langue latine* (Paris).

—— (1991). *Le Vocabulaire latin de l'anatomie* (Paris).

ANDRÉS, G. de (1979). 'Los códices del conde de Miranda, en la Biblioteca Nacional', *Revista de archivos, bibliotecas y museos*, 82: 611–27.

*APPELMANN, C. (1872). *Studia papiniana* (Demmin).

ASHBY, T. (1929). *Some Italian Scenes and Festivals* (London).

ABFAHL, G. (1932). *Vergleich und Metapher bei Quintilian* (Stuttgart).

ASTIN, A.E. (1978). *Cato the Censor* (Oxford).

AUSTIN, R. G. (1968). '*Ille ego qui quondam . . .* ', *CQ*, NS 18: 107–15.

AXELSON, B. (1945). *Unpoetische Wörter* (Lund).

BABEȘ, M. (1977). 'Peuce — Peucini', *Peuce*, 6: 79–85.

BAEHRENS, E. (1873). 'Emendationum in Statii Silvas Particula I', *RhM*, NF 28: 250–63.

BAEHRENS, W. A. (1922). *Sprachlicher Kommentar zur vulgärlateinischen Appendix Probi* (Halle).

BALSDON, J. P. V. D. (1979). *Romans and Aliens* (London).

BARCHIESI, A. (1998). 'The Statue of Athena at Troy and Carthage', in Knox and Foss (1998), 130–40.

BEAN, G. E. (1965). *Side kitabeleri: The Inscriptions of Side* (Ankara).

BEHOTIUS, A. (1602). *Apophoretorum libri tres* (Paris).

BELOCH, J. (1890). *Campanien* (Breslau).

BÉRARD, F. (1997). 'Bretagne, Germanie, Danube: mouvements de troupes et priorités stratégiques sous le règne de Domitien', *Pallas*, 40: 221–40.

BERGER, H. (1880). *Die geographischen Fragmente des Eratosthenes* (Leipzig).

BILLANOVICH, G. (1958). ' "Veterum vestigia vatum" nei carmi dei preumanisti padovani. Lovato Lovati, Zambono di Andrea, Albertino Mussato e Lucrezio, Catullo, Orazio (*Carmina*), Tibullo, Properzio, Ovidio (*Ibis*), Marziale, Stazio (*Silvae*)', *Italia medioevale e umanistica*, 1: 155–243.

BIRLEY, A. R. (1981). *The Fasti of Roman Britain* (Oxford).

—— (1992). *Locus virtutibus patefactus? Zum Beförderungssystem in der Hohen Kaiserzeit* (Opladen).

—— (2000). 'The Life and Death of Cornelius Tacitus', *Historia*, 49: 230–47.

BIRLEY, E. (1953). *Roman Britain and the Roman Army* (Kendal; repr. 1961).

BIRT, T. (1882). *Das antike Buchwesen in seinem Verhältnis zur Literatur* (Berlin; repr. 1974).

BIVILLE, F. (2002). 'The Graeco-Romans and Graeco-Latins: A Terminological Framework for Cases of Bilingualism', in J. N. Adams, M. Janse, and S. Swain (eds.), *Bilingualism in Ancient Society: Language Contact and the Written Text* (Oxford), 78–102.

BOARDMAN, J. (1980). *The Greeks Overseas*, rev. edn. (London).

BONESCHANSCHER, E. J. (1982). 'Procne's Absence Again', *CQ*, NS 32: 148–51.

BONNER, S. F. (1977). *Education in Rome from the Elder Cato to the Younger Pliny* (Berkeley).

BOXHORN, M. (1662). *Epistulae et Poemata* (Amsterdam).

BOYANCÉ, P. (1964). 'La science d'un quindécimvir au Ier siècle après J.-C.', *REL* 42: 334–46.

BOYLE, A. J., and DOMINIK, W. J. (eds.) (2003). *Flavian Rome: Culture, Image, Text* (Leiden).

BRANDES, W. (1885). 'Zu Statius', *Zeitschrift für die österreichischen Gymnasien*, 36: 573–83.

BRAUND, D. (1994). *Georgia in Antiquity: A History of Colchis and Transcaucasian Iberia 550 BC–AD 562* (Oxford).

—— (1996). *Ruling Roman Britain: Kings, Queens, Governors and Emperors from Julius Caesar to Agricola* (London and New York).

BRIGHT, D. F. (1980). *Elaborate Disarray: The Nature of Statius' Silvae* (Meisenheim am Glan).

BROWN, J. (1994). 'Into the Woods: Narrative Studies in the *Thebaid* of Statius with Special Reference to Books IV–VI' (Diss. Cambridge).

BROŻEK, M. (1965). 'De Statio Pindarico', *Eos*, 55: 338–40.

—— (1994). 'Quo tempore Statii epicedium patris conscriptum sit', *Eos*, 82: 53–4.

BRUNO, V. J. (1977). *Form and Color in Greek Painting* (New York).

BUCHNER, G., MORELLI, D., and NENCI, G. (1952). 'Fonti per la storia di Napoli antica', *PP* 7: 370–419.

BURESCH, K. (1894). 'Die griechischen Trostbeschlüsse', *RhM*, NF 49: 424–60.

BURN, A. R. (1960). *The Lyric Age of Greece* (London).

BURTON, G. P. (1975). 'Proconsuls, Assizes and the Administration of Justice under the Empire', *JRS* 65: 92–106.

BUTTREY, T. V. (1980). *Documentary Evidence for the Chronology of the Flavian Titulature* (Meisenheim am Glan).

CAIRNS, F. (1972). *Generic Composition in Greek and Roman Poetry* (Edinburgh).

—— (1979). *Tibullus: A Hellenistic Poet at Rome* (Cambridge).

—— (1992). 'The Power of Implication: Horace's Invitation to Maecenas (*Odes* 1.20)', in A. J. Woodman and J. G. F. Powell (eds.), *Author and Audience in Latin Literature* (Cambridge), 84–109.

CALDELLI, M. L. (1993). *L'Agon Capitolinus: storia e protagonisti dall'istituzione domizianea al IV secolo* (Studi pubblicati dall'Istituto Italiano per la Storia Antica, 54; Rome).

CAMERON, A. (1995). *Callimachus and his Critics* (Princeton).

CAMPBELL, B. (1975). 'Who were the "Viri Militares"?', *JRS* 65: 11–31.

CANCIK, H. (1965). *Untersuchungen zur lyrischen Kunst des P. Papinius Statius* (Hildesheim).

—— (1972). Review of Håkanson (1969), *Gnomon*, 44: 85–8.

—— (1973). 'Römischer Religionsunterricht in apostolischer Zeit: Ein pastoralgeschichtlicher Versuch zu Statius, Silvae V 3, 176–184', in H. Feld and J. Nolte (eds.), *Wort Gottes in der Zeit: Festschrift Karl Hermann Schelke zum 65. Geburtstag dargebracht von Kollegen, Freunden, Schülern* (Düsseldorf), 181–97.

CANINA, L. (1853). *La prima parte della Via Appia dalla Porta Capena a Boville*, 2 vols. (Rome).

CARRADICE, I. (1983). *Coinage and Finances in the Reign of Domitian* (British Archaeological Reports International Series, 178; Oxford).

CARRAI, S. (1990). *Ad Somnum: l'invocazione al sonno nella lirica italiana* (Padua).

CARTAULT, A. (1903). Review of Vollmer (1898), *Journal des savants*, NS 1: 626–35, 666–77.

—— (1904). Review of A. Klotz, *P. Papini Stati Silvae* (Leipzig, 1900), *Journal des savants*, NS 2: 515–29, 561–9.

CARTLEDGE, P. (1979). *Sparta and Lakonia* (London).

CARUSO, C. (2003). 'Una nota sulle *Silvae* di Stazio nel medioevo', *Italia medioevale e umanistica*, 44: 303–7.

CERRATO, L. (1881). 'De Claudii Claudiani fontibus in poemate De Raptu Proserpinae', *RFIC* 9: 273–395.

CESARINI MARTINELLI, L. (1975). 'Le *Selve* di Stazio nella critica testuale del Poliziano', *SIFC* 47: 130–74.

—— (1978). *Angelo Poliziano: Commento inedito alle Selve di Stazio* (Florence).

—— (1982). 'Un ritrovamento polizianesco: il fascicolo perduto del commento alle Selve di Stazio', *Rinascimento*, 22: 183–212.

CIRILLI, R. (1913). *Les Prêtres danseurs de Rome: étude sur la corporation sacerdotale des Saliens* (Paris).

CITRONI, M. (1988). 'Pubblicazione e dediche dei libri in Marziale', *Maia*, 40: 3–39.

—— (1989). 'Marziale e la letteratura per i Saturnali (poetica dell'intrattenimento e cronologia della pubblicazione dei libri)', *ICS* 14: 201–26.

CLARK, A. C. (1899). 'The Literary Discoveries of Poggio', *CR* 13: 119–30.

CLAUSEN, W. V. (1964). 'Callimachus and Latin Poetry', *GRBS* 5: 181–96.

—— (1994). *A Commentary on Virgil: Eclogues* (Oxford).

CLINTON, K. (1972). 'Publius Papinius ST[—] at Eleusis', *TAPhA* 103: 79–82.

COARELLI, F. (1981). *Dintorni di Roma* (Rome and Bari).

COLEMAN, K. M. (1986). 'The Emperor Domitian and Literature', *ANRW* II 32. 5: 3087–115.

—— (1988). *Statius: Silvae IV. Edited with an English Translation and Commentary* (Oxford).

CORNELISSEN, J. (1877). 'Ad Statii Silvas', *Mnemosyne*, 2nd ser. 5: 277–94.

CORNELL, T. J. (1995). *The Beginnings of Rome. Italy and Rome from the Bronze Age to the Punic Wars (c. 1000–264 BC)* (London).

COTTON, H. M. (1981). 'Military Tribunates and the Exercise of Patronage', *Chiron*, 11: 229–38.

—— (1984). 'The Concept of *indulgentia* under Trajan', *Chiron*, 14: 245–66.

COULTER, C. (1959). 'Statius *Silvae* V,4 and Fiametta's Prayer to Sleep', *AJP* 80: 390–6.

COURTNEY, E. (1966). 'On the *Silvae* of Statius', *BICS* 13: 94–100.

—— (1968). 'Emendations of Statius' *Silvae*', *BICS* 15: 51–7.

—— (1971). 'Further Remarks on the *Silvae* of Statius', *BICS* 18: 95–7.

—— (1980). *A Commentary on the Satires of Juvenal* (London).

—— (1984). 'Criticisms and Elucidations of the *Silvae* of Statius', *TAPhA* 114: 327–41.

—— (1987). 'Imitation, chronologie littéraire et Calpurnius Siculus', *REL* 65: 148–57.

—— (1988). 'Problems in the *Silvae* of Statius', *CPh* 83: 43–5.

—— (1990). *P. Papini Stati Silvae* (Oxford).

—— (1993). *The Fragmentary Latin Poets* (Oxford).

CRAWFORD, M. H. (ed.) (1996). *Roman Statutes*, 2 vols. (London).

CREMA, L. (1959). *L'architettura romana* (Turin).

CROSBY, J. O., and LERNER, L. S. (1986). 'La silva "El sueño" de Quevedo: génesis y revisiones', *Bulletin of Hispanic Studies*, 63: 111–26.

CROWTHER, N. B. (1978). 'Horace, Catullus, and Alexandrianism', *Mnemosyne*, 4th ser. 31: 33–44.

CROWTHER, N. B. (1979). 'Water and Wine as Symbols of Inspiration', *Mnemosyne*, 4th ser. 32: 1–11.

CUMONT, F. (1942). *Recherches sur le symbolisme funéraire des Romains* (Paris).

CURCIO, G. (1893). *Studio su P. Papinio Stazio* (Catania).

CURTIUS, E. R. (1953). *European Literature and the Latin Middle Ages*, tr. W. R. Trask (Princeton).

DAM, H.-J. VAN (1984). *P. Papinius Statius: Silvae Book II. A Commentary* (Leiden).

D'AMBRA, E. (1996). 'The Calculus of Venus: Nude Portraits of Roman Matrons', in Kampen (1996*b*), 219–32.

—— (2000). 'Nudity and Adornment in Female Portrait Sculpture of the Second Century AD', in D. E. E. Kleiner and S. B. Matheson (eds.), *I Claudia II: Women in Roman Art and Society* (Austin), 101–14.

DANIELSSON, O. A. (1897). 'De loco Statiano, Silv. V, 5, 69 sq.', *Eranos*, 2: 43–5.

D'ARMS, J. H. (1970). *Romans on the Bay of Naples* (Cambridge, MA).

DARWALL-SMITH, R. H. (1994). 'Albanum and the Villas of Domitian', *Pallas*, 40: 145–65.

—— (1996). *Emperors and Architecture: A Study of Flavian Rome* (Brussels).

DAVIES, P. J. E. (2000). *Roman Imperial Funerary Monuments from Augustus to Marcus Aurelius* (Cambridge).

DEBRU, A. (1996). *Le corps respirant: la pensée physiologique chez Galien* (Leiden).

DELARUE, F. (1968). 'Sur deux passages de Stace', *Orpheus*, 15: 13–31.

—— GEORGACOPOULOU, S., LAURENS, P., and TAISNE, A.-M. (1996) (eds.), *Epicedion: Hommage à P. Papinius Statius, 96–1996* (Poitiers).

DELLA PORTELLA, I, PISANI SARTORIO, G., and VENTRE, F. (2004), *The Appian Way from its Foundation to the Middle Ages* (Los Angeles).

DELZ, J. (1992). 'Zu den "Silvae" des Statius', *MH* 49: 239–55.

DENCH, E. (1995). *From Barbarians to New Men: Greek, Roman, and Modern. Perceptions of Peoples of the Central Apennines* (Oxford).

DENNISTON, J. D. (1959). *The Greek Particles*, 2nd edn., corr. repr. (Oxford).

DEWAR, M. J. (1991). *Statius: Thebaid IX: Edited with an English Translation and Commentary* (Oxford).

DICKEY, E. (2002). *Latin Forms of Address from Plautus to Apuleius* (Oxford).

DIONISOTTI, A. C. (1982). 'From Ausonius' Schooldays? A Schoolbook and its Relatives', *JRS* 72: 83–125.

DIONISOTTI, C. (1968). 'Calderini, Poliziano e altri', *Italia medioevale e umanistica*, 11: 151–85.

DIXON, S. (1991). 'The Sentimental Ideal of the Roman Family', in B. Rawson (1991*b*), 99–113.

DOMASZEWSKI, A. VON (1967). *Die Rangordnung des römischen Heeres*, 2nd edn. rev. B. Dobson (Cologne).

DOMINIK, W. J. (1994). *The Mythic Voice of Statius: Power and Politics in the Thebaid* (Leiden).

DUBOURDIEU, A. (1989). *Les Origines et le développement du culte des Pénates à Rome* (Collection de l'École française de Rome, 118; Rome).

DUBUISSON, M. (1981). '*Vtraque lingua*', *AC* 51: 274–86.

DUNSTON, A. J. (1967). 'What Politian Saw: Statius, *Silvae* I.4.88', *BICS* 14: 96–101.

—— (1968). 'Studies in Domizio Calderini', *Italia medioevale e umanistica*, 11: 71–150.

DURRY, M. (1950). *Éloge funèbre d'une matrone romaine (Éloge dit de Turia)* (Paris).

DUTOIT, E. (1936). *Le Thème de l'adynaton dans la poésie antique* (Paris).

ECK, W. (1970). *Senatores von Vespasian bis Hadrian: Prosopographische Untersuchungen* (Vestigia, 13; Munich).

—— (1972–3). 'Über die prätorischen Prokonsulate in der Kaiserzeit: Eine quellenkritische Überlegung', *Zephyrus*, 23–4: 233–60.

—— CABALLOS, A, and FERNÁNDEZ, F. (1996). *Das senatus consultum de Cn. Pisone patre* (Munich).

ELLIS, R. (1885). 'Some Passages of Statius' *Silvae*', *JPh* 13: 88–97.

—— (1892). 'An Oxford MS of Statius' *Silvae*', *JPh* 20: 17–24.

—— (1900). 'A Conjecture on Stat. *Silv.* V.3.94', *CR* 14: 259–60.

—— (1910). 'Adversaria, VI.', *JPh* 31: 44–9.

ERSKINE, A. (2001). *Troy between Greece and Rome: Local Tradition and Imperial Power* (Oxford).

ESKUCHE, G. (1890). 'Die Elisionen in den letzten Füssen des lateinischen Hexameters, von Ennius bis Walahfridus Strabo', *RhM*, NF 45: 236–64, 385–418.

ESTEVE-FORRIOL, J. (1962). *Die Trauer- und Trostgedichte in der römischen Literatur* (Munich).

EYBEN, E. (1972), 'Antiquity's View of Puberty', *Latomus*, 31: 677–97.

FANTHAM, E. (1972). *Comparative Studies in Republican Latin Imagery* (Toronto).

—— (1999). '*Chironis exemplum*: On Teachers and Surrogate Fathers in Achilleid and Silvae', *Hermathena*, 167: 59–70.

FARNELL, L. R. (1896–1909). *Cults of the Greek City States*, 5 vols. (Oxford).

FEDELI, P. (1983). *Catullus' Carmen 61* (Amsterdam).

FERA, V. (2002). 'Pomponio Leto e le *Silvae* di Stazio', *Schede umanistiche*, 16/2: 71–83.

FERGUSON, J. (1978). 'China and Rome', *ANRW* II 9. 2: 581–603.

FINLAY, V. (2002). *Colour: Travels through the Paintbox* (London).

FITZMYER, J. A. (1993). *Romans: A New Translation with Introduction and Commentary* (The Anchor Bible; New York, London, Toronto, Sydney, Auckland).

FITZPATRICK, D. (2001). 'Sophocles' *Tereus*', *CQ* NS 51: 90–101.

FLETCHER, G. B. A. (1961). 'The Suffix *Met* in Post-Virgilian Poetry', *Hermes*, 94: 254–6.

FLOWER, H. I. (2001). 'A Tale of Two Monuments: Domitian, Trajan, and Some Praetorians at Puteoli (*AE* 1973, 137)', *AJA* 105: 625–48.

FORBES IRVING, P. M. C. (1990). *Metamorphosis in Greek Myths* (Oxford).

FORBIGER, A. (1877). *Handbuch der alten Geographie*, 2nd edn., 3 vols. (Hamburg).

FORREST, W. G. (1980). *A History of Sparta: 950–192 BC*, 2nd edn. (London).

FOWLER, D. P. (2000). *Roman Constructions: Readings in Postmodern Latin* (Oxford).

FRAENKEL, E. (1932). 'Selbstmordwege', *Philologus*, 87: 470–3 [= id., *Kleine Beiträge zur klassischen Philologie*, 2 vols. (Rome, 1964), i. 465–7].

—— (1957). *Horace* (Oxford).

FRANK, E. (1968). 'Struttura dell'esametro di Stazio', *Rend. Ist. Lomb.* 102: 396–408.

FRASER, P. M. (1972). *Ptolemaic Alexandria*. 3 vols. (Oxford).

FREDERIKSEN, M. W. (1984). *Campania*, ed. N. Purcell (Rome).

FRIEDLAENDER, L. (1921). *Darstellungen aus der Sittengeschichte Roms*, 10th edn.. 4 vols. (Leipzig).

FRIEDLÄNDER, P. (1932). 'Statius An den Schlaf', *Die Antike*, 8: 215–28.

FRIEDRICH, G. (1908). 'Zu Martial', *Hermes*, 43: 619–37.

FRIEDRICH, H. (1963). 'Über die Silvae des Statius (inbesondere V,4 Somnus) und die Frage des literarischen Manierismus', in H. Meier and H. Sckommodau (eds.), *Wort und Text: Festschrift für Fritz Schalk* (Frankfurt), 34–56.

GALE, M. R. (1994). *Myth and Poetry in Lucretius* (Cambridge).

GALINSKY, G. K. (1996). *Augustan Culture: An Interpretive Introduction* (Princeton).

GAUDEMET, J. (1962). *Indulgentia principis* (Conferenze romanistiche, 6; Trieste).

GEER, R. M. (1935). 'The Greek Games of Naples', *TAPhA* 66: 208–21.

GEORGACOPOULOU, S. (1996). 'Ranger/déranger: catalogues et listes de personnages dans la *Thébaïde*', in Delarue et al. (1996), 93–129.

GEYSSEN, J. W. (1996). *Imperial Panegyric in Statius: A Literary Commentary on Silvae 1.1* (New York).

GIBSON, B. J. (1995). 'A Commentary on Statius, *Silvae* 5.1–4' (D.Phil. thesis, Oxford).

—— (1996). 'Statius and Insomnia: Allusion and Meaning in *Silvae* 5.4', *CQ*, NS 46: 457–68.

—— (2001). Review of Laird (1999), *PVS* 24: 139–46.

—— (2004). 'The Repetitions of Hypsipyle', in M. R. Gale (ed.), *Latin Epic and Didactic Poetry: Genre, Tradition and Individuality* (Swansea), 149–80.

GIGANTE, M. (1966). 'Il logos erodoteo sulle origini di Elea', *PP* 21: 295–317.

GIRARD, J.-L. (1981a). 'La place de Minerve dans la religion romaine au temps du principat', *ANRW* II 17. 1: 203–32.

—— (1981b). 'Domitien et Minerve: une prédilection impériale', *ANRW* II 17. 1: 233–45.

GOETTE, H. R. (1988). 'Mulleus—Embas—Calceus: Ikonografische Studien zu römischem Schuhwerk', *JDAI* 103: 401–64.

GRADEL, I. (2002). *Emperor Worship and Roman Religion* (Oxford).

GREWING, F. (1997). *Martial, Buch VI: Ein Kommentar* (Hypomnemata, 115; Göttingen).

GRIFFIN, M. T. (1984). *Nero: The End of a Dynasty* (London).

—— (2000). 'The Flavians', in *Cambridge Ancient History*, xi, 2nd edn. (Cambridge), 1–83.

GRISET, E. (1962). 'Il problema della "Silva" V,3 di Stazio', *RSC* 10: 128–32.

GSELL, S. (1893). *Essai sur le règne de l'empereur Domitien* (Paris).

GUHL, C. (1969). *Die Fragmente des alexandrinischen Grammatikers Theon* (Diss. Hamburg).

HABICHT, C. (1975). 'New Evidence on the Province of Asia', *JRS* 65: 64–91.

—— (1994). *Athen in hellenistischer Zeit* (Munich).

HÅKANSON, L. (1969). *Statius' Silvae: Critical and Exegetical Remarks with Some Notes on the Thebaid* (Lund).

—— (1973). *Statius' Thebaid: Critical and Exegetical Remarks* (Lund).

HALL, J. B. (1969). *Claudian. De Raptu Proserpinae* (Cambridge).

HANI, J. (1985). *Plutarque: Consolation à Apollonios*, in *Plutarque: œuvres morales*, ii (Paris), 1–89.

HANSON, W. S. (1987). *Agricola and the Conquest of the North* (London).

HARDIE, A. (1983). *Statius and the Silvae: Poets, Patrons and Epideixis in the Graeco-Roman World* (Liverpool).

—— (2003). 'Poetry and Politics at the Games of Domitian', in Boyle and Dominik (2003), 125–47.

HARDIE, P. (1993). *The Epic Successors of Virgil* (Cambridge).

HARRISON, S. J. (1989). 'Augustus, the Poets and the *Spolia Opima*', *CQ*, NS 39: 408–14.

—— (1991). '*Discordia Taetra*: The History of a Hexameter-Ending', *CQ*, NS 41: 138–49.

—— (1995). '*Discordia Taetra*: Appendix', *CQ*, NS 45: 504.

HATTO, A. T. (1965). *Eos* (London).

HAUPT, M. (1876). 'Beiträge zur Berichtigung der Gedichte des P. Papinius Statius', in id., *Opuscula*, iii/1 (Leipzig), 126–36.

HEATH, M. (1998). 'Was Homer a Roman?' *PLLS* 10: 23–56.

HENDERSON, J. (1991). 'Statius *Thebaid*/Form premade', *PCPhS*, NS 37: 30–80.

—— (1998a). *A Roman Life: Rutilius Gallicus On Paper & In Stone* (Exeter).

—— (1998b). *Fighting for Rome: Poets and Caesars, History and Civil War* (Cambridge).

HERRMANN, P. (1981). 'Teos und Abdera im 5. Jahrhundert v. Chr.', *Chiron*, 11: 1–30.

HERSHKOWITZ, D. (1998). *Valerius Flaccus' Argonautica: Abbreviated Voyages in Silver Latin Epic* (Oxford).

HEYWORTH, S. J. (1988). 'Horace's Second Epode', *AJP* 109: 71–85.

—— (1993). 'Horace's *Ibis*: On the Titles, Unity and Contents of the *Epodes*', *PLLS* 7: 85–96.

HEYWORTH, S. J. (1994). 'Some Allusions to Callimachus in Roman Poetry', *MD* 33: 51–79.

HILL, D. E. (1996). '*Thebaid* I Revisited', in Delarue et al. (1996), 35–54.

—— (2002). 'Statius' *Nachleben*: The First Few Hundred Years', *Schede umanistiche*, 16/2: 5–28.

HIND, J. G. F. (1983). 'Caledonia and its Occupation under the Flavians', *PSAS* 113: 373–9.

HINDS, S. (1998). *Allusion and Intertext* (Cambridge).

—— (2001). 'Cinna, Statius and "Immanent Literary History" in the Cultural Economy', in *L'Histoire littéraire immanente dans la poésie latine* (Fondation Hardt, Entretiens sur l'antiquité classique, 47; Vandœuvres-Geneva), 221–57.

HOBLEY, A. S. (1989). 'The Numismatic Evidence for the Post-Agricolan Abandonment of the Roman Frontier in Northern Scotland', *Britannia*, 20: 69–74.

*HOEUFFT, J. H. (1807–8). *Pericula critica* (Breda).

HOLFORD-STREVENS, L. A. (1993). '*Vtraque lingua doctus*: Some Notes on Bilingualism in the Roman Empire', in H. D. Jocelyn (ed.), *Tria Lustra: Essays and Notes Presented to John Pinsent* (Liverpool), 203–13.

—— (2000). 'In Search of Poplios Papinios Statios', *Hermathena*, 168: 39–54.

—— (2003). *Aulus Gellius: An Antonine Scholar and his Achievement*, rev. edn. (Oxford).

HÖLSCHER, T. (1967). *Victoria Romana* (Mainz).

HOPKINS, K. (1983). *Death and Renewal* (Cambridge).

HORDERN, J. H. (2004). *Sophron's Mimes. Text, Translation, and Commentary* (Oxford).

HORNBLOWER, S. (1991). *A Commentary on Thucydides, Volume I: Books I–III* (Oxford).

HUDSON-WILLIAMS, A. (1980). 'Some Passages in Virgil's *Eclogues*', *CQ*, NS 30: 124–32.

HUMBERT, M. (1972). *Le Remariage à Rome* (Milan).

HUMPHREY, J. H. (1986). *Roman Circuses: Arenas for Chariot Racing* (Berkeley and Los Angeles).

HUNINK, V. (1999). 'Sleep and Death (Lucan 9,818)', *MD* 42: 211–13.

HUNT, E. D. (1984). 'Travel, Tourism and Piety in the Roman Empire: A Context for the Beginnings of Christian Pilgrimage', *ÉMC* 28 (NS 3), 391–417.

HUTCHINSON, G. O. (1988). *Hellenistic Poetry* (Oxford).

—— (1993). *Latin Literature from Seneca to Juvenal* (Oxford).

IMHOF, A. (1859). *De Silvarum Statianarum condicione critica* (Halle).

—— (1867). *Emendationes Statianae* (Halle).

JONES, B. W. (1992). *The Emperor Domitian* (London).

JONES, C. P. (1998). 'Joint Sacrifice at Iasus and Side', *JHS* 118: 183–6.

JONES, F. M. A. (1996) *Nominum Ratio: Aspects of the Use of Personal Names in Greek and Latin* (Liverpool).

KACHARAVA, D. D., and KVIRKVELIYA, G. T. (1991). *Goroda i poseleniya Prichernomor'ya antichnoy epokhi* (Tbilisi).

KAHRSTEDT, U. (1959). 'Ager Publicus und Selbstverwaltung in Lukanien und Bruttium', *Historia*, 8: 174–206.

KAJANTO, I. (1965). *The Latin Cognomina* (Helsinki).

KAMBYLIS, A. (1965). *Die Dichterweihe und ihre Symbolik* (Heidelberg).

KAMPEN, N. (1996a). 'Omphale and the Instability of Gender', in ead. (1996b), 233–46.

—— (1996b) (ed.). *Sexuality in Ancient Art* (Cambridge).

KARSTEN, H. T. (1899). 'Spicilegium Statianum', *Mnemosyne*, 2nd ser. 27: 341–77.

KASER, M. (1996). *Das römische Zivilprozeßrecht*, 2nd edn. rev. K. Hackl (Munich).

KASSEL, R. (1958). *Untersuchungen zur griechischen und römischen Konsolationsliteratur* (Zetemata Monographien, 18; Munich).

—— (1977). 'Nachtrag zum neuen Kallimachos', *ZPE* 25: 51.

KELLER, G. A. (1946). *Eratosthenes und die alexandrinische Sterndichtung* (Diss. Zurich).

KENNEDY, D. (1998) (ed.). *The Twin Towns of Zeugma on the Euphrates: Rescue Work and Historical Studies* (Journal of Roman Archaeology Supplementary Series, 27; Portsmouth, RI).

KENNEDY, G. (1972). *The Art of Rhetoric in the Roman World* (Princeton).

KER, A. (1953). 'Notes on Statius', *CQ*, NS 3: 1–10.

KIERDORF, W. (1980). *Laudatio Funebris: Interpretationen und Untersuchungen zur Entwicklung der römischen Leichenrede* (Meisenheim am Glan).

*KLOTZ, A. (1896). *Curae Statianae* (Diss. Leipzig).

—— (1903). 'Iubatus. Abolefacio', *ALL* 13: 286.

KNOX, P. (1985). 'Wine, Water, and Callimachean Polemics', *HSCPh* 89: 107–19.

—— (1998). 'Ariadne on the Rocks', in Knox and Foss (1998), 72–83.

—— and FOSS, C. (eds.) (1998). *Style and Tradition: Studies in Honor of Wendell Clausen* (Stuttgart and Leipzig).

KONSTAN, D. (2001). *Pity Transformed* (London).

KÖSTLIN, H. (1876). 'Besserungen und erläuterungen zu P. Papinius Statius', *Philologus*, 35: 493–533.

KÖVES-ZULAUF, T. (1990). *Römische Geburtsriten* (Zetemata, 87; Munich).

KÜHL, E. (1913). *Der Brief des Paulus an die Römer* (Leipzig).

LAGUNA MARISCAL, G. (1990). 'La *Silva* 5.4 de Estacio: plegaria al sueño', *Habis*, 21: 121–38.

—— (1992) *Estacio: Silvas III. Introducción, Edición Crítica, Traducción y Comentario* (Madrid).

LAGUNA MARISCAL, G. (1998). *Estacio* (Madrid).

LAIRD, A. J. W. (1999). *Powers of Expression, Expressions of Power* (Oxford).

LA PENNA, A. (1996). 'Modelli efebici nella poesia di Stazio', in Delarue et al. (1996), 161–84.

LATTIMORE, R. (1942). *Themes in Greek and Latin Epitaphs* (Urbana).

LEBERL, J. (2004). *Domitian und die Dichter: Poesie als Medium der Herrschaftsdarstellung* (Göttingen).

LE BŒUFFLE, A. (1962). 'Vénus "étoile du soir" et les écrivains latins', *REL* 40: 120–5.

LEFKOWITZ, M. R. (1981). *The Lives of the Greek Poets* (London and Baltimore).

LEIGH, M. G. H. (1994). 'Servius on Vergil's Senex Corycius: New Evidence', *MD* 33: 181–95.

—— (1997). *Lucan: Spectacle and Engagement* (Oxford).

LEIWO, M. (1995). *Neapolitana: A Study of Population and Language in Greco-Roman Naples* (Helsinki).

LEO, F. (1892). *De Stati Silvis commentatio* (Göttingen).

LETTA, C. (1972). *I Marsi e il Fucino nell'antichità* (Milan).

LEUMANN, M. (1947). 'Die lateinische Dichtersprache', *MH* 4: 116–39.

—— (1977). *Lateinische Laut- und Formenlehre* (Munich).

LIGHTFOOT, J. L. (1999). *Parthenius of Nicaea* (Oxford).

LILLO REDONET, F. (2001). *Palabras contra el dolor: la consolación filosófica latina de Cicerón a Frontón* (Madrid).

LINDERSKI, J. (1986). 'The Augural Law', *ANRW* II 16. 3: 2146–312.

LING, R. (1991). *Roman Painting* (Cambridge).

LITCHFIELD, H. W. (1914). 'National *exempla uirtutis* in Roman Literature', *HSCPh* 25: 1–71.

LIVREA, E. (1979). 'Das Lille-Kallimachos und die Mäusefallen', *ZPE* 34: 37–42.

—— (1980). 'Polittico callimacheo: contribuiti al testo della Victoria Berenices', *ZPE* 40: 21–6.

LÖFSTEDT, B. (1958). 'Zum Gebrauch der lateinischen distributiven Zahlwörter', *Eranos*, 56: 71–117, 188–223.

*LOHR, F. (1876). *De infinitivi apud P. Papinium Statium et Juvenalem usu* (Diss. Marburg).

LOMAS, H. K. (1993). *Rome and the Western Greeks 350 BC–AD 200: Conquest and Acculturation in Southern Italy* (London).

LOTITO, G. (1974–5). 'Il tipo etico del liberto funzionario di corte (Stazio *Silvae* III,3 e V,1)', *Dialoghi di archeologia*, 8: 275–383.

LOVATT, H. (2001). 'Mad about Winning: Epic, War and Madness in the Games of Statius' *Thebaid*', *MD* 46: 103–20.

—— (2005). *Statius and Epic Games: Sport, Politics and Poetics in the Thebaid* (Cambridge).

LUGLI, G. (1965). *Fontes ad topographiam ueteris urbis Romae pertinentes*, vi (Rome).

LUNDSTRÖM, V. (1893). *Quaestiones Papinianae* (Uppsala).

LUTZ, C. E. (1947). 'Musonius Rufus "The Roman Socrates"', *YCS* 10: 3–147.

LYNE, R. O. A. M. (1980). *The Latin Love Poets* (Oxford).

—— (1998). 'Love and Death: Ladoamia and Protesilaus in Catullus, Propertius and Others', *CQ*, NS 48: 200–12.

MACNAGHTEN, H. (1891). 'Some Passages of the *Silvae* of Statius', *JPh* 19: 129–37.

McCRUM, M., and WOODHEAD, A. J. (eds.) (1961). *Documents of the Flavian Emperors* (Cambridge).

McGANN, M. J. (1975). 'Lucan's "De Incendio Urbis"', *TAPhA* 105: 213–17.

MACKAIL, J. W. (1895). *Latin Literature* (London).

McNELIS, C. (2002). 'Greek Grammarians and Roman Society during the Early Empire: Statius' Father and his Contemporaries', *CA* 21: 67–94.

*MADVIG, J. N. (1834). *Opuscula academica*, i (Copenhagen).

MALTBY, R. (1991). *A Lexicon of Ancient Latin Etymologies* (Leeds).

MARASTONI, A. (1961). *P. Papini Stati Silvae* (Leipzig).

MARKUS, D. D. (2000). 'Performing the Book: The Recital of Epic in First Century C.E. Rome', *CA* 19: 138–79.

—— (2003). 'The Politics of Epic Performance in Statius', in Boyle and Dominik (2003), 431–67.

MARTIN, A. (1987*a*). 'Domitien *Germanicus* et les documents grecs d'Égypte', *Historia*, 36: 73–82.

—— (1987*b*). *La Titulature épigraphique de Domitien* (Frankfurt am Main).

—— (1988). 'Domitien et les documents égyptiens de l'an 3', *Proceedings of the XVIII International Congress of Papyrology*. 2 vols. (Athens), 465–70.

MATTINGLY, H. (1910). *The Imperial Civil Service of Rome* (Cambridge).

MAYER, A. (1954). 'Die lateinischen Ortsbezeichnungen auf -etum', *Glotta*, 33: 227–38.

MERKELBACH, R. (1963). 'Die Erigone des Eratosthenes', in *Miscellanea di studi alessandrini in memoria di Augusto Rostagni* (Turin), 469–526.

—— (1974). 'Zu den Festordnung für die Sebasta in Neapel', *ZPE* 15: 192–3.

MILLAR, F. G. B. (1992). *The Emperor in the Roman World*, 2nd edn. (London).

MILLER, J. I. (1969). *The Spice Trade of the Roman Empire* (Oxford).

MINGAZZINI, P. (1954). 'Velia: scavi 1927. Fornace di mattoni ed antichità varie', *Atti e memorie della Società Magna Grecia*, 1: 21–60.

MIRANDA, E. (1982). 'I cataloghi dei *Sebasta* di Napoli: proposte ed osservazioni', *RAAN* 57: 165–81.

MOMMSEN, Th. (1887/8). *Römisches Staatsrecht*, 3rd edn., 2 vols. (Leipzig).

MORGAN, L. (2000). 'Metre Matters: Some Higher-Level Metrical Play in Latin Poetry', *PCPhS*, NS 46: 99–120.

MORGAN, T. (1998). *Literate Education in the Hellenistic and Roman Worlds* (Cambridge).

MRATSCHEK-HALFMANN, S. (1993). *Divites et praepotentes: Reichtum und soziale Stellung in der Literatur der Prinzipatszeit* (Historia Einzelschriften, 70; Stuttgart).

MUELLER, L. (1894). *De re metrica poetarum latinorum praeter Plautum et Terentium libri VII*, 2nd edn. (St Petersburg and Leipzig).

MÜLLER, O. (1861). *Quaestiones Statianae* (Berlin).

MÜNZER, F. (1920). *Römische Adelsparteien und Adelsfamilien* (Stuttgart).

MUSITELLI, S. (1980). 'Ancora sui φώλαρχοι di Velia', *PP* 35: 241–55.

MUSTI, D. (1966). 'Le fonti per la storia de Velia', *PP* 21: 318–35.

MYERS, K. S. (2000). '"*Miranda fides*": Poet and Patrons in Paradoxographical Landscapes in Statius' *Silvae*', *MD* 44: 103–38.

NAGY, G. (1973). 'Phaethon, Sappho's Phaon and the White Rock of Leucas', *HSCPh* 77: 137–77.

NAUTA, R. (2002). *Poetry for Patrons: Literary Communication in the Age of Domitian* (Leiden).

NEWLANDS, C. (1991). '*Silvae* 3.1 and Statius' Poetic Temple', *CQ*, NS 41: 438–52.

—— (2002). *Statius' Silvae and the Poetics of Empire* (Cambridge).

NEWMYER, S. T. (1979). *The Silvae of Statius: Structure and Theme* (Leiden).

NIELSEN, H. S. (1990). '*Delicia* in Roman Literature and in the Urban Inscriptions', *Analecta Romana Instituti Danici*, 19: 79–88.

NIJF, O. van (2001). 'Local Heroes: Athletics, Festivals and Elite Self-Fashioning in the Roman East', in S. Goldhill (ed.), *Being Greek under Rome: Cultural Identity, the Second Sophistic and the Development of Empire* (Cambridge), 306–34.

NÍ MHEALLAIGH, K. (2005). 'Lucian's Self-Conscious Fiction: Theory in Practice' (Diss. Trinity College, Dublin).

NISBET, R. G. M. (1978). '*Felicitas* at Surrentum (Statius, *Silvae* 2.2)', *JRS* 68: 1–11 [= id., *Collected Papers on Latin Literature*, ed. S. J. Harrison (Oxford, 1995), 29–47.]

NODELL, J. A. (1787). *Flavii Aviani Fabulae* (Amsterdam).

NORDEN, E. (1913). *Agnostos Theos: Untersuchungen zur Formengeschichte religiöser Rede* (Berlin; repr. Stuttgart, 1956).

NORDH, A. (1949). *Libellus de regionibus urbis Romae* (Lund).

OAKLEY, S. P. (1998), *A Commentary on Livy, Books VI–X*, ii: *Books VII–VIII* (Oxford).

ÖNNERFORS, A. (1974). *Vaterporträts in der römischen Poesie unter besonderer Berücksichtigung von Horaz, Statius und Ausonius* (Stockholm).

ORCHARD, A. (2003). *Pride and Prodigies: Studies in the Monsters of the Beowulf-Manuscript*, rev. edn. (Toronto).

OTTO, A. (1887). 'Zur Kritik von Statius' Silvae', *RhM*, NF 42: 362–73, 531–46.

—— (1890). *Die Sprichwörter und sprichwörtlichen Redensarten der Römer* (Leipzig).

PAGE, D. L. (1951). *Alcman: The Partheneion* (Oxford).

—— (1953). *Corinna* (London).

PANIN, N. (1983). 'Black Sea Coast Line Change in the Last 10,000 Years: A New Attempt at Identifying the Danube Mouths as Described by the Ancients', *Dacia*, 27: 175–84.

PARKE, H. W. (1978). 'Castalia', *BCH* 102: 199–219.

PARSONS, P. J. (1977). 'Callimachus: Victoria Berenices', *ZPE* 25: 1–50.

PETRINI, M. (1997). *The Child and the Hero: Coming of Age in Catullus and Vergil* (Ann Arbor).

PICKARD-CAMBRIDGE, A. (1962). *Dithyramb, Tragedy and Comedy.* 2nd edn. rev. T. B. L. Webster (Cambridge).

PISTOR, H.-H. (1965). *Prinzeps und Patriziat in der Zeit von Augustus bis Commodus* (Freiburg im Breisgau).

POLLINI, J. (2003). 'Slave-Boys for Sexual and Religious Service: Images of Pleasure and Devotion', in Boyle and Dominik (2003), 149–66.

POLSTER, L. (1878). 'Quaestionum Statianarum Particula I', *Abhandlung zum VI. Jahresbericht des königlichen Gymnasiums zu Wongrowitz, Schuljahr 1877–78* (Wongrowitz [Wągrowiec]), 3–12.

—— (1884). 'Quaestionum Statianarum Particula III', *XVIII. Programm des königlichen Gymnasiums zu Ostrowo* (Ostrowo), 1–14.

—— (1890). 'Quaestionum Statianarum Particula IV', *Königliches Gymnasium zu Inowrazlaw* (Inowrazlaw [Inowrocław]), 1–18.

POMEROY, A. J. (1986). 'Somnus and Amor: the Play of Statius, *Silvae* 5,4', *QUCC* NS 24: 91–7.

POMEROY, S. B. (ed.) (1999). *Plutarch's Advice to the Bride and Groom and A Consolation to his Wife* (New York and Oxford).

PORSIA, F. (1976). *Liber monstrorum: Introduzione, edizione, versione e commento* (Bari).

POSTGATE, J. P. (1905). 'Ad silvas Statianas silvula', *Philologus*, 64: 116–36.

POWELL, J. G. F. (1988). *Cicero: Cato Maior de Senectute* (Cambridge).

PULLEYN, S. J. (1997). *Prayer in Greek Religion* (Oxford).

QUINN, K. (1963). *Latin Explorations: Critical Studies in Roman Literature* (London).

RADERMACHER, L. (1916). 'Ein Nachhall des Aristoteles in römischer Kaiserzeit', *WS* 38: 72–80.

RADITSA, L. F. (1980). 'Augustus' Legislation Concerning Marriage, Procreation, Love Affairs and Adultery', *ANRW* II 13: 278–339.

RASCHKE, M. G. (1978). 'New Studies in Roman Commerce with the East', *ANRW* II 9. 2: 604–1378.

RAWSON, B. (1991a). 'Adult–Child Relationships in Roman Society', in ead. (1991b), 7–30.

—— (1991b) (ed.) *Marriage, Divorce and Children in Ancient Rome* (Oxford and Canberra).

RAWSON, E. (1969). *The Spartan Tradition in European Thought* (Oxford).

REEVE, M. D. (1977*a*). 'Politian and Statius' *Silvae*', *SIFC* 49: 285–6.

—— (1977*b*). 'Statius' *Silvae* in the Fifteenth Century', *CQ*, NS 27: 202–25.

—— (1983). 'Statius', in L. D. Reynolds (1983) (ed.). *Texts and Transmission: A Survey of the Latin Classics* (Oxford), 394–9.

RHEINHOLD, M. (1970). *History of Purple as a Status Symbol in Antiquity* (Collection Latomus, 116; Brussels).

RIBUOLI, R. (1981). *La collazione polizianea del codice Bembino di Terenzio* (Rome).

RICH, J. W. (1996). 'Augustus and the Spolia Opima', *Chiron*, 26: 85–127.

RIDGWAY, D. (1992). *The First Western Greeks* (Cambridge).

RIVOIRA, G. T. (1921). *Architettura romana: costruzione e statica nell'età imperiale* (Milan).

ROBERT, L. (1930). 'Études d'épigraphie grecque', *RPh* 56: 25–60.

ROBERTSON, C. M. (1975). *A History of Greek Art*, 2 vols. (Cambridge).

ROSATI, G. (2002). 'Muse and Power in the Poetry of Statius', in E. Spentzou and D. P. Fowler (eds.), *Cultivating the Muse: Struggles for Power and Inspiration in Classical Literature* (Oxford), 229–51.

ROSEMAN, C. H. (1994). *Pytheas of Massalia: On the Ocean* (Chicago).

ROSS, D. O. (1975). *Backgrounds to Augustan Poetry: Gallus, Elegy and Rome* (Cambridge).

ROTHSTEIN, M. (1900). 'Ad Statii silvas observationes criticae', in W. von Hartel (ed.), *Festschrift Johannes Vahlen zum siebenzigsten Geburtstag* (Berlin), 497–522.

RUSTEN, J., and CUNNINGHAM, I. C. (2002). *Theophrastus, Characters; Herodas, Mimes; Sophron and other Mime Fragments* (Cambridge, MA, and London).

RUTHERFORD, R. B. (1989). *The Meditations of Marcus Aurelius: A Study* (Oxford).

SACKETT, L. H., HANKEY, V., HOWELL, R. J., JACOBSEN, T. W., and POPHAM, M. R. (1966). 'Prehistoric Euboea: Contributions toward a Survey', *ABSA* 61: 33–112.

SAENGER, G. (1907). 'Zamietki k latinskam tekstam', *Zhurnal Ministerstva Narodnago Prosvieshcheniia*, NS 9 [June 1907]: 267–314.

—— (1910). 'Zamietki k latinskam tekstam', *Zhurnal Ministerstva Narodnago Prosvieshcheniia*, NS 30 [December 1910]: 523–69.

SALOMIES, O. I. (1992). *Adoptive and Polyonymous Nomenclature in the Roman Empire* (Helsinki).

SANDSTRÖM, C. E. (1878). *Studia critica in Papinium Statium* (Diss. Uppsala).

SARKISSIAN, J. (1983). *Catullus 68: An Interpretation* (Leiden).

SAUTER, F. (1934). *Der römische Kaiserkult bei Martial und Statius* (Stuttgart and Berlin).

SCARCIA PIACENTINI, P. (1984). 'Note storico-paleografiche in margine all'Accademia Romana', in *Le chiavi della memoria: Miscellanea in occasione del I centenario della Scuola Vaticana di paleografia, diplomatica e archivistica, a cura della Associazione degli ex-allievi* (Vatican City), 491–549.

SCHEID, J. (1978). 'Les prêtres officiels sous les empereurs julio-claudiens', *ANRW* II 16. 1: 610–54.

SCHRÖDER, B. (1902). 'Studien zu den Grabdenkmälern der römischen Kaiserzeit', *BJ* 108: 46–79.

SCHRÖDER, B.-J. (1999). *Titel und Text: Zur Entwicklung lateinischer Gedichtüberschriften. Mit Untersuchungen zu lateinischen Buchtiteln, Inhaltsverzeichnissen und anderen Gliederungsmitteln* (Berlin).

SCHULZE, W. (1933). *Kleine Schriften* (Göttingen; 2nd edn. 1966).

SCHÜRER, E. (1973–87). *The History of the Jewish People in the Age of Jesus Christ*, rev. G. Vermes and F. G. B. Millar (Edinburgh).

SCHWARTZ, E. (1889). *Coniectanea* (Rostock).

SCODEL, R. (1980). 'Hesiod Redivivus', *GRBS* 21: 301–20.

SCOTT, K. (1931). 'The Significance of Statues in Precious Metals in Emperor Worship', *TAPhA* 62: 101–23.

—— (1936). *Imperial Cult under the Flavians* (Berlin).

SCOURFIELD, J. H. D. (1993). *Consoling Heliodorus: A Commentary on Jerome Letter 60* (Oxford).

SCULLARD, H. H. (1970). *Scipio Africanus: Soldier and Politician* (London).

SEAGER, R. J. (1983). 'Two Notes: I. Horace, *Odes* 1.17: II. Statius, *Silvae* 5.2', *LCM* 8.4: 51–3.

SHACKLETON BAILEY, D. R. (1987). 'The *Silvae* of Statius', *HSCPh* 91: 273–82.

SHAW, B. D. (2001). 'Raising and Killing Children: Two Roman Myths', *Mnemosyne*, 4th ser. 54: 31–77.

SHERWIN-WHITE, A. N. (1963). *Roman Society and Roman Law in the New Testament* (Oxford).

SIHLER, A. L. (1995). *New Comparative Grammar of Greek and Latin* (New York and Oxford).

SINCLAIR, P. (1991). ' "These are my Temples in your Hearts" (Tac. *Ann.* 4.38.2)', *CPh* 86: 333–5.

SIRNA, F. G. (1973). 'Alcmane εὑρετὴς τῶν ἐρωτικῶν μελῶν', *Aegyptus*, 53: 28–70.

SKIADAS, A. D. (1965). *Homer im griechischen Epigramm* (Athens).

SKUTSCH, F. (1901). 'Grammatische-lexikalische Notizen', *ALL* 12: 199–200.

SLATER, D. A. (1907). 'Conjectural Emendations in the *Silvae* of Statius', *JPh* 30: 133–60.

—— (1908). *The Silvae of Statius: Translated with Introduction and Notes* (Oxford).

—— (1909). 'Conjectures', *CR* 23: 248–9.

SLATER, W. J. (1974). '*Pueri, turba minuta*', *BICS* 21: 133–40.

SMITH, W. (1856) (ed.). *Dictionary of Greek and Roman Geography* (London).

SNELL, B. (1931). 'Sapphos Gedicht φαίνεταί μοι κῆνος', *Hermes*, 66: 71–90.

—— (1943). *Leben und Meinungen der Sieben Weisen* (Munich).

SOLIN, H. (1982). *Die griechischen Personennamen in Rom: Ein Namenbuch* (Berlin).

SOLMSEN, F. (1947). 'Eratosthenes' *Erigone*: A Reconstruction', *TAPhA* 78: 252–75.

SOMMERSTEIN, A. H. (1989). *Aeschylus: Eumenides* (Cambridge).

SPEIDEL, M. A. (1998). '*Legio IIII Scythica*, its Movements and Men', in D. Kennedy (1998), 163–204.

SPRENGER, B. (1962). *Zahlenmotive in der Epigrammatik und in verwandten Literaturgattungen alter und neuer Zeit* (Diss. Münster).

STAFFORD, E. J. (1991–3). 'Aspects of Sleep in Hellenistic Sculpture', *BICS* 38: 105–21.

STINTON, T. C. W. (1990). *Collected Papers on Greek Tragedy* (Oxford).

STROBEL, K. (1989). *Die Donaukriege Domitians* (Bonn).

STUPPERICH, R. (1977). *Staatsbegräbnis und Privatgrabmal im klassischen Athen* (Diss. Münster).

SWAIN, S. (1996). *Hellenism and Empire: Language, Classicism and Power in the Greek World AD 50–250* (Oxford).

SYME, R. (1939). *The Roman Revolution* (Oxford).

—— (1958). *Tacitus* (Oxford).

—— (1980). *Some Arval Brethren* (Oxford).

SZEMERÉNYI, O. (1956). 'Latin tantus quantus and the Genitive of Price: With an Excursus on Latin quandō and Gk. πηνίκα', *Glotta*, 35: 92–114.

TAISNE, A.-M. (1996). 'Échos épiques dans les *Silves*', in Delarue et al. (1996), 215–34.

TALBERT, R. J. A. (1984). *The Senate of Imperial Rome* (Princeton).

TANNER, R. G. (1986). 'Epic Tradition and Epigram in Statius', *ANRW* II 32. 5: 3020–46.

TARRANT, R. J. (1985). *Seneca's Thyestes* (Atlanta).

TAYLOR, L. R. (1931). *The Divinity of the Roman Emperor* (Middletown, CT).

THOMAS, R. F. (1983). 'Callimachus, the *Victoria Berenices*, and Roman Poetry', *CQ*, NS 33: 92–113.

THOMPSON, D'ARCY W. (1936). *A Glossary of Greek Birds*, 2nd edn. (Oxford).

THOMPSON, L. (1984). 'Domitianus Dominus: A Gloss on Statius *Silvae* 1.6.84', *AJP* 105: 469–75.

TOYNBEE, J. M. C. (1971). *Death and Burial in the Roman World* (London).

TRAGLIA, A. (1964). 'De Statii *Silva* ad Somnum', *Latinitas*, 12: 7–12.

TREGGIARI, S. (1984). 'Digna Condicio: Betrothals in the Roman Upper Class', *EMC* 28 (NS 3), 419–51.

—— (1991). *Roman Marriage* (Oxford).

—— (1996). 'Social status and social legislation', in *Cambridge Ancient History*, x, 2nd edn. (Cambridge), 873–904.

TUPLIN, C. J. (1981). 'Catullus 68', *CQ*, NS 31: 113–39.

UNGER, R. (1868). *P. Papinii Statii Ecloga ultima: emendatiorem edidit Robertus Unger. Accedunt ejusdem de Statii locis controversis conjectanea* (Neustrelitz).

VAQUERIZO GIL, D., and NOGUERA CELDRÁN, J. M. (1997). *La Villa de El Ruedo (Almedinilla, Córdoba), decoración escultórica e interpretación* (Murcia).

VENINI, P. (1971). *Studi staziani* (Pavia).

VERMEULE, E. (1979). *Aspects of Death in Early Greek Art and Poetry* (Berkeley and Los Angeles).

VESSEY, D. W. T. C. (1971). Review of Håkanson (1969), *CPh* 66: 273–6.

—— (1973). *Statius and the Thebaid* (Cambridge).

—— (1986). 'Style Preserved: Style and Theme in Statius' *Silvae*', *ANRW* II 32. 5, 2754–2802.

VIDMAN, L. (1980). *Corpus Inscriptionum Latinarum: Voluminis Sexti Pars Sexta. Indices. Fasciculus Secundus. Index Cognominum* (Berlin and New York).

VOLLMER, F. (1893). 'Ad Statii silvas symbolae II', *JbClPh* 147: 825–43 (includes conjectures by F. Skutsch).

—— (1896). 'Textkritisches zu Statius', *RhM*, NF 51: 27–44.

—— (1898). *P. Papinii Statii Silvarum libri* (Leipzig).

WACKERNAGEL, J. (1920). *Vorlesungen über Syntax mit besonderer Berücksichtigung von Griechisch, Lateinisch und Deutsch* (Basel).

WAGNER, J. (1976). *Seleukeia am Euphrat/Zeugma* (Wiesbaden).

WALBANK, F. W. (1967). 'The Scipionic Legend', *PCPhS* 193, NS 13: 54–69.

WALDSTEIN, W. (1964). *Untersuchungen zum römischen Begnadigungsrecht: Abolitio — Indulgentia — Venia* (Innsbruck).

*WALLER, W. (1885). 'Excursus criticus in P. Papinii Statii Silvas' (Diss. Breslau).

WARREN, L. BONFANTE (1970). 'Roman Triumphs and Etruscan Kings: The Changing Face of the Triumph', *JRS* 60: 49–66.

—— (1973). 'Roman Costumes: A Glossary and Some Etruscan Derivations', *ANRW* I 4: 584–614.

WATSON, P. A. (1995). *Ancient Stepmothers: Myth, Misogyny and Reality* (Leiden).

WATT, W. S. (1988). 'Notes on Statius' *Silvae*', *WJA* 14: 159–70.

WEAVER, P. R. C. (1994). 'Confusing Names: Abascantus and Statius, *Silvae* 5.1', *ÉMC* 38 (NS 13), 333–64.

WEBSTER, G. (1979). *The Roman Imperial Army*, 2nd edn. (London).

WELLESLEY, K. (1964). '*Facilis descensus Averno*', *CR*, NS 14: 235–8.

WEST, M. L. (1970). 'Corinna', *CQ*, NS 20: 277–87.

—— (1983). *The Orphic Poems* (Oxford).

—— (1997). *The East Face of Helicon* (Oxford).

WEST, S. (1983). 'Notes on the Text of Lycophron', *CQ*, NS 33: 114–35.

WHEELER, E. L. (1988). *Stratagem and the Vocabulary of Military Trickery* (Leiden).

WHITE, K. D. (1970). *Roman Farming* (London).

WHITE, P. (1973). 'Notes on two Statian ΠΡΟΣΩΠΑ', *CPh* 68: 279–84.

—— (1974). 'The Presentation and Dedication of the *Silvae* and the *Epigrams*', *JRS* 64: 40–61.

WHITE, P. (1998). 'Latin Poets and the *carmen Capitolinum*', in Knox and Foss (1998), 84–95.

WHITEHOUSE, J. E. G. (1975). 'Golden Statues in Greek and Latin Literature', *GR* 22: 109–19.

WIEDEMANN, T. (1989). *Adults and Children in the Roman Empire* (London).

WILAMOWITZ-MOELLENDORF, U. von (1913). *Sappho und Simonides* (Berlin).

WILKES, J.J. (1983). 'Romans, Dacians and Sarmatians in the First and Early Second Centuries', in B. Hartley and J. Wacher (eds.), *Rome and her Northern Provinces* (Gloucester), 255–89.

WILLIAMS, G. D. (1994). *Banished Voices: Readings in Ovid's Exile Poetry* (Cambridge).

WILLIAMS, J. H. C. (2001). *Beyond the Rubicon: Romans and Gauls in Republican Italy* (Oxford).

WILLS, J. (1996). *Repetition in Latin Poetry* (Oxford).

WIMAN, G. (1937). 'Papiniana', *Eranos*, 35: 1–21.

WIMMEL, W. (1960). *Kallimachos und Rom* (Hermes Einzelschriften, 16; Wiesbaden).

WINTER, T. (1907). *De ellipsi uerbi esse apud Catullum, Vergilium, Ovidium, Statium, Iuvenalem obvia capita duo* (Marburg).

WISSMANN, H. VON (1976). 'Die Geschichte des Sabäerreichs und der Feldzug des Aelius Gallus', *ANRW* II 9. 1: 308–544.

WISSOWA, G. (1912). *Religion und Kultus der Römer* (Munich).

WÖLFFLIN, E. (1898–1900). 'Zur Geschichte der Pronomina demonstrativa', *ALL* 11: 369–93.

WOOD, J. R. (1980). 'The Myth of Tages', *Latomus*, 39: 325–44.

WOODMAN, A. J. (1975). 'Questions of Date, Genre and Style in Velleius: Some Literary Answers', *CQ*, NS 25: 272–306.

—— (1997). 'The Position of Gallus in *Eclogue* 6', *CQ*, NS 47: 593–7.

WREDE, H. (1971). 'Das Mausoleum der Claudia Semne und die bürgerliche Plastik der Kaiserzeit', *MDAI(R)* 78: 125–66.

—— (1981). *Consecratio in formam deorum: Vergöttlichte Privatpersonen in der römischen Kaiserzeit* (Mainz).

—— (1988). 'Zur Trabea', *JDAI* 103: 381–400.

ZANKER, P. (1968). *Forum Augustum: Das Bildprogramm* (Tübingen).

—— (1988). *The Power of Images in the Age of Augustus* (Ann Arbor).

—— (1999). 'Eine römische Matrone als Omphale', *MDAI(R)* 106: 119–31.

ZEUGMA: Interim Reports (2003). *Journal of Roman Archaeology Supplementary Series*, 51 (Portsmouth, RI).

ZWICKY, H. (1944). *Zur Verwendung des Militärs in der Verwaltung der römischen Kaiserzeit* (Zurich).

INDEXES

References in italics in the form of e.g. '*p. xv*' or '*pp. 312–17*' are to page numbers, almost always either in the General Introduction, or in the introductions to individual poems. References in roman type in the form of e.g. '5.2.163n.' or '5.3.76–9nn.' are to the commentary on the line or passage in question, with 'n.' signifying a single note to be consulted, and 'nn.' more than one note on a particular passage.

GENERAL INDEX

This index includes proper names, *Realien*, and other subjects and topics of interest. Readers are also alerted to the presence of various items grouped under the heading of 'themes and motifs'.

INDEX OF LATIN WORDS
AND PHRASES

INDEX OF PASSAGES

This index does not cover every reference to an ancient text in this book, but lists passages quoted or referred to more fully, and references to what may be less obvious passages.